Leicester and the Court

Essays on Elizabethan politics

SIMON ADAMS

Manchester
University Press
Manchester and New York

distributed exclusively in the USA by Palgrave

Published by Manchester University Press
Oxford Road, Manchester M13 9NR, UK
and Room 400, 175 Fifth Avenue, New York, NY 10010, USA
http://www.manchesteruniversitypress.co.uk

Distributed exclusively in the USA by
Palgrave, 175 Fifth Avenue, New York, NY 10010, USA

Distributed exclusively in Canada by
UBC Press, University of British Columbia, 2029 West Mall,
Vancouver, BC, Canada V6T 1Z2

British Library Cataloguing-in-Publication Data
A catalogue record for this book is available from the British Library

Library of Congress Cataloging-in-Publication Data applied for

ISBN 0 7190 5324 2 *hardback*
      0 7190 5325 0 *paperback*

First published 2002

10 09 08 07 06 05 04 03 02   10 9 8 7 6 5 4 3 2 1

Typeset in Scala with Pastonchi display
by Graphicraft Limited, Hong Kong

Printed in Great Britain
by Bookcraft (Bath) Ltd, Midsomer Norton

DATE DUE

Leicester and the Court

MANCHESTER
UNIVERSITY PRESS

Politics, Culture and Society in Early Modern Britain

General Editors

PROFESSOR ANN HUGHES

DR ANTHONY MILTON

PROFESSOR PETER LAKE

This important series publishes monographs that take a fresh and challenging look at the interactions between politics, culture and society in Britain between 1500 and the mid-eighteenth century. It counteracts the fragmentation of current historiography through encouraging a variety of approaches which attempt to redefine the political, social and cultural worlds, and to explore their interconnection in a flexible and creative fashion. All the volumes in the series question and transcend traditional inter-disciplinary boundaries, such as those between political history and literary studies, social history and divinity, urban history and anthropology. They thus contribute to a broader understanding of crucial developments in early modern Britain.

IN MEMORY
OF MY PARENTS

Contents

Contents

Preface

M y primary debt is to the editors of this series, especially Peter Lake, for considering the contents of this volume worthy of re-publication. My second is to the editors of the various volumes or journals where the essays first appeared, in particular Juliet Gardiner, Christopher Haigh, Ronald Asch, John Guy, George Bernard, Marcel Aymard and Marzio Romani, David Starkey, Paul Hofthijzer, David Dean, Gordon Marsden, Richard Cust and John Watts.

Specific acknowledgements will be found in most of the chapters (and numerous others must await a further occasion), but three general obligations should be recorded here. The first is to the staffs of the numerous archives, record offices and libraries where I have worked over the years. I owe a particular debt to the owners of the private collections that have played such a large role in my research: the Marquess of Bath, the Marquess of Salisbury, the Marquess of Anglesey, the Viscount De L'Isle, the Berkeley Trustees and the Evelyn Trustees (although now in the British Library, the Evelyn Papers were still on deposit at Christ Church, Oxford, when I first worked on them). No less crucial has been the financial support provided on a number of occasions by the British Academy, the Carnegie Trust for the Universities of Scotland and the Wolfson Trust, a vital supplement to such research funds as the University of Strathclyde has been able to supply.

Edinburgh

Acknowledgements

The articles and essays collected here were originally published in the following places and are reprinted by the kind permission of the original publishers.

Chapter 1   *History Today*, xxxii (December 1982), pp. 33–9.

Chapter 2   *The Reign of Elizabeth I*, ed. Christopher Haigh (Macmillan, 1984), pp. 55–77.

Chapter 3   *The Tudor Monarchy*, ed. John Guy (Edward Arnold, 1997), pp. 253–74, and initially in *Princes, Patronage and the Nobility: The Court at the Beginning of the Modern Age, c.1450–1650*, ed. Ronald G. Asch and Adolf M. Birke (German Historical Institute Studies, Oxford University Press, 1991), pp. 265–87.

Chapter 4   *The Reign of Elizabeth I: Court and Culture in the Last Decade*, ed. John Guy (Cambridge University Press, 1995), pp. 20–45.

Chapter 5   *Transactions of the Royal Historical Society*, 6th ser., vii (1997), pp. 247–65.

Chapter 6   *La Cour comme Institution Economique*, ed. Maurice Aymard and Marzio A. Romani (Editions de la Maison des sciences de l'Homme, 1998), pp. 127–36.

Chapter 7   *Rivals in Power: Lives and Letters of the Great Tudor Dynasties*, ed. David Starkey (Macmillan, 1990), pp. 146–73.

Chapter 8   *The Tudor Nobility*, ed. G. W. Bernard (Manchester University Press, 1992), pp. 241–65.

Chapter 9   *The Dutch in Crisis, 1585–1588: People and Politics in Leicester's Time. Papers of the Annual Symposium held on 27 November 1987*, ed. Paul Hofthijzer (Leiden, Sir Thomas Browne Institute, 1988), pp. 7–34.

Chapter 10   *Parliamentary History*, viii (1989), pp. 216–39.

Chapter 11   *History Today*, xl (January 1990), pp. 14–19.

Chapter 12   *Welsh History Review*, vi (1974), pp. 129–47.

Chapter 13   *Bulletin of the Board of Celtic Studies*, xxvi (1976), pp. 479–511.

Chapter 14   *Transactions of the Denbighshire Historical Society*, xxv (1976), pp. 92–113.

Chapter 15   *Midland History*, xx (1995), pp. 21–74.

Chapter 16   *The End of the Middle Ages? England in the Fifteenth and Sixteenth Centuries*, ed. John L. Watts (Sutton Publishing, Fifteenth Century Series VI, 1998), pp. 155–97.

Abbreviations and conventions

I t is nearly impossible to standardise the notes in a range of essays written over a quarter of a century and employing a variety of house styles. They have therefore been left in their original form. Chapters 2, 3, 4, and 16, however, were published in collections employing standard abbreviations across the volume and these are reproduced below. Cross-references to essays included in this volume have the original source replaced, in the initial citation, by the chapter reference in square brackets; subsequent citations employ the chapter reference exclusively. Page references have been similarly amended, as have those in cross-references within chapters.

As noted in several of the chapters, after 1981 I followed the spelling of surnames employed in *The History of Parliament: The House of Commons 1559–1603*; where necessary those found in the older essays have been amended. There is one exception, Sir John Huband, where the form Hubaud has been adopted in the last two chapters (see p. 350 below). In the case of works originally noted as in press or forthcoming (whether my own or by others), publication details have been supplied silently.

Correction of spelling, typographical and grammatical errors has been undertaken silently. Where it has been necessary to correct errors of fact this has been done in square brackets at the end of the subsequent note, or, in those chapters which did not include notes in the original version, by introducing an alphabetical series of references.

AGR	Brussels, Archives Générales du Royaume
PEA	Papiers d'Etat et de l'Audience
AMRE	Paris, Archives du Ministère des Relations Etrangères [temporarily Extérieures]
CPA	Correspondence Politique, Angleterre
APC	*Acts of the Privy Council of England*, ed. J. R Dasent *et al.* (46 vols, 1890–1964)
BIHR	*Bulletin of the Institute of Historical Research*
BL	British Library
Lansd. MSS	Lansdowne Manuscripts
Add. MSS	Additional Manuscripts
Bod. Lib.	Oxford, Bodleian Library
CPR	*Calendar of the Patent Rolls*
CSPF	*Calendar of State Papers, Foreign Series*
CSPSc	*Calendar of State Papers relating to Scotland and Mary, Queen of Scots*
EcHR	*Economic History Review*
EHR	*English Historical Review*
HA	Historical Association

Abbreviations and conventions

Haynes and Murdin	*Collection of State Papers . . . left by William Cecil, Lord Burghley*, ed. S. Haynes and W. Murdin (2 vols, 1740–59)
HJ	*Historical Journal*
HMC	Historical Manuscripts Commission
H of C, 1509–58	*The History of Parliament. The House of Commons 1509–1558*, ed. S. T. Bindoff (1982)
JBS	*Journal of British Studies*
PRO	Public Record Office
C	Chancery
E	Exchequer
LC	Lord Chamberlain's Department
LS	Lord Steward's Department
PCC	Prerogative Court of Canterbury
PROB	Probate
SP	State Papers
Rel. Pol.	*Relations Politiques des Pays Bas et de l'Angleterre sous le règne de Philippe II*, ed. J. M. B. C. Kervyn de Lettenhove (11 vols, Brussels, 1882–1900)
RO	Record Office
STC	*A Short Title Catalogue of Books Printed in England . . . 1475–1640*, ed. A. W. Pollard and G. R. Redgrave (1969, 2nd ed., 3 vols, 1986–94)
TRHS	*Transactions of the Royal Historical Society*

Introduction

This volume is the result of a flattering invitation by Manchester University Press to publish a collection of my essays in the Politics, Culture and Society in Early Modern Britain Series. Although the original invitation was made in 1996, other pressures have delayed preparation of the collection. But this delay, however irritating, has made it possible to include three papers initially delivered at conferences in 1996 and 1997.

Sixteen essays or articles have been selected from the fifty that I have produced since 1974. Given that collections of this type serve as a work of reference, and that I have criticised others in reviews for failing to make clear their principles of selection, it is best to begin with reasons for the present choice. The subject, Robert Dudley, Earl of Leicester and the Elizabethan Court, was proposed by the editors of the series, and the precise selection reached by negotiation between us. Essays on foreign, naval or military policy have been relegated to a possible further volume, among them three that could have been included here.[1] Also excluded are three relevant, but lesser, pieces: a note on land tenure in Denbighshire, a short essay on the nobility and the Court, and an article on Leicester's daily life based on my edition of his household accounts.[2] The most substantial omissions are five articles on Leicester's papers. But since the main series of articles on that subject is not yet complete, these have been left for possible re-publication in another form.[3] The editors' initial selection also included two unpublished conference papers, but they have been replaced here by the three conference papers mentioned above (chapters 5, 6 and 16), which were published in 1997 and 1998. It was also an editorial request that this collection be accompanied by a fuller introduction than is normally found in volumes of essays.

With the exception of the articles on Leicester's papers, the sixteen chosen can be fairly said to include the more substantial of my essays on Leicester or the Court. Chapter 3 has already been reprinted and at that point a postscript bringing it up to date was added; this is the version published here. The temptation to do the same with the others has had to be resisted if this volume was ever to go to press, and therefore they have been reprinted in their original form, with corrections limited to typographical, grammatical, spelling and factual errors. In an effort to supply a logical order, the chapters have been arranged in three groups, those dealing with the Court and Court politics, those dealing with the Earl of Leicester and his affinity in general, and those dealing with Leicester's territorial interest.

The last group contains my earliest published essays and they and most of the other Leicester essays are the product of research towards my forthcoming biography, presently under contract with Yale University Press. The subjects covered in them were dictated by the rhythms of my research and there is no pretence of providing a general biographical coverage. There is in fact only one specifically biographical essay (chapter 7), a short contribution to a collection of the letters of the greater Tudor noble dynasties edited by David Starkey. A number of the other Leicester essays and all of the essays on the Court were originally contributions to collections commissioned by the editor or published conference papers. These invitations have had the beneficial effect of forcing me to leave the minutiae of Leicester's life and to address a number of wider questions posed by the recent revival of interest in the political history of the sixteenth and seventeenth centuries: in particular the nature and role of clienteles, noble affinities and factions, and the structure and politics of the Court.[4]

It would be an exaggeration to say that when I began research on Leicester in the early to mid-1970s hardly anything was known about him, for that would do a disservice to the two pioneers of the re-appraisal of Leicester's place in Elizabeth's reign, Eleanor Rosenberg and Patrick Collinson.[5] But it was certainly widely believed then that his papers had disappeared and therefore a full-scale biography was not possible. The situation is now very different. Apart from my own work, since the mid-1970s three popular biographies and a scholarly edition of *Leicester's Commonwealth* have been published.[6] More recently David Loades has written a biography of his father and Steven Gunn has published a very valuable and quite moving letter by his mother.[7]

The fact that the earliest essays (chapters 12–14) deal with Wales is not accidental. They are the product of an experiment I undertook during my tenure of a University of Wales research fellowship at UCW Bangor in 1973–75 to see what evidence survived of Leicester's extensive estates in north Wales. The result was the discovery not just of the extensive collection of his papers at Longleat House, but also (for the Welsh estates) of the large body of estate muniments in the Public Record Office and the Chirk Castle collection in the National Library of Wales.[8] It was clear that the 'disappearance' of his papers needed to be re-examined and over the next twenty years other big

Leicester collections emerged. There were two particularly exciting moments along the way. The first was to find quite by accident that my previous guess that a large section of the Elizabethan papers in the Cottonian Manuscripts were in fact Leicester's was correct.[9] The second was the discovery by Sally-Beth McLean, editor of *Records of Early English Drama*, of Leicester's disbursement book for 1584–86 among the Evelyn Papers. She was kind enough to let me publish it in the *Household Accounts*.[10]

The essay on Leicester and the West Midlands (chapter 15) was written nearly twenty years after the Welsh chapters. By then I was far more knowledgeable about Leicester, his men and his estates. Possibly too knowledgeable, for it could be (as has been) said that it attempts to cover too much ground for a single essay. Be that as it may, between them chapters 13–15 survey the two main concentrations of his estates, for the lands he held elsewhere were peripheral. Thanks to the loss of most of the contents of the 'evidence house' at Kenilworth Castle, we know less about the management of the West Midlands estates than about the Welsh.[11] But in compensation we have *The Black Book of Warwick*, which contains some of the most vivid accounts of dealing with Leicester that we possess. Leicester was, of course, essentially an absentee landlord. But if he visited Wales only once (in 1584), he did holiday annually at Kenilworth between 1570 and 1585, with the single exception of 1583, when his departure was called off at the last minute by the discovery of what later became the Throckmorton Plot. The West Midlands estates had an almost emotional significance for him, for it was through their descent from the Suttons, Lords Dudley, and the Beauchamps, Earls of Warwick, that the Tudor Dudleys claimed to be members of the ancient nobility. The Welsh estates were far more remunerative and Leicester might be considered a more exploitative landlord there. Nevertheless, the tenurial reformation he undertook in the lordships of Denbigh and Chirk reveals an administrative ability that has often been overlooked. This was an ambitious resolution of a long-standing problem, and, so far as I know, without parallel in Elizabeth's reign.[12]

My initial research in Wales also inspired an attempt to identify and reconstruct his affinity, the results of which can be found in a number of these essays. Quite early on I came to appreciate two aspects of the affinity that have shaped my subsequent approach to it. The first was the close connection between his estate administration and that of his brother, Ambrose, Earl of Warwick. Both employed more or less the same body of legal advisors and administrators in both Wales and the Midlands (see chapters 14 and 15). This was a family, as much as an individual, affinity, a subject also addressed in chapter 8. The second is an unusual piece of evidence. Leicester's household is discussed in detail in the *Household Accounts*, where such lists of his household as survive, together with a livery list and the lists of his funeral attendants, have been printed. Also included there is a biographical index of his servants, though it is necessarily limited to the periods covered by the accounts, i.e. 1558–61 and 1584–87. However, for the wider affinity there are also the lists of the cavalry contingent of his Netherlands Expedition in 1585, which, thanks to the way in which it was recruited, supply a unique snapshot of those Leicester considered to be his 'good friends and servants'. A consolidated list can be found in the appendix to chapter 16, but earlier discussions are found in chapters 5, 12, and 15.

The essays in Part II look at certain wider aspects of the affinity and its position in Elizabethan society. Chapter 8 deals with the particular issue of the continuity of personnel between the households of the Duke of Northumberland and his son, which not only strengthens the case for a Dudley affinity but in turn brings up the wider question of continuity between Edward VI's reign and Elizabeth's.[13] To what extent was an 'Edwardian restoration' an issue in 1558–59?[14] Looked at from an Edwardian perspective, Leicester was not an unknown adventurer at the beginning of Elizabeth's reign, but one of its central figures. An important aspect of the wider Dudley affinity was its military wing, which can be traced back to the 1540s. The Newhaven (Le Havre) expedition of 1562 was the connecting link. If its senior figures began their careers under Northumberland, the younger ones were to be Leicester's protégés. The outlines of his military patronage between 1562 and 1585 are surveyed in chapter 9.

A more complex issue, or series of issues, Leicester's affinity in the House of Commons is raised by chapter 10. In 1981 the Elizabethan section of the *History of Parliament* was published.[15] This is a major work, which remains the indispensable guide to the Elizabethan political elite, but so far as Leicester is concerned, it is seriously out of date. Far too many of his men are either un- or mis-identified and the extent of his parliamentary patronage greatly under-estimated. Part of the purpose of chapter 10 was to fill in the gaps left by the *History of Parliament*. In the process, however, a number of very curious things appeared. The evidence for Leicester's electioneering is, for a variety of reasons, scrappy, yet what does survive suggests a burst of activity in the final parliament, that of 1584, in which he was able to play a direct role. This I thought in 1989 (and am now convinced) was not an illusion created by the accidents of archival survival. Rather it reflects a deliberate attempt, shared with other privy councillors, to ensure a House of Commons that would support a military intervention in the Netherlands.[16]

If this evidence suggests a far greater interest in the direct influencing of elections on at least one occasion during Elizabeth's reign than heretofore thought, another curious phenomenon also emerged. Chapter 10 was written when the revisionist approach to Elizabethan parliaments championed by the late Sir Geoffrey Elton was in vogue. Elton argued then that M.P.s were primarily interested in local matters, that high politics was only introduced into the House of Commons through the actions of Court factions and that the key figures in the House were the 'men of business' of the leading privy councillors. A large number of Leicester's own men of business sat in the House thanks to his patronage, yet very few of them were active parliamentarians. The problems of squaring Elton's analysis of parliamentary politics with what we know about Leicester's affinity in the House are addressed in chapter 5.

The remaining chapter in Part II deals in an admittedly very brief way with Leicester's religious patronage. Despite Patrick Collinson's work, which revealed Leicester's role in Elizabethan puritanism, it is still widely assumed that he was a political opportunist of no strong religious allegiance, whose espousal of 'extreme' puritanism in the 1580s was the result of his loss of influence following the Anjou marriage. Yet the identification of his chaplains and an analysis of his major religious patronage reveal the essential continuity of his religious allegiances. Unlike Lord Burghley, Leicester appears to have employed chaplains on an annual rotating basis, which made him the direct patron of a very wide range of clergymen. His chaplains in 1559 and 1560 (the earliest we know of) were both former Marian exiles, and a substantial number of those he employed subsequently became bishops or heads of university colleges. Leicester certainly protected radicals like Thomas Cartwright, but they were far from being the sole recipients of his patronage, even in the 1580s. This went overwhelmingly to the more cautious 'moderate puritans'.

Of the six essays on the Court and high politics, chapters 2 and 6 survey the Elizabethan Court as institution. The others (chapters 1 and 3–5) address a particular aspect of the revival of interest in the Court in the 1980s and 1990s: the nature of factional politics. The historiography is covered in these chapters and needs only to be summarised here. There is the contemporary Catholic claim, found in *Leicester's Commonwealth*, that Leicester and his 'faction' dominated the Court, subsequently refuted by defenders of Elizabeth. The modern interest began with Conyers Read's discovery of a factional dispute over foreign policy beginning in the late 1570s. This was followed by Sir John Neale's attempt to apply Sir Lewis Namier's analysis of the politics of patronage to the sixteenth century. Most recently we have Elton's and Conrad Russell's explanation of parliamentary politics through the workings of Court factions. Elton is also often given credit for initiating the new interest in the Court in his three 'Points of Contact' lectures of 1974–76. But he was, to some extent at least, influenced by the research of David Starkey, although Starkey's work did not appear in print until the end of the 1970s. In turn, Starkey's appreciation of the significance of the institutional geography of the Court owes much to a very clever article published by Hugh Murray Baillie in 1967.[17]

My doubts about the factional explanation of Elizabethan politics began to emerge when, in the course of working through Leicester's affairs, I simply failed to find the evidence for a struggle over patronage with Burghley, which thanks to Neale's influence had been regarded almost as axiomatic. It was clear that a more sophisticated politics of patronage was necessary. This has set my appreciation of Elizabethan Court politics at odds with Starkey's, for whom a factional struggle for patronage remains at its centre. The case for political factionalism at Elizabeth's Court in the years prior to Leicester's death in 1588 hinges on the interpretation of the two episodes when a major internal upheaval appeared to be in the offing. The first was the attempted overthrow of Cecil in 1569 and the second the attempted overthrow of Leicester during the Anjou marriage in 1579. Neither of these episodes is discussed in any detail here, so only limited comment can be made. What they have in common is that the most lurid accounts are supplied by Catholic ambassadors. They were not eyewitnesses to the events they described, but they had an interest in such an upheaval and to a considerable extent tried to instigate it. To date we lack an adequate account of the events of 1569.[18] 1579 has been the subject of some important recent work, in particular a thesis by Mitchell Leimon, which, though unpublished, has had a considerable influence on two recent accounts of the Anjou marriage.[19] For Leimon the episode is a classic example of factional politics, in this instance Burghley using the Anjou negotiations to regain his pre-eminence in the formulation of policy that he had lost to Walsingham and Leicester in the later 1570s. Much of his argument, however, is very unconvincing, not just the questions of whether Burghley had indeed lost his pre-eminence and precisely how committed he was to the Anjou marriage, but also his superficial identification of factions.[20]

These episodes apart, there are two general weaknesses in the case for an intense factional politics. The first is the role of the crown. To argue that factions predominate is to argue that the monarch was essentially their plaything and not in control of the Court. This is all very well when dealing with a monarch who was mentally deranged (like Henry VI) but it was hardly the case with Elizabeth.[21] One of the difficulties with the factional interpretation of the Anjou marriage is, as Wallace MacCaffrey perceptively noted, that the running was made by Elizabeth.[22] Whatever her motives, the overthrow of Leicester was not one of them. The only privy councillor who supported the marriage with any degree of enthusiasm was the Earl of Sussex, and his enthusiasm was not shared by Burghley. However, this aspect of the Anjou marriage does confute the argument I made in chapter 2, that Elizabeth did not go behind the back of the privy council. Elizabeth revived the marriage herself in May 1578, using Sussex as an intermediary with the French ambassador.[23]

The other problem is the very tightness of the Elizabethan establishment and the centrality of Leicester's place in it. The Elizabethan court, for all its tensions, was composed of a relatively small number of closely related men and women. They came to power together in 1558 and they grew old together. This is perhaps the real significance of Leicester's position as favourite. At the end of the day Leicester's wider position was derived from Elizabeth's favour. However extensive his regional interests, this was not where his power lay. This does not mean that he was necessarily playing at being a member of the territorial nobility, rather his ambition was to make permanent the Dudley position among them. What he undoubtedly regarded as his personal tragedy was his failure to produce the legitimate heirs to ensure it.

But if he was Elizabeth's creature, it was no less significant that she chose someone from the existing protestant political elite, no matter how controversial his family. This is what distinguished Leicester from Sir Christopher Hatton, Sir Walter Ralegh, or (to cite a Jacobean example) George Villiers, all of whom had to create such affinities as they possessed from nothing. It even distinguishes him from Essex, for although on one level the Devereux position among nobility was more substantial than the Dudley, they were not heretofore in the first rank. Having said this, there is one important revision to be made to the argument in chapter 2 that we need to look to the rise of Essex and Ralegh at the end of the 1580s to discover the really discordant elements at the Elizabethan Court. This, as John Guy has observed, was the rise of Archbishop Whitgift after 1583.[24] Whitgift was as much a shaper of what is now being termed the 'second reign' as Ralegh or Essex. By the same token Leicester was as central a figure to the 'first reign' as Burghley. To study Leicester and his men, as I have tried here, is to study the Elizabethan establishment.

NOTES

1 'The Count of Feria's Dispatch to Philip II of 14 November 1558', ed. with M. J. Rodríguez-Salgado, *Camden Miscellany XXVIII* (Camden Society, 4th ser., xxix, 1984), 302–44; 'The Release of Lord Darnley and the Failure of the Amity', in Michael Lynch (ed.), *Mary Stewart: Queen in Three Kingdoms* (Oxford, 1987), pp. 123–53, and 'A Patriot for Whom? Stanley, York and Elizabeth's Catholics', *History Today* xxxvii (July 1987), 46–50.

2 'Military Obligations of Leasehold Tenants in Leicesterian Denbigh', *Transactions of the Denbighshire Historical Society*, xxv (1975), 205–8; 'La Noblesse et la Cour sous Elisabeth', in André Stegmann (ed.), *Pouvoir et Institutions en Europe au XVIème Siècle* (Paris, 1987), pp. 163–71; 'At Home and Away: The Earl of Leicester', *History Today*, xlvi (May 1996), 22–8.

3 'The Papers of Robert Dudley, Earl of Leicester: I–III', *Archives*, xx (1992), 63–85, xx (1993), 131–44, xxii (1996), 1–26; 'The Lauderdale Papers, 1561–1570: The Maitland

of Lethington State Papers and the Leicester Correspondence', and 'Two "Missing" Lauderdale Letters', *Scottish Historical Review*, lxvii (1988), 28–55 and lxx (1991), 55–7.

4 In order to avoid taking up this introduction with yet another discussion of the vexed terminology of factions and affinities, the reader is referred to the comments in chapter 16 (p. 376).

5 Eleanor Rosenberg, *Leicester, Patron of Letters* (New York, 1955). Patrick Collinson, 'Letters of Thomas Wood, Puritan, 1566–76', in *Godly People: Essays on English Protestantism and Puritanism* (London, 1983), pp. 45–108, and *The Elizabethan Puritan Movement* (London, 1967).

6 Alan Kendall, *Robert Dudley, Earl of Leicester* (London, 1980); Derek Wilson, *Sweet Robin* (London, 1981); Alan Haynes, *The White Bear* (1987). Dwight C. Peck (ed.), *Leicester's Commonwealth: The Copy of a Letter written by a Master of Art of Cambridge (1584) and related documents* (Athens, Ohio, 1985).

7 David Loades, *John Dudley, Duke of Northumberland* (Oxford, 1996). S. J. Gunn, 'A Letter of Jane, Duchess of Northumberland, in 1553', *English Historical Review*, cxiv (1999), 1267–71.

8 To be strictly truthful I knew something of the Longleat collection from a day working there in 1971, but it was not until 1974 that I was able to work on it extensively. It might be recalled that the Historical Manuscripts Commission, *Calendar of the Manuscripts of the Marquess of Bath V: Talbot, Dudley and Devereux Papers 1533–1659* was not published until 1980. The Leicester collection at Longleat is discussed in detail in 'Leicester Pap. III'; see p. 19 for the surrender of the lordship of Denbigh 'books' to the crown, which explains why they are presently in the PRO.

9 This was the discovery c.1990 of a note in Sir Robert Cotton's hand: 'Papers of my Lord of Lecestre and Mr Herls that I had of Sir Arthur Atye', see 'Leicester Pap. II', p. 132.

10 *Household Accounts and Disbursement Books of Robert Dudley, Earl of Leicester, 1558–1561, 1584–1586* (Camden Society, 5th ser., vi, 1995), see p. 4.

11 Some of the records from Kenilworth may now be in Longleat, see below, pp. 311–12.

12 In the 1970s I did not have sufficient familiarity with the Close Rolls to appreciate that the filling of entire rolls with the deeds from one estate was unique.

13 As noted below, p. 67, n. 99, David Loades does not concur with this conclusion, but see my review of *Northumberland, Parliamentary History*, xvi (1997), 361–3. Given the scarcity of sources for this subject, one recent discovery deserves to be mentioned here. Among the more interesting of Leicester's clients (encountered regularly below) was the Norfolk lawyer William Grice (or Le Grice). His father Gilbert was a bailiff of Great Yarmouth with some connection to Northumberland. At the time chapter 8 appeared, J. D. Alsop published the records of a case brought by Gilbert Grice in the High Court of Admiralty in 1555, which reveal that he had been the commander of the ships that Northumberland sent to Lowestoft to stop Mary in 1553. See J. D. Alsop, 'A Regime at Sea: The Navy and the 1553 Succession Crisis', *Albion*, xxiv (1992), 577–90.

14 This issue has recently been approached from a different perspective by Diarmaid MacCulloch; see *Tudor Church Militant: Edward VI and the Protestant Reformation* (London, 1999), p. 185.

15 P. W. Hasler (ed.), *The History of Parliament: The House of Commons 1558–1603* (1981).

16 I shall be discussing this more fully in my forthcoming *The Road to Nonsuch: The Netherlands in Elizabethan Diplomacy 1575–85*.

17 'Etiquette and the Planning of State Apartments in Baroque Palaces', *Archaeologia*, ci (1967), 169–99. Starkey's views are most fully expressed in his introduction to *The English Court from the Wars of the Roses to the Civil War* (London, 1987).

18 The most recent attempt can be found in Stephen Alford, *The Early Elizabethan Polity: William Cecil and the British Succession Crisis, 1558–1569* (Cambridge, 1998), ch. 8, but this ignores the role of Don Guerau de Spes entirely.

19 M. M. Leimon, 'Sir Francis Walsingham and the Anjou Marriage Plan 1574–1581' (unpublished Cambridge Ph.D. thesis, 1989). See the references to this thesis in Susan Doran, *Monarchy and Matrimony: The Courtships of Elizabeth I* (1996), pp. 159–60, and Blair Worden, *The Sound of Virtue: Philip Sidney's Arcadia and Elizabethan Politics* (New Haven and London, 1996), chs 3–6. I shall be discussing the Anjou marriage in detail in my forthcoming *The Road to Nonsuch*.

20 See below, p. 93, n. 106.

21 An interesting approach to this problem can be found in Diarmaid MacCulloch's *Thomas Cranmer: A Life* (London, 1996). MacCulloch suggests that Henry VIII deliberately manipulated conservatives and evangelicals in order to maintain a middle ground for himself, see pp. 212, 216.

22 'The Anjou Match and the Making of Elizabethan Foreign Policy' in Peter Clark *et al.* (eds), *The English Commonwealth 1547–1640: Essays in Society and Politics* (Leicester, 1979), pp. 63–4.

23 Susan Doran discovered this important point; see *Monarchy and Matrimony*, p. 147. Owing to *lacunae* in the French sources (discussed in *The Road to Nonsuch*) the precise circumstances are not entirely clear. She also notes, quite accurately, that Burghley was distinctly unhappy about the conduct of the marriage negotiations, which completely undercuts Leimon's thesis, though several pages later she cites him with approval.

24 See below, p. 62.

Part I

The Elizabethan Court

Chapter 1

Faction, clientage and party: English politics, 1550–1603[a]

'FACTION', EITHER AS A NOUN OR IN its adjectival form 'factious', was one of the most over-used words in the Elizabethan political vocabulary. What was meant by it, on the other hand, was less clear. 'I have never loved or favoured factious dealing, nor have used it in my whole course of this action' declared Robert Dudley, Earl of Leicester, Chancellor of Oxford, in a letter to the convocation of the University in April 1577, defending (at great length) his role in the recent disputed election to the rectorship of Lincoln College. He went on to accuse two of the Fellows of having rigged the election for their personal advantage. The term was used in a similar sense by Sir Henry Sidney in 1572, when he stated that J.P.s should execute their offices 'uncorruptly without partiality or faction'. But it could also refer to a mere personal emnity or a refusal to co-operate: 'a very unsound and factious fellow' was how Leicester described the Cambridge don Everard Digby during the course of another University *cause célèbre* in 1588. At times it was used in something approaching the modern sense of a political alliance or following. In 1572 Thomas Digges argued that the delay in executing the Duke of Norfolk following his trial for treason 'augmenteth his well-willers and increaseth his faction'; a decade later Leicester considered that the recent revival of Catholicism had created 'a manifest faction in [the] realm'. Yet on other occasions, when we might have expected 'faction' to be used, Sir William Cecil would describe alliances and followings simply as 'friends'.

The widespread contemporary use of the term creates difficulties for the historian. 'Faction' clearly implied that personal advantage or connection were being placed above equity, a greater good, or straightforward behaviour. Faction was the dark side of the system of personal loyalties and dependence that the society prized so much. But when did an otherwise legitimate or even politically neutral connection become a faction, and an act of patronage become factious? Obviously, it was something one's opponents did: faction was a term of abuse, similar to the contemporary use of the word 'Puritan'. Just as few advanced Protestants accepted the description Puritan, so would few Elizabethan politicians have considered themselves as the leaders of factions.

For some years there has been a running debate over whether a broad or a narrow definition of a Puritan is the more accurate; the current interest in factional politics has, as Dr Starkey has suggested, raised similar questions about the use of 'faction'. There is a great danger of trivialising contemporary political disputes by considering them all to have been factional. Ultimately one must decide whether to use the term loosely or strictly. I shall argue here for a narrow definition. A faction was not the same thing as a clientage; nor was it the exercise of patronage; nor was it the taking of sides on a major political issue: a faction was a personal following employed in direct opposition to another personal following. A faction struggle could involve disputes over patronage or debate over matters of state, but its essence was a personal rivalry that over-rode all other considerations.

At the risk of appearing to explain the entire phenomenon away, I would argue further that there were only two periods in the later sixteenth century in which English politics was dominated by faction struggles: the middle years of Edward VI's reign (1548 to 1552) and the 1590s. Factional struggles occurred at these points for very specific reasons; and the factions involved were quite distinct from other forms of political and social association. Much of the confusion over the role of faction in Tudor politics has been caused by the fact that the relationship between Court politics and local politics underwent significant changes during the course of the sixteenth century. Dr Starkey has focused his article on the changing institutional structure of the Court of Henry VIII and the dramatic turnover in its personnel. In his portrait of faction-struggle at Court, the older picture of a battle between the crown and the territorial nobility, the 'overmighty subject' of legend, has completely diasappeared. Significantly, few of the greater noble families – the Howards provide the main exception – played much of a role in Court politics. The great families that fell foul of Henry VIII were a limited group: the Percies (for whom the Tudors entertained an undying suspicion – they were never able to do anything right), the northern families implicated in the Pilgrimage of Grace and those families who had the misfortune to possess royal blood: the Staffords, Courtenays and Poles. The great majority of noble families – the Stanleys, Earls of Derby, Talbots, Earls of Shrewsbury or Somerset, Earls of Worcester, for example – continued to rule in their 'countries'. The substructure of their territorial power – the loyalty and allegiance of the country gentlemen, who, in turn, acted as local magistrates and J.P.s – once known as 'bastard feudalism' also underwent little change. The earlier practice of retaining may have declined during the course of the century, but the underlying patron–client relationship remained intact.

The relative stability of the greater nobility was as much a part of Henrician politics as the tumult at Court. Provided that there was reasonably competent governance on the part of the crown, that their legitimate interests were safeguarded and that no attempt was made (as by Cardinal Wolsey on several occasions) to undercut them, the greater nobility were content to let the court run itself. Nor was their power a cause of instability in the regions. This was more likely to be the product either of two great families in a single county – Leicestershire, where the battles between the Greys and the Hastings can be traced from the 1550s to the Civil War, provides a classic example – or of the absence of noblemen of weight altogether. Thanks to the researches of Dr Alan Hassell Smith, we know a great deal about the politics of Elizabethan Norfolk and its bitter feuds and rivalries. Often overlooked, however (though not by Dr Smith), is that after the execution of the 4th Duke of Norfolk in 1572 the country was run solely by its gentry and could fairly be described as a gentry republic. Despite the traditional picture of the belligerent nobleman, the gentry were as much, if not more, to blame for instability as the nobility: the tail very often wagged the dog. The origins of the early Tudor concern with retaining, livery and maintenance lay not so much in the fear of noble factions as in the danger that personal disputes among the gentry would be settled by the intervention of noblemen, obliged to maintain their reputations as lords and patrons, rather than by process of law.

During the second half of the sixteenth century this pattern of politics became increasingly transformed by the Protestant Reformation. On the one hand the self-identification of Protestants as 'the godly' created a new type of social allegiance, while at the same time Protestantism tended to reduce the differing degrees of the ruling society into a single class of 'magistrates', who were all expected to execute their offices in the advancement of God's cause. The Court, council and parliament took on a new importance, for they now became the means through which a godly policy would be formulated. Who would define God's cause in a given situation was a moot point, but there emerged a novel pressure group of Protestant divines and evangelical laymen more than willing to give kings and magistrates advice. A new type of client – the ideologically committed – was created, and the danger of the nobleman being led by his followers took on a new significance. The evangelical impact was first felt during the reign of Edward VI. The Dukes of Somerset and Northumberland were barraged by sermons from Hugh Latimer and other popular preachers. At the time of his overthrow in October 1549, Somerset was considered to have been led into unsound policies by a group of evangelical intellectuals. Northumberland was faced with the thankless task of trying to resolve the growing tension in the church between Archbishop Cranmer and hot gospellers like John Hooper and John Knox.

During the reign of Elizabeth the now 'Puritan' pressure group became far more active and there was real danger of the magistrate losing control entirely. The Puritan lawyer Robert Snagge made the first open parliamentary attack on the Church Settlement of 1559 in the House of Commons in 1572; at the time he was also the Earl of Leicester's steward at Kenilworth. It is extremely doubtful that Snagge was following Leicester's instructions; rather, the incident shows that even Leicester could not fully control his own household servants. What strengthened the position of the advanced Protestants was the further fact that the Reformation had also introduced a new definition of loyalty – 'soundness in religion' – and they could thereby wrap themselves in the flag of being the Queen's most loyal subjects.

Under this new pressure the nature of aristocratic clientages began to change and they became more openly religious in orientation, a trend which was increased by the tendency of Protestants to intermarry. The followings of both Somerset and Northumberland in the 1540s and 1550s already possessed a markedly evangelical bias. During the reign of Mary, the tensions created by the Queen's decision to embark on the active persecution of heretics brought the system of religiously neutral clientages to the breaking point. The story of how Sir John Perrot came to blows with his patron, the Earl of Pembroke, over his refusal to enforce the statutes against heresy may be apocryphal; but the grovelling letter of Sir Thomas Gargrave to his patron the Earl of Shrewsbury, apologising for voting against the crown's bill for confiscating the lands of exiles in 1555, survives. The process quickened during Elizabeth's reign. By the 1580s, Leicester's clientage, originally inherited from his father, was beginning to adopt something of a party ethos; loyalty to the Earl himself was increasingly overshadowed by his identification with the cause. In 1581 the fervent Puritan Sir Richard Knightley informed him that

> you have lightened many a godly man's heart and I am sure you have thereby gotten you such friends as would be ready to venture their lives with your lordship in a good cause, even such as would not do it so much in respect of your high calling, as for that they espy in your lordship a zeal and care for the helping and relieving of the poor church.

The impact of these changes in the broader context of politics was, in turn, very much conditioned by significant transformations in the structure of the court during the reigns of Edward VI, Mary and Elizabeth. These made it very difficult to play one part of the Court off against another and prevented it from becoming the battleground for religiously-based factions. Most deeply affected was the Privy Chamber, which ceased to be an independent political body. During the reign of Edward VI its composition reflected the balance of power in the council. During the reigns of Mary and Elizabeth its personnel were largely female, occasionally reflecting outside male influences, but incapable of acting as political figures in their own right. Important changes also occurred in the relationship between the household and the council. As we know from Dr Dale Hoak's work, the Edwardian council ruled supreme in a way that it had neither before nor has since. Mary and Elizabeth, on the other hand, had extensive experience in running independent households as princesses. It is not surprising that, when they came to the throne, the personnel of their princely households became the core of the royal household. The household, as a body of trusted intimate servants and friends, retained a continued importance.

The continued importance of the household had a significant effect on the role of the council. Since the emergence of the Privy Council in the early decades of the sixteenth century, household and council had overlapped, for a substantial proportion of councillors were always household officers. But in Mary's reign there was a distinct difference between her relationship to such household officers as Sir Robert Rochester and Sir Henry Jerningham and the leading officers of state. The latter were mainly former Henrician and Edwardian councillors, whom she never really liked nor trusted. This was particularly the case with the most active of the officers of state, William, Lord Paget. The tension between household and council was widely observed; but, while there were major personal clashes and disputes over policy, factional struggles did not result. In part this was due to Philip II's desire to mediate the disputes in the interests of stability; but it was also the case that the major political issues of the reign (the Habsburg marriage and alliance and the attack on heresy) cut across institutional boundaries.

For the greater part of Elizabeth's reign this potential tension was resolved, whether by accident or design, through her reliance upon men who were both leading household officers and major political figures. The central position was held by Sir William Cecil, Secretary of State until 1572 and then Lord Treasurer, who combined the roles of household servant (he had first been appointed to her household in 1550) and principal administrator. Moreover, Cecil never attempted to convert the secretaryship into an independent power-base but exercised it very much in household terms. His well-known refusal to come down decisively on major issues was in part due to his desire to act as the Queen's advisor and mouthpiece rather than as a policy-maker like Wolsey or Cromwell. But Cecil was not the only key figure: Leicester too combined personal intimacy, household office and a significant political role. The traditional picture of Leicester as a courtier-adventurer who rose to great heights through the Queen's misguided affection is based on a fundamental misconception. From the earliest years of the reign he was the inheritor of his father's following, and it was this that gave significance to his position as intimate and potential consort. Throughout the first three decades of the reign (until Leicester's death in 1588) the relationship between Cecil, Leicester and the Queen remained more or less unchanged. In the mid-1570s Sir Francis Walsingham, Sir Christopher Hatton and, until his death in 1583, the 3rd Earl of Sussex became part of this inner ring, although Cecil and Leicester remained the most important councillors. The existence of a stable inner ring deprived the council as a body of decisive influence, as was revealed by the failure of attempts to play the council off against the Queen (most notably by Mr Secretary Davison over the execution of Mary, Queen of Scots, in 1587). Conciliar votes counted for little: policy was made by the Queen in consultation with her intimates.

As a result, faction on the council was not an issue; nor did it really appear in the Court itself (if we except hostile comments on Leicester or Cecil). The true courtiers of the reign – men who rose from obscurity through royal favour alone – were Hatton and Sir Walter Ralegh. Neither possessed more than a microscopic following; their positions were purely individual ones. Sussex might have played the role of faction leader, and may briefly have tried to in 1565, but in the main he too possessed a very small following. The Duke of Norfolk was perhaps in the strongest position to do so, for he possessed a regional base, a wide aristocratic connection and the prestige of his house. However, to the despair of those who, like the Spanish ambassadors, wanted him to take up the leadership of a conservative alliance, Norfolk, until his last years, was not really interested in high politics and preferred a domestic life. A widespread conservative coalition was certainly in the making in 1568–69, but Norfolk's indecision prevented it from rallying under his banner and the most vulnerable members, the Northern Earls, were left to rise in rebellion alone.

Any serious discussion of faction at Elizabeth's Court in this period must, therefore, revolve around the question of whether the relationship between Leicester and Cecil was a factional one. Sir John Neale certainly believed it was, but in his essay *The Elizabethan Political Scene* all he could produce in the way of evidence were a few comments from that notoriously unreliable libel *Leicester's Commonwealth*. Indeed, most of his evidence for faction at all was drawn from the 1590s. The relationship between the two was certainly a complicated one. There were serious political disagreements – over Elizabeth's marriage, over the fate of Mary, Queen of Scots, in 1568–69 and over foreign policy in the later 1570s and 1580s – although in the main they agreed over the broader aims of a Protestant policy. Neither may have liked the other greatly, but the evidence for warm and sympathetic relations is more substantial than generally acknowledged. The evidence for Leicester's attempt to overthrow Cecil at the beginning of 1569 is suspect and must be regarded with scepticism. In recent years there has been a tendency to see a difference over religious policy, with Cecil patronising the conformists and Leicester the Puritan radicals, but the distinction has been very much overdrawn. Many of Leicester's clerical protégés proceeded to impeccably respectable careers, while Cecil can be found patronising such men as the former separatist Robert Browne and the presbyterian theorist Walter Travers.

More significantly, there is little evidence for competing patronage, whether lay or clerical, at any level. Both men acted as patrons to the same broad body of advanced Protestants. 'In these cases I take you to be as one' wrote Henry Killigrew, a life-long Dudley partisan and Cecil's future brother-in-law, to Dudley in 1562. The relationship had its symbiotic elements. Cecil may have been at the centre of the administration but he lacked noble rank and a wider connection. This Leicester provided. Only by the 1580s, did the relationship undergo something of a transformation. After he entered the peerage himself as Baron of Burghley in 1571, Cecil appears to have changed his view of his own position. More importantly, the extended debate over intervention in the Netherlands polarised opinion and Cecil appears to have acted as a protector for those who opposed it, while Leicester championed the interventionist cause.

The tensions in the Cecil–Dudley relationship do not, however, add up to a factional conflict and the distinction becomes apparent when the real faction-struggles are examined. Edward VI's reign contains many still unexplained political events: chief amongst them is the origin of the factional struggle between Edward Seymour, Duke of Somerset, and the future Duke of Northumberland, then Earl of Warwick, between 1549 and 1551. Recent research has made clear the disagreements between Somerset and the more conservative councillors in 1549: the disasters attending his foreign policy, the bankrupting of the crown, his liberal religious policy, apparent tolerance of peasant rebellion and high-handed mannner of government. Less understandable was why Warwick, who shared Somerset's religious views and was an old friend (as one contemporary put it, 'being fellows together with the Cardinal and after was made knights in France'), joined in the *coup* against him. Whether or not Warwick had, as some contemporaries alleged, been plotting against the Seymours for some time, by 1549 there is evidence of personal antagonism and disputes over patronage.

The faction-struggle proper, however, followed on Somerset's release in 1550. Despite an attempt to repair the breach by a marriage between his daughter and Warwick's heir, Somerset was intent on revenge. Following the discovery of evidence that Somerset was planning a *coup*, Warwick made a preemptive strike which resulted in Somerset's trial and execution for felony in January 1552. The evidence for Somerset's attempted *coup* reveals the depths of the struggle, for it involved not only the creation of a faction against Warwick (which may have included plans for Somerset to exploit his popularity in the City of London) but also the use of the next parliament to call him to account. Warwick in turn was prepared to fabricate a capital charge against his rival, to which he confessed on the eve of his own execution in 1553 and, to clear his conscience, requested forgiveness from Somerset's sons. This posthumous element was not a formality, for despite Northumberland's attempts to win over Somerset's former followers (William Cecil, for example), many of them remained either openly unreconciled or, in his own moment of crisis in 1553, stood on the sidelines or defected to Mary.

The vendetta to some degree split the leadership of Edwardian Protestantism and showed signs of continuing into Elizabeth's reign. One of Elizabeth's first acts was to restore Somerset's son to his father's earldom of Hertford, and about him soon rallied the core of the surviving Seymour faction. A second round of the Dudley–Seymour feud might have resulted had not Hertford destroyed his chances of retaining royal favour by his un- or ill-advised marriage to Lady Catherine Grey in the winter of 1560–61. His fall left the Seymour partisans leaderless and by the later 1560s most of them are found in Leicester's following. One such was the future Sir William Pelham, who left England to enter the service of the Regent of the Netherlands after Somerset's second arrest, and later warned Mary against Northumberland. After an active military career under Elizabeth, he died in 1587 as one of the Earl's 'very good friends' and marshal of the camp to his army in the Netherlands.

The course of the faction-struggle of the 1590s is easier to follow. Its origins lay in the attempt of Robert Devereux, Earl of Essex, to take over Leicester's mantle as leader of the interventionist party. On Leicester's death, the well-known Puritan Sir Francis Hastings had urged him to

> employ your whole forces both in honour and credit to advance God's truth . . . Now is the time come wherein you should put this in practice, in that He hath taken from us that honourable worthy gentleman, whom He used many times as a notable instrument.

About him rallied the former Leicesterians, partly out of personal loyalty and partly out of loyalty to the cause. As Sir Robert Sidney (Sir Philip's younger brother) put it,

> For though I were in no way tied unto you for your own particular favours, as long as you have these ends you now have, you cannot separate me from following your course.

But Essex lacked the confidence of the Queen, and she and Burghley (who shared a deeply engrained suspicion of military over-extension) regarded sceptically his proposals for an offensive strategy on the continent. The failure of the Rouen campaign of 1591–92, in which Essex commanded the

English contingent, marked the turning point of his career. He believed the failure to be due to lack of support at home or even, in his darker moments, deliberate sabotage. His response was to seek to take control of the Court in order to provide himself with a firmer political base in the future. After 1593 he challenged every major Court appointment: patronage became a factional issue. He met with almost total failure, which caused him to redouble his efforts, for patronage now became a demonstration of influence irrespective of the importance of the office. Local office also became the subject of his attentions and for the first time in Elizabeth's reign local disputes became closely linked to a factional contest at Court. The patronage disputes also changed the complexion of the factions, for the pressure on office-holders created a pro-Cecilian alliance of 'ins', while Essex's following became something of a coalition of 'outs'.

By 1598–99 he had both split the Court (though his following there was a clear minority) and created two factions whose influence had spread deep into the country. But any remaining hopes he may have had of winning the struggle were effectively destroyed by his ill-advised return from Ireland in 1599. The near total destruction of his influence led him to plot his *coup d'état* against Sir Robert Cecil; but at the same time it caused the more substantial members of his faction, particularly the old Leicesterians like Sidney, Lord Willoughby D'Eresby or Sir William Russell, to stand back. In 1599 Sidney was warned by one of his own clients that he was regarded at Court as having been 'for many year most inward and great in all secrecies and factiously great with the Earl of Essex . . . you are not to be trusted'. The *coup* was mounted by only a rump of his old faction: a handful of personal intimates, like the Earl of Southampton, and former army officers who had nowhere else to turn.

Despite the fifty years that separated them, there are basic similarities between the two faction struggles. Both involved deep personal emnities, the creating of personal factions, and the attempt to rally the country against the court. Like Somerset, Essex counted heavily on his popularity in the city of London (which played an important role in his plans for the *coup d'état*). He may also have hoped to employ parliament in the struggle. He certainly engaged in extensive borough-mongering, but occasion did not serve, for the only parliamentary session he might have employed occurred in 1597 when he was embarked on the expedition to the Azores. Like Somerset, Essex enjoyed a posthumous continuation of his popularity and the aura of having been unfairly, and through faction, put to death. The Essex faction also survived. Ralegh's notorious advice to Robert Cecil to remove Essex entirely while he had the chance and not fear a future vendetta was, like much of Ralegh's advice, very wide of the mark. The reverberations of the Essex–Cecil feud continued long into the reign of James I – in 1613 Southampton was still trying to rally men through the use of Essex's name. Of this second phase, Ralegh, as the outcome of the Bye Plot of 1604 showed, was himself to be the first victim.

Perhaps the most significant parallel between Somerset and Essex, however, is found in their attitude towards the crown. They went to the block for having attempted *coups* against rivals, not against the crown directly. This distinguishes them from Norfolk, who was executed for a treasonable conspiracy against the crown itself. But the mere fact that they could expect to succeed in such a *coup* also reflects a weakness in royal leadership. In Somerset's case there was a boy king, who could be won over, in Essex's case Elizabeth's failure to make clear to him the limits of her tolerance encouraged him to believe that he might turn her against the Cecils. The weakness of the crown also explains the survival of factional struggles into the seventeenth century. The periods most dominated by faction, the reign of James I or the first decades of the Restoration, were precisely those in which the king was either indecisive or sufficiently ambiguous in his politics and in his relationship to his ministers to encourage a belief that a factional victory was possible.

By contrast, both Mary, and Elizabeth during the first three decades of her reign, were sufficiently stable in their personal relationships to discourage factional contests. The role of the weakness of the crown in factional struggles also provides the best counter to the argument that it was endemic. Clientages or party battles over issues were not in themselves factious, nor were gentry quarrels. In neither of the great sixteenth-century factional struggles were party issues of major importance; by the same token the semi-party association created under Leicester and Cecil was not of itself factious. Faction may have been widely considered a disease of the body politic, but it was a disease with very specific causes.

NOTES

a This chapter was originally the second in a four-part series on faction in Tudor and Stuart England. The first in the series was David Starkey, 'From Feud to Faction: English Politics *c.* 1450–1550', *History Today*, xxxii (Nov. 1982), 16–22, to which reference is made on p. 14.

FURTHER READING

There are two excellent, if occasionally conflicting, studies of the politics of the reign of Edward VI: M. L. Bush, *The Government Policy of Protector Somerset* (Edward Arnold, 1975), and Dale Hoak, *The King's Council in the Reign of Edward VI* (Cambridge University Press, 1976). Extensive and up-to-date surveys of the reigns of Mary and Elizabeth (to 1588) are provided by D. M. Loades, *The Reign of Mary Tudor* (Ernest Benn, 1979), and Wallace T. MacCaffrey, *The Shaping of the Elizabethan Regime* (Princeton University Press and Jonathan

Cape, 1969) and *Queen Elizabeth and the Making of Policy, 1572–1588* (Princeton University Press, 1981). A. Hassell Smith, *County and Court: Government and Politics in Norfolk, 1558–1603* (Oxford University Press, 1974), is a first-rate local study, while Peter Clark, *English Provincial Society from the Reformation to the Revolution: Religion, Politics and Society in Kent, 1500–1640* (Harvester Press, 1977), contains valuable chapters on the later sixteenth century. The author has published a study of one aspect of the Earl of Leicester's clientage, 'The Gentry of north Wales and the Earl of Leicester's Expedition to the Netherlands, 1585–86' [Ch. 12] and has others in preparation.

Chapter 2

———◆———

Eliza enthroned? The Court
and its politics[1]

It is one of the curiosities of recent Elizabethan scholarship that the local-
ities have received much more attention than either the Court or the central
government. While counties and towns have been the subject of an impressive series of sophisticated monographs, research on the Court has stag-
nated. The standard account of its institutional structure was written by Sir
Edmund Chambers some sixty years ago as an introduction to his work on
the Elizabethan stage: since then we have had only the valuable, yet impress-
ionistic, essays of Sir John Neale, Professor Wallace MacCaffrey, Professor
G. R. Elton and, most recently, Dr Penry Williams. Lacking is either the
major survey of its personnel that Professor G. E. Aylmer has provided for
the reign of Charles I, or the sustained analysis of its institutions that Dr
David Starkey has undertaken for the earlier Tudors.

The politics of the Court retain, therefore, an enigmatic quality. Many key
episodes – the approaches made by Lord Robert Dudley and Elizabeth to
Philip II in 1561, the attempted overthrow of Sir William Cecil in 1569,
Leicester's acceptance of the governor-generalship of the Netherlands in 1585,
or Essex's return from Ireland in 1599, to cite but a few examples – still
await adequate explanation. Most accounts of the Court have tended to emphasise factional strife and a vicious atmosphere of place-seeking, enmity
and competition surrounding an alternatively goddess-like or hag-like queen.
It has been easy to paint the picture in the most lurid colours. Yet, as I have
suggested elsewhere, much of the evidence for factional strife has been drawn
from the 1590s and by no means reflects the reality of the previous decades.
The Court was never completely free from conflict, but such conflict was less
the product of faction among courtiers than of disputes between an able,
charming, yet imperious and idiosyncratic queen, and councillors and intimates who generally shared a high degree of social, political and cultural
homogeneity. Whatever Elizabeth may have desired, even her closest servants

could not be isolated from outside pressures, whether the more immediate ones of family or clients, or those arising from the wider concerns of the post-Reformation world. Our primary concern here will be, therefore, to assess the impact of such tensions on political dynamics of the Court. It is to its institutions and personnel that we should turn first; then to the social and political composition of its membership; and finally to a more specific examination of its relationship to the Queen.

I

'The Court', declared Sir James Croft (Comptroller of the Household, 1570–90) in 1583, 'is divided into two governments, the Chamber and the Household'. It is similarly described in the only full source for its permanent membership, the surviving subsidy assessments of the Household.[2] The ambiguous nature of this description becomes apparent, however, when it is observed that not only were two other major departments – the Stables and the Privy Chamber – subsumed within the Chamber and the Household, but also such civil servants as the Principal Secretaries of State, the clerks of the Council, the signet and the privy seal, and the French and Latin secretaries were included among the members of the Chamber. There are fundamental difficulties in defining the boundaries of the Court, and a clear distinction between the courtier and the bureaucrat is almost impossible to draw.

Further ambiguities emerge when the more mundane aspects of the Court's domestic economy are considered. Overall expenditure ranged between £70,000 and £90,000 a year, but further accuracy is almost impossible. The spending of certain departments varied from year to year, each department accounted separately to the Exchequer, and certain minor items such as the annuities of the gentlemen pensioners or the annual Christmas present of £100 to the grooms of the Chamber were paid by the Exchequer directly.[3] Furthermore, it is particularly difficult to assess the overall impact of the Crown's various economy drives: a steady inflation-led increase in expenditure should not be assumed. The largest department was the Household, presided over by the Board of Green Cloth or Compting House. It received a statutory annual assignment of £40,027 in 1563, but its expenditure rose from £45,000–50,000 a year in the first half of the reign to £50,000–60,000 at the end. The largest part (usually in excess of £40,000 per annum) was taken up by the diets provided for those in attendance, bouge of court, and the wages of the Household and Privy Chamber.[4] Second in rank was the Chamber, whose Treasurer received annual assignments of about £15,000, from which he paid the wages of members of the Chamber, the Yeomen of the Guard and such miscellaneous servants as the Queen's boatmen, mole-

and ratcatcher, together with her alms and the expenses of messengers and diplomatic couriers.[5] For the third great department, the Stables, there are no surviving accounts prior to 1638, but its running-costs cannot have been less than £5000 per annum.[6] Lesser departments – the Wardrobe, the Revels or the Works – spent more erratically: the expenses of the Wardrobe, for example, depended very much on the ceremonial engaged in during the year. Finally there was the Privy Purse, of which the account of only one of its two keepers – John Tamworth (1559–69) – survives. He received a total of £26,675 and disbursed £26,701. His functions, however, were still undefined: apart from providing for items of immediate personal use – the Queen's lute-strings for example – Tamworth occasionally paid wages within the Privy Chamber, and once channelled a loan of £5000 to the Earl of Moray.[7]

The Household was the largest regular spending-department of the Crown, and its expenses were the subject of constant review by Queen and Council. Economy campaigns took place at regular intervals, but particularly in 1564, 1569, 1576, 1582–83, 1589–90, 1598 and 1602. The primary targets were its basic running-costs, especially the diets and bouge of court. Both the Household officers and Lord Burghley appreciated that inflation was making an impact upon the price of foodstuffs, but the Queen was less easy to convince. At the end of 1602 she claimed to her Clerk Comptroller that the increase in Household expenditure was primarily due to excessive dining at her expense:

> I was never in all my government so royally with numbers of noble men and ladies attended upon, as in the beginning of my reign . . . and all those then satisfied with my allowance. . . . And shall these that now attend and have the like allowance not rest contented? I will not suffer this dishonourable spoil and increases that no prince before me did, to the offence of God and great grievance of my loving subjects. . . .[8]

The issue had, however, been repeatedly discussed in the past. The book of diets had been drawn up in 1560, and extensive comparisons with current costs (together with those of the reign of Henry VIII) made in 1576, 1583 and 1591. In 1576 it was observed that the annual cost of diets exceeded the authorised scales by £6000, and in 1583 Croft reported that the annual expenditure on food and other commodities had risen by £10,000–12,000 since the beginning of the reign. Moreover, despite the increased cost of living, the wages of the ordinary staff had been frozen, which had led to exploitation and embezzlement. Only the Yeoman of the Guard and the Stables staff are known to have received any increase in wages during the course of the reign.[9] The quality of the food served in the Hall did not help: 'for almost few or none in this house . . . likes their ordinary diet, for that they are grown to such delicacy that no meat will serve them but that which cometh from her Majesty's board'. The result was much dining in private chambers on food from the Queen's kitchens, while Hall food was wasted. The reforms that Lord Burghley proposed, however, verge on the comical: he wished to see room service terminated at eight o'clock, a halt to the filling of private bottles at the Buttery and measures to prevent the removal of the Queen's crockery from the Hall.[10]

Yet two more significant problems were less easy to remedy. The first was that the Queen herself, whatever her fussing, was the chief offender. Her own diets had increased more than anyone else's, while she was primarily responsible for another major source of expense: the annual summer progress.[11] Elizabeth did not invent the royal progress, but she always enjoyed playing to the crowd and she employed progresses in a striking manner. The impact on the nobility and gentry has been the subject of much recent comment. Less noted (except by Dr David Palliser) has been the fact that each progress usually contained at least one entry into a major corporate town. There she would be greeted by cheering, if well staged, crowds: to them, as at Worcester in 1574, she responded 'with a heartiness that did her honour, [and] threw up her cap and said "I say God save you all, my good people"'.[12] The cost of transporting the Court fell on the Crown: in 1576 Burghley noted that the last 'overlong progress' had cost an extra £2000, and he also complained of the expense incurred through the Queen's frequent changes of itinerary. It is probable that attempts to economise on progresses lay behind their relatively limited range (one to York was certainly planned in 1574 and 1575), and their suspension between 1580 and 1589.[13]

II

'Hard to be observed' was Burghley's comment on possible solutions to the other great problem of the Court economy: lack of control over the numbers living there, particularly the servants of noblemen and gentlemen in attendance. The reiteration of this complaint was a reflection of the fact that the Court was (to paraphrase Conrad Russell's now-famous description of Parliament) almost as much an event as an institution, and that its population fluctuated from week to week. At the centre of the Court were the Queen's servants, who swore an oath to her and took her wages. Yet (in the absence of the archives of most of the major Court officers) they are difficult to identify with assurance.[14] While the Household subsidy assessments provide the best overall guide, we possess an annual record of the permanent waged members of only one department, the still-mysterious Privy Chamber. But even this does not establish its full membership. The waged servants of the Privy Chamber consisted of a limited body of women, ladies or chamberers, of whom the four senior were known as the Bedchamber, and a smaller group of men, either gentlemen or grooms. Yet we know of a further group of women – among them Lady Mary Sidney, Anne, Countess of Warwick, and the two marchionesses of Northampton – who did not receive wages, but were also members of the Privy Chamber, personally close to Elizabeth and in frequent attendance. Of these women, however, there is only one complete list: the Coronation roll of 1559, which identifies them either as 'the Privy Chamber without wages', or 'extraordinary of the Privy Chamber, when the queen's majesty calleth for them'.[15]

On a more significant level, the composition of the Court remains difficult to define because its structure was still fluid and determined more by certain idiosyncrasies of the Queen than by any formal hierarchy. It is true that Elizabeth made only minor changes in Court organisation – distinguishing the Bedchamber from the Privy Chamber in 1559 and abolishing the Henchmen in 1565 – but this static structure reveals little about the actual functioning of the Court.[16] Nor does the book of officers and fees, often cited in the past, provide an accurate guide to its personnel: it is simply a copy of the Edwardian survey of 1552 made in 1576–78.[17] A central defining idiosyncrasy was the Queen's extremely conservative attitude towards office and rank, which can be seen very clearly in her reluctance to expand the peerage. Equally conservative was the composition of the Court. In its lower posts the Household possessed a recognised internal system of promotion (to the level of cofferer) and there was an established body of Household families whose position Elizabeth did little to disrupt. The same also appears to have been the case with the personnel of the Chamber and such attached bodies as the gentlemen pensioners: the one Elizabethan esquire of the body whose career has been studied – Roger Manners – had been appointed by Mary.[18] Among the senior personnel, there was only one purge of significance, and that followed Elizabeth's accession in 1558.[19] Thereafter men and women served until removed by death or incapacity. New blood entered only when vacancies were created, and the Court aged steadily with the Queen. The key to the process was Elizabeth's use of office as a reward rather than as a means of advancement: service was not dependent on office-holding so much as award of office followed on years of service. Croft could therefore defend the private sale of a recently awarded Household office on the ground that, since the recipient had obtained his reward, it did not matter in which form he received the benefit. Men such as Charles Howard of Effingham and Thomas Sackville, sons of councillors and major office-holders, spent long years at Court before receiving any significant office themselves. Moreover, Elizabeth's loyalty to 'old servants' (whether her own or those of her father, mother and brother) was pronounced, although it was also a widely respected social convention. Thus Bishop Cox was told in the midst of his disputes with Lord

North in 1575 that 'she hath borne with me and put up with many complaints against me, in consideration of my age and for that I was her father's and brother's servant'.[20]

The static nature of the Court was further compounded by Elizabeth's tendency to leave offices vacant or held jointly by one person for long periods of time. The most striking instance was the vacancy in the Secretariat between the death of Sir Francis Walsingham in 1590 and the appointment of Sir Robert Cecil in 1596, but further examples are plentiful. No Lord Privy Seal was appointed throughout the reign, while the mastership of the Court of Wards was granted to a favoured existing office-holder: in turn, Sir Thomas Parry, Sir William Cecil and Sir Robert Cecil. Sir Francis Knollys, Sir Thomas Heneage and Sir John Stanhope all combined at some stage the offices of Vice Chamberlain and Treasurer of the Chamber, while Knollys and Sir Christopher Hatton combined the vice-chamberlaincy and the captaincy of the guard. Walsingham, Heneage (possibly the greatest pluralist of the lot) and Sir John Fortescue all held the chancellorship of the Duchy of Lancaster in conjunction with another office. Lord Stewards were rarely appointed: Leicester (1584–88) alone made any impact on the Household, and his reforms were limited by his simultaneous employment as Master of the Horse and Captain-General in the Netherlands.[21]

The consequences of the system were significant. First, competition for a tightly restricted range of offices became an issue in its own right and the Queen's parsimony with office as well as land and money was repeatedly commented upon. Secondly, a vast gap was created between those, such as Burghley, Leicester, Hatton and – on a lesser scale – Heneage, who received the full benefit of the Queen's favour and those who did not. For most servants reward took the form of grants that did not place a direct burden upon the Queen's purse: customs concessions or farms, wardships, leases in reversion, and a variety of licences were most commonly employed. In the late 1570s patents and monopolies became favoured. As their use expanded, such grants became increasingly controversial and by the 1590s were very much a public issue.[22]

A further consequence of the structure of the Court was the effect on its relationship with the Privy Council. Elizabeth's privy councillors fall into three distinct groups: the major officers of the Household, the major officers of state, and a more amorphous body of men not holding office of importance. For those in the first two categories appointment to the Council was practically *ex officio*: only the two masters of the Horse, Dudley and Essex, had to wait several years for membership. Other offices – the captaincy of the guard, or the regional lord presidencies, for example – did not involve automatic membership of the Council. In some cases appointment to the Council followed; but this was not (as with Sir Henry Sidney or the Earl of Warwick) necessarily a consequence of the office held. There was, therefore, always a group of men prominent at Court who were not members of the Council, while some councillors, particularly in the first decade, were hardly important men at Court (Dr Nicholas Wotton and Sir William Petre fall into this category). Only one leading Court figure – Sir Walter Ralegh – was never appointed to the Council, but several had to wait for some time: the Duke of Norfolk was not appointed until 1562, the Earl of Sussex until 1570, Hatton until 1577, and Heneage until 1587.

These considerations therefore raise the very important question of how far the politics of the Court were subsumed within those of the Council. The Council clearly regarded consideration of matters of state and the Queen's business as its concern. Burghley was very unhappy about public discussion of affairs of state within the Court, while Leicester warned Francis Walsingham in 1573 not to discuss his negotiations in France with others 'being no councillors'.[23] Yet the Council had no power to enforce its monopoly and its success in so doing lay in the fact that within it there was a distinct inner ring of councillors who were also the leading members of the Court. The key figures were Burghley and Leicester. Burghley's genius lay in his ability to expand his position as the Queen's man of business to approach in stature the great ministers of Henry VIII. His power did not come from his offices; rather, his personal relationship to the Queen extended their potential functions. Unlike his predecessor as Lord Treasurer, he did not operate within a relatively restricted sphere. Burghley displayed little hesitation in supervising the reform of the Household, an area where Winchester, in common with other officers, was markedly reluctant to intervene.[24]

Yet Burghley's pre-eminence was not total. Until 1588 it was always limited by the influence of Leicester, and it is revealing that the clashes between them arose in the main from Leicester's resentment of Burghley's monopolistic tendencies.[25] Yet a sustained struggle for power was prevented by their similar outlook in religion and agreement on most matters of state, together with a mutual appreciation of their joint intimacy with the Queen. About them existed a group of councillors who were clearly more deeply involved in matters of state than others, and who can legitimately be characterised as an inner ring. Once again office was of less significance than personal relationships both to each other and to the Queen. During the 1560s the inner ring included Sir Thomas Parry (until his death in December 1560) and, intermittently, Sir Nicholas Bacon, Winchester and Pembroke. From the mid 1570s to the end of the 1580s the pre-eminent members (together with Leicester and Burghley) were Walsingham, Hatton and (until his death in 1583) Sussex. At the end of the reign the key councillors were clearly Robert Cecil, Buckhurst and Nottingham.[26] Only in the mid 1590s was the composition of the inner ring in any real dispute; and it was on this issue that the great faction fight between Essex and Cecil centred, a struggle which was fought out in both Court and Council.

III

The tightly restricted nature of the Court's inner circle and its close relationship to the structure of power within the Council raise several important questions about its composition and recruitment. Was it as representative of the nobility and upper gentry as Professor Elton and Dr Williams have suggested? Was it a meeting-place for divergent views and interests? Was there, as Dr MacCulloch and Dr Williams have proposed, 'more than one road to Westminster'?[27] Such a picture of the Court rests, however, on the assumption that there was a fairly constant balance of factions there throughout the reign, which in turn permitted a certain religious diversity. This assumption should not be accepted uncritically: a more complex situation is revealed when we examine the relationship between changes in personnel and major political debates of the day. The most dramatic aspect of the post-accession purge of the Court was the transformation of Elizabeth's previous household. On her accession, Elizabeth's servants and friends were already a well-defined and closely knit group, as the frequent references to her 'old servants' and the 'old flock of Hatfield' make clear.[28] As had been the case on Mary's accession, the women became the new Privy Chamber and the men received their reward in appointment as officers of the Court and Household: Sir Thomas Parry as Treasurer of the Household and Master of the Court of Wards, Sir Thomas Benger as Master of the Revels, Sir William St Loe as Captain of the Guard, Sir John Fortescue as Master of the Wardrobe, and John Ashley as Master of the Jewels. The creation of the new Privy Council was a more complicated process. The Council in 1559 consisted of nine (originally eleven) former Marian councillors and nine new men, several of whom had previously served on the Council of Edward VI. The surviving Marians had also been councillors of Edward, but, more importantly, they appear to have intervened on Elizabeth's behalf at some point in Mary's reign. This was clearly the case with the one Marian Household officer – Sir John Mason (Treasurer of the Chamber, 1557–66) – to be retained in post.[29] The new men were a more disparate body, but the majority were either members of her household, relatives, or men with an existing personal connection. There is only one apparent exception: the former member of Edward VI's Privy Chamber, Sir Edward Rogers (Vice Chamberlain and then Comptroller of the Household to 1568), the nature of whose earlier association with Elizabeth remains unclear.

Both Court and Council were thus bound to the new queen by direct personal ties, an aspect of the Court which was to remain a constant feature throughout the reign. Yet such connections could not fully resist the impact of political debate. The first cracks appeared in 1559. Two members of the Council (Winchester and Shrewsbury) voted against the Act of Uniformity and several (Winchester again, Arundel, Sir Nicholas Bacon, Petre, Wotton and Mason) opposed the intervention in Scotland, although only Arundel remained adamant. The Queen began to conduct her affairs with the assistance of the inner ring (Cecil, Parry and, possibly, Dudley), a course which drew further complaint from the excluded councillors. Conciliar opposition to the Queen's policies in turn provoked criticism from the more radical Protestants.[30] At this stage the radical wing of the Protestant laity was composed of former Edwardians, who sought restoration to office lost in 1553, the settling of old scores with their political enemies, and a more actively Protestant policy. They looked for leadership to Cecil and Dudley, the son of their old patron. For reasons that have never been entirely clear, a number of the older Edwardians (Sir Peter Carew, Sir William Pickering and Sir Nicholas Throckmorton, for example) did not receive the offices they might have expected, but the younger men soon became diplomatic agents and officers of the major military operations, beginning with the Newhaven Voyage of 1562 and Sir Henry Sidney's expedition to Ireland in 1566.[31] Simultaneously, age took its toll, particularly among the former Marian councillors, while others retired from the Court. Arundel resigned as Lord Steward in 1564, while Petre stopped attending the Council in 1567. The Crown also carried out one further purge: the removal of the Percies and the northern nobility from offices of military or political importance, undercutting their local power base in the process. A more difficult problem was posed by the Duke of Norfolk, who preferred a domestic life to that of the Court, but expected deference to his rank and disliked the trend of Elizabeth's policies. His promotion to the Privy Council (though not to major office) simultaneously with Dudley in the autumn of 1562 was engineered by Cecil – despite the Queen's reservations – probably as an act of pacification when Norfolk opposed the expedition to Newhaven.[32]

During the mid 1560s the underlying political tension came to focus on the settlement of the succession, the question of the Queen's marriage to the Archduke Charles, and further intervention in Scotland. It took its most dramatic form in the running battle between Norfolk and Sussex on the one hand and Leicester on the other through the winter of 1565–66, in which Cecil and the Queen attempted to maintain a mediating position.[33] The collapse of the negotiations with the Archduke in 1568 – which ended any hope of obtaining a conservative king and a moderating influence at Court – together with the arrival of Mary, Queen of Scots, in England triggered the major eruption of 1569. This confused series of events was the product of the interaction of three overlapping political groupings: the Percies and their allies among the northern nobility (who had been pushed so far that plotting the overthrow of Elizabeth had become their only hope); a wider body of semi-Catholic nobles led by Arundel and Lumley, who wished to see Cecil dismissed for risking a war with Philip II through the seizure of his treasure-ships; and a party headed by Leicester and Throckmorton who sought (with Cecil's knowledge) to compensate for the Queen's hesitation over the fate of the Queen of Scots by arranging a Protestant marriage with Norfolk. The failure of their allies at Court to alter the Queen's policies led to the desper-ate rising of the northern earls, which in turn compromised the wider body of conservative nobles irretrievably.

The drift towards more open ideological confrontation was further im-pelled by the publication of the papal bull of deposition in 1570, Norfolk's participation in the Ridolfi Plot of 1571 and then the massacre of St Bartholomew's Day of 1572. Appointments to office and the Council in these years gave both Court and Council a more distinctly Protestant tone, begin-ning with Sir Walter Mildmay and the veteran Sir Ralph Sadler in 1567, Sir Thomas Smith in 1572, Leicester's brother Warwick and brother-in-law Sidney, together with Walsingham, in 1573 and then Dr Thomas Wilson in 1577. The only exceptions to the trend were the more ambiguous Croft and Sussex in 1570, and the Queen's cousin Lord Hunsdon and Hatton in 1577.

From the early 1570s both Council and Court thus displayed a degree of political homogeneity previously unknown. The religiously conservative nobility no longer played any role there and, hamstrung by the conflict of loyalties created by their rank, either retired to their houses, went into exile or dabbled hesitantly in the plots of the early 1580s. This new wave of plot-ting was, however, in part a response to the new question that came near to dividing the Court itself: the long debate over intervention in the Nether-lands from 1572 (or possibly more accurately 1576) to 1585, to which the clashes over the proposed marriage to the Duke of Anjou were closely re-lated. The most outspoken opponent of intervention was Sussex and the issue revived the older tensions between him and Leicester (the leading interventionist): disputes between them became particularly marked in the early 1580s.[34] Burghley, trapped between his basic sympathy for Protestant politics and his equally fundamental dislike of military overextension, played a more cautious role as a councillor than heretofore. The decision to inter-vene in 1585 did not, however, bring the debate to an end; rather the years of Leicester's governor-generalship in the Netherlands (1586–87) created a novel dual focus for Elizabethan politics and brought to the surface the ambiguities of Elizabeth's foreign policy. Elizabeth reacted very strongly to rumours that Leicester was establishing an alternative court at the Hague, while the milit-ary and political failures of the expedition encouraged the anti-interventionists at Whitehall. Whether or not Burghley employed Leicester's absence to strengthen his own position, the appointment of new anti-interventionist councillors at the beginning of 1586 (Archbishop Whitgift, Buckhurst and Lord Cobham) marked a reversal of the trend of the 1570s.[35]

The 1585 intervention did, on the other hand, precipitate the war that dominated the remainder of the reign. Elizabeth and Burghley were united on a cautious and largely maritime strategy; after the deaths of Leicester in 1588 and Walsingham in 1590, the spokesman for the continental strategy and the heir of the old interventionist party was the much less powerful Essex. Their agreement with the Queen over strategy gave the Cecils (Burghley and his son Robert) a stronger hold over the Court and the Council than they had previously possessed. Essex's attempts to wrest control of the Court from them during the mid 1590s and then his attempt to appeal to the country against the Court merely made his position worse: the Court became a battle-ground for factional struggle, and his efforts to obtain office for his allies and followers were almost uniformly unsuccessful. Elizabeth, aging unhappily and increasingly withdrawn, resented Essex's 'presumption' and gave Robert Cecil a control over access not previously achieved by any other councillor.[36] The anti-Essex coalition was led by Cecil, Nottingham and Ralegh (united by their shared interest in a maritime war as well as by personal enmity to Essex), while the leading Court officers of the period were drawn from the established Court families. The old courtiers Nottingham (Lord Admiral since 1585, Lord Steward from 1597) and Buckhurst (Lord Treasurer in 1599) were now those closest to the Queen. Established Household officers such as Heneage (Vice-Chamberlain and councillor from 1587) and Fortescue (Chancellor of the Exchequer and councillor from 1589) rose to prominence, while sons of earlier courtiers – George, 2nd Lord Hunsdon (Lord Chamberlain from 1597), or Sir William Knollys (Comptroller of the Household from 1596, Treasurer from 1602) – succeeded their fathers. Only one new family entered: the Stanhopes, who had been associated with the Cecils since the protectorate of the Duke of Somerset. Sir John Stanhope became Treasurer of the Chamber in 1596 and then Vice-Chamberlain in 1601; his brother Michael was appointed a gentleman of the Privy Chamber in 1598. Against this solid phalanx, Essex could count on few allies: his uncle Knollys (fitfully) and the elderly ex-friend of Leicester, Roger, Lord North (Treasurer of the Houshold, 1596–1600). Even allowing for his paranoia, his claim that the coup he attempted in 1601 was mounted against a Court dominated by his enemies was not without justification.

IV

Given this pattern of Court politics, certain conclusions can be drawn. Faction needs to be much more closely defined. Too much has been made, for

example, of the enmity between Leicester and Sussex; there were bitter disputes in the mid 1560s and early 1580s, but during most of the 1570s their
relations were quite amicable. Even their disputes cannot accurately be termed
factional, because there never was a Sussex faction of any size.[37] Indeed, until
the Essex–Cecil struggle of the 1590s, politics could be said to have intruded
into the Court rather than extruded from it. These intrusions took either the
form of major questions of state – generally of foreign policy, with ideological
overtones – or else of local squabbles among the clients of great men, which
then ran back up the ladder of clientage to the Court. In this context the
barriers between 'Court' and 'country' were very slight indeed: when Croft
penned a long defence of his conduct as Comptroller of the Household in
1587, he spent the greater part of it attacking his enemy in Wales, the 2nd
Earl of Pembroke. Usually these local quarrels could be mediated informally
by leading councillors, though often it was necessary to proceed more formally through the Court of Star Chamber. On rare occasions the Queen herself
would act as arbitrator, as she did in the long-running soap opera of the Earl
of Shrewsbury's divorce, which one wit wagered would outlast the Dutch
Revolt.[38] Leicester very specifically defined his role as that of honest broker:
'I have never been willing to make quarrels in this Court nor to breed any.
Mine own honour and poor credit always saved, I neither have nor will be a
peace breaker but a peace maker.'[39]

The relative internal cohesion of the Court to a large extent prevented
debates over policy or disputes over clients from developing into true
factionalism. With the exception of Arundel, Norfolk and the brief appearance of the Earl of Oxford in the mid 1570s, few members of the older noble
families played even a minimal role there. Almost all its members came
from established Tudor Court families, and the web of intermarriage and
family connection was extremely tight: they were practically all each other's
cousins in the most literal sense. Even the apparent shift in the ideological
outlook of the Council in the 1570s took place within a comparatively narrow
compass; it was accomplished mainly through the promotion of several of
Leicester's relatives and protégés. The succession of fathers and sons in
office, or mothers and daughters in the Privy Chamber, is striking. The sons
of Cecil, Sir Richard Sackville, Lord William Howard of Effingham, Hunsdon
and Sir Francis Knollys, who had been among Elizabeth's first appointments
or creations, all obtained major office by the end of the reign. Hunsdon's
daughter Catherine, who married Lord Charles Howard, the later Earl of
Nottingham, was the senior lady of the Privy Chamber throughout the 1590s.
Both Essex and Sir Philip Sidney were to some degree surrogate sons of
Leicester.

By contrast, only two real outsiders were able to break into the Court's
upper ranks: Hatton and Sir Walter Ralegh. Hatton, from a minor-gentry

family without previous Court connections, came to the Queen's notice, we are told, during the Inner Temple Revels of 1561; only in 1577 did he become Vice-Chamberlain and a member of the Council. His steady but slow rise appears to have been without immediate political significance; he did not participate in a major debate prior to the negotiations over the Anjou marriage in 1578–79 and there was never a Hattonian faction. His career was solely owing to the Queen's personal favour – as the frequent sneers about the 'dancing Chancellor' make clear – yet when he entered higher Court circles he was on equally friendly terms with Leicester, Sussex, Walsingham and Burghley. His success at Court may be attributed simply to his good nature and easy manners: Burghley informed him that 'I find you readier to change offence taken than any other with whom I have had like occasion.'[40] The rise of Ralegh was equally solitary (there was no Ralegh faction either), but meteoric by comparison. He also came from a minor-gentry family and in 1581 was still an officer of the Irish garrison; in 1587 he was appointed Captain of the Guard. His rise was due to his concentrated assault on the Queen, but his manner of proceeding was bitterly resented and Ralegh uniformly disliked.[41] He survived until 1603, despite his bitter vendetta with Essex, through a mixture of effrontery and ability.

The two outsiders were *sui generis*, yet their prominence has always provided evidence for those who have wished to portray the Court as a meeting-place for divergent opinions. Their religious views in particular have suggested that the Puritan patronage of Leicester, Walsingham and Burghley was by no means shared by the Court as a whole. But to portray this as religious factionalism is to overstate the case. A basic confusion has been caused by the Queen's comparative liberalism or agnosticism. Apart from the oath of supremacy, she always resisted pressure from Parliament and Council for the establishment of a narrower religious test, so it remained possible for a religious conservative such as the 4th Earl of Worcester to progress at Court. Yet even he took the supremacy oath 'on his knees' on appointment as Master of the Horse in 1601.[42] There were a few conservative councillors (the ex-Marians or the more ambiguous Croft, Hatton and Norfolk) and looser connections (the second Keeper of the Privy Purse, Henry Seckford, was the son-in-law of the Marian Vice-Chamberlain, Sir Henry Bedingfield), while several women of the Privy Chamber married men of conservative outlook (Margaret Willoughby and Sir Matthew Arundel provide one example), yet these hardly amounted to a coherent conservative party.

The perspective shifts, however, if the attitude towards Puritanism is taken into account. When portrayed as the factious and nonconformist proceedings of the lower clergy, Puritanism certainly created enemies at Court. Here the lines were drawn between those, such as Leicester, Walsingham and, less clearly, Burghley, who were prepared to overlook the preciseness of 'godly ministers and the queen's best subjects' and those, such as Hatton, who shared the views of the Archbishops Parker and Whitgift that the maintenance of order was the first priority. Thus there were always potential pro- and anti-Puritan parties at Court; but their influence depended on the Queen's attitude at the time.[43] While she could be panicked into a crackdown on nonconformity, she was also receptive to godly preachers and numbered such Puritan patrons as Leicester and the Countess of Warwick among her intimates. It has generally been agreed that Puritanism lost its foothold at Court after the deaths of Leicester and Walsingham, but the promotion of so many of Leicester's former chaplains and clerical protégés to bishoprics in the 1590s suggests that the strength of the reaction can be overplayed.

V

If the social and political homogeneity of the Court shaped one dimension of its political dynamics, the relationship of the Court to the Queen created the other. There was never any doubt as to who was the dominant personality: Elizabeth's notorious vanity permeated all aspects of Court life. Her sexual jealousy not only embittered her relations with women of royal blood (Mary, Queen of Scots, the Countess of Lennox or Lady Catherine Grey) and made the lives of her gentlewomen miserable, but also threatened the careers of favoured men when they made marriages of which she did not approve.[44] Her vanity also affected her attitude towards the public position of courtiers: she alone could play to the crowd. Essex's attempts to cultivate his popular standing in the mid 1590s only worsened his relations with the Queen. Leicester had been more cautious, but when he played the role of popular political leader in the Netherlands the effect was equally disastrous.[45] Elizabeth's influence was more than merely emotional, however. Some features of the Court can possibly be attributed to a sense of feminine identity: her fixation with Household management may reflect a conception of good housewifery, while foreign envoys commented upon the prominence of women at formal diplomatic receptions.[46] The Court also reflected her intellectual and artistic tastes. The influences of her education – a mixture of early Italianate Court humanism and Protestant evangelism – created a distinct cultural context. Together with her pleasure in music and the dance, she took her scholarship seriously. In the 1590s her favourite reading is said to have been Seneca, while in 1593 she had it recorded that she had translated Boethius's *De Consolatione Philosophae* in a total of twenty-four hours.[47] Under her encouragement, therefore, spread the Elizabethan fascination with allusive prose, poetry and pageantry. After 1580 Court culture entered a particularly intense phase, coinciding both with the spread of the Gloriana cult (and her own acceptance of the role) and the growing formality of ceremonial. Under the auspices of Sir Henry Lee (Master of the Armoury from 1580) a particular form of entertainment, the Accession Day tilts, developed from comparatively informal jousts to elaborate rituals and pageants, while foreign ambassadors of the period were struck by the careful staging of receptions by ranked members of the Court in the various chambers leading to the Presence Chamber.[48]

Yet essential to Elizabeth's self-image were also the vision of herself as the Senecan princess and her own application to the business of state. Central to the conduct of affairs was – as the more sophisticated students of the early modern Court have noted – the question of access. It was widely recognised – not the least by Elizabeth herself, who considered the privilege part of their reward – that those in immediate personal attendance, however humble their rank, had the greatest opportunity to advance suits.[49] In earlier Tudor reigns this opportunity had led to the increased importance of the Privy Chamber; but under a female sovereign, a Privy Chamber staffed by women became an inner sanctum impenetrable to most of the Court. Elizabeth's careful choice of personal friends and established servants further strengthened the barriers. No foreign ambassador was able to penetrate her Privy Chamber in the way Thomas Randolph did that of Mary, Queen of Scots, in 1565.[50] Yet the women could not be completely isolated: the great majority of them were connected by marriage or family to the leading men at the Court. That they provided Elizabeth with information is clear. In 1569 Leicester complained of the leaking to the Queen by 'some babbling women' of news of the proposed marriage between Norfolk and Mary, Queen of Scots.[51] There is also considerable evidence that members of the Privy Chamber could do their friends favours, either by providing them with access (as William Killigrew did for Sir Robert Carey in 1597) or by advancing their suits (as the Countess of Warwick did for John Dee in 1592). But whether this amounted to political influence is another question. Here we possess a categorical statement by a knowledgeable witness: Rowland Vaughan, the nephew of one of the most long-serving women of the Privy Chamber, Blanche Parry. When complaining of the Court of James I, he noted that

> I remember in Queen Elizabeth's days, my lady of Warwick, Mistress Blanche and my lady Scudamore in little lay matters would steal opportunity to serve their friends' turns . . . because none of these (near and dear ladies) durst intermeddle so far in matters of commonwealth.[52]

The Queen's toleration of personal patronage by members of the Privy Chamber should therefore not be construed as an acceptance of independent political involvement on their part. On this issue Elizabeth had made her position clear in the early years of the reign. The complaints of her newly appointed gentleman usher, Dru Drury, and his brother Sir William about her relations with

Lord Robert Dudley at the end of 1559 earned them both a spell of imprisonment. A milder form of the same punishment was suffered by her favourite
gentlewoman, Catherine Ashley, and her husband for their assistance to the
suit of Eric XIV of Sweden in 1561 and 1562. Yet only Catherine Ashley
appears to have had such confidence in her knowledge of 'her highness
nature by long continuance of time'; after her death in 1565, none of the
other gentlewomen displayed a similar initiative.[53] So the influence of the
Privy Chamber could be discounted by the Queen's leading ministers, confident that their monopoly over the conduct of affairs of state would be
upheld. Even the success of the complaints of William Carmarden against
Customer Thomas Smythe in 1589 may owe more to the recent appointment
of Fortescue as Chancellor of the Exchequer than, as often claimed, to Elizabeth's receptivity to backstairs criticism.[54] Nor, unlike in the previous and the
succeeding reigns, did foreign ambassadors play much of a role at Court.
The only continuous embassy was that of the kings of France, and until 1587
French ambassadors were compromised by their function of protecting the
interests of the Queen of Scots. Spanish ambassadors were distrusted and
kept at arms length: in 1562 the Bishop of Aquila defended his reliance on
Catholic informants on the ground that the Queen and Council would tell
him nothing of importance.[55] Protestant envoys, with the possible exceptions
of Paul Choart de Buzenval, agent of the King of Navarre in 1586–87, and
Noel de Caron, Dutch agent from 1590, generally held too low a status and
too brief a commission to exert much influence.

Yet Elizabeth's dealings with her councillors were never entirely straightforward. She rarely attended Council meetings and was more than willing to
delegate minor and routine matters to them. Major questions were reserved
for discussion with the inner ring of councillors, and there is considerable
evidence that she enjoyed playing them off against each other. Their opinions
were sought individually and then relayed to the others.[56] It was widely known
that she could not keep a secret: in 1587 Thomas Wilkes was worried that
Walsingham would impart his criticisms of Leicester's government in the
Netherlands to Elizabeth, 'who as your honour knoweth can hold no secrets'.
Burghley provides further evidence of her tactics. When Leicester accused him
of going behind his back with complaints over financial maladministration
in the Netherlands, he protested that 'her Majesty many times chargeth me
that I conceal, I flatter, I dare not speak anything that you should mislike'.[57]

Yet Elizabeth's playing off of councillors against each other had its limits.
The comparative unanimity of the inner ring of councillors provided for a
basic political consensus, and maintenance of a common front against the
Queen became a pronounced feature of the Council's advisory function.
Thus Cecil advised Sir Henry Sidney in 1566 that, while persuasion might
take some time, 'I have good hope that her majesty will, with the good

importunity of her Council, stick at nothing devised in this behalf.'[58] The correspondence of Leicester, Burghley and Walsingham in the 1570s and 1580s is very much concerned with their attempts to concert their approaches to Elizabeth and then to hammer away at her. Here they were rarely success-ful, as the long debates over intervention in the Netherlands, or the execu-tion of Mary, Queen of Scots, show. Frequently the Queen would simply lose her temper and the matter would rest in suspension. A very revealing picture of the Elizabethan government at work in the early 1580s is provided in the report of the agent sent by the city of Geneva to negotiate a loan in 1582. His initial contacts were with Leicester and Walsingham, but Walsingham advised waiting for a more propitious moment because Elizabeth was presently averse to spending more money on the Protestant cause. He spent a year in London and, in the end, despite the sympathy of the Council and the support of the Puritan nobility, gentry and clergy, never saw the Queen and only received permission to raise a voluntary collection through the Church.[59] What would spur Elizabeth in action – temporarily – was less pressure from her councillors than a panic or an emotional reaction, but for such a reaction a sufficient dan-ger was necessary. It was for this reason that the uncovering of the various Catholic conspiracies of the 1570s and 1580s became an essential feature of the campaign to persuade Elizabeth to reach a decision over the fate of the Queen of Scots.

On the other hand, attempts to maintain a common front against the Queen did not amount to an independent position for the Council. The reign saw at least four major attempts to play off the Council against the Queen in order to force her into agreeing to measures she opposed: the parliamentary appeal for the establishment of the succession in 1566; Archbishop Grindal's refusal to co-operate in the disbanding of prophesyings in 1576; Leicester's acceptance of the governor-generalship of the Netherlands in 1586; and William Davison's dispatch of the warrant for the execution of the Queen of Scots in 1587. In each case those responsible knew that they were in some sense defying the Queen, but expected that the backing of the Council would cause her to retract. In none of them were they successful, though her initial anger may have been moderated by the Council's stand.

The tensions that doing business with Elizabeth created fed the recurrent complaints against the Court. Backbiting, 'whereof that place indeed is too full', was constantly complained of, yet apparently universally practised. Much of the leading councillors' time was spent in protecting their absent friends and clients, particularly those (such as the lord deputies of Ireland) conducting expensive military operations. It is not surprising to find some of the strong-est criticisms of Court life from men at its centre.[60] Yet compared to that of Henry VIII Elizabeth's governance was, without flattery, mild and merciful. Leicester commented during his quarrel with Sir John Norris in 1587 that 'in

King Henry the 8th's time his doings for sure would have cost him his pate'.[61] Elizabeth may have been imperious, vain and sharp of temper, but she was unwilling to go to extremes, as her agonising over the executions of Norfolk and Essex revealed. For those who experienced it, the Court of Elizabeth I, like the Queen herself, evoked an ambiguous response. In 1602 her godson, Sir John Harington, looked forward to the imminent accession of a king instead of 'a lady shut up in a chamber from her subjects and most of her servants, and seldom seen but on holy days'; yet, as his sardonic account of the drunken shambles that attended the reception of Christian IV of Denmark in 1606 and his later affectionate portrait of the aged Queen show, his mood soon turned to nostalgia.[62]

NOTES

1 The research on which this essay is based was made possible by generous grants from the University of Strathclyde, the British Academy and the Carnegie Trust for the Universities of Scotland. I should like to thank the Marquess of Bath for permission to employ the Dudley MSS at Longleat House. I am extremely grateful to the editor of this volume, Patrick Collinson, Geoffrey Elton, David Loades, Geoffrey Parker, Mia Rodríguez-Salgado, David Starkey and Penry Williams for their invaluable comments and criticisms.

2 BL Lansd. MS 34, fo. 95. The best surviving Household subsidy rolls are those for 1559 (BL Lansd. MS 3, fos 193–200), 1567 (PRO E 179/69/82) and 1576 (PRO E 179/69/93).

3 BL Egerton MS 2723, fos 32v, 33v.

4 5 Eliz. I, c. 32 (An Act of Assignment of Certain Sums of Money to Defray the Charges of the Queen's Majesty's Household). The Cofferer's accounts are PRO E 351/1795–96.

5 PRO E 351/541–3. During the first years of the reign the Treasurer's ordinary annual expenditure lay in the region of £11,500; see E 351/541, and BL Cotton MS. Vespasian C xiv (1), fos 68–75.

6 In 1576 Burghley computed Stables expenses at £4148 (BL Harleian MS 709, fos 19v, 22). In 1590 the wages bill alone came to an annual £2100; see M. M. Reese, *The Royal Office of Master of the Horse* (1976) p. 163. Total expenditure on 'incidents' for both Household and Stables was £15,188 in 1573 (BL Lansd. MS 21, fo. 127).

7 The Wardrobe account for 1559, for example, records an expenditure of £14,439, exclusive of the £17,662 the department spent on Mary's funeral (see PRO LC 5/32, p. 59). Tamworth's Privy Purse account for 1559–69 (BL Harleian Roll 609) is printed in J. Nichols, *The Progresses and Public Processions of Queen Elizabeth*, iii (1805) B–C, 1–9.

8 PRO LS 13/280/82, see also fo. 134. For the latest discussion of the impact of inflation on foodstuffs see D. M. Palliser, *The Age of Elizabeth. England under the Later Tudors, 1547–1603* (1983) pp. 140–2.

9 The 1576 survey is now BL Harleian MS 609, largely printed in Nichols, *Progresses*, i (1788) A–F, 1–37. For other documents relating to the 1576 reforms see below, nn. 10

and 14. For the problem of staff wages, see BL Lansd. MSS 34, fos 95–6 (1583) and 86, fo. 108 (1598).

10 For Hall food, see BL Lansd. MS 21 fos 133, 139r–v. For Burghley's proposed reforms, BL Lansd. MSS 86, fos 107–8, 34, fos 91r–v, 45, fo. 49.

11 BL Lansd. MS 21, fos 124, 129, 139. See also R. C. Braddock, 'The Royal Household, 1540–1560: A Study in Office-Holding in Tudor England' (Northwestern University Ph.D. thesis, 1971) p. 35.

12 There are numerous references to Elizabeth's appeal to popularity: see 'The Count of Feria's Dispatch to Philip II of 14 November 1558', ed. M. J. Rodríguez-Salgado and S. Adams, *Camden Miscellany*, XXVIII (1984) 315 n. 1; BL Add. MS 34,563 fo. 11; *The Letters and Epigrams of Sir John Harington*, ed. N. E. McClure (Philadelphia, 1930) p. 122; *Elizabeth of England. Certain Observations concerning the Life and Reign of Queen Elizabeth by John Clapham*, ed. E. P. and C. Read (Philadelphia, 1951) p. 69. For Elizabeth's urban receptions, see the comments of Palliser, *Age of Elizabeth*, pp. 235–6, and, for Worcester, Nichols, *Progresses*, I, 1–O, 94 n. 4.

13 BL Lansd. MSS 21, fos 130, 139v, 34, fo. 95. For the proposed 1574 progress, see AGR PEA 361, fo. 78v, printed in *Rel. Pol.*, VII, 122; and, for the 1575, BL Lansd. MS 20, fo. 128, printed in T. Wright, *Queen Elizabeth and Her Times* (1838) II, 11.

14 The surviving order book of the Compting House (PRO LS 13/168) begins in 1598. See on this question, A. P. Newton, 'Tudor Reforms in the Royal Household', in *Tudor Studies presented . . . to Albert Frederick Pollard*, ed. R. W. Seton-Watson (1924) p. 249. For Burghley's comments, BL Lansd. MS 21, fo. 130; cf. fo. 139v, and MS 34, fo. 95.

15 The Coronation roll is now PRO LC 2 4/3, see pp. 104–5; a garbled list of the Privy Chamber in 1559 can be found in Bod. Lib. MS English Hist. C 272, fo. 95. For the waged members of the Privy Chamber, see the Cofferer of the Household's accounts, PRO E 351/1795 *passim*. BL Lansd. MS 3, fo. 192, is a copy of the first warrant of January 1559; MS 59, fo. 43, gives the state of the Privy Chamber on 22 May 1589.

16 For discussion of the structural stability of the post-Henrician Court, see G. R. Elton, *The Tudor Revolution in Government* (Cambridge, 1953) p. 370; D. R. Starkey, 'The King's Privy Chamber, 1485–1547' (Cambridge University Ph.D. thesis, 1974) pp. 415, 419; and Braddock, 'Royal Household', p. 35.

17 The book of fees of 1576–8 is printed in *A Collection of Ordinances and Regulations for the Government of the Royal Household* (1790) 250–74; see also D. E. Hoak, 'The King's Privy Chamber, 1547–1553', in *Tudor Rule and Revolution: Essays for G. R. Elton from his American Friends*, ed. D. J. Guth and J. W. McKenna (Cambridge, 1983) p. 89 n. 7.

18 On Household promotions, see Newton, 'Tudor Reform', pp. 254–5, and the qualifications by Braddock, 'Royal Household', p. 213. On Manners, see L. C. John, 'Roger Manners, Elizabethan Courtier', *Huntington Library Quarterly*, XII (1948) 57–84.

19 *H of C*, *1509–58*, II, 103 (on Sir Francis Englefield) and 354 (Sir Richard Southwell). For a comment on the purge, see AMRE CPA, XIII, fo. 256, A. de Noailles to Montmorency, 7 June 1559.

20 BL Lansd. MS 20, fo. 164. For Croft's defence of sale of office, BL Royal MS 18 A XLVI, fos 3v–4.

21 A. Woodward, 'Purveyance for the Royal Household in the Reign of Queen Elizabeth', *Transactions of the American Philosophical Society*, n. s., XXXV, no. 1 (Philadelphia, 1945)

pp. 8, 14, 58. [There are two errors in this paragraph. Firstly, Elizabeth did in fact appoint a single Lord Privy Seal, William, Lord Howard of Effingham, for the brief period from July 1572 till his death in 1573. Secondly, Leicester was not appointed Lord Steward in 1584, but at some point in 1587, probably 18 June.]

22 See *inter alia*, G. D. Duncan, 'Monopolies under Elizabeth I, 1558–1585' (Cambridge University Ph.D. thesis, 1976) p. 116; C. J. Kitching. 'The Quest for Concealed Lands in the Reign of Elizabeth I', *TRHS*, 5th ser., xxiv (1974) 66.

23 PRO SP 52/10/120; Haynes & Murdin, ii, 764; D. Digges, *The Compleat Ambassador* (1655) p. 322.

24 BL Lansd. MS 7, fos 123–4; cf. PRO SP 12/126/13.

25 BL Lansd. MSS 21, fo. 75, and 102, fo. 230r–v; HMC, *Salisbury MSS*, ii, 610; PRO SP 12/125/151–2.

26 For Buckhurst, see *Harington Letters*, pp. 90–1; for Nottingham, *The Memoirs of Robert Carey*, ed. F. H. Mares (Oxford, 1972) p. 59.

27 D. MacCulloch, 'Anglican and Puritan in Elizabethan Suffolk', *Archiv für Reformationsgeschichte*, lxii (1981) 280–1; P. Williams, 'Court and Polity under Elizabeth I', *Bulletin of the John Rylands University Library*. lxv (1983) 265, 267; G. R. Elton, 'Tudor Government: the Points of Contact. iii. The Court', *TRHS, 5th ser.*, xxvi (1976) 219, 224–7.

28 See, *inter alia, Sir John Harington's 'A New Discourse of a Stale Subject called the Metamorphosis of Ajax'*, ed. E. S. Donno (1962) p. 252; P. Collinson, *The Elizabethan Puritan Movement* (1967) p. 134; PRO PCC 11 Daughtry; and Dudley MS i, fo. 46.

29 For Mason, see 'Feria Dispatch', p. 319 n. 3; for an interesting general reflection on this aspect of the Court of 1559, see AMRE CPA, xiii, fo. 258v, memoir of M. de Gondran, 15 June 1559 (transcribed in PRO 31 3/24/51).

30 N. L. Jones, *Faith by Statute. Parliament and the Settlement of Religion, 1559*, Royal Historical Society Studies in History xxxii (1982) p. 72 n. 50; PRO SP 12/7/190. See also A. Teulet, *Papiers d'état . . . relatifs à l'histoire d'Ecosse au 16ᵉ siècle*, i (Paris, 1852) 361. For Protestant discontent see PRO SP 12/12/1 and HMC, *Salisbury MSS* i, 679; cf. Dudley MS i, fo. 90.

31 The best account of this process to date is N. Canny, *The Elizabethan Conquest of Ireland: A Pattern Established, 1565–76* (Hassocks, Sussex, 1976) pp. 70–1. I have taken up aspects of the question in an unpublished paper, 'The Dudley Clientage, 1553–1563' [now Ch. 8].

32 BL Cotton MS Titus MS B ii, fo. 31; PRO SP 12/31/23; AGR PEA 360/207, printed in *Rel. Pol.*, iii, 153.

33 For reliable information on these clashes, see Haynes & Murdin, ii, 760–1.

34 For Sussex's views on foreign policy, see *Illustrations of British History*, ed. E. Lodge (1791) ii, 161–2, 177–86. For an eyewitness account of a clash with Leicester on 12 July, 1581, see *The Private Diary of John Dee*, ed. J. O. Halliwell, Camden Society xix (1842) p. 11. For Leicester's support for Protestant interventionism see S. L. Adams, 'The Protestant Cause: Religious Alliance with the West European Calvinist Communities, 1585–1630' (Oxford University D.Phil. thesis, 1973) pp. 37–9, 46–7. Conyers Read's portrait of a Council factionalised by the debate ('Walsingham and Burghley in Queen Elizabeth's Privy Council', *EHR*, xxviii (1913) 34–58) is overdrawn.

35 Adams, 'Protestant Cause', p. 61; *The Correspondence of Robert Dudley, Earl of Leycester*, ed. J. Bruce, Camden Society xxvii (1844) esp. pp. 142–5.

36 Williams, 'Court and Polity', 263; cf. *Carey Memoirs*, pp. 42–3.

37 For evidence of good relations between Leicester and Sussex in the mid-1570s see BL Lansd. MS 21, fo. 75; BL Harleian MS 6991, fo. 27; and PRO SP 12/126/20. See also Susan Doron, 'The Political Career of Thomas Radcliffe, 3rd Earl of Sussex (1526–1583)' (London University Ph.D. thesis, 1977) pp. 153, 334–5, 393, 396, 403; M. B. Pulman, *The Elizabethan Privy Council in the Fifteen-Seventies* (Berkeley, Calif., 1971) p. 49. On the other hand, Leicester did refer to Sussex posthumously as a liar (*CSPF*, xxi (3) 233).

38 See John, 'Manners', 69–75, esp. 71 n. 71. For Croft's comments on Pembroke see BL Royal MS 18 A xlvi, fos 6–8v. [Croft's enemy was not Pembroke, but Sir Henry Sidney; the reference was a retrospective one.]

39 PRO SP 12/126/20–1.

40 E. StJ. Brooks, *Sir Christopher Hatton. Queen Elizabeth's Favourite* (1946) p. 19.

41 See, *inter alia*, the comments of Clapham, *Observations*, pp. 92–3. For Ralegh's rise, see W. R. Wallace, *Sir Walter Raleigh* (Princeton, NJ, 1959) pp. 25–30.

42 PRO LS 13/168/24. For Elizabeth's attitude, see J. E. Neale, *Elizabeth I and her Parliaments*, i: *1559–1581* (1953) pp. 191–3.

43 See Archbishop Parker's comments to Burghley, 11 April 1575, BL Lansd. MS 20, fo. 149.

44 For examples of Elizabeth's treatment of her women, see *Harington Letters*, pp. 124–5, and C. A. Bradford, *Helena, Marchioness of Northampton* (1936) pp. 65–7.

45 For Essex's attempt to exploit his popularity after the Cadiz voyage and its effects, see Adams, 'Protestant Cause', pp. 138–9.

46 See for example AGR PEA 361/26, printed in *Rel. Pol.*, v, 505; and 362/145.

47 For Elizabeth's studies, see L. V. Ryan, *Roger Ascham* (Stanford, Calif., 1963) p. 223 (I owe this reference to Gail Stedward); *Harington Letters*, p. 123; and Nichols, *Progresses*, i, xi.

48 R. Strong, *The Cult of Elizabeth. Elizabethan Portraiture and Pageantry* (1977) pp. 30–1, 130–3; F. A. Yates, 'Elizabethan Chivalry: The Romance of the Accession Day Tilts', in *Astrea. The Imperial Theme in the Sixteenth Century* (Harmondsworth, Middx, 1977) pp. 88–111; AGR PEA 362/145, 150.

49 Starkey, 'Privy Chamber', pp. 51, 63; Williams, 'Court and Polity', 270–1; Braddock, 'Royal Household', p. 36; PRO LS 13/280/82.

50 National Library of Scotland, Advocates MS 1.2.2., art. 39.

51 *CSPSc*, iv (1905) 36.

52 *Rowland Vaughan, his Book, Published 1610: The Most Approved and Long-Experienced Waterworks*, ed. E. B. Wood (1897) p. 57; 'The Compendious Rehearsal of John Dee . . . A° 1592, November 9', printed in *Johannis Confratis et Monachi Glastoniensis Chronica*, ed. T. Hearne (Oxford, 1726) ii, 499; *Carey Memoirs*, pp. 42–3.

53 PRO SP 70/39/110; see also BL Add. MS 48,023, fos 352, 353v, 366.

54 H. A. Lloyd, 'Camden, Carmarden and the Customs', *EHR*, lxxxv (1976) 781.

55 AGR PEA 360/273.

56 *Harington Letters*, pp. 123–4; for evidence of delegation to the Council, see PRO SP 12/103/97, and *CSPSc*, v (1907) 266.

57 *Correspondentie van Robert Dudley, Graaf van Leycester . . . 1585–1588*, ed. H. Brugmans, Werken van het Historisch Genootschap, 3rd ser., LVI–LVIII (Utrecht, 1931) II, 230, 310.

58 PRO SP 63/16/197v.

59 Geneva, Archives d'Etat, Pièces Historiques, 2066, report of Jean Maillet, Oct. 1582–Oct. 1583. An edition of this document is presently being prepared for publication by the Camden Society.

60 PRO SP 12/140/46–7; cf. Bod. Lib., Perrot MS 1, fos 163v–166v, and *Correspondentie van Leycester*, II, 227.

61 *CSPF*, XXI (3), 233.

62 *Sir John Harington. A Tract on the Succession to the Crown (AD 1602)*, ed. C. R. Markham, Roxburghe Club (1880) p. 51; *Harington Letters*, pp. 118–26.

Chapter 3

Favourites and factions at the Elizabethan Court

As the household of a virgin queen regnant, the Court of Elizabeth I was all but unique for the sixteenth century. The limited exceptions of her sister's essentially female Privy Chamber and the Court of Mary Stuart in Scotland between 1561 and 1565 prove, as it were, the rule. In institutional terms, Elizabeth's Court was simply a restricted version of its predecessors. The Privy Chamber, central to the Courts of Henry VII and Henry VIII, was reduced to a feminine inner sanctum similar to that of Mary Tudor.[1] As if in compensation, however, the reign produced a controversial novelty: the male favourite, whose leading characteristic was his physical and personal attraction for the Queen. Unlike the 'favourites' of Henry VIII (or, for that matter, those of Francis I), these men were neither a large nor a transient series of companions. Rather, they were individuals who both occupied the central positions at the Court, and enjoyed an apparently unequalled degree of intimacy with and indulgence by the Queen.

By the end of Elizabeth's reign there was general agreement that there had been four favourites of this rank: Robert Dudley, Earl of Leicester, Robert Devereux, Earl of Essex, Sir Christopher Hatton, and Sir Walter Ralegh. But 1603 did not bring the era of favourites to an end. The homosexual affections of James I led to the rise of two men, Robert Kerr, Earl of Somerset, and George Villiers, Duke of Buckingham, whose influence and position were as great if not greater than those of their Elizabethan predecessors.[2] By the date of the assassination of Buckingham (1628) there had been nearly 60 years of favourites; by then also their role had become both the subject of major controversy and a political issue in its own right.[3] This debate has in turn had a major influence on all later comment on the Court of Elizabeth I.

In a perceptive survey of the present state of Tudor studies, Ralph Houlbrooke has drawn attention to a recent revisionist emphasis on 'harmony' in Elizabethan politics. He refers in particular to the work of Sir

Geoffrey Elton and Norman Jones on Parliament, which has disputed the presence of 'a powerful puritan opposition', and to an earlier essay of mine on the Court, which 'denies the existence of destabilising factional rivalries at any time before the 1590s'. The latter, he feels, might have gone 'too far in playing down the volatility of court politics'. The comment is a fair one, for the classic image of the Elizabethan Court, as established in such works as Sir John Neale's essay 'The Elizabethan Political Scene', is one of intense rivalry and factionalism.[4] Indeed, it has been considered one of Elizabeth's strengths that she was able in the main to 'manage' this factionalism to her own advantage. What has not been sufficiently appreciated, however, is the way in which this image of the Court was a product of the contemporary debate on favourites. Even less understood is the way in which the Stuart context of the later stages of the debate came to influence the portrayal of Elizabeth's reign.[5] The result has been a confused tapestry in which myth and reality have been deeply interwoven.

About one point there is no real controversy. During the 1590s the Court was nearly torn apart by a factional struggle of major proportions that culminated in an attempted *coup d'état*. The antagonism between the Earl of Essex and Sir Robert Cecil spread into the country at large, and left scars on the English body politic for at least a generation. Less clear, however, is the relationship between the politics of this decade and the three that preceded it. Was the difference one of degree or of kind? If the former, was there a 'controlled' factionalism in the earlier period that degenerated in the latter? If the latter, did the Essex–Cecil rivalry initiate a new political world quite unlike the earlier years?

Any study of the Elizabethan Court prior to the 1590s must focus on the Earl of Leicester, who, as the leading favourite, was at its centre. Moreover, it was Leicester rather than Essex who inspired the controversy over the favourite. Essentially there were two extreme arguments. Was Leicester an all-powerful, hegemonic, or monopolistic force or was he but one of a number of personalities or factions competing in a more fluid environment? The manner in which these questions were phrased is best revealed if the debate is set in its immediate context, and the ways in which the issues it raised were exploited for later political and polemical ends are examined. Although the debate was primarily concerned with the structure of power at the Elizabethan Court, its implications were much wider. At its heart lay the impact of the Reformation on the English political system.

I

The central document in the controversy is the most notorious of Elizabethan political libels: *The Copy of a Letter written by a Master of Arts of Cambridge* of

1584, better known as 'Leicester's Commonwealth'.[6] It was not, however, *sui generis*. Rather, it formed part of a particular strand of Elizabethan Catholic polemic that included two other important tracts: *A Treatise of Treasons against Q. Elizabeth* of 1572, and *A Declaration of the True Causes of the Great Troubles presupposed to be intended against England* of 1592.[7] Like 'Leicester's Commonwealth', these were celebrated enough to receive familiar titles, 'The Papists' Commonwealth' and 'Burghley's Commonwealth'. In all three cases the putative author or authors are still disputed.[8]

These tracts are distinguished from the main body of Elizabethan Catholic literature by their concern with the structure of politics. They share an initial premiss common to many other sixteenth-century Catholic interpretations of the Reformation: the argument that heresy had been introduced by new men, whose intentions were political revolution. These men were 'machiavellian' in the sense made explicit in *A Treatise of Treasons*: 'it is that I call a Machiavellian state and regiment: where religion is put behind in second and last place, where civil policie, I meane, is preferred before it.' Thus 'to set up a lawless faction of Machiavellian Libertines . . . a new religion was pretended'.[9]

The argument was itself a variant on the old theme of evil councillors. Its significance lies in the identification of the supporters of the Reformation as new men, and the attribution of machiavellian motives to them. In this way the cause of the Catholic Church was linked to that of the 'ancient nobility', an association that had first been made in the 1530s. The attacks on Thomas Cromwell by the rebels of the Pilgrimage of Grace of 1536 and then by Cardinal Pole in 1539 had made explicit both the threat to the ancient nobility and the machiavellianism of the new men.[10] The charge was revived during the rebellion of the northern earls in 1569. In the Darlington proclamation of 16 November the Earls of Northumberland and Westmorland identified their enemies as

> diverse newe set up nobles about the Quenes Majestie, [who] have and do dailie, not only go about to overthrow and put down the ancient nobilitie of this realme, but also have misused the Queens Majesties owne personne, and also have . . . mayntayned an new found religion and heresie . . .'[11]

This argument was taken up more extensively in *A Treatise of Treasons*, which was published on the eve of the trial of the 4th Duke of Norfolk for his involvement in the Ridolphi plot of 1571. Its immediate purpose was to defend Norfolk and Mary, Queen of Scots, from the charges against them. To do so it associated Mary's cause with that of the Catholic Church and the ancient nobility. The link was forged by a common threat: the attempt to eliminate Mary from the succession 'under the title of a third family' by 'two Catalines'.[12] The two are not named, but there are sufficient personal allusions to identify them clearly as Lord Burghley and Sir Nicholas Bacon, the Lord Keeper. Their aim was said to be 'a new crew and the setting up of a partie Protestant', by means of a puppet monarchy first under Elizabeth, who had been kept unmarried deliberately, and then under the children of the Earl of Hertford and Lady Catherine Grey. Their control of the Court provided them with the means to do so, for Elizabeth had been isolated and 'al accesse of those that would intimate it unto her is by one crafte or other restrained and prohibited from her'.[13]

A number of subsidiary accusations were also made – financial malversation and corruption, the encouragement of foreign immigration that drove Englishmen out of work, and a major change in foreign policy, which involved the alienation of old allies, the stirring-up of panics of foreign invasions, and the encouragement of rebellion abroad – though little evidence was advanced to support the charges. However, the tract does contain a detailed account of the complex events of 1569.[14] This is of major importance, for the events described were the one apparent example of a major power struggle in Elizabeth's Court. The *Treatise* distinguishes between two separate intrigues. One was the proposed marriage of Norfolk and the Queen of Scots, which it claims was agreed to by all the Privy Council except Bacon. The earls of Arundel, Pembroke, and Leicester, and Cecil himself are specifically mentioned. The second was the attempt to overthrow Cecil, organised by Norfolk 'and the other nobility'. In the belief that the Queen was 'but Queen in name', it was 'at length decided and resolved by a general consent of many both of the council and other nobility . . . in removing from her by some good mean, twoo or three persons of meane birth and condition'.[15] Having discovered this conspiracy, Cecil and Bacon then turned Elizabeth against Norfolk. His subsequent imprisonment led the northern earls to fear a wider attack on the nobility, and thus forced them into rebellion – not against the Queen but against her evil councillors.

It does not perhaps need to be emphasised how important the events of 1569 are to any study of Elizabethan Court politics. The significance of this interpretation lies in the theme of the supplanting of the ancient nobility by the new men. The key figures are Cecil and Bacon; Leicester plays hardly any role at all. He is mentioned as a supporter of the Norfolk marriage, but is not included by name among those who sought to overthrow Cecil. In 'Leicester's Commonwealth' the emphasis is reversed, and Leicester rather than Cecil becomes the villain of the piece. The events of 1569 are overtaken by a number of new issues that emerged in the 12 years that separated the two tracts – the execution of Norfolk in 1572, the failure of the Queen's possible marriage to the Duke of Anjou in 1578–81, the spread of Puritanism, and the passing of more severe legislation against papal allegiance – yet many of the basic arguments remain. The threat to the Crown is the central political issue. Leicester is said to be seeking a puppet monarchy for his brother-in-law, the Earl of Huntingdon. To that end, the Queen has been kept unmarried (his own efforts in that direction having failed), and the Stuart succession blocked. Leicester is also the enemy of the old nobility and the betrayer of Norfolk. He was less obviously a baseborn new man (despite an attempt to blacken the Dudley ancestry in passing), but his notorious father and grandfather provided a more effective line of attack.[16] In seeking to usurp the Crown Leicester was simply trying to realise his father's earlier ambition. Leicester's influence on the new foreign policy is not so obvious, although he too is accused of exploiting fears of nonexistent foreign threats.[17]

It is, however, for reasons other than its defence of the Stuart succession that 'Leicester's Commonwealth' obtained its notoriety. The intensity of the personal vilification is noteworthy even by contemporary standards. A few themes – notably cowardice and duplicity – are found in the earlier attack on Cecil, but others, Leicester's spectacular sexual appetites and his skill as a poisoner, are unique. More significant, however, is the description of Leicester's dominance of the Court. His 'reign is so absolute in this place (as also in all other parts of the Court) as nothing can pass but by his admission'.[18] The charge is supported by details of a number of incidents of tyranny and corruption, which reveal a considerable knowledge of events at Court between 1575 and 1584. His position had been equalled only by the notorious fourteenth-century favourites, Piers Gaveston, Hugh Despencer, and Robert de Vere. A few councillors, Burghley, Bacon, and Thomas Radcliffe, Earl of Sussex, had been able to remain independent, but they were powerless to halt him. Sussex (who was not mentioned in *A Treatise of Treasons*) is here portrayed as the surviving representative of the ancient nobility at Court.[19]

Yet Leicester was more than simply a Court figure, for he had been able to create a faction that dominated the realm as well. This was the 'Puritan faction', which serves an important polemical purpose in 'Leicester's Commonwealth' and was to some extent its creation. In a novel variant of the machiavellian argument, 'Leicester's Commonwealth' makes an unusual plea for toleration for Catholics, on the ground that they were less of a danger to the Crown than Leicester and his followers. Burghley (it is implied) was open to argument; the real advocate of persecution was Leicester, acting as patron of the Puritans.[20] Puritanism thus drives a wedge between Leicester, on the one hand, and Burghley and Bacon, the earlier 'Catalines' of Protestantism, on the other. (There is scarcely any reference to Sir Francis Walsingham, it might be noted.) It also provides the vital cement that holds Leicester's faction together, for without it Leicester was too odious to retain any man's allegiance. As befits the machiavellian emphasis, his purpose in patronising Puritanism was to exploit religion to advance his own political ends. It is revealing that the tract has little otherwise to say about Leicester's involvement in the Church, apart from the claim that the University of Oxford had been ruined by his chancellorship.[21]

'Leicester's Commonwealth' therefore replaces the Protestant faction of *A Treatise of Treasons* with a hegemonical favourite exploiting internal Protestant divisions. 'Burghley's Commonwealth' combined the monopolist of the former with the themes of the latter. The emphasis is very much on foreign policy. Burghley had led England into a series of military adventures and a disastrous war with Spain. Seeking to make himself *dictator perpetuus*, he had overthrown the nobility and ruled all. Recent events confirm his hegemony: 'for better contriving of the whole domination to himself he hath lately brought in his second son to be of the Queen's council and keeper of her privy seal'. Leicester and Walsingham, both dead by 1592, appear only peripherally, and then as tools of Burghley's: his 'chiefest actors'.[22]

Whatever their differences, the three tracts advance the central proposition that the Elizabethan Court had been dominated by a monopolistic figure who had treated the Queen as a puppet. This, Francis Bacon noted in his observations on 'Burghley's Commonwealth', was an old tactic, 'for this hath some appearance to cover undutiful invectives, when it is used against favourites or upstarts and sudden risen councillors'. Moreover, the employment of the charge against more than one of Elizabeth's councillors had weakened the force of the argument: 'When the match was in treating with the duke of Anjou . . . all the gall was uttered against the Earl of Leicester'. Lastly, it was an inaccurate description of the relationship between the Queen and her ministers:

> it is well known that . . . there was never counsellor of his lordship's [i.e. Burghley's] long continuance that was so applicable to her majesty's princely resolutions; endeavouring always, after faithful propositions and remonstrances . . . to rest upon such conclusions as her majesty in her own wisdom determineth . . .[23]

The prominence of Ralegh and Essex in the 1590s and the open factionalism of the decade weakened the argument for the hegemony of the favourite. There were now several favourites whose relationship both to each other and to the Cecils needed to be explained. John Clapham, in his unpublished 'Observations' written immediately after the accession of James I, took the extreme position of playing down the importance of the favourites as a group. A former servant of Burghley's, he saw no shame in the *regnum Cecilianum*. Burghley had ordered 'the affairs of the realm in such manner, as he was respected by his enemies, who reputed him the most famous councillor of Christendom in his time; the English government being then commonly termed by strangers Cecil's Commonwealth'. Clapham refers to a mysterious (though undated) plot to overthrow Cecil by 'diverse councillors of noble birth, pretending that he went about by suppressing them to establish his own greatness', but also relates that Cecil surmounted this and other intrigues 'by advised patience'. The prominence of the four favourites he attributes to the weakness of the Queen, who, he claims, was too susceptible to flattery. Leicester and Hatton were primarily self-interested courtiers; Ralegh and Essex, on the other hand, were at least men of ability and heroic ambition.[24]

The contrast between Leicester's 'domestical greatness' and Essex's martial actions had the paradoxical effect of strengthening the growing legend of Leicester the master courtier.[25] By the end of the reign he was being seen more and more as an intriguer of unrivalled skill.[26] A Welsh author considered 'how wise and politike was the late Earl of Leicester in all the course of his actions' one of the major questions of the day, but refrained from comment on the ground

> it concerneth an honourable personage, the greatest subject of late days in England and now dead. And I do take that it is rather my part and duty being but a poor gentleman to honour his memory in the grave than to discourse of his life and actions . . .[27]

In 1599 a Court observer wrote of Leicester's influence as a model for others: 'I am credibly made beleve . . . that at this Instant the Lord Admirall is able to doe with the Queen as much as my Lord Lester was . . .'[28]

Simultaneously, a second aspect to the legend emerged as the machiavellian patron of Puritanism of 'Leicester's Commonwealth' was taken up by Anglican apologists and employed for their own purposes. During the 1570s and 1580s the standard charge against clerical Puritanism and presbyterianism had been that of political subversion.[29] In the 1590s a new theme can be detected. Puritanism was now depicted as a front for lay attempts to complete the expropriation of the wealth of the Church; the motive for lay patronage of Puritan clergy was the hope that, in the confusion created by attacks on the government of the Church, the remaining ecclesiastical estates would fall into their hands. Leicester had been simply seeking to continue his father's expropriations of 1552–53. The threat to the Church was made explicit by Archbishop Whitgift in 1585.[30] An early example of the use of the machiavellian portrait of 'Leicester's Commonwealth' to explain the danger to the Church can be found in William Harrison's manuscript 'Chronologie', written between Leicester's death in 1588 and Harrison's own in 1593. Leicester was

> the man of grettest powre (being but a subject) which in this land, or that ever had bene exalted under any prince sithens the times of Peers Gavestone & Robert Vere . . . Nothing almost was done, wherein he had not, either a stroke or a commoditie; which together with his scraping from churche and commons . . . procured him soche inward envie & hatred.[31]

In 1602 even one of Leicester's former clerical protégés, the Archbishop of York, Matthew Hutton, could write of his designs on ecclesiastical estates.[32] The very range of Leicester's ecclesiastical patronage, of which Hutton himself had been a beneficiary, strengthened the depth of his machiavellianism. Sir John Harington, who was himself no admirer of Leicester, observed at the beginning of James I's reign that, if Leicester 'made no great conscience to spoyle the church lyvings no more than did his father, yet for his recreation [he] would have some choyse and excellent men for his chaplayns'.[33]

II

The growing confusion surrounding Leicester and the Elizabethan Court was not clarified by the Stuart commentary, least of all by William Camden's *Annals*.[34] It has been claimed that Camden 'went out of his way to paint the blackest possible picture' of Leicester.[35] This may be an exaggeration, but it is also clear that Camden's much-praised objectivity did not apply in his case. The reasons have been less obvious, owing in part to the controversy that still surrounds the composition of the *Annals*. It is now accepted that the first three books were not rewritten by James I or Henry Howard, Earl of Northampton, but what can be attributed to the influence of Burghley, who first commissioned the work, is still to be decided.[36] The consistency of Camden's emphasis on Leicester's malignant influence makes its source a question of no small importance.

Camden's observation that 'evill speakers tooke occasion to tugge and tear at him continually, during the best of his fortune, by defamatory libels, which contained some slight untruths', reveals both a knowledge of, and a certain distancing from, 'Leicester's Commonwealth'.[37] The latter is revealed in his handling of two important episodes. The death of Amy Robsart is passed over very rapidly. More striking is the long passage devoted to refuting the charge that Leicester poisoned Walter Devereux, Earl of Essex, in 1576, which 'Leicester's Commonwealth' made much of as evidence for Leicester's plot to destroy the nobility.[38] Yet a number of incidents from 'Leicester's Commonwealth' are found in very similar form in the *Annals*: the disgrace and death of Sir Nicholas Throckmorton, the suspension of Archbishop Grindal in 1577, the fall of Sir John Throckmorton, the Somerville affair, and the attempted assassination of the Duke of Anjou's agent Jehan Simier. There are also a number of further malign intrigues. Several, like Leicester's ambition to become ruler of the Low Countries in 1586–87, or his advice that Mary, Queen of Scots, be poisoned instead of being executed in 1587, occurred after 'Leicester's Commonwealth' was published. Others, however, did not: Leicester's plot against Sir Nicholas Bacon for encouraging the Grey succession tracts in 1564, his involvement in the release of Lord Darnley in 1565, and his sabotaging of the Austrian marriage negotiations in 1565–67.

The accuracy or inaccuracy of Camden's version of these incidents cannot be discussed here.[39] What can be suggested, however, is that they serve a very important purpose. By establishing Leicester as the evil genius of the Court, a number of awkward episodes in the reign can be explained away. This is particularly the case with regard to the two major concerns that Camden shares with 'Leicester's Commonwealth': the cause of Mary, Queen of Scots, and the cause of the ancient nobility. Elizabeth's treatment of Mary provided him with his most difficult problem, and the disproportionate amount of space devoted to her in the *Annals* has been commented on.[40] Thus by emphasizing Leicester's role in the release of Darnley, or his poisoning proposal, for example, Camden is able to defend the Queen's innocence and moderation, and transfer the blame elsewhere.

Camden's loyalty to the ancient nobility comes into play in his account of the tension between Leicester and Sussex in 1565: 'Sussex inuriously despised him as an upstart, and, to detract him, would say, that hee could cite onely to of his pedigree, that is to wit his Father and Grand-father, both being enemies to their Countrey.'[41] From this perspective his account of the events of 1569 is of particular interest. His source (as was probably also the case for Clapham) for the attempted *coup* against Cecil appears to have been *A Treatise of Treasons*, for 'Leicester's Commonwealth' has little to say on the subject.[42] But Camden also provides a much more detailed account of the marriage negotiations between Norfolk and Mary, clearly derived from the text of Norfolk's later confession.[43] It is also heavily edited to convict Leicester of betraying Norfolk. Leicester's revelation of the marriage scheme to the Queen at Titchfield in the summer of 1569 was caused by fear, 'beholding his blood and vitall senses to shrink in himselfe'. Sir Nicholas Throckmorton's involvement in these intrigues is attributed to his being Cecil's 'ambitious emulator'. His disgrace and sudden death, 'eating salads' at Leicester's house, are portrayed as the consequence of allying with the favourite.[44]

Similarly, the attribution of the fall of Archbishop Grindal, 'because hee condemned as unlawfull the marriage of Iulius an Italian Physician, with another man's wife, which much distasted the Earle of Leicester', to a Court intrigue rather than the dispute over prophesyings serves to obscure an otherwise awkward moment in the Queen's government of the Church.[45] Camden's hostility to Puritanism leads him to give the machiavellian theory the full weight of authority. Archbishop Whitgift's attempts to restore unity in the Church in 1583 were hindered by 'certaine Noblemen; who by placing men unfit in the Church encreased their estate, or else had hopes upon the goods of the Church'.[46] The Puritan Court faction was thus established, as can be seen in a more elaborate form in Peter Heylyn's later history of the presbyterians. Heylyn explained the growth of Puritanism in the 1560s and 1570s by the secret favour of some great men in the Court who greedily gaped after the Remainder of the Churches patrimony. It cannot be denied but that this faction received much encouragement underhand from some great persons near the Queen; from no man more than from the Earl of Leicester, the Lord North, Knollys, Walsingham; who knew how mightily some numbers of the Scots, both lords and gentlemen, had in short time improved their fortune, by humouring the Knoxian Brethren in their Reformation; and could not but expect the like in their own particulars, by a compliance with those men, who aimed apparently at the ruine of the bishops and Cathedral Churches.[47]

The faction nearly enjoyed a revival in the 1620s. Both Heylyn in his biography of Archbishop Laud, and John Hacket in his life of Laud's rival John Williams, give their respective heroes the credit for dissuading the Duke of Buckingham from a similar plot to expropriate Church lands in 1624–25.[48]

Camden also strengthened Clapham's distinction between Leicester the courtier and Essex the hero. In phrases echoed by several Stuart commentators, Camden doubted whether Essex was a courtier at all: 'indeed he seemed not a man made for the Court, being not easily induced to any unhandsome Actions . . . No man was more ambitious of glory by vertuous and noble deeds, no man more careless of everything else.'[49] Leicester by contrast 'was reputed a compleat Courtier', who 'was wont to put up all his passions in his pocket'.[50] Yet by posing this contrast Camden did create other problems. However unsuccessful Leicester's intrigues may have been, the malignant favourite still raised doubts about Elizabeth's wisdom and judgement. Camden evaded the problem in part by employing the standard trope of the Court as the seat of underhanded behaviour, and thus the natural environment for Leicester.[51] But he is also quick to deny that Elizabeth was a puppet Queen; her favour was a product of her 'rare and royal clemency'. Thereafter he disappears into astrology:

> whether this might proceed from some secret instinct of those vertues apparant in him, or out of common respect, they both being prisoners under Queene Marie, or from their first procreation, by a secret coniunction of the Planets at the houre of their birth combining their bearts in one, no man can easily conceive.[52]

His conclusion 'it is most certain, that onely Destinie causeth Princes to affect some, and reiect others', may legitimately be termed evasive.[53] Camden's primary concern with *res gestae* absolved him from the need to draw any explicit wider political deductions from his history. Nevertheless he was clearly unhappy with a Leicesterian monopoly of the Court and moved tentatively towards a more open environment. Leicester's attempt to obtain a 'general lieutenancy under the Queen' in 1588 was halted by Burghley and Hatton, and the Queen 'betimes prevented the danger which might have ensued in giving too much power to one man'.[54] Similarly, Elizabeth herself attempted to extinguish the Leicester–Sussex quarrel of 1565, 'For she condemned dissension among Peeres, and that old proverbe used by many, *Divide et Impera . . .'.*[55]

The publication of the *Annals* had a major influence on the Stuart debate over favourites. The comparisons drawn between Essex and Buckingham in the late 1620s were based in the main on Camden's portrait of Essex.[56] Despite his ultimate obscurity on the relationship between factions and favourites, his portrait of the Elizabethan Court provided evidence for the argument for a 'balanced' Court. In the final version of his essay on 'Faction', Bacon revealed the contemporary concern. Princes should not govern their estates 'according to the respect of factions'; yet the instability of factions enables monarchs to control them.[57] It was, however, Sir Robert Naunton's *Fragmenta regalia* that delivered the most open attack on the tradition of 'Leicester's Commonwealth', and painted the most radical portrait of Elizabeth's Court.

Naunton was nothing if not explicit about his position; Elizabeth was puppet-mistress, never a puppet.

> The principal note of her reign will be that she ruled much by faction and parties, which she herself both made, upheld and weakened as her own great judgement advised, for I disassent from the common and received opinion that my lord of Leicester was absolute and alone in her grace and favour.

The hegemonical favourite had never existed.

> Her ministers and instruments of state . . . were favourites and not minions, such as acted more by her own princely rules and judgement than by their own will and appetites; which she observed to the last, for we find no Gaveston, Vere or Spencer to have swayed alone during forty-four years.[58]

Given the probable date of completion of the *Fragmenta* (1633), and the comparison between Elizabethan and Caroline Parliaments, the implicit contrast between the Elizabethan and the Stuart Court (of which Naunton himself had first-hand experience) is clear. By making this comparison, Naunton's work played a role in the creation of the Elizabethan legend second only to the *Annals*. Yet Naunton also described the Elizabethan Court in terms unlike anything encountered previously.[59] The 22 portraits of the leading men of the reign are divided into two categories, *togati* and *de Militia*, which owe more to classical parallels than historical reality. The portraits include extensive borrowings from Camden, both directly, and indirectly through Wotton's *Parallel* between Essex and Buckingham, but Naunton's most dramatic and frequently quoted anecdotes have no prior source. These include the famous 'I will have here but one mistress and no master' speech (employed to put Leicester in his place), Sussex's deathbed denunciation of the gypsy, Leicester's claim that the Queen's relations were of 'the tribe of Dan', and the Marquess of Winchester's excuse 'ortus sum ex salice non ex quercu'. It may be going too far to dismiss them completely as artistic inventions, but they can be regarded as no more than Elizabethan apocrypha.

Naunton's defence of Elizabeth from the charge of taking into her favour 'a mere new man or a mechanic' on the ground that 'it was part of her natural propensity to grace and support ancient nobility' also reflects the earlier debate.[60] Yet the attempt to restore the nobility to the Court is equally suspect. Nor can the importance he assigns to his characters be accepted outright. His personal animus against Sir Christopher Hatton and defence of Sir John Perrot are well known. Why the relatively obscure Sir John Packington was included, when a number of leading Court figures (like Sir Thomas Heneage) were omitted, remains a mystery.[61] The Knollys–Norris feud to which he gives such prominence is also difficult to trace elsewhere. These biographical details would not in themselves deserve much attention were it not for the profound effect Naunton's picture of a volatile and faction-ridden Court that the Queen manipulated to her advantage has had on so many later accounts of the reign.

III

By the middle of the seventeenth century Naunton's Queen Elizabeth had become the model of political wisdom. As the republican Francis Osborne, who regarded favourites as an 'Epidemical mischief', put it, Elizabeth's inconstancy of favour was a virtue, for it created 'the double and contrary interests of a divided party, no vertue was excluded or vice admitted'.[62] This was not, however, the view of nineteenth-century scholarship. J. A. Froude's portrait of the Queen as an overly indulgent woman was deeply influenced by his discovery of the Spanish ambassadorial reports of the matrimonial intrigues of the 1560s. These led him to view Elizabeth as 'dashed with a taint which she inherited with her mother's blood'. The successes of the reign were to be attributed to the 'policy' of Burghley and the 'skill' of Walsingham. Leicester, consumed by his ambition to marry the Queen, was an ornamental, if malignant, figure:

> he combined in himself the worst qualities of both sexes. Without courage, without talent, without virtue, he was the handsome, soft, polished, and attentive minion of the Court. The queen . . . selected her own friends; and in the smooth surface of Dudley's flattery she saw reflected an image of her own creation . . .[63]

Froude had little to say about faction as an aspect of Elizabethan politics; this was the discovery (or rediscovery) of Conyers Read. Read's research into the conduct of foreign policy in the later 1570s and early 1580s led him to query Froude's description of the relationship between Burghley and Walsingham.[64]

Instead of a single 'policy' there were now distinct rival policies. More pro-found, however, was his positing of an 'inveterate antagonism [between] Burghley and Leicester' that decisively shaped the politics of the reign. 'It is certain that each one continually tried to displace the other from his position of influence. The contest between them began at the very beginning of Eliza-beth's reign and ended only with Leicester's death.'[65] Arising from these tensions was a central factional division in the Court. Burghley 'the Erastian' led a conservative coalition with Sussex, who 'hated Leicester with all the fervour of a passionate nature' as his deputy. Leicester was the patron of what was a more sophisticated version of the puritan faction of 'Leicester's Commonwealth', 'not because of his abilities, which were mediocre at best, but because his commanding position beside the Queen gave them an advoc-ate and won for their ideas a consideration which they could hardly otherwise have got'. Walsingham 'supplied the brains and framed the policy while Leicester furnished the court influence of the faction'.[66]

Read's factional division was essentially one over policy. A more radical approach to the role of faction was taken by Sir John Neale. Not only was it of the essence of Court life – 'competition at the court was ceaseless' – but it was less concerned with policy than patronage. 'The place of party was taken by faction, and the rivalry of the factions was centred on what mattered supremely to everyone: . . . control of patronage.'[67] Neale's Elizabeth, who 'played the factions one against the other', is openly Naunton's (an 'astute' observer, who is accepted uncritically), garnished with examples drawn mainly from the 1590s.[68] Between them Read and Neale established factionalism as the central phenomenon of Elizabethan Court politics, yet the bases for their factions – policy or patronage – were fundamentally different. The difficulties thus posed can be seen in Wallace MacCaffrey's two volumes. MacCaffrey also posits an antagonism between Burghley and Leicester, but one more active in the 1560s when it was provoked by Leicester's efforts to marry the Queen. However, once Leicester abandoned this ambition in the early 1570s, factionalism diminished.[69] Patronage does not appear to play much of a role one way or the other, except in the Church. MacCaffrey sees the growing division over Puritanism in the 1580s leading to the increased prominence of Hatton, to whom he assigns more importance than his predecessors have done, as the patron of the more conservative clergy.[70]

MacCaffrey's account of Court politics has, if nothing else, raised major doubts about Read's conception of factionalism over policy. There have been similar problems with the role of patronage. In his later work Read was frequently forced to admit that the evidence for the antagonism between Burghley and Leicester was not as clear-cut as he would have liked.[71] Sir Geoffrey Elton, though prepared on balance to accept the existence of factions, has injected an important note of scepticism in the observation that 'we have grown so familiar with the notion of faction . . . that we forget how little the structure of those groupings has been studied'.[72] The difficulty of explaining the dynamics of Court politics in conventional terms is revealed in essays published since 1979. Eric Ives comments, 'Burghley and Leicester – Elizabeth's closest confidant and her most intimate courtier – were recognised rivals, but there was never a complete breakdown of relations.'[73] Pam Wright rephrases it slightly:

> [after 1572] the principal contenders for power seem to have decided that while competition was healthy, full-blown factional disputes were a destructive and time-consuming diversion . . . This *modus vivendi* among the leaders chimed nicely with the instinct of everyone else to run with the hare and hunt with the hound.[74]

In other words, hard evidence for the central argument that factionalism and patronage were the central constituents of Court politics has so far been lacking. In some cases factions have been created out of thin air – the 'too blatant a vendetta' that William, Lord Cobham, is said to have conducted against Leicester, for example.[75] Equally dubious has been the attempt to build the authors of 'Leicester's Commonwealth' into a 'catholic Court faction'.[76] Patronage struggles within the Court between Burghley and Leicester have been noteworthy by their absence. In fact the opposite is the case. In a number of cases – for example, those of Walsingham himself, Henry Killigrew, Robert Beale, William Herle – clear lines of allegiance have been very difficult to draw. Central to the argument for a struggle between Burghley and Leicester has been Leicester's putative involvement in the attempted overthrow in 1569. Yet the evidence for this incident is very thin. Apart from the tradition of *A Treatise of Treasons*, discussed in this essay, which does not mention Leicester, the only other source is the notorious Roberto Ridolphi, who is scarcely reliable.[77] This does not mean that Cecil looked upon a marriage between Leicester and the Queen with enthusiasm, that they did not disagree over foreign policy, or adopt different approaches to ecclesiastical policy, but these instances must be weighed against the major areas of agreement.

Once the Burghley–Leicester hostility is queried, then the role of the favourite becomes clearer. The favourites, like the other central figures of the Court, were there ultimately by the Queen's choice. Unlike the favourites at the Court of Henry III of France, for example, their rise was neither overtly political nor factional.[78] Yet, unlike Hatton and Ralegh (or the Stuart favourites), Leicester did not come from a minor gentry family, but from the leading family of the Edwardian Court, however notorious it may have become after 1553. Thus, although Elizabeth's attraction to him may have been purely personal, he was a choice of a major political consequence. Much of his relationship to Burghley can be explained by this, for, however much Burghley may have disliked and feared the revival of old enmities that Leicester's rise might threaten, they were at the end of the day men from a similar political milieu, with a similar range of friends and associations. In this respect the Leicesterian monopoly of the Elizabethan Court was a mirage, for it reflected the hegemony of a broader political élite of which both Burghley and Leicester were part. The older Catholic polemic was to this extent correct, for there had occurred in the decades that preceded the accession of Elizabeth a major reshaping of the English political élite in which religious allegiances clearly played a part. This in turn created the social and political basis of the Elizabethan Court. The central figures were all recipients of the Queen's favour, and, however they may have disagreed, they had too much in common for permanent antagonisms to be established. The terms favourite and faction obscure as much of the reality of the Elizabethan Court as they explain.

BIBLIOGRAPHICAL POSTSCRIPT

The first version of this essay was a paper delivered to the conference on 'The Court at the Beginning of the Modern Age', organised by the German Historical Institute, London, and held at Madingley Hall, Cambridge, in 1987. It was published in the collected papers from that conference in 1991. I have resisted the temptation to make major revisions, and therefore the text and notes are unchanged, with the exception of the correction of some of the punctuation, two typographical errors, and a few of the more egregious solecisms. However, years since it was published there have been a number of important additions to the literature on the subject, and therefore the following brief survey has been added for the benefit of the reader who may wish to pursue points made here further.

As I hope the text has made clear, this essay was intended as a historiographical sequel to my earlier essay on the Court in Christopher Haigh's collection *The Reign of Elizabeth I.* One theme I wished particularly to address was the failure of the existing literature to distinguish between factional disputes over policy and those over patronage. I have since discussed the political role of patronage more fully in an essay published in 1995.[79] Since 1989 substantial sections of my research on the Earl of Leicester have also appeared, which both modify and expand upon points made here. Excluding lighter pieces, these comprise the reconstruction of his surviving papers[80] and the editing of his household accounts[81], three studies of his clientele – one on its Edwardian origins,[82] one on its activities in the House of Commons,[83] and a third on its major regional aspect[84] – and a brief survey of his role in ecclesiastical politics.[85]

A number of lesser points made here can also be expanded upon. A fuller discussion of the contemporary disparagement of Leicester's ancestry can be found in ' "Because I am of that Countrye" '.[86] The reappraisal of the circumstances of the writing of Camden's *Annals* that Dr McGurk initiated has been further developed by D. R. Woolfe in a most exciting way.[87] In discussing Naunton's indebtedness to Camden I overlooked an important piece of evidence: Camden's *Remains* is the source for Winchester's famous description of himself as a willow.[88] It is also clear that my brief comments on the importance of the Elizabethan 'puritan faction' to seventeenth-century Anglican historiography only scratched the surface of a fascinating subject. The theme can be found in numerous works ranging from Sir John Harington's tract on the succession to Izaak Walton's *Life of Mr Richard Hooker*.[89] No less interesting is the role 'Leicester's Commonwealth' continued to play in political debate. An unfortunately anonymous letter of Queen Anne's reign claimed that the recent publication of a new edition of the tract was part of a Tory attack on the Duke of Marlborough as a 'single minister'.[90] This in turn reopens the question of whether the reprinting of 'Leicester's Commonwealth' in 1641 was an example of contemporary anti-Puritan polemic.

The wider debate on the role of factions in Tudor Court politics as a whole shows no signs of diminishing. To date the 1530s remain the most hotly disputed subject, particularly the fall of Anne Boleyn, where the earlier theories that a factional struggle was responsible for her demise and the outbreak of the Pilgrimage of Grace (advanced by Eric Ives, Sir Geoffrey Elton, and David Starkey) have been challenged by George Bernard.[91] Even if the question of Anne's 'guilt' remains unproven, Dr Bernard has effectively queried much of the evidence on which the factional argument rests.[92] The Elizabethan debate has been less dramatic, but, as Steven Gunn has perceptively suggested, what provides a continuity between the reigns is the issue of monarchical independence: were decisions made by the monarch for his or her own reasons or under factional pressure?[93]

The issue in Elizabethan politics that has attracted most attention recently has been the distinction drawn between the collegiality of the years to 1590 and the factionalism of the final decade. Susan Doran has continued to argue the case for the importance of factional politics in the earlier period, particularly over the Queen's marriage, though, by simultaneously arguing that the Queen took her decisions independently, she has muddied the waters somewhat.[94] The 1590s have been examined in detail in the contributions to the volume, published in 1995, that John Guy has edited. Paul Hammer argues that policies rather than patronage were the key to the struggles between Essex and the Cecils.[95] Natalie Mears advances a similar case: that the Cecil–Essex struggle was a dispute between martial and civilian codes rather than an attack on a *regnum Cecilianum* by those excluded.[96] An underlying theme in both these essays (and much of the rest of the volume from which they come) is that of a growing loss of control by Elizabeth, a subject to which Dr Hammer has returned in an interesting paper on the rise of Ralegh and Essex in the later 1580s delivered to the conference 'The World of the Favourite' that Sir John Elliott held at Magdalen College, Oxford, in March 1996.[97]

Two further subjects are also relevant. One is the rise of Archbishop Whitgift and the effects of the new tone of ecclesiastical government in the 1590s. In this respect it could be argued that Whitgift's appointment as Archbishop of Canterbury in 1583 was a more important turning point in Elizabethan politics than 1588–90.[98] The other is the growing interest in the intermediate level of Elizabethan government and the question of a united political élite, which underpins the case for collegiality. This interest has manifested itself both in the arguments for the continuity of a Protestant élite from the reign of Edward VI[99] and in the debate surrounding the role of the 'men-of-business'.[100] These are important topics to be addressed in any further study of the politics of the Court.

NOTES

1 On the structure of the court, see S. L. Adams, 'Eliza Enthroned? The Court and its Politics' [Ch. 2], and P. Wright, 'A Change of Direction: The Ramifications of a Female Household, 1558–1603', in D. Starkey (ed.), *The English Court from the Wars of the Roses to the Civil War* (London, 1987), pp. 147–72.

2 N. Cuddy, 'The Revival of the Entourage: The Bedchamber of James I, 1603–1625', in Starkey (ed.), *The English Court*, pp. 173–225. R. Lockyer, *Buckingham: The Life and Political Career of George Villiers, First Duke of Buckingham, 1592–1628* (London, 1981), pp. 17, 21–2, makes the sexual connection explicit.

3 R. P. Shepheard, 'Royal Favorites in the Political Discourse of Tudor and Stuart England', Ph.D. thesis, Claremount (1985), surveys the literature but draws different conclusions from those advanced here.

4 R. Houlbrooke, 'Politics and Religion in Tudor England', *Historian*, 17 (1987–8), pp. 10–11. See J. E. Neale, 'The Elizabethan Political Scene', in his *Essays in Elizabethan History* (London, 1958), pp. 59–84.

5 See, however, Haigh's comments in the introduction to *The Reign of Elizabeth I*, pp. 1–25, at pp. 6–11.

6 The excellent recent edition by D. C. Peck, *Leicester's Commonwealth: The Copy of a Letter written by a Master of Art of Cambridge (1584) and Related Documents* (Athens, Oh., 1985), supersedes all earlier ones.

7 STC nos. 7601 and 10005. Neither title has been published in a modern edition.

8 For the debate over the authorship of 'Leicester's Commonwealth', see Peck (ed.), *Leicester's Commonwealth*, pp. 25–32. *A Treatise of Treasons* is generally attributed to John Leslie, Bishop of Ross, the agent of Mary, Queen of Scots; *A Declaration of the True Causes* to Richard Verstegan. The tracts are briefly discussed in P. J. Holmes, *Resistance and Compromise: The Political Thought of the Elizabethan Catholics* (Cambridge, 1982), pp. 25–6, 138, 141.

9 *Treatise*, sigs. [a5], a4.

10 See art. 4 of the York Articles and art. 8 of the Pontefract articles, and the advice of Sir Thomas Tempest, printed in A. Fletcher, *Tudor Rebellions* (3rd edn, London, 1983), pp. 105, 109, 111. Cf. W. G. Zeeveld, *The Foundations of Tudor Policy* (Cambridge, Mass., 1948), pp. 196–200, and G. R. Elton, 'The Political Creed of Thomas Cromwell', in his *Studies in Tudor and Stuart Politics and Government* (4 vols, Cambridge, 1974–92), pp. 216–20.

11 C. Sharp, *The Rising in the North: The 1569 Rebellion*, ed. R. Wood (Shotton, 1975), p. 42. The extent to which the rebellions of 1536 and 1569 were revolts of a self-conscious 'old nobility' cannot be adequately discussed here. Certainly the Earl of Westmorland came close to seeing his actions in 1569 in this light. The general point is touched on in passing in M. R. James, *English Politics and the Concept of Honour, 1485–1642, Past and Present*, supp. 3 (1978), pp. 32–43, repr. in James, *Politics and Culture: Essays in Early Modern England* (Cambridge, 1986), pp. 308–415. The long-running debate over the causes of both rebellions has revealed the difficulty of isolating a single issue.

12 *Treatise*, sig. a3^v, fo. 84.

13 *Ibid.*, sig. [a6^v].

14 The familiarity with the 1569 intrigues supports the case for the authorship of the Bishop of Ross, whose involvement in them was considerable.

15 *Treatise*, fos. 11^v–12^v, 29^v–30^v.

16 Peck (ed.), *Leicester's Commonwealth*, pp. 172–4, 193. Cf. p. 111.

17 *Ibid.*, p. 186.

18 *Ibid.*, p. 95, cf. pp. 93, 98–9.

19 *Ibid.*, pp. 103, 92.

20 *Ibid.*, p. 73, cf. pp. 67–9, 104–5.

21 *Ibid.*, pp. 115–17.

22 *A Declaration of the True Causes*, pp. 10, 52–3, 70.

23 'Certain Observations made upon a Libel Published this Present Year 1592', in *The Letters and Life of Francis Bacon*, ed. J. Spedding *et al.* (7 vols, London, 1861–74), I, pp. 197–8.

24 E. P. Read and C. Read (eds), *Certain Observations Concerning the Life and Reign of Queen Elizabeth by John Clapham* (Philadelphia, 1951), pp. 75–7, 90–4.

25 The phrase used in a letter of 1 July 1591, PRO SP 12/239/70.

26 See, for example, Sir Walter Raleigh, *Works* (8 vols, Oxford, 1825), VIII, pp. 758–9, 769–70, Lord Henry Howard to Sir R. Cecil, *c.* 1602.

27 Huntington Library, Ellesmere MS 1598, Treatise by R. Griffith, *c.* 1598–1600, fo. 17^v. I should like to thank the Huntington Library for permission to cite this manuscript.

28 A. Collins (ed.), *Letters and Memorials of State in the Reigns of Queen Mary . . . from the Originals at Penshurst* (2 vols, London, 1746), II, p. 122, R. Whyte to Sir R. Sidney, 12 Sept. 1599.

29 See, for example, the two anti-Puritan tracts of Richard Bancroft, *Daungerous Positions and Practices* and *Survay of the Pretended Holy Discipline* (both London, 1593).

30 BL Lansdowne MS xlv, fo. 98, Whitgift to Burghley. The question of the truth of the charges demands more space than can be devoted to it here. In 1588 Leicester received a grant of episcopal estates in recompense for his expenditure in the Netherlands. This was supported by both Walsingham and Burghley, see BL Cotton MS, Titus B. vii, fo. 32, and Lansdowne MS xxxi, fo. 103 (misdated to 1580). Leicester's secretary, Arthur Atye, later commented on the 'novelty of it', Longleat House, Dudley MS ii, fo. 261, to Leicester, 27 Aug. 1588. The Welsh separatist John Penry proposed to Essex in 1593 that the Queen should abolish the bishops and 'employ their livings for the benefit of hir crown and the support of hir subjects' (A. Peel (ed.), *The Notebook of John Penry 1593* (Camden Society, 3rd ser., 67; London, 1944), p. 89).

31 F. J. Furnivall (ed.), *Harrison's Description of England* (New Shakespeare Society, 6th ser., I; London, 1877), pp. lviii–ix; cf. pp. lix–lx for Harrison's fears of attacks on Church lands in the Parliaments of 1589 and 1593.

32 HMC, *Calendar of the Manuscripts of the . . . Marquess of Salisbury*, XII (1910), p. 113, to Sir R. Cecil, 17 Apr. 1602.

33 Sir John Harington, *Nugae Antiguae* (2 vols, London, 1804), II, p. 268.

34 The editions employed here are the Abraham Darcie translation of 1625 (*Annales, The True and Royal History of Elizabeth, Queene of England*) for the first three books (1558–88) and the 1688 translation (*The History of the Most Renowned and Victorious Princess Elizabeth*) for bk IV (1589–1603). Although the Darcie translation is clumsier, it is less influenced by later commentary.

35 W. Camden, *The History of the Most Renowned and Victorious Princess Elizabeth*, ed. W. T. MacCaffrey (Chicago, 1970), p. xxxviii.

36 Camden, *History*, ed. MacCaffrey, pp. xxxv–xxxvi, cf. p. xxvii. H. R. Trevor-Roper, 'Queen Elizabeth's First Historian: William Camden', in his *Renaissance Essays* (London, 1985), pp. 121–48, at pp. 134–5. The only sources Camden specifically mentions are Sir John Fortescue and Essex's secretary Henry Cuffe. See bk IV, pp. 438, 624.

37 Camden, *History*, ed. MacCaffrey, bk III, p. 288.

38 *Ibid.*, bks I–II, pp. 100, 366–7. Cf. Peck (ed.), *Leicester's Commonwealth*, pp. 82–4.

39 I have examined one of them in 'The Release of Lord Darnley and the Failure of the Amity', in M. Lynch (ed.), *Mary Stewart: Queen in Three Kingdoms* (Oxford, 1988), pp. 123–53.

40 J. McGurk, 'William Camden: Civil Historian or Gloriana's Propagandist?', *History Today*, 38 (Apr. 1988), pp. 47–53, at p. 52.

41 Camden, *Annales*, bk I, p. 121.

42 See Peck (ed.), *Leicester's Commonwealth*, pp. 172–3.

43 Printed in W. K. Boyd (ed.), *Calendar of State Papers Relating to Scotland and Mary, Queen of Scots*, IV (Edinburgh and Glasgow, 1905), pp. 32–40. Cf. Camden, *Annales*, bk I, pp. 208–13.

44 Camden, *Annales*, bk I, p. 199; bk II, p. 256. Cf. Peck (ed.), *Leicester's Commonwealth*, pp. 84–5. The reference to salads may reflect a well-known taste of Leicester's. See his attempt to hire a French cook to make salads in the winter of 1584–5: Huntington Library, MS HM 21714, to J. Hotman, 2 Nov. 1584, and Paris, Archives du Ministère

des Relations Extérieures, Correspondance Politique, Hollande, II, fo. 215, to Hotman, 4 Jan. 1585.

45 Camden, *Annales*, bk III, p. 45. Cf. P. Collinson, *Archbishop Grindal 1519–1583* (London, 1979), pp. 253–6.

46 Camden, *Annales*, bk III, p. 46.

47 *Aerius Redivivus; or the History of the Presbyterians* (London, 1670), p. 258.

48 P. Heylyn, *Cyprianus Anglicanus or, The History of the life and Death . . . of William . . . Lord Archbishop of Canterbury* (London, 1668), p. 123; J. Hacket, *Scrinia Reserata: A Memorial offer'd to . . . John Williams* (London, 1693), pp. 204–6.

49 Camden, History, bk IV, p. 624. Cf. Sir H. Wotton, 'The Parallel of R. Devereux, earl of Essex and George Villiers, duke of Buckingham', and [E. Hyde], 'The Difference and Disparity between . . . George Villiers, duke of Buckingham and Robert, earl of Essex', *Reliquiae Wottonianae* (London, 1685), pp. 175, 186–7.

50 Camden, Annales, bk III, p. 288; Wotton, 'Parallel', p. 175.

51 See, for example, Camden, *History*, bk IV, pp. 509–43.

52 Camden, *Annales*, bk I, p. 57; cf. bk III, p. 288.

53 *Ibid.*, bk I, p. 57.

54 *Ibid.*, bk III, p. 288.

55 *Ibid.*, bk I, p. 121.

56 See the Wotton and Hyde essays cited in n. 49 above.

57 *The Works of Francis Bacon*, ed. J. Spedding *et al.* (7 vols, London, 1857–9), VI, pp. 498–50.

58 Sir R. Naunton, *Fragmenta regalia; or Observations on Queen Elizabeth her Times and Favourites*, ed. J. S. Cerovski (Washington, 1985), pp. 40–1.

59 Shepheard, 'Royal Favorites', p. 134, describes Naunton's portrait of the Court as 'idiosyncratic'; cf. p. 139.

60 Naunton, *Fragmenta regalia*, pp. 69, 72.

61 There is a seventeenth-century life of Packington which portrays him as a defender of the lands of the Church against Leicester: Cambridge University Library, MS MM.i.39, see fo. 224^v.

62 *The Works of Francis Osborne . . . in four several parts* (10th edn, London, 1701), pp. 562, 559.

63 J. A. Froude, *The Reign of Elizabeth* (Everyman edn, 5 vols, n.d.), I, p. 60.

64 Conyers Read, 'Faction in the English Privy Council under Elizabeth', *Annual Bulletin of the American Historical Association* (1911), pp. 111–19.

65 Read, 'Faction', p. 113.

66 Read, 'Faction', p. 116; Read, 'Walsingham and Burghley in Queen Elizabeth's Privy Council', *English Historical Review*, 28 (1913), pp. 34–58, at pp. 39–41.

67 Neale, 'Elizabethan Political Scene', p. 70. The argument is also developed in W. T. MacCaffrey, 'Place and Patronage in Elizabethan Politics', in S. T. Bindoff, J. Hurstfield, and C. H. Williams (eds), *Elizabethan Government and Society: Essays presented to Sir John Neale* (London, 1961), pp. 95–126.

68 Neale, 'Elizabethan Political Scene', p. 79 and *passim*.

69 W. T. MacCaffrey, *Queen Elizabeth and the Making of Policy, 1572–1588* (Princeton, NJ, 1981), pp. 458–9.

70 *Ibid.*, pp. 452–4. However, cf. P. Collinson, *The Elizabethan Puritan Movement* (London, 1967), pp. 313–14.

71 See, for example, Conyers Read, *Lord Burghley and Queen Elizabeth* (New York, 1960), p. 375.

72 G. R. Elton, 'Tudor Government: The Points of Contact: III. The Court', *Transactions of the Royal Historical Society*, 5th ser., 26 (1976), pp. 211–28, at p. 224.

73 Eric Ives, *Faction in Tudor England* (Historical Association, Appreciations in History, 6; 1979), p. 22.

74 Wright, 'A Change of Direction', p. 170.

75 P. Clark, *English Provincial Society from the Reformation to the Revolution: Religion, Society and Politics in Kent, 1500–1640* (Hassocks, 1977), p. 129. This is based on a misreading of D. B. McKeen, '"A Memory of Honour": A Study of the House of Cobham of Kent in the Reign of Elizabeth I', Ph.D. thesis, Birmingham (1964), pp. 202, 253. Cf. p. 496.

76 Peck (ed.), *Leicester's Commonwealth*, pp. 13–25. P. Roberts, 'Elizabeth and her Dazzling Court', in R. Smith (ed.), *Royal Armada, Guide to the 400th Anniversary of the Sailing of the Armada* (London, 1988), pp. 70–88, at p. 76.

77 See the correspondence printed in J. M. B. C. Kervijn de Lettenhove (ed.), *Relations politiques des Pays-Bas et de l'Angleterre sous le règne de Philippe II* (11 vols, Brussels, 1882–1900), V, p. 307.

78 For Henry III, see J. Boucher, *Société et mentalités autour de Henri III* (4 vols, Lille, 1981), I, pp. 199, 208–9.

79 'The Patronage of the Crown in Elizabethan Politics: The 1590s in Perspective' [Ch. 4].

80 S. L. Adams, 'The Papers of Robert Dudley, Earl of Leicester I–III', *Archives*, 20 (1992), pp. 63–85; 20 (1993), pp. 131–44; 21 (1996), pp. 1–26. Part IV is in preparation.

81 *Household Accounts and Disbursement Books of Robert Dudley, Earl of Leicester, 1558–1561, 1584–1586*, ed. S. L. Adams (Camden Society, 5th ser., 6; London, 1995).

82 'The Dudley clientele, 1553–1563' [Ch. 8].

83 'The Dudley clientele and the House of Commons, 1559–1586' [Ch. 10].

84 '"Because I am of that Countrye & Mynde to Plant Myself There": Robert Dudley, Earl of Leicester and the West Midlands' [Ch. 15].

85 'A Godly Peer? Leicester and the Puritans' [Ch. 11].

86 Ch. 15 below, pp. 312–15.

87 D. R. Woolfe, *The Idea of History in Early Stuart England* (Toronto, 1990), see pp. 215–19.

88 William Camden, *Remains Concerning Britain* (1870 edn), p. 313 (under 'Wise Speeches').

89 Harington, for example, comments, 'Those we call Puritans seemed to adhere to the Earl of Huntingdon's title . . . This faction died with my lo. of Leicester' (*Sir John Harington. A Tract on the Succession to the Crown (A. D. 1602)*, ed. C. R. Markham (Roxburgh Club, 1880), p. 41). I hope to explore the whole subject more fully when occasion serves.

90 Lambeth Palace Library, MS 933, art. 93, 'A letter concerning the memoirs of Robert Dudley, Earl of Leicester, now published by Dr Drake'. This was James Drake's edition, entitled *The Secret Memoirs of Robert Dudley*, and published in 1706 and 1708. The letter, which from internal evidence was written before Godolphin's dismissal in 1710, is an informed commentary on both the contemporary context and its background.

91 The best guide to the now extensive literature on this subject is Steven Gunn, 'The Structures of Politics in Early Tudor England', *Transactions of the Royal Historical Society*, 6th ser., 5 (1995), p. 59 n. 1. I discuss Sir Geoffrey Elton's contribution to the debate in my paper on 'Politics', which was delivered to the Royal Historical Society conference 'The Eltonian Legacy' in March 1996 [Ch. 5].

92 See his comments in G. Bernard, 'The Fall of Anne Boleyn', *English Historical Review*, 106 (1991), pp. 591–5.

93 Gunn, 'Structures of Politics', pp. 59–60.

94 Susan Doran, 'Religion and Politics at the Court of Elizabeth I: The Habsburg Marriage Negotiations of 1559–1567', *English Historical Review*, 104 (1989), pp. 908–26, and more generally in Doran, *Monarchy and Matrimony: The Courtships of Elizabeth I* (London, 1996).

95 Paul Hammer, 'Patronage at Court, Faction and the Earl of Essex', in Guy (ed.), *The Reign of Elizabeth I*, pp. 65–86.

96 Natalie Mears, '*Regnum Cecilianum*? A Cecilian perspective of the Court', in Guy (ed.), *The Reign of Elizabeth I*, pp. 46–64.

97 Paul Hammer, '"Absolute and Sovereign Mistress of her Grace"? Queen Elizabeth I and her Favourites, 1581–1592', in J. H. Elliott and L. W. B. Brockliss (eds), *The World of the Favourite, c.1550–c.1675* (New Haven, 1999), pp. 38–53. Although the conference itself was chiefly concerned with the seventeenth century, many of the wider issues raised at it are relevant here.

98 See Guy, 'The Elizabethan Establishment and the Ecclesiastical Polity', in Guy (ed.), *The Reign of Elizabeth I*, pp. 126–49, and the literature cited there.

99 The case for intellectual and religious continuity was made in W. S. Hudson, *The Cambridge Connection and the Elizabethan Settlement of 1559* (Durham, NC, 1980), and N. L. Jones, *Faith by Statute: Parliament and the Settlement of Religion 1559* (London, 1982). In Ch. 8 below (see n. 82 above) I seek to add a further dimension. David Loades has challenged the case for the continuity between Northumberland's and Leicester's clienteles made there in the epilogue to his biography of Northumberland (*John Dudley, Duke of Northumberland, 1504–1553* (Oxford, 1996)), but he overlooks much of the evidence.

100 See, in general, Michael A. R. Graves, *Thomas Norton: The Parliament Man* (Oxford, 1994), and Patrick Collinson, 'Puritans, Men of Business and Elizabethan Parliaments', in his *Elizabethan Essays* (London, 1994), pp. 59–86.

Chapter 4

The patronage of the crown in Elizabethan politics: the 1590s in perspective[a]

I

In February 1597, after learning of the initial discussions of the naval operation that would become known as the 'Islands Voyage', Sir Francis Vere observed to Sir Robert Sidney: 'Of my Lord of Essex's going to sea, I am sorry to hear, unless I could persuade myself that before his going he would furnish the court with offices, for that it will else prove his adversaries work whilst he is absent.'[1] These comments were no doubt an allusion to the events of the previous summer, when Sir Robert Cecil was finally successful in obtaining formal appointment as Principal Secretary of State while Essex was absent on the voyage to Cadiz, but their general import is no less interesting. They contain several of the apparent truisms of Elizabethan Court politics: the competition for patronage, the need for a constant presence at Court, and the dual function of office under the crown as both the prize and the instrument of politics. Such commentary is found throughout Sidney's correspondence, which since its publication in 1746 has been one of the best-known sources for the Court politics of the 1590s. The editor, Arthur Collins, then noted to a friend that in the Sidney Papers 'the intrigues of Queen Elizabeths court [are] more fully set forth than has been published and which shows how the Cecilian Faction Reigned'.[2]

Quite ironically, perhaps, this eighteenth-century perception of the relationship between the patronage of the crown and Elizabethan Court factions is shared by the most advanced modern scholarship. Yet this scholarly consensus is not completely convincing; if the underlying arguments are examined the relationship between patronage and faction is by no means so clear cut, and a number of questions are posed that have yet to receive answers. The earliest modern analysis of Elizabethan politics in factional terms was that outlined by Conyers Read in the first decades of this century

68

during the preparation of his study of the career of Sir Francis Walsingham. In what was essentially a revision of J. A. Froude's portrait of the dedicated Walsingham and Lord Burghley managing the country on behalf of a wayward queen, Read pointed to a serious difference of opinion between the two over the conduct of foreign policy, about which the rest of the Privy Council divided. But this factional dispute was inspired specifically by the debate over intervention in the Netherlands, which was limited to the decade 1575–85. The conciliar factions were to some extent shaped by religious allegiances and clashes of personality, but they were not otherwise concerned with issues of domestic politics. Nor was Read himself then interested in whether this factional division was continued into the succeeding decade or came to an end in the years 1585–88.[3]

The connection between patronage and factional politics was first drawn by Sir John Neale in his Raleigh Lecture of 1948. In what was a reappraisal of the sixteenth century inspired by Sir Lewis Namier's earlier re-interpretation of eighteenth-century parliamentary politics, Neale argued that 'The place of party was taken by faction, and the rivalry of the factions was centred on what mattered supremely to everybody: influence over the Queen, and, through that influence, control of patronage with its accompanying benefits.'[4] If the distinction between party and faction was ultimately derived from Namier, Neale was nonetheless clear that the battleground was the Court, not Parliament: 'As we should expect, clientage reached its fullest expression at Court. Here was the Mecca of patronage: place and profit incomparable to be had through the favour of the great ones of the land.'[5] Yet while Namier had supplied a carefully articulated case for the importance of the patronage of the crown to eighteenth-century politics, Neale took it more or less as proven.[6] Similarly the assumption that the motor of faction was the pursuit of patronage was also taken for granted. The relationship between factions of this type and Read's 'ideologically driven' factions was never explored.

Neale did, however, develop several further very influential theories about the politics of Elizabethan patronage. He argued that patronage also gave the crown a potent instrument for political control and manipulation; careful exploitation of its powers of patronage could thus become the key to successful monarchical government. Elizabeth's skilful control of Court factions, an argument Neale drew from Sir Robert Naunton's seventeenth-century commentary *Fragmenta regalia*, by means of patronage thus became an important theme in his revision of the queen's reputation.[7] Yet he also recognised that if this type of politics had worked successfully during the first thirty years of the reign, the same could not be said for the final decade. Precisely why there was a deterioration in the 1590s was less clear, however, and he attributed it variously to the weakening powers of the ageing queen, the strains of the war with Spain, and the possibility that 'the standard of public morality was declining sharply in the last decade or so of the reign'. He then confused the issue by drawing almost all the examples of patronage disputes cited in 'The Elizabethan Political Scene' from the 1590s, and, as he himself admitted, by relying heavily on the correspondence of Michael Hickes, which was largely concerned with the administration of the Court of Wards.[8]

Subsequent work on Elizabethan politics has in the main elaborated these themes. Wallace MacCaffrey has argued that there was a deliberate employment of patronage to cement loyalty to the crown; that this was a Tudor rather than a specifically Elizabethan policy; and that it helped to transform the 'dynastic factionalism' of the fifteenth century into the Court- and patronage-centred politics of the seventeenth. The successful exploitation of patronage was a central element in the stability of Elizabeth's reign, for which the credit went both to Burghley, whom he described as a 'patronage minister', and to the queen, who created 'a rough system', for, by 'refusing to limit her favour to a single favourite, she kept open a number of channels to her bounty'. Unlike Neale, MacCaffrey did attempt an assessment of the actual resources of patronage at the crown's disposal and having noted the limited number of offices of profit available suggested that other forms of 'royal bounty' may have been more significant than office-holding.[9] Lawrence Stone advanced a similar thesis. While he accepted Neale's general argument that patronage gave the crown 'great powers of leverage over the nobility', he was also influenced by the contemporary debate over the 'General Crisis' of the seventeenth century, and the rôle of the expansion of an essentially parasitic Court. This led him to suggest that the 1590s saw the emergence of a specific crisis of patronage in which pressure on the finite patronage resources of the crown from a growing population had by the end of the sixteenth century created an imbalance between supply and demand that neither Elizabeth nor the first two Stuarts were able to resolve.[10]

This 'concentration on the politics of patronage' Christine Carpenter has defined as a characteristic of 'the "new history" of the period'.[11] For Linda Peck, 'The basis of English politics in the sixteenth and seventeenth centuries was the patron-client relationship between the monarchy and the most important political groups in the state, the peerage and the gentry.'[12] Even Christopher Haigh, a critic of Neale on other issues, advances the impeccably Nealean observation that 'the Court was the clearing-house for royal patronage, and the distribution of patronage was a key to political power'.[13] The 'patronage system' features prominently in textbooks on the period.[14] More recently the relationship between factional politics and patronage has been a leading issue in the debates over early-Tudor Court politics, and, specifically, the apparently ideological factional struggles of the 1530s.[15] The connection between the two has been argued most strongly by Eric Ives, who claims that patronage 'produced the simplest form of Tudor faction, the patron and the clients who depended on him and on whom he depended'.[16] But he and Pam Wright have also detected an apparent reduction in factional tension over patronage in the middle years of Elizabeth's reign. This stability he considers to have been an anomaly; the factionalism of the 1590s was not so much a novel deterioration of standards as a return to the Tudor norm.[17]

II

I have elsewhere advanced the argument that factional politics were not endemic to the Elizabethan Court and must be seen as quite specific responses to certain political conjunctures.[18] Such an interpretation would therefore fly in the face of this general agreement on the centrality of patronage-based factions. A resolution is to be found in a re-phrasing of the question. There is no need to dissent from the general agreement over the factionalism of the 1590s; the issue is really the nature of the equally gener- ally perceived distinction between the 1590s and the previous decades, if not the rest of the century. Had the patronage of the crown taken on new signi- ficance during the course of Elizabeth's reign, or were the 1590s simply a return to normal Tudor politics? The answer that will be advanced here is a two-fold one: first, there had been a major re-shaping of the patronage of the crown during the course of the century, and second, the 1590s saw a dram- atically different style of political behaviour. The conjunction between the two created a new politics of patronage.

It is important to start by laying aside the assumption that the employ- ment of patronage by the crown was political in inspiration, and to address the subject instead from the contemporary perspective of the reward of ser- vice. The issues involved were outlined succinctly by the Earl of Salisbury on behalf of James I in 1608:

> For as no Sovereign can be without service, nor service without some reward, so we confess no prince is more desirous than we are to reward the merits of our servants and other subjects in things that might be fitting for us to give, provided always that the same be not prejudicial either to the main part and limbs [sic] of any revenue which we are desirous to leave to our posterity.[19]

The basic definition of service was extremely loose. Claims for reward could be framed in terms of service either rendered in the past, or to be rendered in future, or both simultaneously. Henry VIII granted Sir Thomas Poynings a barony in 1545 'as well for some declaration of our goodness towards him, as also to encourage him to serve us the better'.[20] Service could be either specific and contractual, or general. It was not necessarily directly remunerated: wages were a descendant of the provision of board and lodging in the household, and, as the transitional phrase 'board-wages' reveals, were a consequence of the decline of the household, and therefore intended primarily for those who could not maintain themselves on private means.[21] Nor were the fees attached to offices necessarily intended to supply adequate reward for the services rendered; indeed they may have served primarily as a formal symbol of the relationship between servant and master. This would account for the widespread sixteenth-century practice of supplementing offices with annuities.[22]

Office was not therefore assumed to be its own reward. The pattern was more likely to be one of long periods of un-, or poorly, paid service in expectation of a substantial reward at the end. The universally desired reward was an estate of inheritance, for, as a medieval poet put it, 'servise is non heritage'.[23] Since this estate could be obtained most easily through a direct grant, the late-medieval and Tudor monarchy faced the dilemma of paying for generosity in reward through the alienation of its own landed estate. For this reason policy towards patronage was an aspect of the crown's overall financial policy, and changes in one had an immediate impact on the other. The dilemma took on a particular form at the beginning of the sixteenth century owing to three quite specific developments of the past two centuries. The earliest was the final severance during the fourteenth century of land held in feudal tenure from any meaningful obligations of service; thus the crown was forced to reward the service of those who were nominally its chief tenants.[24] The second was the disappearance in 1453 of the crown's possessions in France as a source of reward.[25] Ireland remained a potential alternative, but Irish lands were not attractive, and in the sixteenth century they were largely reserved for service in the Irish administration and garrison, or for those prepared to settle or reside there.[26] The third was the new concern to maintain the revenue from the Crown estate that began with Henry IV's retention of the duchy of Lancaster in 1399, and reached its highpoint under Edward IV and Henry VII.[27]

The clearest illustration of the relationship between the politics of patronage and financial policy can be seen in promotions to the peerage, which is all the more striking given Elizabeth's reputation for parsimony in the creation of peers. Underlying promotions was the unwritten assumption that a peerage was an absurdity without sufficient landed wealth to maintain the estate, and further that there should be a clear distinction in stature between the various ranks of the peerage. Liberal creations of senior peers would therefore necessitate substantial alienations from the crown estate, and it was precisely for this reason (give or take other political motives) that the creations of Richard II and Henry VI were so strongly criticized.[28] Elizabeth's parsimony is in fact an illusion caused by viewing her reign from the perspective of the Stuarts, who essentially revolutionised the peerage.[29] Between 1400 and 1603 the peerage was largely static both in overall numbers, roughly between fifty and sixty, and in its internal composition, the norm being a handful of non-royal Dukes and Marquesses, between ten and twenty Earls, another handful of Viscounts, and (in the sixteenth century at least) upwards of thirty Barons.[30]

Although there is no evidence that any figure either for overall size or composition was ever established as optimal, it is difficult to avoid the conclusion that the result was not wholly accidental. In other words the size of the peerage was determined by the availability of estates. Replacing political casualties posed no real problem in this respect, for the forfeited estates of the victims could simply be re-granted to their successors. More difficult was the failure of male lines through natural causes and the subsequent dispersal of the estates through female inheritance. Thus while at law earldoms and above descended only in tail male, there was nonetheless a general willingness to accord some recognition to female descents, and many of the leading families of the Tudor 'new nobility' claimed historic titles in this way: the Dudleys and the Grey viscountcy of Lisle and the Beauchamp earldom of Warwick, Sir Anthony Browne and the Neville viscountcy of Montague, and the Devereux and the Bourchier earldom of Essex being the most obvious examples.[31]

Recruitment followed a consistent pattern. Leaving aside certain specific exceptions, such as marital connections with the royal family (which accounted for the ennobling of Charles Brandon and Edward Seymour), new creations were made at the level of baronies, while the upper ranks were replenished by the promotion of the wealthier barons and viscounts to earldoms.[32] In 1525 Lords Roos, Clifford and Fitzwalter became the Earls of Rutland and Cumberland and Viscount Fitzwalter. In 1529, in the largest single burst of creations in Henry VIII's reign, seven new Barons were created and Viscount Fitzwalter, Viscount Rochford and Lord Hastings became the Earls of Sussex, Wiltshire and Huntingdon. For all that is written about the great plundering under Edward VI, the creations of his reign followed his father's practice.[33] During 1547 an Earl holding the office of Lord Protector and directly connected to the royal house became a Duke (Somerset), and a second, brother to the queen dowager, a Marquess (Northampton); a Baron and a Viscount became Earls (Southampton and Warwick); and four Barons (Rich, Paget, Sheffield and Seymour of Sudeley) were created. In 1550 two more Barons became Earls (Bedford and Wiltshire), and a third a Viscount (Hereford).[34] In April 1551 on his appointment as Lord Chamberlain of the Household, Sir Thomas Darcy received a barony, and (significantly) 'for maintenance whereof he had given him 100 marks to his heirs general and 300 to his heirs male'.[35] October 1551 saw the last creations of the reign: the Earl of Warwick became Duke of Northumberland ostensibly on appointment as Warden General of the Marches (and on receiving many of the Percy lands); the Marquess of Dorset became Duke of Suffolk, a title to which he possessed a claim through his wife; the Earl of Wiltshire, Marquess of Winchester; and Sir William Herbert, Earl of Pembroke, a title to which he possessed a claim through an illegitimate descent.[36] Mary's major creations were restorations of the victims of Henry VIII: the dukedom of Norfolk and the earldoms of Devon and Northumberland. Her other creations consisted of one Viscount (Montague) and five Barons.[37]

At her accession Elizabeth was also faced with an issue of restoration, in this instance the attainted Edwardian peers. At her coronation she made two restitutions – the Marquess of Northampton and Somerset's son, the Earl of Hertford – and created three new peers: two Barons (Hunsdon and St John of Bletso) and one Viscount (Howard of Bindon).[38] More complicated was the position of the two surviving Dudley brothers. In 1561 and 1562 they received portions of their father's estate, and the barony of Lisle and the earldom of Warwick went to Ambrose, the elder brother, in 1561. Robert, the more politically significant, needed a separate and new creation. His endowment on creation as Baron of Denbigh and Earl of Leicester in 1564 was the most generous single grant of a landed estate in the reign – he was also the only man Elizabeth promoted directly to an earldom.[39] Only one further creation was made in the decade: the promotion of Sir Thomas Sackville, heir to the notoriously wealthy Sir Richard Sackville, to the barony of Buckhurst in 1567.

The years 1570–72 saw the largest series of creations of the reign. The upper peerage was replenished by the promotion of Lord Clinton and Viscount Hereford to the earldoms of Lincoln and Essex, ostensibly for service in the rebellion of 1569, and the 'restoration' of the Earl of Kent. One Baron (De La Warre) was restored, and four (Burghley, Norris, Compton and Cheyney) created. Cecil's barony may have been a consequence of his services, but, despite his protests, he could certainly afford the dignity. Norris had old associations with Elizabeth and had been ambassador in France, but baronies were not usually awarded for diplomatic service and 'his living is known to be great'– his wife was a co-heiress of Lord Williams of Thame.[40] Compton and Cheyney were devoid of political significance, but they were the descendants of leading men of Henry VIII's Court and notably wealthy. No less significantly, Sir Henry Sidney refused a barony in 1572 without a grant of lands from the crown, on the ground that his own estate could not bear the dignity.[41] The first Lord Howard of Effingham was under consideration for an earldom, but was rejected, apparently, because 'he hath not an earl's living'.[42] Similar concerns can also be found in the proposals for a new series of creations in 1589, when lists of Barons (all of them principal officers of the crown) and wealthy gentlemen 'meet to be advanced' were drawn up.[43] Nothing was done then, but the two creations of the 1590s were men on these lists: the second Lord Howard of Effingham became an Earl (Nottingham) and Lord Thomas Howard (the Duke of Norfolk's second son) became Lord Howard de Walden. It is probable that a similar pattern can be traced in the bestowing of knighthoods, although the process would be more complex. In her instructions for Essex in 1599, Elizabeth warned that knighthoods were only to be awarded to those who deserved it by 'some notorious service' or those who had 'in possession or reversion sufficient living' and claimed that sufficient moderation had not been employed in the past – no doubt a reference to the 'Cadiz knights' of 1596.[44]

The conclusion to be drawn from this survey is that honours, with certain specific exceptions, were granted only to those who could already afford them. The scales were weighted heavily in favour of the cadet lines of greater families (the Howards being the greatest beneficiaries) and the descendants of certain major office-holders: five baronies (Rich, North, Williams of Thame, Buckhurst and Norris) were granted to families whose fortunes were founded by officers of the Court of Augmentations. One effect of this policy was almost to detach peerages and honours from any 'patronage system', since they were so rarely awarded for service. Attempts to find a political motive behind specific creations, for example those of 1529, 1559 or 1570–72, may be misdirected.[45] The crown's hand may only have been forced by the desire to promote individuals to great offices of state that were normally expected to be held by peers, thus Burghley's promotion following his appointment as Lord Treasurer, or Lord Darcy's as Lord Chamberlain in 1551. Elizabeth's conservatism did, however, create a specific tension over claims through the female line to extinguished peerages, for fourteen peerages died out during the reign. Robert Sidney's vociferous and obsessive pursuit of the Dudley earldoms of Warwick and Leicester during the 1590s is a case in point. Yet there were quite valid reasons for resisting his claims – notably the existence of two widowed countesses and the dispersal of Leicester's estate owing to his debts to the crown and his bequest to his illegitimate son – and we can query whether Sidney's lack of success was the work of political enemies.[46]

III

If Elizabeth's 'policy' towards the peerage was very much within the Tudor norm, her reign did see a major transformation of the patronage of the crown. This, however, was as much the consequence of changes in financial policy as in the politics of patronage itself. Here the distinction between Henry VIII's policy and his daughter's becomes most apparent, for Henry employed a specific type of patronage that came to an end in the financial collapse of the late 1540s, while Elizabethan practice was shaped by the mid-century response to that collapse.

Henrician patronage was dominated by the 'royal affinity', a subject that has only recently received serious attention.[47] The Tudor royal affinity was the product of two major trends of the fifteenth century: the crown's attempt to gain a monopoly over liveried retaining by creating its own retinue or affinity, and the use of the crown estate to support this affinity.[48] Patronage was supplied by leases, annuities, rent charges and, most importantly, offices, particularly stewardships of crown lands, rather than alienations. Offices of this type provided the crown with further specific forms of service, in administration of the estate, in local government and in war. The significance of the royal affinity to the raising of armies was made clear by a statute of 1495, which stated that while all subjects owed military service, it was 'specially suche persones as have by hym [i.e. the king] promocion or avauncement, as grauntes and giftes of offices, fees and annuities, which owe and verily be bounden of reason to gif their attendaunce upon his roiall person to defend the same'.[49] The employment of offices in this way was advocated by Sir John Fortescue in his proposals for re-endowing the crown.[50] As a policy it was pursued more or less consistently by Edward IV, Henry VII and Henry VIII.[51] Under Henry VIII stewardships of royal estates became one of the most widely employed types of reward. Many of the key figures of the Court in its first three decades – Sir William Compton, Sir Ralph Egerton and William Brereton are the most closely studied to date – built up long strings of crown stewardships, frequently in their counties of origin or settlement, which made them figures of major local influence.[52]

Grants in fee simple or fee tail were, by contrast, 'an exceptional favour', as Helen Miller has observed for the reign of Henry VIII.[53] A statute of 1504 drew a further distinction between those merely possessing life interests, and those holding land of the king's gift, 'by reason they are more bounden', in qualifying the obligation to military service.[54] The fact that these were grants at pleasure or for life worked to the crown's advantage politically as well as financially, for they made local influence very much dependent on the good will of the king and on a position as the king's servant, as was the case in the attachment of the stewardships of the Crown estates in the northern counties to the wardenships of the Marches.[55] There is even evidence from Henry VIII's reign of this patronage being exploited to manage the House of Commons. During the debate on the subsidy in the Parliament of 1523, it was reported that: 'There has been suche hold that the Hous was like to have bene disseuered; that is to sey the Knights being of the Kings Counsaill, the Kings servaunts and gentilmen, of the oon partie, whiche in soo long tyme were spoken with and made to sey ye; it may fortune, contrarie to their hert, will, and conscience.'[56] But this form of patronage also accounted for two of the more prominent features of Tudor Court life: the attempt to establish some form of semi-heritable interest – the long lease, or reversions and grants in survivorship of offices or leases – and the scramble for those life grants that became available on the death of an office-holder.[57]

John Guy and David Starkey have described Henry VIII's royal affinity as a wide network, encompassing almost the entire political nation during the 1520s and 1530s.[58] Guy estimates that during the latter years of his reign Henry had between 1000 and 1200 significant paid offices at his disposal.[59] These were very much under the king's direct control, moreover he had little regard for the convention that officers could appoint their own subordinates.[60] No general record (outside the Patent Rolls) appears to have been kept of the king's grants, at least under Cardinal Wolsey. When Compton died in 1528, no one had any idea of the extent of his offices and fees and a search in Chancery had to be undertaken.[61] Wolsey's attempts to control the Privy Chamber suggest that he had no monopoly of influence over the crown's patronage. It may be of significance that such a charge did not figure among those brought against him by the council in December 1529.[62]

In its military rôle, the royal affinity reached its apogee in the expedition to Boulogne in 1544.[63] There is some ground, therefore, for considering the capitulation of Boulogne (14 September 1544) as marking the end of an era. The reasons for the collapse of the royal affinity after 1544 were both financial and military. The financial problem was created by the fact that although the funding of the affinity avoided permanent alienation of the crown estate, it created its own dangers by burdening it with fees and offices. Despite the scanty evidence for the administration of the land revenue in the first half of Henry's reign, there is some indication that by the early 1530s it was unable to meet the demands placed upon it.[64] The last Parliament of Edward IV (1483) had seen the passing of a statute assigning the revenues of certain crown estates to the support of the household, in order to assure payment to tradesmen and other suppliers.[65] Similar statutes were passed in the first Parliaments of Richard III, Henry VII and Henry VIII. Henry VIII's statute (1510) declared explicitly that it was intended to prevent the revenues of the named estates being used for rewards.[66] This concern is also reflected in the Act of Resumption of 1515, which noted that 'your lands . . . being so greatly minished by reason of the manifold gifts, grants and releeves . . . that the residue thereof now remaining . . . no wise sufficeth . . . to bear or maintain your great charges'. To this end a number of grants – annuities not connected to office-holding, reversions to offices and absentee officers – were abolished.[67] A second statute of assignment for the household was passed in 1531, specifically transferring the burden from the land revenue to the customs so that more of the estate could be used for patronage.[68]

The expropriation of the monastic lands should have rectified the situation, for, not being considered part of the crown's inherited estate, they could be employed to relieve the burden of patronage.[69] There is also evidence – the shadowy 'King's Book' of the 'names of such persons to whom the king's majesty will now give any lands, fees or offices' projected in 1537

– that at the same time Thomas Cromwell was seeking to obtain a greater (if not monopoly) control over grants.[70] However, Cromwell's plans died with him and the military and financial crisis of 1544–45 overwhelmed the land revenue by massive overseas borrowing and land sales; the continuation of the war to 1550 made it impossible to recoup. Moreover, the war itself amounted to a minor military revolution, for it was fought in the main with fortresses and permanent garrisons employing firearms, for which the retinues provided by the royal affinity were of little use. As a military institution, the retinue did not disappear overnight, but its replacement during the course of the second half of the century by the revived militia and the standing garrison led to pressure for new forms of remuneration and reward for the professional officer.[71]

In providing permanent employment and a career structure a standing army does at least resolve the question of reward. In its absence the crown was faced with recurrent demands for other forms of reward for its military servants. Part of the Edwardian crisis was the increase in demands for military rewards combined with diminished revenues and increased basic military expenditure. The lower level of Elizabethan military activity prior to 1585 reduced the pressure, but even so the demands created by such standing forces as Elizabeth consented to maintain were considerable. The annuity of £1100 that Lord Hunsdon received as governor of Berwick was compared favourably to the potential profits of the lord chamberlaincy.[72] After 1585 military rewards once again became a major issue. The establishment of the permanent English contingent in the Netherlands did provide a partial alleviation, but compared to the overall forces raised during the 1590s it was only a limited one.[73]

Faced with near-bankruptcy in August 1550 the Privy Council announced a moratorium on all suits 'in any man's behalf for land to be given, reversion to offices, leases of manors or extraordinary annuities, except for certain captains who served at Boulogne, their answer being deferred to Michaelmas next'.[74] There followed a debate over financial reform that lasted over the course of the decade and which shaped policy for the remainder of the century.[75] The victory went to the marquess of Winchester, thanks largely to his survival into Mary's reign. Winchester's solution was to restore the value of the crown estate by halting alienations, more economic management, and reducing the burden of offices both on the estates and in the household, while simultaneously increasing the yield of the customs. The best known of his 'reforms' were the 1558 book of customs rates and the absorption of the combined Court of Augmentations and General Surveyors by the Exchequer. However, the wider consequences on the use of office-holding for patronage were of major importance. The new policy led initially to the great survey of the crown's office-holders of 1552.[76] It may also have inspired the statute of

1553 prohibiting sale of offices involved in the administration of justice or services of trust.[77] The Court of Augmentations had possessed a substantial bureaucracy, both central and local. Winchester's reforms involved the elimination of most of these offices – although their immediate incumbents were compensated by generous pensions.[78] At the same time, the circumstances of Mary's accession caused many of the chief recipients of Edwardian military patronage to lose their offices and rewards.[79]

It may not be stretching the point to suggest that the collapse of the royal affinity and the financial crisis of the 1550s created a 'mid-Tudor crisis in patronage', and that the chosen solution involved the elimination of office-holding as the major instrument of royal patronage for the remainder of the century, in direct contrast to France.[80] The frequently commented-upon absence of a national royal bureaucracy was not an accident but a deliberate act of policy. The other relevant consequence of Winchester's reforms was the enhancement of the potential rôle of the Lord Treasurer – who now controlled directly all the major sources of the land revenue (with the exception of the Duchy of Lancaster) – as a patronage minister. Winchester appears to have obtained from Mary 'a promise not to determine the gift of any land without [my] consent', and may have been successful in practice in holding her to it.[81]

IV

Elizabeth's awareness of the financial restraints on patronage was signalled by Sir Nicholas Bacon – albeit highly rhetorically and with an element of special pleading – in his opening speech to the Parliament of 1559. After referring to the 'marvellous decays and waste of the revenue of the crown', he drew attention to the 'huge and most wonderful charge, newly grown' of fortifications and the navy, which 'in mine opinion . . . doth exceed the ancient yearly revenue of the crown', and then drew the conclusion: 'The necessity and need of this ragged and torn state . . . should by force so bridle and restrain the noble nature of such a princess, that she is not able to show such liberality and bountifulness to her servants and subjects, as her heart and inclination disposeth her highness to.'[82] Given the increased power of the Lord Treasurers after 1554 it is tempting to see policy as demarcated by the succession in office of Winchester, Burghley and Lord Buckhurst, yet the central figure remained the queen. Whatever her parsimony in other respects, Elizabeth took pride in 'her old wont, which is always to hold both ears and eyes open for her good servants'.[83] Like Henry VIII, she took a close and detailed interest in the minutiae of patronage.[84] No officer of the crown appears to have controlled the sign manual in the way that Cromwell had sought. While the secretaries of state possessed lists of offices and fees, there is no evidence of a 'queen's book' of grants as Cromwell in the reign of Henry VIII and Salisbury in the reign of James I attempted to establish.[85]

The two treatises on the secretaryship written by Robert Beale and Nicholas Faunt in 1592, both of which probably reflect Walsingham's influence, are more concerned with matters of state than patronage. Faunt says nothing on the subject, while Beale's advice is almost to avoid becoming involved. As much as possible suits were to be referred 'unto others of the Chamber or the household under whom they serve'; members of the queen's kin and the privy chamber were to be pleasured, but with regard to the latter 'yet yield not to their importunity for suits'. Ordinary suits were to be dealt with by the masters of requests. Since bills for lands and leases needed the signatures of the Lord Treasurer, the Chancellor of the Exchequer, and the Attorney- and Solicitor-General, Beale's treatise can be seen as a recognition of the Lord Treasurer's central rôle, with the Secretary of State playing purely a bureaucratic one.[86]

The evidence of the process of suing reveals two important features. In general it was up to the suitor to make his own case, yet there appears to have been a convention that to sue directly for oneself was 'not commendable'.[87] This applied at the highest level and contributed to the pronounced degree of collegiality among the Privy Council which is characteristic of the first three decades of the reign. Examples are extensive, but one is very revealing of the consequent difficulty in establishing direct 'patronage-broking'. In 1571 William Fitzwilliam, Sir Walter Mildmay's son-in-law, was appointed a gentleman pensioner, and W. J. Tighe in his study of the gentlemen pensioners drew the natural conclusion that the appointment reflected Mildmay's influence. In fact it was obtained by the Earl of Leicester as a favour to William Fitzwilliam's father, Sir William Fitzwilliam, then Lord Justice in Ireland.[88] No less important is the impression that the suitor's main difficulty lay in persuading the queen to go through with verbal agreements. She appears to have been more than ready to halt proceedings for second thoughts and to haggle extensively. The process from verbal agreement to the passing of letters patent under great seal could take months.

A well-documented example of the process as a whole is Leicester's conduct of a major exchange of lands with the queen in 1566. His pressing need for financial assistance having been discussed for some months, he received a verbal agreement from Elizabeth in February 1566, and then left the Court to visit in the country. He did not return until early April, having been delayed by the illness of his sister, the countess of Huntingdon, much to Elizabeth's growing annoyance. He left his suit to be negotiated by Cecil in his absence, in whom he appears to have placed complete confidence. It was the queen herself who decided that the original proposal was unfavourable to her, and referred it to the auditors of the Exchequer for renegotiation; it was not until 29 June that the letters patent were finally sealed.[89]

Where the Lord Treasurers were most influential was in the relationship of patronage to wider financial policy. Winchester initially appears to have attempted to continue his Marian policy of reorganising the crown estate, and the statute of 1563 assigning revenues to support the household drew mainly on the land revenue.[90] During the middle of the 1560s he concentrated on improving the administration of the customs. Burghley's succession to the office does seem to have initiated a new policy. Several of his memoranda reveal an appreciation of the political advantages of patronage. In April 1572, he regretted the queen's failure to erect and advance 'to estates and degrees multitudes of chosen and faithful persons to assure herself thereby'.[91] In January 1580 he advised Elizabeth in the event that she rejected the Anjou marriage: 'That you gratyfye your nobylyte and the principall persons of your realme to bynde them faste to you with such things as have heretofore bene cast away upon them that in tyme of neede can serve you to no purpose; whereby you shall have all men of value in your realme to depend only upon you.'[92]

No less importantly, Burghley also appears to have presided over a major re-shaping of the financial basis of the crown's patronage. Recent work on the Elizabethan crown estate has suggested that under Burghley there was something of a return to the Henrician exploitation of the estate for patronage purposes, although there is no evidence for an overall policy.[93] In Lincolnshire the estate consisted of a large number of small ex-monastic properties, which were difficult to administer effectively, and David Thomas has argued that the crown gave up any attempt to realize the financial value of its lands and employed them purely for patronage.[94] Katherine Wyndham, on the other hand, suggests that in Somerset, where the crown estate was also not extensive, there was a serious effort to retain the major portions of it.[95] More recently it has been argued that it was only after Buckhurst took office in 1598 that there was a sustained attempt to improve the return on the crown's lands.[96] More significant, and characteristic of Burghley's administration, was the employment of new types of grant, first seen in the 1560s, but far more prominent after 1570: favourable leases, leases in reversion, exchanges, grants in fee-farm and searches for concealed ex-monastic lands.[97]

Where Burghley appears to have had a more dramatic impact was on the real novelty of Elizabethan patronage: the exploitation of the customs revenues through farming, various import and export concessions and monopolies. Winchester opposed customs farming and tried to block the earliest proposals in 1568–69. The major farms were all established in the 1570s with the leading crown servants – Leicester, Hatton, Walsingham and then Essex – being the recipients.[98] No less important were export concessions, particularly of wool or cloth. The first major recipient had been Leicester in 1560–63, when they were clearly intended as a temporary source of income while his estate was resolved.[99] Thereafter they became a regular feature of the crown's patronage. Burghley has been considered a leading encourager of monopolies, both of imported commodities and of domestic manufactures. Initially the latter were intended to support a policy of import substitution, but after about 1572 monopolies began to feature prominently as rewards.[100]

By the 1580s, therefore, a major re-shaping of the patronage of the crown had in fact taken place. If the treatment of the crown estate has similarities to its use under Henry VIII, the novel exploitation of the customs and the creation of monopolies can be considered the Elizabethan equivalent of the contemporary French exploitation of sale of office. The main characteristic of the new sources of reward was the limited pressure they placed on the crown's landed resources. Like the Henrician use of offices, they possessed the benefit for the crown of being temporary or life-grants, which could be reclaimed on death or loss of favour. Elizabeth's largess to Leicester could thus be justified as a subsidy for his attendance at Court in the requisite style. Once he died she considered herself equally justified in cancelling his patents and calling in his debts. The new rewards did not resolve the issue of heritable interests and the scramble for vacancies remained a regular feature of Court life. Yet unlike the Henrician offices, the Elizabethan concessions did not involve regional power; instead they created what Robert Ashton has called the 'concessionary interest'.[101] This can be considered a form of centralisation by default, but here the City of London was as important as the Court and the most important consequence was the strengthening of a central financial nexus. The concessions also fell heavily on the consumer, inspiring a major body of criticism by the end of the reign. In this respect, the revival of the demand that the king should 'live of his own' was a response not simply to increased parliamentary taxation, but also – and more specifically – to the shifting of the burden of the reward of its servants from the crown to the commonwealth. There is a certain irony in the fact that the main targets of Salisbury's proposed reforms of the patronage of the crown after 1608 were precisely those devices that his father had encouraged.[102]

V

As important to late-Elizabethan patronage as the employment of the new sources of reward were new attitudes towards service. The brevity of the reigns of Edward and Mary inhibited the creation of a new type of royal affinity. Elizabeth's raises more complex questions, for there is some evidence to suggest that her accession marked the triumph of an affinity. A large number of her grants in 1559, both of offices and of lands, were bestowed on men identified simply as the queen's servants, with no particular office attached. Some of these men were clearly minor household figures, but there were also a number of greater significance: Sir John Perrot, Thomas Fisher of Warwick, John Harington of Stepney, Simon Musgrave, Sir Thomas Chaloner and Sir George Howard.[103] Some later obtained office, but others did not. The scanty evidence of the mobilisation of support in the autumn of 1558 has long been known; it may be that these grants were the subsequent rewards.

Thereafter, however, a distinct royal affinity is difficult to discover, though an echo of the Henrician policy may be detected in Burghley's memoranda of 1572 and 1580. One reason may be the consistent hostility Elizabeth displayed towards any manifestation of liveried retaining, which greatly encouraged the decline of retaining in general during the reign.[104] Yet elements of such an affinity may be reflected in the collegiality of the Privy Council on matters of patronage. Not the least interesting aspect of Leicester's 1566 exchange is the evidence it supplies for querying whether absence from Court was indeed dangerous and colleagues on the Privy Council not to be relied upon. The collegiality within the Privy Council, and particularly that between Burghley and Leicester, is an essential element in the politics of patronage prior to 1588. For all that has been written of the 'Leicester–Burghley rivalry' hard evidence for patronage contests has been difficult to come by. When their various efforts at advancing suits are studied, the beneficiaries turn out to be much the same people, the central core of the crown's servants. In 1585 Burghley became quite upset at gossip that he monopolised patronage and considered himself maligned by the *regnum Cecilianum*.[105] Nor is there evidence of Leicester possessing an access to the queen behind Burghley's back. This does not mean that there were no disagreements over policy, or that either was slack at pursuing his own interests, but disputes over policy did not transform themselves into disputes over patronage.[106] Indeed a certain mutual sympathy over their respective financial positions can even be detected. In 1571, Burghley, reflecting on the borrowing he was forced to undertake to support 'my fond humour of Building', observed 'And so I had rather do, my lord, and leave my heir less land to repay than by bribery in any office I have to set up one brickstone, or by being too importunate to her majesty to seek further relief of her majesty. You see of what disease I labour, not unlike your own in my opinion.'[107] In 1575 Leicester wrote in a similar vein: 'I know your lordship's charge to be as mine and as your place requireth.'[108]

What helped to reinforce this collegiality were two novel approaches to service. The first was a demand for religious allegiance which can be detected at the beginning of the reign in the purge of the Court, and then in the removal of the Earl of Northumberland from the wardenships of the East and Middle Marches at the end of 1559, following Sir Ralph Sadler's doubts about his loyalty.[109] The second was a more self-consciously classical definition of service. By the mid-1580s Walsingham was employing the phrase 'public service' regularly, most clearly in the context of the Netherlands expedition. In September 1585 he informed Leicester: 'But yf your lordships requests shall mynister matter of charge, thowghe yt be for publycke servyce, the impedyment wyll be fownde in her majestye . . .'[110] In the summer of 1587 he commented, 'Sorry I am to see men so unwilling and discomforted to be employed in any public service.'[111] There are echoes of Fortescue's *regnum politicum et regale* here; Leicester, for example, distinguished in 1573 between his 'private good will to yourself and for public respect of my country and the queen's majesty's service'.[112] The commonwealth tradition may also have had an influence, but it employed a terminology of private commodity and the common weal, while this use of 'public service' would appear related to the increasing use of 'the state'.[113] The significance of such a definition of public service lay in its qualification of the crown's powers to define service at will. There were now public criteria to be taken into account, and some types of service would be more worthy than others. This provided both a basis for claims of merit and a basis for criticism of the crown's choice. One consequence of the new emphasis on merit may be the 'memoirs of services' that begin to survive from the 1570s. The longest and best known is that supplied by Sir Henry Sidney to Walsingham in 1583, but the earliest surviving one was drawn up by Henry Killigrew some time after 1573. A second (and later) one by Killigrew has also survived, as have others by Sir James Croft and Sir Thomas Wilkes, while Sir Robert Carey provides a Jacobean example.[114] These have generally been consulted for the valuable biographical information they often uniquely contain, but their purpose was not that of a private memoir, but to support a claim for reward.

In its combination of the pressures of war, particularly on a patronage 'system' now heavily dependent on the profits of trade, and the revived demand for military patronage, the 1590s saw a return to the tensions of the reign of Edward VI. But there was a major novelty in the public identification of the Earl of Essex with the conduct of an aggressive war against Spain, and his efforts, as the self-proclaimed spokesman for this military interest, to arrogate to himself a monopoly of military patronage.[115] Moreover this military interest adopted the rhetoric of public service which was being deprived of its due reward. Instead of a broad band of royal servants presided over by a collegial council, a division into military and civil factions, reflected in the pseudo-Plutarchianism of Naunton's *Fragmenta regalia*, was encouraged.[116] It is in this context that Essex's impact on Elizabethan politics should be assessed. The neo-feudal and neo-chivalric aspect is deceptive, for it is in Essex's circle that the growing classicisation of politics becomes explicit.[117]

The pressure on conciliar collegiality was further heightened by Essex's radical identification of friends and enemies at the level of both county and

Court and his open use of his influence to advance one or depress the other. A good example is his decision in February 1597 to support Robert Sidney against Lord Cobham as Warden of the Cinque Ports on the latter's father's death. There were several legitimate reasons against the appointment of Sidney, as Essex himself appreciated; his motive was purely to stop Cobham: 'such hath his base villanies bene towards me, which to all the world is to well known, that he shalbe sure never to have yt if I can keepe him from yt'.[118] Such efforts to monopolise the patronage of the crown to conduct private vendettas created an edge to factionalism not seen before. With this came a political language of controlling the Court, as Vere's comments, quoted at the beginning, illustrate. Essex was thus the first Elizabethan political figure to equate control of patronage with power, and his pressure on patronage at all levels created hostility even among those who were previously his friends.[119] Only after Essex lost his influence at Court did he adopt the rhetoric of popular discontent with the concessionary interests.

The 1590s therefore saw the emergence of a politics of patronage which had not been present earlier. It was not so much the result of a demographic crisis of supply and demand, as a reflection of the novel political significance of patronage in those years. The crisis of supply and demand arose in the mid-Tudor decades; to this Elizabeth and her councillors had found a temporary resolution in the new devices of the 1570s and 1580s. But this resolution in turn created a new framework in which the wealth generated by the concessionary interest became essential for anyone seeking to play a major political rôle. It was also accompanied by a redefinition of service. During the first half of the century service had been defined by the crown at will; in Elizabeth's reign it became increasingly subject to wider criteria, which created a new justification for criticism and discontent, the more so since the burden of reward was now borne by a wider public. In the course of this process, the relationship between faction and patronage was transformed. Patronage became both a means to an end and a demonstration of political power; factions became the norm of Court politics rather than the exception. The politics of collegiality were replaced by the politics of competition.

NOTES

a This chapter has been revised in the light of works published since 1991, the most important being R. W. Hoyle (ed.), *The Estates of the English Crown 1558–1640* (Cambridge, 1992). Earlier versions were delivered to a seminar at the University of Birmingham in 1988 and a conference on Patronage, Politics and Literature 1550–1660 at the University of Reading in 1989. Reference to the Penshurst Papers, the Dudley Papers at Longleat House, the Cecil Papers at Hatfield House and the Pepys MSS is by kind permission of the Viscount De L'Isle, the Marquess of Bath, the Marquess of Salisbury and the Pepysian Librarian.

1 L. Howard (ed.), *A Collection of Letters* (2 vols., London, 1753), I, p. 388, 8 February 1596/7. This letter is not included in A. Collins (ed.), *Letters and Memorials of State . . . transcribed from the originals at Penshurst Place* (2 vols., London, 1746) [hereafter Sidney Papers].

2 Maidstone, Centre for Kentish Studies, K[ent] A[rchives] O[ffice], U 1475 [Penshurst Papers]/C 236/art. 26, Collins to William Pervy, 3 Sept. 1744.

3 For a fuller discussion and references, see S. Adams, 'Favourites and Factions at the Elizabethan Court' [Ch. 3], pp. 57–9.

4 'The Elizabethan Political Scene', reprinted in *Essays in Elizabethan History* (London, 1958), p. 70.

5 *The Elizabethan House of Commons* (London, 1949), p. 23.

6 Namier's case can be found in *The Structure of Politics at the Accession of George III* (London, 1965 edn), pp. 16–17.

7 'Eliz. Political Scene', pp. 78–9. Future reference to Naunton's *Fragmenta regalia* will be made to J. S. Cerovski's edition (Washington, DC, 1985). For reservations about the reliability of the *Fragmenta*, see Ch. 3, above, pp. 56–7.

8 'Eliz. Political Scene', p. 74.

9 'Place and Patronage in Elizabethan Politics', in S. T. Bindoff *et al.* (eds), *Elizabethan Government and Society* (London, 1961), pp. 108–9. The argument is rehearsed with little modification in 'Patronage and Politics under the Tudors', in L. L. Peck (ed.), *The Mental World of the Jacobean Court* (Cambridge, 1991), pp. 21–35.

10 *The Crisis of the Aristocracy 1558–1641* (Oxford, 1979 edn), chap. 8. For further elaboration of this argument, see also Stone, 'Office under Queen Elizabeth: The Case of Lord Hunsdon and the Lord Chamberlainship in 1585', *HJ*, 10 (1968), 279; R. C. Braddock, 'The Rewards of Office-Holding in Tudor England', *JBS*, 14 (1975), 29–30; L. L. Peck, 'Corruption at the Court of James I: The Undermining of Legitimacy', in B. C. Malament (ed.), *After the Reformation* (Manchester, 1980), pp. 77–8.

11 C. Carpenter, *Locality and Polity: A Study of Warwickshire Landed Society, 1401–1499* (Cambridge, 1992), p. 4.

12 L. L. Peck, 'Court Patronage and Government Policy: The Jacobean Dilemma', in G. F. Lytle and S. Orgel (eds), *Patronage in the Renaissance* (Princeton, NJ, 1981), pp. 28–9. For further recent general comment, see Peck, '"For a King not to be bountiful were a fault": Perspectives on Court Patronage in Early Stuart England', *JBS*, 25 (1986), 31–61, and A. Maczak, 'From Aristocratic Household to Princely Court: Restructuring Patronage in the Sixteenth and Seventeenth Centuries', in Asch and Birke (eds), *Princes, Patronage and Nobility* (Oxford, 1991), pp. 315–28. V. Morgan, 'Some Types of Patronage, mainly in Sixteenth- and Seventeenth-Century England', in A. Maczak (ed.), *Klientelesysteme im Europa der Frühen Neuzeit* (Schriften der Historischen Kollegs, Kolloquien IX, Munich, 1988), pp. 91–115, on the other hand, does not address this subject.

13 *Elizabeth I* (London, 1988), pp. 88–9.

14 See, for example, A. G. R. Smith, *The Government of Elizabethan England* (London, 1967), chap. v, 'The Patronage System'; and his *Tudor Government* (HA, New Appreciations in History, no. 20, 1990), pp. 10–12.

15 For the disputed rôle of patronage-based factions in the fall of Anne Boleyn, see G. W. Bernard, 'The Fall of Anne Boleyn', *EHR*, 106 (1991), 591–5, and R. M. Warnicke, 'The Fall of Anne Boleyn Revisited', *EHR*, 108 (1993), 653–65, and the references cited there.

16 E. Ives, *Faction in Tudor England* (HA, New Appreciations in History, no. 6, 1986), p. 7. A similar approach is found in K. Sharpe, 'Faction at the Early Stuart Court', *History Today*, 33 (Oct. 1983), 39–46. Cf. Sharpe's reference (p. 39) to patronage as 'the cynosure . . . of early modem government'.

17 Ives, *Faction*, p. 21. P. Wright, 'A Change in Direction: The Ramifications of a Female Household, 1558–1603', in D. Starkey (ed.), *The English Court from the Wars of the Roses to the Civil War* (London, 1987), esp. p. 170. This point has also been made to me more explicitly by Professor Ives in conversation.

18 See Ch. 3 above, S. L. Adams, Faction, Clientage and Party. English Politics, 1550–1603' [Ch. 1] and 'Eliza Enthroned? The Court and its Politics' [Ch. 2].

19 PRO, SP 14/37/145v, also quoted, though in slightly different form, in L. L. Peck, *Northampton: Patronage and Politics at the Court of James I* (London, 1982), p. 29.

20 Quoted in H. Miller, *Henry VIII and the English Nobility* (Oxford, 1986), p. 34.

21 On board-wages in the sixteenth century, see Braddock. 'Rewards', 38. The decline of the noble household is a theme of both J. M. W. Bean, *From Lord to Patron: Lordship in Late Medieval England* (Manchester, 1989), and K. Mertes, *The English Noble Household, 1250–1600* (Oxford, 1988).

22 Annuities had been the most 'open-ended' form of reward since the thirteenth century, see Bean, *Lord to Patron*, pp. 13–14. By the sixteenth century they were used both to remunerate officers, see e.g. the 1515 Act of Resumption (below, p. 77), MacCaffrey, 'Place and Patronage', pp. 114–15, and Stone, 'Hunsdon', and as compensation for surrendered offices, see e.g. W. C. Richardson, *History of the Court of Augmentations 1536–1554* (Baton Rouge, La., 1961), pp. 181, 254–5, 258.

23 Quoted in S. J. Gunn, *Charles Brandon, Duke of Suffolk 1485–1545* (Oxford, 1988), p. 224. For further sixteenth- and seventeenth-century illustrations of this crucial distinction, see D. Thomas, 'Leases of Crown Lands in the Reign of Elizabeth I', in Hoyle, *Estates of the English Crown*, p. 183.

24 K. B. McFarlane, 'Bastard Feudalism', in *England in the Fifteenth Century: Collected Essays* (London, 1981), p. 24. The running debate over bastard feudalism is not directly relevant to this essay, but S. L. Waugh, 'Tenure to Contract: Lordship and Clientage in Thirteenth-Century England', *EHR*, 101 (1986), 811–39, contains a valuable discussion of this point.

25 For their earlier importance, see R. Massey, 'The Land Settlement in Lancastrian Normandy', in A. J. Pollard (ed.), *Property and Politics: Essays in Later Medieval History* (Gloucester, 1984), pp. 76–96.

26 The complaints of lord deputies when it was violated testify to the 'general rule', see e.g. PRO, SP 61/3/97, 187, Sir James Croft to the Duke of Northumberland, 27 July, 18 Nov. 1551.

27 R. A. Griffiths (ed.), *Patronage, the Crown and the Provinces in Later Medieval England* (Gloucester, 1981), intro. p. 11. B. P. Wolffe, *The Crown Lands 1461–1536* (London, 1970) and *The Royal Demesne in English History* (London, 1971).

28 See, for example, the seventeenth-century observations by the Marquess of Newcastle, quoted in Peck, 'For a King not to be bountiful', p. 59.

29 As noted by Stone, *Crisis*, pp. 97–8, though this is not reflected in his further comments.

30 For the composition of the peerage in the sixteenth century, see the tables in Stone, *Crisis*, p. 99 and Appendix VI, p. 758. In the fifteenth century the numbers were slightly inflated by baronies by writ, see K. B. McFarlane, *The Nobility of Later Medieval England* (Oxford, 1973), pp. 175–6.

31 The Dudley claim came through Edmund Dudley's marriage to Elizabeth, the Grey heiress. See PRO, SP 10/1/104, Warwick to Paget, 24 March 1547. For the Devereux, see P. E. J. Hammer, '"The Bright Shining Sparke": The Political Career of Robert Devereux, 2nd Earl of Essex', unpublished Cambridge Ph.D. dissertation (1991), p. 17. (I am most grateful to Dr. Hammer for giving me a copy of his thesis.) For Browne, see J. A. Froude, *History of England* (London, 1893 edn), VI, p. 153, though no source is given. On the complications created by female heirs, see B. Coward, 'Disputed Inheritances: Some Difficulties of the Nobility in the Late Sixteenth and Early Seventeenth Centuries', *BIHR*, 44 (1971), 194–215, esp. 194–5, 198–9.

32 Miller, *Henry VIII*, pp. 11–12. Members of the royal family, however broadly defined, had the first claim on the patronage of the crown (see McFarlane, *Nobility*, pp. 156–8), but since this was not an issue in Elizabeth's reign, it need not be pursued here.

33 E.g. H. Miller, 'Henry VIII's Unwritten Will: Grants of Lands and Honours in 1547', in E. W. Ives *et al.* (eds), *Wealth and Power in Tudor England* (London, 1978), pp. 87–105. Note, however, the initial rejection of Henry's 'deathbed' promotions by those proposed, 'thinkeng the land to litle for their mayntenaunce which was appoynted to them' (p. 88). The limited expansion of the Edwardian peerage is noted in M. A. R. Graves, *The House of Lords in the Parliaments of Edward VI and Mary I* (Cambridge, 1981), p. 12.

34 Lords Russell and Paulet had received their baronies together with William Parr, the future Marquess of Northampton, on 9 March 1539. Russell was unusual in the extent to which his estate was composed of ex-monastic property (D. Willen, *John Russell, First Earl of Bedford: One of the King's Men* (London, 1981), p. 122), but Paulet could not have been far behind.

35 *The Chronicle and Political Papers of King Edward VI*, ed. W. K. Jordan (London, 1966), p. 57.

36 W. K. Jordan, *Edward VI: The Threshold of Power* (London, 1970), p. 53. It might also be noted that through his wife Suffolk was a member of the royal house as well. Pembroke was the only man to rise directly to an earldom in the reign.

37 Mary's policy is discussed in G. W. Bernard, 'The Fourth and Fifth Earls of Shrewsbury: A Study in the Power of the Early Tudor Nobility', unpublished Oxford D.Phil. dissertation (1978), pp. 229–30, and D. Loades, *The Reign of Mary Tudor* (2nd edn, London, 1991), pp. 52–3.

38 Hertford had been restored in blood by Mary in 1553. On 7 May 1559 he received a licence to enter upon lands entailed by his father (*CPR, Elizabeth I* (9 vols., London, 1939–86), *1558–60*, p. 100); he did not receive a further endowment. Hunsdon was an immediate Boleyn relation and had been a gentleman of Elizabeth's household in 1554 (*APC, 1554–5*, p. 25). Stone considers St. John and Howard of Bindon also to have been royal cousins (*Crisis*, p. 98), but they were of minimal political importance.

39 The complexities of the Dudley restoration are discussed in S. Adams, 'The Dudley clientele, 1553–1563' [Ch. 8], p. 163.

40 PRO, SP 12/74/43, Walsingham to Cecil, 22 Oct. 1570. Walsingham described Norris this way in requesting financial assistance if he was to succeed him in Paris, on the ground that he was otherwise in danger of being 'charged above my calling'.

41 PRO, SP 12/86/159–v, Mary Sidney to Burghley, 2 May 1572. In April 1582, when Sidney was approached about serving as Lord Deputy in Ireland for a third time, he demanded both a peerage and an augmentation of his estate as the price, see KAO U 1475/C 7/art. 4.

42 PRO, SP 52/23/art. 6, Hunsdon to Burghley, 7 May 1572.

43 PRO, SP 12/222/32, 46–7.

44 J. S. Brewer (ed.), *Calendar of the Carew Manuscripts* (6 vols., London, 1867–73), III, p. 295.

45 It has been argued (e.g. Miller, *Henry VIII*, pp. 22–3) that the purpose of the mass creation of 1529 was to create a majority of temporal peers in the Lords. However, Henry Pole, Lord Montague, or John, Lord Hussey, were odd choices if peers hostile to the church were sought.

46 The discussion of Sidney's pursuit of the Dudley earldoms and estates in M. V. Hay, *The Life of Robert Sidney, Earl of Leicester (1563–1626)* (Washington, DC, 1984), is inadequate. Peregrine Bertie managed to establish a claim to the barony of Willoughby d'Eresby by a female descent in 1580–1, but only after considerable lobbying, see PRO, SP 12/144/51, R. Bertie to Leicester, 11 Nov. 1580, and BL, Lansdowne MS 31, fo. 36, to Burghley, 13 Nov. 1580. Richard Fiennes and Edward Neville were unsuccessful in their respective claims to the baronies of Saye and Sele and Burgavenny; see HMC, *Manuscripts of the Marquess of Bath*, V, p. 91, and *Manuscripts of the Marquess of Salisbury*, III, pp. 251–2. Neville is also discussed in Coward, 'Disputed Inheritances', 199–201. Sidney, Fiennes and Neville were among those proposed for baronies in 1589, see PRO, SP 12/222/32.

47 J. A. Guy, *Tudor England* (Oxford, 1988), pp. 165–8. D. Starkey, 'Intimacy and Innovation: The Political Rôle of the Privy Chamber, 1485–1547', in *The English Court*, pp. 87–91.

48 C. Given-Wilson, *The Royal Household and the King's Affinity* (New Haven, Conn., 1986), esp. chap. iv. Bean, *Lord to Patron*, pp. 205, 207, 210–11.

49 11 Henry VII, c. 18, quoted in Miller, *Henry VII*, p. 133. The military function of the affinity is further discussed in S. Adams, 'The English Military Clientèle, 1542–1618', Charles Giry-Deloison and Roger Mettam (eds), *Patronages et clientélismes 1550–1750 (France, Angleterre, Espagne, Italie)* (Lille, 1995), pp. 217–27.

50 *The Governance of England by Sir John Fortescue* (ed. C. Plummer, Oxford, 1926), pp. 143–4, 150–3.

51 For Edward IV, see D. A. L. Morgan, 'The House of Policy: The Political Rôle of the Late Plantagenet Household, 1422–1485', in Starkey, *The English Court*, pp. 63–7. For Henry VII, M. Condon, 'Ruling Elites in the Reign of Henry VII', in C. Ross (ed.), *Patronage, Pedigree and Power in Later Medieval England* (Gloucester, 1979), pp. 109–42, and Bean, *Lord to Patron*, pp. 220–1, 226.

52 E. W. Ives, 'Court and County Palatine in the Reign of Henry VIII: The Career of William Brereton of Malpas', *Transactions of the Historic Society of Lancashire and Cheshire*, 123 (1971), 1–38; 'Patronage at the Court of Henry VIII: The Case of Sir Ralph Egerton of Ridley', *Bulletin of the John Rylands Library*, 52 (1969–70), 346–74.

G. W. Bernard, 'The Rise of Sir William Compton, Early Tudor Courtier', *EHR*, 96 (1981), 745–77. See also Gunn, *Suffolk*, pp. 178–9, and for a Yorkist example, I. Rowney, 'Resources and Retaining in Yorkist England: William, Lord Hastings and the Honour of Tutbury', in Pollard, *Property and Politics*, pp. 139–55.

53 *Henry VIII*, p. 224.

54 19 Henry VII, c. 1, quoted in Miller, *Henry VIII*, p. 134.

55 See, for example, the assignment of crown stewardships to Sir Thomas Wharton on appointment as deputy-warden of the West March in 1537, M. E. James, 'Change and Continuity in the Tudor North: Thomas First Lord Wharton', in *Society, Politics and Culture* (Cambridge, 1986), p. 121, though James does not give prominence to the crown's lordships in the North in his studies of the northern nobility. See also the comments of G. W. Bernard in 'The Fall of Anne Boleyn', *EHR*, 106 (1991), 594–5.

56 Quoted in J. A. Guy, 'Wolsey and the Parliament of 1523', in C. Cross, *et al.* (eds), *Law and Government under the Tudors* (Cambridge, 1988), p. 3.

57 For an example of the pressure for reversions, see Ives, 'Egerton', 365. The creation of a semi-heritable interest through father and son holding office in survivorship was an established tactic, see, for example, A. J. Slavin, 'Sir Ralph Sadler and Master John Hales at the Hanaper: A Sixteenth-Century Struggle for Property and Profit', *BIHR*, 38 (1965), 46–7. A major scramble for offices occurred on the death of Sir William Compton in 1528; the best account is in P. Gwyn, *The King's Cardinal: The Rise and Fall of Thomas Wolsey* (London, 1990), pp. 196–8.

58 Guy, *Tudor England*, pp. 167–8.

59 *Ibid.*, p. 166.

60 See, e.g., Richardson, *Augmentations*, pp. 192, 225, Miller, *Henry VIII*, p. 179, and *State Papers . . . Henry VIII* (11 vols., London, 1830–52), I, p. 651, the Duke of Norfolk to the Council, 16 Oct. 1540.

61 Bernard, 'Compton', 761–2.

62 For the charges against Wolsey, see BL, Cotton MS Vespasian F IX, fos. 175–7v. The best account of Wolsey and the patronage of the crown is in Gwyn, *King's Cardinal*, pp. 190–201. Cf. Bernard, 'Compton', 775. Starkey, 'Intimacy and Innovation', does not discuss the subject.

63 Discussed in Adams, 'English Military Clientèle', pp. 220–1.

64 J. D. Alsop, 'The Theory and Practice of Tudor Taxation', *EHR*, 97 (1982), 21–2. Wolffe, *Crown Lands*, pp. 82–3, 85–6.

65 A. R. Myers (ed.), *The Household of Edward IV: The Black Book and the Ordinance of 1478* (Manchester, 1959), p. 36.

66 1 Henry VIII, c. 16; c. 17 was a similar act passed for the Wardrobe.

67 6 Henry VIII, c. 25. This was derived from earlier acts of Resumption, see Miller, *Henry VIII*, p. 198 and S. J. Gunn, 'The Act of Resumption of 1515', in D. Williams (ed.), *Early Tudor England* (Woodbridge, 1989), pp. 87–106. Gunn's comments on the patronage of the crown in the early years of Henry's reign on pp. 98–104 are valuable.

68 22 Henry VIII, c. 18.

69 Miller, *Henry VIII*, pp. 224–5.

70 BL, Cotton MS Titus B I, fo. 457. On the 'King's Book', see D. Starkey, 'Court and Government', in C. Coleman and D. Starkey (eds), *Revolution Reassessed* (Oxford, 1986), pp. 53–4, and 'Tudor Government: The Facts?', *HJ*, 31 (1988), 922.

71 See Adams, 'English Military Clientèle', pp. 218–20.

72 Stone, 'Hunsdon', 283–5. For examples of the claims of professional officers for rewards, see BL, Lansdowne MS 12, fo. 216, C. Vaughan to Cecil, [1560–62], and Magdalene College [Cambridge], Pepys MS 2502, p. 553, Sir J. Croft to Leicester, 28 February 1566.

73 The importance of the Netherlands regiments is discussed in Adams, 'English Military Clientèle', pp. 219, 226–7.

74 *Chronicle of Edward VI*, p. 45.

75 The best discussion so far is C. Coleman, 'Artifice or Accident? The Reorganization of the Exchequer of Receipt, c. 1554–1572', in *Revolution Reassessed*, pp. 163–98, but see also Hoyle, 'Introduction: Aspects of the Crown's Estate, c. 1558–1640', in *Estates of the English Crown*, pp. 33–9.

76 BL, Stowe MS 571, discussed in D. Hoak, 'The King's Privy Chamber, 1547–1553', in D. J. Guth and J. W. McKenna (eds), *Tudor Rule and Revolution* (Cambridge, 1983), p. 89, n. 7. See also J. Alsop, 'The Revenue Commission of 1552', *HJ*, 22 (1979), 511–33, which notes (p. 526) that although the commission began in the misplaced belief that there were extensive debts to the crown outstanding, it soon focussed on offices as the main source of potential economies.

77 5 & 6 Edward VI, c. 16.

78 Richardson, *Augmentations*, pp. 207, 220–6, 246–7. The importance of the Augmentations bureaucracy is emphasised by D. L. Thomas, 'The Administration of the Crown Lands in Lincolnshire under Elizabeth I', unpublished London Ph.D. thesis (1979), pp. 16–17, 46.

79 The subject of the displaced Edwardians is addressed in Ch. 8 below, pp. 157, 163–5; see also Slavin, 'Sadler and Hales', pp. 38–40.

80 For the thrust of Winchester's policy, see the answers to the 'articles propounded for the diminution of charges and safe answering of the revenue of the crown' of 1555, BL, Cotton MS Titus B IV, fos. 129–31. M. Gray, 'Power, Patronage and Politics: Office-Holding and Administration on the Crown's Estates in Wales', in Hoyle, *Estates of the English Crown*, pp. 137–62, argues for the continued importance of local office-holding in Wales, but elides officers of the crown estate and noble estates, cf. Hoyle, in *ibid.*, pp. 44–5.

81 BL, Cotton MS Titus B II, fo. 136, 4 July 1555[?]. See also Richardson, *Augmentations*, p. 260, for Winchester's influence on leases.

82 T. E. Hartley (ed.), *Proceedings in the Parliaments of Elizabeth I*, I: *1558–1581* (Leicester, 1981), pp. 37–8.

83 MSS of the Marquess of Salisbury, Hatfield House, Cecil Papers 11, fo. 97 (calendared in HMC, *Calendar of the MSS of the Marquis of Salisbury*, II, p. 403), Leicester to Walsingham, 30 July 1581.

84 Thomas, 'Lincolnshire', pp. 16, 44. She could be as cavalier as her father in appointing to under-offices nominally in the gift of a superior. For an example, see PRO, SP 12/105/163, Leicester and Walsingham to the Earl of Shrewsbury, 15 Nov. 1575.

85 The proposal to regulate approaches of suitors to the masters of requests in February 1594 (PRO, SP 12/247/98–9) was inspired by a concern for security at the court, not by a desire to systematise patronage.

86 Beale's treatise is printed in C. Read, *Mr. Secretary Walsingham and the Policy of Queen Elizabeth* (3 vols., Oxford, 1925), I, pp. 421–43, esp. pp. 437–8. Faunt's was published by C. Hughes in *EHR*, 20 (1905), 499–508.

87 Magdalene College, Pepys MS 2503, p. 307, Archbishop Parker and Bishop Grindal to Leicester, 2 June 1569. Although this comment referred to ecclesiastical patronage, the general point was made by Sir Geoffrey Elton in discussion during the Anglo-German Conference on the Early-Modern Court at Madingley Hall, Cambridge, in 1987.

88 W. J. Tighe, 'The Gentlemen Pensioners in Elizabethan Politics and Government', unpublished Cambridge Ph.D. thesis (1983), p. 189. Cf. Bodleian Library, MS Carte 57, fo. 212, Mildmay to Fitzwilliam, 15 Dec. 1571.

89 See PRO, SP 12/39/105, 125, Leicester to Cecil, 20 Feb., 20 March 1566; SP 15/13/11–13, 14–15, John Dudley to Leicester, 29, 31 March.

90 5 Eliz. c. 32. Of the £40,000 assigned, only some £13,000 came from customs receipts. For Winchester's policy towards the crown estate in the early 1560s see R. W. Hoyle, 'Customary Tenure on the Elizabethan Estates', in *Estates of the English Crown*, pp. 198–9, and S. Adams, 'The Composition of 1564 and the Earl of Leicester's Tenurial Reformation in the Lordship of Denbigh' [Ch. 13], pp. 263–4.

91 J. Bain *et al.* (eds), *Calendar of State Papers, Scotland* (13 vols., Edinburgh, 1898–1969), IV, p. 272.

92 W. Murdin (ed.), *A Collection of State Papers . . . left by . . . Lord Burghley* (London, 1759), p. 340.

93 D. Thomas, 'The Elizabethan Crown Lands', in Hoyle, *Estates of the English Crown*, pp. 78–81.

94 *Ibid.*, p. 63, and 'Lincolnshire', p. 382.

95 K. H. S. Wyndham, 'The Redistribution of Crown Land in Somerset by Gift, Sale and Lease, 1536–1572', unpublished London Ph.D. thesis (1976), p. 266, and 'Crown Land and Royal Patronage in Mid-Sixteenth Century England', *JBS*, 19 (1980), 33.

96 Hoyle, ' "Shearing the Hog": The Reform of the Estates, c. 1598–1640', in *Estates of the English Crown*, pp. 204–62.

97 Thomas, 'Elizabethan Crown Lands' and 'Leases of Crown Lands in the Reign of Elizabeth I', in Hoyle, *Estates of the English Crown*, pp. 79, 169–90. See also Thomas, 'Leases in Reversion on the Crown's Lands, 1558–1603', *EcHR*, 2nd ser., 30 (1977), 67–72, and C. J. Kitchin, 'The Quest for Concealed Lands in the Reign of Queen Elizabeth I', *TRHS*, 5th ser., 24 (1974), 63–78.

98 F. C. Dietz, 'Elizabethan Customs Administration', *EHR*, 45 (1930), esp. 41–5, 117. For a good example of the combination of grants received by senior privy councillors, see S. Doran, 'The Finances of an Elizabethan Nobleman and Royal Servant: A Case Study of Thomes Radcliffe, 3rd Earl of Sussex', *Historical Research*, 61 (1988), esp. 290, 293.

99 *CPR, 1558–60*, p. 321, *1560–63*, pp. 244–5, 270–1, 361.

100 G. D. Duncan, 'Monopolies under Elizabeth I, 1558–1585, unpublished Cambridge Ph.D. thesis (1976), esp. p. 116.

101 R. Ashton, *The City and the Court 1603–1640* (Cambridge, 1979), pp. 12ff.

102 See PRO, SP 14/37/152.

103 See *CPR, 1558–60*, pp. 27, 45, 59, 86, 90, 93.

104 See Adams, 'English Military clientèle', p. 220.

105 PRO, SP 12/181/138v, 158–60, W. Herle to Burghley, 11 Aug., Burghley to Herle, 14 Aug. 1585. This appears to have been the earliest use of the term, which became more common during the 1590s.

106 M. M. Leimon, 'Sir Francis Walsingham and the Anjou Marriage Plans 1574–1581', unpublished Cambridge Ph.D. thesis (1989), has attempted to revive this connection, by arguing (pp. 77ff) that Walsingham exploited his influence on patronage to create an ideologically sympathetic following in the Irish administration, while Leicester and Burghley played a 'passive rôle'. However, Leimon did not examine Leicester's extensive Irish correspondence, which reveals that many of the men he claims to have been Walsingham's clients (Sir Nicholas Maltby, for example), were already Leicester's. Leicester's Irish correspondence is discussed in S. Adams, 'The Papers of Robert Dudley, Earl of Leicester. II. The Atye-Cotton Collection', *Archives*, 20 (1993), 136–8.

107 MSS of the Marquess of Bath, Longleat House, Dudley Papers, II, fo. 57, 10 Aug. 1571.

108 BL, Harleian MS 6992, fo. 11, 28 June 1575. The one discordant note is the complaint of Leicester on Burghley's failure to help him relayed by the Earl of Northumberland to Burghley in February 1576, see BL, Lansdowne MS 21, fo. 75.

109 For the removal of Northumberland, see A. Clifford (ed.), *The State Papers and Letters of Sir Ralph Sadler* (2 vols., Edinburgh, 1809), I, pp. 409, 460, 470–1.

110 J. Bruce (ed.), *Correspondence of Robert Dudley, Earl of Leycester* (Camden Soc., XXVII, 1844), p. 9.

111 BL, Cotton MS Galba D I, fo. 47, to Leicester, 8 June 1587.

112 Bodleian Library, MS Carte 56, fo. 221, to Sir William Fitzwilliam, 26 Oct. 1573.

113 Some of the earliest uses of 'the state' are found in Irish correspondence, as, for example, 'this state here erected', in BL, Addit. MS 32,091, fo. 57v, Sir J. Perrot to Leicester, 20 April 1572.

114 The most accessible version of Sidney's memoir is found in *Cal. Carew MSS*, II, pp. 334–60. Killigrew's earlier memoir is BL, Lansdowne MS 106, fo. 132. His second and Wilkes' are printed in Howard, *Collection of Letters*, I, pp. 184–5, and II, pp. 518–21. Croft's has been published by R. E. Ham, 'The Autobiography of Sir James Croft', *BIHR*, 50 (1977), 48–57, and Carey's by F. H. Mares, *The Memoirs of Robert Carey* (Oxford, 1972).

115 See the complaints of Lord Grey in 1598, HMC, *Salisbury MSS*, VIII, p. 269, and also James, 'At a Crossroads of the Political Culture: The Essex Revolt, 1601', in *Society, Politics and Culture*, pp. 427–9.

116 I.e. the distinction between the *togati* and the *militia*, see Sir R. Naunton, *Fragmenta regalia*, p. 48.

117 The neo-feudal and neo-chivalric case is made in James, 'Crossroads', pp. 416–65, and R. C. McCoy, *The Rites of Knighthood* (Berkeley, Calif., 1989), chap. 4. For the neo-classical tone, see e.g. the correspondence between Essex and Lord Willoughby in 1599, HMC, *Salisbury MSS*, IX, pp. 9–11, 34–5.

118 Collins, *Sidney Papers*, II, p. 20, R. Whyte to Sidney, 27 Feb. 1597, see also I, p. 115, *ibid.*, 4 March 1597.

119 For examples, see HMC, *Salisbury MSS*, VI, p. 197, VIII, p. 233; and H. Ellis (ed.), *Original Letters* (London, 1824–46), 3rd ser., IV, pp. 112–17, R. Beale to Burghley, 24 April 1595.

Chapter 5

The Eltonian legacy: politics[a]

The legacy of Sir Geoffrey Elton to the study of Tudor politics can only be described as paradoxical. For all his reputation as a doyen of what has been termed the Cambridge school of high political history, studies of politics comprise but a small section of his *œuvre*. He never wrote a substantial account of an episode in high politics in the manner of Maurice Cowling or J. C. D. Clark.[1] If one excludes his textbooks, political subjects are treated primarily in his essays.[2] Even these, though, are not numerous. The section 'Tudor Politics' in *Studies* 1 contains eleven essays and papers. Four are reviews, two are introductions to reprinted biographies, two are essays on Thomas More and two are the famous studies of Henry VII and Henry VIII ('Rapacity and Remorse' and 'King or Minister?'), which are essentially analyses of personality. Only one article, the early 'Decline and Fall', deals with a specific political episode. For a man whose doubts about biography as an exercise are well known, there is a striking amount of biographical material here. Elton's real contribution is to be found in his later essays. *Studies* 3 contains the 'Points of Contact' trilogy, 'Pilgrimage of Grace' and 'Arthur Hall'. 'Hall', 'Piscatorial Politics' in *Studies* 4 and the final section of *Parliament of England* form a distinct corpus of Elizabethan political studies.

In the very attempt to categorise his works in this fashion we encounter a further paradox, the difficulty of establishing precisely what Elton was writing about. This difficulty may be attributed in large part to his celebrated, even notorious, combativeness, for in almost every one of his major works there are actually two subjects: the announced one and the sub-text, which is invariably a tilt at his target of the moment. In the Elizabethan studies the attack on Sir John Neale is open and explicit. In others no names are mentioned, but those under attack are not difficult to identify.[3] To some extent these sub-texts give his works a dated air; his sparring with eminences of the past, A. F. Pollard for example, seems of limited relevance now.[4]

Elton's two commentaries on history, *Practice* and *Political History*, are also of significance here. They were written nearly thirty years ago when he had reached a plateau of eminence. While they do not appear to have been written as a pair, retrospectively they very much read as one. Both share a strikingly defensive tone. One aspect of this defensiveness has a definite period flavour: the alarm with which he reacted to the putative student rebellion of the late 1960s.[5] More important, though possibly not unrelated, was the defensiveness over his subject. 'A good many people', he wrote in *Political History*, 'think of political history as a very old-fashioned way of looking at the past, even as a boring form of study and as not very civilised.'[6] 'Pilgrimage of Grace' begins in a similar fashion: 'Few scholars these days like to be called political or constitutional historians: it is widely held that those have ceased to be useful occupations.'[7] His unhappiness over the rise of sociology and social history permeates *Practice*.[8] Although he was determined to go down fighting (and take a few opponents with him), a distinct fatalism can be detected in both books. A decade later he referred to *Political History* 'as the one of my books which practically nobody seems to have read . . . No doubt the book justifies the neglect, but I confess to an affection for this runt of the litter.'[9]

Yet these books do constitute a very real legacy in the form of his now famous emphasis on the mastery of the archive and its technical problems. It may be claimed that this is not particularly novel, yet nowhere else in recent historiographical literature is it so clearly and elegantly described. There is also a curiously prophetic note: the almost passing reference at the end of *Political History* to the 'new narrative'.[10] It might legitimately be asked how much narrative history Elton himself had written; he admitted in *Political History* that 'I tried with limited success to write such narrative in my *Reformation Europe* . . . but I may add that I remain ambitious to do more of this sort of thing, and do it better.'[11] Nine years later, however, Lawrence Stone detected 'evidence of an undercurrent which is sucking many prominent "new historians" back again into some form of narrative'.[12] There is no reference in this article to *Political History*, but towards the end Elton is described as urging on 'the new British school of young antiquarian empiricists'.[13] It is not my purpose here to discuss Elton's role in any revival of political history over the past twenty years, nor to speculate on the potential influence of this 'antiquarian empiricism' on the future of the subject. Suffice it to say that *Political History* initiated Elton's own venture into specifically political history. As he observed in 'Pilgrimage of Grace', it was 'the editor of this volume, who encouraged me to reinforce my assertions by a practical demonstration'.[14]

Elton's emphasis on the mastery of the archive raises one final paradox. It is probably not coincidental that he cut his teeth, as it were, on administrative history. Here the archives are by their nature straightforward, and if the technical problems they pose are frequently demanding, they are also obvious. Although his command of the broad range of British historical literature both past and contemporary was formidable, he only mastered two archives: the Cromwell papers and other records of the central administration for Henry VIII's reign, and what he defined, somewhat idiosyncratically, as the archive for the parliaments of 1559 to 1581.[15] He never worked in foreign, diplomatic, local, ecclesiastical or manorial archives. His one excursion into local history, 'Piscatorial Politics', was based, as he acknowledged, on the research of David Dean.[16] He could make some quite basic mistakes when commenting on Elizabethan archival sources. I have referred to two elsewhere, and a possibly more significant one will be mentioned below.[17]

The works relevant to this theme can therefore be reduced to three roughly chronological groups: those relating to Thomas Cromwell, what can be termed the 'middle period' essays and the Elizabethan parliamentary studies. Certain postulates and problems first encountered in the books on Cromwell dominate the *œuvre* as a whole. The middle period essays – the 'Points of Contact' series and 'Pilgrimage of Grace' – are the slightest in volume, but perhaps the most influential. This is not simply because they are the most specifically political, but also because they outline the broader interpretation of Tudor politics that informs the Elizabethan studies.

The Thomas Cromwell books form a discrete group not least because he himself brought his work on that subject formally to an end in *Reform and Renewal*, where he announced that 'this is to be my last engagement with Thomas Cromwell'.[18] It is not my purpose here to speculate as to why he never wrote or even contemplated a biography of Cromwell, but it does mean that an Eltonian overview of Cromwell's career is lacking and his place in Henrician politics remains to some extent undefined.[19] One has only to turn to the more recent work on Cromwell by David Starkey, Susan Brigden and Mary Robertson to see what is missing.[20] Moreover, looking at the three Cromwell books, *Tudor Revolution*, *Policy and Police* and *Reform and Renewal*, in this context, it is the sub-texts that are the most revealing. The formal subject of *Tudor Revolution* needs no description here, but the sub-text is clear: it is a sophisticated revival of the old 'new monarchies' thesis. Indeed, Elton was quite explicit about this: 'Talk of a "new monarchy" in the sixteenth century has become a little unfashionable of late . . . But in some ways the reaction has gone too far; as regards political and social structure, the sixteenth century produced something quite new in England.'[21] In the introduction he was equally explicit in defining his subject as the transition from medieval to modern: 'Where it mattered most a change had occurred which entitles us to speak of a revolution from the medieval to the modern state.'[22] On the surface, *Policy and Police* is perhaps the classic example of the Eltonian method: there is a discrete archive, a discrete subject, 'the enforcement of the Reformation', and a detailed analysis of methods and procedures. Yet *Policy and Police* is really an attack on the 'Tudor despotism'. For reasons of his own, he deliberately ignored Joel Hurstfield's essay on the subject, which he had criticized two years earlier in *Political History*.[23] Instead, he posed the rhetorical question 'was there a reign of terror?', and then attacked Pollard and H. A. L. Fisher for claiming that there had been no significant resistance to the break with Rome.[24] *Reform and Renewal* is basically an attack on the existence and influence of the Edwardian Commonwealthmen, a favourite theme to which he returned in a later essay.[25] It is difficult not to see R. H. Tawney as the target here.

Are these studies in Tudor politics? *Tudor Revolution* is so explicitly concerned with administration that it is tempting to say that politics were deliberately excluded. However, Elton was fully aware not only that the thrust of his argument was that the Cromwellian Revolution separated government from the court and administration from politics, but also that this might be too radical a step. He manoeuvred himself out of this potential trap by a not altogether successful compromise: 'The political life of the country centred on the court, but administration rested in the hands of agencies divorced from the household, though often in those of men not strange to court life, and the household concerned itself only with its specialised tasks.'[26]

The problems created by the 'administrative' approach are also encountered in *Policy and Police*. The conclusion of the chapter on 'Police' includes a comment on Cromwell's dependence on the co-operation of individuals over whom he had no direct control: 'he depended in the last resort on the willingness, prejudices and private ends of men over whom he had no hold except what general adjurations and warnings could add to general loyalty and the desire to stand well with the fountain of patronage'.[27] This would appear to be an admission that the patronage of the crown played a major role in the enforcement of the Reformation. We might legitimately ask for more on this important subject. However, there is no entry for patronage in the index, and my (admittedly brief) skimming of the text has turned up only one further reference. In the introduction to the chapter in which he discusses how Cromwell kept in touch with the various parts of the realm, Elton notes:

> It needs to be stressed that the matters that here interest us were in life mingled with a great many other necessary occupations: foreign policy . . . [etc.] and especially the laborious details of patronage on the effective use of which Cromwell in great part depended for his power and survival.[28]

This is a substantial concession. Yet nowhere in this book does Elton discuss patronage.[29] A major aspect of the story – the carrot as against the stick – has simply been omitted.

The near antithesis between policy and politics found in both *Tudor Revolution* and *Policy and Police* is if anything more explicit in *Reform and Renewal*.

This is a study in the formulation of policy, but policy very narrowly defined and – in its emphasis on social and economic concerns – almost anachronistically modern. The 'policy' was formulated in very intellectual terms – to all intents and purposes it was a political programme – and it was the work primarily of Cromwell and a few intimates. Here again there is a revealing aside: 'Cromwell's connection with the City of London . . . needs more study than I can give it here.'[30] It is not unfair to suggest that in any study of the formulation of economic or commercial policy this connection ought to be crucial.

Yet it was the very programmatic nature of Cromwell's ministry that Elton regarded as the measure of his greatness, as he states more or less openly in 'Redivivus', and the distinction between 'the business of government' and politics, so explicit in the Cromwell books, is never absent from the later political studies.[31] As a result, the important and influential middle period essays also have their problematic side. The strength of these essays is found in their emphasis on the political importance of the centre, an important and timely corrective to the provincialism and localism so prevalent in the 1960s, and also to the negative role played by the Court and the central government in the various 'general crisis' theories.[32] The three 'Points of Contact' essays address a single rather idiosyncratic theme: was there something in the central institutions under the Tudors that served a representative function responsible for stability in the sixteenth century, which then broke down in the seventeenth? The assumption that this representative function would be served by institutions rather than by less formal means is typically Eltonian. The initial essay on parliament is straightforward enough except for the rather odd argument at the end that membership of the House of Commons might have been a first stage in political advancement. To support this case Elton made a series of comparisons of dates of entry into parliament with dates of appointment to the council. But nowhere does he supply positive evidence that the latter was a consequence of the former. This would appear to be a flagrant example of *post hoc ergo propter hoc*, and Elton certainly appreciated the danger, but his disclaimer verges on the disingenuous: 'I am not prepared to say that membership of the House had become a necessary prerequisite for elevation to the Privy Council, but it looks very much as though it had become a very useful first step.'[33]

'Council' poses the very interesting paradox that if a large council served a representative function, a small one was clearly more efficient. Yet the issue of absolute size may be irrelevant, given the general agreement that within the councils of Henry VII, Henry VIII (excluding the periods of Wolsey and Cromwell) and Elizabeth I, a clear 'inner ring' operated.[34] 'Court' is both the most adventurous of the series and the most vulnerable. The vulnerability is clearly evident in one of the best-known passages in the essay: 'We need no more reveries on accession tilts and symbolism, no more pretty pictures of gallants and galliards; could we instead have painful studies of Acatry and Pantry, of vice-chamberlains and ladies of the Privy Chamber?'[35] Beneath the rhetorical antithesis is of course the old Eltonian distinction between business and frivolity. The side-swipes at Francis Yates, Roy Strong and Sidney Angelo are in the classic mould. Yet anyone who has ever worked on the Elizabethan Court knows that the archives of the Court and household departments are thin on the ground at best.[36] Nor, assuming that it were possible, is there any evidence to suggest that a detailed study of the Acatry would enhance our knowledge of Elizabethan politics in any substantial respect. However, the most influential aspect of this essay was undoubtedly its discussion of factional politics, especially the argument that the Court was where 'the battle of politics' was fought out. Here Elton found the distinction between Tudor and early Stuart politics. Under the Stuarts, 'conflict was forced out of court into a public arena; but this was new'. Under the Tudors, the Court maintained its centrality: 'the factions in the Country linked to members of the Court; Court faction spread its net over the shires'.[37]

This argument informs all his subsequent work on Tudor politics, beginning with 'Pilgrimage of Grace'. 'Pilgrimage of Grace' is an undoubted triumph. Without entering into the long historiography of this complex episode, the immediate background is worth noting. As well as 1960s localism, recent debate on the subject had been very much influenced by A. G. Dickens's essay 'Secular and Religious Motivation in the Pilgrimage of Grace'.[38] This was itself a controversial work, both in Dickens's pursuit of a popular Protestantism in the North of England and in his attempt to portray the Pilgrimage as something other than a revolt of northern Catholicism. Elton's essay was not definitive, and he probably would not have claimed that it was. But it did restore a political dimension to the Pilgrimage and brought to the fore the issue of the politics of faction.[39]

The conclusion of the essay is, however, curiously qualified: 'On this occasion a court faction transferred its power base to the country, a step most unusual in the sixteenth century. It had to do so because it had lost all hope of victory by conventional means.'[40] The implication that this was a rare phenomenon poses wider questions that Elton never addressed. The factional interpretation of the events of 1536 was first advanced in Eric Ives's article 'Faction at the Court of Henry VIII: The Fall of Anne Boleyn', which was followed by an unpublished paper by David Starkey.[41] Yet the description of the faction behind the Pilgrimage as the 'Aragonese Faction' appears to have been of Elton's coining. Ives refers simply to the conservative faction, while Starkey in his later published work refers to both the conservative and the Aragonese faction.[42] Elton had in fact employed the term Aragonese on two earlier occasions.[43]

The difficulty with the argument that the Pilgrimage was the work of the Aragonese faction lies in the fact that the main evidence for the discontents of those identified as members of the faction prior to 1536 comes from Eustace Chapuys's reports of his conversations with Lords Darcy and Hussey in 1534 and 1535. In these conversations Hussey held Henry VIII personally responsible for the break from Rome; therefore, if he was plotting anything he was plotting deposition.[44] If this was the case, then the Pilgrimage was not the result of one Court faction seeking to oust another. The deposition of Henry VIII does not, of course, feature in any of the Pilgrims' public statements. Why it did not is one of the major mysteries of the whole affair. The localist interpretation actually explains its absence better, but if the Pilgrimage is to be linked to an Aragonese conspiracy then a different explanation is necessary.[45] However not only does Elton fail to address the issue of deposition, but he is quite vague about what precisely the conspirators expected to achieve and how they intended to go about it. At one point he refers simply to the conspirators 'plotting violence as their only hope'.[46] Later on he states: 'in the main the northern risings represent the effort of a defeated court faction to create a power base in the country for the purpose of achieving a political victory at court'.[47] Neither what would constitute such a political victory nor how this 'power base' would achieve it are explained.

'Pilgrimage of Grace' was Elton's last major contribution to the study of Henrician politics. Several years after it was published a serious challenge to the 'Tudor Revolution' was mounted in the form of David Starkey's reappraisal of Court politics, which only received widespread attention in the 1980s.[48] The reasons why a serious Starkey–Elton debate never got beyond the exchange in *The Historical Journal* in 1987–88 do not need rehearsal here, but its absence has left a number of questions unresolved.[49] Elton had, however, moved on to his final great project, *Parliament*. The personal motive for this work is sufficiently notorious and does not need further comment. Nor are the specifically parliamentary aspects relevant here, except to note that Elton's approach to the parliamentary history of Elizabeth's reign both subsumed his old distinction between serious business and ephemeral politics within the wider revisionist emphasis on the greater importance of parliamentary business as opposed to constitutional or political conflict and combined it with his new interest in factional politics. Political conflict was now to be explained by the activities of Court factions taking their opposition into the parliamentary arena. As he put it:

> Without the monarch, the Lords and Commons had no power; without the Council, they even lacked the means for organising themselves for any political purpose or for initiating a policy. This degree of powerlessness, this dependence on sources of power outside itself, had always been the truth about the Parliament [*sic*] as a participant in national politics.[50]

Leaving aside the wider aspects of this interpretation of parliamentary politics, what needs examination here is the argument that, to quote from 'Arthur Hall', 'Like so many other parliamentary events in the reign of Elizabeth, the demolition and restoration of Arthur Hall reflected the politics of council factions rather than strictly House of Commons matters.'[51] Or to quote from his essay on 'Parliament' in Christopher Haigh's collection *The Reign of Elizabeth I*:

> The agitation over the Queen's marriage and the uncertain succession even more clearly demonstrates the real meaning of protest in Parliament. In 1563 and 1566, led by councillors despairing of any chance of pressing their policy in Council, both Houses were mobilised to urge the Queen to act . . . Similarly, the pressure for the executions of Norfolk and the Queen of Scots . . . exhibits not the opposition of religious extremists, but a rift within the government itself, as some courtiers and councillors, having failed at Court, tried to use Parliament to press their policies upon the Queen.[52]

Elton's motive for seeking to discredit what he termed 'the myth of opposition' needs no discussion here. Our concern is with the positive case he made for the Court factional explanation. He did so in three specific instances: 'Arthur Hall' and the accounts of the debates on the succession in 1563 and 1566 in the section 'Great Affairs' in *Parliament*. His arguments rest not only on his own wider theories about Court factions, but also on two new interpretations of Elizabethan parliamentary history advanced very much under his influence. The first was N. L. Jones's reappraisal of the religious settlement of 1559 and the second M. A. R. Graves's 'men of business' thesis.[53]

In his 'grasp of historical context' Arthur Hall is a true Eltonian hero. Yet what Elton wished to explain in 'Arthur Hall' was the hostility to Hall in the Commons in 1581, and specifically that of Thomas Norton. While admitting that 'the hunting of Arthur Hall sprang from motives linked to the obscure politics of the City [of London]', Elton, very much influenced by Graves's argument that Norton was the privy council's man-of-business, also detected the council's hand at work.[54] However, the ample evidence that Burghley had a soft spot for Hall and that the attack on Hall was led by Sir Thomas Wilson and Sir Walter Mildmay, with Sir Christopher Hatton playing a somewhat obscure role in the background, suggested a factional rather than a conciliar explanation. Hall was the victim of factional politics within the council: 'This would seem to clinch it: the real target for the council group in pursuit of Hall was Hall's sole friend in high places, Burghley himself.'[55]

Ironically, given his reliance on the man-of-business thesis, Elton's interpretation of this affair has caused Graves considerable difficulties. In his recent biography of Norton, Graves has emphasized Norton's connection to Burghley, and therefore he has had to work hard to find a convincing explanation for Norton's siding with Burghley's enemies on this occasion.[56] No less problematic is the composition of Elton's conciliar faction. If Sir Thomas Wilson had an established connection with the Earl of Leicester, and Hatton was very much his own man, Mildmay was not the most obvious participant in an intrigue against Burghley. Elton finds the explanation for his involvement in somewhat mysterious disagreements with Burghley over the Anjou marriage.[57] Yet even if they held different views over the Anjou marriage, there was a general appreciation among the Elizabethan council that disagreements over policy were legitimate and Mildmay worked closely with Burghley for many years both before and after 1581. No more obvious is the answer to the question what – if their target was Burghley – did the faction hope to gain by attacking Hall? All Elton could come up with was 'if Hall had had to suffer the punishment imposed by the House the loss of face would certainly have extended to his patron'.[58] This raises the immediate supplementary questions what did 'loss of face' mean and how would it have extended to Burghley? It is difficult to avoid the suspicion that an elaborate framework is being erected on some rather shaky foundations.

The succession debates in 1563 and 1566 are notoriously difficult affairs and on one level Elton's interpretations are as valid as any of the others advanced to date. The possibility that there was a genuine faction involved in the 1563 debates in the form of various Seymour partisans advancing the case for Lady Catherine Grey Elton rejected out of hand. He did so partly (one suspects) because Sir John Neale had suggested there was parliamentary agitation in favour of the Grey claim, but also because the very existence of this type of faction assumed a degree of political organisation within the Commons not directly instigated by a member of the council.[59] Instead Elton placed Lord Robert Dudley at the centre: 'the future earl of Leicester and his supporters offer themselves as the most likely Council faction to work up steam for the general hope [*sic*] that Elizabeth might act' and 'the "party" calling for action came together from a mixture of motives and under the guidance of a councillor (Dudley) who was not even a member'.[60] Lord Robert's motive in mobilising support in the Commons was marriage: 'Lord Robert had reason to think that a call to the Queen to marry might promote himself into a royal consort.'[61] His evidence for the 'Dudley faction', on the other hand, consists of the suggestion that Alexander Nowell, the Dean of St Paul's, who preached at the opening of parliament, 'belonged to the clientage of the Dudley family', and that the release Lord Stafford obtained from the Lords for ill health was obtained by Dudley.[62]

This line of argument involves conflating the debate on the succession with the pressure on the queen to marry. It is instructive to compare Elton's case with the more recent treatment by Susan Doran. She too sees Dudley at the centre of the agitation, but criticises her predecessors, including Elton, for failing to appreciate that marriage rather than the succession was the issue at stake.[63] Her case rests primarily on sources that Elton did not employ, and she is less persuaded of the involvement of a Dudley faction.[64] She argues that if Nowell was acting for anyone, it was for the council rather than Dudley himself, but (like Michael Graves) she draws attention to the role played by Richard Gallys, the mayor of Windsor, whom she identifies as one of Dudley's men-of-business.[65] However, Gallys is said to have initiated a debate on the succession on 16 January 1563. Doran's explanation of how a debate on the succession resulted in a petition to marry by the 26th is an idiosyncratic one: the assumption that marriage (in general terms) was less contentious an issue than the succession.[66]

One central conundrum that neither Elton, Doran nor Graves has been able to resolve was the role of Thomas Norton, who read the Commons draft petition to the House, but who was also the author of *Gorboduc* a year earlier.[67] The traditional reading of *Gorboduc* as a succession commentary would place Norton among the Grey supporters.[68] More recently discovered evidence suggests that *Gorboduc* may have been a marriage tract written in Dudley's favour.[69] This would cast Norton as a possible supporter of a Dudley marriage in 1563, but his long and active career supplies no other evidence of an association with Dudley.[70] Including him in a Dudley faction is highly debatable.

The high politics of the parliament are central to any argument for conciliar factions. The parliament was summoned to raise money for the Le Havre expedition, and Elizabeth's unwillingness to have either marriage or the succession discussed publicly was well established and clearly known to her councillors. From her perspective the parliament was therefore a calculated risk, particularly given her desire at this juncture to maintain friendly relations with the Queen of Scots, whose interests were most threatened by a possible limitation of the succession. Given Dudley's apparent commitment to the Queen of Scots's interests and Cecil's equally well-established caution, the council had no desire to rock the boat.[71] The Earl of Huntingdon's surviving letter on the subject makes clear his unhappiness at his name being used.[72] The only people to have a clear interest in making the succession a public issue were those who wished to bar Mary.[73] The case for Dudley rests solely on the assumption that he had an interest in encouraging agitation for Elizabeth to marry. Yet neither Elton nor Doran are able to discover evidence for a sustained campaign to pressure the queen into agreeing to marry – indeed Doran's concession that the ultimate petition for marriage represented an evasion of the difficulties posed by the succession blunts the thrust of her argument. Moreover, given Elizabeth's dislike of this type of public debate, open encouragement of parliamentary agitation would do Dudley's chances little good, as Elton recognised in his further suggestion that the proposal of

Dudley as a husband to Mary was 'one of Elizabeth's cruel jokes' to pay him back. Unfortunately this argument is difficult to maintain in the face of Elizabeth's sustained commitment to this scheme in 1564–5.[74]

The situation in 1566 is far more confused – indeed I must confess that I still do not fully understand it. Elton claimed that initially the 'great matter [the succession] which everyone expected to come up again remained dormant . . . The real cause appears to have been a division in the Privy Council where Leicester apparently favoured the Queen of Scots while Norfolk supported Catherine Grey.[75] This situation was transformed by Molyneux's motion. In a novel argument, Elton suggested that Molyneux's motion was engineered by Cecil in 'a conciliar manoeuvre which accepted that if the money bill was to go forward marriage and the succession would have to be allowed back on the agenda'.[76] His general argument, that the course of the session was punctuated by a series of Cecilian manoeuvres, has been convincingly challenged by J. D. Alsop.[77] However, Alsop's claim that 'Few, if any, scholars would accept the [Spanish ambassador's] assertion that Elizabeth had not dared summon Parliament in the years following the 1563 session' can be queried.[78] On the contrary, Elizabeth's desire to avoid a revival of parliamentary pressure on the succession is the best explanation for the prorogations of parliament between 1563 and 1566. The reactions of the Queen of Scots are very revealing. She took parliament's possible role in the succession so seriously that as soon as she learnt that one was about to meet, she immediately sent an ambassador to London to safeguard her interests. This was why Maitland of Lethington was sent in 1563 and Robert Melville in 1566, but it was also the real reason for the well-known embassy of Melville's brother James Melville of Halhill in the autumn of 1564.[79] The decision to summon parliament in the autumn of 1566, when the birth of the future James VI had if anything heightened the tension surrounding the Stuart succession, therefore becomes all the more curious, and Elton's argument that financial needs forced the crown to take a calculated risk (or uncalculated gamble) over the succession becomes more substantial.

By associating the M.P. John Molyneux with Cecil, Elton revised an earlier tentative identification of him as a follower of Leicester's. In his reinterpretation of the 1566 session, Alsop has reopened this question: 'In view of the fact that Molyneux's brother was secretary to Sir Henry Sidney in the later 1560s, it may be worth considering the possibility that his concerns lay with the Leicester clique.'[80] As with Richard Gallys in 1563, Molyneux's possible associations have a direct bearing on any factional interpretation of parliamentary politics. In Gallys's case the fact that he also initiated the debate on the Queen of Scots in 1572 is significant, for here we have a clearly active parliamentarian. The more difficult issue is the nature of his association with Leicester. Both Doran and Graves have rested their case that Gallys was one of Leicester's 'men-of-business' on the biography in *The History of Parliament*, but this does not mention any connection to Leicester.[81] In 1563 Gallys was mayor of New Windsor, and in that office signed the patent appointing Dudley, who had been granted the constableship of Windsor Castle the previous autumn, high steward of the borough on 9 September 1563.[82] Gallys was also a tenant of the castle, but the only evidence suggestive of a closer relationship is a reference in the 1588 inventory of Leicester's wardrobe to a short sword 'which was Gallecies of Windsor'.[83] Leicester certainly exercised electoral patronage at Windsor, but Gallys's stature in the borough did not make him dependent on it.[84] Molyneux presents a greater problem, for a 'Molynex' is included in Cecil's well-known list of Leicester's friends of 1565–67.[85] However, no further evidence has yet been discovered to establish the connection, nor even to supply 'Molynex's' Christian name, despite the survival of two long lists of men given Leicester's badge and livery in 1567.[86]

In 'The Dudley Clientele and the House of Commons' I concluded by noting that while certain of Leicester's followers (William Grice, Thomas Digges and Robert Snagge in particular) were very active parliamentarians, the great majority – including his leading household officers and servants – left little or no trace in the records of the Commons, and therefore the existence of an organised 'Dudley faction' was doubtful.[87] In essays published at roughly the same time on the House of Lords in the 1640s and the parliamentary patronage of Robert Cecil, Earl of Salisbury, both J. S. A. Adamson and Stephen Hollings reached strikingly similar conclusions. To quote Adamson:

> Indeed, there is no evidence that peers ever attempted to demand the adherence (or the votes) of M.P.s who were their servants and stewards . . . Far more important as potential allies of peers were those members of the Commons who were figures of standing and repute within their own House.[88]

Hollings's verdict was more or less the same: 'Being a client of the Earl of Salisbury did not commit you to support the Earl or government in Parliament, and . . . this was understood by both the Earl and his clients.'[89]

Slightly earlier in his essay Adamson supplied a reason for his conclusion:

> It was in the nature of such arrangements that peers should strive to leave the independence of the privilege-conscious House of Commons apparently unviolated. It hardly availed an M.P., when moving a question in the Commons, to announce that he had been put up to making his speech at the request of a member of the Lords. Sponsors of legislation in which they had a vested interest took pains to cover their tracks.[90]

There is some early Stuart evidence to support this argument, notably Robert Cecil's possible regular use of unofficial agents to raise matters in the

Commons.[91] There is also the negative example of 'Goring's motion' in 1621.[92] However, Adamson's argument raises the broader question: if their servants were so unimportant, why then did the peers go to such lengths to get them elected to the Commons?

In Leicester's case a basic reliability may have been the reason. His electioneering in 1571–72 was undertaken partly under the umbrella of a general conciliar instruction that lords-lieutenants should ensure the election of reliable men in their counties. There is also evidence that in 1584 he and Walsingham engaged in an extensive electioneering campaign to ensure support for intervention in the Netherlands in the Commons.[93] On one level Gallys and Molyneux would appear to be suitable agents for theories of parliamentary intervention through indirect means, though one could also ask why – if indirect means were being employed – Leicester would use men with any connection at all? More important, though, is the question what did Leicester hope to gain by having these motions moved? In arguing for the attribution of the 1566 speech on the succession to Molyneux, Alsop has noted that here too, as he did in his account of 1563, Elton conflated marriage and the succession.[94] While we might argue for a personal interest on Leicester's part in bringing marriage forward, his attitude towards the succession is less clear. There is sufficient evidence to suggest that until 1571–72 Leicester was more willing to come to terms with Mary than Cecil. Therefore there is some substance in the argument that Leicester took Mary's side in the succession debates. But in 1566, as in 1563, Mary's interests were best served by avoiding discussion. Thus Leicester, on the face of it, would have had no interest in stimulating a debate on this subject.

For all the difficulties of the factional explanation of Elizabethan parliamentary politics, Elton's separation of politics from business has led – almost by accident – to a reconsideration of a hitherto neglected subject, the national politics of the corporate towns. This took the form of a series of battles both against each other and against London for commercial interests and monopolies, battles that were fought out in parliament, before the council, at Court and in the law courts. One aspect, the 'decline of the outports', has long been known, but Neale's assumption of the electoral supineness of the towns has helped to obscure the full extent of the urban dimension.[95] In his study of the Yarmouth interest at work in 'Piscatorial Politics' Elton has provided a valuable description of one parliamentary campaign.[96] The Earl of Leicester's patronage of boroughs reveals how interwoven urban interests were with the wider politics of aristocratic clienteles and factions.[97] The whole subject deserves investigation.

The 'Points of Contact' articles are now twenty years old, but the study of Tudor factions and interests is still in its infancy. However, Elton's general theory about factional politics, at least in the terms in which he framed it, can be challenged. There is a final paradox here, in that Elton was at his boldest and most adventurous in a subject – Elizabethan politics – in which his command of the sources and evidence was at its weakest. By seeking to reduce all political discontent and 'opposition' to the workings of obscure aristocratic intrigues and Court factions he ran the risk of erecting complex edifices on shaky foundations. Not only did he make little effort to study the factions themselves, but the explanations he supplied for their motives, as in 'Arthur Hall', were on a level that he would have been the first to criticize if advanced by anyone else. Possibly at the heart of the problem is the fact that Elton never escaped the influence of his early distinction between govern-ment and politics. He was never particularly interested in political behaviour as such and made no real attempt to explore it. He never examined the problems of patronage and his conception of factions was quite basic and old-fashioned. Yet despite the critical tone to this paper, the Eltonian legacy is not, overall, a negative one. At the end of the day Elton was a true heavy-weight; he can always be read for profit and even when he is wrong his errors are stimulating. The questions he posed are questions that need ad-dressing and the issues he tackled are important ones. This seriousness of purpose is his true legacy. He is still the ultimate reader of any scholarly work of Tudor history.

NOTES

a This chapter was originally published as part of the proceedings of a conference on the influence of Sir Geoffrey Elton, which employed a standardised series of abbreviations for his various works. Those referred to here are (in order of citation): *F. W. Maitland* (1985) (*Maitland*), *Studies in Tudor and Stuart Politics and Government* (4 vols., Cambridge, 1974–92) (*Studies*), *Political History: Principles and Practice* (1970) (*Political History*), *The Practice of History* (1967) (*Practice*), *Reform and Renewal: Thomas Cromwell and the Common Weal* (Cambridge, 1973) (*Reform and Renewal*), *The Tudor Revolution in Government* (Cambridge, 1953) (*Tudor Revolution*), *Policy and Police: The Enforcement of the Reformation in the Age of Thomas Cromwell* (Cambridge, 1972) (*Policy and Police*), and *The Parliament of England 1559–1581* (Cambridge, 1986) (*Parliament*).

1 E.g. Maurice Cowling, *The Impact of Hitler* (Cambridge, 1975), or J. C. D. Clark, *The Dynamics of Change* (Cambridge, 1982).

2 The textbooks, specifically *Tudors*, *Reformation* and *Reform and Renewal*, will not be discussed here in any detail. It could be argued that omitting them weights the scales unfairly, but ultimately they are works of synthesis.

3 For examples, see pp. 98, 100 below.

4 See, for example, p. 98 below, and *Maitland*, 63, as well as his assessment of Pollard in the introduction to the reprint of *Wolsey*, *Studies* 1 (6), 110–15.

5 E.g. *Political History*, 129, 150–1.

6 *Ibid.*, 4.

7 *Studies* 3 (36), 183.

8 See especially 35ff.

9 'Pilgrimage of Grace', *Studies* 3, 184 n. 1.

10 *Political History*, 178–9.

11 *Ibid.*, 179.

12 Lawrence Stone, 'The Revival of Narrative', *Past and Present*, 85 (1979), 3–24, see p. 3.

13 *Ibid.*, 20.

14 *Studies* 3, p. 184 n. 1. The reference is to Barbara Malament, editor of *After the Reformation: Essays in Honor of J. H. Hexter* (Manchester, 1980), in which the essay first appeared.

15 His command of the literature is best displayed in *Political History* and *Practice*, but see also his archival survey *England, 1200–1640* (1969), in the series 'The Sources of History', of which he was general editor.

16 *Studies* 4 (57), see p. 119 n. 32.

17 The reference to the 'disastrous disappearance of Leicester's papers' in 'Court', *Studies* 3 (33:3), 53, is noted in S. Adams, 'The Papers of Robert Dudley, Earl of Leicester. I', *Archives*, 20 (1992), 63. Elton was surprised to find Welsh Elizabethan parliamentary papers in the MSS of the Duke of Northumberland ('Wales in Parliament', *Studies* 4, 98). For the explanation of their presence there, see my review of *Studies* 4, *History*, 79 (1994), 137. The third example is found on p. 100 below.

18 *Reform and Renewal*, vii.

19 'Redivivus', *Studies* 3 (46), is the nearest approach to an overview.

20 David Starkey, *The Reign of Henry VIII: Personalities and Politics* (1985). Susan Brigden, 'Thomas Cromwell and the "Brethren"', in *Law and Government under the Tudors*, ed. Claire Gross *et al.* (Cambridge, 1988), 31–49. M. L. Robertson, 'Profit and Purpose in the Development of Thomas Cromwell's Landed Estates', *Journal of British Studies* [hereafter *JBS*] (1990), 317–46.

21 *Tudor Revolution*, 425–6.

22 *Ibid.*, 8.

23 *Political History*, 56.

24 *Policy and Police*, 2, 4.

25 'Commonwealth-Men', *Studies* 3 (38).

26 *Tudor Revolution*, 373. In the later review 'Tudor Government', *Historical Journal* [hereafter *HJ*], 31 (1988), 428, he was more categorical: 'Now the book on the Tudor revolution was not about politics; as its subtitle explained, it was about administration.'

27 *Policy and Police*, 382.

28 *Ibid.*, 164.

29 Nor anywhere else for that matter.

30 *Reform and Renewal*, 65.

31 E.g. 'Cromwell worked in ways that became almost schematical', and 'the subjection of the Church was only part of Cromwell's great political programme', 'Redivivus',

Studies 3, 380–1. The programmatic emphasis can also be found in the work of members of Elton's school, e.g. Brendan Bradshaw, *The Irish Constitutional Revolution of the Sixteenth Century* (Cambridge, 1979).

32 The classic description of the parasitical 'Renaissance Court' is to be found in H. R. Trevor-Roper, 'The General Crisis of the Seventeenth Century', in *Crisis in Europe 1560–1600*, ed. Trevor Aston (1965), esp. 68–78. The pervasive influence of 1960s provincialism can easily be seen in the first edition (1968) of Anthony Fletcher's very successful textbook *Tudor Rebellions*.

33 'Parliament', *Studies* 3 (33:1), 20.

34 Elton used the term himself to describe the councils of Henry VII and early Henry VIII, see *Tudor Revolution*, 34–5, and *Constitution* (1982), p. 90. The Elizabethan inner ring is discussed in Adams, 'Eliza Enthroned? The Court and its Politics' [Ch. 2], pp. 30, 32.

35 'Court', *Studies* 3, 53.

36 See Ch. 2 above, pp. 25–7.

37 'Court', *Studies* 3, 56.

38 *Studies in Church History*, 4 (1967), 39–64.

39 A dramatic illustration of the effect of Elton's reappraisal of the Pilgrimage can be found in the comparison of the relevant section (pp. 17–39) of the third edition of Fletcher's *Tudor Rebellions* (1983) with the first two.

40 'Pilgrimage of Grace', *Studies* 3 (36), 211.

41 E. W. Ives, 'Faction at the Court of Henry VIII. The Fall of Anne Boleyn', *History*, 57 (1972), 169–88. Starkey's general line of argument can be found in the relevant chapters of *Reign of Henry VIII*. Reference is made to both in 'Court' and 'Pilgrimage of Grace', *Studies* 3, 51 n. 87, and 210 n. 71.

42 Ives, 'Faction', 182. Starkey, *Reign of Henry VIII*, 118, and *idem* (ed.), *The English Court from the Wars of the Roses to the Civil War* (1987), 110–11.

43 'Court', *Studies* 3, 50, and *Reform and Reformation*, 267. 'Pilgrimage of Grace' may well have been written by the time they were published.

44 The main reports of the conversations are found in Chapuys's despatches of 30 September 1534, 23 March 1535 and 11 July 1535, *Letters, Despatches and State Papers, Relating to the Negotiations between England and Spain*, V, pt 1 [1534–35] (1886), 608–11, 470–1, 512. It might be argued that deposition is not mentioned explicitly, but the references to Charles V declaring war on Henry VIII and executing a bull of excommunication can mean little else. In his account of the plotting (*Studies* 3, 209–10), Elton employed the summary of the despatch of 30 Sept. 1534 in *Letters and Papers, Foreign and Domestic, Henry VIII*, VII (1883), art. 1206.

45 The fall of Anne Boleyn in the interval may have altered the situation. There is a hint of such an argument in 'Pilgrimage of Grace', *Studies* 3, 210.

46 *Ibid.*, 209.

47 *Ibid.*, 212.

48 The reappraisal is to be found in *Reign of Henry VIII*, *English Court*, and explicitly in Christopher Coleman and David Starkey, ed., *Revolution Reassessed* (Oxford, 1986).

49 The public exchange was limited to Elton's reviews of *Revolution Reassessed* and *English Court*, 'A New Age of Reform?' and 'Tudor Government', and Starkey's reply, 'Tudor Government: The Facts?', *HJ*, 30 (1987), 709–16, 31 (1988), 425–34, 921–31. The underlying issue is the distinction between Court and government. Both Elton's criticism of Starkey for writing the history of the Tudor Court solely in terms of the Privy Chamber and Starkey's argument that the Tudor revolution was one-sided are valid.

50 *Parliament*, 377.

51 'Arthur Hall', *Studies* 3 (39), 266.

52 *Reign of Elizabeth I*, 99. As I observed in my review of *Studies* 4 (see n. 17 above), no reason is given for the omission of this essay from that volume.

53 N. L. Jones, *Faith by Statute: Parliament and the Settlement of Religion 1559*, Royal Historical Society, Studies in History, xxxii (1982). The latest version of Graves's thesis can be found in *Thomas Norton the Parliament Man* (Oxford, 1994).

54 'Arthur Hall', 260.

55 *Ibid.*, 262.

56 *Thomas Norton*, 361–2.

57 'Arthur Hall', 261.

58 *Ibid.*, 266.

59 J. E. Neale, *Elizabeth I and her Parliaments I. 1559–1581* (1965 edn), 103–4. See also the discussion of the numerous Grey supporters sitting for Seymour seats in 1563 in S. T. Bindoff's chapter, 'Parliamentary History 1529–1688', in *The Victoria History of Wiltshire*, V (1957), 129.

60 *Parliament*, 358–60.

61 *Ibid.*, 358.

62 *Ibid.*, 358, 361. Elton does not identify the peer, but he was clearly the 11th Lord Stafford. 'The Dudley faction' is referred to on p. 362.

63 Susan Doran, *Monarchy and Matrimony: The Courtships of Elizabeth I* (1996), 60.

64 *Ibid.*, 60–1, 64. She relies heavily on the reports of the Spanish ambassador, Alvaro de La Quadra, particularly that of 15 November 1562. Elton was sceptical of ambassadors as sources for parliamentary proceedings, see his comments on Chapuys's reports on the parliament of 1532 in 'Commons Supplication', *Studies* 2 (25), 112–13. Doran's caution about the Dudley faction was derived in part from my conclusions in 'The Dudley Clientele and the House of Commons, 1559–1586' [Ch. 10].

65 *Monarchy and Matrimony*, 61, 64. *Norton*, 106.

66 *Monarchy and Matrimony*, 64.

67 *Parliament*, 358–9. *Monarchy and Matrimony*, 56–7, 61–2. *Norton*, 95–7.

68 Marie Axton, *The Queen's Two Bodies: Drama and the Elizabethan Succession*, RHS Studies in History (1977), 46.

69 See Adams, 'The Release of Lord Darnley and the Failure of the Amity', in *Mary Stewart: Queen in Three Kingdoms*, ed. Michael Lynch (Oxford, 1988), 137 n. 117, and *Monarchy and Matrimony*, 55–7.

70 Graves accepts the connection between Dudley and *Gorboduc* and denies categorically that Norton and Sackville were members of a Grey faction (p. 97), but other than that Dudley appears only peripherally in *Norton*. See my review, *History*, 81 (1996), 656–7.

71 This argument can be found in 'Release of Darnley', 136–7.

72 *Ibid.*, 137 n. 117.

73 *Ibid.*, 136.

74 *Parliament*, 33. Cf. 'Release of Darnley', 128, 138–42.

75 *Parliament*, 365.

76 *Ibid.*, 367.

77 J. D. Alsop, 'Reinterpreting the Elizabethan Commons: The Parliamentary Session of 1566', *JBS*, 29 (1990), 216–40.

78 *Ibid.*, 221.

79 'Release of Darnley', pp. 126, 138. For Robert Melville, see also Neale, *Elizabeth and her Parliaments I*, 158–9.

80 'Reinterpreting the Commons', 239. Wallace MacCaffrey suggested that Molyneux may have been a partisan of Leicester's in *The Shaping of the Elizabethan Regime* (Princeton, 1968), 211.

81 P. W. Hasler, ed., *The House of Commons 1558–1603* (3 vols., 1981), II, 163.

82 The original of the patent is now Longleat House, Dudley Papers, Box II, art. 12. The Dudley Papers are cited with the kind permission of the Marquess of Bath.

83 For Gallys's tenancy, see the Windsor Castle accounts for the period 1562–74, Public Record Office, Special Collections 6/Elizabeth I/136–47. Gallys is not found among the officers of the Castle listed in these accounts. For the reference to his sword, see Longleat, Dudley Papers XIII, fol. 21.

84 This was my conclusion in Ch. 10 below, pp. 206–8, 214. Given the disappearance of the New Windsor records for the reign of Elizabeth I, we are dependent on Elias Ashmole's transcriptions (Bodleian Library, MS Ashmole 1126). Ashmole (fol. 46) notes the election in 1572 of Gallys and Edmund Dockwra, lieutenant of the Castle, and a letter of recommendation from Leicester. This certainly applied to Dockwra, but it is not clear whether it included Gallys as well.

85 Hatfield House, Cecil Papers, MS 155, art. 28 (cited with the kind permission of the Marquess of Salisbury). See the discussion in Adams, 'The Dudley Clientèle, 1553–1563' [Ch. 8], p. 152, in which I suggested Mollynex was probably Edmund rather than John. On the basis of further study of the internal evidence, I would now date this document to 1565.

86 The lists are published in Adams, ed., *Household Accounts and Disbursement Books of Robert Dudley, Earl of Leicester, 1558–61, 1584–86*, Camden Society, 5th ser., vi (1995), 432–8. To be fair, Molyneux's absence from these lists proves only that he was not a member of Leicester's household.

87 Ch. 10 below, p. 212.

88 J. S. A. Adamson, 'Parliamentary Management, Men-of-Business and the House of Lords, 1640–49', in *A Pillar of the Constitution. The House of Lords in British Politics, 1640–1784*, ed. Clive Jones (1989), 21–50, see 45–6.

89 Stephen Hollings, 'Court Patronage, County Governors and the Early Stuart Parliaments', *Parergon*, n.s. 6 (1988), 121–35, see 122–3.

90 'Parliamentary Management', 32.

91 N. R. N. Tyacke, 'Wroth, Cecil and the Parliamentary Session of 1604', and Pauline Croft, 'Serving the Archduke: Robert Cecil's Management of the Parliamentary Session of 1606', *Historical Research*, 50 (1977), 120–5, and 64 (1991), 289–304.

92 Negative in the sense that Goring was immediately identified as speaking on Buckingham's behalf. See Adams, 'Foreign Policy and the Parliaments of 1621 and 1624', in *Faction and Parliament*, ed. Kevin Sharpe (Oxford, 1978), 163, Conrad Russell, *Parliaments and English Politics 1621–1629* (Oxford, 1979), 133–5, and Roger Lockyer, *Buckingham* (1981), 108–11.

93 Ch. 10 below, pp. 199, 213. I intend to explore the 1584 electioneering in further detail in my planned study *The Decision to Intervene: England and the Revolt of the Netherlands 1584–85*.

94 'Reinterpreting the Commons', 239.

95 See the famous chapter on the 'invasion of the boroughs by the country gentlemen', in J. E. Neale, *The Elizabethan House of Commons* (1963 edn), 133–54.

96 'Piscatorial Politics', *Studies* 4 (54), 112–13, 124–5. See also Robert Tittler, 'Elizabethan Towns and the "Points of Contact": Parliament', and David Dean, 'London Lobbies and Parliament: The Case of the Brewers and Coopers in the Parliament of 1593', *Parl. Hist.*, 8 (1989), 275–88, 341–65.

97 Ch. 10 below, pp. 200–3. I have explored this subject further in a paper, 'The Elizabethan Earl of Leicester as a Patron of Boroughs', delivered to the Tudor seminar at Cambridge University in 1991.

Chapter 6

The Court as an economic institution: the Court of Elizabeth I of England (1558–1603)

In institutional terms, the English Court of the sixteenth century had evolved without a significant hiatus since 1066. As a result there was a definite continuity in the development of its constituent elements. Yet this evolution had not been insular. French influence had been continual since 1066 and Burgundian influence particularly strong in the latter half of the fifteenth century.[1] The most dramatic phase of the court's institutional development, however, occurred during the reign of Henry VIII (1509–47), which basically established its structure for the remainder of the century.[2] This too was not insular, for many of Henry VIII's innovations were the products of his famous rivalry with François I.[3]

However, Courts are also to a greater or lesser degree the mirrors of the personality of the reigning monarch, and therefore any meaningful discussion of the Elizabethan Court as an institution must begin by recognising its unique features. These were derived less from Elizabeth's sex, for the precedents for the Court of a queen regnant had been provided by her sister's brief reign, than from her virginity. Of direct relevance to the present theme is the basic fact that Elizabeth's Court was peculiarly economical. There was no royal family, nor were there any royal Dukes, the English equivalent of princes of the blood. This had an immediate impact on the overall personnel of the Court, which was substantially smaller than the personnel of the Courts of her predecessors and successors.

CONCENTRATION, GEOGRAPHY

The sixteenth century saw a significant reduction in the mobility of the English Court. Since late Anglo-Saxon times, Westminster, lying to the west of the City of London, had been the site of the main royal palace, but as late as the reigns of Richard III (1483–85) and Henry VII (1485–1509) the Court was still highly itinerant. Both of these kings resided for considerable periods of time at Nottingham Castle, Kenilworth Castle in Warwickshire (close to the geographical centre of the kingdom), and Woodstock in Oxfordshire (the greatest of the royal hunting lodges).[4] The reduction in mobility was to some extent initiated in the later years of the reign of Henry VII, but became more pronounced during the reign of Henry VIII. Although Henry VIII made a famous progress to York in 1541 for an abortive meeting with James V of Scotland, his increased corpulence caused a substantial restriction of his movements in the last years of his reign. This took a highly visible form in 1539–40, when he created the honour of Hampton Court, an extensive hunting ground near to London served by three new royal palaces, Hampton Court, Oatlands and Nonsuch, which saved him the journey to Woodstock.[5]

An immediate consequence of the reduction in the Court's mobility was the expansion of the number of palaces along the Thames and in the immediate environs of London. Greenwich (to the east of London) and Richmond (to the west), the greatest of these new palaces, were substantially the work of Henry VII. In his early years Henry VIII was not a major builder, and was over-shadowed by Cardinal Wolsey. However, after Wolsey's fall in 1529 the king took over and expanded Wolsey's two great houses, Hampton Court and Whitehall, and then launched his own extensive building programme, which included the construction of two further substantial palaces, Oatlands and Nonsuch. He became, in fact, the greatest palace-builder of all English monarchs.[6] But, as also occurred with the Navy, this scale of activity could not be sustained, and in the reigns of his successors Henry's extravagances were pared back. The succession of first a boy and then a woman who did not like travel made many of the more outlying royal houses redundant.[7] Nonsuch was sold to the Earl of Arundel, Beaulieu or Newhall in Essex to the Earl of Sussex and, most famously, Kenilworth Castle was given to the future Earl of Leicester in 1563.[8]

Elizabeth I was notoriously uninterested in building, and indeed made a virtue of it.[9] She resided almost exclusively in the greater Thames-side palaces: Whitehall, which since the 1530s had been the seat of the Court, Greenwich, Richmond and to a lesser extent Hampton Court. The Court's wider mobility was reduced to the annual summer progress, usually beginning in July and ending in September or early October. The traditional view that these progresses were intended solely for pleasure has recently been challenged and a definite political motive in maintaining contact with the regions has been detected. Although their initial range was limited, between 1566 and 1575 they went a considerable distance, with Kenilworth, which the queen visited in 1566, 1568, 1572 and 1575, featuring prominently.[10] No less significant is the fact that between 1576 and 1592 their range was restricted once again, more or less to Henry VIII's old circuit of Hampton Court, Oatlands and Nonsuch, but now specifically for reasons of economy.

The reduction in the number of outlying royal houses and the poor state of repair of the remainder meant that the housing of the Court on progress devolved on courtiers and the local nobility. This was a direct inspiration for the construction of numerous houses large enough to accommodate the Court in the late 1560s and 1570s.[11] The near-permanent location of the Court in close proximity to London had a number of other important consequences. Most of the major Court figures also acquired substantial town houses and these, rather than their country properties, became their main residences. The regular presence of the courtiers in London produced a close intermingling with the urban and commercial elite, a significant feature of Elizabethan politics and society.[12]

From the fifteenth century the Court possessed a permanent institutional structure of two main departments, the Household and the Chamber, presided over by the Lord Steward and the Lord Chamberlain. The only exception occurred in 1540 when, copying French practice, Henry VIII renamed the Lord Steward the Lord Great Master and gave him overall charge of both departments. However, this office was abolished in 1554 and the Court returned to its traditional structure. There were also a number of smaller departments, which had originated in the Chamber, but became semi-independent (in the sense of being funded directly from the Exchequer rather than through the Chamber) during the sixteenth century.[13] The Household was probably the largest single secular institution in the country, and the principal officers of both the Household and the Chamber remained at the centre of both Court and government, for they supplied the core of the membership of the Privy Council. There was no distinction between the service of the crown and the service of the state. Although a vocabulary of the state was in increasing use by the end of Elizabeth's reign, it is doubtful whether in fact an Elizabethan 'state' existed.[14]

The erratic survival of the archives of the various departments of the Court makes precise statistics difficult.[15] Therefore any computation of their personnel and by extraction the size of the Court can only be on the level of an estimate. However, a complement of some 250 for the Household and 250 for the Chamber, Privy Chamber, and Stables, and between 100 and 200 for the other departments would not be unreasonable. The overall total of the permanent staff of the Court would thus be in the region of 600 to 700. This total, however, excludes the (relatively small) Guard and more importantly the extraordinary members, whose existence makes any close discussion of Court size almost impossible. It was distinctly smaller than the contemporary French Court.[16] On the other hand, it was dramatically larger than the English noble household, the average size of which declined substantially during the course of the sixteenth century. The Earl of Leicester's household at its peak was no more than 100–150, and those of his peers were of similar size.[17]

Service in the Court departments had two potentially contradictory aspects. Heritable offices did not exist in any formal sense, but there were informal methods of ensuring the succession of sons (particularly grants in survivorship) and numerous Court dynasties can be discovered. On the other hand there was also a meritocratic and careerist element, especially in the technical branches of the Household, and this included recruitment from the households of courtiers.[18] However, the great majority of Elizabeth's Court servants at all levels came from families found in the Court of Henry VIII, though it is less clear whether they went further back.[19] Wages were employed only for the lesser offices, the more honorific were limited to fees, which in many cases were little more than nominal, and may have been kept low deliberately. Those officers were thus dependent on more indirect forms of reward.[20]

THE ORGANISATION OF SUPPLY

With the reduction of the Court's mobility in the sixteenth century self-sufficiency became less of an issue. The Court could draw easily upon the skills available in London and a number of London tradesmen became in effect suppliers of goods and services to the crown. As a customer of the luxury goods market the Court now became fully integrated with the City.[21] Foodstuffs and similar provisions were supplied under the prerogative right of purveyance (pre-emptive purchase).[22] This was a particularly sophisticated function of the Household and it is not surprising to find purveyors also employed in the supplying of naval and military expeditions.[23] Purveyance itself became an increasingly controversial issue during Elizabeth's reign owing to the decision (apparently taken by the queen herself) to pay less than the market rate (which was the established practice) in an effort to economise on the running of the Court. This can be seen as a definite shift away from financial self-sufficiency and an increase of the burden on the public. The supply of other commodities was largely the responsibility of the Wardrobe and its various branches – the least studied of the departments of the Tudor Court.

There was a marked decline in the scale of direct patronage of the arts by Elizabeth in comparison with her father – building, the most expensive form of artistic patronage, being the best example.[24] The main Court spectacle was the accession day tournament (17 November), particularly in the latter two decades of the reign.[25] There was a well-known patronage of the theatre, but it was by no means monopolistic.[26] Patronage of the arts was basically governed by the queen's tastes, which were limited to a few poets, musicians and portrait painters. With regard to styles of dress we are faced with the difficulty that the image presented by her portraits was clearly a fanciful one, and it is not easy to establish how she dressed on a daily basis. The relevant financial records are fragmentary and other evidence largely anecdotal.[27] However, it can be safely said that she did not engage in the informality of Louis XI, Henri IV or William of Orange. Her role in the setting of fashions is not clear. Fashions in dress certainly changed during the four decades of her reign, but the influences may have been continental rather than domestic.

There was, therefore, no effective royal monopoly over artistic patronage. The patronage of architecture was largely undertaken by courtiers – particularly in the building of houses suitable for entertaining the queen on progress. This raises the question of the extent to which they – especially the Earl of Leicester and to a lesser extent the Earl of Essex – acted as surrogates for the queen in this area as in many others. The range of Leicester's patronage – artistic, literary, ecclesiastical and military – the expense of his dress and his consumption of luxury goods would certainly appear to support such an argument, though the extent to which he set fashions is less clear.[28] The wider context of the arts in the reign was shaped by two apparently contradictory trends. The first was the continued dependence on the continent for luxury goods and works of arts throughout the century. There is evidence of the encouragement of domestic production (frequently involving continental artisans), which included patronage by courtiers, but the overall balance does not appear to have shifted.[29] The second is the well-known argument for an insularity of taste caused by the severing of contact with the Catholic world.[30] The severing of contact can be over-stated; the insularity may once again have reflected the personal tastes of the queen.[31] There is no evidence of a rivalry between the Elizabethan and contemporary Courts similar to the one between Henry VIII and François I in the first half of the century.

FINANCIAL FLOWS

The financial structure of the Court was complex. After 1563 the Household was funded by means of a statutory assignment (5 Eliz. I, c.32) of £40,027 drawn from the revenues of specific crown estates and the customs. This was an established procedure first employed in the fifteenth century as a means of providing assurance to creditors. As noted above, the other departments were financed separately by the Exchequer. According to the Cofferer of the Household's accounts the Household spent between £45,000 and 50,000 annually in the first decade of the reign, and between £50,000 and 60,000 in the 1580s and 1590s.[32] The Chamber, the next largest department, spent between £10,000 and 15,000 annually.[33] The other departments pose greater problems, for their accounts (where they survive) are in many cases fragmentary. My own rough estimate is that in the first decade of the reign the direct cost of the Court was slightly over £70,000 a year, and by the end of the reign slightly under £90,000 a year.[34] This would appear to be roughly a third of the crown's ordinary (non-parliamentary) revenue. Although the ordinary revenue is no less difficult to compute, the best estimates give roughly £200,000 in the early years of the reign, and possibly £300,000 at the end. The proportion of revenue devoted to the Court thus remained relatively constant, as both Court costs and revenue increased during the course of the reign.[35]

This proportion is greater than that found in the later years of the reign of Henry VII, when the court (costing about £25,000) absorbed about a quarter of the annual ordinary revenue of £100,000.[36] Inflation is probably the main explanation for the difference. Henry VIII's reign remains something of a mystery owing to major *lacunae* in the surviving accounts, but there is some evidence of a crisis in the ordinary revenue in the early 1530s, which was relieved by various expedients, most famously the expropriation of the monastic lands.[37] The costs of the Court may have contributed to this crisis, but recent research has given greater weight to the increased burden of the subsidising of the government of Ireland from the English ordinary revenue from the 1530s onwards.[38] This was no less a problem for Elizabeth.

The Court was the primary target in the general campaign of the queen and her ministers to control expenditure, and, apart from various apparently ineffectual economy drives, this campaign led to the exploitation of purveyance (referred to above), limitation of offices and the increased use of fiscal perquisites as rewards for members of the Court.[39] The queen's personal contribution was her self-restraint in building. As mentioned earlier, her clothing expenses are not known, but even if we credit her with a certain extravagance, it was not on a scale to have serious financial repercussions. In the 1590s her fiscal devices became the subject of open parliamentary complaint (purveyance in fact had been raised in parliament as early as 1563), and similar complaints would be a regular feature of Stuart parliaments.[40] It is fair to say that Elizabeth's reign (and possibly Henry VIII's as well) saw a definite shifting of the expenses of the Court from the prince to the public, and as a result inspired a new level of public criticism of the Court.

MANAGEMENT

The nominal management structure consisted of the Lord Steward and his chief officers (known collectively as the Board of Green Cloth) presiding over the Household and the Lord Chamberlain presiding over the Chamber. The reality, however, was more fluid and less formal. For most of her reign

Elizabeth did not appoint a Lord Steward (the office was only occupied in 1558–64, 1569–70 and 1587–88), and the functioning of the lord chamberlaincy depended very much on the personality of the incumbent Lord Chamberlain. The Earl of Sussex (1572–83) appears to have been a more active and interventionist Lord Chamberlain than his predecessor, the 1st Lord Howard of Effingham (1558–72).[41] The Board of Green Cloth effectively ran the Household throughout the reign, although Lord Burghley (Lord Treasurer 1571–98) intervened regularly.[42] Similarly the ceremonial of the Court (in theory the responsibility of the Lord Chamberlain) may have been usurped to a considerable extent by the Earl of Leicester, Master of the Horse 1558–87 and Lord Steward 1587–88. There was no master of ceremonies (as there would be in the seventeenth century) and the role of the Revels Office was a limited one.

The Court calendar was set by the queen, though to some extent in consultation with her leading councillors, for Elizabeth ran her Court in much the same way as she conducted other business. Unlike her grandfather, Henry VII, she does not appear to have acted as her own accountant, so effective control of Court finances was, as noted above, in the hands of the Lord Treasurer. Since Elizabeth did not succeed her father directly and the Court had undergone several reshapings in the interval, there was no entrenched old guard of established courtiers. Her relations with her sister's Court had been largely determined by religion, and thus her reign began (as her sister's had done in 1553) with a fairly sweeping purge of the upper levels of the Court. She was thus able to remodel and repopulate the Court in her own image.[43] She retained a close control over the social life of the Court; her interest in Court marriages was notorious.

FUNCTIONALITY

Elizabeth's sex and personality were the decisive influences over the functioning of the Court. The department most affected was undoubtedly the Privy Chamber, which had been of major political importance in the reign of Henry VIII. This now became a female inner sanctum, another precedent set by her sister.[44] On the other hand her male favourites had major public roles. There was no distinct group of companions of pleasure or little people as was found in the Courts of Henri IV or Charles II in the later seventeenth century, though it is possible that the women of the Privy Chamber were expected to act as companions of relaxation. There is some anecdotal evidence to this effect, but so little is known of the daily routine of the Privy Chamber that no definitive account of its function can be provided. This was a very private world, and there is evidence of complaints in the last decade of the reign that Elizabeth had become too private.[45]

The key figures in the Court were her four male favourites, who remain its most controversial personalities.[46] They were not the companions of war or pleasure of a male sovereign, or the tools of faction, but men who enjoyed extremely close and highly individual relationships with the queen in which sexual and/or romantic attraction on her part was the major element. If the Earl of Leicester was a surrogate husband and the Earl of Essex a surrogate son or nephew, Sir Christopher Hatton was a loyal admirer and Sir Walter Ralegh a flamboyant companion. Moreover, these relationships once established remained unaltered – Elizabeth's fickleness is a myth. Leicester, Essex and Ralegh did temporarily damage the relationship when they married (Hatton remained a bachelor), but Elizabeth took her anger out on their wives rather than on them.

The impact of the favourites on the Court brings up the vexed subject of factionalism. Their relationships with each other varied. Essex was Leicester's godson and stepson and to some extent his heir. An initial defensiveness on Leicester's part about Hatton's rise in the course of the 1570s can be detected, but by the end of the decade they had become firm friends. There is no evidence of tension between Hatton (who died in 1591) and Essex. Ralegh, on the other hand, was in this as in other areas a discordant element. Initially one of Leicester's protégés, he became one of his critics in 1585–88 and a serious antagonist of Essex's at the same time. Their mutual antipathy became a key element in the factionalism of the 1590s.[47] On the wider issue of factionalism between the favourites and other members of the court there is some debate. The factionalism of the 1590s associated with Essex is not disputed, but the earlier decades pose more of a problem.[48] The previously accepted belief that a factional contest between Leicester and Burghley dominated the reign can be queried, and the tension between Leicester and the Earl of Sussex, if undoubted, was sporadic. The only occasion prior to the 1590s when the Court appeared to divide was immediately prior to the Northern Rebellion in 1569, but what precisely went on then, and whether Leicester attempted to overthrow Burghley at that point, is by no means clear.

There are several wider aspects of the Elizabethan Court of major significance in this context. The first was the absence in England of a clear distinction between the robe and the sword, which removed a major source of tension. Similarly, great churchmen had been eliminated from Court politics by the Reformation, although there was an exception here in the major political role played by Archbishop Whitgift (the only Bishop to sit on the Privy Council in Elizabeth's reign) after 1583.[49] Secondly, there were no princes of the blood or royal dukes, a leading source of discord in England in the previous century as well as in contemporary France. There was only one major noble 'house', the Howards, but its various branches do not appear to have co-operated very effectively as a unit, and they were related to the queen through her mother.

Moreover, the Howards went into eclipse after the fall of the 4th duke of Norfolk in 1572, although there was a significant revival of the house in the 1590s, which reached its fruition in the following reign. Lastly, the small size (50–60) of the English titled nobility (the peerage) needs to be taken into account.[50] A considerable proportion of the adult peers was known personally to the queen.

Essentially the Court was composed of people the queen wanted there; she was the dominant personality and given the permanency of her personal relationships, courtiers operated in roles she determined for them. The fact that she did not condone attempts to interfere with her choices meant that there was in fact little advantage in intriguing to unseat each other. Moreover, the relatively small size of the English landed elite meant that the Court was bound together by many layers of intermarriage and family connection. Marriage was undoubtedly a leading concern of the Court, with the leading courtiers as well as the queen playing major roles in the making of politically significant marriages. If there was a policy behind them, it was to bind the elite closer together and to integrate the heirs of Catholic nobles into it. A number of the latter type of marriages were to be disasters for those involved, the classic example being the marriage of Burghley's daughter Anne to the 17th Earl of Oxford.[51]

The tightly-knit social structure of the Court raises interesting questions about its representative function, because there was a distinct section of the peerage who were not regularly present. Except for those peers who held Court offices, attendance at Court by the nobility was erratic (it was fullest during parliaments), and residence at Court considered an expensive duty. This was not in itself a novelty, but during Elizabeth's reign religion came to play a major role in determining participation at Court.[52] Although there were some favoured individual Catholics, the non-attendant nobles were the more Catholic in sympathy; it is difficult to find examples of 'Puritan' nobles similarly excluded.[53] To the extent that exclusion from the Court was a factor in one major rebellion of the reign (the Northern Rebellion of 1569), a risk was possibly being run over representation.

Court politics certainly involved the representation of wider interests, but the process was a complex one. Parliament, which met regularly, if erratically, throughout the reign, did to some extent challenge the Court's monopoly. During the past two decades several leading historians of parliament have emphasised the role of 'private acts' (legislation to serve particular interests) and the degree of brokerage involved.[54] However, the most recent study of this particular subject suggests that the significance of private acts may be exaggerated.[55] The crown remained the font of patronage and lobbying in the Court remained the most effective means of benefiting from it. The more difficult question is the nature of the brokerage. The key figures were the queen's chief ministers and favourites, who were Leicester and Burghley during the first thirty years of the reign. Given the degree of intimacy with the queen that both possessed, it is difficult to establish whether one was clearly a more effective broker than the other. As Lord Treasurer after 1572 Burghley could not be circumvented where financial grants were involved, but even as Secretary of State between 1558 and 1572 he possessed a degree of influence similar to the great ministers of Henry VIII.[56]

Leicester's potential influence as a broker was certainly recognised by those towns who appointed him to the otherwise honorific office of high steward.[57] Yet it is difficult to find clear evidence of his ability to circumvent Burghley or of his acting as an openly alternative patron, or even of one of the two gaining advantages in brokerage over the other. The evidence points to a large degree of co-operation rather than competition. They occupied a curious position with regard to each other; there was a mutual appreciation that they were the beneficiaries of an unusual degree of royal generosity. Both began the reign with quite small clienteles, in which their immediate families played large roles. Leicester's expanded more dramatically than Burghley's and was possibly more traditional in structure, but they were not rivals. Indeed there is a possible element of robe and sword in the composition of their respective clienteles – Burghley numbered few soldiers among his followers, while Leicester was the leading military patron of the reign.[58] Their correspondence reveals both their awareness of their roles as brokers and the efforts that they made to satisfy certain key regional magnates (the Earls of Derby and Shrewsbury for example). In this respect the Elizabethan Court benefited from a political sensitivity that counter-balanced its unrepresentative aspects.

The more difficult question is that of the role of lobbying and brokerage in the factional struggles of the 1590s, which has yet to be analysed in any detail. However, given that both lobbies and English clienteles in general were driven by interest rather than sentiment, those with something to lose did not back losers. Thus Essex was abandoned as soon as his sun appeared to have set. A final issue is whether lesser courtiers or the women of the Privy Chamber acted as alternative brokers. The attempts made to argue the case have not, to date, been convincing.[59] If the evidence is largely anecdotal, the overall impression is left that the queen did not tolerate rivals to her leading ministers on major issues, and such influence over patronage as the others possessed was limited to minor suits.

To the extent that we can talk of an inherent institutional tension in Courts between their function as the royal household and their function as a public body, the former most accurately describes the Elizabethan Court. Despite its historical reputation, it was not the battleground of faction until the final decade, and then the Earl of Essex's attempts to factionalise it and to challenge the queen's assignment of roles were the direct causes of his downfall. The internal politics of the Court were essentially those of conciliation. If a wider representative function was sacrificed, it also served as the centre of a formidable political elite grouped round its leading figures.

THE COURT AS A MODEL

As a model the Court was without rival, for there were no regional or princely Courts. The nearest to a regional Court was possibly the Duke of Norfolk's household at Kenninghall in Norfolk, but that died with him.[60] Nor, despite Lord Hunsdon's well-known complaint that the North of England knew 'no prince but a Percy', is there any evidence that the Earl of Northumberland's household acted as a regional focus.[61] Mary, Queen of Scots, did attempt to create a Scottish Court in exile during her 'imprisonment' in the 1570s, but Elizabeth refused to subsidise it.[62]

As a model of behaviour, the Court was once again decisively shaped by Elizabeth's sex. If her parsimony was notorious and the subject of almost public humour, there was also a general perception that she was milder than her father, not least because women were expected to be more merciful – there are even some hints that her mildness was seen as one of the weaknesses of female rule.[63] Although she hunted regularly in the early years of the reign, hunting lacked the obsessive quality found elsewhere. There was also a public temperance in behaviour: drunkenness and duelling were frowned on and duels are not encountered until the late 1580s.[64] Sexual behaviour is a particularly interesting subject, given Elizabeth's virginity, her sexual jealousy and the fact that she was to some extent compromised in one of the greater scandals of the reign – the death of Leicester's first wife in 1560. Overall the level of sexual scandal at the Court was very low; a number of extra-marital liaisons are known (often the result of failed politically-arranged marriages), but they were carried on very discreetly. The younger courtiers of the 1590s (Ralegh, Essex and the Earls of Southampton and Pembroke, for example) were more openly sexually active than their predecessors, but this cost them the queen's favour, temporarily in the case of Essex and Ralegh, but more permanently in the case of Southampton and Pembroke.[65]

The 'Gloriana' aspect of Court culture, which flourished in the last two decades of the reign, can be seen as a feminising of an earlier chivalric culture, and its prominence must reflect the queen's appreciation of it, even if she did not actively patronise it.[66] The queen's desire for privacy also encouraged a certain formalising of Court routine, as the accounts of foreign visitors testify.[67] The public facade was undoubtedly considered impressive, but to some extent that was an open admission of Elizabeth's uniqueness.

If the Court of Elizabeth I became one of the most famous in Europe, rivalling that of Louis XIV in historical reputation, its domestic reputation was very much the product of English politics in the following century. As an institutional model its immediate relevance disappeared with the restoration of a male monarch and a royal family in 1603 – the more so since this was also a foreign dynasty. If there was some discontent with female government by the end of the reign, favourable comparisons, both behavioural and functional, grew as the reign of James VI and I progressed. But there was also a major division of opinion that originated in the politics of Elizabeth's reign and underlay the civil wars of the seventeenth century. Those who saw Elizabeth as the model were the descendants of the political elite formed by her Court. Their opponents saw Elizabeth as the tool of a faction that sought to destroy the church and the old nobility. The Elizabethan Court thus became one of the battlegrounds over which Whig and Tory historians fought.[68]

In the development of the English political economy Elizabeth's Court occupied an important if far from straightforward position. As an economic institution it supplied a considerable amount of glamour for a relatively low price, but this sleight of hand could not be repeated with a 'normal' royal family. Moreover, the queen's celebrated parsimony was in itself an almost ironic comment on expectations of princely munificence. The reign also saw the shifting of a greater amount of the financial burden onto the wider public. The tension this would ultimately produce was lessened in the immediate term by the way in which the Court brought together the leading forces in the national economy – Sir Thomas Gresham was as at home at Court as in the City. Close personal relations between the courtiers and the City elite were widespread. The Court did not self-consciously foster an aristocratic – as opposed to a bourgeois – culture; Elizabethan drama linked both. Instead the Court acted as the centre for a wider political elite, focused on London and the Southeast of the country. The partial displacement of this elite and the restoration of the old nobility under the Stuarts accounted for much of the growing institutional and political tension surrounding the monarchy in the following century.

NOTES

1 An excellent discussion of the influence of the Burgundian court on that of Edward IV (1461–83) can be found in Thurley, Simon, 1993, *The Royal Palaces of Tudor England: Architecture and Court Life 1460–1547*, London, Yale University Press: 11–24.

2 The study of the Court of Henry VIII and by extension the Tudor Court in general has been transformed by the work of David Starkey. See in particular: Starkey, David, 1985, *The Reign of Henry VIII. Personalities and Politics*, London, George Philip; Starkey, David (ed.), 1987, *The English Court from the Wars of the Roses to the Civil War*, London,

Longman; and Starkey, David, 1997, 'Representation through Intimacy: A Study in the Symbolism of Monarchy and Court Office in Early Modern England', and 'Court and Government', in Guy, John (ed.), *The Tudor Monarchy*, London, Arnold: 42–78, 189–213. No less important, as a study of the physical aspects of the Court, is Thurley, *The Royal Palaces*.

3 The rivalry is the theme of Starkey, David (ed.), 1991, *Henry VIII: A European Court in England*, London, Collins & Brown; see also Thurley, *Royal Palaces*: 70, 85–6. Henry VIII's experiments with his guard, all modelled on the contemporary French guard, are also a good example, see Adams, Simon [1995], 'The English Military Clientele, 1542–1618', in Charles Giry-Deloison and Roger Mettam (eds), *Patronages et clientélismes 1550–1750 (France, Angleterre, Espagne, Italie)*, Lille, Université Charles de Gaulle (Lille III): 218.

4 On the general subject, see Thurley, *Royal Palaces*: 1–37, 67–72. For Richard III, see the itinerary in Gillingham, John (ed.), 1993, *Richard III: A Medieval Kingship*, London, Collins & Brown: 66. Henry VII was at Kenilworth for two months in 1493, and at Woodstock for long periods in 1494, 1495 and 1497, see Arthurson, Ian, 1994, *The Perkin Warbeck Conspiracy 1491–1499*, Gloucester, Alan Sutton: 65, 81, 111, 165.

5 Thurley, *Royal Palaces*: 60–1.

6 Thurley, *Royal Palaces*, is the now definitive account; he attributes the king's new interest in building in the 1530s to the possible influence of Anne Boleyn, see p. 49. For Wolsey, see also Thurley, Simon, 1991, 'The Domestic Building Works of Cardinal Wolsey', in Gunn, S. J. and Lindley, P. G. (eds), *Cardinal Wolsey: Church, State and Art*, Cambridge, Cambridge University Press: 76–102.

7 Edward VI began his first progress in the summer of 1552, but it had to be called off owing to his ill health, see MacCulloch, Diarmaid, 1996, *Thomas Cranmer*, London, Yale University Press: 517. As queen, Mary I did not leave the outskirts of London except to journey to Winchester to meet Prince Philip on his arrival in 1554.

8 For Leicester and Kenilworth, see Adams, Simon, 1995, ' "Because I am of that Countrye & mynde to plant myself there": Robert Dudley, Earl of Leicester and the West Midlands' [Ch. 15]. He also obtained another former royal house, the manor of Langley near Woodstock, where the hunting was regarded as particularly good, see Adams, Simon (ed.), 1995, *Household Accounts and Disbursement Books of Robert Dudley, Earl of Leicester, 1558–1561, 1584–1586*, Camden Society, 5th ser. 6: 188, n. 391 (hereafter *Leicester Accounts*); and Thurley, *Royal Palaces*: 60.

9 See n. 24 below.

10 For Kenilworth and the progresses, see Ch. 15 below, pp. 323–4, 327–8.

11 On the progresses in general, see Cole, Mary Hill, 1985, The Royal Travel: Elizabethan Progresses and their Role in Government, Ph.D. thesis, University of Virginia, now published as *The Portable Queen: Elizabeth I and the Politics of Travel* (Amherst, Mass., 1999).

12 For examples, see Adams, *Leicester Accounts*.

13 For the structure of the Court in the reign of Elizabeth, see Adams, Simon, 1984 'Eliza Enthroned? The Court and its Politics' [Ch. 2], pp. 25–7. For a more general account, see Loades, David, 1992, *The Tudor Court*, Bangor, Headstart: 38–72.

14 For a brief discussion of the emergence of the 'vocabulary of the state', see Adams, Simon, 1995, 'The Patronage of the Crown in Elizabethan Politics: The 1590s in Perspective' [Ch. 4], pp. 83–4.

15 See Ch. 2 above, pp. 25–8.

16 See Adams, Simon, 1987, 'La noblesse et la cour sous Elisabeth', in André Stegmann (ed.), *Pouvoir et institutions en Europe au XVIᵉ siècle*, Paris, J. Vrin: 164.

17 See Adams, *Leicester Accounts*: 29–30.

18 For examples from the Earl of Leicester's former servants, see the index of servants in Adams, *Leicester Accounts*: 461–88.

19 Ch. 2 above, p. 35.

20 Ch. 4 above, esp. p. 72.

21 For examples, see the tradesmen listed in Leicester's household account for 1559–61 in Adams, *Leicester Accounts*: 119–34.

22 The established account is Woodworth, Allegra, 1945, *Purveyance for the Royal Household in the Reign of Queen Elizabeth, Transactions of the American Philosophical Society*, new ser. 35, 1, though there are a number of sources she did not employ.

23 The purveyor James Quarles (d. 1599) organised the supplying of the expedition to relieve Sluys in the summer of 1587 and later in the year was appointed Surveyor of Naval Victuals. He held overall responsibility for provisioning the fleet in the campaign against the Armada in 1588. In 1592 he was appointed a Clerk Comptroller of the Board of Green Cloth. The official responsible for the victualling of Drake's squadron (and ultimately the whole fleet) at Plymouth in 1588 was the clerk-avenor of the Stables, Marmaduke Darrell.

24 Elizabeth's abstention from 'superfluous and sumptuous buildings of delight' was cited by Sir Nicholas Bacon, the Lord Keeper, as a prime example of her concern for economy in his opening speeches to Parliament in both 1563 and 1571, Hartley, T. E. (ed.), 1981, *Proceedings in the Parliaments of Elizabeth I*, vol. 1, 1558–81, Leicester, Leicester University Press: 85, 186. The absence of royal patronage of architecture during the reign is also commented on in Girouard, Mark, 1983, *Robert Smythson and the Elizabethan Country House*, London, Yale University Press: 3–4.

25 The fullest discussion is found in Young, Alan, 1987, *Tudor and Jacobean Tournaments*, London, George Philip, See also Sir Roy Strong's earlier essays reprinted in Strong, Roy, 1977, *The Cult of Elizabeth*, London, Thames & Hudson.

26 See the perceptive comments of David Starkey in Starkey, David, 1984, 'An English Renaissance?' in Simon Adams (ed.), *Queen Elizabeth I: Most Politic Princess*, London, History Today: 48–51.

27 The disappearance of most of what records the Privy Chamber kept makes it difficult to comment on the queen's personal wardrobe. One of the most valuable survivors, entitled 'Book of the stuffe of the Queens Majesties wardrobe' and covering the years 1561 to 1585, is found among the Scudamore papers deposited with the Masters in Chancery in the nineteenth century in what is known as the Duchess of Norfolk's Exhibit, Public Record Office, C 115/L2/6697. It has been published: Arnold, Janet, 1980, *Lost from her Majesties Back*, London, Costume Society. A number of miscellaneous wardrobe warrants survive in what were once private collections: one group can be found in British Library, Additional MS 5751, a stray warrant of 1565 for the

delivery of petticoats to the queen is now Washington D.C., Folger Shakespeare Library, MS Xd 265.

28 Evidence of the range of Leicester's patronage can be found throughout Adams, *Leicester Accounts*. He was not, however, a builder on the scale of some of his peers.

29 For example of his purchases, see Adams, *Leicester Accounts*, and Longleat House, Dudley Papers, Box V, fos. 146–50v, an extensive bill from the leading Genoese merchant and banker Benedict Spinola including a range of purchases in the Low Countries and France during the period 1562–66. In later years Leicester employed English diplomatic agents and military officers to purchase household furnishings and works of art for him in the Netherlands. See, for example. British Library Cotton MS, Galba C VII, fos. 59–60, 157, Thomas Cotton to Leicester, 28 Aug. 1580 and 3 Dec. 1581.

30 Strong, Roy, 1986, *Henry, Prince of Wales and England's Lost Renaissance*, London, Thames & Hudson: 86–8 and 184–6 makes the case. See also Girouard, *Robert Smythson*: 2–4.

31 There was close contact with France throughout the reign; the possible cultural interchange is a theme of Woodhuysen, H. R., 1981, 'Leicester's Literary Patronage: A Study of the English Court, 1578–1582', D.Phil. thesis, Oxford University. Sir Philip Sidney spent a considerable period of time in Venice and Vienna in the mid-1570s.

32 Public Record Office, E 351/1795.

33 Taken from the Treasurer of the Chamber's accounts, Public Record Office, E 351/541–2.

34 Ch. 2 above, pp. 56–7.

35 There is some confirmation of this estimate of the ordinary revenue for the first decade of the reign in Folger Shakespeare Library MS Xd. 112; a survey of the revenue for the first half of the year dated 1 June 1563. This gives a total of revenue owing for the half year as £77,831. As there are categories of revenue missing, an annual income of between £150,000 and £200,000 would appear to be correct. I am not entirely convinced by the figure of £300,000 for the last years of the reign.

36 This figure was reached by an extrapolation from the expenditure on the Household of between £14,000 and 15,000 p.a., given in Myers, A. R. (ed.), 1959, *The Household of Edward IV: The Black Book and the Ordinance of 1478*, Manchester, Manchester University Press: 45–7.

37 Discussed in Alsop, J. D., 1982, 'The Theory and Practice of Tudor Taxation', *English Historical Review*, 97: 1–30.

38 See Hoyle, R. W., 1994, 'Crown, Parliament and Taxation in Sixteenth-Century England', *English Historical Review*, 109: 1174–96, esp.: 1190–1.

39 See Ch. 2 above, pp. 26–31, and Ch. 4 above, pp. 81–2.

40 The most recent discussion can be found in Dean, David, 1996, *Law Making and Society in Late Elizabethan England: The Parliament of England, 1584–1601*, Cambridge, Cambridge University Press: 80–5.

41 This conclusion rests on what is to some extent anecdotal evidence, provided by the survival of a considerable body of Sussex's correspondence dealing with Court business and the absence of anything by Howard. For examples of Sussex's correspondence, see Public Record Office C 115/M19/7543, Sussex to Mary Scudamore, 9 Oct.

1576, and British Library, Cotton MS Titus B II, fo. 302, Lady Mary Sidney to Sussex, n.d. (1573–76).

42 Ch. 2 above, p. 30.

43 *Ibid.*, pp. 31–2.

44 Some general comments can be found in *ibid.*, pp. 27–8, 38. Fuller accounts can be found in Wright, Pam, 1987, 'A Change in Direction: The Ramifications of a Female Household, 1558–1603', in Starkey (ed.), *The English Court*: 147–72, and Merton, Charlotte, 1992, '"The Forgotten Crowd of Common Beauties", the Women who Served Queen Mary and Queen Elizabeth', Ph.D. thesis, Cambridge University.

45 See the complaints of Sir John Harington about 'a lady shut up in a chamber from her subjects', quoted in Ch. 2 above, p. 41.

46 Adams, Simon, 1997, 'Favourites and Factions at the Elizabethan Court' [Ch. 3].

47 On this see also Hammer, Paul, 'Absolute and Sovereign Mistress of her Grace? Queen Elizabeth I and her Favourites, 1581–1592', in Elliott, J. H. and Brockliss, L. W. B. (eds), *The World of the Favorite, c. 1550–1675*, London, Yale University Press, 1999: 38–53.

48 On the 1590s, see Mears, Natalie, 'Regnum Cecilianum? A Cecilian Perspective of the Court', and Hammer, Paul, 'Patronage at Court, Faction and the Earl of Essex', in Guy (ed.), *The Reign of Elizabeth I*: 46–64, 65–86, as well as Ch. 2 above, pp. 33–4.

49 Guy, John, 'The Elizabethan Establishment and the Ecclesiastical Polity', in Guy (ed.), *The Reign of Elizabeth I*: 126–49.

50 See the discussion in Ch. 4 above, pp. 72–5.

51 It is interesting in this context that Burghley rejected Philip Sidney as a possible husband. Leicester was no less active as a matchmaker and was responsible for another marital disaster: the marriage of Penelope Devereux and the grimly Puritan 3rd Lord Rich.

52 Bernard, George (ed.), 1992, *The Tudor Nobility*, Manchester, Manchester University Press: introduction, 20–2.

53 The best examples of favoured Catholics are Anthony Browne, Viscount Montague and Sir Thomas Cornwallis.

54 Sir Geoffrey Elton in particular, see Elton, G. R., 1984, 'Parliament', in Haigh (ed.), *Reign of Elizabeth I*: 79–100, and Elton, G. R., 1986, *The Parliament of England*, Cambridge, Cambridge University Press.

55 Dean, *Law-Making and Society*: 217–58.

56 See the discussion in Ch. 4 above, pp. 79–82.

57 Leicester's borough patronage is outlined in Adams, Simon, 1989, 'The Dudley clientele in the House of Commons, 1559–1586' [Ch. 10]. A fuller account will be found in a still unpublished paper, 'The Earl of Leicester as a Patron of boroughs'.

58 Leicester's clientele is discussed in Ch. 10 and Ch. 15 below, *Leicester Accounts*; and Adams, Simon, 1992, 'The Dudley Clientele 1553–63' [Ch. 8]. The best discussion of Burghley's clientele can be found in Morrison, G. R., 1990, 'The Land, Family and Domestic Following of William Cecil, Lord Burghley. c.1550–98', D.Phil. thesis, Oxford University.

59 The argument for the influence of the Privy Chamber can be found in Wright, 'Change of Direction' and Merton 'Forgotten Crowd'; a more sceptical one in Ch. 2 above, pp. 38–9. I have not yet seen any evidence advanced to cause me to revise my opinion.

60 Some idea of the regional importance of the Duke of Norfolk's household at Kenninghall can be found in the records of his visits there in 1561 in the household account of Sir Thomas Cornwallis for 1560–61. Suffolk Record Office, HA 411 (Iveagh MSS: Cornwallis Papers), Box 3, art. 2.

61 See the comments on this much-quoted 'dictum' in James, Mervyn, 1986, *Society, Politics and Culture: Studies in Early Modern England*, Cambridge, Cambridge University Press: 291–3.

62 The best account of the funding of Mary's 'Court' can be found in Greengrass, Mark, 1988, 'Mary, Dowager Queen of France', in Lynch, Michael (ed.), *Mary Stewart: Queen in Three Kingdoms*, Oxford, Basil Blackwell: 171–94.

63 For comments on female rule, see Ch. 2 above pp. 40–1.

64 The earliest confirmed and lethal Elizabethan duel that I know of involved two army officers and took place in the Netherlands in September 1587, see *Calendar of State Papers, Foreign Series Elizabeth I*, 21.(3), 1929: 321. This does not mean that there were not disputes that involved violence or threats of violence earlier, but the discussion of duelling and aristocratic violence in Stone, Lawrence, 1979, *The Crisis of the Aristocracy 1558–1641*, Oxford, Oxford University Press: 223–34, 242–7, is exaggerated. Even Stone (p. 245) admits that there were few duels before the 1590s.

65 An extremely perceptive assessment of Pembroke in the last years of Elizabeth's reign can be found in Gebauer, Andreas, 1987, *Von Macht und Mäzenatentum: Leben und Werk William Herbert, des Dritten Earls von Pembroke*, Heidelberg, Carl Winter: 38–53.

66 There is no direct evidence of Elizabeth's reaction to Edmund Spenser's *Faerie Queene*, but the fact that he was one of the two poets pensioned by the queen is not irrelevant. I owe this point to the late Professor W. A. Ringler.

67 Ch. 2 above, p. 38.

68 For the historiographical debate, see Ch. 3 above, pp. 53–7.

Part II

The Earl of Leicester
and his affinity

Chapter 7

Queen Elizabeth's eyes at Court: the Earl of Leicester

W hatever else may be said of them, the Duke and Duchess of Northumberland produced a large and happy family. Of their thirteen children, seven were alive at the time of the Duke's execution. The five boys – John, Earl of Warwick, Lord Ambrose, Lord Guildford, Lord Robert (born on 24 June 1532) and Lord Henry – were also tried and found guilty of participating in their father's treason. The elder of the two girls, Mary, married to Sir Henry Sidney, escaped with her husband from the full effects of the disaster. The eight-year-old Catherine, though already betrothed to Henry, Lord Hastings, was still living with her mother.[a]

Tudor opinion was divided on whether the sins of the father should be visited on the children. On the one hand it was the very principle upon which acts of attainder, whereby the descendants of traitors were barred from inheritance of land or title, were based. Yet one of Henry VIII's Councillors recalled from an earlier case 'the difference between the king's laws and an instinct or law that is in nature' that permitted children to be spared. At his trial, John Dudley appealed for mercy for his sons, and some speculated that it was the hope of saving his children that lay behind his forswearing of his religion.

Only Lord Guildford followed his father to the block. He was executed with his wife Lady Jane Grey in February 1554. The other Dudleys received the Queen's clemency. The Duchess was able to retain most of her dower lands and a substantial estate of inheritance. Sir Henry Sidney went to Spain in 1554 to plead with Philip 'for the liberty of John, Earl of Warwick, and his brethren'. Thanks partly to his efforts, the four remaining brothers were released from the Tower and then pardoned in January 1555. But liberty came too late for Warwick, who died in October from the effects of imprisonment.

He was followed three months later by his mother. Her will, written in the weeks before her death, is a poignant document. Long and rambling, it is a testimony to her efforts to save what was left of her family.

Will of Jane, Duchess of Northumberland   December 1554–January 1555

> Here followeth my last will and testament written with mine own hand. First I bequeath my soul unto Almighty God and my body unto the earth and to be buried without any solemnity, for my will is rather to have my debts paid and my children and servants considered than my body that is but meat for worms. I do commit unto the hands of my executors . . . all the whole lands of mine inheritance as my house of Halesowen for the behalf of my children for to inherit my lands, the Queen's highness showing her mercy and the King's majesty to my sons their pardons that they may enjoy my lands . . . I give my lord Don Diego de Acevedo the new bed of green velvet with all the furniture to it, beseeching him even as he hath in my lifetime showed himself like a father and a brother to my sons, so I shall require him no less to do now their mother is gone . . . I give to the duchess of Alba my green parrot; I have nothing worthy for her else . . .

King Philip's clemency was not entirely disinterested; he now possessed a direct claim to the personal loyalty of the Dudley brothers. The debt was repaid in 1557 when the three surviving brothers took part in the siege of St Quentin. There, before his own eyes, Lord Robert later declared, Lord Henry was killed. Thanks possibly to his death, the four remaining Dudley children were restored in blood by the Parliament of 1558.

In Lord Robert's case restoration did not stop there. The origins of his personal relationship with Queen Elizabeth have been the subject of much curiosity, but reliable evidence is very sparse. For all the speculation about a romance in the Tower in 1554, the only statement by either Elizabeth or Dudley on the subject describes a childhood friendship beginning in 1540–41. Other than that, all that can be established is that Lord Robert was included among Elizabeth's friends in the report made by Philip's Councillor, the Count of Feria, of an interview with her a week before she came to the throne.

Count of Feria to Philip II   14 November 1558
London

> I have also been told (although not directly by her) of certain others with whom she is on very good terms. They are the Earl of Bedford, Lord Robert, Throckmorton, Peter Carew and Harrington. I have also been told for certain that Cecil, who was King Edward's Secretary will also be Secretary to Madam Elizabeth. He is said to be an able and virtuous man . . .

It is quite likely that Dudley was with Elizabeth at Hatfield House when she received the news of her sister's death in the morning of 17 November 1558. One of her earliest acts was to appoint him Master of the Horse. His brother, Lord Ambrose, was appointed Master of the Ordnance shortly afterwards, while his sister, Mary Sidney, had become one of the Gentlewomen of the Privy Chamber by the time of the coronation. The Dudleys were thus at the centre of Elizabeth's Court from the first days of the reign.

By the summer of 1559 the closeness between Elizabeth and Dudley was the subject of widespread gossip and innuendo. What increased the potential for scandal was the fact that he was already married. When his wife died in mysterious circumstances on 8 September 1560, the rumours appeared confirmed. The reasons for his marriage in 1550 to Amy Robsart, the only child of the middling Norfolk gentleman-farmer Sir John Robsart, remain unclear. Nor is much known of their married life. For still unexplained reasons Amy Dudley spent most of 1558–60 near Abingdon in Berkshire – latterly at the former religious house at Cumnor where she died, thus giving rise to speculation that Dudley was deliberately keeping his wife in seclusion. She has left only two letters. One, probably written in 1558, deals with the management of the estates in Norfolk that she had inherited from her father. The other was written to her London dressmaker a fortnight before her death, and he attached it to the bill that he later sent to Dudley for payment. When it was discovered a century ago among Dudley's financial documents at Longleat House, its ordinariness destroyed the legend of the 'prisoner of Cumnor'.[b]

Amy Dudley to [John] Flowerdew   7 August [?1558]
Mr. Hyde's [Denchworth, Berks]

Mr. Flowerdew, I understand by Grice that you put him in remembrance of that you spoke to me of concerning the going of certain sheep at Syderstone. Although I forgot to move my lord thereof before his departing, he being sore troubled with weighty affairs and I not being altogether quiet for his sudden departing, yet notwithstanding . . . I neither may nor can deny you that request in my lord's absence . . .

Amy Dudley to William Edney   24 August [1560]
Cumnor

[I] . . . desire you to take the pains for me to make this gown of velvet which I send you with such a collar as you made my russet taffeta gown . . .

Little is known of the circumstances of Amy Robsart's death. Lord Robert himself was then at Windsor with the Court, which had just completed a summer progress in Hampshire. The day before, he had written to the 3rd Earl of Sussex in Ireland to order horses for the Queen. This letter helps to explain Sir William Cecil's complaint at the time that Dudley was encouraging Elizabeth to take up dangerous sports.

Lord Robert Dudley to the Earl of Sussex   7 September 1560
Windsor

My good Lord, the Queen's majesty thanks be to God is in very good health and is now become a great huntress and doth follow it daily from morning till night. She doth mean out of hand to send into that country [Ireland] for some hobbies [everyday riding horses] for her own saddle, specially for strong good gallopers, which are much better than her geldings, whom she spareth not to tire as fast as they can go . . .

For the events at Cumnor we are dependent upon a series of letters between Dudley and his chief household officer, Thomas Blount of Kidderminster. They survive only as copies made in 1567 when Amy Dudley's half-brother, John Appleyard, claimed that Dudley had failed to investigate her death fully. The letters reveal the efforts that Dudley made to establish the truth – accident, foul play or suicide being suspected – though there is always the possibility that they were doctored. The first of the series gives Dudley's reaction to the news; the wandering grammar may reflect his shock.

Lord Robert Dudley to Thomas Blount 9 September [1560]
Windsor

Cousin Blount, immediately upon your departure from me there came to me Bowes, by whom I do understand that my wife is dead and as he sayeth by a fall from a pair of stairs. Little other understanding can I have of him. The greatness and the suddenness of the misfortune doth so perplex me until I do hear from you how the matter standeth, or how this evil should light upon me, considering what the malicious world will bruit, as I can take no rest. And because I have no way to purge myself of the malicious talk that I know the wicked world will use, but one, which is the very plain truth to be known . . .

Particularly cryptic is a hastily scrawled (and undated) note from Dudley to Cecil, probably in the week after his wife's death, when he had retired from the Court to his house at Kew. Whether this was at his own volition or under orders from the Queen is still debated, as is the nature of his request to Cecil in the letter. Nevertheless, Cecil's visit, and the implied moral support he offered, helps to explain why Dudley's career at Court was not destroyed at this point.

Lord Robert Dudley to Sir William Cecil [?13 or 14 September] 1560

Sir, I thank you much for your being here, and the great friendship you have showed towards me I shall not forget. I am very loath to wish you here again, but I would be glad to be with you there. I pray you let me hear from you what you think best for me to do. If you doubt, I pray you ask the question, for the sooner you advise me thither, the more I shall thank you.
 I am sorry so sudden a chance should breed me so great a change, for methinks I am here all the while as it were in a dream, and too far, too far from the place I am bound to be, where methinks also this long idle time cannot excuse me for the duty I have to discharge elsewhere. I pray you help him that seems to be at liberty out of so great bondage. Forget me not though you see me not, and I will remember you and fail ye not . . .

Amy Dudley's death by misadventure may have freed Dudley to marry Elizabeth, but it also overshadowed their relations with scandal. During the winter of 1560–61 Elizabeth's intentions were the subject of much speculation; by the end of 1561 this had died down. Nor was Dudley's ambition to marry the Queen his only iron in the fire. Equally important was the final restoration of his house, as his pleasure when the Queen granted his father's old titles to his brother Ambrose in December 1561 reveals.

Lord Robert Dudley to George, Earl of Shrewsbury   27 December 1561
The Court

> ... I thought good ... to participate unto your lordship these comfortable news which are that it hath pleased the queen's majesty of her great bounty and goodness to restore our house to the name of Warwick, and as yesterday hath created my said brother earl hereof ...

Soon afterwards both brothers readopted the bear and ragged staff device made famous by the Beauchamp Earls of Warwick in the fifteenth century and revived by their father when he became Earl of Warwick in 1547. They also received many of his former estates. However, Robert Dudley's own promotion to the peerage did not occur until Michaelmas Day 1564, when Elizabeth, after considerable debate about his title, created him Earl of Leicester and Baron of Denbigh.

In October 1562, shortly after recovering from her near-fatal attack of smallpox, Elizabeth appointed both Dudley and the fourth Duke of Norfolk to her Privy Council. Dudley was already deeply involved in the making of foreign policy, and in particular with the maintaining of good relations with Mary, Queen of Scots. A letter he wrote then to the Scottish Secretary, William Maitland of Lethington, alludes to the great debate over the succession provoked by the Queen's illness.

Lord Robert Dudley to William Maitland of Lethington   27 October [1562]

> My Lord, either I wrote in a piece of my last letter unto you that I wished you here for sundry causes to have spoken with you, or I meant to have written so to you. But to say truth, the extremity of our case was such that as I wot not well what I wrote of that woeful case. Thanks be to Almighty God, He has well delivered us for this present, for the Queen's majesty is now perfectly well out of all danger and the disease so well worn away as I never saw any in so short [time]. Doubtless, my Lord, the dispair of her recovery was once marvelous great, and being so sudden the more perplexed the whole state, considering all things, for this little storm shook the whole tree so far as it proved the strong and weak branches. And some rotten boughs were so shaken as they appeared plainly how soon they had fallen. Well this sharp sickness hath been a good lesson, and as it hath not been anything hurtful to her body, so I doubt not but it shall work much good otherwise. For ye know seldom princes be touched in this sort, and such remembrances are

necessary in His sight that governeth all. As further occasions and respects moveth me, I intend to write further by the next to you, for that my leisure is presently such as this bearer can tell. And shall pray you to use my writings when they come as I required you, for that I will be more frank with you than any other there, and do wish her Majesty [Mary, Queen of Scots] had two Lethingtons that she might spare one here. Fare you well and wish you humbly kiss her Majesty's hand on my behalf. In haste this 27 of October.

Your assured,
R. Dudley

As important as any formal position as a councillor was Dudley's intimacy with Elizabeth. She was extremely possessive of his company and refused for many years to allow him to take up embassies or military commands abroad. Even his temporary absences from the Court were begrudged, and his 'often sending' to her when away was expected. Elizabeth saved many of these private letters, and about twenty of them survive. Those that she wrote to him, on the other hand, appear (with the exception of the letter on p. 148) to have been destroyed.

The earliest of Dudley's involved an awkward explanation. He had left the Court in August 1563 to greet his wounded brother on his return from commanding the expedition to Le Havre (a post that Dudley himself had wanted), despite the fact that many of the survivors were infected with the plague. After 1562 Elizabeth was very frightened by disease.

Lord Robert Dudley to Queen Elizabeth   7 August 1563
Bagshot

My most humble thanks, my most dear Lady, I must render as most bound for all, but in particular for this your gracious advertisement which I have received by your own handwriting . . . And yet ten hundred deaths would I more suffer rather than by my evil chance the fear of any such sickness should happen to that dear person. And albeit to my judgement all doubt had been past, for the later and more perilous passengers hath been lightlier by others accounted of repairing to your presence, notwithstanding the natural care and love toward my brother might well much sooner have provoked me to desire the sight of him, yet surely both care of your person for fear of such danger and the occasion thereby to be absent from it, which thereby must force me, had been enough the least of both to have made me fast from the dearest and best sight that this world could show me. Wherefore my own Lady pardon me, though otherwise it will be painful enough to be so long from you, that I should do anything that might seem to any others careless of so great care as I am bound to have more than any other in this case . . . So remaining your farther pleasure always [sic], I humbly take leave. From Bagshot this Saturday.

Most bounden for ever and ever,
R.D.

In 1564 the relationship between Dudley (now Earl of Leicester) and the Queen came to the fore again, when a marriage to the Archduke Charles of Styria, son of Ferdinand I, the Holy Roman Emperor, was proposed. This was the most serious of Elizabeth's 'courtships', and it dominated Court politics between 1564 and 1568.

The long debates over marriage to the Archduke involved two distinct issues. At the beginning of the reign Elizabeth had made public her desire to remain single. What was not clear was whether her decision was an absolute one, or whether new circumstances might influence it. Should she change her mind, then the question of whether she should choose a foreign or a native husband arose. Against the established preference for a husband of royal blood was the memory of the widespread anxiety that her sister's marriage to Philip II of Spain had caused. This and Elizabeth's obvious affection for him were the strongest arguments in Leicester's favour.

During the progress of 1566 he gave his own views to a French diplomatic agent. This statement may, of course, have been made for foreign consumption, but it remains the most explicit surviving description of his relationship with the Queen.

Jacob de Vulcob, sieur de Sassy to   6 August 1566
Jacques Bochetel de La Foret
Stamford

I told him [Leicester] that their Majesties [Charles IX and Catherine de Medici] did not believe that she [Elizabeth] wished to choose a foreign prince for her husband. That point he would not concede to me at all, but showed nevertheless that he believed it to be so. Then speaking less guardedly he told me that his true opinion was that she would never marry. To convince me he added that he considered that he knew her Majesty as well as or better than anyone else of her close acquaintance, for they had first become friends before she was eight years old. Both then and later (when she was old enough to marry) she said she never wished to do so. Thereafter he had not seen her waver in that decision. However, if by chance she should change her mind and also look within the kingdom, he was practically assured that she would choose no one else but him, as she had done him the honour of telling him so quite openly on more than one occasion, and furthermore he enjoyed as much of her favour now as he had ever done.

The case against Leicester as Elizabeth's consort was outlined by Cecil in a memorandum he drafted in either 1566 or 1567 (excerpts of which are printed below).[c] His own prejudice is evident. He constructs a damning indictment of Dudley, but he also displays a considerable amount of wishful thinking about the Archduke, and says nothing about the crucial issue of religion.

The Earl of Leicester and his affinity

Sir William Cecil, memorandum   1566 or 1567

Reasons against the Earl of Leicester
1. Nothing is increased by marriage to him either in { riches
                                          { estimation
                                          { power
2. It will be thought that the slanderous speeches of the Queen with the Earl have been true.
3. He shall study nothing but to enhance his own particular friends: to wealth, to offices, to lands and to offend others.
4. He is infamed by the death of his wife.
5. He is far in debt.
6. He is like to prove unkind or jealous of the Queen's majesty.

To be considered in the Marriage

Carolus	Earl of Leicester
in birth	
nevew	born a son of a knight
brother of [an] Emperor	his grandfather but a solicitor
in degree	
an archduke born	an earl made
in wealth	
by report 3,000,000 ducats	all of the Queen and in debt
by year	
in education	
amongst princes	always in England
in reputation	
honoured of all	hated of many
named to the empire	his wife's death

But though Leicester never became Elizabeth's husband, he always remained one of her intimates. This gave him an influence that most of her other councillors lacked. 'You know the Queen and her nature best of any man,' a member of the Court wrote in 1586. Much of his later reputation as a 'politician' came from his careful manoeuvring of her. A revealing insight into the way this was done is provided by his advice to the French Protestant envoy, the cardinal of Châtillon, who arrived in England with a number of French exiles after the outbreak of the third 'War of Religion' in France in the autumn of 1568. The problem was Elizabeth's well-known reluctance to countenance rebels, 'those who have to do with princes' – even when those princes were hostile to her.

Earl of Leicester to Sir Nicholas Throckmorton   3 October 1568

Sir Nicholas, My Lord Steward [the 1st Earl of Pembroke], Mr. Secretary [Cecil] and I have written to you for an advice to be given to the cardinal upon the great resort and repair we hear from all parts that are come lately into the realm out of France, praying you to use our advice in such sort to him as he perceive no evil in our meaning either toward himself or his nation, for that in very deed there is no cause at all but only our chief respect is toward him that we may continue and show our good affections toward him the more largely. And without all doubt I know assuredly her Majesty hath a marvellous liking of him and one thing more than I looked for, which is her liking to hear of his wife, and is very desirous to see her and hath sent one expressly to visit her. But what her general opinion is to show public receiving of those that have to do with their princes you know as well as I, which causeth us to foresee lest too much open show may cause her in time to grow more weary of the cardinal, for that all the repair will now come to him. Wherefore it is reason they repair and deal with him, so we wish that he deal warily and wisely that he may do good in the cause. And when he will treat with her Majesty, that he come but in his former sort to her, that the open company appear not, that the [French] ambassador take not just cause to challenge the Queen's majesty for the maintenance of the King's adversaries and so to cause a stay, where we wish by little and little to have it so increase as it may break forth as it should indeed and must do if we look to her own safety and the realm's surety. Now you know my mind and ours, I doubt not of your wise handling thereof, our chief respect being to have the cardinal to keep his credit and recourse hither, who I trust shall do most good. In haste, 3 October.

Your assured,
R. Leycester

Leicester's support for the 'Protestant Cause' became more pronounced as Protestant rebellions spread in both France and the Netherlands in the 1570s. His reaction to the notorious assassination of the Admiral Coligny (brother of the Cardinal of Châtillon) and the massacre of the French Huguenot leadership in Paris on St Bartholomew's Day 1572 reflects the growing trend towards religious politics. More particularly, Leicester was also using the Massacre to support the Protestants (and English) party in Scotland, as opposed to the Catholic (and French).

Earl of Leicester to the Earl of Morton   7 September 1572
Woodstock

My lord, I think your lordship is not ignorant of the late most shameful and most cruel fait [deed] used in France against the Admiral and all others, the chief of the religion, being many hundred worthy and noble gentlemen murdered and slain in one day and night besides many thousands of zealous and good people likewise guiltlessly at the same time put to the sword. And as the act is most horrible to all true Christians so is it more to be lamented that it should hap to be done by the consent of such a prince [Charles IX] as hath so openly professed sincerity and with good and gracious dealings so entrapped the hearts of all good men to trust or rather to believe in his princely and upright meaning . . .

These my lord be good warnings to all those that be professors of the true religion to take heed in time, for how great hope there was of this prince's indifference that way or rather good affection, I refer to your lordship that hath heard I am sure no less than we have done, which now seeing it to fall out as we do, we are to look more narrowly to our present estate. We cannot but stand in no small danger except there be a full concurrence together of all such as mean faithfully to continue such as they profess. And having always for my own part made no less reckoning of your lordship's good devotion toward the advancement of God's true religion than of my own which I know best, I think it my part upon these considerations to impart with your lordship so frankly thereof as the necessity of the case doth require . . .

Your lordship's assured loving friend,
R. Leycester

By the 1570s Leicester had also become a leading domestic patron – artistic, literary and economic as well as political. In his journal the town clerk of Warwick, John Fisher, recorded an interview with him in 1571. It reveals both the pressure of lobbying on Privy Councillors as well as Leicester's benevolent response. Warwick and Coventry, which bordered his own estate at Kenilworth, had a particularly close association with him.

Journal of John Fisher   27 November 1571

At Greenwich on Wednesday being the 27th of the same month the Queen's majesty riding abroad and the said earl among other lords attending her highness the said Fisher had good opportunity and took such time as the said earl heard him at length . . . and asked what good trade there was in the said town and how the poor were relieved. To which the said Fisher answered that the number of the poor was great . . . 'I marvel [said the earl] you do not devise some ways among you to have some special trade to keep your poor on work as such as Sheldon of Beoley [Worcestershire] devised, which methinketh should not be only very profitable but also a means to keep your poor from idleness, or the making of cloth or capping or some such like. But I do perceive that every man is only careful for himself . . . I could wish there were some special trade devised wherewith having a good stock both reasonable profit might arise and your poor set on work. Whereunto I would be glad to help, and in mine opinion nothing would be more necessary than clothing or capping to both which occupations is required many workmen and women and such may be employed as in no faculty else, for though they be children they may spin and card, though they be lame they may pick and free wool and do such things as shall keep them from idleness and whereof some commodity may grow. And therefore many such poor as I perceive you have, I would to God you would some ways devise that they might in sort be relieved and your commonwealth profited. And because I am of that country and mind to plant myself there I would be glad to further any good device with all my heart.'

The 'commonwealth' rhetoric Leicester used to Fisher commanded universal consent; a far more controversial aspect of the Earl's patronage was his encouragement of Puritan preachers. Both as a Councillor and as Chancellor of Oxford University (to which he was elected in 1564) he had a major influence on the Church. During the 1570s growing attacks on the bishops by the Puritans ('uncharitable preaching') and the bishops' aggressive response frequently placed him in a difficult position, as an official letter to the University in 1580 shows.

Earl of Leicester to the Vice-Chancellor   13 October 1580
and Convocation of Oxford University
The Court

After my right hearty commendations. Complaints have been made unto me by the space of these two or three years from time to time almost continually, touching disorderly and uncharitable preachings among you by some of the younger sort, which though I have much misliked, yet I have not much dealt in reprehension or reformation thereof for two causes: the one that I thought the men to be young that were named so to overshoot themselves [and] would in time see their own faults and amend them, the other that I would not seem to discourage any from preaching, knowing the great want of preachers everywhere. But now the fault, as it is informed, increasing daily and by example of sufferance to be more general and the complaint thereof not reaching to myself alone but to many others of the best sort, I was as well by further authority enforced as bound in respect of mine office there among [you] to look into it. And therefore to be as well informed more fully of the disorders as advised for the remedies, I sent for two or three of the preachers which had offended that way and for some five or six of the wiser and graver sort of the University whose advice I might use for redress.

In conference with all whom I do find indeed disorders so great as it grieved me to hear and think the preachers that were here were themselves sorry. But for redress I have by advice of those doctors I sent for and other men of authority and wisdom here devised the enclosed orders, which I send and commend unto you as those that being well observed will, I hope, in time work some good reformation in this point, requiring you Mr. Vice-Chancellor and you the whole house to confirm them with your consents and authority . . .

Your loving friend and Chancellor,
R. Leycester

By the end of the 1570s the long-standing relationships between the Queen and the leading figures of the Court found expression in numerous private jokes and allusions which are not always easy to understand now. The best-known of them were Elizabeth's nicknames for her intimates – her 'eyes' in Leicester's case (see p. 148). In 1577 Leicester and his brother Warwick initiated what would become an extensive Court patronage of the medicinal baths at Buxton in Derbyshire. This provoked a bantering exchange with the

Queen, a great believer in her own herbal remedies, but sceptical of the benefits of the baths. Early in June she dictated to Sir Francis Walsingham a letter of thanks to the Earl and Countess of Shrewsbury for Leicester's entertainment. Much of the humour is derived from the implicit allusion to her disputes with Shrewsbury over the household expenses ('diets') of Mary, Queen of Scots. This letter may not have been sent, for a more formal version dated the 25th is now among Shrewsbury's papers. Even that pleased him so much that he endorsed it 'to be kept as the dearest jewel'.

Elizabeth I   4 June 1577
to the Earl and Countess of Shrewsbury

Right trusty etc., being given to understand from our cousin of Leicester how honourably he was lately received and used by you our cousin the Countess of Shrewsbury at Chatsworth and how his diet is discharged by you both at Buxton . . . we think it meet . . . to prescribe unto you a proportion of diet, which we mean in no case you shall exceed, and that is to allow him by the day two ounces of flesh, referring the quality to themselves, and for his drink the twentieth part of a pint of wine to comfort his stomach, and as much of St. Anne's sacred water as he listeth. On festival days, as is fit for a man of his quality, we can be content you shall enlarge his diet by allowing unto him for his dinner the shoulder of a wren, and for his supper a leg of the same, besides his ordinary ounces. The like proportion we mean you to allow our brother of Warwick, saving that we think it meet that in respect that his body is more replete than his brother's, that the wren's leg allowance on festival days be abated, for that light suppers agree best with rules of physic.

But however entrancing these courtly games, Leicester was growing increasingly unhappy about the absence of a Dudley heir. Both Warwick (as Cecil had unkindly pointed out in 1566) and the Earl and Countess of Huntingdon were similarly childless, which left the Sidney children as the nearest heirs. He also became emotionally involved with two widows. The first, Douglas, Lady Sheffield, bore him a son, Robert Dudley, in 1574. The circumstances of this affair are as mysterious as any episode in Leicester's life. In 1605 during a Star Chamber case over the inheritance to his estates between her son, Leicester's widow and Sir Robert Sidney, Lady Sheffield claimed that she and Leicester had made a secret marriage. This she was unable to prove; but among the papers of the case is an undated letter from him, possibly the most personal to survive.

Earl of Leicester to [Douglas, Lady Sheffield]   [undated]

My good friend, hardly was I brought to write in this sort unto you lest you might conceive otherwise thereof than I mean it, but more loath am I to conceal anything from you that both honesty and true good will doth bind me to impart unto you.

I have, as you well know, long loved and liked you, and found always that faithful and earnest affection at your hand again that bound me greatly to you. This good will of mine, whatsoever you have thought, hath not changed from that it was at the beginning toward you. And I trust, after your widowhood began upon the first occasion of my coming to you, I did plainly and truly open unto you in what sort my good will should and might always remain to you, and showing you such reasons as then I had for the performance of mine intent as well as ever since . . . And so without difference or question ever since it passed between us, till as you can remember this last year at one time upon a casual doubt you pressed me in a further degree than was our condition, wherein I did plainly and truly deal with you. Some unkindness began and after, a greater strangeness fell out, though, as I have told you since, for other respects, for notwithstanding that first unkindness we did often meet in friendly sort and you resolved not to press me more with that matter . . . If I should marry I am sure never to have favour of them that I had rather yet never have wife than lose them, yet is there nothing in the world next that favour that I would not give to be in hope of leaving some children behind me, being now the last of our house . . . To carry you away for my pleasure to your more great and further grief hereafter were too great a shame for me, when being too late known, the lack could not so easily be supplied as now it may, having both time and occasion offered you, neither should my repentance be excusable when no recompence could be made on my part sufficient to make satisfaction . . .

Several years later, Leicester's desperation for an heir led him to take the step he had refused Douglas Sheffield. In a discreet ceremony in September 1578, attended only by a small group of family and friends, Leicester married Lettice, Countess of Essex, mother of the second Earl. In the winter of 1580–81 a son was born; and when the little Robert, Lord of Denbigh, died in 1584 Leicester was shattered.[d]

His marriage also coincided with a major debate over foreign policy. Elizabeth had recently rejected a proposal of military intervention in support of the Dutch rebels (which Leicester himself had offered to command), but instead sought to aid them in alliance with the French king's brother, the Duke of Anjou – an alliance that might be sealed by her marriage to Anjou. As he wrote to the English agent in the Netherlands, Leicester was himself at a loss to understand whether Elizabeth was serious.

Earl of Leicester to William Davison   26 February [1579]

Cousin Davison, I perceive the matters there [the Netherlands] goeth not well, which I am right sorry for and I am not deceived in my expectation, for I neither looked for better since her Majesty's forces joined not with them . . . Now touching the other matter at home here for Monsieur [Anjou], which you desire to understand of, for that many speeches are of it, I think none but God can let you know yet. Only this I must say. Outwardly there is some appearance of good liking, for the messengers are very well used and her Majesty's self doth seem to us all that she will marry if she may like the person and if the person adventure without condition or assurance to come. If she then like him, it is like she will have him. His ministers say he will adventure his coming and stand upon that matter of liking &c. And this is all I assure you that can yet be said to you. For my own opinion, if I should speak according to former disposition, I should hardly believe it will take place. And yet if I should say conjecturally, by that I newly hear or find in her deep consideration of her estate and that she is persuaded nothing can more assure it than marriage, I may be of mind she will marry if the party like her. But till the issue come for that point, I can say little nor any more else I believe; yet thus much shortly shall we know certainly, whether he will come or no . . . In some haste this 26 of February.

Your loving cousin and friend,
R. Leycester

Leicester was, however, widely regarded as the leading opponent of the match, and Anjou's agents were believed to have informed Elizabeth of his own secret marriage in the autumn of 1579 in an effort to destroy his influence. Her notorious sexual jealousy exploded. Leicester stood his ground, but his resentment at what he considered unfair treatment emerges clearly in a letter he wrote to Lord Burghley at the time.

Earl of Leicester to Lord Burghley   [late November 1579]

My lord, I have desired my Lord of Pembroke to excuse me to you and to pray your lordship to help to excuse my not coming this day. I perceive by my brother of Warwick your lordship hath found the like bitterness in her majesty towards me that others (too many) have acquainted me lately withal. I must confess it grieveth me not a little, having so faithfully, carefully and chargefully served her Majesty these twenty years as I have done. Your lordship is a witness I trust that in all her services I have been a direct servant unto her, her state and crown, that I have not more sought my own particular profit than her honour.

Her Majesty I see is grown into a very strange humour all things considered towards me, howsoever it were true or false as she is informed, the state whereof I will not dispute. Albeit I cannot confess a greater bondage in these cases than my duty of allegiance oweth, your lordship hath been best acquainted next myself to all my proceedings with her Majesty and I have ere now broken my very heart with you . . . I ever had a very honourable mind in all my actions as near as my capacity might direct me (and with modesty be it spoken) toward her service in my poor calling. Even so was it never abased in any slavish manner to be tied in more than unequal and unreasonable bonds. And as I carried myself almost more than a bondman many a year together, so long as one drop of comfort was left of any hope, as yourself my lord doth well know, so being acquitted and delivered of that hope and by both open and private protestations and declarations discharged, methinks it is more than hard to take such an occasion to bear so great displeasure for. But the old proverb sayeth, they that will beat a dog will want no weapon . . . God Almighty direct her Majesty and grant her many happy and prosperous years and your lordship as well to do as myself. In haste this Tuesday afternoon.

Your lordship's faithful friend,
R. Leycester

In time Elizabeth relented and, probably out of sympathy for the death of his son, appointed Leicester Lord Steward of the Household in the autumn of 1584.[e] But her bitterness towards his wife remained. This cast a major shadow over the crowning and most controversial episode in his career: his command of the English expeditionary force in the Netherlands in 1585–87. By the summer of 1585 Elizabeth was left with no alternative but to aid the Dutch directly. Leicester's willingness to lead an army there was long established, but for a mixture of personal and political reasons she hesitated about sending him, and only gave way after learning of the surrender of Antwerp to the Spaniards in August. Leicester was laid up by a riding accident near Kenilworth when he received the news.

Earl of Leicester to Sir Francis Walsingham   28 August 1585
Stoneleigh

Good Mr. Secretary, I have this day received two letters from you, both much to one effect, and the substance being of her Majesty's good resolution now to proceed effectually in the causes of the Low Countries . . . and that her Majesty did promise to send some nobleman to be their chief as heretofore was treated of, whom you thought should be myself, but first her Highness willed you to understand my own disposition now, whether I do remain in the same mind Antwerp being lost which I did before to be employed in that service. Truly Mr. Secretary that which moved me heretofore to be willing and ready to do her Majesty service in those parts was wholly and chiefly in respect of the cause offered which concerned God and her Majesty: God, touching religion which in my opinion is a sufficient cause for all true Christians to adventure their lives for; her Majesty, touching her safety as hath been to my seeming flatly and resolutely set down by all her Councillors, that there was never cause that happened in any prince's days whose estate both for their person and kingdom that was more nearly to be touched than her Majesty's, which for my part I have so assuredly conceived to be true, as if I be either a good Christian toward God or a faithful subject to her Majesty, I cannot but rest still of that mind.

Leicester's trials in the Netherlands – his acceptance of the governor-generalship against Elizabeth's opposition, his attempt to combat the leading army of Europe with small and under-funded forces, the difficulties of trying to deal with both Elizabeth and the Dutch, and the sadness caused by the death of Sidney – revealed him at his best and worst. Despite Elizabeth's savage repudiation of his governor-generalship, the extensive correspondence from this campaign contains the draft – the only one to survive – of a personal letter from the Queen to her favourite. In it the royal plural is abandoned and the 'mask of royalty' dropped.

Elizabeth I to Earl of Leicester   19 July 1586

Rob: I am afraid you will suppose by my wandering writings that a midsummer moon hath taken large possession of my brains this month, but you must needs take things as they come in my head, though order be left behind me . . . I have fraught this bearer full of my conceits of those country matters and imparted what way I mind to take and what is fit for you to use: I am sure you can credit him and so I will be short with these few notes . . . If there be fault in using soldiers or making of profit by them, let them hear of it without open shame, and doubt not but I will well chasten them therefore. It frets me not a little that the poor soldier that hourly ventures life should want their due that well deserve rather reward . . . And if the treasurer be found untrue or negligent, according to desert he shall be used, though you know my old wont that love not to discharge from office without desert, God forbid . . . Now will I end that do imagine I talk still with you and therefore loathly say farewell ô ô [i.e. 'Eyes' – his nickname] though ever I pray God bless you from all harm and save you from all foes with my million and legion of thanks for all your pains and cares.

As you know, ever the same,
E.R.

Provoked beyond endurance by England's direct intervention in the Netherlands, Philip II decided to launch a direct attack on England. The Spanish Armada sailed in May 1588 and Leicester was given the command of the main army raised for the defence of London. Worn out by his exertions, he left the Court for Kenilworth and Bath at the end of August, having drafted a letter describing the victory (not altogether accurately) to an old friend in France, Henry, Duke of Montmorency.

Earl of Leicester to Henry, Duke of Montmorency   22 August 1588
St. James's Palace

Monsieur my brother, you already know that the king of Spain has been assembling a great fleet during the last few years, which recently he sent forth to conquer this kingdom, as the prisoners who have fallen into our hands have testified and admitted; but it pleased God, who governs the hearts of kings, to permit him no advantage over us and to favour the good and just cause, so that this fleet (whose smallest ship carried at least five hundred men) has been so met by ours and saluted by such cannon fire that few ships escaped damage and more than 5000 soldiers were killed. Don Pedro de Valdes is a prisoner here, and in Holland Don Diego de Pimentel, *Maestre de Campo* of the *Tercio* of Sicily, which was composed of thirty companies of Spaniards and many members of the nobility; Don Pedro de Toledo escaped to Nieuport at night. We have certain news of seventeen great ships, some taken, some sunk; the others have been so scattered towards the north that we are sure that their force and fury has passed for this year. And because it was their intention that the Prince of Parma should embark at Dunkirk with another army to make a landing here while that from Spain was attacking our fleet, her majesty appointed me lieutenant-general of her forces to await the Duke of Parma with so good and able an army that the triumph for his *joyeuse entrée* [triumph] was already arranged; but now that the duke has seen the judgement God has delivered on the fleet, we believe that his plans, which were based on its arrival, will come to nothing, or even if the desire is still there, the means are lacking, so that in a short time God has revealed that it is He, the God of hosts, who disposes the plans and designs of men to His will. May this example serve as a solace and comfort to you in your daily trials and tribulations, for we need not doubt that God, for his glory, will give a happy outcome to the enterprises and just defence of Christian princes. To whom I pray, Monsieur, to grant you in good health a long and very happy life. From the Court at St. James the 22nd of August 1588.

Your very loving brother to do you humble service . . .

On 29 August he wrote briefly to Elizabeth, who endorsed it 'his last letter'. Six days later he died from malaria at Cornbury in Oxfordshire.

Earl of Leicester to Elizabeth I   29 August 1588
Rycote

I most humbly beseech your Majesty to pardon your poor old servant to be this bold in sending to know how my gracious lady doth and what ease of her late pains she finds, being the chiefest thing in this world I do pray for and for her to have good health and long life. For my own poor case I continue still your medicine and it amended much better than with any other thing that hath been given me . . . I humbly kiss your foot . . .

R. Leycester

Leicester's death was overshadowed by the celebration of the victory over the Armada, and he was buried quietly (as he had requested) in the Beauchamp Chapel of St Mary's, Warwick, where his son and 'sundry of my ancestors do lie'. By 1590 one of the greatest Tudor dynasties was extinct. In the finest of the literary tributes to him, Edmund Spenser saw in the suddenness of Leicester's demise a proof of the transitory nature of being.

Edmund Spenser, 'The Ruins of Time'

He now is dead, and all is with him dead,
Save what in Heaven's storehouse he uplaid:
His hope is failed, and come to pass his dread,
And evil men, now dead, his deeds upbraid:
Spite bites the dead, that living never baid [bit].

He now is gone, the whiles the fox is crept
Into the hole, the which the badger swept.
He now is dead, and all his glory gone,
And all his greatness vapoured to nought,
That as a glass upon the water shone,
Which vanished quite, so soon as it was sought.
His name is worn already out of thought,
Ne [nor] any Poet seeks him to revive;
Yet many Poets honoured him alive.

NOTES

a Catherine Dudley was certainly under twelve in 1553, but her date of birth presents a number of problems, see *Household Accounts*, pp. 43–4, n. 35.

b See *Household Accounts*, appendix I, for a major revision of this paragraph. Amy Dudley never lived in Berkshire before she moved to Cumnor in early 1560, but appears to have spent 1557–59 mainly at Throcking in Hertfordshire. Her letter to Flowerdew was probably written in 1557 rather than 1558 and refers to her husband's departure on the expedition to St. Quentin.

c As noted on p. 112, n. 85 above, internal evidence now suggests a date of 1565 for this memorandum.

d The Lord of Denbigh was born on 6 June 1581, see p. 390 below.

e For the revision of the date of Leicester's appointment as Lord Steward, see p. 43, n. 21 above.

Chapter 8

The Dudley clientele, 1553–63

At some point in 1567 Sir William Cecil composed a well-known memorandum on the greater suitability of the Archduke Charles of Styria as a
consort for Elizabeth I rather than Robert Dudley, Earl of Leicester. Fourth in
the list of arguments against Leicester was the danger that 'he shall study
nothing but to enhance his own particular friends: to wealth, to offices, to
lands and to offend others'. As if to illustrate the point Cecil then added the
names of nineteen individuals.[1] The possible significance of the members
of this Dudley faction has not gone unnoticed. Conyers Read and Wallace
MacCaffrey have drawn attention to their prominence in the Newhaven
(Le Havre) expedition of 1562–63.[2] David Loades has observed that Cecil's
list 'reads like a roll call of the rebels and conspirators of the previous reign'.[3]
Nicholas Canny discovered that many of the Newhaven survivors accompanied
Sir Henry Sidney to Ireland in 1565–66, and saw in their presence there the
victory of Leicester in a factional struggle with the 3rd Earl of Sussex.[4] In the
best of the three recent biographies of Leicester, Derek Wilson has argued
that his association with the former conspirators gave him a greater political
importance in the first years of Elizabeth's reign than has been previously
appreciated.[5]

There is, however, a further, and less-discussed, aspect to this Dudley
faction. David Loades also noted that many of the leaders of the Wyatt and
Dudley conspiracies had 'held office in the previous reign'.[6] This point deserves further attention. If these men had indeed been followers of John
Dudley, Duke of Northumberland, then their association with his son in Elizabeth's reign could be seen as the reforming of an earlier Dudley clientele
rather than the creation of a new faction.[7] Two very interesting hypotheses
would then arise. The participation of these men in the Marian conspiracies
would suggest that as a group they retained a certain cohesion between 1553
and 1558. Secondly, their allegiance to Lord Robert in the new reign may not

have been solely the result of his prominence at Court. The reverse may well have been the case. His personal closeness to the queen may have derived some of its notoriety from his leadership of an existing faction.

If these hypotheses can be proved, they would add a new dimension to the politics of the first years of Elizabeth's reign. Lord Robert's position at Court would make possible a restoration of the lands and offices the Dudley family and its clients had lost after 1553. The extent to which such a restoration occurred has never been explored. This chapter will examine the evidence for and ramifications of both the continuity of the Dudley clientele from 1553 to 1563 (a terminal date suggested by the Newhaven expedition), and the Dudley restoration. Its first section will establish more clearly the identities of the clientele of the early 1560s and trace, where possible, their Edwardian connections. Its second section will reconstruct Lord Robert's activities in the reign of Mary. Its final section will assess the place of the Dudley clientele in a wider 'Edwardian restoration' in 1559.

I

The great majority of the nineteen names that Cecil noted in 1567 are easily identified. Relations by blood or marriage formed a central group: Leicester's brother Ambrose, Earl of Warwick, the master of the Ordnance, his brother-in-law Sir Henry Sidney, president of the Council in the Marches of Wales and lord deputy of Ireland, Sir Francis Jobson, who married his father's half-sister, and John Appleyard, half-brother to Amy Robsart. Four cousins were also included: Sir James Croft, Sir Henry Dudley and the brothers Thomas and John Dudley.[8] Thomas Wilson, Henry Killigrew, Henry Middlemore, Edward Horsey and Thomas Leighton had already served Elizabeth in either a civil or a military capacity, and would do so more prominently in future. Robert and George Christmas, Anthony Forster and Richard Ellis were, like the Dudley brothers, among Leicester's men of business. Only four prove more elusive. 'Colshill' may be either Robert, the gentleman pensioner, or his brother Thomas, surveyor of the customs. 'Wysman' was probably Thomas, son of the Exchequer official John Wiseman. 'Mollynex' was probably Sidney's future secretary Edmund Molyneux, rather than either of the M.P.s in the 1563–66 parliament.[9] 'Middleton' has been tentatively identified as Richard, the captain of Denbigh Castle.

The main reason for the obscurity of the last four is the fact that they were not otherwise prominent among Leicester's followers. This raises doubts about the accuracy of Cecil's list, which are reinforced by some obvious omissions. Why, for example, were his other brother-in-law Henry Hastings, Earl of Huntingdon, and Sir Nicholas Throckmorton, widely regarded as his political brain at that time, not on the list, when Throckmorton's cousin

Middlemore, for whom he was constantly soliciting office, was there?[10] Cecil's motive in compiling the list was clearly to reinforce the argument that a domestic marriage for the queen would create factions. He had already advanced it at an earlier stage in the revived negotiations with the Archduke Charles, when he told an agent of the Duke of Württemberg in 1564 that the English nobility feared that a royal consort drawn from their ranks would 'favour his family and oppress others'.[11] It may simply have been the case that these were the first names that came to mind, possibly because Leicester had recently given his assistance to suits they had submitted.

The list is not therefore a definitive guide to Leicester's following. To establish its wider membership, other methods must be employed. In doing so it should first be noted that, with the exception of immediate household servants, Leicester and his brother Warwick employed the same pool of officers, lawyers and 'men of business' throughout the first three decades of Elizabeth's reign. This was a Dudley clientele, rather than Leicester's personal following.[12] In the absence of a satisfactory study of the duke of Northumberland, let alone his household and clientele, the previous history of these men is not always easy to trace.[13] It is simplest to proceed through a series of categories relevant to both father and son.

The immediate households present the fewest difficulties. The survival of two volumes of Robert Dudley's household accounts (20 December 1558–20 December 1559 and 22 December 1559–30 April 1561), wages and livery lists for 1559–60, together with a number of tradesmen's bills and other financial documents from the period 1558–66, makes it possible to identify the members of his household and his chief men of business in those years.[14] Neither Northumberland's nor Ambrose Dudley's household accounts have been discovered, but we do possess the records of the crown's commissioners who wound up Northumberland's estate after his execution, which can be supplemented by some miscellaneous correspondence.[15] The surviving wardrobe inventories of his heir, John, Viscount Lisle (Earl of Warwick from 1551 to 1554), also give some idea of the persons in the Dudley entourage between 1545 and 1550.[16]

Robert Dudley's household in the early 1560s appears to have been fairly fluid in structure; formal offices are not encountered until the end of the decade, possibly because his estate did not assume its full shape until the period 1563–72. Only Richard Ellis, compiler of the second volume of accounts, is described in passing as Dudley's 'paymaster'.[17] William Chauncy, who drew up the first volume, is not encountered again after 1559. 'There was, however, a distinct group of men of business dealing with Dudley's affairs at Elizabeth's accession, most of whom remained in his service on a permanent basis for the rest of their lives. Chauncy's account was audited by John Dudley, William Kynyat and Richard Horden. Thomas Blount of

Kidderminster, Anthony Forster, two Chester lawyers – William Glasier and John Yerwerth – and two men of Norfolk background, the lawyer William Grice (clerk of the Stables by 1564) and the London merchant William Hogan or Huggins, were the most prominent of their colleagues in 1559.[18] After 1562 Horden disappears; Dudley's wages account for 1559–61 was audited by Kynyat, Ellis, Blount, and the otherwise unknown Richard Overton. In the period 1564–66 the auditors were Dudley, Kynyat, Blount, Forster, Glasier and George Christmas.[19] Dudley, Kynyat and the lawyer Thomas Rolfe were the surveyors of the lands granted to Robert Dudley by Elizabeth in 1563; Dudley, Kynyat, Glasier and Yerwerth for those of 1566. Blount and John Somerfield were the attorneys for the livery of seisin of Kenilworth in 1563; Dudley, Rolfe, Glasier and Yerwerth were the commissioners in the settlement with the tenants of the lordship of Denbigh in the following year.[20]

Two of these men had been among Northumberland's leading household officers. Blount (whose position under Leicester appears to have been a similar one) was his comptroller in 1553.[21] Kynyat was one of his three general surveyors in 1548–49, and was described retrospectively as his auditor.[22] John Dudley and Hogan can be identified as his servants; Somerfield was a cousin of the Duchess of Northumberland and an executor of her will; Forster and Ellis had some form of association with his household.[23] Grice, whose father Gilbert (bailiff of Great Yarmouth) had some connection to Northumberland, is referred to in Lisle's wardrobe inventory.[24] Glasier cannot be traced directly to Northumberland, but he was doing business with Robert Dudley on the eve of Edward VI's death.[25]

Several of Northumberland's household officers in 1553 – John Holmes, his secretary, Charles Tyrell, his master of the horse, or Henry Brooke, his general receiver, for example – are not encountered among his son's servants. It is therefore possible that we may be giving those who survived to the 1560s a greater retrospective importance than they deserve. By the same token many of Northumberland's household servants may have obtained a more independent stature by Elizabeth's reign, and their relationship to Leicester would have become a less formal one. Only one man is found in both the list of the gentlemen of Northumberland's household in 1553 and Robert Dudley's wage and livery lists for 1559–61: John Dudley's younger brother Thomas, Leicester's comptroller by 1571.[26] Another of the household gentlemen of 1553, Henry Killigrew, was a secretary to Sir Nicholas Throckmorton in Paris in 1559.[27] The Lisle wardrobe accounts refer to Killigrew, Blount, Grice, one of the Dudley brothers, one of the Aglionbys, Sir Richard Verney and Sir George Blount.[28] Other sources identify at least three further men associated with Leicester in the 1560s as Northumberland's servants in 1553: Sir John Throckmorton, his brother Clement, and the captain of Bewcastle in Cumberland, Simon Musgrave. The career of Thomas Wilson, the future secretary of state, also spans both households.[29]

As in any other sixteenth-century affinity, the family formed the core. Northumberland's brother Sir Andrew, who died unmarried in 1559, was prominent in his entourage. So too was Jobson, whose wife Elizabeth was the daughter of Northumberland's mother through her second marriage to Arthur Plantagenet, Viscount Lisle. Northumberland's other half-sister, Bridget, married the brother of Sir Thomas Cawarden. Sidney and Hastings were brought into the Dudley connection by Northumberland's marriage manoeuvres for his children in the last years of Edward's reign. John Appleyard was the main figure to enter Robert Dudley's clientele through the Robsart marriage. However, the example of William Hogan, whose sister was married to Appleyard, reveals that a clear distinction cannot be drawn between Northumberland's clientele and Robert Dudley's Norfolk connection.[30]

Given the extent of intermarriage among the mid Tudor political nation, the importance to be assigned to cousins can be exaggerated. The case of Sir James Croft, however, provides clear evidence of the role it played in the formation of Northumberland's military clientele. In his 'autobiography' Croft records how, as a relative of Dudley's wife, he was invited by him to serve in the expedition to Leith in 1544 'as a private man'; later in the year he was given the command of 100 of Dudley's household men at the siege of Boulogne. Thereafter he became an officer of the garrison (water-bailiff and under-marshal), and then obtained further rapid promotion in the military service of the crown.[31] It is probable that the military career of the notorious Sir Henry Dudley (son of John Sutton, Lord Dudley, of the senior branch of the family) followed a similar pattern. Thomas and John Dudley came from a junior branch, domiciled at Yanwath in Cumberland. The Worcestershire Blounts (Thomas of Kidderminster and Sir George of Kinlet), always addressed as cousins, were probably related to Northumberland's mother. However, it is not clear how important family connections were to other prominent members of Northumberland's clientele, Sir Nicholas and Sir Ralph Bagnall or Sir Henry Gates, for example.[32]

The officers of the Boulogne garrison, where he was lieutenant in 1544–45, were possibly the most significant element in Northumberland's military clientele. The garrison was the first substantial body of English troops to be armed extensively with arquebuses. The officers were therefore the most professional the mid Tudor period could boast.[33] Their later careers are of equal interest, for both Sir Henry Dudley and many of the central figures of Wyatt's rebellion (Sir Thomas Wyatt himself, Croft, Sir George Harper, Sir Nicholas Arnold, Cuthbert Vaughan and Alexander Brett) were former Boulogne officers. It was precisely the element of a military coup rather than a provincial rising which distinguished the Marian conspiracies from the other rebellions of the century, with the significant exception of Essex's revolt. The senior officers of the Newhaven garrison of 1562–63 were also veterans of Boulogne: both the first knight-marshal, Sir Adrian Poynings, and his successor, Sir Hugh Paulet, the treasurer (Sir Maurice Dennys), the comptroller (Cuthbert Vaughan) and the clerk of the council (the later Puritan activist, Thomas Wood). Croft was expected to have joined them, but his appointment was blocked by the Duke of Norfolk.[34]

The Boulogne connection suggests that to label the Wyatt rebels and the Newhaven officers as 'gentlemen adventurers' is to miss the point. They were in fact key figures from the Edwardian military establishment who had enjoyed the benefits of Northumberland's patronage. Lord Robert's involvement in the preparation of the Newhaven expedition (and the expectation that he would command it) made possible their reemployment by Elizabeth, for only a few of the former Edwardian officers had served in the expedition to Scotland in 1560. Newhaven provided the occasion for the revival of Dudley military patronage, with which Leicester would be identified until his death. No list of appointments specifically made by him survives, but a number of Dudley followers can be found among the sixty-two men who held either captaincies or staff appointments in the expedition.[35] This total excludes the Earl of Warwick and those who, like Sidney, Sir Richard Lee and Sir Francis Knollys, were sent to Le Havre for brief periods of inspection, but does include Sir Thomas Finch, who drowned in the sinking of the *Greyhound* en route, and Killigrew and Leighton, who commanded the companies sent to Rouen in October 1562. Apart from the senior officers already referred to, four of the men on Cecil's list were among them: Killigrew, Leighton, Edward Horsey, and John Appleyard. William Saule, lieutenant of the Ordnance, and Arthur Heigham, the water-bailiff, are both found in Dudley's 1559–60 livery lists.[36] Nicholas Maltby (Warwick's secretary), John Fisher of Packington (the gentleman porter), and Edward Driver can also be definitely identified as Dudley clients.[37] Together they constitute about a quarter of the total.

Two further aspects of the Newhaven expedition deserve consideration. It also served to expand and consolidate the Elizabethan Dudley clientele, for not all the officers later associated with the Dudleys had been among Northumberland's immediate followers. Horsey, for example, had originally been a client of Lord Clinton.[38] Moreover, the Edwardian military establishment had been bitterly divided by the fall of the Duke of Somerset. William, Lord Grey de Wilton's, treatment of Northumberland at his surrender in 1553 is well known. William Pelham, Wyatt rebel, captain of the pioneers at Newhaven and Warwick's lieutenant of the Ordnance from 1567, had left England for the service of the queen of Hungary in the Netherlands after Somerset's arrest in 1551, and did not return until after Mary's accession.[39]

The simultaneous assembly of the parliament of 1563 made the New-haven officers and the M.P.s mutually exclusive bodies. Since many of the Newhaven survivors would sit in later parliaments, the Dudley clientele present in the House of Commons in 1563 may have been smaller than it otherwise would have been. Nevertheless, Blount, Glasier, Grice, Yerwerth, Wilson and John and Thomas Dudley, Lord Robert's leading men of business, were all to be found in the House. With the exception of Blount they sat for boroughs, in some cases with the possible patronage of Dudley himself. Also in the House was a group of older Dudley followers: Jobson, Ralph Bagnall, Clement Throckmorton, Ellis Price, Arnold, Gates and Croft. They, on the other hand, sat for counties or for boroughs where they possessed their own influence; most of them had been M.P.s either in 1559 or before.[40]

II

The fifty-odd men identified above do not represent the whole of the Dudley clientele of the early 1560s, let alone that of Northumberland. But it is doubtful that many of the significant Elizabethan figures have been excluded. They are not easy to trace in Mary's reign, for the slightly paradoxical reason that the disaster of July 1553 had only a limited impact on most of Northumberland's followers. If the Duke himself, Sir John Gates and Sir Thomas Palmer were executed, and his sons and several peers imprisoned and attainted, the others suffered mainly loss of office or (later) former episcopal lands. Wyatt's rebellion, by contrast, had far more widespread consequences. These, however, the Dudley brothers, with the exception of the unfortunate Lord Guildford, were able to escape. The research of Richard McCoy has now established that Lord Robert and Lord Ambrose took part in one of the Anglo-Spanish tournaments of the winter of 1554–55.[41] A petition to Philip drafted by Roger Ascham for Lord Ambrose's wife, Lady Elizabeth Tailboys, on 8 November 1554 reveals that he alone was still in the Tower by then. His brothers were probably released in October, immediately prior to the death of the eldest, John, Earl of Warwick, at Penshurst on the 21st.[42] There is no reference to them as prisoners in the Privy Council registers after September 1554, and no contemporary source includes them among those released ceremoniously on 18 January 1555. With the exception of Sir Andrew Dudley, the latter were all former Wyatt rebels.[43]

As the well-known passages in her will reveal, the Duchess of Northumberland had made considerable efforts to obtain the release of her sons. In her campaign she was assisted by Sir Henry Sidney, who later claimed to have joined the embassy to Spain of his brother-in-law Viscount Fitzwalter (the future 3rd Earl of Sussex) at the beginning of 1554 for that purpose.[44] It is also not impossible that some of Mary's Councillors, Sir Thomas Cornwallis,

Lord Hastings of Loughborough, and Lord Paget in particular, may have regarded their case with sympathy. Despite Northumberland's role in Paget's disgrace in 1552, good relations between the families had continued. Robert Dudley was a close friend to Sir Henry Paget (the future 2nd lord), and later informed the 3rd Lord Paget that he had loved his father and brother 'as dearly as any friends as ever I had'.[45] As Dudley frequently acknowledged, however, the key role was played by the new king.[46] Charity was not Philip's only, or even his primary, motive. It was in his interest to win over both the Dudleys and the former Wyatt rebels by a gesture that gave him a claim to their future personal loyalty and service. For Croft and Edward Randolph, release was followed by inclusion in his list of pensioners, with, in the case of Randolph, the significant rank of colonel.[47]

Philip's benevolence is of central importance to the participation of both the Dudley brothers and many of the other former prisoners in the St Quentin expedition of 1557. This expedition was both mounted at Philip's request and financed by him.[48] Its members 'went out to serve the king', their service being less the rallying to the crown of a 'deeply divided ruling class', than the honouring of a personal debt.[49] It is revealing that the unpardoned rebels then in France (Sir Henry Dudley, Henry Killigrew and Edward Horsey, for example) did not return.[50] What has further complicated the issue has been the persistent belief that Robert Dudley was a member of Philip's household in Brussels after 1555.[51] This has been derived from a single reference in Henry Machyn's diary to Dudley's arrival at the Court on 17 March 1557 with letters 'from King Philip from beyond the sea' advising of his impending departure from Calais on his final visit to England.[52] There is also evidence that Dudley met both Cardinal Granvelle and Lazarus von Schwendi prior to 1559, but he probably did so at St Quentin.[53] He was not a member of Philip's English household, nor can an extended absence abroad be deduced from other sources.[54] His presence at Calais in March 1557 can be explained by membership of the entourage of the Earl of Pembroke, who had been sent to inspect the fortress in December 1556 and remained there to escort the king to England.[55]

Several months after their release, the former prisoners were pardoned: the Dudley brothers on 22 January 1555, the others during the following spring.[56] But their attainders were not repealed, nor was their property automatically restored. However, the Dudleys thereafter received several further demonstrations of royal generosity, culminating in their restitution in blood in the parliament of 1558.[57] The latter may be explained by the death of Lord Henry in the assault on St Quentin. The reasons for the earlier are less immediately obvious, though they may have been inspired by the same motives that underlay the kindness that Mary showed to the duchess of Northumberland in 1553–54. They also made possible the initial rebuilding of the Dudley clientele.

It is important at this point to resolve the confusion that has arisen over Lord Robert's claim to the Robsart estate: the Norfolk manors of Syderstone, Bircham Newton and Great Bircham, and the Suffolk manor of Bulkham. Under the terms of the marriage settlement made between Sir John Robsart and Northumberland on 24 May 1550, Robert and Amy Dudley would inherit the Robsart estate only after the deaths of both Sir John and his wife. To support the young couple, Northumberland obtained from the crown the lands of the former priory of Coxford which had been confiscated from the 3rd Duke of Norfolk.[58] They lay close to the Norfolk manors of the Robsart estate, and Northumberland intended that when the two were combined Robert Dudley would possess a substantial landed interest in the county. In 1553 he added the manor of Hemsby near Great Yarmouth, so that his son 'might be able to keep a good house in Norfolk where he had married him'.[59] These lands were lost in Dudley's attainder, and therefore on his release he was propertyless. Sir John Robsart had died on 8 June 1554, but his widow, Lady Elizabeth, was alive as late as the winter of 1557–58.

About the time her sons received their pardons, the duchess of Northumberland herself died.[60] Through a series of exchanges with the queen, she had been able to retain a life interest in part of her jointure and an estate of inheritance composed of properties inherited from her own family, together with the lands of the former monastery of Hales Owen in Worcestershire and Shropshire.[61] Under the terms of her will (drafted in the months between her sons' release and their pardon) Hales Owen was to descend to Lord Ambrose, with fifty marks' worth of other lands to both the surviving younger brothers. As attainted traitors, however, they were unable to inherit, so Hales Owen was left to her executors (Sidney, Sir George Blount, John Somerfield and the Warwickshire lawyer Thomas Marrow) to be used for the benefit of her children.[62]

On 4 May 1555 the queen, in the first of her further acts of generosity, waived her rights to the estate and permitted Ambrose Dudley to inherit it despite his attainder.[63] This in turn made possible a remarkable family compact. On 20 November 1555 the duchess's executors, Lord Ambrose, Lord Henry and Sir Andrew Dudley agreed that Lord Robert, 'left with nothing to live by and having most need of [ ] friendly and brotherly [love?]', could inherit the whole of Hales Owen in exchange for the settlement of the duchess's debts, provision of an estate of fifty marks p.a. for Lady Katherine Hastings, and payments to Lord Ambrose of £800 and Sir Andrew of £300.[64] This agreement was confirmed and livery of seisin performed on 6 March 1556.[65] In those involved the first stage of the Dudley restoration can be detected. Lord Robert's attorneys were his men of business William Glasier and William Grice. The attorneys for the tenants were Northumberland's former servants Thomas Blount and George Tuckey, who had been granted extensive leases of lands from the Hales Owen estate during the 1540s. Tuckey was also the bailiff of Hales Owen, and Lord Robert appointed Blount its chief steward.[66]

This is not the place to attempt a reconstruction of Robert Dudley's tangled finances. However, one or two points should be noted. By the summer of 1557 parts of Hales Owen had been heavily mortgaged. Dudley borrowed £400 from the London merchant William Bird in December 1556, and then another £340 from the brothers William and Robert Bowyer on 31 May 1557.[67] There is some evidence these loans may have been used to repay earlier debts, as one bond made in May 1556 was cancelled in February 1557.[68] The same may also be true of the mortgage of all of Hales Owen to Anthony Forster on 11 July 1557, which appears to have been employed to redeem the earlier one to the Bowyers.[69]

Dudley's decision to exploit Hales Owen in this manner may have been influenced by a second act of royal favour. On 30 January 1557 both Hemsby and his rights of inheritance to the Robsart estate were restored to him despite his attainder, together with such of his chattels still in the possession of the crown.[70] It was probably as a consequence of this grant that he persuaded Lady Elizabeth Robsart in May 1557 to permit him to sell the outlying Robsart manor of Bulkham to Robert Armiger under the condition that his wife was assigned certain lands of the Hales Owen estate for her jointure.[71] The reasons for the large-scale raising of money between May and July 1557 cannot be fully established. It may have been intended to equip a retinue for the St Quentin expedition.[72] The contemporary rumours that Dudley supplied Elizabeth with money during Mary's reign remain unconfirmed.[73]

In 1558 his position underwent a further transformation. At some point during the winter of 1557–58 Lady Elizabeth Robsart died, and by the summer the three Norfolk manors of the Robsart estate had descended to Dudley and his wife. Thanks to the letters patent of January 1557, the descent of the Robsart estate did not depend on the restitution in blood in the first session of the parliament of 1558, though the latter did restore to Northumberland's four surviving children their full rights of inheritance.[74] The inheritance of the Robsart estate probably lay behind the decision to sell Hales Owen to Blount and Tuckey on 27 March 1558 for £3000.[75] Despite the formal processes gone through, there is some reason to suspect the sale was a fictitious one, but it enabled Dudley to raise the capital to repay Forster.[76] More decisive was the further sale of Hales Owen to John Lyttleton of Frankley for £2000 by Blount and Tuckey on 22 October, a sale in which Dudley clearly had a hand.[77]

The traditional picture of Dudley greeting the accession of Elizabeth as a Norfolk squire is therefore very much a myth. The manor house of Syderstone was uninhabitable, and Sir John Robsart himself had lived at Stansfield, a house in which his wife had been left a life interest by her first husband, Nicholas Appleyard. On her death it descended to John Appleyard, her son by that marriage. Dudley faced his father-in-law's difficulty in the summer of 1558, and his earliest surviving letter (22 July) deals with the possible purchase of the manor of Flitcham 'if I am to live in that country'.[78] Between 1556 and 1558 Hales Owen was given as his residence on legal documents, though there is no evidence that he ever lived there.[79] He probably spent most of the time in one or other of two houses in London: Sir Andrew Dudley's in Tothill Street, Westminster, and the mansion of Christchurch in the liberty by St Bartholomew the Grand, which Lord Henry Dudley's wife had inherited from her father.[80] Other than that, he may have been peripatetic until Elizabeth granted him the house at Kew on 29 December 1558.[81] Amy Dudley's own roamings at the beginning of 1559 from Lincolnshire to Denchworth and then Cumnor in Berkshire may not therefore have had any sinister implications.[82]

The Hales Owen estate did, however, make possible a continued Dudley connection with the West Midlands during the reign of Mary. It is revealing that the two leases of Robert Dudley's to survive were both to former servants of Northumberland.[83] If the mutual support the members of the immediate Dudley family provided for each other might have been expected, the continued association of Sidney, Blount and Forster, whose own interests might appear to have been better served by distancing themselves from so discredited a cause, is the more noteworthy.[84] Less clear is the political significance of the connection during Mary's reign. Wyatt's Rebellion caused a substantial dispersal of the clientele, for many of those who, like Killigrew, went abroad in 1554 did not return until the accession of Elizabeth. Nor is the extent to which they maintained a correspondence known.[85] The best-known reference to some form of 'political' association is the report of the Venetian ambassador in July 1555 of the lord chancellor's order that the Dudley brothers and the released Wyatt rebels should leave London.[86] The possible connection between these gatherings and the Dudley Plot of 1555–56 remains obscure. In April 1556, immediately after the conspiracy was broken and the first arrests made, the French ambassador reported a rumour that 'les enfans du duc de Northumberland sont tous fugitifs et que l'on a fait une grande diligence pour les prendre'.[87] Arnold and Cawarden were temporarily arrested, and Killigrew, Leighton and Horsey (then in France) were implicated. Anthony Forster was tried in July 1556 (and pardoned in January 1557) for misprision of treason.[88] John Appleyard was placed under a recognisance in May.[89] The threat of misprision frightened Sir Nicholas Throckmorton into fleeing to France, and possibly Sir Ralph Bagnall as well.[90] Sir Henry Sidney's decision to serve in Ireland at this point, 'neither liking nor liked as I had been', may not have been unrelated.[91]

Misprision was probably the significant aspect. If anything the plot was focused about Edward Courtenay, Earl of Devon; it may have been less the case that the Dudleys and their immediate friends were actively involved in the conspiracy, than that their natural associations were with those who were.[92] Robert Dudley's later connection to the former Marian conspirators was not confined to those on Cecil's list. Six captains had led the 'white-coats' who defected to Wyatt at Rochester in January 1554. The three who survived Mary's reign (William Pelham, Brian Fitzwilliam and Robert Perceval) all received Dudley's patronage in the years that followed.[93] It is also reveal-ing to encounter Dudley dining in May 1559 at Arundel's, the tavern opposite St Lawrence Eastcheap which Croft had made his headquarters at the end of 1553 and where the Dudley plotters met in late 1555.[94]

III

It was not until April 1559 that the extent of Dudley's personal closeness to Elizabeth I became open knowledge, but on the eve of the accession he was included among those expected to form the inner circle of her Court.[95] There are one or two hints that he had had some contact with the household at Hatfield before then, and he was certainly part of the new Court by the time of the move to London on 22 November 1558. He was proposed by Cecil as a possible ambassador to Philip II to announce the accession, but on being given responsibility for the Stables was replaced by Lord Cobham.[96] His family was soon equally well entrenched in Elizabeth's Court. Mary Sidney was a gentlewoman of the privy chamber 'without wages' by the time of the coronation. Lord Ambrose was named master of the Ordnance by the end of 1558, though he did not receive his letters patent until the beginning of 1560. Sidney himself become lord president of the Council in the Marches after his return from Ireland in the middle of 1559.[97]

Dudley's membership of the new Court was seen from the start as part of Elizabeth's general rejection of Mary's household and return to the former Edwardians. In recent work the 'Edwardian' influence on the religious settle-ment of 1559 has been accorded much greater importance than it has in the past.[98] The wider political dimension deserves similar attention. The use of the 1552 prayerbook as the basis for that of 1559, and the refusal of the Marian Bishops to accept the royal supremacy, which left the crown with no alternative but to recruit a new episcopate from the middle ranks of the Edwardian hierarchy, made the Edwardian influence on the new church relatively straightforward. Yet there were also two further aspects to the 'res-toration of religion' of no less significance. The first was the attempt in the parliament of 1559 to obtain restitution by statute for those 'bishops and spiritual persons' deprived under Mary.[99] The second was the demand

encountered both in 1559 and later for the punishment of the bishops associated with the Marian persecutions, particularly Edmund Bonner: 'by his
willing cruelty no few number of the saints of God hath lost their lives . . . yet
through her mercy he liveth at such liberty as he himself considering his
own cruel faits I think could not have hoped for'.[100]

The twin themes of restoration and revenge are central to any discussion
of the Edwardian influence on the politics of the accession. It has been
suggested that Sir Thomas Cawarden's intervention in the Surrey election of
1559 may have been inspired by revenge for his treatment by Lord Howard of
Effingham after the discovery of the Dudley Plot.[101] In April 1560 Lord John
Grey of Pirgo (another significant figure) criticised Elizabeth's failure to purge
the former Marians from her Privy Council.[102] It is now clear that most of the
leading members of the new royal household, both male and female, came
from the household at Hatfield. It is also probably the case that support for
Elizabeth during Mary's reign lay behind the choice of those retained from
the previous Court and Council.[103] Yet the appointment of Cecil as secretary
of state was also seen by one correspondent as a return to 'your old room'.[104]
Similarly, Lord Robert's appointment as Master of the Horse could also be
considered a restoration, for his brother Warwick had held the office in
1553.[105]

The Dudley family could expect to be central figures in an Edwardian
restoration. Yet the process took much longer than might have been expected,
particularly when Edward Seymour was restored to the earldom of Hertford
and William Parr to the marquessate of Northampton at the coronation. Not
until December 1561 were the viscountcy of Lisle and the earldom of Warwick
restored to Ambrose Dudley, or, as Robert Dudley put it, Elizabeth 'restored
our house to the name of Warwick'.[106] He himself readopted the celebrated
device of the bear and ragged staff in the following spring, but his own entry
into the peerage was delayed until September 1564.[107] Nor was there an
immediate restoration of Northumberland's estate. Except for Knebworth
Beauchamp in 1559, Warwick did not receive anything until 1562 and 1564.
Robert Dudley obtained the house at Kew at the beginning of the reign, and
the site and demesne lands of the former priory of Watton in the East Riding
of Yorkshire in 1560, but no substantial grants until 1561 and 1563.[108] In the
meantime he began negotiating the purchase of the stewardship of the borough of Warwick from Sir Robert Throckmorton and (less successfully) revived his father's old campaign for the lands of the Suttons, Lords Dudley.[109]

The clientele had an equal interest in a Dudley restoration. Lord Robert's
surviving correspondence for 1559–60 contains frequent references to suits
of old Dudley servants, such as the unnamed 'gentleman's widow, whom my
lord your father (whose soul God pardon) favoured well', recommended by
Croft from Berwick in April 1559, or Lady Joan Poyntz's request for a prebend

for 'my man Freeman, the which was once servant to my lord your father, whom I think your lordship knoweth well'.[110] On one level this was expected filial piety, similar to his private gift 'to a poor woman that named herself your lordship's father's nurse', but there was also a political aspect.[111] In the West Midlands the Dudley re-forming preceded the restoration of Northumberland's lands. Lord Robert's tenure of the lord-lieutenancy of Warwickshire (jointly with Sir Ambrose Cave) and Worcestershire in 1559–60 saw Thomas Blount, John Fisher of Packington and Sir Richard Verney rise to prominence in local administration.[112] A similar process occurred in the East Riding of Yorkshire, where Simon Musgrave offered to 'provide your lordship yearly of three or four geldings as I did to my lord's grace your father' in return for his 'patent of Beverley', a suit obtained when Lord Robert was granted the lordship of Beverley in 1561.[113]

The Dudley connection was also the key to Lord Robert's religious patronage in 1559–60. Two prominent former Edwardians, Edwin Sandys and John Aylmer, both of whom may have had some association with Northumberland's household, were the main recipients.[114] Sandys became Bishop of Worcester (a possibly significant choice of diocese); Aylmer, whose participation in Wyatt's rebellion may have been regarded suspiciously, only obtained the archdeaconry of Lincoln. More revealing, perhaps, were Dudley's household chaplains: Thomas Willoughby in 1559 and the émigré Scot Alexander Craik in 1560.[115] Both appear to have been Marian exiles, but equally importantly, both had been chaplains to Northumberland.[116] Their household service to Lord Robert was followed by promotion in the church, Willoughby to be a canon of Canterbury and Craik the Bishop of Kildare.

More controversial was the question of episcopal lands. In the summer of 1559, following the deprivation of the Bishop of Durham, Ralph, Lord Eure, wrote to Dudley to request the restoration of a stewardship to some of the bishopric's temporalities he had held under Edward VI, 'for that it may appear to my countrymen that the queen's highness hath me in no less estimation than her majesty's brother had'.[117] Better known, thanks to the work of N. L. Jones, were the attempts in the parliament of 1559 to regain episcopal estates obtained under Edward and forfeited under Mary. Both Sir Francis Jobson and Sir John Throckmorton had been forced to surrender lands to the Bishop of Worcester, and Jobson to the Bishop of Durham as well. Thomas Fisher had similar interests in Coventry and Lichfield.[118] It is revealing of the way in which the Dudley restoration was pursued that Robert Dudley later obtained episcopal leases for Jobson (and possibly Throckmorton also) in compensation for the failure of their bill.[119]

The Bagnalls advanced an equally awkward demand for restitution. Immediately after Elizabeth's accession Sir Ralph Bagnall petitioned the Privy Council for restoration of his former Irish lands and offices. These he claimed he had lost through his opposition to the re-establishment of papal authority in the parliament of November 1554.[120] His brother, Sir Nicholas, took up the case in a letter to Dudley in July 1559, requesting as well the restoration of his own marshalcy of Ireland, which he had lost to Sir George Stanley in 1553–54.[121] Restoring the Bagnalls, however, would involve undercutting the Earl of Sussex's administration in Ireland. It did not occur until Sidney's appointment as lord deputy at the end of 1565, which was thus as much an aspect of the Dudley restoration as a revolution in Irish government.

The Dudley clientele were not alone in seeking restitution. Other former Edwardians, Sir Ralph Sadler and Sir Thomas Smith, for example, submitted similar requests or held similar expectations on Elizabeth's accession.[122] However, the potential ramifications of the Dudley restoration were considerably greater and they account for much of the tension surrounding Lord Robert's relationship to the queen. When he left London for Cambridge in July 1553, Northumberland was said to have warned the Privy Council: 'If ye meane deceat, thoughe not furthwith yet hereafter, God will revenge the same'.[123] Would his son be the instrument of that revenge? Pius IV heard something to this effect in 1561:

> the greater of part of the nobility of that island take ill the marriage which the said queen designs to enter into with the Lord Robert Dudley. His father was beheaded as a rebel and usurper of the crown and they fear that if he becomes king, he will want to avenge the death of his father, and extirpate the nobility of that kingdom.[124]

Domestic echoes can also be detected. In the same year Thomas Trollope proposed to Dudley to publish a tract to 'take away the infamies passed against your father and grandfather', and with 'a probable reason to prove their unjust and innocent deaths procured through envy and malice'.[125]

The death of Northumberland was not the only potentially contentious issue. There was also the older question of Northumberland's role in the fall of Somerset, a subject that exercised several minds in the early 1560s.[126] The danger that factional disputes arising from old quarrels and revenge for old injuries might tear apart the new Court was thus very real. In this context an otherwise cryptic comment of Elizabeth reported by Sir Humphrey Ratcliffe in November 1560 takes on considerable significance: 'I learned of a friend of mine in secrecy that the queen's majesty should in commendation of my Lord Robert upon questions moved say that he was of a very good disposition and nature, not given by any means to seek revenge of former matters past, wherein she seemed much to allow him'.[127] Other contemporary references to Lord Robert's open nature and generosity may therefore reflect more than sycophancy or compliment. The extent to which Dudley may have made a conscious effort to let bygones be bygones and to bury old quarrels is an aspect of his career in the Elizabethan Court that still needs exploration. He certainly appears to have sought good relations with the Seymours, as his efforts to mitigate the queen's anger against Hertford for his marriage, his later patronage to Pelham and Arthur, Lord Grey, and his kindness to John Hales reveal.[128]

The political fears created by the threat of a Dudley restoration may account for the long time it took Elizabeth to grant Northumberland's lands to his sons. They may also have inspired Cecil's reflections on the archducal marriage. Yet by the time Cecil compiled his list, many of the men included (the main exception being Sir Henry Dudley) had become established figures in Elizabethan governing circles. They were neither a faction of outsiders, nor even enemies of his. He enjoyed very good relations with Sidney and Thomas Wilson, and Henry Killigrew (albeit after some initial hostility on Cecil's part) became his brother-in-law. Dudley was on similar friendly terms with former Edwardians like Smith or Sadler, who are normally regarded as allies of Cecil. The impression Cecil's list gives of a distinct faction may well be a distortion.

The significance of the Dudley clientele is possibly best explained by its social composition. The Dudley family itself is revealing. For all their claims of descent from the Suttons, Lords Dudley and the Beauchamp Earls of Warwick (through Northumberland's mother, Elizabeth Grey), their prominence was the result of legal and military service to the crown. The background of their clients was quite disparate. If their connection included some members of established gentry families (the Blounts, Sidney or Croft), the social antecedents of others (the Bagnalls, Forster or Jobson, for example) were highly questionable. Cawarden, like Sir Nicholas Arnold and Sadler, had originally been a member of Thomas Cromwell's household. Nor should the military bias obscure the importance of the lawyers and men of business found among them, many of whom (like Glasier or Grice) were also important local political figures. The wide geographical base is equally striking: the connection extended to Cumberland, Chester, the East Riding, East Anglia and Cornwall, as well as the West Midlands. Essentially we are seeing the initiation of a third phase in the post-Reformation reshaping of the social basis of the Tudor political nation. The first began with Thomas Cromwell in the 1530s, the second took place in the Court of Edward VI: the early years of Elizabeth's reign saw its consolidation.

The Dudley clientele was thus a curious hybrid. The impressive degree of mutual loyalty displayed after 1553 was not dissimilar to that found in other affinities. If the clients provided support (financial as well as moral) in bad times, they would expect their reward in prosperity. Yet because 1559 saw a Dudley restoration rather than the formation of a new faction, there were bounds to their ambitions. To regain offices and lands they had lost, or to obtain compensation for them, was their immediate aim. Furthermore, because they were as much a section of a former governing elite as a personal faction led by Lord Robert, they were rapidly integrated into Elizabethan government. Lord Robert's direct influence cannot be discounted, as, for example, in the Newhaven expedition, but given the central role the Dudley clientele had played in the reign of Edward VI, they could not be excluded in an Edwardian restoration. Lord Robert was as much the spokesman for their interests as they were the supporters of his.

NOTES

Early versions of this chapter were delivered to seminars at the Universities of Durham and York and the Institute of Historical Research. The research was made possible by generous grants from the British Academy, the Carnegie Trust for the Universities of Scotland, the Wolfson Foundation, and the Universities of Wales and Strathclyde. I should like to thank the Most Honourable the Marquesses of Bath and Anglesey for permission to employ the Dudley MSS at Longleat and the Paget MSS. The microfilms of the Cecil MSS at Hatfield House deposited at the British Library are used with permission of the Marquess of Salisbury.

Note: Place of publication is London unless otherwise stated.

1 Hatfield MS 155, art. 28, printed with the omission of 'Wilson' in S. Haynes (ed.), *A Collection of State Papers . . . left by William Cecil, Lord Burghley* (1740), p. 444. Haynes dated the memorandum April 1566, though it was endorsed by Cecil Anno 9° Eliz. [But see p. 112, n. 85 above for a revised dating of 1565.]

2 C. Read, *Mr Secretary Cecil and Queen Elizabeth* (New York, 1955), p. 260; W. T. MacCaffrey, *The Shaping of the Elizabethan Regime* (Princeton, NJ, 1968), pp. 96–7 and 129–30.

3 D. M. Loades, *Two Tudor Conspiracies* (Cambridge, 1965), pp. 246–7.

4 N. Canny, *The Elizabethan Conquest of Ireland: A Pattern Established 1565–1572* (Hassocks, Suss., 1976), pp. 42–3, 70–1.

5 D. Wilson, *Sweet Robin: A Biography of Robert Dudley, Earl of Leicester, 1533–1588* (1981), pp. 104–5, see also the comments on pp. 318–19.

6 Loades, *Two Tudor Conspiracies*, p. 16. A stronger connection is drawn in K. R. Bartlett, 'The English exile community in Italy and the political opposition to Queen Mary I', *Albion*, xiii (1981), 223–41.

7 A point made by Wilson, *Sweet Robin*, p. 105, though he sees the resort to Leicester as a consequence of his prominence at Court.

8 Cecil's note can be read either Tho or Jho Dudley, but since both the brothers were in Dudley's service both are included here.

9 For the controversy surrounding Molyneux, the M.P. who moved the linking of the petition on the succession to the subsidy bill in the parliament of 1566, see P. W. Hasler (ed.), *The History of Parliament: The House of Commons, 1558–1603* (1981), iii, 60–3, and G. R. Elton, *The Parliament of England 1559–1581* (Cambridge, 1986), pp. 365–6.

10 For Throckmorton's advancing of Middlemore, see J. E. Neale, 'Sir Nicholas Throckmorton's advice to Queen Elizabeth on her accession to the throne', *E[nglish] H[istorical] R[eview]*, lxv (1950), 91.

11 V. von Klarwill, *Queen Elizabeth and Some Foreigners* (1928), p. 190.

12 Discussed in more detail in S. Adams, 'The Dudley clientèle and the House of Commons, 1559–1586' [Ch. 10], p. 197, n. 6.

13 I am very grateful to Mr A. J. A. Malkiewicz of the University of Edinburgh for his generous help and advice on the sources for Northumberland's followers. R. C. Braddock, 'The composition and character of the duke of Northumberland's army', *Albion*, vi (1974), 342–55, refers in passing to one or two of the men discussed here.

14 The accounts are now [Longleat], Dudley MSS XIV, XV; the wages list Dudley MS III, fos. 2–17v; the bills and the livery lists are found in Dudley Box V, the livery lists being fos. 280–3. [Now published in *Household Accounts*.]

15 P[ublic] R[ecord] O[ffice], L[and] R[evenue Office] 2/118; S[tate] P[apers] 46/163/53–74.

16 Bodl[eian Library], MS Addit[ional] C. 94.

17 Dudley MS III, fo. 114, bill of Hans Frank (pre-1564). In his account of receipts for December 1559–February 1561 (*ibid.*, fo. 27ᵛ), Ellis is simply styled servant.

18 All of them appear in Chauncy's account, Dudley MS XIV. For Grice, Blount, Yerwerth and Glasier, see Ch. 10 below, pp. 202, 205–6; for Hogan nn. 23, 30 below.

19 Based on a study of the bills found in Dudley Box V. George Christmas died on 23 February 1566. His brother Robert was Leicester's treasurer in 1570–1, see Ch. 10 below, p. 207.

20 The two surveys are now Dudley MSS XVI-II; for the seisin of Kenilworth see Dudley Box II, art. 11; for the Denbigh commissioners, S. Adams, 'The composition of 1564 and the earl of Leicester's tenurial reformation in the lordship of Denbigh' [Ch. 13], pp. 255, 264.

21 J. R. Dasent (ed.), *A[cts of the] P[rivy] C[ouncil]* (32 vols., 1890–1907), iv, 323–4.

22 See *ibid.*, p. 330; *C[alendar of the] P[atent] R[olls], Philip and Mary* (4 vols., 1936–39), ii, 116; PRO, SP 46/124/77 and C[hancery] 78/17/10 (Robert Dudley vs. Hugh Ellis, decided on 27 November 1559); B[irmingham] R[eference] L[ibrary], [Lyttleton of] Hagley Hall MSS 351597–8. In T. Kemp (ed.), *The Black Book of Warwick* ([Warwick], 1989), p. 8, he is described as auditor to Ambrose Dudley in 1565.

23 The duchess's will is PRO, PROB 11/37/194–5; much is omitted in the synopsis published in A. Collins (ed.), *Letters and Memorials of State . . . written by Sir Henry Sidney* (2 vols., 1746) [hereinafter *Sidney Papers*], i, 33–6. For John Dudley and North-umberland, see his will, PRO, PROB 11/63/117ᵛ–8; for Hogan, B[ritish] L[ibrary], Harleian MS 353, fos. 121–2ᵛ. Clear references for Forster and Ellis are not available, though Ellis's brother Hugh is identified as a servant of Northumberland's in PRO, C 78/17/10.

24 See Ch. 10 below, p. 218, n. 35. Bodl. MS Addit. C 94, fo. 2.

25 Glasier and Dudley received a grant of miscellaneous lands on 27 June 1553, see PRO, SP 10/18/49 (a draft) and *CPR, Edward VI* (5 vols., 1924–29), iv, 221. This was enrolled in Chancery by Dudley on 1 April 1555 (PRO, C 54/509).

26 PRO, LR 2/118 and Dudley Box V, fo. 282. He also served in the household of the duchess of Northumberland in 1553–55 and was left an annuity of £5 in her will (PRO, PROB 11/37/194ᵛ). In 1560 he was receiving one of £6/13/4 from Lord Robert (Dudley MS XV, fo. 10). See also Ch. 10 below, p. 220, n. 61.

27 He was referred to as 'next the queen's majesty wholly your lordship's' in Dudley MS I, fo. 116, Throckmorton to Dudley, 27 February 1560.

28 For Edward and Thomas Aglionby and Sir George Blount, see Ch. 10 below, pp. 204, 207–8.

29 *Ibid.*, p. 204 (John Throckmorton), p. 204 (Clement Throckmorton), p. 221, n. 81 (Musgrave). I should correct here the implication in the above that Clement Throckmorton's connection with the Dudleys included office-holding at Kenilworth. He was in fact appointed constable of Kenilworth by Mary on 19 September 1553, following the deprivation of Ambrose Dudley. However, John Throckmorton was receiver of the castle under Dudley. See PRO D[uchy of] L[ancaster] 42/23/97 and 29/464/7594–5. For Wilson, see the dedicatory epistle to *A Discourse Uppon Usurye* (ed. R. H. Tawney, 1925), p. 185. In December 1560 he was expected to become Dudley's 'chancellor' (PRO, SP 70/21/61).

30 Hogan was a son of Robert Hogan of East Bradenham and brother to Thomas, the servant of the fourth duke of Norfolk, and Robert, the servant of Philip II who acted as an English intelligencer in Spain during the 1560s. Edmund, the Spanish and Barbary merchant, was also a member of this family. Like the Ellises, the Hogans were related to Sir Thomas Gresham, whose own career reveals the difficulties of distinguishing a metropolitan from an East Anglian nexus.

31 See R. E. Ham (ed.), 'The Autobiography of Sir James Croft', *Bulletin of the Institute of Historical Research*, 1(1997), 50.

32 For the Bagnalls and the Dudleys, see Ch. 10 below, p. 219, n. 46.

33 Discussed in S. Adams, 'The Dudley clientele and the earl of Leicester's expedition to the Netherlands, 1585–1586' [Ch. 9]. For the identities of the Boulogne officers see C[alendar] of S[tate] P[apers], Foreign [series], Edward VI (1861), pp. 292–355, and PRO, SP 68/15 191.

34 For Croft, see 'Autobiography', p. 56. Warwick also wanted Thomas Wilson at Newhaven (PRO, SP 70/44/163). I intend to re-examine the early life of Thomas Wood in a further essay.

35 Derived from Hatfield MS 154, art. 47, 'Names of such as served at Newhaven Anno 1563', supplemented by the correspondence in SP 70/40–61 and SP 12/24–29.

36 For Heigham, see PRO, SP 70/47/140; for Saule, SP 70/49/87.

37 For Maltby, see PRO, SP 70/44/37. He had been associated with the exiles in France in 1554: [Paris], A[rchives du] M[inistère des] R[elations] E[xtérieures], C[orrespondence] P[olitique], A[ngleterre], IX, fo. 271. Fisher is discussed below, nn. 84, 112. For Driver, see PRO, SP 70/54/92.

38 P. Forbes (ed.), *A Full View of the Public Transactions in the Reign of Elizabeth* (2 vols., 1740–41), i, 161, Throckmorton to Cecil, 13 July 1559.

39 For Pelham, APC, iii, 391. C[alendar of] S[tate] P[apers], Span[ish], 1553 (1916), pp. 351–2, 354. For Grey, AMRE, CPA, XII, fo. 40ᵛ, Noailles to Henry II, 20 July 1553.

40 See Ch. 10 below, pp. 205–6.

41 R. C. McCoy, 'From the Tower to the tiltyard: Robert Dudley's return to glory', *H[istorical] J[ournal]*, xxvii (1984), 425–35. The Dudley brothers appear on an undated tournament score cheque. There were four major Anglo-Spanish tournaments, dated 14 and 18 December 1554, 23 January and 25 March 1555 by McCoy, and 4 and 8 December, 24 January and 25 March by A. Young, *Tudor and Jacobean Tournaments* (1987), p. 31. It has not been possible to establish the one to which it belongs. David Loades, 'Philip II and the government of England', in C. Cross, D. Loades and J. J. Scarisbrick (eds), *Law and Government under the Tudors* (Cambridge, 1988), p. 193, assigns it to that of 23 January.

42 J. A. Giles (ed.), *The Whole Works of Roger Ascham* (3 vols., 1865), i, 419–20. For Warwick's death, see J. G. Nichols (ed.), *The Diary of Henry Machyn* (Camden Society, xlii, 1848), p. 72 and AMRE, CPA, XIII, fo. 270ᵛ, Noailles to Henry II, 26 October 1554.

43 *APC*, v, 72. Lists of those released can be found in *Machyn's Diary*, p. 80; *APC*, v. 90–1; AMRE, CPA, IX, fo. 635ᵛ and XII, fo. 320; and J. Stow, *The Annales of England* ([1592]), p. 1061. The Dudley brothers were first included by John Strype, *Ecclesiastical Memorials* (3 vols., 1721), iii, 208, to whom the error can be traced. Cf. McCoy, 'Tower to tiltyard', 425.

44 PRO, PROB 11/37/194–5 *passim*. For Sidney's role, see his 'Memoir' of 1 March 1583, in *Calendar of the Carew Manuscripts* (6 vols., 1867–73), ii, 359; it is also commented upon by Noailles in his letter of 26 October 1554, see n. 42 above.

45 [Plas Newydd], Paget MSS, X, art. 12, 25 May [1574]; Paget in turn referred to the affection the duchess had borne him (*ibid.*, art. 57). She left gifts to the 1st lord and his wife in her will. The possible role of Cornwallis and Hastings is suggested by Dudley's help for them in 1559: see Dudley MS I, fos. 16, 54.

46 See, *inter alia*, PRO 31, 3/3/25, fo. 134, Paul de Foix to Catherine de Medici, 23 January 1565; *CSP Span.*, *Elizabeth* (4 vols., 1892–99), ii, 314; [Brussels], A[rchives] G[énérales du] R[oyaume], P[apiers d'] E[tat et de l'] A[udience] 361, fo. 156, Champigny to Requesens, 15 February 1576.

47 Copies of the cedulas are now in A[rchivo] G[eneral] de S[imancas], C[ontaduría] M[ayor de] C[uentas], Primera Epoca, leg. 1345, n.f. The original of Randolph's is now BL, Stowe MS 142, fo. 19.

48 See D. M. Loades, *The Reign of Mary Tudor* (1979), p. 373. Loades's surmise is confirmed by the account of Philip's paymaster, see AGS, CMC, Iª Epoca, leg. 1231.

49 PRO, SP 11/11/12. Cf. Croft, 'Autobiography', p. 54, 'divers Elected persons were chosen thereunto', and J. M. Osborn (ed.), *The Autobiography of Thomas Wythorne* (Oxford, 1961), p. 85, Lord Ambrose Dudley 'waz kalled to serv the prins in her warz'. The argument of C. S. L. Davies, 'England and the French War, 1557–9', in J. Loach and R. Tittler (eds), *The Mid-Tudor Polity c. 1540–1560* (1980), p. 163, overlooks the personal nature of the relationship to Philip.

50 As noted by Loades, *Reign*, pp. 470–1, and K. R. Bartlett, ' "The misfortune that is wished for him": the exile and death of Edward Courtenay, Earl of Devon', *Canadian Journal of History*, xiv (1979), esp. 19–21.

51 Most recently in McCoy, 'Tower to tiltyard', 430, from Wilson, *Sweet Robin*, p. 71.

52 *Machyn's Diary*, p. 128.

53 The letter of recommendation for Philip Sidney sent to an unnamed German on 23 July 1573 (Cambridge University Library, University Archives, Letters 8, p. 160), recalling 'nostra benevolentia recordatione iam inde a Sancti Quintini obsidione', was undoubtedly addressed to Schwendi. In his letter to Requesens of 15 February 1576 (AGR, PEA 361, fo. 156ᵛ), Champigny reports Leicester's references to courtesies received from 'Monsr. d'Arras lequel il avait cogneu avant qu'il fut Cardinal'.

54 He is not found in any of the lists of Philip's English household, e.g. AGS, CMC, lᵃ Epoca, leg. 1184, or E[stado] 811, fo. 122.

55 For Pembroke's visit to Calais, see AMRE, CPA, XX, fo. 349, F. to A. de Noailles, 20 December 1556, and *C[alendar of] S[tate] P[apers]. Ven[etian]*, vi (2) (1881), p. 835.

56 *CPR, Philip and Mary*, ii, 150–1, 158–9. Sir Andrew Dudley did not receive his pardon until 5 April (p. 42), Sir Nicholas Arnold until 4 March (p. 47).

57 4 & 5 Philip and Mary c. 12. On the subject of reversal of attainders, see Elton, *Parliament of England*, pp. 303–5.

58 Dudley Box II, art. 12, published in J. E. Jackson, 'Amy Robsart', *Wiltshire Archaeological and Natural History Magazine*, xvii (1878), 81.

59 Quoted in Robert Dudley vs. Hugh Ellis (PRO, C 78/17/10).

60 The date of the duchess's death is not clear: the inquisitions post mortem give 15 January 1555, her funeral monument in Chelsea Old Church, 22 January. See G. E. Cockayne, *Complete Peerage* (rev. edn, 13 vols., 1910–49), ix. 726.

61 Northumberland obtained Hales Owen from the crown in 1538 and settled it on his wife in 1539. The duchess received further jointures in 1546 and 1552. See BRL, Hagley Hall MS 351609 and *CPR, Edward VI*, iv, 431. For the settlement with Mary, see Edinburgh University Library, Laing MS 634/2 and *CPR, Philip and Mary*, i, 129. The manorial court of Hales Owen was held in her name in 1554, BRL, Hagley Hall MS 357332.

62 PRO, PROB 11/37/194. Marrow was an MP for Warwickshire in October 1553. The overseers included Jobson and Sir Thomas Cawarden.

63 *CPR, Philip and Mary*, ii, 121. Lady Tailboys petitioned Philip for the restoration of her own estates on 22 February 1555; Giles, *Works of Ascham*, i, 429–30.

64 BRL, Hagley Hall MS 351613, badly damaged by damp. Lord Henry apparently wanted nothing. His generosity may be attributed to the fact that he was married to a major heiress, Margaret, daughter of Thomas, Lord Audley, whose lands the queen permitted them to inherit when Margaret came of age in July 1556. See *CPR, Philip and Mary*, iii, 11. Dudley MS XX [Schedule of Evidences], fo. 55ᵛ, refers to a release by a further executor, the minor Gloucestershire gentleman, Gabriel Blike. He is not mentioned in any of the other Hales Owen muniments, but did have a later association with Leicester, see Ch. 10 below, p. 218, n. 34.

65 BRL, Hagley Hall MS 351614. The view of frankpledge was taken in Lord Robert's name in April 1556, MS 346500.

66 For Tuckey's lease of the manor house of Hales in 1549, see BRL, Hagley Hall MS 351598. He was one of Northumberland's household gentlemen in 1553 (PRO, LR 2/118). Blount is identified as chief steward in two of the Hales Owen court rolls of 1556: Hagley Hall MSS 346501 and 346869.

67 William Bowyer, keeper of the records in the Tower in the 1650s, wrote an *Heroica Eulogia* in 1567 to celebrate Robert Dudley's creation as Earl of Leicester. This is now [San Marino, Calif.] Huntington Library MS HM 160. The recognizances for the loans from the Bowyers are PRO, C 54/529, m. 26, and 531, mm. 32 and 44; from Bird, C 54/533, mm 8, 20.

68 PRO, L[ord] C[hamberlain's Department], 4 [Recognizances]/188/287.

69 PRO, C 54/546, m. 6. See also n. 76 below. Forster may have leased the estate back to Dudley on the 16th, see Dudley XX, fo. 58^v.

70 *CPR, Philip and Mary*, iii, 250–1.

71 PRO, C[ommon] P[leas], 40 [feet of fines, enrolled deeds]/1170/17, 1171/9^v–10; CP 26/1/94; C 54/531, m. 45. See also C 78/68/11, Arthur Robsart vs. John Lyttleton and George Tuckey, 1578.

72 For his raising of money on 16–17 July 1557, see PRO, LC 4/188/369^v–70. M. Waldman, *Elizabeth and Leicester* (1944), p. 60, refers to a sale of lands to equip a retinue that failed to assemble, but provides no evidence. Cf. Wilson, *Sweet Robin*, pp. 71–2.

73 They are discussed in Wilson, *Sweet Robin*, p. 73.

74 Their petition of 20 January 1558 (PRO, C 89/6/5) referred to their disablement from inheriting lands of their father, their wider family or their ancestors. [The date of Lady Elizabeth Robsart's death has now been revised to the spring of 1557; see *Household Accounts*, p. 13, n. 52.]

75 The indenture of sale is BRL, Hagley Hall MS 351493; the licence to alienate (24 March), *CPR, Philip and Mary*, iv, 345.

76 See the release of Forster of his interest in Hales Owen, 28 March 1558, BRL, Hagley Hall MS 351494; the bill for the redemption of the mortgage, PRO, C 54/546, m. 6; and the related recognizances, LC 4/188/415–^{v}, 432. The argument for a fictitious sale is made in N. D. Fourdrinier, 'Amy Robsart' (unpublished typescript, c. 1957, now Norfolk Record Office, MS MC 5/33), p. 135.

77 For the date, see BRL, Hagley Hall MS 351621; for the licence to alienate (3 November 1558), *CPR, Philip and Mary*, iv, 440–1. Some idea of the circumstances can be found in the badly worn response of John Lyttleton (PRO, C 3/50/120), the only document from the case of Dudley vs Lyttleton (1560) to survive.

78 BL, Harleian MS 4712, fo. 273, to John Flowerdew.

79 His coat and conduct money for the St Quentin expedition was paid to and from Hales Owen: see BL, Stowe MS 571, fos. 101–^{v}, 121.

80 *CPR, Philip and Mary*, iii, 10–11. Robert Dudley had books delivered to Christ Church in 4 Mary (1556–57), Dudley Box V, art. 3, and belongings moved from there in early 1559, Dudley MS XIV, fo. 6^v. For Sir Andrew Dudley's house, see his will (drafted on 21 July 1556), *Sidney Papers*, i, 30. [The location given for Christ Church is erroneous: it was adjacent to St. Katherine Cree; see *Household Accounts*, p. 43, n. 28.]

81 For the grant of Kew, *CPR, 1558–1560* (1939), p. 60.

82 Her movements can be traced through references in Dudley MS XIV. [See the revisions to Amy Dudley's movements on p. 150 above.]

83 BRL, Hagley Hall MSS 351612, 351619.

84 Sidney and John Fisher of Packington also stood surety for Lord Ambrose in the reign of Mary, see the bonds enrolled in PRO, C 54/505 and 539.

85 Thomas Wood referred to corresponding with Croft from Germany while the latter was in the Tower in 1554. PRO, SP 70/45/5ᵛ, to Cecil 17 November 1562.

86 *CSP Ven.*, vi(i), 137. See Loades, *Two Tudor Conspiracies*, pp. 177–8.

87 AMRE, CPA, XII, fo. 502, avis au roi, 29 April 1556. See also *APC*, v, p. 263, an order on 18 April to stay the process of seizure of Ambrose Dudley's goods.

88 *CPR, Philip and Mary*, iii, 453.

89 *APC*, v, 274–5.

90 See Throckmorton's letters of 30 September 1556, BRL, Baker MS 2/2, n.f.; for Bagnall, Loades, *Two Tudor Conspiracies*, p. 214. It is worth noting that the French wished the English exiles to use a cover story that they were fleeing their creditors. See AMRE, CPA, IX, fo. 609, Montmorency to Noailles, 21 March 1556.

91 'Memoir', *Cal. Carew MSS*, ii, 359.

92 On Courtenay, Bartlett, '"Misfortune"', pp. 19–21.

93 Pelham was identified as a follower of Leicester's in 1568 ([Paris], Bibliothèque Nationale, fonds français 15971, fo. 143, La Forêt to Charles IX, 19 July). For Fitzwilliam, see Bodl, MS Carte 56, fo. 194, Leicester to Sir W. Fitzwilliam, 21 October 1573, for Perceval, PRO, SP 70/49/158, 60/97, Sir T. Smith to Cecil, 2 January, 19 July 1563. Of the other three, Alexander Brett was executed following Wyatt's Rebellion and William Sturton after the Dudley Plot, while Sir George Harper appears to have died between 1555 and 1559.

94 Dudley MS XIV, fo. 10.

95 M. J. Rodríguez-Salgado and S. Adams (eds), 'The count of Feria's dispatch to Philip II of 14 November 1558', *Camden Miscellany XXVIII* (Camden Society, 4th ser., xxix, 1984), pp. 332, 341n. For his position as favourite, AGS, E 812, fo. 28, Feria to Philip II, 18 April 1559.

96 'Feria dispatch', p. 341n. For Dudley's associations with Hatfield, see Dudley MS I, fos. 27, 26, Sir Nicholas Bagnall to Dudley, 12 July 1559, Sir Thomas Benger to Dudley, 23 July.

97 For Mary Sidney, see the 'coronation roll': PRO, LC 2/4/3, fo. 104. The young countess of Huntingdon does not appear to have been as close to Elizabeth at the beginning of the reign as she was in the 1590s.

98 W. S. Hudson, *The Cambridge Connection and the Elizabethan Settlement of 1559* (Durham, NC, 1980); N. L. Jones, *Faith by Statute: Parliament and the Settlement of Religion 1559* (1982).

99 See Elton, *Parliament of England*, p. 121, and Jones, *Faith by Statute*, pp. 156–7.

100 Dudley MS I, fo. 90, the duchess of Suffolk to Dudley, [? October 1559]. For later examples see J. E. Neale, *Elizabeth I and her Parliaments, 1559–1581* (pb. ed., 1965), pp. 121, 180.

101 C. G. Bayne, 'The First House of Commons of Queen Elizabeth', *EHR*, xxiii (1908), 467–8. See also the petition he submitted to Elizabeth on her accession for compensation for damages suffered under Mary: A. J. Kempe (ed.), *The Loseley Manuscripts* (1835), pp. 140–4.

102 PRO, SP 12/12/1; Haynes, *Burghley Papers*, p. 295, to Cecil, I, 20 April 1560.

103 S. Adams, 'Eliza enthroned? the court and its politics' [Ch. 2], pp. 31–2. Loades, *Reign of Mary Tudor*, pp. 459–61.

104 PRO, SP 63/1/12, J. Alen to Cecil, 16 December 1558.

105 The staff of the Edwardian Stables were still in post in 1559. Compare BL, Stowe MS 571, fo. 37^v and PRO, E 101/427/8–^{v} (the establishments of 1552 and 1553) with the household subsidy rolls for 1559 (BL, Lansdowne MS 3, fo. 200) and 1564 (PRO, E 179/69/81).

106 E. Lodge (ed.), *Illustrations of British History* (3 vols., 1791), i, 347, Dudley to the Earl of Shrewsbury, 27 December 1561. [Ambrose Dudley did not receive the viscountcy of Lisle, only the barony, see p. 357, n. 71 below.]

107 BL, Addit. MS 35831, fo. 32, R. Jones to Sir N. Throckmorton, 25 May 1562.

108 These were all lands formerly held by Northumberland, with the exception of Kew and some of the manors granted to Robert Dudley in 1563 and to Warwick in 1564. See *CPR, 1558–60*, pp. 86, 288, *1560–63* (1948), pp. 189–90, 291–3, 534–43, *1563–1566* (1960), p. 59. For Watton, see also A. G. Dickens (ed.), 'Archbishop Holgate's Apology', *EHR*, lvi (1941), 456–8, and Dudley MS I, fo. 44. Yerwerth to Dudley, 19 July 1559.

109 For the stewardship of Warwick, see Ch. 10 below, p. 218, n. 33. Northumberland had bought out John Sutton, Lord Dudley, in the reign of Henry VIII; these lands were restored to Edmund, the 4th lord, by Mary (*CPR, Philip and Mary*, ii, 22–3, iii, 34–7). For Robert Dudley's efforts to purchase them, see Dudley MS I, fos. 84, 108, 171, Lord Dudley to Dudley, [? Aug.] 1559, 30 January, 25 November 1560.

110 Dudley MS I, fos, 13, 74, Croft to Dudley, 10 April, Poyntz to Dudley, 29 August 1559.

111 Dudley MS XIV, fo. 15. The rewarding of old Dudley servants was an extensive process, see, for example, the correspondence over 'my dear lord and father-in-law's old servant' Hugh Shadwell, Dudley MS II, fo. 131, Sidney to Leicester, 2 March 1573.

112 Dudley MS I, fos. 36, 121, 158, Cave to Dudley, 16 July 1559, Fisher to Dudley, 18 March, 29 August 1560.

113 Dudley MS I, fo. 118, 6 March 1560. See Humberside R.O., B[everley] C[orporation] Records], II/7/2 [Minute Book of the Governors, 1558–1567], fos. 66, 76^v, tolls paid to Mr Musgrave, 1564–65.

114 For Aylmer, Dudley MS I, fos. 106, 172. For Sandys, *ibid.*, fo. 139, and BL, Addit. MS 32091, fo. 185. The 'list of divines' dated 1559 in Historical Manuscripts Commission, *Report on the Pepys MSS* (1911), p. 2, relates to the Vestiarian Controversy and should be assigned to 1565–6.

115 Dudley MSS XIV, fo. 15, XV, fo. 24^v. For Craik, see also Greater London Record Office, P92/Sav/1957, Craik to Dudley, 10 January 1562. How this letter strayed into the St Saviour's parish records is a mystery.

116 For Willoughby, see Dudley MS I, fo. 70, Ambrose to Robert Dudley, 17 August 1559. For Craik and Northumberland, see PRO, SP 10/14/144, Northumberland to Cecil, 11 December 1552. I am very grateful to Dr John Durkan of Glasgow University for information about Craik.

117 Dudley MS, I, fo. 28.

118 See N. L. Jones, 'Profiting from religious reform: the land rush of 1559', *HJ*, xxii (1979), 287–8.

119 PRO, SP 15/12/88, Sir John to Sir Nicholas Throckmorton, 29 December 1565. For Jobson's claims in the bishopric of Durham, see also SP 12/20/62, Bishop Pilkington to Cecil, 14 November 1561.

120 PRO, SP 63/1/20.

121 Dudley MS I, fos. 27–8.

122 For Sadler, see PRO, SP 15/12/109 and Dudley MS I, fo. 181, to Dudley, 24 January 1561; for Smith, *CSP Foreign, Elizabeth*, vi, p. 186.

123 J. G. Nichols (ed.), *The Chronicle of Queen Jane* (Camden Society, xlviii, 1850), pp. 7, 9. At his trial, Sir Thomas Palmer accused his judges of being equally guilty of treason, *CSP Span.*, *1553*, p. 185.

124 To the cardinal of Ferrara, July 1561, printed in J. H. Pollen (ed.), *Papal Negotiations with Mary Queen of Scots* (Scot. Hist. Soc., xxxvii, 1901), pp. 60–1.

125 Dudley MS I, fo. 207. William Hayworth took up the same theme in 1573: 'how Judasly your dear father was betrayed by trusting too much to the children of man'. *CSP Scotland, 1571–74* (1905), p. 631.

126 Notably the anonymous compilers of the 'histories' of Edward VI's reign now BL, Addit. MSS 48023, fos. 350–69ᵛ, and 48126, fos. 6–16. [These are presently being prepared for publication by the Camden Society. The author of MS 48023 may have been John Hales.]

127 BL, Cottonian MS Titus B XIII, fo. 28, to the Earl of Sussex. The first page has disappeared, obscuring the immediate circumstances of the remark.

128 For Grey, see *Sidney Papers*, i, 282, Sidney to Grey, 17 September 1580; for Hales, RL, Addit. MS 32091, fo. 248, Hales to Leicester, 28 July 1571. Northumberland is said to have sought a reconciliation with Somerset's sons on the eve of his own execution: see *CSP Span.*, *1553*, p. 185.

Chapter 9

A Puritan crusade? The composition of the Earl of Leicester's expedition to the Netherlands, 1585–86

One of the most important developments in Elizabethan studies over the last thirty years has been the reappraisal of the most controversial personality of the reign, Robert Dudley, Earl of Leicester. No longer can he be dismissed simply as the beneficiary of the queen's misplaced favour or the evil genius of the Court; he has emerged increasingly as a political figure of major significance. The credit for initiating the reassessment belongs rightly to Eleanor Rosenberg.[1] It was, however, Patrick Collinson, in his edition of the *Letters of Thomas Wood, Puritan*, who first subjected Leicester's religious patronage to serious examination. In the introductory essay, which remains the best survey of Leicester's role in the Elizabethan church, Professor Collinson observed that Leicester's 'Puritan friends' regarded his Netherlands expedition of 1585 'as a crusade for the Gospel'.[2] Four years later the expedition itself received a novel treatment in Roy Strong and Jan van Dorsten's *Leicester's Triumph*.[3] Whatever ultimate assessment is made of Leicester's government in the Netherlands, recognition of both his puritan sympathies and his long-standing support for the Dutch cause has made it impossible now to regard his appointment to the command of the expeditionary force as a mere whim of Elizabeth's.[4] Likewise, the expedition as a whole has come to be seen as something more than a limited military and diplomatic manoeuvre.[5]

The central concern of Strong and Van Dorsten was the nature of Leicester's reception in the Netherlands, but they also compiled a valuable table of the membership of the 'train' that accompanied him in December 1585.[6] In the early 1970s, while exploring the sources for Leicester's estates in north Wales, I discovered in the National Library of Wales a document that provides a key to the assembly of the train. This is a letter from Leicester to the Caernarvonshire gentleman John Wynn of Gwydir of 26 September 1585, requesting him to attend him with horse and armour for service in the Low Countries.[7] Its significance lies in the fact that it was clearly one of over two hundred letters that Leicester had sent (so he informed Sir Francis Walsingham on the 27th) 'to my servants and sundry my friends'.[8] The letter to Wynn gave a new importance to the train. Firstly, it was not primarily ceremonial in purpose, but was in fact the cavalry contingent of the expedition. Secondly, if the cavalry was raised by Leicester directly from among his friends and followers, then its composition should enable us to identify his clientele at this key point in his career. Having done so, we would then be in a position to reach firmer conclusions about its religious and political orientation, and to assess the extent to which the expedition was indeed Elizabethan puritanism in arms.

These hypotheses were tested in a study of those of Leicester's followers in north Wales who could be identified as members of the expedition in the table in *Leicester's Triumph*.[9] Further progress, however, would depend on learning more about the composition of his following, and therefore it seemed best to do so as part of a wider reconstruction of Leicester's papers and his clientele as a whole.[10] This research is now sufficiently advanced to allow some provisional conclusions to be drawn. It also emerges, however, that the recruiting of the Netherlands expedition was a much more complicated process than has been previously acknowledged. The infantry, who preceded Leicester's train to the Netherlands in the summer of 1585, also demand consideration. It has recently been argued that there were in fact two separate expeditions, one of professionals and then a later one of gentlemen amateurs.[11] This thesis, however, ignores Leicester's influence as a military patron. It is therefore necessary to begin with a reappraisal of the military background to the expedition.

Our present knowledge of the Elizabethan military system is derived mainly from two monographs: Lindsay Boynton's *The Elizabethan Militia*, and George Cruickshank's *Elizabethan Army*.[12] The latter deserves some comment, because it has had an (unwittingly) unfortunate influence. It began as an Oxford thesis on the recruiting of the big amphibious expeditions of the 1590s. When it was expanded into a general study, it took as its central theme the very important subject of the constitutional sleight of hand whereby Elizabeth introduced what amounted to a system of conscription for overseas service. What Cruickshank was less interested in, and does not devote much attention to, were the permanent forces of the crown: the Irish garrison and the forces maintained in the Netherlands after 1585. These were the products of a process of professionalisation that can be traced back to the first half of the century. It is clear from much recent work that the growth of standing armies in the sixteenth century can be linked very directly to the need for permanent garrisons, which in turn were a consequence of the widespread adoption of the bastioned fortress. Since they lacked the extensive land frontiers of the continental monarchies, the English lagged behind – but not entirely. At the beginning of the century England possessed a major fortress at Calais. Calais was a pale, a fortified zone with a standing garrison commanded by a military officer who possessed both civil and military authority. During the course of the first half of the century the pale system was expanded. In the 1530s it was introduced into Ireland; between 1546 and 1550 large standing garrisons were employed at Boulogne and Scotland; after 1550 a third pale was created around the new bastioned fortress at Berwick-upon-Tweed.[13]

By continental standards the scale of manpower employed was limited: possibly no more than 15,000 men were involved in the years of greatest military expansion during the attempted conquest of Scotland in the later 1540s. But there are two aspects of the mid-Tudor garrisons whose importance has not been sufficiently grasped. Much has been made of the apparently sentimental attachment to the longbow in the sixteenth century and the military obsolescence that ensued. It has, however, recently been argued that the superiority of the arquebus was by no means absolute during the first half of the century. The longbow possessed a higher rate of fire, for example, and only over time did its weaknesses become apparent. A key failing was the fact that longbows could not be fired effectively through loopholes or embrasures, and were therefore useless in fortresses.[14] The garrisons of the 1540s and 1550s thus became the first English troops to be armed primarily with firearms.[15]

If the professional importance of the garrisons was much greater than their numbers would suggest, the political significance of their officers also demands reconsideration. In the 1540s they were the central figures in the clienteles of the two rising military commanders of the decade, Edward Seymour, Duke of Somerset, and John Dudley, Duke of Northumberland. Northumberland's former followers were precisely the men we find surrounding the young Lord Robert Dudley at the beginning of Elizabeth's reign.[16] Equally pronounced was their protestantism, which is clearly observable in the reign of Edward VI. These men were the central figures in the rebellion of Sir Thomas Wyatt against the Spanish marriage in 1554, which in some respects was little more than a conspiracy of old Boulogne officers. The revived and restored Dudley clientele was first employed in the expedition to Le Havre (Newhaven) in 1562–63. In both its Dudley leadership and its religious ambiance the Newhaven expedition was the direct precursor of the Netherlands expedition of 1585.

Many of the Newhaven survivors are next encountered in Sir Henry Sidney's campaign against Shane O'Neill in Ireland in 1566–67.[17] At the beginning of the next decade, however, a major change of generations can be detected. The attrition rate among these officers (who were never very numerous at any stage) was high, and the survivors were becoming distinctly middle-aged.[18] In the 1570s a younger generation emerged, whose careers were shaped largely by the wars in the Netherlands. The nature of this involvement deserves a brief introduction. The first English troops to serve in the Netherlands were the 300 foot, commanded by Thomas Morgan, that William of Orange raised in 1572, apparently through funds provided by the émigré congregation in London.[19] Another 600 foot under the command of Sir Humphrey Gilbert and paid for by the queen occupied Flushing temporarily between July and October 1572. Orange raised further English troops in 1573, but lack of money forced him to dismiss both them and Morgan's company at the end of the year.[20]

1575 saw Orange recruiting in England again, but a more important military relationship was formed in the winter of 1577–78. Following the failure of the Perpetual Edict, full-scale English intervention under Leicester's command was very nearly agreed on. Elizabeth chose instead to pursue the indirect course of providing a loan to enable Orange to raise a large body of English troops. By the summer of 1578 a force of 3000 men led by John Norris had entered his service. Norris's troops, frequently reinforced, remained in the Netherlands until the beginning of 1584. In the summer of 1584 the Estates of Brabant raised a new regiment of 1500 foot under Morgan to reinforce the garrison of Antwerp. This regiment served throughout the winter of 1584–85; its survivors were then incorporated into the new expedition in the summer of 1585.[21]

Although these soldiers were technically mercenaries, the adventuring element can be exaggerated. Apart from those committed politically to the Dutch cause, men seeking military careers were encouraged by the crown to train with the leading continental armies. By the 1570s neither the Spanish nor the French armies were suitable. Service in the Dutch wars was more challenging than guerilla warfare in Ireland, and it helped to cure the endemic English shortage of officers experienced in the handling of large bodies of men. The pride (if not arrogance) of the Low Countries officers in their own professional superiority emerges clearly in Roger Williams's 'history' *The Actions of the Lowe Countries.*[22] Nor were the Dutch and the queen's service mutually exclusive. The 1572 troops were raised (so Williams claimed) from veterans of Berwick, Le Havre and Ireland.[23] Gilbert had served at Le Havre and in Ireland; Morgan (like Roger Williams) had originally followed the 1st Earl of Pembroke, possibly at St. Quentin in 1557, and possibly in Ireland. After leaving the Low Countries in 1573 Morgan and his company were sent immediately to Ireland. Norris's career began in Ireland in 1575–76; he returned there as lord president of Munster in 1584.

Nor did the change of generations lessen Leicester's military patronage; if anything, his advocacy of the Orangist cause enhanced it. Morgan and Williams gravitated to him after Pembroke's death in 1570. Norris was his special protégé. After their quarrel in 1587, Leicester wrote (and Norris never denied): 'It is well known that the said earl hath always been a good friend to Sir John Norris his house and that he brought him up. He procured his first credit in that country; he caused him to be sent for out of Ireland for that service.'[24] It was Leicester (together with Walsingham) who in the early 1580s mediated Norris's quarrels with his fellow commanders, the forerunners of the notorious disputes that came near to dividing the expeditionary force in 1586–87, and continued undiminished long after Leicester's death.[25]

The overall scale of the military intervention that began in 1585 was of a different order to anything the Elizabethan government had previously attempted. Between 1585 and 1587 18,000 Englishmen and 1000 Irishmen were recruited for service in the Netherlands.[26] They were, however, doled out by Elizabeth in small numbers. The prolonged debate over military assistance to the States General following the assassination of William of Orange in July 1584 need not be rehearsed here. However the term under which the expeditionary force was finally dispatched deserves some comment. The Anglo-Dutch negotiations of July and August of 1585 culminated in the four separate agreements (2 and 10 August, 2 and 22–23 September) known collectively as the treaty of Nonsuch. The States General wanted an English force of 10,000 foot and 2000 horse, but were prepared to compromise on half that number.[27]

Elizabeth initially offered 4000 men for the relief of Antwerp (the provisional treaty of 2 August), but then agreed to supply 4000 foot and 400 horse on a permanent basis (the contract of 10 August). After the surrender of Antwerp she raised the limit of those she would pay to 5000 foot and 1000 horse. This treaty (the additional convention or amplification treaty) was signed by the English council on 2 and 3 September. When it was ratified by the States General on 22–23 September (becoming thereby the act of amplification), the English agent, William Davison, made a further concession by agreeing that the 1400 foot needed to garrison the Cautionary Towns would be supplementary to, and not drawn from, the 5000 foot of the treaty.

Although the commissioners from the States General did not arrive until the end of June 1585, English preparations for the expedition began in May. On the 12th Norris was recalled from Ireland to take command.[28] In June the States General requested that a further 2000 (later raised to nearly 3000) English troops be raised at their expense. These voluntary companies became a source of major controversy, but have been all but ignored in most accounts.[29] The queen's troops were raised in July and August, and dispatched in two waves: 2000 in mid-August, and 2450 at the end of the month. The full English force was mustered at Utrecht on 14 September, and numbered 7200 foot in forty-eight companies: twenty-seven in the queen's pay and twenty-one paid by the States General.[30] At the beginning of October, in order to increase the number of queen's troops as required by the act of amplification, most of the States companies were taken into her pay.[31]

The act of amplification also provided for the appointment of an English nobleman to command the expedition and to provide counsel for the States General. Leicester had made clear his willingness to accept such a position in the spring of 1585, but it was not until after the surrender of Antwerp was confirmed in late August that Elizabeth was persuaded to agree.[32] She then went to a series of second thoughts, and it was only at the beginning of December that Leicester was able to depart. With him in the form of the 'train' went the cavalry required under the act.

On Leicester's arrival the English foot companies numbered forty-nine in total – an additional one for Sir Philip Sidney having arrived in the meantime. Of these, eleven were committed to the garrisons of the Cautionary Towns (seven at Flushing and Ramekins, four at the Brill). Furthermore the English had also reinforced the garrisons of Bergen-op-Zoom (nine companies) and Ostend (six), following rumours in the autumn of 1585 that the Duke of Parma was planning to besiege them.[33] Twenty-six companies were thereby effectively immobilised. If, as originally intended, the English were to form part of a field army, reinforcements would be necessary. Since the queen would not increase her total, Leicester began negotiations with the States General to raise further English volunteers in their pay. Owing to the dispute over the governor-generalship, the recruiting of this force did not begin until April and May 1586. On 31 May 1586 the English total was thirty-nine queen's companies (6400 at full strength) and twenty-one States'; by the end of August the States' companies numbered fifty (7500 at full strength).[34] Following the conclusion of the Zutphen campaign most of the new companies were broken up, some being absorbed into those remaining, and some returning to England. When Leicester himself returned in November 1586 he left in the Netherlands an English contingent of thirty-nine queen's and twenty-three States' companies.[35]

There was no shortage of officers for the expeditionary force. By 1585 a considerable number of men with Low Countries experience were available, as well as those older officers who had served in Ireland, Le Havre or Berwick. There were over fifty Irish pensioners alone.[36] From the lists of captains compiled during the summer of 1585 the process of selection can be deduced to some extent.[37] A combination of officers with and without experience was sought, but those officers already holding positions of responsibility at home, such as muster-masters of county militias, were steadily weeded out. This decision would appear to reflect Elizabeth's frequently-expressed determination not to denude the realm of trained men.[38] Of the captains of the forty-eight companies of the Utrecht muster, approximately two-thirds were experienced.

In the twenty-seven queen's companies, ten captains were inexperienced, seventeen experienced. Five of the twenty-one States companies were commanded as second companies by captains of the queen's companies (Norris and his brothers in the main). Of the remaining sixteen, twelve were experienced, four apparently not. It has not been possible to trace the careers of all the twenty-nine captains described as experienced, but at least sixteen had served previously in the Low Countries, eight in Ireland and two at Berwick. The fourteen inexperienced captains were not necessarily less competent, for many of them (Charles Blount, the future Lord Mountjoy, or Robert Sidney) were to have impressive military careers in the 1590s.

The sixteenth-century custom whereby generals and colonels had the prerogative of appointing their subordinates seems to have been as violated as much on this occasion as on many others. From a memorandum presented by Norris in July it would appear that the privy council reserved the final decision on the captains of the queen's companies.[39] Norris may have retained more control over the States companies. One of the few letters on the subject to survive reveals Sir Philip Sidney obtaining from him the captaincy of a States' company for his brother Robert.[40] There was certainly a substantial Norris contingent present; between them Norris and his brothers Henry and Edward held the captaincies of six companies. At least four other captains were Norris's immediate followers, in all over a fifth of the total.[41] Morgan may have had a similar influence, for six captains had been officers of his 1584 regiment.[42] No direct evidence survives of Leicester's involvement; indeed, given his long-standing patronage of so many of the senior officers, he did not need direct influence. One captain (Digory Hender) can be identified as a follower of Walsingham's, and another (John Boroughs) may have been patronised by Burghley.

The recruiting of the companies raises more questions than can be answered easily. The traditional method of recruiting for overseas service, dating back to the Hundred Years War, was recruiting by retinue, an ostensibly voluntary process relying on the influence of noblemen and gentlemen over their 'servants and tenants'.[43] This could involve the formal process of retaining (which will be discussed below), or the employment of military service clauses in leases, a practice still widespread in Elizabeth's reign.[44] The last expedition completely recruited by retinue was that sent to aid Philip II at the siege of St. Quentin in 1557.[45] The system had however been breached in a major way in 1544 when Henry VIII levied sizeable numbers of men for service in France.[46] Elizabeth's use of impressment for overseas service was initiated in the expedition to Le Havre in 1562. Captains were assigned a particular county and local magistrates were then instructed to aid them in levying a stated number of men. The novelty caused considerable comment at the time, but between 1563 and 1585 the burden was limited to irregular reinforcements for Ireland.[47] Only when impressment became a regular occurrence after 1585, and especially in the 1590s, did it become a source of major discontent. Moreover, it could also be combined with the earlier system, which probably helped to mitigate its effects. How this could be done was outlined by a Norfolk gentleman, John Peyton (who himself commanded one of the 1586 companies), in a letter to Walsingham in the summer of 1585.

> And sure it is right honourable that if any gentleman of the county of whose moderation in government the people have any good liking should be employed in this action, this county will voluntarily furnish unto that service five hundred men . . . the gentlemen of the counties are the only captains to draw the persons or the purses of the common sort into martial actions, and most sure it is that persuading without pressing will carry most and make the best soldiers.[48]

In a commission drafted on 19 July the Privy Council stated a preference for men who had previously served in the Low Countries, but how successful this was is unknown.[49] It is possible to identify the counties where twenty-four of the twenty-seven queen's companies were raised. In at least twelve cases the captain was connected to the leading gentry, and one may suspect that Peyton's advice was taken in practice. The recruiting of the States companies remains a more mysterious process, for since the English government was not directly concerned it had no interest in recording the details. Impressment should not have been used for they were not technically in the queen's service, but how 'voluntary' they were is unclear, given the desire of local authorities to clear the gaols and the poorhouses. On 27 August 1585 Harwich submitted a bill to the council for £167 14s. 8d. for the shipping of 300 masterless men to the Low Countries; these could not have been the only victims.[50]

Leicester's complaints about the quality of many of the men are well-known, but they should be seen in perspective. A spectrum of companies, from those managed with classic Tudor paternalism to those of unhappy pressed men exploited by unscrupulous or unconcerned captains, would probably be a more accurate picture. The fragmentary evidence we possess of local recruiting supports this impression. On 17 August 1585 the official supervising the embarkation at Gravesend reported that the Kentish company of John Scott had arrived in 'very good order', supplied with carts to carry their equipment. Scott was the son of a leading Puritan county magistrate, and his company included the large number of twelve gentlemen volunteers. The Sussex company which embarked at the same time was led by the lieutenant of a non-resident captain (who did not in fact take up the command in the end), had been badly equipped, and was in a state of near mutiny.[51]

In Suffolk, the outspoken Puritan Sir Robert Jermyn of Rushbrook, who would himself accompany Leicester, commented that:

> the soldiers are ready and forward and thanks be to God well instructed from the mouth of the preachers in these counties even at their departure to use this calling and profession of a soldier in their duty to God and their sovereign. I wish the same were done in all places where soldiers be leaving.[52]

Such encouragement also appears to have been very much a matter of local initiative. The limited nature of the English domestic propaganda campaign is striking, especially when compared to the scale of Leicester's reception in the Netherlands. There are one or two references to preachers praying for the success of the expedition, but the surviving literature consists of a manuscript tract by the Puritan divine Oliver Pig, 'Part of a Letter sent to a Christian knight . . . the service . . . of the Low Countries, 1585' (which may indeed have been an item of private correspondence), and the anonymous *A most Necessary and Godly Prayer for the Preservation of the Earle of Leicester*.[53] This is the more surprising given that Leicester had been the dedicatee of a number of earlier propaganda tracts, and had been accused of tuning the pulpit on more than one occasion. The answer probably lies in the unwillingness of Elizabeth to encourage an open war with Spain, either explicitly or implicitly, as her own published *Declaration* on the intervention reveals.

The 1000 cavalry to be supplied under the act of amplification were not in fact raised until Leicester dispatched his 200 circular letters on 25 and 26 September. In the letter to Wynn of Gwydir, Leicester requested the horse to assemble in London on 15 or 16 October. The further delays caused by the queen's hesitations meant that he and the train did not leave London until 4 December. At some point before then a muster was held at Tothill Fields near Westminster; a second one was held at the Hague on 10 January. According to a letter written several years later by Leicester's secretary Arthur Atye, 400 horse were present at the first muster. A further 250 had joined by the date of the second.[54]

The letter to Wynn is the only one of the two hundred I have encountered so far. Nor have any of the answers survived. For the identification of the cavalry we are therefore dependent on the surviving lists of the train. Strong and Van Dorsten compiled their table from five separate lists: two sets of billeting lists, one from Leiden, the other from the Hague (6 January 1586);[55] a list drawn up in January 1586 by Henry Goodere, which turns out to be two, one of Leicester's guard of halberdiers (of which Goodere was captain), and one of Leicester's household in 1587;[56] a list of gentlemen who accompanied Leicester printed in the *Calendar of State Papers, Spanish*;[57] and, lastly, 'The whole number of the horsemen at the Hague the xth of January 1586'.[58] Since the publication of *Leicester's Triumph* two further lists have come to light in the Bodleian Library. One, 'The checkrole of the earl of Leicesters followers when he went into Holland An 1585', is bound into a volume of miscellaneous papers in the Rawlinson MSS; the other, 'A particular of the earl of Leicester's followers both gentlemen and servants into the Low Countries, 1584 [*sic*]', is part of a collection formerly belonging to the nineteenth-century Norfolk antiquary Hudson Gurney.[59]

The two Bodleian lists, the 'number of horsemen at the Hague', and the 'Spanish' list are the most important for our purposes. All consist of lists of names with numbers of men or horses attached. They are not lists of individuals, but of the retinues brought by men whom Leicester summoned. The 'number of horsemen at the Hague' is a copy of the roll of the muster held on 10 January 1586, immediately prior to the organisation of the cavalry into cornets or companies. The other three probably originate from a further missing list. Although the total of names is different, there are large sections in each three where the names appear in the same order, and that for no apparent reason. (This is not the case with the Hague muster-roll.) Their provenance is therefore of some importance. The 'Spanish' list is a translation of an English original sent to Philip II by his ambassador in Paris, Don Bernardino de Mendoza, early in January 1586. It is possible that Mendoza obtained the original list from one of his agents, though there is no proof.[60] This list alone indicates the ships in which the men were transported to the Netherlands in December 1585, which suggests that the English original may have been an embarkation list.[61] The Gurney list can be traced to the manuscript collection of Sir Henry Spelman; its earlier history is unknown.[62] That in the Rawlinson MSS may have come from a sale of Pepys manuscripts in the eighteenth century and thereby ultimately from the important collection of Leicester's papers left by his servant Richard Browne.[63] In the absence of any evidence to the contrary, it may be assumed that both these lists and the embarkation list were derived ultimately from the roll of the first muster at Tothill Fields.

The Hague muster-roll gives a total of 744 horsemen in 199 retinues. The difference between this total and the 650 horse reported by Leicester's secretary is accounted for by references to forty more supplied by Leicester and a further fifty by Robert Devereux, Earl of Essex.[64] Of the other three lists, the Spanish is the smallest: it includes 542 horse in 122 retinues. The two Bodleian lists are roughly similar in total: the Rawlinson has 754 horse in 169 retinues, the Gurney 757 horse in 164 retinues, which would suggest that whatever their original derivation, they had been amended following the Hague muster. If we can assume that some 750 horse were present in January 1586, the cavalry was still only three-quarters its treaty strength, the cause of another future dispute with the States General. The fault lay with the queen, who had taken the cavalier attitude that since the cavalry would not be needed until the spring and summer of 1586, it did not have to be brought up to strength until then.[65]

In its structure, therefore, the 'train' was thus a giant retinue, composed of a number of smaller retinues. The individual retinues varied from single persons to the fifty men brought by the Earl of Essex and Sir Thomas Cecil. An internal list of Cecil's retinue survives.[66] The total of fifty lances consists of seventeen lances brought by seven gentlemen 'as go voluntary with me', five from Burghley's household, and the remainder from Cecil's own. The existence of these subsidiary retinues also raises the question of the extent to which the expedition was indeed Leicester's. At the beginning of September 1585 he had declared to Walsingham 'if I should [go] so I would carry the best I can of every degree'.[67] Since the one man we know to have been summoned (Wynn of Gwydir) did not in the event take part in the expedition, the extent to which Leicester obtained the men he wanted is a matter of speculation. Elizabeth herself refused to release a number of his choices, and over two experienced officers in particular – the lieutenant of the Ordnance, Sir William Pelham, and the former lord deputy of Ireland, Arthur, Lord Grey de Wilton – a considerable struggle ensued. In Pelham's case Leicester was eventually successful, in Grey's he was not. The final composition of the expedition was therefore not necessarily what Leicester would have wanted had he had a free hand.

The key figures in the train, the men who brought their own retinues, amount to just under 200 individuals. So far I have been able to identify 133 of them, and have discovered clear evidence of some form of association with Leicester in the case of 105. It is reasonable to assume that those still unidentified will prove to have been among the more obscure of Leicester's followers. Moreover, since many would probably have been fairly young, they may also have been the younger sons, brothers and nephews of better-known men. Nevertheless we are still dealing with an important section of the Elizabethan political nation. Some sixty to seventy of the members of the expedition became members of parliament at some point in their lives. More significantly, perhaps, at least thirty had been M.P.s in the session of 1584–5. Their absence forced Elizabeth, when summoning parliament in the autumn of 1586 to support the execution of Mary, Queen of Scots, to hold a new election rather than recall the earlier parliament, as had been her first intention.[68] Since many of them had been patronised by Leicester in 1584, the expedition therefore comprised the key members of his following.

Apart from Leicester himself, there were four peers. The Earl of Essex, George Touchet, Lord Audley, and Roger, Lord North, accompanied him. Peregrine Bertie, Lord Willoughby, joined directly from his embassy to Denmark in January 1586. Together they comprised a tenth of the Elizabethan peerage, and nearly a fifth of the physically able. The proportion is the more marked if sons of peers (both heirs and younger sons) are included, for Norris and his brothers, Sir Thomas Cecil, Sir William Russell, Charles Blount, and Edward Cromwell all fall into this category. Although he was prevented from obtaining the services of Lord Grey, Leicester may not have wished for further peers. As the correspondence over North reveals, he did not consider that he possessed a sufficient number of suitable offices for them.[69]

The four peers did, however, play prominent roles in the expedition. This was not necessarily the case with the knights. Seventeen knights are found in the Hague muster list, but eight of them were created by Leicester himself during the course of 1586.[70] The remaining nine reveal some interesting common features. Three became leading figures of the expedition: the 2nd Earl of Bedford's son Sir William Russell (Sidney's successor as governor of Flushing), Sir John Conway (the governor of Ostend in 1587), and Sir Thomas Shirley (treasurer after 1586). Most of the other six were considerably older than the great majority of the train. They did not remain in the Netherlands for very long, but returned to England in 1586 to raise the new voluntary companies. They were men of considerable local prominence, and in some cases notoriety. Sir Robert Jermyn was a leading figure in Suffolk, Sir John Harington of Exton (the later guardian of James I's daughter Elizabeth) in Rutland and Northampton, and Sir Arthur Basset in Somerset. Neither Basset nor the other two West Country knights, Sir Henry Berkeley and Sir Richard Dyer, were particularly close to Leicester, nor was this a region where his landed interest was strong. Their appearance, like that of Sir William Russell, may reflect the support for the expedition of Bedford, who had died in August 1585.[71] For two of the knights the expedition also served as a means of regaining the queen's favour. Jermyn had been dismissed from the Suffolk bench several years earlier for being the ringleader in a running battle between the local puritan gentry and the Bishop of Norwich. When he returned from the Netherlands in 1586, he brought with him a recommendation from Leicester for his reinstatement.[72] The case of Sir Robert Stapleton was even more controversial. His celebrated attempt to compromise the Archbishop of York, Edwin Sandys, in 1581 had created a major embarrassment for the Privy Council, for previously he had been regarded as a rising man in the North.[73]

In the three lists derived from the Tothill muster the rest of the train are described simply as the Earl's gentlemen. There is, however, one exception. In the Gurney list forty-five men are identified as gentlemen retainers. This raises the important technical issues of the extent to which Leicester continued to employ formal retaining (the wearing of badges and liveries) and its relationship to the expedition. The successive Tudor monarchs had been remarkably consistent in their efforts, as most recently expressed in a proclamation of 1583, to restrict retaining to members of immediate households, military service commissioned by the crown, or to those specifically licensed.

The practice clearly was declining, and being replaced by less formal relationships, but the stages of its decline are very difficult to delineate.[74] That it was still being employed in the 1580s is illustrated by the chance survival of an order from Anthony Browne, Viscount Montague, to one of his men that following the proclamation of 1583 he was no longer to wear badge of livery or call himself a retainer.[75] In 1588 Leicester himself complained of a major revival of retaining that was playing havoc with the mobilisation of the militia against the Armada.[76]

Not the least of the problems raised by Tudor retaining is the fact that few sixteenth-century lists of retainers have been discovered.[77] The extent of the practice is therefore impossible to gauge. Equally unhelpful is the widespread use of the simple description 'servant', which may or may not be a euphemism for a retainer. The letter to Wynn of Gwydir, for example, is addressed to 'my loving servant', and signed 'your loving master'. In common with several other privy councillors, including Burghley, Leicester had been granted a licence to retain 100 men in 1565; how he employed it is unknown.[78] The only other direct reference to his retainers in the documents of the expedition is the description of several of the halberdiers of his guard as 'your lordship's old retainers' in Goodere's list.[79] This would imply that they were of less than gentry rank. Of the forty-five men of the Gurney list, there is corroborating evidence in the case of twenty-eight that they were either his immediate officers or servants. Among the remainder appear to be two gentlemen pensioners and one member of the staff of the queen's stables.[80] These were servants of the crown who were specifically prohibited from being retained by other individuals, though it has been argued that the prohibition was frequently ignored in practice.[81]

If no firm conclusions can be drawn about the role of retaining the identification of the members of the train does confirm the impression that they were very much Leicester's men. Only Thomas Arundell would appear to have been hostile to Leicester, and it is possible that his presence may be accounted for by his friendship with Sidney.[82] The members of Leicester's household formed the core of the train: twenty-two were found in the 1587 household list, a further sixteen were officers or servants in other capacities.[83] In another twenty-nine cases there was a clear family connection to the Dudleys, either to Leicester or to his brother the Earl of Warwick. Frequently the family association can be traced back over two generations to the following of the Duke of Northumberland. Eighteen of these men took part in Leicester's funeral, as compared to only five (peers excluded) in Sidney's.[84]

Equally striking is the fact that the great majority were not young courtiers, but members of the country gentry. Excluding the peers, and such prominent figures as Sidney, Sir Thomas Cecil and Sir William Russell, so far only twelve men who either held Court office themselves or were the sons of

Court officers can be identified. One was the member of the staff of the queen's stables, and another two the gentlemen pensioners mentioned above. A few sons of privy councillors can be found: Lord Hunsdon's son Edmund Carey (who had been in Leicester's household for some years), and Sir Francis Knollys's son William, both of whom Leicester knighted.[85] The other were sons of less prominent Court figures: Francis Castilion, for example, son of Gian Baptista Castiglione, a groom of the privy chamber and Elizabeth's Italian tutor, Francis Fortescue, son of her long-serving household officer and future chancellor of the exchequer, Sir John Fortescue, or Richard Ward, son of the cofferer of the household of that name.[86]

In about seventy-five cases counties of origin can presently be established. The strongest concentrations reflect the pattern of Leicester's territorial interest. The largest single group (twenty-nine) came from the West Midlands, the centre of the Dudley estates. Twelve came from East Anglia, partly Leicester interest, partly local puritanism. Lancashire and Cheshire (where Leicester was chamberlain of the county palatine) produced nine, Wales about ten. Seven came from the East Midlands, especially Northamptonshire where Leicester was steward of the royal forest of Grafton. Eight can be traced to Somerset and Devon, in some cases Leicester's followers, in others Bedford's.

With so many still to be more fully identified firmer conclusions cannot be drawn, but it is reasonable to assume that when identified the more obscure will probably strengthen the existing concentrations. 'Servants and friends' was how Leicester described the train, a distinction of wider importance to an understanding of the expedition, his clientele as a whole, and to some extent the man himself.

Regardless of the degree of formal retaining involved, it was a giant retinue, drawn from what was a bastard feudal affinity of family, officers and tenantry. These connections, which in many cases can be traced to Northumberland, were its cement. It was the last major military expedition to be recruited in this manner. Yet it was also something more. Like Northumberland, Leicester was a figure of major prominence and his influence was not limited to the territorial. The tradition of Dudley military patronage had brought into its orbit many of the leading professional officers of the day. Equally important was Leicester's patronage of advanced protestantism, and espousal of the international protestant cause. This brought into his following the 'friends', men whose relationship was not a traditional one. The result was untidy and frequently difficult to categorise exactly, but its very fluidity reflects its transitional nature. Leicester (no less than Sidney) cannot be described simply as a late-medieval nobleman, a Renaissance courtier, or an embryonic Whig grandee; he was an awkward combination of all three. His clientele was equally awkward: from one perspective a traditional affinity, from another a primitive political movement. Indeed it is precisely because he was such a transitional figure that Leicester obtains his historical importance.

The complex structure of the expedition also explains its religious orientation. If we exclude the notorious examples of Sir William Stanley and Rowland York, six quasi-Catholics can be detected. Christopher Blount, Leicester's own master of the horse, was one; Sylvanus Scory, the controversial son of the late Bishop of Hereford, was another. Clearly Leicester had a certain soft spot for them, and regarded their personal loyalty a sufficient guide to their political allegiance – a confidence that had disastrous consequences in the case of Stanley and York.[87] The significance of Blount, Scory and York lies in the fact that they were the sons of members of the old Dudley Edwardian connection, whose fathers and families had been associated with Leicester or his father for many years. They thus represented the older bastard feudal affinity, a connection still not completely transformed by religious allegiance.

It is among the 'friends' that a strong religious commitment is to be found. All the peers were markedly Puritan in orientation, even Audley, whose poverty turned him into a semi-professional soldier. Indeed they made up a high percentage of the Puritan peerage not holding major office in England. A similar outlook is found among the knights, particularly those who earlier had been followers of Bedford. In the case of the more obscure provincial gentry the picture is not so clear. Certainly there are figures who appear in Midlands and East Anglian puritanism, but not enough is known about the others to permit definite conclusions. We must once again bear in mind that the expedition was not as Leicester necessarily would have desired it. Those men he failed to obtain certainly shared the Puritan conception of the expedition. So too, in the main, did those whom he promoted to senior positions; to this extent they, like Leicester, contributed to its political difficulties in their shared misreading of the complexities of Dutch politics. The puritanism that would be so pronounced among the English troops in the Dutch service for several generations was a direct inheritance of Leicester's expedition. 'Crusade' may not be the best description of the expedition, but the religious element in the Anglo-Dutch relationship cannot be denied either. Only Leicester possessed the influence and the clientele to mobilise support for the Netherlands on such a scale. To that extent his expedition was as near to 'puritanism in arms' as the Elizabethan political system could provide.

NOTES

This paper was delivered to the annual symposium of the Sir Thomas Browne Institute on 27 November 1987. An early version was given to the Dutch History Seminar of the Institute of Historical Research in 1981. It will in due course become a full-scale study of the composition of the 1585 expedition. For that reason tables have not been included and the notes have been restricted. I am most grateful to the Sir Thomas Browne Institute for their invitation (and their patience in waiting for the text) and the British Council for financing my journey to Leiden. The research, which has extended over ten years, owes much to the generous financial support of the British Academy, the Carnegie Trust for the Universities of Scotland, and the University of Strathclyde. Dates employed are those of the Julian Calendar.

1 *Leicester, Patron of Letters* (New York, 1955).

2 *Letters of Thomas Wood, Puritan, 1566–1577, Bulletin of the Institute of Historical Research,* Special Supplement, 5 (1960); reprinted in *Godly People: Essays on English Protestantism and Puritanism* (London, 1983), pp. 70, 81.

3 R. C. Strong and J. A. van Dorsten, *Leicester's Triumph* (Leiden/London, 1964). Also of importance for the reappraisal is F. G. Oosterhof, 'The Earl of Leicester's Governorship of the Netherlands, 1585–1587' (London University PhD Thesis), W. T. MacCaffrey, *The Shaping of the Elizabethan Regime* (Princeton, 1969), and *Queen Elizabeth and the Making of Policy, 1572–1588* (Princeton, 1981). The three recent biographies – A. Kendall, *Robert Dudley, Earl of Leicester* (London, 1980), D. Wilson, *Sweet Robin: A Biography of Robert Dudley, Earl of Leicester 1533–1588)* (London, 1987), and A. Haynes, *The White Bear: The Elizabethan Earl of Leicester* (London, 1987) – are in the main derivative.

4 Though not by Charles Wilson, *Queen Elizabeth and the Revolt of the Netherlands* (2nd edn, The Hague, 1979), esp. pp. 86ff.

5 J. A. Dop, *Eliza's Knights: Soldiers, Poets and Puritans in the Netherlands, 1572–1586* (Alblasserdam, [1981]).

6 *Leicester's Triumph,* Appendix III, pp. 108–34.

7 National Library of Wales, Wynn of Gwydir MS 9051 E, printed in S. L. Adams, 'The Gentry of north Wales and the Earl of Leicester's Expedition to the Netherlands, 1585–1586' [Ch. 12], pp. 246–7. My first incursion into Leicester's politics can be found in my 1973 Oxford DPhil. thesis, *The Protestant Cause: Religious Alliance with the West European Calvinist Communities as a Political Issue in England, 1585–1630.*

8 J. Bruce (ed.), *Correspondence of Robert Dudley, Earl of Leycester* (Camden Soc., vol. xvii, 1844), p. 5.

9 See Ch. 12 below, *passim.*

10 This will in due course form the basis of a full-scale biography of Leicester. For the reconstruction of a section of his correspondence, see my article, 'The Lauderdale Papers, 1561–1570: The Maitland of Lethington State Papers and the Leicester Correspondence', *Scottish Historical Review,* 67 (1988), pp. 28–55.

11 Dop, *Eliza's Knights,* pp. 153–5.

12 L. Boynton, *The Elizabethan Militia, 1585–1638* (London, 1967). C. G. Cruickshank, *Elizabeth's Army* (2nd edn, Oxford, 1966). J. J. Goring, *The Military Obligations of the English People, 1551–1558* (London University PhD thesis, 1955), though not directly relevant, is in some respects more useful.

13 Discussed in further detail in my essay 'Tactics or Politics? The "Military Revolution" and the Habsburg Hegemony, 1525–1648', in John A. Lynn (ed.), *Tools of War: The Technology and Concepts of War in the West, 1550–1865* (University of Illinois Press, 1989).

14 See J. F. Guilmartin, *Gunpowder and Galleys: Changing Technology and Mediterranean Warfare at Sea in the Sixteenth Century* (Cambridge, 1974), p. 151.

15 See descriptions of the Boulogne garrison in 1550 in British Library [hereafter, BL], Harleian MS 353, ff. 50–3; and the Berwick garrison in 1559 in A. Clifford (ed.), *The State Papers and Letters of Sir Ralph Sadler* (Edinburgh, 1809), II, p. 3.

16 To be discussed in my forthcoming essay 'The Dudley Clientele, 1553–1563' [now Ch. 8].

17 As noted by N. Canny, *The Elizabethan Conquest of Ireland: A Pattern Established, 1565–1576* (Hassocks, Suss., 1976), p. 70.

18 Some came to occupy permanent posts at home; thus Sir William Pelham succeeded Colonel Edward Randolph as lieutenant of the Ordnance after his death in Ireland in 1566, and Sir Thomas Leighton and Sir Edward Horsey became governors of Guernsey and the Isle of Wight.

19 A. Pettegree, *Foreign Protestant Communities in Sixteenth-Century London* (Oxford, 1986), pp. 253–4. See also D. Caldecott-Baird (ed.), *The Expedition in Holland, 1572–1574* (London, 1976).

20 For Orange's recruiting in 1573, see Algemeen Rijksarchief, Eerste Afdeling [hereafter ARA], Collectie Ortell 29 and J. W. Wijn, 'Het Noordhollandse Regiment in de eerste Jaren van de Opstand tegen Spanje', *Tijdschrift voor Geschiedenis*, 62 (1949), pp. 240–1.

21 For the raising of this regiment, see Public Record Office, State Papers [hereafter PRO, SP] 83/22/51, Estates of Brabant to Leicester, 19/29 July 1584, and ARA, Raad van State 3, ff. 3, 7, 152v.

22 J. X. Evans (ed.), *The Works of Sir Roger Williams* (Oxford, 1972), pp. 51–153. Compare the attacks on the Low Countries, officers in the works of that notorious crank, Sir John Smythe, esp. *Certain Discourses Military*, J. R. Hale (ed.) (Ithaca, N.Y., 1964), and his letter to Burghley of 20 May 1590, printed in H. Ellis (ed.), *Original Letters of Eminent Literary Men* (Camden Soc., vol. xxiii, 1843), pp. 59–60.

23 *Actions*, p. 101.

24 BL, Add. MS 48116, f. 77. Cf. Bruce, *Leycester Correspondence*, p. 385 and *Calendar of State Papers, Foreign Series, Elizabeth I* [hereafter *CSPF*], XXI, pt. 3 (London, 1929), p. 38.

25 See BL, Cottonian MSS, Titus B VII, f. 38, Galba C VII, ff. 144, 241, Morgan to Leicester, 2 June and 30 June 1581, and Leicester to [the Duke of Anjou], 12 May 1582.

26 BL, Add. MS 48084, ff. 134–6.

27 ARA, Staten Generaal 8299 (Rapport of the ambassadors in England, ff. 32v–33 (13/23 July 1585).

28 Bodleian Library, St. Amand MS [Norris Papers] 8, f. 57, Walsingham to Norris, 12 May 1585. Norris had earlier indicated his willingness to serve, see PRO, SP 63/115/86v, to Walsingham, 31 March 1585.

29 The negotiations for these troops appear only fleeting in the English government's archives. See ARA, Raad van State, 3, ff. 223v, 226v, 304, and Regeringsarchieven van de Geünieerde . . . Provinciën, IX-8. BL, Cottonian MS Galba C VIII, f. 78, J. Ortell to Leicester, 8 June (NS?) 1585, and Harleian MS 6993, f. 80, Walsingham to Burghley, 21 May 1585. *CSPF*, XXIX (London, 1916), pp. 506–7.

30 BL, Harleian MS 168, f. 159v. In the Poole Borough Archives there is a file (PBA 71(26)–89(45)) relating to the dispatch to Flushing of the three hundred men of the

Somerset and Dorset companies. The Privy Council's orders to the deputy-lieutenants to raise the men and to the borough to prepare the shipping were sent on the 1st of August. Poole received its instructions at 5.00 in the afternoon of the 4th. The first hundred men were embarked on the 13th, the remainder on the 19th.

31 PRO, SP 84/3/57, Walsingham to William Davison, 4 Sept. 1585.

32 Leicester acknowledged the queen's decision in letters to Walsingham and Burghley on 28 August, PRO, SP 12/181/222–23v and Historical Manuscripts Commission [hereafter HMC], *Calender of the Manuscripts of the . . . Marquess of Salisbury*, III (London, 1889), p. 108. For his earlier willingness, see ARA, Regeringsarchieven, I-90B, J. Ortell to States General, 28 April/8 May 1585.

33 PRO, SP 84/5/107.

34 BL, Add. MS 48084, f. 119.

35 PRO, SP 84/10/270v.

36 PRO, SP 63/115/131–71, Irish Establishment List, 1584–85. See also C. G. Cruickshank, 'An Elizabethan Pensioner Reserve', *English Historical Review*, 56 (1941), pp. 637–9.

37 See esp. PRO, SP 15/29/53, 55.

38 See Bodleian Library, St. Amand MS 8, f. 59, Elizabeth to Norris, 31 October 1585.

39 PRO, SP 12/180/88r–v. Cf. SP 15/29/75.

40 Bodleian Library, St. Amand MS 8, f. 69, Robert Sidney to Norris, dated merely 'this Wednesday'.

41 Norris's uncle Richard Hurleston (the treasurer), John Price, John Hill, and Richard Wingfield.

42 Emanuel Lucar, Edward Morgan, Edward Udall, William Ince, Francis Littleton, and Thomas Watson.

43 Goring, 'Military Obligations', pp. 12, 17, refers to this as a quasi-feudal system, which was superseded by the end of Mary's reign.

44 See Goring, 'Military Obligations', pp. 93ff, 146, 149, 175; L. Stone, *The Crisis of the Aristocracy, 1558–1641* (Oxford, 1979), pp. 214–16; J. P. Cooper, 'Retainers in Tudor England', in *Land, Men and Beliefs: Studies in Early-Modern History* (1983), pp. 91–2; and, for Leicester, Adams, 'Military Obligations of Leasehold Tenants in Leicesterian Denbigh', *Transactions Denbighshire Historical Society*, 24 (1975), pp. 205–8.

45 HMC, *Savile Foljambe MSS* (London, 1897), pp. 5–6.

46 Goring, 'Military Obligations', pp. 47–8. H. Miller, *Henry VIII and the English Nobility* (Oxford, 1986), pp. 159–60.

47 The novelty is commented on in an anonymous history of the first years of the reign, BL, Add. MS 48023, ff. 365v–66.

48 PRO, SP 12/182/36, 19 Sept. 1585.

49 PRO, SP 12/180/80–5.

50 PRO, SP 12/181/220. Cf. Cruickshank, *Elizabeth's Army*, p. 27.

51 PRO, SP 12/181/192, John Wanton to Walsingham; SP 12/181/48, muster of the Kent company. P. Clark, *English Provincial Society from the Reformation to the Revolution:*

Religion, Politics and Society in Kent, 1550–1640 (Hassocks, Suss., 1977), p. 222, comments on the Sussex mutiny but not the Kentish success.

52 Bodleian Library, Tanner MS 78, f. 73, to William Davison, 25 Aug. 1585. Cf. PRO, SP 12/18/199, W. Herle to Burghley, 21 Aug.

53 Cambridge University Library, MS Dd.2.76, ff. 21–5. The only surviving copy of the prayer (*Short Title Catalogue of English Books, 1475–1649*, item 7289) is found in the library of Emmanuel College, Cambridge.

54 BL, Lansdowne MS 61, art. 81, to Burghley, 9 Dec. 1589, printed in H. Ellis, *Original Letters Illustrative of English History*, 3rd ser., 4 (1846), p. 76.

55 The Hague billeting list is BL, Cottonian MS Vespasian C XIV, ff. 321–8; for the Leyden list see Strong and Van Dorsten, p. 107.

56 BL, Cottonian MS Galba C VIII, ff. 96v–97, 98–102.

57 *Calendar of State Papers, Preserved in the Archives of Simancas, 1580–1586* (London, 1896), pp. 553–6.

58 PRO, SP 84/6/79ff, printed in E. M. Tenison, *Elizabethan England* (14 vols., Leamington Spa, 1933–61), VI, pp. 45–7.

59 Bodleian Library, Rawlinson MS B. 146, f. 235r–v, MS Eng. Hist. C 272, pp. 82–7. The latter was calendared among the Gurney collection in HMC, *XIIth Report*, pt. 9 (London, 1981), p. 146.

60 Archivo General de Simancas, Estado K 1564, f. 4, entitled 'El sequito del Conde de Lestre', sent with Mendoza's dispatch of 29 Dec./8 Jan. (f. 2). In *CSPSpan.*, p. 556, a further list of volunteers raised in 1586 (f. 19) is added incorrectly to this list.

61 Leicester himself commented on the number of 'tyckettes' originating from London and circulating in the Netherlands giving the names of those who accompanied him in December 1585. Bruce, *Leycester Correspondence*, p. 27.

62 It was included in volume IX of the eighteen volumes of Spelman manuscripts Gurney purchased in the sale of the library of the Rev. Cox Macro in 1820. See Adams, 'Lauderdale Papers', pp. 35–6.

63 For a brief discussion of Browne's Leicester Papers, see Adams, 'Lauderdale Papers', pp. 32–3.

64 PRO, SP 84/6/79ff.

65 Bruce, *Leycester Correspondence*, pp. 228, 236.

66 PRO, SP 84/5/3.

67 PRO, SP 12/182/1.

68 R. C. Gabriel, 'The Members of the House of Commons, 1586–7' (unpublished London University MA diss., 1954), pp. 6–9.

69 North reveals the difficulties of simplistic interpretations of recruiting. Although he was one of Leicester's closest friends, he was in fact sent on the expedition at Elizabeth's order, and against Leicester's wishes. See Bruce, *Leycester Correspondence*, p. 75.

70 This reveals the document to be a copy rather than the original.

71 For Basset and Bedford, see J. C. Roberts, 'The Parliamentary Representation of Devon and Dorset, 1559–1601' (unpublished London MA diss., 1958), p. 40.

72 D. MacCulloch, *Suffolk and the Tudors: Politics and Religion in an English County, 1500–1600* (Oxford, 1986), pp. 206–8.

73 The queen, in fact, did not want Stapleton to go, see *CSPF*, XX, p. 589, Leicester to Stapleton, 30 April 1586.

74 Cooper, 'Retainers', pp. 78–96. M. James, *English Politics and the Concept of Honour 1485–1642, Past and Present*, Supplement 3 (1978), pp. 20–21.

75 Henry E. Huntington Library, San Marino, Battle Abbey MS 56, f. 6. (I am grateful to the Huntington Library for permission to cite this manuscript.)

76 PRO, SP 12/213/40, to Walsingham, 24 July 1588.

77 Cooper, 'Retainers', p. 93.

78 *Calender of the Patent Rolls, 1563–1566* (London, 1960), p. 206, 3 Aug. 1565.

79 BL, Cottonian MS Galba, C VIII, ff. 96v–97.

80 The pensioners were Henry Barington and John Wotton, the Stables officer was Thomas Harrison.

81 W. J. Tighe, 'The Gentlemen Pensioners in Elizabethan Politics and Government' (unpublished Cambridge PhD diss., 1983), p. 126.

82 See his complaints against Leicester, HMC, *Salisbury*, III, p. 433, to Burghley, 28 Sept. 1589. Cf. Sidney to Walsingham on Arundell. *The Prose Works of Sir Philip Sidney*, III (ed. A. Feuillerat, Cambridge, 1963), p. 157.

83 For the 1587 household list see n. 56. No 1586 list can presently be traced. Leicester's Netherlands household account for 1586 was destroyed in the Birmingham Reference Library fire of 1879. A small extract is printed in E. H. Knowles, *The Castle of Kenilworth: A Guide for Visitors* (Warwick, 1872), pp. 46–50. [The extract is reprinted in *Household Accounts*, pp. 367–75, together with the 1587 household list.]

84 For the attendants at Leicester's funeral, see Bodleian Library, Ashmole MS 818, f. 38.

85 Carey provides an example of the difficulties of identification; should he be considered a servant of Leicester's or a member of a Court family?

86 Castilion has left a letterbook covering the period of his Low Countries service, now in the Beinecke Library of Yale University.

87 For Stanley and York, see my article, 'A Patriot for Whom? Stanley, York and Elizabeth's Catholics', *History Today*, 37 (July 1987), pp. 46–50.

Chapter 10

The Dudley clientele and the House of Commons, 1559–86[a]

I

The 'parliamentary patronage' of Robert Dudley, Earl of Leicester, has been the subject of debate since the eighteenth century.[1] In *The Elizabethan House of Commons* Sir John Neale provided what is now the established account, but it is one very much influenced by his preconceptions about the nature of Elizabethan politics. On the one hand Neale saw the pre-industrial House of Commons as an institution dominated by the political and social ambitions of the country gentry. He was close to being a county federalist, the 'federation of counties' being 'a misnomer' he felt that 'conveys a valuable truth'. On the other hand he also accepted the all-pervading influence of 'clientage', which was ultimately centred on the Court. He attempted to resolve the inherent contradiction by an artificial distinction (found throughout the book) between counties dominated by the leading gentry, and counties and boroughs patronised (for largely social rather than political reasons) by established peers. The influence of Leicester, the Court favourite, who 'unlike the great territorial magnates ... was promiscuous', was attributed to his novel exploitation of borough high stewardships.[2]

P. W. Hasler's article on Leicester in *The House of Commons, 1558–1603* is based on a draft by Neale. Not surprisingly, we find that Leicester's patronage was 'based not upon vast inherited estates, but upon borough lordships and high stewardships acquired through being a courtier and a royal favourite'. Hasler concludes, however, that 'considering Leicester's temperament and the fact that he was determined to gather into his hands as many borough nominations as he could, his achievement was moderate'.[3] In more recent work on the membership of the Commons Leicester's patronage has not been of major concern, but some important wider considerations have been raised. Although Mark Kishlansky follows Neale on the central importance of the social ambitions of the gentry, he poses the interesting question of the degree to which nominations by high stewards were part of the internal process of borough government rather than acts of external patronage and influence.[4] The importance given to 'men-of-business' by M. A. R. Graves and Sir Geoffrey Elton can be pushed to extremes, but it has also drawn our attention to the concern of the economically significant boroughs with parliamentary business.[5] We can no longer assume a willingness to sacrifice their very real interests in representation to social deference.

The present essay began as an attempt to establish more clearly the identities of Leicester's followers who sat in the House of Commons, about whom the compilers of the *House of Commons, 1558–1603* revealed an understandably limited knowledge. In the process, a number of broader questions have emerged, to which, in the absence of studies of comparable activity by other Elizabethan peers, only tentative answers can be advanced. The first is the possibly distorting effect of an emphasis on patronage, for patronage in the direct sense may have been only a last resort to place men who could not enter the House under their own auspices. In Leicester's case there is also the specific problem of the influence of his brother Ambrose, Earl of Warwick, who employed many of the same officers and agents, and whose role in the creation of any Dudley party in the House cannot be discounted.[6] This consideration accounts for the present title. Secondly, to what extent was Leicester's intervention undertaken as a Privy Councillor, rather than as a private individual or faction leader? Thirdly, to what extent is the assumption that high stewardships possessed an explicit electoral influence justified, and to what extent should they be seen as part of a wider pattern of land- and office-holding and borough patronage?

This essay will be divided into three sections. The first will review the evidence for Leicester's electioneering, and the circumstances under which it occurred. The second will examine the areas of his potential influence, the pattern of land- and office-holding, and the importance of the high stewardships. The last will survey the members of the Dudley clientele elected to the Parliaments of 1559 to 1584 on a Parliament by Parliament basis. Given the irregularity of Elizabethan elections prior to the 1590s, continuity of 'patronage' was of doubtful importance.[7] In this context Parliament was undoubtedly an event rather than an institution.

II

The surviving evidence of Leicester's electioneering is not extensive. For the Parliament of 1571, there is the draft answer of Chester to his nomination.[8] For 1572 we have the well-known letter to Denbigh and a reference to a recommendation at Windsor.[9] Nominations to by-elections were made at

Chester and Liverpool in 1582–83.[10] Only for the Parliament of 1584 is evidence available in any quantity. There are the letters requesting nominations sent to Andover and Gloucester, together with the decision taken by Gloucester, and a following letter to Maldon.[11] For Poole, Southampton and Tamworth (the last retrospectively) electoral agreements survive.[12] Requests also appear to have been made to Chester and St Albans.[13]

Leicester's wider correspondence yields only two references to electioneering. On 14 March 1571 Henry Goodere recommended a kinsman to him: 'if your lordship have any burgess-ship yet ungiven, your lordship may do well to bestow one on him, for he is a meet man of his years for the place.'[14] The second is found in an undated letter of 1580 from an officer of the Kenilworth staff, Anthony Dockwra, answering charges made against him by his colleague Henry Besbeche. One was Dockwra's conduct in the Warwickshire by-election of 1579:[15]

> that I have absented myself from Warwick when the knights of the shire should be chosen, being a freeholder within this shire, because I would not give my voice with Mr. Digby, for the good will I bear to Mr. Goodere. This last only I will answer now . . . George Turville told me he heard Henry Besbeche when he told your lordship this matter of Goodere. Now what opinion I have of long time had and yet have and shall while I live of him, for the cutting of the poor man's ears at Warwick, your lordship knoweth, and again for my freehold in the county of Warwick I will give it to Mr. Besbeche even for I have none at all and therefore he was to blame to trouble you with that untrue matter . . .

Both letters contain significant implications. The first suggests that Leicester was known to be a collector of burgessships by 1571, but also that he might be prepared to grant them to unknown third parties. The second leads to the conclusion that Leicester's officers (and by extension tenants) were expected to vote for specific candidates in county elections. But the further hint that there was some form of contest between Goodere and the successful candidate, George Digby, both of whom were among Leicester's leading followers in Warwickshire, also suggests that he had no absolute control over the shire election.

We can expect therefore to find significant electioneering on Leicester's part in the Parliaments of 1571, 1572 and 1584. Those of 1559, 1563 and 1586, however, demand a more cautious approach. The first two will be discussed below; 1586 can be resolved at this stage. The Queen's decision to summon a new Parliament on 15 September 1586 rather than recall the prorogued Parliament of 1584–85 was taken on the discovery that a significant number of its Members were 'employed in her majesty's service overseas'. Of these the greatest number (33 by one calculation) were with Leicester in the Netherlands.[16]

Before concluding from this (admittedly fragmentary) evidence that 1584 witnessed the culmination of a steadily expanding campaign of borough-mongering, another aspect of the elections of 1571, 1572 and 1584 must be considered. Each of these saw substantial intervention by the Privy Council. For 1571 and 1572 lists of recipients of circular letters survive, together with evidence to show that they were acted on. In 1571 Leicester was given respons-ibility for Berkshire and Worcestershire; in 1572 for Berkshire alone. Warwick-shire was assigned to his brother in both years.[17] The Council register for 1584 has not survived, but we do know it intervened in at least two Cinque Port elections.[18] Leicester's own electioneering in that year is therefore of considerable interest. Both his surviving initial requests (to Gloucester and Andover) were dated the day the writs were issued (12 October).[19] Only two days previously, the Privy Council, after a major conference on the question of assistance to the Netherlands, had recommended as 'most necessary':[20]

> to have a parliament called with speed which may by good order begin by the 20 or 23 of November and end before the 20 or 23 of December in which parliament beside the request of a subsidy, many other necessary provisions may be made for her majesty's more surety.

The purpose of the session (the Bond of Association (dated the 19th) being a secondary concern), and the haste in which it was summoned, sug-gest a major reappraisal of the evidence for the elections. Of Leicester's eight known approaches, in one (Andover) he was unaware that the borough did not possess the franchise; in another five (Gloucester, Poole, Southampton, St Albans and Maldon) his request appears to have been a novelty. In the cases of Gloucester, Andover, and (possibly) Maldon, he asked initially for a blank return, which he does not appear to have done in 1571 or 1572, though the evidence is not sufficient to establish the point. Yet this apparent exten-sion of his interest was not unique. At the same time Sir Francis Walsingham was making equally novel and ignorant requests (at Colchester and Christ-church, for example), with similar mixed success.[21]

In the absence of further research on the election as a whole, the conclu-sion must be provisional, but it would appear that Leicester and Walsingham, and possibly further members of the Council, were engaged in a massive and hasty trawl through the boroughs, regardless of previous connexion. Their intention was to place men who could be relied upon to support inter-vention in the Netherlands; private patronage was a secondary concern.[22] This would explain both the initial request for blanks and the marked confu-sion the surviving evidence reveals. At Poole Leicester nominated Walsing-ham's secretary Laurence Tomson. When it was discovered Tomson intended to sit for Melcombe Regis, he was replaced by another of Walsingham's secretaries, Francis Milles.[23] Yet Leicester himself possessed at least one prominent Dorset client, Robert Gregory (who sat for Poole in 1588), while his own secretaries, Arthur Atye and Alexander Neville, sat for Liverpool through the patronage of the Earl of Derby, and Christchurch through the patronage of the Earl of Huntingdon.[24] The correspondence between the Council, Lord Cobham and Hythe is equally instructive. Having first required Cobham simply to ensure that adequate men be chosen, several days later the Council specifically requested the nomination of Thomas Bodley, apparently unaware that Bodley was also being returned by Portsmouth.[25]

III

Given the fragmentary state of the evidence for electioneering, a brief survey of Leicester's territorial and borough influence is necessary. On Elizabeth's accession Lord Robert Dudley possessed four Norfolk manors (Hemsby near Great Yarmouth and Syderstone, Bircham Newton and Great Bircham from the Robsart estate), and had recently sold the ex-monastic complex of Hales Owen in Worcestershire and Staffordshire. The estate he assembled during the course of the reign was formed from a series of grants from and exchanges with the Crown in 1561, 1563, 1564, 1566, 1572 and 1574, the resolution in his favour of the Berkeley land case, and a number of private purchases, beginning with Watton (Yorks.) in 1559, and including Wanstead (Essex), initially leased in 1569, and Drayton Bassett (Staffs.) in 1579. From the Crown he also obtained a number of offices of territorial influence: the lieutenancy and constableship of Windsor Castle (1559–62), the chamberlaincy of the county palatine of Chester (2 July 1565), the chamberlaincy of Anglesey, Caernarvonshire and Merioneth (1578), the stewardship of the honour and forest of Grafton (1571), and the custodianship of the New Forest (1580).

By the mid-1570s, his estate had two main sections: a central core in the West Midlands (in Warwickshire, Worcestershire, Staffordshire, and to a lesser extent Shropshire), and four marcher lordships in Wales (Denbigh and Chirk in Denbighshire, Arwystli and Cyfeliog in Montgomeryshire). In a further four counties (Gloucestershire, Norfolk, the East Riding of Yorkshire and Essex) there were pockets of significance. In Cheshire and Berkshire, and, to a lesser extent, in Northamptonshire and Hampshire he was a major office-holder but possessed little if any land. He was lord lieutenant of Worcestershire and Warwickshire (the latter jointly with Sir Ambrose Cave) in Elizabeth's first experiment with lieutenancies in 1559–60, of Berkshire during the second (1569–70), of Leicestershire in 1584, and, after the permanent establishment in 1585, of Hertfordshire and Essex. With certain important exceptions (the Welsh lordships and Wanstead, for example) Leicester's estate was largely composed of lands that had previously belonged to the Duke of Northumberland. The restoring of 'the Dudley estate' was one of his more under-appreciated ambitions, and one that had two immediately relevant consequences. Since his brother Warwick also received former lands of their father's, the two estates were closely intermeshed, and, with the main exception again of the Welsh lordships, neither was in fact an intruder. Rather the early years of Elizabeth saw old alliances reforming and old enmities reviving.[26]

Leicester became the high steward of some 13 boroughs: Windsor (9 September 1563), Abingdon (?1566, 8 August 1581), Reading (?1566, 20 November 1567), Wallingford (20 February 1569), Bristol (20 April 1570), Great Yarmouth (10 June 1572), King's Lynn (18 June 1572), Andover by 1574, Tewkesbury by 1575, Harrow-on-the-Hill after 9 July 1575, St Albans after 1579, and from an unknown date Evesham and possibly Barnet.[27] This was not, however, the only dimension to his urban patronage. He was recorder of Maldon after 1583, lord of the manor at Beverley between 1561 and an exchange with the Crown in 1566, and possibly also at Tamworth and Denbigh. In Chester his influence was derived from the chamberlaincy of the palatinate, in Southampton from the farm of the customs on sweet wines.[28] It is revealing of the complexity of these relationships, though, that he held no office in Coventry, the city to which he was otherwise closest.[29]

Only at Bristol and King's Lynn does sufficient evidence survive to make possible a partial reconstruction of the process of appointment. Bristol had had two previous high stewards, the Duke of Somerset and the first Earl of Pembroke, both of whom had combined local and conciliar prominence. When Pembroke died in March 1570, the office was solicited by his heir, Somerset's son the Earl of Hertford, and Lord Chandos. The city council retired into a special session on 22 March, and emerged having chosen Leicester and established an ordinance that all future high stewards were to be Privy Councillors.[30] Leicester was King's Lynn's first high steward. The borough had paid annuities to Northumberland, but not apparently to the Duke of Norfolk, although he was frequently consulted on local affairs. After Norfolk's trial in 1572, the town council requested the advice of the recorder, Robert Bell, on whether to appoint a high steward, and whether the office should be offered to Leicester or to Burghley.[31] For the other towns we are reduced to supposition. It is assumed that the appointment at Windsor arose from the constableship of the castle, and that the other three Berkshire boroughs (who operated closely together) simply followed suit.[32] At Warwick, as at Great Yarmouth (where he had been succeeded by Norfolk), Northumberland had been high steward. After his fall Sir Robert Throckmorton of Coughton had obtained the constableship of Warwick Castle and stewardship of the borough. In 1562, after two years of negotiation, Robert Dudley purchased the offices from Throckmorton, but then either gave or sold them to his brother, who had become Earl of Warwick in the meantime.[33]

Warwick (which may have been a special case) provides the only example of Leicester deliberately collecting a high stewardship. It is not impossible, however, that a 'spontaneous' offer might have been engineered by local partisans, though in neither Bristol nor King's Lynn can they be clearly identified. Some minor figures have been suggested, such as Gabriel Blike in Cirencester and Tewkesbury, but the clearest evidence survives for the trio of Anthony Forster in Abingdon, William Glasier in Chester and William Grice (or, as he preferred, Le Grice) in Yarmouth.[34] All three were old Dudley followers, who were in Lord Robert's service at Elizabeth's accession; in the case of Grice (Clerk of the Stables, an office in Leicester's gift, by 1564) and Glasier (vice-chamberlain of the palatinate and customer of Chester from May 1559) this was combined with office-holding under the Crown.[35] All sat as M.P.s for their respective boroughs, but only Grice, who has been described as occupying 'an ideally suitable position' as a spokesman for Yarmouth's interests, was a prominent Member of the House.[36] Glasier, by contrast, was notoriously quarrelsome and the cause of much tension within Chester.

There is therefore no direct connexion between Leicester's high stewardships and parliamentary patronage. No rights of nomination are specified, as they were to be later, in his surviving patents of appointment.[37] In the case of Bristol, no attempt to nominate appears to have been made. Nor is there any evidence of a campaign of enfranchisement. Of the 32 boroughs that obtained the franchise during Elizabeth's reign, only three have been attributed to Leicester (and that purely by supposition): the resumption by Beverley in 1563, Cirencester in 1572 and Andover in 1586.[38] Many of the boroughs with which he was associated (Bristol, Coventry, Chester, King's Lynn, Yarmouth and Southampton being the most obvious) were leading urban centres, with long traditions of municipal government and important economic interests. They took parliamentary business seriously, but also clearly saw in Leicester a potentially powerful advocate at Council and Court, whom it would be worth gratifying on occasion. The smaller boroughs (Beverley, the Berkshire towns, Denbigh, Tamworth, Maldon and St Albans, for example) may have been more obliging and more malleable (though not necessarily), but here the relationship was more that of a lord of the manor than a high steward.

Two further general aspects of borough 'patronage' should be raised here. The first is that of the return of his officers or followers by boroughs where there was no obvious connexion. Three – Lichfield, Droitwich and Cirencester – were on the periphery of the West Midlands nexus, while the Buckinghamshire boroughs of Aylesbury and Chipping Wycombe may have borne a similar relationship to Berkshire.[39] In the case of the two followers who sat for Colchester (Sir Francis Jobson and Robert Christmas) direct patronage by Leicester may have been unnecessary, since both were local men. More curious is the election of Arthur Atye by Liverpool in 1583. In January 1582 the Earl of Derby obtained the agreement of Liverpool to the election of Atye to replace an existing M.P. on grounds of illness. In April Leicester recommended Atye to Chester in a by-election there, but in June Atye was admitted a burgess of Liverpool, and then a burgess of the Parliament following the death of the sitting Member in April 1583. Although it was perfectly clear who Atye was, Leicester was never mentioned in the correspondence, which remained a private affair between Derby and Liverpool.[40] The Cornish boroughs form a separate category of their own. Clients of Leicester's, none of whom were residents, sat for at least six Cornish boroughs between 1563 and 1586, in some cases for more than one election. In Henry and William Killigrew Leicester possessed important Cornish followers, but otherwise he held neither land nor office in the county. The Killigrews possessed some influence at Helston and Truro, but it is difficult to avoid the impression that Leicester was making use of a system whereby the Cornish boroughs, by means of blank indentures possibly managed by the 2nd Earl of Bedford, were employed as a reserve for members of the Privy Council.[41]

The second general point is the degree to which Leicester's nominations took local associations into account. The standard method of evading the statutory residence requirement for boroughs was the device of admitting the future M.P. to the burgess-ship on the eve of election.[42] The debate in the House in 1571 over the repeal of the relevant statutes (1 Hen. V, c. 1. and 23 Hen. VI, c. 14) reveals considerable anxiety over interference by noblemen, possibly inspired by the Council's circular.[43] However inconclusive the result of the debate, continued restiveness is detectable at (for example) Windsor, Gloucester and Yarmouth.[44] Leaving out the obvious examples of Forster, Grice or Glasier, Leicester's practice is not easy to determine. The request for blanks in 1584 may have been the result of the specific circumstances of that election, rather than (with the exception of the Cornish boroughs) the norm. Richard Browne was recommended to Maldon as 'your countryman', but, on the other hand, neither Thomas Digges at Southampton nor Milles at Poole were local men. In the absence of further letters of nomination no firm conclusions can be drawn; but Leicester may have made some effort to uphold the principle of local representation.

IV

Possibly the most difficult aspect of this section, and the most controversial feature of the essay, is the treatment of those Dudley clients whose immediate association with Leicester is clear, but in whose election no involvement can be found. The emphasis here is on the minor figures; men of individual prominence (like Sir Philip Sidney) have been excluded. No attempt has been made to quantify the size of the clientele in each Parliament, for there are too many marginal cases.

1559

In 1559 Lord Robert Dudley was returned as knight of the shire for Norfolk, a seat he had held in the Parliament of March 1553. His small estate would limit any wider influence, despite his recent appointment as Master of the Horse.[45] No evidence of his intervention survives, nor were any of his men-of-business returned. Yet on the other hand a significant body of earlier Dudley partisans can be found, many of whom had been excluded voluntarily or otherwise from most of the Marian Parliaments. They were, however, men of local prominence in their own right, and could obtain seats without Lord Robert's help, though the influence of the general political climate of the new reign cannot be discounted.

The process can be seen most clearly in the West Midlands. For Staffordshire and Newcastle-under-Lyme the two Bagnall brothers, Sir Ralph and Sir Nicholas, were returned. Both had been prominent clients of Northumberland and are found in his son's following early in Elizabeth's reign, as was the recorder of Coventry, Sir John Throckmorton, who sat for the city as he had done regularly throughout Mary's reign.[46] Other important former Edwardians sat for Gloucester (Sir Nicholas Arnold), Warwick borough (Thomas Fisher), and Bridgnorth (Sir George Blount, one of the executors of the Duchess of Northumberland's will).[47] A scattering of former Dudley clients can be found elsewhere. Sir Francis Jobson and Edward Aglionby sat for Colchester and Carlisle, as they had done in March 1553.[48] Sir Henry Gates was returned for the Duke of Norfolk's borough of Bramber, Walter Haddon for Poole, where Bedford was the immediate patron, and Clement Throckmorton (who had sat for Warwick borough in March 1553) for Sudbury, a Duchy of Lancaster borough.[49] Less clear is the connexion to Dudley of the brothers Robert and Thomas Colshill who sat for Mitchell and Knaresborough.[50]

Only the election for Worcestershire of his cousin Thomas Blount of Kidderminster may reflect Lord Robert's influence. Blount, formerly comptroller to Northumberland and a household officer to Dudley, served as his deputy lieutenant for the county later in the year, but had not sat as an M.P. before. His sudden prominence is suspicious.[51] There is no evidence of these men acting in any united manner during the session, except in one regard: a desire either for restitution in blood or compensation for losses suffered in 1553.[52] Jobson was directly involved in two bills for the restoration of episcopal estates in the dioceses of Worcester and Durham obtained in Edward's reign and lost in Mary's, a concern shared by Sir John Throckmorton and Fisher.[53] A Dudley restoration had much to offer them.[54]

1563

By 1563 the Dudleys had to some extent been re-established in the West Midlands, through Lord Ambrose's restoration to the earldom of Warwick, and the grants made to him and Lord Robert in 1561–62.[55] Lord Robert was also constable of Windsor Castle, lord of Beverley and (since 10 October 1562) a Privy Councillor. Sir Geoffrey Elton has 'discerned' a Dudley faction active in the Commons debates on the Queen's marriage and the Succession. Yet the absence of direct evidence for electioneering forces any analysis to be based on inference.[56] Nor is the role of the Privy Council clear. It certainly intervened in the Essex shire election, but whether it did so more widely cannot be established.[57]

A number of the 1559 Members are found again: Blount for Worcestershire, Jobson for Colchester, Arnold for Gloucester, Ralph Bagnall (this time for Newcastle-under-Lyme), Gates (this time for Scarborough), Clement Throckmorton (Warwickshire) and Thomas Colshill (Aylesbury). Sir James Croft now sat for Herefordshire; Henry Goodere (Stafford) may or may not have been a Dudley follower at this time.[58] The novel aspect is the return of several of Lord Robert's 'men-of-business'. Great Yarmouth provides the most dramatic evidence of possible electioneering. On 22 November 1562 Walter Haddon and William Grice were admitted to the burgess-ship, an entry afterwards scored out. On 7 January 1563 Grice and Thomas Timperley, one of Norfolk's officers, were elected first to the burgess-ship and then as burgesses of the Parliament. Haddon was later admitted to the burgess-ship and granted an annuity; he was returned for Warwick.[59] Although the writs were not issued until 5 December 1562, it looks suspiciously as though Dudley had (possibly through Grice) attempted to obtain both Yarmouth seats, but had backed down before Norfolk. Haddon's seat at Warwick appears to have been compensation. His colleague, the principal burgess John Butler, was later one of the chief officers of Kenilworth, and may already have been in the Dudley orbit.[60] Both of Coventry's M.P.s (Thomas Dudley and Richard Grafton) had close associations with Lord Robert. Unusually for a major city, neither was a resident.[61]

Dudley also placed two men-of-business in Cornish boroughs: John Dudley (the brother of Thomas, and M.P. for Carlisle in March 1553) at Helston and William Glasier at St Ives.[62] He may also have been responsible for the election of Thomas Wilson at Mitchell and John Harington at St Ives.[63] Since Henry Killigrew was then a prisoner of war in France, Bedford seems the most obvious local influence. One of Chester's M.P.s, the clerk of the Pentice,

John Yerwerth, was also a legal agent of Lord Robert's.[64] One Welsh M.P., Dr Ellis Price of Merioneth, was an old Dudley partisan, but his connexion at this stage is unclear.[65]

However, before we can see these elections as evidence of deliberate faction-building, some contradictory examples must be taken into account. There is no reason to doubt that Dudley was behind Beverley's resumption of the franchise, yet neither of the M.P.s was prominent in his entourage. Little is known about the Gentleman Pensioner Robert Hall. Nicholas Bacon, the Lord Keeper's son, may have been in Dudley's household, or his return may have been a favour to his father.[66] The situation in Berkshire is equally vague. Dudley did not become high steward of Windsor until the following autumn, though the close connexion between the town and castle would make a formal relationship less important. The mayor who granted the high stewardship, Richard Gallys, is said to have initiated the debate on the succession on 16 January 1563, but there is no evidence that it was at Dudley's behest.[67] Abingdon was represented by Oliver Hyde, the vice-master of Christ's Hospital, whose relationship to Dudley remains speculative.[68] Hyde was replaced by Anthony Forster after his death in 1566, but the writ for the by-election was not issued until 24 October, after the second session had begun, and then by order of the House.[69] The younger Henry Knollys, a servant of Dudley's in 1559, sat for Reading, but given Lord Robert's closeness to his family and his father's own prominence, assignment of specific influence is impossible.[70] A significant number of Dudley followers were certainly Members of the House, whether by his means or their own, but there is no evidence that they acted as a coherent faction, and Lord Robert does not appear to have employed his 'patronage' to create one.

1571

Despite the loss of the returns, the 1571 Parliament presents fewer problems than its predecessors. Leicester's estate was now largely established, there was clear intervention from the Privy Council, and evidence of electioneering survives. An important generational change is also observable, as the older Dudley partisans died off and a younger body of men emerged who were more directly protégés of Leicester and Warwick. The process is most clear in the West Midlands, where four men – (Sir) John Huband, (Sir) Henry Goodere, (Sir) George Digby and Edward Boughton – rose to local prominence in the 1570s and 1580s as officers of both Earls. Their significance has been obscured by the fact that only Goodere outlived Leicester and Warwick by any length of time. The most important of them was Huband who not only succeeded Thomas Blount (*d.* 28 November 1568) as constable of

Kenilworth in 1572, but by the end of the 1570s had become Leicester's leading officer in Wales as well.[71]

In accordance with the Council's instructions, Warwick intervened directly in the borough of Warwick to make the unexceptional nomination of the recorder, Edward Aglionby. The burgesses offered the second seat to the town clerk, John Fisher, an open follower of Leicester's.[72] Huband became the junior knight of the shire, his predecessor (and brother-in-law) Clement Throckmorton sitting for West Looe. Goodere sat for Coventry, either through his own influence or Leicester's. In Staffordshire a more complicated situation is revealed. Leicester's chief allies in the county had been the Bagnalls (Sir Ralph sat again for Newcastle-under-Lyme), but he had also been on good terms with both the 1st and 2nd Lords Paget, though with the 3rd Baron relations deteriorated steadily during the 1570s. The shire election of 1571, which turned into a contest between Bagnall and the Harcourts (who appear to have been the backbone of gentry Catholicism), and saw the election of Thomas Trentham, later to be one of Leicester's followers, may have contained a deeper significance.[73] Likewise some influence may be detected in several of the borough elections. Lichfield, which had been dominated by the Pagets, now returned Edward Fitzgerald, Lieutenant of the Gentlemen Pensioners, while Tamworth returned Edward Lewkenor.[74] Sir Nicholas Poyntz, whose family had strong Dudley connexions, sat for Gloucestershire and Gabriel Blike for the newly enfranchised Cirencester.[75]

In view of the council's circulars, Worcestershire and Berkshire deserve joint consideration. The death of Thomas Blount removed the leading Dudley follower in Worcestershire, and no direct connexion can be established to the two knights of the shire. However, the M.P. for Droitwich, the minor poet Francis Kinwelmersh, may have been one of Leicester's secretaries at this time.[76] Berkshire (where Leicester was now high steward of the four parliamentary boroughs) was, on the other hand, the scene of considerable activity. The knights of the shire (Sir Henry Neville and Richard Ward) and the burgesses for Windsor (John Thompson and Humphrey Mitchell) were all members of the castle staff and may reflect his influence.[77] At Abingdon Anthony Forster was returned; at Wallingford, Thomas Dudley; while Reading elected Henry Knollys the younger again and John Hastings.[78] There was also a spill-over into Buckinghamshire, where Edward Dockwra, another Windsor Castle officer, was returned for Aylesbury, and Robert Christmas, Leicester's treasurer, for Chipping Wycombe.[79]

At Chester we possess evidence of Leicester's nomination of William Glasier, whom the city agreed to elect only as a gesture to him. Interestingly enough, the city's original choice had been another of his officers, the lawyer Robert Snagge, whom he had recommended for a burgess-ship in 1569.[80] Snagge sat in the end for Lostwithiel. This, the case of Clement Throckmorton, and possibly Robert Colshill at Newport provide the only clear examples of Leicester's use of Cornish boroughs in this Parliament. Elsewhere a range of his followers are found returned for seats through their own influence: Grice again for Yarmouth, Henry Killigrew for a family borough (Truro), Gates for Yorkshire, Sir Simon Musgrave and his son Christopher for Cumberland and Carlisle respectively, and Edward Horsey, captain of the Isle of Wight, for Southampton.[81] In Merioneth there was a contest involving his ally Ellis Price; this became part of a larger power struggle in north Wales the following year, but there is no evidence that Leicester was involved at this stage.[82]

1572

The solid body of Dudley officers and clients returned for the Parliament of 1571 are found again in the House in 1572. The proximity of the two elections provided the one opportunity for continuity of patronage, but both reshuffling of seats and omissions are discovered. The Council's circulars may have played a similar role, though the significance of the removal of Worcestershire from Leicester's commission (if it was more than a copyist's error) is unclear.

To begin with the West Midlands, Clement Throckmorton was returned again as junior knight for Warwickshire. Huband did not sit, though he replaced his brother-in-law in the by-election following Throckmorton's death in 1575. In the borough, Warwick replaced Aglionby with Thomas Dudley, though John Fisher continued as his partner. At Coventry, on the other hand, both M.P.s were townsmen. There appears to have been no Dudley activity in Worcestershire; Kinwelmersh sat for Bossiney instead. In Staffordshire, Fitzgerald sat again for Lichfield, but this time one of Leicester's legal councillors, John Nuthall, for Tamworth.[83] Arnold was returned as junior knight for Gloucestershire, but there is no evidence of Leicester's involvement in Cirencester.

In Berkshire, Leicester may have been involved in the election of William Foster as junior knight. Anthony Forster was returned again for Abingdon; Leicester nominated Edward Dockwra at Windsor (his partner was Gallys); at Wallingford Thomas Digges replaced Thomas Dudley. Another of Sir Francis Knollys's sons sat for Reading, but so did Francis Alford, to whom Leicester had no obvious connexion.[84] Further afield, Glasier was returned again for Chester; Grice for Yarmouth; Musgrave for Cumberland. Gates sat for Scarborough, Horsey for Hampshire, Christmas for Colchester and Robert Colshill for Portsmouth. It would appear that Leicester may have used Beverley again, for of the two M.P.s, Thomas Aglionby was his servant, and Richard Topcliffe regarded himself as one of his followers.[85] Two Norfolk lawyers, Edward Flowerdew and Charles Calthrope, who were later Leicester's deputies at Great Yarmouth, sat for Castle Rising and Eye, but since Leicester did not become high steward until after the Parliament no significance can be attached to their presence.[86] Snagge and Killigrew sat again for their Cornish boroughs of 1571, but now William Killigrew for Helston and Kinwelmersh for Bossiney. None of his other officers can be found, though he may have been involved in the placing of Thomas Randolph at St Ives, Henry MacWilliam at Liskeard, and William Knollys at Tregony.[87]

The explosion at Denbigh should not be taken out of its local context, about which there has been a major misconception. It had less to do with borough-mongering on Leicester's part than a growing struggle for power with the leading county family, Salusbury of Lleweni, that came into the open in the borough's parliamentary and aldermanic elections in 1572. The reference to his goodwill was more than mere rhetoric, for he had recently given the town the land to build a new shire hall.[88] Nor was the tone unusually sharp for the period.[89] Leicester had apparently nominated the auditor of the lordship of Denbigh, Henry Dynne, but the borough had returned Thomas Salusbury, whose name appears in one of the Crown Office lists.[90] On the indenture itself, the original name has been erased and Richard Cavendish substituted.[91] At what stage Leicester had the election reversed, and why he substituted Cavendish for Dynne, are unclear. He does not appear to have intervened in any other Welsh election, though Price may have been again successful in Merioneth.

The three sessions of the Parliament also created a number of by-elections. At Abingdon Anthony Forster (who died in November 1572) was replaced in 1576 by the Stables officer Richard Beake.[92] After Kinwelmersh died in 1581, no further use was made of Bossiney, but the efforts made on behalf of Atye, Leicester's new chief secretary, at Chester and Liverpool in 1582–83 suggest a serious concern to place him in the House. In Warwickshire Huband was returned after the death of Clement Throckmorton in 1575; in 1579 George Digby replaced Sir William Devereux. In 1574 Leicester's rising follower William Thomas replaced John Gwynne in Caernarvonshire.[93] Other by-elections are less clear: the return of John Peyton for King's Lynn in 1579–80, the Lord Keeper's son Edward Bacon for Yarmouth in 1576, and Fulk Greville for Southampton in 1581 may reflect Leicester's influence but the surmise cannot be substantiated. More mysterious still is Coventry's choice of Bartholomew Tate, a minor Northamptonshire squire, in 1573.[94]

1584

The circumstances of Leicester's interventions in 1584 have already been discussed. Equally important is the departure of so many of these M.P.s (indicated below by an asterisk) on the Netherlands expedition in the following year. While all the members of the expedition cannot be described as Leicester's immediate followers, the core certainly were.[95]

In Warwickshire George Digby* was returned again for the shire together with Sir Thomas Lucy. The now established pattern was repeated in the borough with the election of Thomas Dudley and John Fisher. At Coventry Edward Boughton* (who may have had his own contacts with the city) was returned for the first time.[96] In Worcestershire Jasper Chomley* sat for Droitwich.[97] Three of Leicester's followers are found sitting for Staffordshire boroughs: Clement Fisher* (Tamworth), Richard Browne* (Lichfield) and Peter Warburton (Newcastle-under-Lyme). In the case of Tamworth, Leicester is known to have received one nomination; Browne and Warburton had been unsuccessful nominees elsewhere.[98] The M.P. for Much Wenlock (William Baynham) was one of his auditors, but in this instance local connexions may have been at work.[99]

Berkshire presents a novel picture. Sir Henry Neville was senior knight for the county; his son (and Killigrew's son-in-law) sat for New Windsor. Sir Francis Knollys's sons Robert and Richard sat for Reading and Wallingford; Edward Norris* sat for Abingdon. Only one of Leicester's men-of-business sat for a local seat: John Morley, a surveyor of the customs, at Chipping Wycombe.[100] This apparent revival of the power of the local gentry families has been seen as a withdrawal by Leicester from the county. Though the absence of a circular from the Council may have been significant, the extent of the 'withdrawal' can be exaggerated. Neville was deputy constable of the castle and all the families were on good terms with Leicester at the time.

In the absence of any clear previous association with Gloucester on which Leicester could base his request, it is difficult to avoid the surmise that it may have had something to do with the resolution of the dispute with Bristol over Gloucester's customs house. In 1576, when the dispute began, Bristol had appealed for, and obtained, Leicester's assistance as their high steward. Thereafter Burghley, to whom as Lord Treasurer matters involving the customs pertained, had been the principal mediator of the affair. But Leicester's influence may also have been at work. The customer of Gloucester, Kennard Delaber, may have been the man of that name arrested at King's Lynn in 1553 as one of Lord Robert's party.[101] Thomas Throckmorton of Totworth, the leader of the panel of local gentry commissioned as mediators in 1582, was close to Leicester. His nephew Sir John Tracy, the senior knight in 1584, was a former servant of Leicester's, and several of Tracy's sons served in the Netherlands.[102]

Leicester was markedly more successful in the north-west and Wales. If he was baulked at Chester, Hugh Cholmondley*, the junior knight for Cheshire, may have been a former member of his household.[103] In Lancashire his 'old servant' Richard Bold* was returned as a knight of the shire in a

by-election after the beginning of the session, and Atye* sat for Liverpool.[104]
Richard Cavendish* was returned again for Denbigh, while the county seat
went to Evan Lloyd* of Bodidris, steward of the lordship of Chirk, the first
open follower of Leicester's to sit for the shire.[105] William Thomas* sat again
for Caernarvonshire, while Ellis Price continued to dominate Merioneth,
whose M.P. was his grand-nephew Cadwaladr Price*.

King's Lynn and Yarmouth returned Peyton* and Grice. Beverley chose
the otherwise obscure Suffolk Puritan lawyer Robert Wrote, who served Leicester as a legal agent.[106] If Leicester was apparently unsuccessful at St Albans
and Maldon, the south coast and Cornish boroughs proved more amenable.
Thomas Digges* now sat for Southampton on Leicester's nomination, as did
Milles for Poole; Alexander Neville sat for Christchurch and Thomas Bodley
for Portsmouth.[107] In Cornwall Leicester's influence may be suspected at St
Germans, which returned Henry Dynne, his unsuccessful candidate at
Denbigh in 1572, at St Ives (Dr John James*) and possibly at Mitchell (Edward
Barker*?).[108] The lawyers William Lewis (Helston) and William Clerk*
(Saltash) may also have received his backing.[109]

V

In 1586 Warwick was an active patron, the more so since he also controlled
the Bedford influence as guardian to the 3rd Earl. He may have undertaken
to replace some of the men then with Leicester in the Netherlands, as, for
example, at Lichfield where John Goodman, a lawyer who worked for both
Earls was returned, or Denbigh where the M.P. was now Robert Wrote.[110]
Other Dudley officers like William Baynham at Much Wenlock, Thomas
Dudley at Warwick and Grice at Yarmouth continued to sit for their old
seats. Yet despite their presence and the fact that Warwick would nominate
again in 1588–89, the Dudley clientele in Parliament ceased to be of importance after 1585.

The central conclusion suggested by the evidence presented here is that
Leicester's concern was less to control seats than to place certain individuals
in the House. If these men possessed their own influence, so much the
better; his own 'patronage' and that of the Crown he was able to tap provided
a reserve. A narrow definition of patronage is therefore less than useful, for
it excludes the very substantial body of men who though followers sat for
their own seats, servants of his who were also servants of the Crown, and
third-party nominations, whether on his behalf or provided by him. It is also
difficult to avoid the impression that the Privy Council's attitude towards
parliamentary elections (as expressed in the circular letters in particular) was
one of collegiality rather than the advancing of private factions. In this respect both the Dudley clientele and the 'Council's men-of-business' were less

the instruments of a single individual or individuals than members of the body of 'discrete and wise men' (as the 1571 circular put it) that the Council wished to see in the House.

Conciliar intervention may, therefore, have been more significant than previously accepted. It may also have contributed greatly to the Protestant bias of the house, less in the patronizing of a specifically Puritan faction or factions, than in the exclusion of others deemed less loyal. County elections may have been less the result of the independent manoeuvres of 'county governors', for their position too (as for example in Warwickshire or Denbighshire) was in flux. Having said this, however, no clear patterns to Leicester's interventions emerge. The problem of nomination of locals has already been raised; it is equally difficult to establish whether he usually asked for only one seat. He appears to have tried for both at Gloucester and Andover in 1584, but the circumstances may have been unusual. Nor is there any evidence that he encouraged the rotation of Members to educate the gentry as the 2nd Earl of Pembroke claimed to have done.[111]

The activities of both Leicester and the Dudley clientele within Parliament demand a more extensive treatment than can be given here. But some lines of approach emerge. Possibly the most striking aspect of the Dudley clientele in the House is the minimal impact so many of them made on its proceedings. Even Arthur Atye, for whom Leicester was so concerned to find a seat in 1582–83, played a minor role at best in the session of 1584–85. The clientele included a small group of prominent and active parliamentarians (Digges, Robert Snagge and Grice being the obvious examples), but they appear to have been a minority. The advancing of legislation could not, therefore, have been Leicester's primary concern in electioneering. He himself put through only one private act: the 1571 statute (13 Eliz. I, c. 17) for the incorporation of a hospital at either Kenilworth or Warwick. This was an uncontroversial measure that would not involve the mobilization of support.[112]

A more complicated issue is his possible involvement in the parliamentary business of the boroughs with which he was associated. The surviving evidence is, however, inconclusive. In 1576 Bristol made strenuous efforts to defeat the bill which they claimed would lead to 'the inhabitants of Gloucester . . . obtaining of landing and discharging places for merchandises and wares'. This appears to have been Burghley's abortive bill to extend landing places. Later in the year the city presented Leicester with a tun of gascon wine 'in consideration of his pains that he took to move my Lord Treasurer of the indirect dealings of the deputies of the custom house of Gloucester and for his favour and furtherance that he shewed them at the last parliament'. But it was to their M.P.s, also rewarded with wine, that they attributed 'the overthrow' of the bill 'which was put in and passed by the lords house'.[113]

No clearer is Leicester's connexion to the 1581 'fisheries act' (23 Eliz. I, c. 7). The bill received its first reading in the Lords on 16 February and was brought down to the Commons on 4 March. However on 30 January Thomas Digges had already proposed a motion 'for maintenance of the navy and mariners' which had been referred to a committee of Privy Councillors and interested M.P.s.[114] Elton has suggested that this committee was allowed to lapse 'no doubt aware that the Upper House was about to consider cognate proposals'.[115] But the chain of events can equally well be explained by the adoption of Digges's proposals by the Councillors on the committee and the introduction of a bill to that effect in the Lords with their general blessing.[116] Thus the involvement of both Digges and Grice in the successful passage of the bill need not imply Leicester's orchestration. Yarmouth did not acknowledge any particular favour by Leicester at this Parliament, though they may not have considered it necessary, having decided in the previous year to make regular gifts of fish to such lords of the Council 'who hath been good and gracious to this town to the end this town shall not be found ungrateful'.[117]

The limited reference to Leicester's parliamentary support is in striking contrast to the open recognition given to his intervention on behalf of his boroughs with the Queen and Council.[118] His offers of assistance were couched in broad terms; he assured Maldon in 1584 that Richard Browne '(if your occasions shall serve) shall have my help at any time to do your town what convenient pleasure may be'.[119] Leicester may well have encouraged his clients to attend to local issues, for the activities of Grice on behalf of Yarmouth were not unique. Christ's Hospital, Abingdon, gave Anthony Forster presents in 1571 on his 'going to the parliament about the business of the hospital'; Southampton entertained and rewarded Digges for his services in 1584.[120] But the implication remains that parliamentary business was regarded as the primary concern of the borough's M.P.s and as a House of Commons matter; Leicester operated on a conciliar level.

Most difficult is the possible relationship between electioneering and the use of Parliament in matters of state. The argument presented here that Leicester's electioneering in 1584 may have been motivated by a desire to ensure support for intervention in the Netherlands in the House raises the question of whether it was a unique episode. The proposed benevolence to finance the intervention in 1587 would appear to have been the logical outcome of such a view of Parliament, and Neale has argued that Leicester was behind it.[121] His role is still unclear, but for reasons also discussed here the success of the benevolence in the House cannot be attributed to the strength of a Dudley faction there during that session. However close to the Dudley nexus Job Throckmorton may have been, his election at Warwick in 1586 was a purely personal initiative.[122]

In the case of the Parliaments of 1571 and 1572 the issue is obscured by the Privy Council's circular letters. The role of Digges in the debates over Mary, Queen of Scots, in 1572 raises the question of whether the new M.P.s Leicester may have nominated in 1572 were chosen for a purpose; but the others (Aglionby and Topcliffe at Beverley and Nuthall at Tamworth) left no mark on the proceedings of the House. 1563 and 1566 are clearly the most intriguing, given that the petitioning of the Queen to marry would appear to have been very much in Leicester's interest. However, Leicester's slowness to take advantage of the vacancy at Abingdon in 1566 is hardly evidence of a concern to pack Parliament with his supporters. The evidence of electioneering in 1563 is more suggestive, but in this session the central issue was the Succession not the Queen's marriage, and Dudley's involvement in Anglo-Scots relations would have predisposed him against bringing the issue into the open.[123] Support for the expedition to Le Havre would have been a more straightforward motive for electioneering in 1562–63.

It is also revealing that the M.P. who is said to have initiated the Succession debate of 1563 – Richard Gallys, the mayor of Windsor – also initiated the debate on Mary, Queen of Scots, in 1572.[124] That so provincial a figure could have been so outspoken leads one, in the absence of further evidence, back to a Whiggish conclusion. Active Elizabethan parliamentarians were active because they wanted to be, not because they were the instruments of faction or the men-of-business of the Council. This would apply to Leicester's clients as much as anyone else. It may well be that he made no real attempt to dictate or co-ordinate the activities of his followers in the House, as has recently been argued for the Earl of Salisbury in the early Parliaments of James I.[125] His influence on the House would therefore have been an indirect one. It was less the positive directing of a discrete interest than the creation of a climate of benevolent tolerance towards Parliament-men (similar to his tolerance towards Puritan agitators) which encouraged them to express their views without fear of the consequences. If things could (and did) get out of hand, that was in the nature of a free Parliament, not the product of factional politics.

POSTSCRIPT

While working on the Evelyn MSS. in Christ Church Library, Oxford, shortly before receiving the proofs of this article, I was informed that Leicester's household accounts for Oct. 1584–Dec. 1585 had recently been discovered by the Canadian literary scholar S.-B. MacLean among papers relating to the Evelyn family (see her note 'Leicester and the Evelyns: New Evidence for the Continental Tour of Leicester's men', *Review of English Studies*, XXXIX [1988], 487–93). Prior to this only the two volumes for 1558–61 (now Dudley MSS.

XIV–XV) were known to be extant, though several others, which were once among the Evelyn MSS., survived until 1879 (see above notes 79 and 109). [Now published in *Household Accounts*.]

The page for 12 Oct. 1584 contains a single reference to the dispatch of a messenger. He was sent to Portsmouth, but his purpose is not described, and we cannot assume it was related to Bodley's election there. The absence of others supports the suggestion made above that Leicester's letters of nomination were sent with the pursuivants carrying the writs. The accounts confirm the attachment to Leicester's household and service of a number of the M.P.s discussed here: Arthur Atye, Thomas Dudley, Alexander Neville, Edward Boughton, Richard Browne, Richard Cavendish, Gabriel Blike, Richard Topcliffe, and the sons of Sir John Tracy. To them should be added three further Members of the 1584 Parliament: Richard Drake (Castle Rising), Richard Knollys (Reading) and the younger Frances Knollys (Oxford). Richard Lloyd, Leicester's junior secretary, may have been the otherwise unidentified M.P. for Flint Boroughs. One further prominent member of the household, 'Mr. Sandys', presents greater difficulties. He was probably not Miles Sandys (M.P. for Abingdon, 1586), who was then a legal officer of the Crown. His son Edwin (M.P. for Andover, 1586) is more likely, but we cannot rule out his nephew the future Sir Edwin.

NOTES

a The research on which this essay is based was made possible by grants from the British Academy, the Wolfson Foundation and the Carnegie Trust for the Universities of Scotland. I should also like to thank the Most Honourable the Marquess of Bath for permission to employ the Dudley MSS. at Longleat House, and the archivists of numerous county and borough record offices (and in particular those of Chester, Poole, Abingdon and Norfolk) for their generosity with their time. P. W. Hasler, *The House of Commons 1558–1603* (3 vols., 1981 [hereafter *HP 1558–1603*]) is now the indispensable biographical source. To avoid unnecessary notes, reference will be made to it only when I cannot confirm the source employed. The notes are used for biographical information not to be found there. In the interests of uniformity I have followed its spelling of surnames.

1 His letter to Andover of 12 Oct. 1584 was published in *The Gentleman's Magazine*, I (1731), 319–20, in the course of a dispute over the conduct of elections with Bolingbroke in *The Craftsman*. It was reprinted in H. A. Merewether and A. J. Stephens, *The History of Boroughs and Municipal Corporations in the United Kingdom* (2 vols., 1835), II, 1393–94. Its present location is unknown: no reference is found in the *Catalogue of Andover Borough Records* (Andover, 1974). The notorious letter to Denbigh of 30 Apr. 1572 survives in two eighteenth-century copies: one among the Wynn of Gwydir MSS. in the National Library of Wales (see *Calendar of Wynn (of Gwydir) Papers 1515–1690* [Cardiff, 1926], p. 7); the other, Clwyd R.O., Plas Heaton MS. DD/PH/150. The text is published (probably from the former copy) in J. Williams, *Ancient and Modern Denbigh* (Denbigh, 1856), pp. 98–9. [The source for the printed versions of the letter to Andover is a copy in 'The Bromley Precedent Book' in the House of Lords R.O.]

2 (Penguin edn, 1963), pp. 19 (for gentry), 22–3 (clientage), 201–3 (Leicester and high stewardships).

3 *HP 1558–1603*, II, 62–3. Cf. C. Haigh, *Elizabeth I* (1988), p. 90: 'his parliamentary patronage seems surprisingly restricted'.

4 M. A. Kishlansky, *Parliamentary Selection: Social and Political Choice in Early Modern England* (Cambridge, 1986), pp. 12–13, 39–40. D. Hirst, *The Representative of the People? Voters and Voting in England under the Early Stuarts* (Cambridge, 1975) concentrates on the larger boroughs and specifically excludes the influence of the nobility: see p. 139.

5 The 'Mr Melvyn' who appears as a Commons man-of-business in M. A. R. Graves, 'The Management of the Elizabethan House of Commons: The Council's "Men-of-Business"', *ante*, II (1983), 19, was in fact the Scottish ambassador, Robert Melville. G. R. Elton, 'Piscatorial Politics in the Early Parliaments of Elizabeth I', *Business Life and Public Policy. Essays in Honour of D. C. Coleman*, eds. N. MacKendrick and R. B. Outhwaite (Cambridge, 1986), pp. 1–20, contains some valuable observations; see also his *The Parliament of England 1559–1581* (Cambridge, 1986), p. 76 ff.

6 For examples of their dual employment of officers, see S. L. Adams, 'Office-Holders of the Borough of Denbigh and Stewards of the Lordships of Denbighshire in the Reign of Elizabeth I' [Ch. 14], p. 296. Many of the men described as Warwick's officers in *The Black Book of Warwick*, ed. T. Kemp (Warwick, [1899]) were also Leicester's, but the disappearance of Warwick's papers makes it impossible to do more than sketch his influence here.

7 On this point, see the observations of Kishlansky, *Parliamentary Selection*, p. 22.

8 Chester R.O., Mayor's Letters, M/L/5/270, [undated].

9 For the letter to Denbigh, see above, n. 1. The Windsor reference is found in Elias Ashmole's notes from the now missing Mayor's Book: Bodl., MS. Ashmole 1126, f. 46.

10 Both concern his secretary Arthur Atye: see Chester R.O., AB/1 (Assembly Book, 1539–1624), f. 182, and *The Liverpool Town Books*, ed. J. A. Twemloe (2 vols., Liverpool, 1918–35), II, 407–8, 416–17, 445–51.

11 For the letter to Andover, see above, n. 1. The Gloucester correspondence is found in Gloucester R.O., GBR B2/1/(Customal, 1486–1648), ff. 189v–90; B3/1 (Common Council Minute Book, 1565–1632), f. 92v, printed in H.M.C., *12th Rept*, Pt. IX, pp. 457–8, 460. The letter to Maldon is now Essex R.O., D/B 3/3/422, art. 9. I am very grateful to Mr Christopher Thompson for supplying me with a photocopy of this document.

12 The Poole agreement (12 Nov.) is now Poole B[orough] A[rchives], 109(66); Southampton (23 Oct.), Southampton City R.O., SC 2/11/5, f. 146v, printed in *The Third Book of Remembrance of Southampton, 1514–1602*, ed. A. C. Merson (Southampton Record Soc., VIII, 1965), p. 34; Tamworth, B.L., Add. MS. 28175, f. 51.

13 The Chester reference is found in R. H. Morris, *Chester in Plantagenet and Tudor Times* (Chester, 1893), p. 191, n. 3. The source is not given and I have been unable to trace it. For St Albans, see *HP 1558–1603*, I, 178.

14 Dudley MSS. (the Marquess of Bath, Longleat House, Wilts.) I, f. 220.

15 Dudley MS. II, f. 40, undated but badly damp-stained, probably early 1580. *HP 1558–1603*, II, 262, gives the date of Digby's election as 30 Nov. 1578; this must be an error, for his predecessor Sir William Devereux did not die until September 1579. My own reading of the badly defaced indenture (P.R.O., C. 219/283/13) gives a date of 1 Nov. 1579.

16 R. C. Gabriel, 'Members of the House of Commons, 1586–7' (London M.A. thesis, 1954), pp. 6–9. Neale, *Elizabethan Commons*, pp. 278–9 omits any reference to this aspect of the election. For the Dudley clientele and the Netherlands expedition, see S. Adams, 'A Puritan Crusade? The Composition of the Earl of Leicester's Expedition to the Netherlands, 1585–86' [Ch. 9].

17 The lists are found in B.L., Add. MS. 48018 [a precedent book compiled by Robert Beale], ff. 282v–3, 293v–4v. Some evidence for implementation can be found in Neale, *Elizabethan Commons*, p. 277.

18 H.M.C., *Salisbury MSS.*, III, 71. See also G. Wilks, *The Barons of the Cinque Ports and the Parliamentary Representation of Hythe* (Folkestone, [1892]), pp. 62–3, and (for New Romney), Kishlansky, *Parliamentary Selection*, p. 45.

19 For the dating of the writs, see those surviving in P.R.O., C. 219/29/ (e.g.) 6, 41, 58. For some valuable comments on communications, see Kishlansky, *Parliamentary Selection*, p. 28.

20 P.R.O., S.P. 83/23/60v (in Burghley's hand), calendared in *C.S.P. Foreign*, 1584–5, p. 98.

21 For Christchurch, P.R.O., S.P. 12/178/140, mayor to Walsingham, 21 Oct. 1584; for Colchester, *HP 1558–1603*, I, 160. At Christchurch Walsingham was unaware that the Earl of Huntingdon possessed the nomination; at Colchester he nominated both M.P.s. The wider circumstances may also have influenced the Hertfordshire election; certainly the surviving correspondence relating to it (B.L., Add. MSS. 40629, f. 33, 40630, ff. 1–8) does not bear out Neale's contention (*Elizabethan Commons*, pp. 26–7) that 'court parties' were involved.

22 It is unfortunate that the identity of the 'adelman van goede qualiteyt ende een van der gecommitteerde van eeniger steden van t'parlament' Leicester sent to reassure the Dutch envoys of Parliament's support in March 1585 was not revealed. See The Hague, Algemeen Rijksarchief, Regeringsarchieven I–90B, J. Ortell and J. Gryse to the States-General, 14/24 Mar. 1585, quoted in J. L. Motley, *History of the United Netherlands* (4 vols., 1876), I, 278.

23 For Tomson, see I. Backus, 'Laurence Tomson (1539–1608) and Elizabethan Puritanism', *Journal of Ecclesiastical History*, XVIII (1977), esp. 24–5. There is no evidence to suggest a personal connexion to Leicester, who probably obtained the nomination from the second Earl of Bedford. A similar agreement made between Bedford and Poole in 1572 (now missing) is referred to in J. Sydenham, *The History of the Town and County of Poole* (Poole, 1839), p. 253, while Warwick nominated in the name of the 3rd Earl in 1586: Poole B.A., 91(47).

24 Gregory's relationship to Leicester is established by his letterbook, now Harvard University, Houghton Library MS. Eng. 757.

25 Wilks, *Hythe*, pp. 62–3. The Council wrote to Cobham on 18 Oct., his final order was dated 25 Oct. For Bodley see Sir Simonds D'Ewes, *A Compleat Journal . . . Both of the House of Lords and House of Commons throughout the Whole Reign of Queen Elizabeth* (1693), p. 334.

26 To be discussed in further detail in my essay 'The Dudley Clientele, 1553–1563' [Ch. 8].

27 Compiled from Leicester's 'schedule' or register of evidences (Dudley MS. XX), the draft (Dudley MS. III, ff. 176 *et seq.*) and the indentures that survive in Longleat

House Dudley Boxes II and III. For St Albans, see *The Corporation Records of St. Albans*, ed. A. E. Gibbs (St Albans, 1879), p. 13. Despite the later date of the indentures, Leicester is described as the high steward of both Abingdon and Reading in the 1566 visitation of Berkshire. See *The Four Visitations of Berkshire*, ed. W. H. Rylands I (Harleian Soc., LVI, 1907), 13–14. At Abingdon he succeeded Sir John Mason, who died in Apr. 1566, and who had already recommended him as his successor as chancellor of Oxford University in 1565.

28 For Southampton and the sweet wines farm, see Merson (ed.), *Third Book*, pp. 71–5.

29 Proximity to Kenilworth was undoubtedly important, but there was also a long standing Dudley benevolence towards Coventry, best reflected in the 'brass lease' of 1571 in St Mary's Hall.

30 *The Great White Book of Bristol*, ed. E. Ralph (Bristol Record Soc., XXXII, 1979), p. 8. Bristol R.O., MS. 04273(2) (Ordinances of Common Council), f. 4v, and MS. 04026(9) (Chamberlain's Accounts: Audit Book 1570–74), pp. 30, 33.

31 Norfolk R.O., K.L./C7/7 (King's Lynn Hall Book, 1569–91), ff. 55, 56, 61v. For Northumberland's fee, K.L./C7/6, f. 135.

32 At Reading and Abingdon the high steward replaced a former monastic steward. The boroughs regularly employed the same officers. Thomas Stampe (for example), recorder of Wallingford from 1582, had previously been recorder of Abingdon and master of Christ's Hospital: A. C. Baker, *Historic Abingdon: Fifty-Six Essays* (Abingdon, 1963), p. 8.

33 For Northumberland's election as high steward of Yarmouth in 1552, see Norfolk R.O., Y/C19/1 (Gt. Yarmouth Assembly Book A, 1550–59), ff. 36–7v. For the stewardship of Warwick, see Dudley MS. I, f. 121, J. Fisher to Dudley, 18 Mar. 1560; Dudley Box II, art. 9; *Black Bk.*, p. 8.

34 Blike became a principal burgess of Tewkesbury immediately after Leicester obtained a charter for the town in 1574; he may well have been involved. See Gloucestershire R.O., TBR/A/1/1 (Tewkesbury Corporation Minute Book, 1575–1626), pp. 361, 376. He may have been Leicester's man 'Bleke' referred to in Bodl., Perrot MS. 1, ff. 64–5, Sir John Perror to Leicester, 12 Feb. 1585.

35 These men are discussed in further detail in Ch. 8 above. Grice's father Gilbert, a bailiff of Yarmouth in 1542, owed money to Northumberland in 1553. On 11 Aug. 1553 he was discommoned for a year, possibly for supporting Lady Jane Grey. See Norfolk R.O., Y/C19/1, ff. 85 [a heavily scored-out entry], 117; C. J. Palmer, *The History of Great Yarmouth* (Gt. Yarmouth, 1856), pp. 199–200; P.R.O., L.R. 2/118. Grice and Glasier were related (P.R.O., C. 78/20/26); Forster and Grice shared a grant of concealed lands in 1564, *Calendar of the Patent Rolls, 1563–66*, pp. 62–7.

36 Elton, 'Piscatorial Politics', p. 11. It was at dinner in 'my good neighbour' Grice's house that Thomas Norton discussed Parliament business in 1581: 'Further Particulars of Thomas Norton', ed. W. D. Cooper, *Archaeologia* XXXVI (1855), 109.

37 At Reading, for example, the first patent of high stewardship to include a right of nomination was that granted to Essex in 1593: *The Diary of the Corporation of Reading*, ed. J. M. Guilding (4 vols., 1892–96), I, 416; J. Man, *The History and Antiquities of the Borough of Reading* (Reading, 1826), p. 380.

38 The evidence on which M. A. R. Graves (*The Tudor Parliaments* [1985], p. 133) bases his claim that Leicester and Huntingdon 'secured' the enfranchisement of five Hampshire boroughs escapes me.

39 Both Chipping Wycombe and Aylesbury were manorial boroughs; Chipping Wycombe was held in part by the dean and canons of Windsor, Aylesbury by the Packingtons. Packington nominations are found from 1572; the act books of the dean and canons do not survive before 1596. See L. J. Ashford, *The History of the Borough of High Wycombe* (1980), p. 108 ff.; R. Gibbs, *A History of Aylesbury with Its Borough and Hundreds* (Aylesbury, 1885), pp. 131–3; *The Chapter Act Books of the Dean and Canons of Windsor, 1430, 1523–1672*, ed. S. Bond (Hist. Monographs Relating to St. George's Chapel, XIII, 1966), pp. xi ff.

40 See above, n. 9.

41 Killigrew had an interest in Helston, where he was appointed bailiff in 1552 (P.R.O., E. 315/224/221, a reference I owe to the generosity of Mr A. J. M. Malkiewicz of Edinburgh University); his brother William was later a constable of the castle there.

42 As, for example, in the case of Atye at Liverpool in 1582.

43 *Proceedings in the Parliaments of Elizabeth I, Volume I: 1558–1581* (Leicester, 1981), pp. 225–31.

44 For Gloucester, see above, n. 11; Windsor (1575), Bodl., MS. Ashmole 1126, f. 49v; Yarmouth (1584), Norfolk, R.O., Y/C19/4, f. 78.

45 Norfolk nominated (for the first time) one M.P. at King's Lynn and Yarmouth: Norfolk R.O., KL/C7/6, f. 325; Y/C19/1, f. 203.

46 For the Dudley loyalty of the Bagnalls, see *Calendar of the Carew Manuscripts*, II, 628; P.R.O., S.P. 15/12/94, Sir R. Bagnall to Sir J. Throckmorton, 31 Jan. 1565. For their associations in 1559–60, see Dudley MS. I, ff. 27, 189. For Throckmorton and Northumberland, see 'Archbishop Holgate's Apology', ed. A. G. Dickens, *E.H.R.* LVI (1941), 456–7, P.R.O., S.P. 12/15/13 and below n. 54.

47 The connexion is not so clear here, though Dudley was seen as responsible for the dispatch of Arnold to Ireland in 1564 and stayed with Fisher during his visit to Warwick in 1571 (*Black Bk.*, p. 29). Blount acted as Dudley's proxy at the christening of one of Sir Francis Jobson's children in the spring of 1559: see Dudley MS. XIV (Household Account, 1558–59), f. 6.

48 Aglionby's colleague in 1553 was John Dudley, the M.P. for Helston in 1563. Jobson, Northumberland's former secretary, was married to his half-sister.

49 Gates was deputy steward for Leicester of the lordship of Pickeringhythe in 1565 (P.R.O., S.P. 15/12, art. 68). Throckmorton may have been an officer of Kenilworth in 1553 (P.R.O., L.R. 2/118). He was associated with Leicester and Warwick in the proposed incorporation of the preachers of the gospel in Warwickshire in 1567 (P.R.O., S.P. 12/44/148).

50 'Colshill' is included among Cecil's list of Leicester's 'most particular friends' in 1567 (Hatfield MSS. [the Marquess of Salisbury, Hatfield House, Hertfordshire] 155, art. 28; microfilm deposited in the British Library used with permission of the Most Honourable the Marquess of Salisbury). Whether this was Robert or Thomas, is unclear; they were not otherwise prominent among Leicester's clients.

51 See *Acts of the Privy Council*, new ser., IV, 324, 342; Ch. 8 above. [For Blount, see the revisions on p. 368, n. 196 below.]

52 Bills for the restitution of Gates, Sir James Croft and Lord John Grey of Pirgo were introduced on 27 Feb.: *C.J.*, I, 55. See also Elton, *Parl. of Eng.*, pp. 303–4.

53 *C.J.*, I, 57; N. L. Jones, *Faith By Statute: Parliament and the Settlement of Religion 1559* (1982), pp. 109–10.

54 For Leicester's role in obtaining leases for Jobson and Throckmorton after the failure of their bill, see P.R.O., S.P. 15/12/88, Sir John to Sir Nicholas Throckmorton, 29 Dec. 1565.

55 *Cal. Pat. Rolls, 1561–63*, pp. 189–91, 291–3.

56 *Parl. of Eng.*, pp. 358–9; the evidence he advances is not up to his usual standard.

57 P.R.O., S.P. 12/25/125, Council to Lord Rich, 27 Nov. 1562.

58 I have not discovered any reference to Goodere's relationship to Dudley prior to 1571.

59 Norfolk R.O., Y/C19/2 (Assembly Book B), ff. 33, 36, Leicester described Haddon as 'one I love so well' in a letter to Sir Thomas Heneage of 18 Sept. 1570: H.M.C., *Finch MSS.*, I, 11.

60 For Butler and Leicester, *Black Bk.*, p. 31, and Dudley MS. II, ff. 4, 9. The *Black Bk.* sheds no light on the election of 1563.

61 Thomas Dudley (a distant cousin) was a member of Northumberland's household in 1553 (P.R.O., L.R. 2/118), and included in Leicester's livery list in 1559 (Dudley Box V, f. 282). He was described as his comptroller in 1571 (*Black Bk.*, p. 34).

62 The indentures for St Ives, Helston and Mitchell were originally blanks (P.R.O., C. 219/27/11, 14, 19). John Dudley was a central figure in both Northumberland and Leicester's households (see his will, P.R.O., Prob. 11/63, ff. 117v–18).

63 For Wilson, see Ch. 8 above. Harington stood surety for Leicester together with Sir Henry Sidney in December 1560: P.R.O., C. 54/584/5.

64 Yerwerth was engaged in Leicester's business in 1559; he, John Dudley and William Glasier were commissioned by Leicester to survey the lordship of Denbigh in 1563; thereafter he was receiver of the lordship. See Adams, 'The composition of 1564 and the Earl of Leicester's Tenurial Reformation in the Lordship of Denbigh' [Ch. 13] p. 265.

65 Price was in Northumberland's service, and steward of the lordship of Denbigh for Leicester from 1581. See Dudley MS. I, f. 307, to Leicester, 22 July [1571]; Ch. 14 below, pp. 296, 298.

66 The minute book of the governors of Beverley 1558–1574 (Humberside R.O., BC/II/ 7/2) yields nothing. The hostility between Bacon and Dudley has been greatly exaggerated: see Adams, 'The Release of Lord Darnley and the Failure of the Amity', *Mary Stewart. Queen in Three Kingdoms*, ed. M. Lynch (Oxford, 1988), pp. 136–7. Hall may have been a client of Leicester's, a 'Master Hall and Mr. Kindelmarsh' Robert Hogan considered 'so convenient messengers ... by whose means I trust that my letters shall come safely unto your honour': Magdalene College, Cambridge, Pepys MS. I, p. 403, to Leicester, 21 June 1565.

67 On Gallys and the Succession debate, see *HP 1558–1603*, I, 163.

68 Abingdon was largely run by the master and governors of Christ's Hospital, formerly the confraternity of the Holy Cross. A. C. Baker, *Historic Abingdon. Fifty-Six Articles*

(Abingdon, 1963), p. 7. The main association between Dudley and the Hydes comes from Amy Dudley's still unexplained residence at Denchworth and Cumnor in 1559–60.

69 *C.J.*, I, 75.

70 He was probably the Henry Knollys included in Dudley's 1559–60 livery lists (Dudley Box V, ff. 280, 282–3); he still regarded himself as a follower in 1581, see B.L., Cottonian MS. Vespasian C VII, ff. 384–5. His uncle, the elder Henry Knollys, was said to be a client of Leicester's in 1568: Bibliothèque Nationale, fonds français 15971, f. 143, Bochetel de La Forêt to Charles IX, 19 July 1568.

71 See Adams 'The Gentry of north Wales and the Earl of Leicester's Expedition to the Netherlands, 1585–1586' [Ch. 12], pp. 244–5. Huband was in Leicester's entourage during the visit to Warwick in 1571 (*Black Bk.*, p. 34), and witnessed Leicester's 1582 will (Dudley Box III, art. 56), to which he and Digby were appointed overseers.

72 *Black Bk.*, pp. 26–8, 34.

73 On the election, *HP 1558–1603*, I, 238. For Trentham, see Pierpont Morgan Lib., MS. Rulers of England, Box III.2, art. 29.5, Leicester to Humphrey Ferrers, 13 Sept. 1578.

74 Fitzgerald leased the manor of Cranbourne from Leicester in 1574 (J. Hutchins, *History and Antiquities of the County of Dorset* [2 vols., 1774], II, 140), and christened his second son Dudley. Lewkenor's appearance at Tamworth in 1572 and then Maldon in 1584 is curious but no direct connexion can be established.

75 Poyntz was regarded as Leicester's local agent in the Berkeley land case: see J. Smyth, *Lives of the Berkeleys*, ed. J. Mclean (2 vols., Gloucester, 1883–85), II, 294. For Blike see above n. 34.

76 This tentative identification rests on references in Bristol R.O., MS. 04026(9) (Chamberlain's Accounts: Audit Book 1570–74), pp. 98, 102, to Leicester's secretary 'Mr. Kyndlemersh'. A 'Mr. Kindelmersh' had some form of association to Leicester in 1565, see above, n. 66.

77 Neville was an officer of the castle by 1573: see his letter to Leicester of 28 Mar. (Dudley MS. II, f. 160).

78 Despite his diplomatic service, no direct association between Hastings and Leicester can as yet be established.

79 For Dockwra and Windsor Castle, see Dudley MS. II, f. 27, Dockwra to Leicester, 17 June 1571. Christmas, who may have been the tenant of the dean and canons of Windsor, was described as Leicester's treasurer in 1571 (*Black Bk.*, p. 36). His account for the period 1570–71 was lot 53 of the Upcott sale at Sotheby's in 1846; it is presumed destroyed with the rest of the Staunton of Longbridge collection in the Birmingham Reference Library fire of 1879.

80 For Snagge's admission as a burgess of Chester, see Chester R.O., AB/1, f. 118. He was steward of Kenilworth and an officer in Wales for both Warwick and Leicester in 1570–71. See Ch. 14 below, p. 296; Dudley MS. II, f. 32, Snagge to Leicester, 23 July 1571.

81 Musgrave had been a servant of Northumberland's in 1553 (P.R.O., S.P. 46/163/60–2); for his relations with Leicester, see his letters of 6 Mar. 1560 (Dudley MS. I f. 118) and 20 May 1573 (Bodl., MS. Tanner 80, f. 36). Horsey had been a Dudley follower since 1562/3. In a letter to Sir William Fitzwilliam of 26 July 1573, Leicester referred to the 'good will I bear to that name' (Bodl., MS. Carte 56, f. 180).

82 Dudley MS. II, f. 307, ᵖrice to Leicester, 22 July [1571].

83 Leicester described Nuthall as 'my solicitor' in a letter to Burghley of 20 July 1574 (B.L., Lansdowne MS. 18, f. 194); by 1580 he was recorder of the lordship of Denbigh (University College of North Wales Lib., Garthewin MS. 2693, view of frankpledge of the lordship of Denbigh, 1580).

84 According to *HP 1558–1603*, I, 116, Leicester was involved in the dispute between Alford and Reading over his expenses. My own examination of the Reading accounts (Berkshire R.O., R/FA 2/74 [Cofferer's Accounts, 1585–6], f. 8) failed to uncover this reference.

85 Leicester obtained a new charter for Beverley in 1573, for which his arms were set on the common hall, Humberside R.O. BC/II/6/30, 32 (Account Rolls, Keepers and Mayors, 1573, 1575). Aglionby was one of his waged servants in 1559–61 (Dudley MS. III, f. 2v), and still in his household in 1578 (Dudley MS. II, f. 183, Aglionby to Leicester, 30 July 1578).

86 Calthrope was a member of Grice's dinner party with Norton in 1581 ('Further Particulars', p. 110). When he was appointed as steward of Yarmouth is unclear, but he was in office by 1573 and was succeeded by Flowerdew when he resigned in 1580 (Norfolk R.O., Y/C19/3, ff. 98v, 192; C19/4, f. 12).

87 Lostwithiel, Bossiney, Truro, St Ives and Tregony were blanks (P.R.O., C. 219/28/19, 20, 30, 22, 32).

88 For a brief account, see Ch. 14 below, pp. 302–3. I intend to publish a fuller study in due course.

89 Cf. Cobham to Hythe in 1571: see Wilks, *Barons*, pp. 53–4.

90 P.R.O., C. 193/32/8. The initial nominee was probably Thomas Salusbury of Denbigh Castle, rather than his nephew the future Babington conspirator. For Dynne, who was possibly an auditor of the Exchequer as well, see Ch. 12 below, p. 245.

91 P.R.O., C. 219/27/198. The original date of the indenture was 16 Apr. Leicester described Cavendish as 'my loving friend' in a letter to the Marquess of Winchester of 25 April 1570: P.R.O., S.P. 46/28/198.

92 Beake was chief equerry to the Queen. The argument by A. C. Baker (*Historic Abingdon*, pp. 31–2) that the date of the purchase of land in the borough was deliberately manipulated to make him eligible for election in 1573 fails to take into account the fact that his election did not take place until 26 Jan. 1576 (P.R.O., C. 219/282/35).

93 Ch. 12 below, pp. 238–9. Leicester described Thomas as his servant in a letter to Sir William Fitzwilliam of 10 July 1574: Bodl., MS. Carte 56, f. 184.

94 For the elections of Peyton and Bacon, see Norfolk R.O. KL/C7/7, ff. 189–90; Y/C19/3, f. 137. No connexion can be made with Tate, who held property within Coventry.

95 See Ch. 9 above, pp. 188–90.

96 Boughton was in Leicester's service by 1579, see B.L., Stowe MS. 150, f. 19.

97 He was working for Leicester in 1573 (Dudley MS. II, f. 156), and was his deputy in the patent for fines of entry in the Hanaper of the Exchequer in 1580 (Dudley Box II, art. 53).

98 The other M.P. for Tamworth was John Britton. Tamworth returned two indentures: Fisher's (P.R.O., C. 219/29/159) appears to be a blank; Britton's is not (C. 219/29/132). Fisher was the son of John Fisher of Packington, and was one of the bearers of the corpse at Leicester's funeral (Bodl., MS. Ashmole 818, f. 38). Warburton was

Leicester and Derby's nominee at Chester (see above n. 13). Why he was rejected is unclear since he was appointed an alderman on their recommendation on 8 Oct. (Chester R.O., AB/1, f. 194), and sat for the city in 1586. Browne, the failed candidate at Maldon, was victualler and steward of Leicester's household in the Netherlands.

99 He was described as Leicester's auditor in 1580 (Dudley MS. II, f. 215, R. Stoneleigh to Baynham, 28 Mar. 1580), and was still in his service in 1588. See H. Ellis, *Original Letters Illustrative of English History*, 3rd ser. (4 vols., 1846), IV, 78.

100 Morley was involved with Leicester in a number of land transactions in the early 1580s: see, for example, Gloucestershire R.O., D 2957/79 (i). Leicester described him as 'my friend' in a letter to Burghley of 4 Dec. 1585: B.L., Lansd. MS. 45, f. 84.

101 See *Acts of the Privy Council*, new ser. IV, 305. For the first stage of the dispute between Bristol and Gloucester, see n. 113 below.

102 In Sept. 1582 the settlement between Gloucester and Bristol was delayed because Throckmorton was visiting Leicester and Warwick at Kenilworth (Gloucestershire R.O., GBR B3/1, f. 100). For Throckmorton and Tracy, see Smyth, *Lives of the Berkeleys*, II, 307–8. Tracy was one of the supporters of the pall at Leicester's funeral (Bodl., MS. Ashmole 818, f. 38).

103 Cholmondley bore the banner at Leicester's funeral (Bodl., MS. Ashmole 818, f. 38).

104 Bold was a supporter of the body at Leicester's funeral. He was described as 'your lordship's old servant' in Sir John Woolley to Leicester, 11 Feb. 1587, calendared in *C.S.P. Scot.*, IX, 297.

105 The Denbigh borough indenture (P.R.O., C. 219/29/24) appears to be a blank. For Evan Lloyd, see Ch. 14 below, p. 296; Ch. 12 below, pp. 239–40.

106 On Wrote, see D. MacCulloch, 'Catholic and Puritan in Elizabethan Suffolk', *Archiv für Reformtationsgeschichte*, LXXII (1981), 243–4. For evidence of his work for Leicester, see Warwickshire R.O., CR 1600LH/125 (Leicester's Hospital Papers); and the patent of 1586 for fines in the Hanaper of Chancery: P.R.O., C. 66/1277.

107 For Neville's entry into Leicester's service, see Dudley MS. II, f. 224, Neville to Leicester, 23 July 1582. He witnessed part of the Kenilworth inventory of 1583 with Boughton: H.M.C., *De Lisle and Dudley MSS.*, I, 296. Leicester described Bodley as 'my old servant' in a letter to Walsingham of 7 Aug. 1586: *Correspondence of Robert Dudley, Earl of Leycester during his Government of the Low Countries*, ed. J. Bruce (Camden Soc., XXVII, 1844), p. 383.

108 The St Ives indenture (P.R.O., C. 219/29/12) is a blank, but granted with consent of the lords of the manor, Mountjoy and the Marquess of Winchester. The St Germans indenture (C. 219/29/29) is also a blank. Barker was recommended by Leicester as registrar of the court of delegates in 1584 (see P.R.O., S.P. 12/175/9: doctors of the Court of Arches to Leicester, 11 Nov. 1584), and referred to as 'your lordship's servant' in *C.S.P. Scot.*, IX, 93. It is not clear whether he served in the Netherlands.

109 Both indentures (P.R.O., C. 291/29/13, 18) are blanks. Clerk was a judge martial in the Netherlands (P.R.O., S.P. 15/29/339, 340v); he may have compiled Leicester's manual of military law: see the fragment of Leicester's 1585–6 household account (also destroyed in the Birmingham Reference Library fire) printed in E. H. Knowles, *The Castle of Kenilworth. A Handbook for Visitors* (Warwick, 1872), p. 50. For Lewis, *HP 1558–1603*, II, 471.

110 Both were returned on blank indentures (P.R.O., C. 219/30/135, 154).

111 Quoted in *HP 1558–1603*, I, 41.

112 Leicester did not choose Warwick as the site of the hospital until his visit there in September 1571; John Fisher, the M.P., was annoyed that the borough did not respond to the passing of the statute by inviting him to do so. *Black Bk.*, pp. 28–9.

113 Bristol R.O., MS. 04026 (10) (Chamberlain's Accounts: Audit Book 1575–79), pp. 87, 89, 92–3.

114 *L.J.*, II, 34. D'Ewes, *Jnl.*, pp. 290, 302.

115 *Parl. of Eng.*, p. 105; 'Piscatorial Politics', pp. 6, 11.

116 Note the recommendation of the bill by the Lords on 17 Mar. D'Ewes, *Jnl.*, p. 307.

117 Norfolk R.O., Y/C/19/4 (Gt. Yarmouth Assembly Book D: 1579–1586), f. 15v. Instructions were sent to Grice and his colleague at the beginning of the session (f. 18v), but they are not described.

118 This important subject will be dealt with in a future essay.

119 Essex R.O., D/B 3/3/422, art. 9.

120 Abingdon, Christ's Hospital Archives, Original Accounts, 1553–89 (unfoliated); Southampton City R.O., SC 5/3/1 (Book of Fines, 1488–1593), f. 193.

121 *Elizabeth I and Her Parliaments* (2 vols., 1953–57), II, 169.

122 *Black Bk.*, pp. 389–91.

123 Outlined briefly in 'Release of Lord Darnley', pp. 136–7. This interpretation differs from that given in Elton, *Parl. of Eng.*, pp. 358–63, but the whole Succession debate needs a re-examination.

124 See above, n. 67, and Hartley (ed.), *Proceedings*, p. 324.

125 S. Hollings, 'Court Patronage, County Governors and the Early Stuart Parliaments', *Parergon*, new ser., VI (1988), 123 *et seq.*

Chapter 11

A godly peer?
Leicester and the Puritans

Unlike many of his peers, Robert Dudley, Earl of Leicester was not a great builder. His main architectural memorial is, to most people, Kenilworth Castle. But he has left two further monuments, which in some respects explain why he remains one of the most hotly debated figures of Elizabeth I's reign. On the hillside between the town and castle of Denbigh lie the ruins of what is known as 'Leicester's Church'. The corner-stone was laid in 1578, but the building was never completed. According to legend, lovingly retold by later romantic antiquarians, the townsmen pulled down at night what the hated lord had erected by day. The real reason is that the project was simply too ambitious. Had it been finished, it would have been the largest church constructed in England and Wales between the Reformation and the rebuilding of St Paul's Cathedral. Leicester had been warned by his surveyors that there was 'no store of great timber' in the county. Three years before his death in 1588 he was forced to send to Ireland for the roof beams.

As striking as its size is the fact that the church was built on a novel open plan, influenced either by the Friars churches or possibly even French Huguenot temples. The focus would have been on the preacher, rather than the traditional altar. Leicester's Church was intended to serve as a preaching centre for the evangelising of north Wales.

The second monument has survived largely intact, though architecturally it owes little to Leicester himself. This is his hospital in Warwick, which employs the buildings of a pre-Reformation guild. We know slightly more about the circumstances of its foundation. In 1571 Leicester obtained a statute licensing him to found a hospital at either Kenilworth or Warwick, 'for the charitable relief and sustentation of poor and needy people'. During a visit to Warwick in September of that year he was persuaded by his favourite architect, William Spycer, that the guildhall would suit his purpose. Since it was then being used as a town hall and grammar school, it took some years for him to find the borough an alternative site, and precisely when the hospital began to function is still unclear. Its surviving statutes were drawn up (and corrected by Leicester himself) on 26 November 1585, a week before he departed for the Netherlands to take up command of the queen's troops there. The hospital was now intended to support old soldiers, and specifically Warwickshire men 'maimed or hurt' in that campaign. It is possible that Leicester had changed his mind about its purpose in the meantime.

The history of both medieval and post-Reformation Christianity provides many examples of generous endowments to religious and charitable institutions by men whose lives were hardly models of piety. Leicester's charitable impulse, if on a grander scale than many of his contemporaries, was in this respect not unconventional. Yet what is equally famous about the hospital was his appointment of Thomas Cartwright, the notorious Puritan and open presbyterian, as its second master. This was only one example of his controversial patronage of Puritan clergymen, who were ostensibly opposed to the religious policies of the queen and the advocates of a moral reformation little in keeping with his own courtly style of life. Leicester was the patron of one of the leading mid-Elizabethan acting companies, yet he also protected the preacher John Field, who directly criticised his intervention 'on behalf of evil men as of late you did for players to the great grief of all the godly'.

Leicester's conduct puzzled his contemporaries as much as it has since perplexed historians. The less than charitable explanation was that his apparent godliness was purely hypocritical. This charge was also laid against Puritans as a group, but in his case two specific political motives were supplied. The earlier of the two can be found in the tract known as *Leicester's Commonwealth*, the famous Catholic polemic against him published in 1584. Here it is argued that his cultivation of Puritans was Machiavellian, a term which contemporaries understood precisely to mean cloaking political manoeuvre with pious rhetoric. Leicester, the author claimed, had deliberately exploited Puritan disquiet over the proposed marriage between Elizabeth and the Duke of Anjou to block the marriage and to create a faction to support the rebellion he was plotting if the marriage had succeeded.

The Machiavellian theory also provided the basis for the second explanation, which did not appear in print until after Leicester's death. It can be found in William Camden's *Annals of Queen Elizabeth* and (thanks partly to Camden's authority) it later became an established feature of seventeenth-century defences of the Church of England. Puritanism was now seen as openly seditious, and what needed to be explained was how it had become so entrenched in the mid-Elizabethan Church. The answer supplied was that Puritan agitation against the Bishops had been deliberately encouraged by Leicester and other courtiers, who sought thereby to bring about the destruction of the Church as an institution so they could expropriate its remaining landed wealth. The Church's defences were weakened by the courtiers' influence over the promotion of Bishops, which enabled them to appoint men of weak character who were open to manipulation. As chancellor of Oxford University, Leicester had more opportunity than most to advance unsuitable men. The Church was saved only by the fortunate appointment of John Whitgift as Archbishop of Canterbury in 1583 and Leicester's death five years later.

Several of the key elements in this picture of the Elizabethan Church have become embedded in the established history of the reign: Leicester was ultimately up to no good; he and his allies were seeking to rob the Church; and there was an organised Puritan political movement that sought to overturn the Elizabethan religious settlement. However, in the last twenty years, thanks largely to the work of Patrick Collinson, Nicholas Tyacke and Peter Lake, a new view of Puritanism has been advanced that makes Leicester's position much more explicable. It was Collinson who first argued that Puritanism was broader than non-conformity: that it should be defined in such terms as to make it possible to talk of Puritan Bishops. What inspired it was an acceptance of Swiss evangelical theology, a belief in the central role of preaching, a concern for moral reformation and a conception of the English Church as part of an international Reformed community.

This does not mean that the issues that inspired non-conformity (vestments, ceremonies, and church government) disappear, but rather that we should see them in perspective. Lake's study of the Cambridge theologians of the 1580s and 1590s, whom he identified specifically as 'moderate puritans', draws our attention to the important body of clergymen, who, while sympathising with the grievances of the nonconformists, refused to leave the Church so long as its theology remained Reformed or Calvinist. They sought to avoid internal disruption and confrontations with potential nonconformists, owing not least to their sense of an overriding need to continue the Reformation and to maintain a common front against a perceived Catholic enemy. Thus the weak Bishops of Anglican legend (Edmund Grindal or the Jacobean George Abbot) are transformed into men who sought to maintain a Low Church consensus.

The significance of what one is tempted to call the 'soft left' lies not only in its strength in the Church, but also in its strength in the Court, and among the queen's servants and her councillors. Three of the earliest members of Elizabeth's Privy Chamber (Catherine Knollys, Elizabeth Sandys and Dorothy Stafford) had been Marian exiles, and in the last years of the reign Leicester's pious sister and sister-in-law, the Countesses of Huntingdon and Warwick, were among Elizabeth's closest intimates. It is here that Leicester's place in the Elizabethan political and religious spectrum is to be found. For all that has been written about his opportunism during the first decade of the reign, his extensive religious patronage was remarkably consistent. Apart from Edmund Campion (whose relationship to him is still unclear), there are only two known examples of clergymen who received his patronage who do not fit into a confirmed Protestant mould. One was the Rector of Lincoln College, Oxford, John Bridgewater, who was one of his chaplains in the early 1560s, but who in 1574 went into exile and joined the Jesuits. The other was the controversial Spanish free-thinker Antonio del Corro, whose case is more complicated, for the tolerance he received from the Elizabethan government as a whole may have had political motives.

There are, however, two specific questions about Leicester that need to be addressed before this argument can be accepted. The first is whether there is any truth in the charge of his designs on Church lands. He certainly obtained a number of leases of episcopal estates both for himself and for his followers. Like many other Elizabethan landowners he also possessed impropriated tithes, though these he assigned to the endowment of his hospital, an approved practice for a semi-religious institution. Only on one occasion did he seek (and obtain) a grant of episcopal lands from the crown. This occurred shortly before his death in 1588 and it was regarded as a special case, since it was intended to help him redeem the debts he had incurred in the Netherlands, and it was backed by both Sir Francis Walsingham and Lord Burghley. Interestingly enough, Leicester's secretary thought he would have difficulty selling the lands to raise capital owing to 'the novelty of the thing'.

This does not mean that the concern over its remaining landed wealth and its financial independence which was clearly strong within the Church in the 1580s was a complete fabrication. There is evidence that Walsingham, for one, would not have opposed expropriation of dean and chapter lands to meet the expenses of war against Spain, and Archbishop Whitgift claimed as much in 1585. But there is no evidence that expropriation inspired Leicester's involvement in ecclesiastical affairs.

The second question is provoked by the patronage of Corro in particular and cannot be answered conclusively here, though it should not be ignored either. How much did Leicester understand about the issues involved, how theologically literate was he? There are numerous examples of Elizabethan laymen whose knowledge of theology was extensive, but we cannot assume such learning to have been general. In Leicester's case we are also faced with the wider problem of an intellectual portrait that is very difficult to paint. To do so we must also take into account his patronage of the theatre, of painting (he possessed one of the largest collections of paintings of any Elizabethan layman), and of literature. Ninety-eight books were dedicated to him (his only rival in quantity was Burghley); he was regarded as a patron of Spenser, Dyer, and the other poets of the Sidney circle; and he possessed an extensive library. About a hundred or so of his books survive, which include a full range of contemporary and early theology as well as classical and contemporary literature.

Yet it is not clear how many of these books he actually read. While research has confirmed his contemporary reputation as a generous patron of learning and learned men, it has been difficult to discover whether this was more than passive. Unlike Burghley or Walsingham, he received neither an academic nor a university education, and unlike them he rarely employed Latin tags in his letters. Intellectually he was much closer to Elizabeth. Though her Latin was much better than his, they both were fluent in Italian and may have shared several of the same tutors as children. So far only one literary composition has been attributed to him: a verse paraphrase of Psalm 94, said to have been written when he was a prisoner in the Tower in 1554. Similarly, the only theological statement we know of is the preface to the will that he drafted at the beginning of 1582. This does, however, include the apparently predestinarian declaration, 'knowing and assuring myself that He hath made me and chosen me for one of His elect, having promised that all which believe in Him shall be saved'.

Whatever the difficulties of Leicester's intellectual portrait, his correspondence does reveal much about his views on the Church. Professor Collinson's discovery and publication of the correspondence between Leicester and the old Puritan soldier Thomas Wood in 1576–77 has been in many respects the basis for the contemporary reappraisal of Leicester. Not the least striking aspect of these letters was the fact that so grand a courtier found it necessary to justify himself to a minor provincial figure at such length. Nor are the letters to Wood unique. A number of similar long disquisitions survive, largely in Leicester's own hand, which suggests they were not drafted by a secretary. Some may have been intended for public consumption, but most were clearly private, and they reveal one of the secrets of Leicester's influence as a patron, a tolerant willingness to debate the issues.

Leicester was certainly aware that discretion was necessary. In an answer in 1571 to a now-missing letter from the diplomat Robert Beale which contained complaints about the bishops, he warned him in future official correspondence to:

> Eschew as much as you can to enter into any cause . . . touching our bishops or state of religion in sort to mislike them. Let it be only of that matter to myself, for that I do use to show your discourses to her majesty, who liketh very well of them and the last I durst not for these respects. Thus friendly I advise you, knowing you will take it well and I mean all for your best.

His tolerance emerges most vividly in a letter to Oxford University in 1580. He had received complaints of:

Disorderly and uncharitable [a contemporary euphemism for public criticism by clergymen of their colleagues] preachings by some of the younger sort, which though I have much misliked, yet have I not much dealt in reprehension or reformation thereof for two causes: the one that I thought the men to be young that were moved so to overshoot themselves [and that they] would in time see their own faults and amend them; the other that I would not seem to discourage any from preaching, knowing the great want of preachers everywhere.

Leicester's attitude towards preaching links his 'church policy' firmly to moderate Puritanism, for the provision and encouragement of preaching was its central concern. This priority helps to explain how it was possible to blur the distinction between moderates and radicals; the commitment to preaching was the primary quality sought in the clergy. Leicester's immediate contribution was the attention he paid to his own household chaplains. His patronage here was extensive. While only seven of Lord Burghley's chaplains are known, twenty-seven (and a probable further six) of Leicester's can be identified. While we do not know precisely how they were recruited (there is some evidence of recommendations by bishops), it is possible to detect a definite (and possibly annual) rotation.

He took no small pride in their intellectual calibre, and even John Harington, the epigrammist, who did not like Leicester very much, admitted 'he would have some choice and excellent men for his chaplains of both universities'. Nine of them became bishops and at least twelve heads of colleges at Oxford or Cambridge. This might at a first glance appear to reflect his influence as a patron, but in fact four of the nine did not enter the episcopate until after his death. Among the chaplains were the leading figures of Cambridge moderate Puritanism (William Fulke, Robert Some and Humphrey Tyndall), and Oxford Calvinism (Tobias Matthew, Thomas Holland and William James). Interestingly enough he took to the Netherlands in 1585 a much more Presbyterian group (John Knewstubbes, Dudley Fenner, Humphrey Fenn, and George Gifford). This appears to have been deliberate, possibly because it was an opportunity for them to demonstrate their loyalty through active service.

Leicester saw his role as Chancellor of Oxford as that of encouraging a preaching clergy. Soon after he was elected (in January 1565), he wrote to Archbishop Parker to request a preaching licence for a recent graduate and claimed:

I doubt not but you shall ere it be long find many such preachers even out of the same tree, that with God's grace shall bring forth the like fruit, I mean this University of Oxford, which I thank God doth well now begin to prosper in the setting forth of the Gospel, a few being weeded out that be hinderers, that for my part by the help of God I will do my best thereto. Your grace I am sure will rejoice and be glad likewise to do all that may everyway advance the same. In nothing can it be more than in cherishing the good and sincere preachers.

His most notorious intervention in the running of the university occurred at the same time, when, after his repeated requests that the university elect a theologian as vice-chancellor were ignored, he appointed future vice-chancellors (all of them theologians) himself.

Not surprisingly Leicester became the recipient of appeals from preachers who had angered the queen by introducing politics into their sermons. This placed him in some difficulty. As he wrote to Bishop Chadderton in 1579, 'I wish in my heart no jot of the authority of preachers to be diminished, and yet I wish them not to presume upon their authority to enter into condemnation of others without some ground'. He made it clear to Thomas Wood and others that he would not support attempts to overturn the existing structure of the Church: 'I am so resolved to the defence of that which is already established as I mean not to be a maintainer or allower of any that would trouble or disturb the quiet proceeding thereof'. He had earlier informed Beale that he considered the dissension within the Church to be caused by trifles, and that he considered both sides equally to blame: 'the higher sort . . . for being over-hard in persuasion of their inferior brethren, so are they of the inferior sort that use more wilfulness in some causes than reason or charity will allow'.

He also claimed to have left no 'means undone that might make reconcilement between them and thereby have sundry times had conferences between them'. One such was the Lambeth Conference of December 1584, which was inspired by Archbishop Whitgift's drive for conformity over ceremonies and the prayerbook. Leicester's main contribution was to regret that 'it was a pitiful thing that so many of the best ministers and painful in their preaching should be deprived for these things'. When these failed he appears to have tried to sponsor individual settlements, in which his patronage acted as a rein on the radicals. Thus, after the notorious former Genevan exile Christopher Goodman received the archdeaconry of Richmond through his means in 1573, Leicester received a delicately worded letter from the Bishop of Chester: 'Percase he [Goodman] is somewhat singular by fervent zeal of God's truth, which now more temperately he useth and by your lordship's good means and advertisement to him will be the more easily reformed.' He appears to have tried a similar manoeuvre to obtain a preaching licence for Thomas Cartwright from Whitgift in 1585: 'for [Leicester claimed] he protesteth and professeth to me to take no other course but to the drawing of all men to the unity of the Church.'

Whitgift's refusal to 'give unto [Cartwright] any further public approbation until I be better persuaded of his conformity' points to one of the barriers to

Leicester's moderation. For Whitgift, like Archbishop Parker before him, public conformity was the priority; not only were private arrangements intolerable, but Leicester's protection of the obstinate was an unwarranted interference in the discipline of the Church. At the other extreme Leicester's influence over the radicals was not absolute. Two of the leading targets of the *Martin Marprelate* tracts, which appeared just after his death, were his own former protégés Robert Some and Thomas Cooper.

Nevertheless the benefit of his activities did not die with him. After the dissolution of the parliament of 1629, Dr Lionel Sharpe advised the secretary of state that good relations between king and parliament in matters of religion might be restored if Charles I adopted what he claimed had been Elizabeth's policy of allowing Leicester to act as the protector of nonconformist clergy. Of this Sharpe could testify from personal knowledge, having been employed as a young man by Leicester 'to get from him to my lord of Canterbury in the behalf of Mr Cartwright, Fenner and Fenn and the gentlemen that favoured them'. Sharpe is not always to be trusted, and we may doubt Elizabeth's involvement, but there is a definite echo here of what we have been describing. Though it is fashionable today to see Elizabeth's 'success' as a seventeenth-century myth, the support Leicester and his colleagues gave to moderate Puritanism and the 'Calvinist consensus' may have done much to provide her government with the broad base of support that was so distinctly lacking in the succeeding reigns.

FURTHER READING

Patrick Collinson, *The Elizabethan Puritan Movement* (Jonathan Cape, 1967); *The Religion of Protestants* (Oxford University Press, 1982); and *Godly People* (Hambledon, 1983); Peter Lake, *Moderate Puritanism and the Elizabethan Church* (Cambridge University Press, 1982); Lawrence Butler, 'Leicester's Church, Denbigh: An Experiment in Puritan Worship', *Journal of the British Archaeological Association*, xxxviii (1974); Simon Adams, 'Favourites and Factions at the Elizabethan Court' [Ch. 3].

Part III

The Earl of Leicester
and the regions

Chapter 12

The gentry of north Wales and the Earl of Leicester's expedition to the Netherlands, 1585–86[1]

The activities of Robert Dudley, Earl of Leicester, in north Wales in the later sixteenth century have been surrounded with scarcely less controversy than has his career in national politics. A substantial reappraisal of his political career has been long overdue. In the history of north Wales the legend of the rapacious courtier lives on (one need only recall the commissions for the encroachment of the forest of Snowdon, the feud with Sir Richard Bulkeley of Beaumaris and the persecution of the gentry of Llŷn). Given this situation it should have been with unmixed relief that the victims of his rapacity viewed his departure for the Netherlands in December 1585. Yet, on that occasion he was accompanied by a sizeable contingent of gentry from north Wales. The composition of this contingent, and the light it sheds on Leicester's relations with the gentry of north Wales, form the subject of this essay.[2]

Essential to an understanding of the contingent is an appreciation of the structure of Leicester's interests in north Wales and of the structure of the army he commanded in 1585–86. The powerful territorial interest that he wielded was based on a series of royal grants of land and offices: the lordships of Denbigh and Chirk (June 1563), the chamberlainship of the county palatine of Chester (July 1565), the chief forestership of Snowdon (late 1560s), and the lordships of Arwystli and Cyfeiliog in Montgomeryshire (April 1572). In June 1564 his brother Ambrose, Earl of Warwick, was granted the lordship of Ruthin (Dyffryn Clwyd).[3] These grants were buttressed by grants of ex-monastic property: the manor of Halton in Denbighshire (formerly of the abbey of Valle Crucis), and lands of the abbeys of Cymer and Bardsey in Merioneth and Caernarvonshire.[4] By the early 1580s the annual rent roll for his estates in north Wales was computed as follows: Merioneth, £142 16s. 10d.; Caernarvonshire, £130 16s. 4d.; Denbigh, £807 18s. 10¼d.; Chirk, £150 3s. 9½d.; Arwystli and Cyfeiliog, £198 3s. 2d.[5]

The army sent to the Netherlands in 1585–86 has so often been described loosely as composed of 'volunteers' that some attention must be devoted to certain features of its composition. Even more than most Elizabethan armies, it was a complex mixture of genuine volunteers, neo-feudal retinues and conscripts. The conscripts (and some of the volunteers) were in Queen Elizabeth's pay, while the majority of volunteers were paid by the States-General. Although English volunteers had served in the Netherlands in varying numbers since the early 1570s, in the period immediately preceeding Leicester's expedition they comprised a regiment of 1500 foot in the pay of the States-General raised by Colonel Thomas Morgan in 1584. The regiment was sent to reinforce the garrison of Antwerp, where it remained until the capitulation of the city to the duke of Parma in August 1585. The surviving remnant, no more than three or four hundred strong, was incorporated into a new force of English volunteers raised in the autumn of 1585.[6]

When Elizabeth first offered the Dutch direct military assistance in the early summer of 1585 for the relief of Antwerp, she was prepared to offer 4000 foot in her own pay. The Dutch requested a substantially larger force on a permanent basis. After considerable negotiation, the two treaties of Nonsuch in early August provided 4000 foot for the immediate relief of Antwerp, to which were to be added 400 horse to provide a permanent auxiliary army in the queen's pay. Elizabeth's expenses were, of course, to be repaid later on the security of the cautionary towns.[7] In September, alarmed by the situation in the Netherlands after the fall of Antwerp, Elizabeth unwillingly agreed to the Dutch request that she increase her troops to 5050 foot and 1000 horse, with another 1350 foot garrison for the cautionary towns. 6400 foot was henceforth to be the basis for the queen's payroll.

The original contingent of 4000 foot was conscripted in the counties of south-eastern England and along the east coast in July and August and were sent to the Netherlands during August.[8] At the same time, however, the States-General entered into negotiations with the commander of the queen's forces, Colonel John Norris, and with Colonel Morgan for the raising of further English volunteers in their pay to accompany the queen's troops. Norris had a commission for 2000 men and Morgan for some 1300.[9] On 14 September 1585 the whole force was mustered at Utrecht in twenty-seven companies of foot (at a nominal strength of 150 men per company) in the queen's pay (4100 men) and twenty-one companies of volunteers in the States' pay (3305).[10] Later in the month the queen's new obligation to increase her forces by 2400 foot caused a transfer of this number of men from the voluntary troops to her forces, because she objected to raising further troops by conscription. From 27 September, to provide garrisons for the cautionary towns, nine voluntary companies (1350 men) were taken into the queen's pay; from 12 November a further six companies were transferred to raise her field force to 5000.[11] Only some 1000 volunteers should have remained in the States' pay, but several further companies appear to have arrived after September. Moreover, the States-General were negotiating with the Earl of Leicester, recently appointed captain-general, to raise a further contingent of volunteers. Leicester later claimed they wished for some 10,000 or 12,000.[12]

The administrative difficulties caused by the dual payrolls were compounded by difficulties in the financial arrangements. Money loaned to the Dutch to raise volunteers in England and charged against the account of the queen's treasurer in the Netherlands was not repaid in time and the Dutch were lax in paying the volunteers.[13] When Leicester arrived in early December, worried more by the state of his army than the state of the accounts, he ordered the volunteers to be paid by the queen's treasurer together with the queen's troops up to 12 December, the day he assumed command. The troops 'in pay' on 12 December, therefore, comprised forty-seven companies – the twenty-seven original queen's foot, the fifteen transferred volunteer companies, and five volunteer companies theoretically in the States' pay.[14] The total is less than the forty-eight companies mustered at Utrecht in September because two companies, composed of the survivors of Morgan's regiment, had been broken up in the meantime. The decision to include the volunteer companies in the queen's pay was to precipitate the host of financial problems which would bedevil Leicester throughout 1586. One underappreciated repercussion needs to be discussed here. Not only were the forty-seven companies of December substantially in excess of the 6400 men of the queen's payroll, but further conscript companies as well as volunteers were to arrive in 1586.[15] The conscript companies and several volunteer companies which Leicester transferred to the queen's pay raised the number even further and it became necessary to return a number of the original transferred voluntary companies to the States' pay. Although the queen's payroll was successfully reduced to 6400 by the autumn of 1586, the reduction was to contribute to the growing dispute between Leicester and Sir John Norris.[16] Whether by accident or design, the 'intruded' companies were commanded by men associated with Leicester, while those 'extruded' were often commanded by followers of Norris, who saw Leicester's action as a deliberate insult.[17]

Three of the intruded companies were Welsh – the only specifically Welsh companies in the army. One was the conscript company of 200 foot raised in the six counties of south Wales in November and December 1585, the only company of Welsh conscripts to serve in the Netherlands during Elizabeth's reign.[18] The company, which arrived in the Netherlands in early 1586 and was in pay from 20 January, was raised for Sir Philip Sidney to provide the core of the garrison of Flushing – hence the need for it to be in the queen's pay. A similar conscript company was raised in England for Sir Thomas Cecil, governor of the Brill.[19]

The raising of a conscript company for Sir Philip Sidney in Wales was probably a result of the influence of Sir Henry Sidney. The officer appointed to conduct them to Flushing, Richard Gwynne of Caernarvon, was a member of the lord president's Welsh following. The son of John Wynn of Bryncir, Caernarvon (high sheriff of Anglesey, 1572–73), Gwynne served Sidney both in Wales and in Ireland and became a professional soldier.[20] By 1584 he was employed by the commissioners for musters in Caernarvonshire and Anglesey to train the militia in the use of firearms and in May 1584 was officially appointed muster-master for Caernarvonshire, Anglesey and Merioneth.[21] After serving as provost-martial of Flushing under Philip Sidney, he returned to north Wales as muster-master and later became a member of the Council in the Marches and a knight.[22] He was probably a friend of William Thomas of Caernarvon, whose widow he married.

The two other intruded companies – those of Captains William Thomas and Lloyd – were each 200 strong and described as Welsh. Sir John Wynn of Gwydir noted that Thomas commanded 200 men out of north Wales.[23] No record remains of conscripts being levied in north Wales, but there is considerable evidence that they were 'volunteers' raised from among Leicester's tenants. At the end of September 1585 Leicester obtained permission, and on 2 October a licence by letters patent, to levy 500 of his own tenants in England and Wales. These, he remarked, would '(in no way) encrease hir majestie's charges'. It is doubtful that the licence referred to the cavalry which Leicester had summoned a week earlier, for he requested 'v or vj^c of my owne tenauntes, whom I wyll make as good reconing of as of 1000 of any as are yett gonn over' – a comparison with the foot in the Netherlands. Furthermore, Leicester usually only referred to the foot as 'tenants'; the horse he described as 'servants'.[24] On 22 January 1586 he wrote to Walsingham again on this subject:

> I wolde be gladde also, to have leave for v^c of my none servants more, not in Wales alone, but of my other tenantes, where I shall think mete; for I took but iiijc of the v^c hir majestie did graunt, and I wyll not gyve these iiijc for the best v^c and l. that I se or can heare of heare, nether shall any man have charge, by my good wyll, but such as shall have good cause to care for his men.[25]

The imputation that the 400 tenants raised were Welsh is confirmed by the fact that although the companies were usually described as those of Thomas and Lloyd, in the list of companies of 11 November 1586 they were described as 'my Lord's two bandes'. Thomas was dead by then and Leicester took personal charge of his company.[26]

The two companies arrived in the Netherlands in March 1586; Thomas was still engaged in quarter-sessions business in Caernarvon on 4 February and their presence is first recorded at Utrecht at the end of March.[27] They remained at Utrecht until the summer and were taken into the queen's pay at the end of May:

> Colonel (George) Digby (one of Leicester's circle of advisors) first practiced to have drawn a regiment out of Sir John Norrey's regiment . . . And since this way he could not compass a regiment ready made without his pains or purse, there is another shift devised. The two Welsh companies, Captain Thomas and Captain Lloyd, each having two hundred, also the sergeant-major's company of three hundred with others shall make him up a regiment . . . and . . . these men shall be put under the Queen's pay and other captains shall be changed from the Queen's pay to the Estates.[28]

The scheme to create a regiment for Digby never materialised and in July Thomas's company was one of those dispatched under Thomas Morgan to reinforce the garrison of Rheinberg, then under siege, while Lloyd's remained with the camp.[29] The relief of Rheinberg, Leicester's goal during the remainder of the campaign, was accomplished in September when the capture of Doesberg forced Parma to raise the siege and retire to face the main English army. Leaving his company at Rheinberg, Thomas rejoined the main army and was killed in the charge at Zutphen.[30]

Both Thomas and Lloyd were among the leading followers of Leicester in north Wales. Although the service of William Thomas of Caernarvon (high sheriff of Caernarvonshire, 1580–81, M.P. for Caernarvonshire, 1573–1585, and deputy-constable of Caernarvon Castle from 1583) in the Netherlands has been known for some time, his relationship to Leicester has not received similar attention. He owed his position in county politics as much to Leicester's support as to the balance of power among the county gentry. In 1581 he and John Nuthall, one of Leicester's legal agents, purchased from Leicester lands in Caernarvonshire formerly belonging to Bardsey Abbey.[31] In return, Thomas served on the commissions for encroachment in the forest of Snowdon in both Caernarvonshire and Anglesey from 1577 and displayed considerable zeal in Leicester's service.[32] He married Ellin, daughter of William Griffith of Plas Mawr, Caernarvon (d. 1587, and high sheriff of Caernarvonshire, 1562–63), whose sisters Margaret and Catherine married Thomas Price of Plas Iolyn and Griffith Vaughan of Corsygedol (Merioneth), both of whose families were of the Leicesterian connection.[33] His brother-in-law, Edward Griffith (M.P. for Caernarvon borough, 1584–85), who was also killed in the Netherlands in 1586, probably served in his company.[34]

The identification of Captain Lloyd is complicated by the question of the participation in the expedition of both Evan Lloyd of Bodidris in Yale

(Denbighshire) (d. 11 February 1587) and his son John (d. 1606), later the famous partisan of the Earl of Essex. In the army lists Captain Lloyd is usually named 'Jehan', transcribed John in printed calendars, but this could be an English transliteration of Jevan (Evan).[35] Evan Lloyd was well-qualified to command a company of the tenantry of the lordships of Denbigh and Chirk. In 1580 he had been appointed one of the commissioners for musters in Denbighshire, for he had both standing in the county (as high sheriff, 1568, 1583, and M.P. for Denbighshire, 1584–85) and martial reputation – he had served in the English contingent in the St. Quentin campaign of 1557.[36] He was also one of the Earl of Leicester's most trusted officers in Denbighshire: steward, if not of the lordship of Chirk, at least of most of its commotes, farmer of lands in the lordship of Denbigh, and commissioner for encroachments.[37] For all these services he was knighted by Leicester in October 1586 and died in London in February upon his return from the Netherlands with his company.[38]

If the references to Captain John Lloyd are seen as transliterations for Jevan, there is no evidence that John Lloyd of Bodidris was in the Netherlands in 1585–86.[39] The reference to a John Lloyd as being knighted by Leicester in 1586 in W. A. Shaw's *Knights of England* is an error, because John Lloyd was knighted by Essex in Ireland in 1599.[40] The Chirk Castle court rolls show, moreover, that John Lloyd of Yale deputised for Evan Lloyd as steward while he was in the Netherlands and succeeded him in that office after his death. Although it is possible that this John was Evan Lloyd's brother John, his succession to the office on Evan's death strongly suggests that he was his son.[41]

A further complication in the problem of the Lloyds in the Netherlands is caused by the presence of Richard Lloyd, a secretary of Leicester's and the Mr. Lloyd who is mentioned in the lists of Leicester's train.[42] Unfortunately, little is known about him. He may have been a nephew or grandson of Fulke Lloyd of Foxhall, Henllan (high sheriff of Denbighshire, 1555, 1567), chief forester of Denbigh and Chirk, and known as 'one of my lord's officers'.[43] He may possibly have been the Richard Lloyd, M.P. for Flint boroughs in 1584–85, about whom nothing is otherwise known.

Although we have no further information about the raising of the companies of tenants, certain aspects of the tenurial arrangements within the lordships of Denbigh and Chirk were probably not without influence on it. By letters patent of June 1567 (Denbigh), June 1570 (Chirk), and July 1576 (general licence for Denbigh, Chirk, Arwystli, and Cyfeiliog), Leicester was permitted to alienate land within the honours in free and common socage of the chief manor of the honour (i.e., Denbigh Castle, Chirk Castle, etc.).[44] This was to cause a substantial reform of the tenurial structure of the honours by commuting obsolete and archaic tenures and services into a monetary rent.[45] In the light of the long-held conception of Leicester's 'extortions' in the lordship of Denbigh, the benefits of this change may be queried, yet it should be noted that in Arwystli and Cyfeiliog an equitable arrangement for all parties was reached.[46] A considerable number of grants were made under these licences to both gentlemen and lesser freeholders and yeomen through-out the 1570s.[47] The only exception to the commutation of services, however, was the customary military service, always important in a former marcher lordship, which was owed to the lord of the honour.[48] It was probably from this class of tenants that the voluntary companies were raised; it was one of the last uses of the military system of the Marches.

The raising of the cavalry for the expedition provides further confirmation of the role of tenurial arrangements and office-holding in Leicester's rela-tionship to the gentry of north Wales. Elizabeth had agreed in the treaties of Nonsuch and later arrangements to provide 1000 English horse in her own pay; volunteer horse was also raised and by mid-1586 the full strength of the English cavalry was 1300 lances (heavy-armed man-at-arms, with several assistants, which was the basic unit of late-medieval cavalry) in fifteen cornets or companies; of these, 300 lances were in the States' pay.[49] The provision of cavalry for overseas service was still the prerogative of the aristocracy and gentry, and they served at the personal summons of the Crown or a greater lord. As a result, their tenants, retainers, and servants had traditionally been exempt from service in the militia, although the Elizabethan government, in its campaign against organised retaining, was making increasing efforts to incorporate them. The instructions for the commission for musters in Denbighshire in 1580, for example, insisted on retainers being mustered, unless they were engaged on their lord's immediate service, although they were not to be included in the militia companies.[50]

The cavalry of the expedition was therefore raised in the traditional manner – through the retinues of the clients and followers of the Earl of Leicester. From the outset he had emphasised that he would throw all his influence into the expedition: 'In very troth yf I should gooe I wold cary the best I can of every degree'.[51] When the queen gave him permission to proceed on 25 September 1585, he spent the next few days in writing 'above iic lettres to my servauntes and sundry my friends, to prepare themselves, according to the order I had myself, with all speed they could possible, to serve hir majestie under me in the Low Countries'.[52] Of these two hundred letters only one appears to have survived – that sent to John Wynn of Gwydir on 26 Septem-ber.[53] The interesting aspect of this letter is Leicester's declared intention of raising the heavy cavalry (demi-lances) from among his more important fol-lowers. As he described them, they were 'most of them gentlemen of good likings and callings in their countries, though my servants'.[54]

The cavalry arrived in the Netherlands during the winter of 1585–86 in groups of the retinues of individual lords and gentlemen, although the largest group – some 600, including 400 gentlemen – came over with Leicester himself early in December 1585.[55] On 10 January the 650 lances present were mustered at the Hague and formed into companies.[56] The muster itself was conducted by retinue, with the gentlemen and the lances they had brought listed individually. The muster-list is therefore a document of considerable importance – possibly the nearest we shall come to an outline of Leicester's following throughout England and Wales.[57] Although John Wynn did not answer Leicester's summons – during the summer of 1586 he was peacefully engaged in quarter-sessions business in Caernarvonshire[58] – the following ten gentlemen did: Piers Holland (1 lance), Thomas Salusbury senior (1), John Wynne Edwards (1), Cadwaladr Price (2), Jenkyn Lloyd (2), Thomas Price (2), Henry Vaughan (1), William Penrhyn (1), Richard Morris (1), and Henry Jones (10). With the exception of Jones, they represent the major areas of Leicester's influence in north Wales.

Attention has already been drawn to the Caernarvonshire circle of William Thomas and the Griffiths of Plas Mawr. For several decades the leading member of this group had been the notorious Dr Ellis Price of Plas Iolyn, steward of the lordship of Denbigh, whose activities ranged throughout the three counties adjacent to his seat and the appearance of two members of his family is not therefore surprising.[59] Thomas Price (?1564–1634), the poet, who referred in his writing to his service on the expedition, was his son and heir, and married Margaret Griffith of Plas Mawr. He went to the Netherlands in Leicester's train in December 1585 and apparently was a member of Robert Sidney's company of horse after 10 January.[60] Cadwaladr Price of Rhiwlas was a grand-nephew of Ellis Price and head of the cadet house of Rhiwlas. M.P. for Merioneth in 1584–85, he was closely associated with Ellis Price in local politics and married Catherine, daughter of Evan Lloyd of Bodidris.[61]

Another family closely associated with this circle were the Vaughans of Corsygedol (Merioneth) and Llwyndyrys (Caernarvonshire). Richard Vaughan of Llwyndyrys (d. *c.* 1588, high sheriff of Merioneth, 1575–76, and of Caernarvonshire, 1577–78) was a follower of Sir Henry Sidney, and an ally of William Thomas and Ellis Price in the Llŷn recusancy case and the pursuit of Thomas Owen.[62] In the late 1570s his heir Griffith Vaughan (high sheriff of Merioneth, 1585, 1604) married Catherine Griffith of Plas Mawr; in the settlement of the marriage William Thomas played a major role.[63] Richard Vaughan's younger son Henry was probably the Henry Vaughan of the expedition.[64] It should be noted, however, that Henry Vaughan, son of Charles Vaughan of Hergest in the hundred of Huntington (Herefordshire), who is noted as being killed in military service in Flanders during the reign of Elizabeth, may have been the Vaughan mentioned.[65]

The gentry of the lordships of Denbigh and Chirk provided a solid contingent. Piers Holland was probably the son of Piers Holland of Kinmel, Abergele

(d. 1593 and high sheriff of Denbighshire, 1578), who is called a soldier in his father's eulogy. The David Holland mentioned in the Spanish list may be his brother, the heir of Kinmel, who is also described as a soldier.[66] In March 1574 the elder Piers Holland had made an agreement with Leicester to hold the lands of his wife by the new tenure at a rent of £6 11s. 5d. per annum, and the service of his sons may have been the result of this tenurial arrangement.[67] Thomas Salusbury, senior (so-called, no doubt, to distinguish him from his nephew, the heir of Lleweni), was generally known as Thomas Salusbury of Denbigh Castle. A younger son of Sir John Salusbury of Lleweni and brother of John Salusbury (d. 1566), he was probably the Thomas Salusbury admitted to the Inner Temple in 1566.[68] He was the 'Mr. Salusbury of Denbigh' whom, with 'Mr. Salusbury of Rûg . . . and the rest of that crew', Catherine of Berain saw conspiring against her in 1577. An active Leicesterian, he was a member of the commission for encroachment in 1580.[69] John Wynn Edwards of Cefn y Wern in Chirkland and Bangor (Flintshire) was a member of the cadet branch of the house of Edwards of Plas Newydd (Chirk). His father, William Edwards, was the second son of William Edwards (d. 1532), constable of Chirk Castle and founder of Plas Newydd. Wynn Edwards was married to his cousin Jane, daughter of John Edwards of Plas Newydd, and supported this branch of the family in the shire elections of 1588.[70] He, his father, and John Edwards all held land in Chirk under the new tenure.[71]

A third contingent came from Montgomeryshire. William Penrhyn of Rhysnant (high sheriff of Montgomeryshire, 1604, keeper of the seal of Denbighshire and Montgomeryshire, 1590) came from a family which had interests in Denbighshire as well. His father, William Penrhyn (escheator of Montgomeryshire, 1566, deputy-sheriff, 1571) was steward of the manor of Glyn in the lordship of Chirk and possibly a member of the commission for encroachments.[72] Richard Morris of Rhiwsaeson, Cyfeiliog (high sheriff of Montgomeryshire, 1579), became steward of Cyfeiliog in 1583. In 1581 he and several other Montgomeryshire gentlemen leased the use of the wastes of Cyfeiliog for what appears to be the large-scale breeding of cattle for the English market.[73] Jenkyn Lloyd of Berthlwyd (c. 1560–1628) came from one of the leading families of Arwystli. His father, David Lloyd Jenkyn (d. 1587, high sheriff of Montgomeryshire, 1574, 1587), and his uncle, Morgan Glynne of Llanidloes (Inner Temple, 1572), were the attorneys for the tenants of Arwystli in the agreement with Leicester in 1578. Jenkyn Lloyd succeeded his father as sheriff of Montgomeryshire in 1587 and 1588 (when his conduct in the shire election caused him to be summoned before Star Chamber), and again in 1606. From 1596 to 1606 he was deputy-steward of Arwystli.[74] His daughter Dorothy married into the Hollands of Kinmel, possibly as a result of associations formed on the expedition.

The largest retinue brought by any Welsh gentleman comprised the ten lances of Henry Jones, who was probably the Henry Jones knighted by Essex at Rouen in 1591 and whose coat of arms shows him to have been a member of the powerful Carmarthenshire family of Abermarlais. He was probably a younger son of Sir Henry Jones, who married into the Salusburys of Lleweni, and the brother of Sir Thomas Jones (d. 1604, M.P. for Carmarthen in 1584–85). The Joneses had a close alliance with the Perrots, and Sir Henry Jones had purchased land from men in Leicester's circle.[75]

As the lists at our disposal are not complete, any study derived from them cannot be comprehensive. William Midleton of Llansannan (Denbighshire) (c. 1550–c. 1600) and Huw Llwyd of Cynfal (Merioneth) (c. 1568–1630?), both of whom referred to their service in their poems, appear in none of the army lists. As Llwyd claimed to have served in a specifically Welsh contingent, he may have been a member of one of the foot companies. A William Midleton was among the gentlemen of Leicester's household in July 1587.[76]

The expedition also contained a number of Englishmen who either personally or through their families were involved in the administration of Leicester's interests in north Wales. As Penry Williams has noted in his study of the Council in the Marches, Leicester was considerably assisted by the fact that the Council contained a number of his allies and followers who could be relied upon to safeguard his interests.[77] Not only was the president, Sir Henry Sidney, his brother-in-law, but both the early vice-presidents, Sir John Throckmorton and Sir William Gerard, considered themselves his followers. Sir William's son, Gilbert Gerard, served in the expedition with a retinue of two. In 1574, at a time when Leicester was paying considerable attention to north Wales, two particularly close associates were appointed to the Council. Sir John Perrot, the great Pembrokeshire landowner, was an ally in both Welsh and English politics – John Wynn called him an 'inward favourite' of Leicester's.[78] In 1573 he was appointed chancellor and chamberlain of Caernarvonshire, Anglesey and Merioneth, and in 1588 deputy-lieutenant for north Wales.[79] Although Perrot could not join the expedition – he was lord deputy in Ireland – he offered Leicester advice and assistance, and his brother Sir Thomas served with a retinue of five.[80] The other new Council member of 1574 had a far greater effect on north Wales. Sir John Huband (d. 1583) of Ipsley (Warwickshire) was one of Leicester's closest servants. Steward of Kenilworth Castle during the 1560s, in 1572 he was appointed constable of Kenilworth and steward of Leicester's lands in Warwickshire, Worcestershire, Shropshire, and of the lordships of Arwystli and Cyfeiliog.[81] M.P. for Warwickshire in 1571 and 1576, he was nominated to the vice-presidency of the Council by Sir William Gerard in 1576 and given a general stewardship over Leicester's interests in Wales at the same time.[82] Huband was undoubtedly the central figure in the commissions for encroachment in Snowdon Forest.[83] Until his death he appears to have been the intermediary for appeals to, and patronage from, Leicester – the Wynn letters of the 1570s are full of references to him.[84] His brother and heir, Ralph Huband (d. 1605, Inner Temple, 1564), was a member of Leicester's train in December 1585 and brought with him a retinue of five.

The core of the administration of Leicester's estates in north Wales was provided by a small group of lawyers and 'men of business' who had been associated with Leicester since the 1560s: John Dudley of Newington (Middlesex) (d. 1580, a cousin and an Inner Templer, joint-clerk of the signet of the Council in the Marches),[85] John Yerwerth (M.P. for Chester, 1563), John Nuthall of Cottenhall (Cheshire) (d. 1586, a sergeant-at-law in Chester, another Inner Templer and a friend of John Dudley),[86] Henry Dynne (queen's auditor for north Wales) and William Glasier. Yerwerth, Nuthall, Dynne, and Glasier served on most of the commissions for encroachment; Dynne, Yerwerth, Glasier, and Dudley made the surveys of Denbigh and Chirk; and all of them at one time or another acted as attorneys for Leicester in his various property transactions in the 1570s and 1580s.[87] All received grants of property in north Wales.[88]

The most important of the 'men of business' was William Glasier of Lea (Cheshire) (d. 1588), vice-chamberlain of the county palatine of Chester from 1559 and a member of the Council in the Marches from 1560.[89] An Inner Templer, where he shared chambers with John Dudley, Glasier was an aggressive lawyer whose squabbles with the city of Chester and the Council in the Marches over the jurisdiction of his vice-chamberlain's court had to be resolved by the Privy Council, where the favourable verdicts for Glasier were probably the product of Leicester's influence.[90] Although various offices gave Glasier some influence in north Wales, he owed most of it to his relationship with Leicester, for whom he had been acting as a legal agent since 1553.[91] His son John Glasier, also an Inner Templer, was a member of Leicester's train in 1585 with a retinue of two. The list of effects attached to Glasier's will included 'a joyned frame with the earle of Leicester's pedigree' and 'a mapp of the Low Countries'.[92] The Piers Aldersey who served in the expedition was probably a member of the important Chester family of that name which was frequently allied with Glasier in city politics.[93]

Another 'servant' of Leicester's in the Netherlands was a participant in one of the more celebrated incidents in Leicester's relations with the borough of Denbigh. His angry letter to the borough on their apparent rejection of his parliamentary nominee, Henry Dynne, in 1572 has often been cited as an example of local resistance to his borough-mongering. Not enough attention has been paid, however, to the successful candidate, Richard Cavendish, who sat for Denbigh until 1585.[94] Cavendish served as an agent of Leicester's in the marriage negotiations involving the duke of Norfolk and Mary, Queen of Scots, in 1568–69.[95] He was one of Leicester's inner circle of advisers in the Netherlands in 1586, and Lord Burghley called him a 'most perfect devoted creature to your Lordship'.[96]

Including Cavendish, almost all the M.P.s for north Wales in the Parliament of 1584–85 served on the expedition.[97] Although their election may have been only the result of local politics – and there is no direct evidence of electioneering by Leicester – there is strong evidence that he was engaged in substantial electioneering in England in 1584.[98] The coincidence is reinforced by a comparison with Anglesey, where Leicester had no connection with the M.P.s and where there was no apparent participation in the expedition: in Anglesey Leicester had neither lands nor tenants.[99]

The contingent from north Wales was probably the most feudal element in the expedition: its dominant characteristics were the obligation of the tenants of a marcher lord to give military service and the allegiance of the officers of the administration of his estates. Unlike the English gentry contingent, the majority of whom shared Leicester's espousal of puritanism at home and defence of the protestant cause abroad, many of the Welsh families represented in the expedition – Lloyd of Bodidris, Holland of Kinmel, Edwards of Chirk – were markedly conservative. Only the circle of William Thomas, the Prices, and possibly the Vaughans, appears to have shared Leicester's political aspirations. If we had more information about the degree of and reason for refusal – the reasons of John Wynn of Gwydir, for example, or of Thomas Salusbury of Lleweni, who, although Leicester's ward and a member of his household, managed to remain in England and plot with Anthony Babington – these political implications might be clarified. Yet, in contrast to the followers of Sir William Stanley, these men were not poverty-stricken, lesser squires seeking a more congenial political climate or a means of recouping their fortunes in war; nor were they primarily young men seeking adventure. Rather were they summoned as servants and followers of whom Leicester could make 'an assured accompte'.

APPENDIX 12.1:
THE SUMMONS OF THE EARL OF LEICESTER TO
JOHN WYNN OF GWYDIR, 26 SEPTEMBER 1585*

An autograph circular letter, addressed on the dorse 'to my loving servaunt John Wynn, Esq.' The punctuation has been modernised and abbreviations expanded.

Wheras yt pleaseth the Queen's Majestie to assist her neighbours of the Lowe Countryes and to lay the charge of that service uppon me, as her highnes lieutenant generall, with expresse commaundment to prepare myselfe for yt, with all convenient speed, in which action I am to make choice of such my good friends and servaunts, as I may make an

* N.L.W. MS. 9051 E; *Calendar Wynn Papers*, p. 100.

assured accompte of, amongst which nomber your self are one. And therefore I doe not doubt, but that according to the shewe of your goodwill allwaies towards me, and my good opinion of yow, yow will now manifest & performe the same, in furnishing your selfe of a good horse and Arms to serve your soveraigne under me in this service of the Lowe Countryes. For my desier is to have as many demy launces to serve in that Country as I can gett amongst my owne servants. And if yow will furnishe any more horse, besides that for your selfe; lett them be good hable light horse, and the men well chosen also, that shall serve uppon them. And I doe earnestlie requier yow that I maye further receave aunswere from yow & your selfe to be with me here at London by the xvth or xvith of the next month yf it be possible, for hir Majestie doth hasten me verye greatlie to take my Journey speedlie. And to the uttermost of my power I will be thankfull & carefull to requite your ready & serviceable good will at this tyme. And soe fare you well. Leycester House this xxvith of September 1585.

Your loving Master
R. Leycester

NOTES

1 I would like to thank Miss Enid Pierce Roberts and Mr W. K. Williams-Jones of the University College of North Wales for their kind assistance and advice.

2 In his important study 'North Wales in the Essex Revolt of 1601', *English Historical Review*, LIX (1944), Professor A. H. Dodd drew attention to the north Welshmen who accompanied Sir William Stanley in his defection in 1587. Stanley, however, had permission to choose his own officers for the 1000 Irish troops he raised, and these men should be seen as followers of Stanley rather than of Leicester. Hence they will not be discussed here. See *Calendar of State Papers, Foreign Series, 1585–86*, p. 253.

3 *Calendar of the Patent Rolls, 1560–63*, pp. 534–43; *1563–66*, pp. 59, 312; *1569–72*, p. 472. No definite grant of the forestership of Snowdon has survived.

4 Halton was granted in June 1566, National Library of Wales, Chirk Castle MS. F.5599. For Cymer Abbey lands, see, e.g., N.L.W., Peniarth Deeds 473; for Bardsey lands, University College of North Wales Library, Nannau MS. 1560.

5 *Historical Manuscripts Commission, De Lisle and Dudley Manuscripts*, I, 301.

6 See *Cal. S.P. For., 1584–85*, pp. 197–9; *1585–86*, p. 128. Public Record Office, State Papers 84 (Holland)/5/107.

7 See W. A. Shaw's introduction to *Hist. MSS. Comm., De Lisle and Dudley MSS.*, III, xiii, xxii.

8 *Cal. S.P. For., 1584–85*, p. 691.

9 *Ibid.*, p. 507; *1585–86*, pp. 63, 80, 294.

10 P.R.O., S.P. 84/5/107.

11 *Cal. S.P. For., 1586–87*, p. 311; Shaw, op cit., p. xviii.

12 *Cal. S.P. For., 1586–87*, p. 191 (Leicester to Elizabeth, 11 October 1586).

13 See J. E. Neale, 'Elizabeth and the Netherlands, 1586–7', *Eng. Hist. Rev.*, XLV (1930), 377 *et seq.*

14 *Cal. S.P. For.*, *1585–86*, pp. 308–9 (R. Hurleston, the treasurer, to Sir Francis Walsingham, 20 January 1586).

15 In September 1586 the voluntary foot in the State's pay numbered 7512. *Cal. S.P. For.*, *1586–87*, p. 176.

16 British Museum, Egerton MS. 1694, ff. 54–5 (list of companies, 11 November 1586).

17 *Cal. S.P. For.*, *1585–86*, pp. 558–9; *1586–87*, pp. 71, 86.

18 P.R.O., S.P. 12 (Domestic, Elizabeth)/181/5; R. Flenley (ed.), *Calendar of the Register of the Council in the Marches of Wales, 1569–1591* (1916), pp. 225–6. These are the 200 men who appear in G. Cruickshank, *Elizabeth's Army* (2nd edn, Oxford, 1968), appendix II.

19 P.R.O., S.P. 84/12/18 (treasurer's account, January 1587).

20 Sir J. Wynn, *History of the Gwydir Family* (Oswestry, 1878), p. 104. Wynn considered Gwynne a 'godly man'. J. E. Griffith, *Pedigrees of Anglesey and Caernarvonshire Families* (Horncastle, 1914), p. 25. See also *N.L.W., Calendar of Wynn Papers*, no. 47, Gwynne to Maurice Wynn, 24 February 1573?; 'my lord' probably refers to Sidney.

21 Flenley, *Calendar*, pp. 218–20.

22 As muster-master he clashed with Sir Richard Bulkeley in 1588. *Acts of the Privy Council, 1588*, p. 118; I. Edwards (ed.), *Star Chamber Proceedings Relating to Wales* (Cardiff, 1929), p. 19.

23 *Hist. Gwydir*, p. 98.

24 J. Bruce (ed.), *Correspondence of Robert Dudley, earl of Leycester . . . 1585 and 1586* (Camden Soc., XXVII, 1844), p. 11, Leicester to Walsingham, n.d. (end of September). Letters patent in T. Rymer (ed.), *Foedera . . .* (1727–33), XV, 799.

25 Bruce, *Corres.*, p. 73.

26 B.M., Egerton MS. 1694, f. 54, and the note of Leicester on f. 53.

27 Caernarvonshire Record Office, quarter-sessions files (Q.S. 2/4), Thomas to bailiffs of Isaf, 4 February 1586; *Cal. S.P. For.*, *1585–86*, p. 495.

28 *Cal. S.P. For.*, *1585–86*, p. 668, Thomas D'Oyley to Lord Burghley, 24 May 1586. The companies were later considered to have been 'in pay' from 11 April. P.R.O. S.P. 84/12/18 (treasurer's account, January 1587).

29 *Cal. S.P. For.*, *1585–86*, pp. 110, 116, 127; P.R.O., S.P. 84/10/28, 41.

30 The muster-list of 22 November lists Thomas's company at Rheinberg; P.R.O., S.P. 84/11/66. His death is noted in the English edition of Van Meteren's *Historia Belgica, A True Historicall Discourse of the Succeeding Gouvernours of the Netherlands* (1602), p. 90.

31 U.C.N.W., Nannau MS. 1560, indenture of assignment, 10 January 1581. For Nuthall, see below, p. 245. For Thomas's position in county factions, see E. Gwynne Jones, 'County Politics and Electioneering, 1558–1625', *Caernarvonshire Historical Society Transactions*, I (1939), 37–8.

32 E. Gwynne Jones, 'The Caernarvonshire Squires, 1558–1625' (unpublished M.A. thesis, University of Wales, 1936), p. 243; 'History of the Bulkeley Family', ed. E. Gwynne Jones, *Anglesey Antiquarian Society Transactions* (1948), p. 25; *Cal. Wynn Pprs.*, p. 93, Ellis Price to William Thomas, 18 June 1580.

33 For Price and Vaughan, see below, pp. 139–40. It was probably because his son and Thomas married sisters that Ellis Price referred to Thomas as 'son-in-law' in his letter of June 1580.

34 Griffith, *Pedigrees*, p. 25, for Plas Mawr family. There is no other mention of Edward Griffith in the Netherlands.

35 P.R.O., S.P. 84/12/18 (treasurer's account, company of Jehan Lloyd). In the list of checks (S.P. 84/12/27) the company is described as that of Jevan Lloyd. S.P. 84/9/60, a list of companies at the camp, refers to the company of John Lloyd.

36 Flenley, *Calendar*, p. 201; N.L.W., Llanstephan MS. 36, pp. 85–6.

37 In the records of the lordship of Chirk, Evan Lloyd is noted as presiding as steward over the manorial courts of Cynllaith in Yarll, Cynllaith Owen, Mochnant, Llangollen, and Is Clawdd. William Penrhyn (see below, p. 243) was steward of Glyn: N.L.W., Chirk Castle MSS. D. 86, court book, 1576–80; D. 113, court roll, 1584–86. See also Chirk Castle MS. F. 13666, ministers' accounts, lordships of Denbigh and Chirk, 1575–80; Cal. *Wynn Pprs.*, p. 93.

38 N.L.W., Llanstephan MS. 36; *Nat. Lib. Wales Journal*, VI (1949–50), 21.

39 For the career of John Lloyd in the 1590s, see Dodd, 'North Wales in the Essex Revolt'.

40 (1905), II, 85.

41 N.L.W., Chirk Castle MSS. D. 87, court book, 1586–87; D. 115–16, estreats of fines, 1585–86, 1586–87. The John Lloyd who farmed a park in the lordship of Denbigh (MS. F. 13666) in the late 1570s may have been either the son or the brother.

42 Bruce, *Corres.*, p. 37; list of gentlemen accompanying Leicester in December 1585, *Cal. S.P. Spanish*, III, 554–6 (hereafter 'Spanish List'); B.M., Cotton MS. Vespasian C XIV, f. 325v, billeting-list at the Hague, 27 December 1585; J. A. Van Dorsten and R. C. Strong, in *Leicester's Triumph* (Oxford, 1964), have attempted to compile a general list of Leicester's train by combining all the existing manuscript lists. Unfortunately, it is badly edited and contains at least one major error. Cotton MS. Galba C VIII, ff. 96–101, is identified as a list of the train drawn up by Henry Goodere in January 1586. In fact it is two lists: ff. 96–7 is a list of the Earl's guard of 10 January, made by Henry Goodere, captain of the guard; ff. 98–102 is a list of Leicester's household in June 1587. The 'Mr. fleete of Yale' (Dutch list of billeting at Leiden during the spring of 1586, *Leicester's Triumph*, p. 116) is Evan Lloyd.

43 L. Dwnn, *Heraldic Visitations of North Wales* (Llandovery, 1846), II, 332–33, Lloyd of Henllan pedigree; N.L.W., Chirk Castle MS. F. 13666. Cal. *Wynn Pprs.*, p. 83, Catherine of Berain to John Wynn, 24 February 1577.

44 *Cal. Pat. Rolls, 1566–69*, p. 145; *1569–72*, p. 10. Two copies of the letters patent of July 1576 exist: N.L.W., Chirk Castle MS. F. 10609, and Powis Castle MS. 11426. Only lands within the lordship held from the Crown by military service were excluded.

45 Quitclaims for the former services were issued: N.L.W., Chirk Castle MS. F. 11.

46 A major agreement was made with the freeholders of Arwystli in 1578; see Powis Castle MSS. 11408, 11414, 12610, 12773; also E. Evans, 'Arwystli and Cyfeiliog in the Sixteenth Century: An Elizabethan Inquisition', *Montgomeryshire Collections*, LI (1949–50), 27.

47 Although many of the indentures, particularly those of Denbigh, exist only in collections of estate papers, e.g. U.C.N.W., Mostyn MS. 1880, Maenan MS. 111, the Chirk

Castle MSS. contain a considerable number of Leicester's copies: F. 12901 (1576), 495 (1578) and 2168 (1579) are grants to gentlemen; F. 12776, 12911 (1571), 10 (1572), 4470 (1576), 9754 (1577), 4129 (1578) are to yeomen.

48 Every indenture I have seen contains this clause.

49 H.M.C., *De Lisle and Dudley MSS.*, III, xxxiii–iv.

50 Flenley, *Calendar*, pp. 202–3; L. Boynton, *The Elizabethan Militia, 1558–1638* (1967), pp. 30–3.

51 P.R.O., S.P. 12/184/1, Leicester to Walsingham, 1 September 1585.

52 Bruce, *Corres.*, p. 5, Leicester to Walsingham, 27 September 1585.

53 Transcibed in an appendix. The form of the letter suggests that the others were identical.

54 *Cal. S.P. For., 1585–86*, p. 178 (to William Davison, 24 November 1585).

55 P.R.O., S.P. 84/5/3, is a note by Sir Thomas Cecil of his retinue of some fifty lances (to which his father Lord Burghley made a contribution), consisting of several lesser gentlemen and their retinues 'as goo voluntary with me' as well as immediate servants and retainers.

56 *Cal. S.P. For., 1585–86*, pp. 222, 308, 332.

57 P.R.O., S.P. 84/6/9. It is reprinted *in extenso* in E. M. Tenison, *Elizabethan England* (Royal Leamington Spa, 1933–61), VI, 45–7.

58 Caerns. R.O., quarter-sessions files, 1586.

59 N.L.W., Ruthin Lordship MS. 54. On the Prices generally, see E. P. Roberts, 'Teulu Plas Iolyn', *Denbighshire Historical Society Transactions*, XIII (1969), 39–110.

60 W. Rowland, *Tomos Prys o Blas Iolyn, 1564?–1634* (Cardiff, 1964), 21–3; Spanish List; G. J. Williams, 'William Midleton a Tomos Prys', *Bulletin of the Board of Celtic Studies*, XI (1944), 113–14.

61 W. Gareth Owen, 'Family Politics in Elizabethan Merionethshire', *Bull. B.C.S.*, XVIII (1958–60), 188.

62 Griffith, *Pedigrees*, p. 271; *Bull. B.C.S.*, VI (1931–33), 72–3; E. G. Jones, thesis, pp. 205–25.

63 U.C.N.W., Mostyn MSS. 1384, 3793, 3891, 3893.

64 *Ibid.*, 395, 3895, for the activities of Henry Vaughan in 1585 and 1588.

65 M. G. Watkins, *History of Herefordshire*, III (Hereford, 1897), 69.

66 N.L.W., Panton MS. 64, p. 31; *Cal. S.P. Span.*, III, 556.

67 U.C.N.W., Kinmel MS. 686.

68 *Members Admitted to the Inner Temple, 1547–1660* (n.d.), p. 60 (erroneously identified as Thomas Salusbury, the conspirator). Like his father, Robert Dudley was a member of the Inner Temple and in 1561 was appointed their 'Lord and Governour' in return for his patronage in several suits; F. A. Inderwick (ed.), *A Calendar of the Inner Temple Records* (1896), I, 215–19. Possibly by coincidence, a substantial number of Leicester's men of business and of north Welsh gentry were Inner Templers also. Those who will not be mentioned in the text included Simon Thelwall (admitted 1559, M.P. for Denbighshire, 1563), Piers Owen (1557, high sheriff of Denbighshire, 1584), John Gwynne (1561, M.P. for Caernarvonshire, 1571–74), Hugh Owen of Dolgelley, Mer.

(1557), John Salusbury (1561), Richard Puleston (1572), and John Wynn of Gwydir (1576). *Members Admitted, passim.*

69 *Cal. Wynn Pprs.*, pp. 83, 93.

70 *Dictionary of Welsh Biography*, p. 183. J. Lloyd, *History of . . . Powis Fadog* (1881), II, 372; J. E. Neale, *The Elizabethan House of Commons* (1949), p. 108.

71 N.L.W., Chirk Castle MSS. F. 372, 470, 5339, 12847, 12880.

72 W. V. Lloyd, *Montgomeryshire Sheriffs, 1540 to 1639* (1876), pp. 292–4; *Cal. Wynn Pprs.*, p. 93. See also note 37 above.

73 *Mont. Sheriffs*, pp. 192–4; W. V. Lloyd, *Pedigrees of Montgomeryshire Families* (1888), pp. 75, 128–9; N.L.W., Powis Castle MS. 12611.

74 *Mont. Collections*, III, 35; V, 413–14; VII, 57. Although Jenkyn Lloyd himself did not go to the Inner Temple (matriculated Balliol, 1577, *Alumni Oxoniensis*, II, 925), several of his sons did. For Lloyd and the election of 1588, see Neale, *Eliz. House of Commons*, ch. IV, *passim.*

75 For the knighting of Henry Jones, see Tenison, *Eliz. England*, VIII, 525. I am most grateful to Miss Enid Roberts for the information about Jones's coat of arms. See also J. Buckley, *Genealogies of Carmarthenshire Sheriffs* (Carmarthen, 1920), I, 34, 50, 65; N.L.W., Chirk Castle MS. F. 4556.

76 Rowland, *Tomos Prys*, p. 23; *Dict. Welsh Biog.*, pp. 593–4; B.M., Cotton MS. Galba C VIII, ff. 98–v.

77 *The Council in the Marches of Wales under Elizabeth I* (Cardiff, 1958), p. 274.

78 *Hist. Gwydir*, p. 93.

79 *Cal. Wynn Pprs.*, p. 115.

80 Bodleian Library, Perrot MS. 1, ff. 131–2, Perrot to the Privy Council, 10 September 1585; T. Wright, *Queen Elizabeth and Her Times* (1838), II, 289–90, Perrot to Leicester, 20 February 1586.

81 W. Dugdale, *Antiquities of Warwickshire* (1730), II, 138–41. [The statement that Huband was steward of Kenilworth during the 1560s is incorrect.]

82 Williams, *Council*, pp. 267–8.

83 'Bulkeley History', *Trans. Anglesey Antiq. Soc.*, pp. 23–8.

84 His name is frequently mis-spelled in the *Calendar* as Luband, Hughband, and Hybbotts. See also Philip Sidney to Leicester, 28 December 1581; *Prose Works of Sir Philip Sidney*, ed. Feuillerat (Cambridge, 1968), IV, 180–1.

85 Inderwick, *Inner Temple Calendar*, I, 215–19, 290; *Cal. Pat. Rolls, 1563–65*, p. 319.

86 Inderwick, op. cit., p. 295; G. Ormerod, *History of the County Palatine and City of Chester* (1882), II, 98–9. He was M.P. for Tamworth (Staffs.) from 1572 to 1581.

87 Survey of Denbigh, in J. Williams, *Records of Denbigh and its Lordship* (Wrexham, 1860), p. 109; of Chirk, N.L.W., Chirk Castle MS. F. 14000. For the activities of these agents, see, e.g., letter of Yerwerth to William Penrhyn, 24 April 1586, bound with a court roll in Chirk Castle MS. D. 113; Powis Castle MSS. 12610, 12773.

88 U.C.N.W., Nannau MS. 1560; N.L.W., Powis Castle MS. 11381; Chirk Castle MSS. F. 4518, 4556.

89 Williams, *Council in the Marches*, pp. 348–9.

90 *Ibid.*, pp. 198–200; Ormerod, I, 235; Inderwick, I, 234.

91 Caerns. R.O., quarter-sessions files, 1586, Glasier to the J.P.s of Caernarvonshire, 10 May 1586; *Cal. Pat. Rolls, Edward VI*, V, 221; N.L.W., Ruthin Lordship MS. 47.

92 *Lancashire and Cheshire Wills and Inventories, Part III* (Chetham Soc., LIV, 1861), pp. 128–34.

93 A. L. Browne, 'Sir John Throckmorton of Feckenham, Chief Justice of Chester', *Journ. of the Chester and N. Wales Archaeological Soc.*, n.s. XXXI (1935), 61–3.

94 Sir John Neale is unable to make up his mind about Leicester's control of Denbigh; *Eliz. House of Commons*, pp. 146, 203. G. Roberts, in his study of 'The Boroughs of North Wales' (unpublished M.A. thesis, University of Wales, 1928), p. 146, is suspicious of the independence of Denbigh. Although he did not examine Cavendish's career, he notes that the M.P. for Denbigh in 1586–87, Robert Wroth of Enfield (Middx.), had strong Leicesterian connections. In 1584–85 Wroth sat for Beverley, a borough in which Leicester had a considerable interest. [This is a mis-identification; the M.P. was Robert Wrote. See p. 211 above.]

95 W. Camden, *Annals* (1688), 128–9.

96 B.M., Cotton MS. Galba C X, f. 49, Burghley to Leicester, 1 October 1586. See also *Cal. S.P. For., 1585–86*, p. 669.

97 The members for Caernarvonshire, Caernarvon boroughs, Denbighshire, Denbigh boroughs, Merioneth and possibly Flint boroughs.

98 *Eliz. House of Commons*, p. 203.

99 Of minimal importance was the legendary feud with Sir Richard Bulkeley. The most recent study of the Bulkeleys, D. C. Jones, 'The Bulkeleys of Baron Hill, 1440–1621' (unpublished M.A. thesis, University of Wales, 1958), rejects the legend almost in its entirety and notes that during the 1560s and 1570s Richard Bulkeley was a client of Leicester's, although their relationship may have cooled after 1580. See especially pp. 157–8, 181.

Chapter 13

The Composition of 1564 and the Earl of Leicester's tenurial reformation in the lordship of Denbigh

The estate papers of Robert Salusbury of Galltfaenan form one of the most important collections of muniments of the gentry of Elizabethan Denbighshire.[1] MS. 1074 is of unique significance, however, for it is the only surviving copy of the Composition between Robert Dudley, Earl of Leicester, and the tenants of the lordship of Denbigh of 26 September 1564. The terms of the Composition provide the key to an understanding of Leicester's policy as lord of Denbigh and are of major importance for the agrarian history of north Wales in the sixteenth century. Only one other copy is known to have survived until modern times; it was discovered in the mid-nineteenth century among the muniments of Robert Myddelton, Esq. of Gwenynog and printed by J. Williams in his *Records of Denbigh and its Lordship*.[2] Examination of the Galltfaenan copy reveals that Williams mis-transcribed or omitted several important passages; for this reason, and because his work is no longer easily obtainable, it has seemed useful to provide a more accurate transcription. The new transcription will, in turn, serve as a preface to an analysis of the importance and ramifications of the Composition based on the manorial records of Leicesterian Denbigh, the great part of which have survived, and relevant material from the other Denbighshire lordships.[3]

Galltfaenan MS. 1074 is a large vellum indenture, written in English and measuring 56 cm. in width and 60 cm. in length. This and the Gwenynog copy were probably only two of a number of copies distributed among the leading tenants of the lordship.[4] In transcribing it I have attempted to make Elizabethan legal phraseology easier on the eye by modernising the punctuation and treating each sentence as a separate paragraph. With the exception of expanded abbreviations, spelling has not been altered. Notes to the transcription have been limited to a few minor points; the terms of the Composition will be discussed at length in the text of the essay.

Apud Denbighe in Northwallia
xxvi° die Septembris Anno Regni
Regine Elizabeth &c Sexto.

Wheras by reason that the yerly Revenewe of the Seygnorie or Lordshippe of Denbighe, whereof the Right honorable the Lord Robert Dudley, knight of the most noble order of the garter, one of the Quenes Majesties Priveye Counsayll and Master of her highnes horsesse,[5] is Rightfull owener and hathe estate of inheritance in fee symple, is presently in great decay; whiche hathe heretofore in auncient tyme bene answered vnto the Lordes and oweners of the sayd Seignory and Lordshippe yearly of a greater some then is presently answered (over and besydes the demayne Landes, parkes, forestes, Chaises, woodes, waistes and Commons, fyshings, fowlings, wardes, marriages and Reliefes, withall other Rialties then in the manuall occupacione of the sayd oweners and Lordes of the sayd Seignorie and Lordshippe for there best use, comoditie and profytte); whiche ought to be issuing and yearly payable out of and by suche porcions of Landes within the sayd Lordship as the nowe tenauntes of the sayd Lordship do occupie at thys present, albeit they nowe pretend to have the Same parcells of inheritaunce by the stewardes grauntes of the sayd Seignorie discharged from the sayd rents nowe decayed as by the Recordes of the premises evidently apperethe.

And furthermore by Collor of a Charter,[6] which the sayd tenauntes and inhabitauntes seme to have of the graunt of the late kinge Henry the viith as they do alleadge, pretendinge themselves therby to be dischardged of dyverse Costomable Rentes, duties and services hereafter mencioned, dowbtinge the validitie therof in Lawe; whiche are commonly Called by the names of Amobr woodwardeth, forestwryth, pro pastu forestarii alias Arien woodward vel arien forestarii aut Arien lliewe; pro pasture ffryth llech deinewell, havod elwey, egyched, pennant, llwyn fryth magon Tervyn; aut pro metiis et bondis de Denmayle, alias vocatur Arien tervyn dynnayle; Arien parva vel Arien vaure; pro reparacione manerii vocatur vwayth llys; de construccione domorum et sexuum, alias vocatur treth gare; de kylch de Dynnale; de pastu Stalion et gartionis, alias vocatur porthiant stalwyn; de pastu lucrarii cum canibus; de operibus molendinorum; de pastu equi ragloti et de pastu Servientis pacis, alias vocatur kilch kais vel arien pensythyd; de pastu pennyacwy et Gwission vechan; et de advocatione, alias vocatur arderk et denarii advocarii, alias vocatur arien arderk; which should amount unto the some of CCxl li. and above.

Therefore for Reformacione whereof (to thende that the sayd seignorie and Lordship with the possessiones, Lands and Tenaments, Rialties and interest of the Same as well one the behalf of the sayd Lord Robert as of the particular tenauntes and occupiers of the same may be relieved and brought to a certen perfection accordingly), THE SAYD Lord Robert, greatlie desiring not onlie the certentie thereof but also the favorable entreatie and great increase of the sayd tenauntes dwellinge within the said Lordship – and also for the greate zeale, Care and Love which he hath of his sayd Tenauntes – is well Contented and pleased not only to Remytt a great parte of the said decayes but utterly for ever to release and dischardge theym of all the sayd strait costomes, Sharpe imposiciones and exaciones.

And myndinge also to forbere Rigor of Lawe to be commenced agaynst the said tenauntes and for the performance thereof, his Lordship of hys honorable good wyll and Carefullnes over them hathe favorably sent by his commission and authorised, nominated and apoynted hys trustie Servauntes and friends John Dudley,[7] William Glasiour,[8] Thomas Rolfe[9] esquiers and John Yerwerth gentleman[10] to survey, viwe and travell the same, by all suche Lawfull and favorable meanes as for Reformacione of the premisses apperteyneth, whiche nowe bene in execucione accordingly.

The Reverende father in God Thomas, Bishoppe of St. Asaphe,[11] ordinary of the same place, Sir John Salusbury knight,[12] Ellis Price doctor of lawe[13] and Robert Wynn ap Kydwalader[14] esquiers, and all other the tenauntes and inhabitants of the sayd seignorie and Lordship, with one hole mynd and assent humbly submyttinge them Selves to a Reasonable Confirmitie and reformacione of the same by the travell and labor of the sayd Reverend father, John Salusbury, Ellis Price and Robert Wynn (who be aucthorised and apoynted by Commission of all the sayd tenauntes to travell in the premisses), have most instantly desired and praied the sayd John Dudley and others the Commissioners of the sayd Lord Robert to accept and Receyve for the use and behoufe of the sayd Lord Robert not onlie there faithfull and most assured hartes and good wylls, but also there duties, services and powers vnto hys honor most redie and vnfaynedly offered, to remayne at hys honors commaundment and apoyntment in all Lawfull Respectes (there duties of alledgaunce vnto the Quenes highnes, her graces heyres and Successors, kings and Quenes of England, alwayes Reserved).

And for the accomplishment of the premisses the sayd suters and peticioners by there sayd attornies, factors and travellors have also hartely desired, and with many dutiefull perswaciones entreated, the sayd John Dudley and others commissioners aforesayd, one the behalf and for the use of the sayd Lord Robert, to accept and take (and by thees presents they for them and theyre heyres and executors do nowe frely give and graunt) unto the sayd Lord Robert and hys heires not only the some of one thowsand pounds – to be payd in the maner and forme followinge: That is to say in the Vigill of St. Andrew nowe next to come fyve hundreth pounds, and in the twentieth day of March then next ensuinge [an] other fyve hundreth pounds in full payment of the saide thowsand pounds – for the Release and discharge of the sayd Chargeable Rents and bondages, Welsh costomes and services, Imagined to be discharged by the sayd supposed Charter which are commonlie Called as is before Recyted; but also the sayd attorneys and factors for the sayd Tenants, and in there names and behalf, have and by thees presents do lykewyse freely geve and graunt for them and there heyres, one yearly Rent of three hundreths thertie and three pounds, vi s., viii d. to be receaved upon the Landes and tenements whiche the sayd tenauntes have and Clayme to have as there inheritance – be they fyne lands, Costomary Landes, excheat landes, relief landes, copy hould landes, bound land or encroachments, or others their inheritances within the said signorie or Lordship, saving suche as hold by speciall Charters and do pay thowld and accustomed Rentes reserved upon the same – every tenaunt to pay his particular parte and porcion yerely at the feastes of thanunciation of our Ladie and St. Michaell thearchaungell for ever from the feast of St. Michaell tharchaungell next cominge; and to Contynewe the same payment yerely unto the sayd Lord Robert and hys heires for ever after – and by a rate whiche amongst themselfes with the assystance of the Lord's Steward or commissioners aforesaid or any of theym shalbe reduced and apoynted – over and besydes the yerely Rentes alredie payd and which is nowe in yerely Revenewe and Charge within the Seignorie and Lordship, and the rent called tunck and other the Reliefes, services, duties and Rialties.

And for the better performance of the same Rentes presently Revyved unto the sayd Lord Robert and hys heires, the sayd attornies and factors on the behalf and for the sayd Tenants have hartely desired that, vpon the sayd Rates for the particular payments therof, It would please the sayd Lord Robert to accept and take the same to be reserved Chargable and yssuing out of the particular parcells of the premisses in theyre Severall occupaciones by suche severall wrytings as by suche Counsell Learned whiche the sayd Lord Robert and the said attornies for the sayd Tenants and inhabitants shall nominate and appoynte shalbe devised and advised.

The sayd Tenants, by there said attornies and by themselves personally by thees presentes, do promise on there part to performe the same.

All whiche suits, peticiones, and requests, and also the offers, guyfts, and graunts before mencioned, the sayd Commissioners on the behalf and for the sayd Lord Robert have heard and – ponderinge depely the Consyderations and Cyrcumstances thereof not onlie for the augmentacion of the honor of the sayd Lord Robert whome they serve in thys behalf, but also for the great benefyt, wealth, and Comoditie of the sayd Tenants which they greatlie desire to be encreased, and Chiefly in accomplishment of the wyll and pleasure of the sayd Lord Robert, according to the great trust in them reposed, for the alteracion of all such bondages and extremities which the sayd Tenants presently stand in danger of and to Remove from them and there issues hereafter suche services, bondages, feblenes of estates, scruple and dowbtes as are manifestly obiected agaynst there dyssents and inheritances of the sayd Landes in every of there possessions which they nowe Clayme to have by inheritaunce before Recited; And most of all for the performaunce of there better good wylles and services unto his honor to be firmely obliged and assured for ever – upon deliberate Consideracion and good advisement have agreed and assented on the behalf and for the sayd Lord Robert and in hys name to accept, Receave, and take for hys Lordship's use the sayd offers, gyftes, and graunts before mencioned.

And also the sayd Commissioners on the behalf and for the sayd Lord Robert and in hys name do promise: That upon a particular book or verdict to be made and yielded up by verdyt of the Juries nowe Sworne for Survey of the premisses or some other sufficient Jurie within the sayd Lordship unto the sayd Steward or unto the sayd Commissioners of every Tenants Landes and possessions within the sayd Lordship which they have by tytle or Collor of any estate of inheritance and wherof they be nowe in possession accordingly, together with suche encroachments and incroached Landes as they and every of theym have made upon that pretended estate of inheritance, THAT the sayd Lord Robert shall make vnto every tenant so to be named and mencioned in the sayd booke or verdit so good, sure, and perfyct Conveyaunce in the Lawe in fee simple, as by the Councell Learned to be apoynted as is before recyted shalbe devysed or advised, with Reasonable Common of pasture as by the said Charter is graunted and geven.

Reservinge vnto the sayd Lord Robert and hys heyres and assignes suche rents in every of the sayd assurances as the booke or verdit shall express so that in the hole the said Rentes do and wyll amount unto yerely the same Revyvall CCC xxxiii^{li} vj^s viij^d per Annum over and above the yearly Rents of the premisses nowe aunswered and payd, and so that the Seignories and Services of the sayd Tenaunts and other Reservacions, Rialties, sutes of court, and other services before mencioned for the use of the sayd Lord Robert and hys heyres be fully reserved and geven; and yearly from henceforth to be observed and come vnto the sayd Lord Robert and hys heires.

And soe that the demesne landes, the parkes of Moylewige, Snodiock, Castell parke, and Postny parke, forestes, Commons, woodes, waters, fyshings, and all other landes called excheat landes, and other hereditaments whatsoever which nowe be in lease or hathe bene in leas syns [the] fyrst day of the Raygne of the Late Kinge Henry the viijth and thereby possessed or injoyed, be not towched or impeyred.

And the sayd commissioners aforesayd one the behalf and for the sayd Lord Robert dothe also promise that every bondman, vyllayn, bondwoman, and neyfes nowe beinge within the sayd Seignorie and there Sequelles shall have at hys and there resonable request and sute to be made unto the sayd Lord Robert or the sayd Commissioners a sufficient manumission or discharge of there bond tenures for them and there Sequelles for ever without any fyne or some of money to be payd therefore other then there contributions for there partes upon the rates before recyted.

In witnesse of the faythfull, trewe, and unfayned performauncie of all and singular thes premisses on either and every partie before mencioned to be well and trewely performed, observed, and kept; as well the sayd Commissioners and attorneys on the behalf and for the sayd Lord Robert hath to thone parte of thys wrytinge indented put to theare seals and subscribed there names, as also the sayd attorneys and factors one the behalf and for the sayd Tenants and inhabitaunts have put ther seales and subscribed there names, the sayd xxvith day of Septembre in the sayd vith yere of the Raigne of our Sayd Soveraigne Ladie Elizabethe by the grace of God of England, Fraunce, and Yerland Quene, defender of the fayth &c.

I

Before proceeding to examine the Composition in detail, we should first consider the state of the lordship of Denbigh prior to the grant in fee simple of the lordships of Denbigh and Chirk to Lord Robert Dudley by letters patent on 9 June 1563.[15] Four documents shed light on conditions within the lordship: the terms of the grant of 1563, a survey of the later years of Henry VIII,[16] an exchequer inquisition of 1561,[17] and the initial survey taken by

Leicester's commissioners in the summer of 1563.[18] The latter two are worth some attention. The roll of the inquisition of 1561 lacks its first membrane and contains only the answers of the jury. Yet in most cases the questions can be deduced; and the context reveals it to have been part of a wider exchequer investigation of the Crown lands in Wales. The survey of 1563 is part of a general survey made by Leicester's agents of the manors granted to him in that year. It is possible that it is only a summary, the original being lost, for it contains neither the presentments of an inquisition, nor full descriptions of the tenurial status of the tenants it lists. On the other hand, it may never have been intended to be more than a summary, the 1561 inquisition being employed initially, with a full survey, as mentioned in the Composition, to be taken later.

Since the fourteenth century the lordship of Denbigh and Denbighland had been an important part of the earldom of March. The earldom had reverted to the Crown on the accession of Edward IV in 1461 and had been maintained as one of the key administrative units of the royal demesne, being granted out only once, namely to Arthur, prince of Wales in 1493.[19] The three other marcher lordships from which the shire of Denbigh was created in 1536, Chirk, Ruthin, and Bromfield and Yale, had had a more varied history, but had also reverted to the Crown at the turn of the century.[20] They were first united in 1531 when granted to Henry Fitzroy, Duke of Richmond.[21] The grant of Denbigh and Chirk to Leicester, and Ruthin to his brother Ambrose, Earl of Warwick, in 1564 therefore reversed a previous policy of keeping the Denbigh lordships within the royal family, and the revival of dormant marcher lordships after the Act of 1536 created a tense political situation in the region.[22]

The formal structure of the lordship of Denbigh in 1563 was little different from that described in the famous survey of 1334. Leicester was granted the three commotes of the cantref of Rhufoniog – Ceinmeirch, Isaled, and Uwchaled – and two commotes of the cantref of Rhos – Isdulas and Uwchdulas. The third commote of Rhos, Creuddyn, had been incorporated with the principality at the Conquest; but a detached portion of this commote, the townships of Penmaen and Llysfaen lying in Isdulas, Leicester was able to restore to the lordship in 1569, although they were again severed, as not being 'parcell of the lordship of Denbigh', after his death.[23] He was also granted the commote or ringildry of Dinmael, which was 'in the lordship of Denbigh but not of it', and continued the long-established practice of leasing it as a separate manor.[24] Dinmael lay outside the purviews of the court baron of the lordship and had its own manorial court, although it appears to have been included within the Composition.

Within the five commotes the core of the demesne comprised the four demesne manors, the parks, and the mills.[25] The four manors included in the grant of 1563 had all been in existence before 1334. Dinorben Fawr (called Talgarth in the grant of 1563) in Isdulas and Ystrad (Astred Owen in 1334) in Ceinmeirch had been *maerdrefi* before 1282. Ystrad Sheephouse (called the manor of Denbigh in 1334) and Kilford had been created by the first lords of Denbigh in the Ystrad valley. They had all been leased since the mid four-teenth century; by 1500 the lessees were usually the leading families of the lordship. In several cases, the Myddeltons with the manor of Ystrad, the Hollands with Dinorben Fawr, and the Salusburys of Lleweni with Kilford, the manors were regarded almost as a family possession.[26] The grant of 1563 recites a list of five parks: Castle or Little Park, Moel-y-wig, and Garth Snodyog in Isaled, Postney and Kilford in Ceinmeirch, all of which had been created between 1282 and 1334.[27] A sixth park, Galch Hill, had been alienated before 1563 and was restored to the demesne only in 1584.[28] The parks were little strain on the economy of the lordship, for by 1540 Galch Hill, Postney, and Kilford had been effectively disparked and leased as pasture.[29] Kilford Park had been created from the manor of Kilford, and its lands

> do entremedle with the grounds and pastures of the manor Kilford, so that by reason the same manor and parke have been letten together. And of so long time in the occupacion of one Farm for the tyme being that the parcells and certeyntye thereof are unknown from the oder . . .[30]

Of the other parks, the inquisition of 1561 described Moel-y-wig as 'a sowre and barren grounde and good for no purpose but for game', and Garth Snodyog as 'being a ragged rocky grounde and for no purpose but for dear'.[31] In 1563 they were in considerable disrepair and the lessees of Moel-y-wig and Castle parks offered to compound with Leicester for their disparking, suc-cessfully in the case of Castle Park.[32] The seigniorial mills in each commote were in a worse condition; the inquisition of 1561 revealed that most were either in ruin or in private hands.[33]

The greater part of the demesne was composed of the former tribal and bond lands which had come into the lord's immediate possession through escheat and forfeiture. These had been regranted in English tenures, a pro-cess which was well advanced in the eastern commotes (Isaled and Ceinmeirch) by the middle of the fifteenth century.[34] The process was accompanied by the demands of the emerging gentry and greater tenants to hold entirely by English tenures, demands which were met in the Charter of 1506 and in the terms of the 'Acts of Union'.[35] Yet if Welsh tenures had been abrogated at law and replaced by the English trinity of freehold, leasehold, and copyhold by 1563, the lands of the greater tenants were not immediately transformed into freehold estates of inheritance.[36] The history of the regranted demesne lands was a complicated subject, of considerable interest to both lord and tenant. For this reason the fate of the demesne and the growth of the new estates were aspects of the same problem and should be examined together.

The most stable, if minor, class of freeholders were those who held by charters of military service, probably survivals of castle-guard tenure, the most honourable of the English tenures of the early years of the lordship.[37] The charterers are mentioned in both the inquisition of 1561 and the Composition. The main Leicesterian rental, compiled in 1583, recites a list of six gentlemen who held land in Isaled 'ut de domino de Denbigh et per serviciam militarem': John Hanmer, Esq., Robert Salusbury of Galltfaenan, Fulk Lloyd, Esq. of Henllan, John Panton, Thomas Salusbury, Esq. (the future conspirator, grandson and heir to Sir John Salusbury of Lleweni), and Henry Chambers.[38] The reserved rents, a total of 2s. 10d. p.a., were the old rents unaffected by the Composition.

These tenancies were only a small, if respected, portion of the estates of the six gentlemen concerned, the greater part of which had accrued in a manner similar to that open to the other tenants. By the mid sixteenth century it was considered a custom of the lordship that regranting of demesne land was a prerogative of the steward. The inquisition of 1561 gives a vivid description of the procedure followed. The court baron had jurisdiction over

> all lands excheated or forfeited or common to the lordes handes by any wayes or meanes. [The steward] used the next court after the seasure thereof to make open proclamation who would come and be the lordes best tenauntes and pay most fyne and the greatest rent to have yt to them and theire heires or in such estat as thei and the lord could agree, doing such suyt to and service to the lord and his courts as appertayned, after whiche proclamation they used to stay the courts; and in that time the lords attorney directed his process to the excheator to impanell a Jurye to viewe and understand how the landes was excheated to the lords handes and of the value thereof. And upon bringing in of this presentment the steward, after a solemn proclamation made in open courte, [with] thadvise of the attorney, the excheator and Receiver, and all other the lordes officers, wold lett the said landes to the most profitt of the lord as they could agree with the tenauntes, whether it were by Coppie of Court Rowle, or fyne to them and to their heires for ever, or for years. And thus hathe yt ben used and contynued time out of mynd.[39]

The lands granted by the steward fall into two main categories: estates of inheritance ('by fyne to them and to their heires for ever'), or leases by copy of court roll ('for years') – leasehold land within the lordship was invariably referred to as term (of years) lands. Since there are no surviving leases by indenture prior to 1563, apart from leases by letters patent discussed below, it is probable that all leases by the steward were by copy. The nature of the estates of inheritance (whether freehold or copyhold) is, on the other hand, a more difficult problem, for the extent of tenure by customary copyhold directly from the lordship (not by the subtenants of the greater tenants) is not easy to learn from the surviving documents. The survey of 1563 does not give information of sufficient precision, while the jurors of 1561 claimed that lack of time prevented them from proceeding to 'the answering of the division of the coppiehould from the freehould'.[40] The best guide is the Henrician survey, which lists customary tenants in the two eastern commotes – Isaled and Ceinmeirch – although in suspiciously small numbers.[41] Leicester's complaint in the Composition about the large amount of land which the tenants 'pretend to have . . . of inheritaunce by the stewardes grauntes of the sayd Seignorie' suggests that the stewards had connived at a widespread (and illicit) transformation of copyhold to freehold.

The role of the steward was central both to the tenurial situation in the lordship and to its politics; the office had been in the possession of the leading landed family, Salusbury of Lleweni, from 1508 to 1563.[42] The 'auctoritie of the Steward' was considered a liberty of the lordship and the powers of the office enabled its possessor to manipulate the administration of the lordship in his own behalf and that of his allies. Not only could favourable grants be obtained, but, with the assistance of a pliant escheator, concealment of escheats and rents could be arranged, estates of inheritance created, and seigniorial rights over commons and wastes allowed to lapse. In 1523 Robert Dolben, clerk of the rolls of the lordship, complained that when he was intimidated by tenants whom he had discovered concealing rents owed to the king, the steward, Sir Roger Salusbury, refused to assist him. Robert Salesbury of Bachymbyd and Rûg, steward of Ruthin, was accused in the later years of Henry VIII of claiming Crown lands as his inheritance.[43]

During the first half of the sixteenth century the monopoly of the steward to set and let freely was increasingly threatened by the practice of obtaining leases directly from the Crown by letters patent or, from 1540 to 1553, from the court of augmentations, or from the exchequer after 1554. Twenty-one-year leases were the norm, although there are examples of 25-, 30-, and 50-year leases in the reign of Mary. The lands involved in such transactions were substantial in extent, the demesne manors, for example, or all the Crown's land in a particular township.[44] Another threat emerged in 1538 when Walter Blount was appointed surveyor of the earldom of March and licensed to let lands in the Crown estates worth under 40s. per annum.[45] This caused considerable turmoil, for not only did Blount deprive the steward of his monopoly, but he also brought into question some of the earlier steward's grants. At the end of the reign of Henry VIII, Robert Salesbury, the steward of Ruthin, was charged in the court of augmentations with preventing Blount from enjoying his licence.[46] In the reign of Edward VI the inhabitants of Bromfield and Yale complained strongly to the court about the growing practice of seeking leases directly from the Crown, which subverted the custom of the lordship and threatened the security of those who held by the steward's grants.[47] The Crown's suspicions about the use to which the steward of Denbigh put his powers can be seen in the inquisition of 1561.[48]

Together with the powers of the steward, the inquisition of 1561 investigated a second area of major concern: the rights of the tenants under the Charter of 1506. If the greater part of the provisions of the Charter had been subsumed within the Acts of Union, two had not: the abolition of bond tenures and the abolition of traditional Welsh duties and renders. Moreover, the tenants of Chirk, and probably those of Denbigh as well, claimed that the Charters of Henry VII also discharged decays in rent.[49] The 1561 inquisition in Denbigh included a question about bondmen and received the answer that 'all suche as have manumission of Henry vijth by his said charter be made meere Englishmen by diverse lawes made by the kinge of famous memory king Henry the Eighth'. A question concerning the renders received the answer: 'for all other exaciones that the lordship were charged we say that the said inhabitauntes be discharged by the said graunt of Henry the viith as aforesaid'; while a further question, probably concerning decays of rent, received a similar answer: 'we be discharged by the said graunt of Henrie the viith'.[50] The evidence suggests that the tenants of the Denbighshire lordships claimed, as did those of the principality, that the manumission by Henry VII converted bondholdings into freeholdings.[51] The Chirk inquisition of 1566 lists tenants as freeholders, leaseholders, copyholders, and freeholders, formerly bondholders.[52] While neither the inquisition of 1561, nor the survey of 1563, provides such information for Denbigh, the Henrician survey includes references to former bond-, now freeholders.[53]

Neither the inquisition of 1561 nor the survey of 1563 discusses encroachment on the commons or wastes; yet they both raise a similar issue, destruction of timber in the parks and commons. The survey of 1563 noted that there was 'no store of great timber' within the lordship and there had been numerous complaints over the previous fifty years about the destruction of woods and game by the lessees of the parks.[54] The inquisition of 1561 received an indignant answer to a question about rights over timber:

> We say that the freehoulders time out of mind have as well used there woodes as there landes to there most commoditie and profitte and knowe of now suche custome. And if there were any suche custome yt was never put into execution and is meere repugnant to the lawes of the Realme.[55]

The conclusions reached by the exchequer commission in 1561 about the steward's authority and the Charter of 1506 can be deduced from the petition of the tenants appended to the inquisition.

> We the tenauntes and inhabitants of the lordshipp of Denbigh most humblie desire you, being the Queenes Majesties commissioners, that it may please you of

your goodness to consider this booke of articles that conteyneth suche matters as you have geven us in charge and our customary conteyned in the same. And because our answer restithe upon the Charter of the king of famous memory King Henry the vijth and the auctoritie of the Steward, the whiche seemeth to you to be dowbtfull; therefore our most humble desire is that yt may please you to be meanes unto the Queenes Majesties most honourable counsaill of thexchequier, that yt may please them of theyr goodness to enforme the Queenes Majestie of her meere clemency and mersie in consideracion of a fyne to her hyghness to be paid to Ratifie and confirme the graunt of the late Kinge Henry the vijth and the auctoritie of the said steward that haithe had contynuance for thys 300 years; and the poore tenauntes and inhabitauntes shall pray to allmighty god for the prosperous estat of her Majestie. The fyne that we are contented to geve to the Queenes Majestie is fyve hundred marks.

And further, we the jurors and a nombre of the gentlemen of the said lordship have subscribed this our verdict and peticion that we will stand unto.[56]

The information from the inquisition enables us to place it in the context of wider developments. There is evidence to suggest a growing dissatisfaction on the part of the Crown with the liberties claimed under the Charters and the decayed revenues of the lordships of north Wales. The commission granted to Walter Blount in the late 1530s may have been part of a wider effort to increase the revenue from the area in an age of growing inflation. It is also possible that the examination of conditions in Wales made at the time of the Acts of Union may have begun the process of reappraisal of the Charters, although the Charter to Denbigh was confirmed in its entirety by letters patent of 8 October 1551.[57]

Action was taken at the beginning of Elizabeth's reign. A document of 1562 refers to 'a general commission being already forth to survey the land in all Wales' granted to the marquis of Winchester, lord treasurer, Sir Richard Sackville, under-treasurer, and Sir Walter Mildmay, chancellor of the exchequer. Under this commission 'speciall inquisitions were delyvered' to local commissioners, of which the Denbigh inquisition of 1561 and one for Bromfield and Yale are known.[58] While the Bromfield and Yale inquisition has not survived, we have a supplementary commission of 1 August 1562 to make a settlement with the tenants and the resultant surveys.[59] The surveys record the judgement that the decays of rent were produced by the effects of Glyndŵr's revolt and 'the neglect of the officers of the Queen's predecessors' – which was considered to be the case in all the Denbighshire lordships. There was also confusion in the tenurial structure, although 'they [the tenants] have alledged charters and other writings which have been considered and cannot be found allowable, notwithstanding the great chardges, sustained about the triall thereof'.[60] Leaving the details of the composition in Bromfield and Yale for later examination, certain points are immediately relevant. First, both the Denbigh and the Bromfield inquisitions were part of a wider effort to resolve the Welsh land problem. Secondly, we can now date the origins of the campaign which would culminate in the judgement of the exchequer of 1603 that the Charters of Henry VII had conferred only a personal manumission and that claims to freehold under the Charters were invalid. Further confirmation of this changed attitude comes from a case involving some Caernarvonshire tenants in 1590 in which both sides accepted that the Charters had been invalid for many years, although the tenants claimed that their freehold had not been queried until 1566.[61]

II

There can be little doubt that the leading families of the lordship had derived considerable advantage from the conditions obtaining in the first half of the sixteenth century. But the confusion in law offered little security once greater powers began to examine closely the situation in the lordship in the 1560s. The conclusions of the exchequer commission of 1561 foreshadow the concerns of Leicester's Composition. It is, however, instructive to examine the making of the Composition in the context of the activities of Leicester's surveyors.

On 10 June 1563, the day following the grant of the lordship, Leicester commissioned John Dudley, Glasier, Rolfe, and Yerwerth to survey the lordship and to initiate, at least, the setting and letting of his lands.[62] Their survey, discussed above, was taken between 29 July and 8 August 1563. Apart from its summary of the rental, the survey also includes the initial revivals of leasehold rents, recommendations concerning the salaries of the officers of the lordship, and estimates that the revival of leasehold rents would increase the revenues by £200, while 'improvement [enclosure] of your lordship's waistes and commons with the contentatione of the tenants' would be worth another £100 per annum.[63] On the other hand, the survey does not allude to any of the issues of the Composition. Nor, as mentioned above, do we know whether an inquisition was taken at this time. The full 'book or verdict' was still to be made at the time of the Composition.[64]

We have no knowledge, moreover, of the course of events between the summer of 1563 and that of 1564; but certain proceedings may be deduced. The surveyors made their initial revivals of leasehold rents 'for a president . . . for we found at fyrst the tenauntes somewhat stubborne and straunge to the same and now more redie upon this example and well affected thereto'.[65] At this stage in the later survey of Chirk the surveyors noted that the revivals could not be made immediately owing to the tenants' invocation of the Charter of Henry VII and it is probable that a similar resistance was encountered in Denbigh. It is revealing that the main series of new leases was not made until 1 October 1564 – after the Composition.[66] Leicester's commissioners do, however, display a certain confidence which suggests that they knew of the conclusions of the exchequer commission. While the fate of the inquisition and petition of 1561 is unknown, the doubts of the exchequer commissioners probably lay behind the attitude of the surveyors of Chirk towards the Charter, 'which we stand in and do think their Charter doubtfull', and behind Leicester's thinly veiled threat in the Denbigh Composition to go to law if necessary.[67] The identity of the resisting tenants is also unknown, but it is probable that they were the wealthier members of the community.[68] It would not be to their advantage to antagonise Leicester too openly, however, particularly when the strength of his legal position was considered, and a compromise was therefore mutually satisfactory. The role played in the Composition by Sir John Salusbury was probably not without significance.

The Composition rehearses the doubts expressed by the commissioners of 1561 concerning the liberties claimed under the Charter and the liberties claimed under the 'auctoritie of the Steward'. With regard to the Charter, the Composition deals directly with the two main provisions not included in the Acts of Union: the customary renders and the manumission of bondmen. Leicester agreed to grant his own discharge of the renders. The list recited in the Composition is identical to that in the Charter. The only Welsh rents retained were *twnc* rents, which were also excluded in the Charter. Leicester also offered free manumission to all bondmen and included former bondland with other lands claimed as estates of inheritance. The offer of manumission does not appear to have had immediate relevance but it may have been included as a reassurance that no tenant need suffer loss of personal status through the Composition.[69] For this part of the Composition Leicester was granted £1000 to be paid on 30 November 1564 and 20 March 1565. The size of the 'gift' may, however, be deceptive. The inquisition of 1561 reveals that it was customary for the lordship to offer a mise of 500 marks on the entry of a new lord for confirmation of their liberties. This had been increased to 700 marks under the Charter of 1506. In 1561 the tenants were prepared to offer the queen another 500 marks: a total of 1200 marks (£800). Part at least of the queen's mise had been paid, for on 6 November 1564 Sir John Salusbury informed Sir William Norris that the 200 marks remaining were to be discharged owing to the mise to be paid to Leicester.[70] In the register of Leicester's papers there is a reference to a composition for his mise made at the same time as the greater Composition.[71] While nothing further is known of this mise, it is not impossible that it provided the greater part of the £1000.

The second part of the Composition was concerned with the decays of rent and encroachments. The decays of rent were mainly attributed to the claims of the tenants 'to have the Same parcells of inheritaunce by the stewardes grauntes of the sayd Seignorie' and not to the Charter of 1506. Leicester's solution was to offer, in exchange for a general increase in rent of £333. 6s. 8d. 'to be reserved Chargable and yssuing out of the particular parcells of the premisses in theyre Severall occupaciones', 'good, sure, and perfyct Conveyaunce in the Lawe in fee simple' of 'the Landes and tenements whiche the sayd tenauntes have and Clayme to have as there inheritance' of whatever origin, together with previous encroachments and reasonable common of pasture as allowed under the Charter. The only lands excluded were the old charter lands, the demesne, and any land granted as leasehold since the first day of the reign of Henry VIII.[72]

The Composition was to be put into effect after the general survey had been completed. The first results of the survey were not, however, surrendered to Leicester's commissioners until 15 September 1566, although the survey had been completed earlier and the results 'kept sealed up in a bagg' by the jurors. In a report attached to this survey in the survey book for 1566, the commissioners described some of the circumstances of the tenants' further resistance.[73] After the jurors' initial refusal to surrender their presentments, the case had gone before the Council in the Marches, where the tenants had stated that they 'onlie had yielded unto the said composition upon respect of our liberall words and promyss touching the decaies and encroachments'. The Council apparently decided in Leicester's favour, for the tenants were ordered to surrender the survey to the Council at Chester on 23 September 1566. Shortly before that date, Leicester's commissioners contrived to be in Denbigh and 'friendlie to debat the cause of there grief'. Sir John Salusbury took the lead in calling for a compromise and claimed that by refusing to honour their part of the Composition the tenants had given Leicester 'by lawe good cause of action against them there chosen commissioners'. On 15 September the tenants agreed to surrender the presentments on the condition that Leicester's commissioners carry a petition to him requesting that he moderate the Composition.

This account is the only one surviving of the making of the Composition and of its immediate consequences. While it is not as explicit as one would have wished, it does appear to indicate that the concern of the tenants lay with the increase of rent rather than the Charter. Their complaint about the promises of Leicester's commissioners suggests that the terms of the Composition were set by them, although the influence of Sir John Salusbury should not be underrated. On the other hand, Leicester's commissioners denied rumours which had circulated among the tenants that they could not or would not perform their part of the Composition. Two of the requests of the tenants are reported. The presentments of the jury had revealed that the decayed rents amounted to £396. 0s. 4¼d., £62. 13s. 8¼d. more than the increase agreed upon in the Composition, and the tenants requested that

Leicester discharge the latter sum. They also wished that he would consider the 'great burden laid upon them' and desired to know 'whether he would abate anything of the composition or nothing'.[74] They appear to have been successful, for examination of the assessments of the increase to be levied on each commote reveals that the total was only some £290.[75]

The next known step was taken by Leicester. On 30 June 1567 he obtained a licence by letters patent to alienate lands in the lordship to be held of the castle of Denbigh in free and common socage.[76] Under this licence he issued the feoffments he had promised in the Composition. Upon enfeoffment each tenant received three documents: an indenture of enfeoffment (also called a charter by contemporaries), a release, and a bond. The clauses of the feoffment refer to a consideration (discussed below), the queen's licence, and Leicester's enfeoffment of X to hold the named lands in free and common socage of the castle of Denbigh, owing only the reserved rent, suit of court (every three weeks), subscription to the mises laid upon the lordship, and the customary military service owed to the lord.[77] Reliefs were set at a year's rent and the Earl was allowed to distrain for arrears in rent. The solution to the question of the commons is found in a clause which grants the tenant 'reasonable common of pasture' yet maintains the lord's pre-eminent right to the commons as well as the appurtenant fishings, huntings, woods, minerals, and regalities. The lands included in the feoffment are described briefly but their previous tenurial status is left vague; they are described only as being in the tenure or occupation of X. The feoffments also contain a record of their enrolment in the close rolls of chancery (discussed below) and, on the dorse, a note of livery of seisin. The release, which was also an indenture, was issued with the feoffment and discharged the Welsh renders and customs abolished in the Composition. Its clauses recited the list of customs, referred to the mise of £1000, and renounced any further claim to them by Leicester.[78] Only one example of the bond has survived. Issued on 12 August 1574 it obliged Robert Salusbury of Galltfaenan to Leicester for £20 that none of the lands which he claimed as freehold and of which he had been recently enfeoffed had previously been leasehold lands of the lordship.[79] The significance of the bond will be discussed below.

In Appendix 13.1 details are given of the nineteen indentures of feoffment which survive in the National Library of Wales, the Library of the University College of North Wales, or the Clwyd Record Office.[80] The earliest was issued in 1568 but few others before 21 May 1571, on which date John Yerwerth, now receiver of the lordship, wrote to Leicester to warn him of rumours among the tenants that he did not intend to complete the enfeoffments. Yerwerth advised Leicester to delay no longer, warning that the attractions of the Composition were being diminished by the delay, so that 'whensoever your Lordship shall be contented to passe the Charters according to your

Lordship's fyrst order . . . they will not be over hastye in procuring them'.[81] Little evidence survives as to the cause of the delay. It does not appear to have been at Leicester's direct order, for in July 1571 Robert Snagge, his commissioner, wrote to the Earl to justify himself in the delay of the enfeoffments in Chirk.[82] Two possibilities suggest themselves. One was a problem of administration, for the officers of Denbigh and Chirk were often the same men, many of whom had further responsibilities in Leicester's other estates, and they were probably overworked. Moreover, William Glasier, steward of Denbigh, was growing increasingly eccentric and difficult to deal with.[83] It may not be coincidental that it was only after Glasier had been superseded by one of Leicester's most trusted followers, Sir John Huband, in 1573 that the majority of Denbigh enfeoffments were completed.[84] More significant might have been the suspicion among Leicester's officers that the Compositions in Denbigh and Chirk had not been entirely advantageous to the Earl. They appear to have sought to delay the conclusion of the Composition to make further investigations. In 1566 the commissioners had hinted that the complaints of the tenants of Denbigh had been feigned. Snagge claimed that Leicester had lost £400 from the Composition in Chirk.[85]

Whatever the causes of the delay, the enfeoffment of the tenants of Denbigh was completed substantially in 1574 and 1575.[86] As can be seen in Appendix 13.1, the estates enfeoffed were of widely varying sizes and would include all lands, with the exception of charter lands and leasehold, to which the tenant laid claim. The feoffments can be divided into three categories according to the nature of the consideration involved. Category A contains no financial consideration but refers to the faithful service of the recipient. The one grant in this category should probably not be included among the feoffments; it records a gift to Edward Conway, for the lands were not previously in his tenure or occupation. It has been included because it is similar to the other indentures in all other respects. Category B includes those feoffments where the consideration was the nominal one of 4*d*. With only one or two exceptions the recipients were gentlemen, although their wealth varied considerably. These estates were probably those claimed as freehold in 1564. Owing to the absence of descriptions of the previous status of the estates, we cannot tell how much of the land could have been proved to have been freehold in 1564 and how much was the product of encroachment. Category C comprises the feoffments where the consideration was the equivalent of one year's rent.[87] With one exception the estates are very small and the rank of the recipient is that of yeoman or clerk. There is sufficient evidence to argue that these were previous copyholdings and it can be stated with some assurance that one effect of the Composition was to transform customary copyhold into freehold. Firstly, the Composition of 1564 included copyhold within its terms and the rental of 1583, compiled at the conclusion of the process of enfeoffment, contains no reference to copyholders, but includes a great number of freeholders. Secondly, in 1566 the tenants of Chirk petitioned Leicester to be 'in the case that Denbighland be', specifically that 'there copyhold land be made freehold'.[88] Finally, the parliamentary survey of the lordship in 1649 refers to 'the tenants in the said Commotes etc. heretofore as Coppiehoulders nowe in free socage teanure according to the grants of the Right Hon. Robert, Earl of Leicester'.[89]

The number of enfeoffments remains to be computed. The nearest approach to a total provided by Leicester's surviving estate papers is a reference in the register to 332 bonds of obligation in a bag.[90] The enrolments in the Close Rolls do not provide much assistance for examination shows them to be incomplete. The earliest enrolments are found in the rolls for 1568; but between then and mid 1574 only ten enrolments can be found. Using our previous system of classification, and the rank of the recipient when indicated, we find the ten are all to freeholders: 2 esquires, 5 gentlemen, and 3 with rank not given.[91] On 15 December 1574 a large number of enrolments were made: 77 feoffments of tenants of Denbigh and 2 of tenants of Chirk. They fill two rolls, which are described in the contemporary index as containing 'only deeds made by therle of Leycester to divers Welshmen of lands in Denbighshire'.[92] These feoffments fall into the following categories: freeholders: 3 esquires, 44 gentlemen, 2 burgesses of Denbigh, 1 servant of Leicester (probably a retainer), 8 yeomen, and 8 with rank not given; copyholders: 2 gentlemen, 8 yeomen, and 1 with rank and tenure not given. To this total of 87 only one further gentleman freeholder can be added, the only surviving enrolment after December 1574.[93] While the indentures in Appendix 13.1 indicate that a number of enfeoffments were made in 1575, they do not appear in any of the existing rolls or indexes.

III

Together with his reformation of the tenurial structure, Leicester also obtained a substantial increase in the revenues of the lordship of Denbigh. We shall begin with freehold rents; increases in leasehold rents present a separate, if related, problem.

The surviving rentals from the Leicesterian period and the years immediately prior to 1563 have been summarised in Appendices 13.2 and 13.3. Owing to substantial differences in the manner of compilation, they deserve individual consideration. The 'pre-Leicesterian' rentals are four: [A.] the assessments employed in the accounts of Simon Thelwall, the Crown's receiver-general for north Wales, for 1553;[94] [B.] a Crown survey of 1559;[95] [C.] the valuation placed by the exchequer on the lordship at the time of the grant to Leicester;[96] [D.] the survey of the lordship conducted by Leicester's commissioners in the summer of 1563.[97] The 'Leicesterian' rentals were all compiled after 1580; no earlier ones have survived. [E.] is the most complete, it was made by the deputy-recorder of the lordship in 1583, on the completion of the process of enfeoffment;[98] [F.] is part of a general survey of Leicester's estates, which internal evidence shows to have been made after 1584;[99] [G.] is the valor compiled by the recorder in 1590 when the lordship reverted to the Crown after the deaths of Leicester (1588) and his brother Warwick (1590).[100] A final source is the assessments and returns of the ministers' accounts for 1581–84, which are summarised in Appendix 13.4.[101]

The most important difference is that between [E.] and the other major rentals. In most cases the leasehold category contains only the larger lease-hold lands; the smaller ones are contained within the commotal totals and are not distinguished from the freehold rents.[102] In [E.], however, all the leasehold lands are placed in a separate category. Thus there is a difference of some £100 (added under leasehold and taken from the commotal totals) between [E.] and [F.] and [G.]. Secondly, certain rents, e.g. those of the bor-ough of Denbigh and the 'manor' of Dinmael, and perquisites of Court are included in some of the rentals and excluded in others. These have been noted and, if excluded, added to the original totals.[103] The commissioners of 1563–64 included in their total the immediate increase from the revival of rents in 1563 (£61. 19s. 7¾d.) and an estimated £20 from perquisites of court. A total of £453. 6s. 5¾d. was to be answered at Michaelmas 1564.[104]

The most complete rentals of the pre-Leicesterian period are [A.] and [D.]. Immediately noteworthy is the distinction between the rents of the commote and the ringildry – obviously the same geographical area. In the absence of contemporary definitions of the distinction, it may be suggested that the commotal rents were those from freehold, leasehold, and copyhold lands, while those of the ringild were from lands still in Welsh tenures and from the surviving traditional renders. This method of assessment was continued in the ministers' accounts of the Leicesterian period, despite the Composi-tion.[105] A further general point should be made about the earlier rentals. It is often stated that Leicester increased the revenues of the lordship from £250 per annum to £800 per annum.[106] While this conclusion may be reached through a comparison of [C.] with [E.], [F.], or [G.], the result is deceptive, for [C.] is a clear valuation, including current deductions. The largest of these were salaries; and when the total for these in 1563 is added to [C.], its total rises to £356, similar to the totals obtained in 1553 and 1559.[107]

The effects of the Composition of 1564 can be seen both in the ministers' accounts and in [E.]. In the ministers' accounts the increase produced by the Composition forms a separate category within the traditional structure of the accounts.[108] The rental of 1583 records the changes made to the rents of individual holdings through the Composition. The individual freehold rents are given, both the old rents and the post-1564 increase, and the new rent owing was the sum of the two. The survey mentioned in the Composition, the subject of the dispute in 1566, was probably the standard survey book compiled whenever large estates changed hands. Only the leasehold portion survives.[109]

The rentals do not, however, provide us with the essential base for an accurate computation of the Leicesterian increases: a statement of freehold and leasehold individually in 1563. At first glance it would appear that a figure for the non-leasehold might be obtained by subtracting the increase of £333. 6s. 8d. from the freehold total in [E.]; this would leave £203. 15s. 6d.[110] Yet on closer examination of the increases actually levied on the commotes, we find that the £333 appears to have been abated by some £40 or £50.[111] This would suggest a total of non-leasehold rents in 1563 of nearly £250. The commotal totals also show that the increases produced by the Composition varied from a rough doubling in the eastern commotes to a tripling in Uwchaled (and by extension Uwchdulas). This would reflect the relative backwardness of the western commotes. But it is also possible that it was the result of an attempt, similar to that which occurred in Caernarvonshire during the Forest of Snowdon case, of the greater eastern squires to place the burden of the increase on more remote areas. Unfortunately, apart from the statement in the Composition that the assessment would be apportioned by the tenants themselves with the assistance of the officers of the lordship, we know nothing of the process actually employed.

Whatever the initial response to the Composition, it can be suggested that its advantages, the enfeoffments, the elimination of copyhold, and the security of rights of common, outweighed its immediate disadvantages. Further controversy between the tenants and the administration of the lordship was primarily produced by certain aspects of Leicester's policy towards leasehold lands. As described above, leasehold demesne lands fall into the categories of greater, the parks and other specified parcels, and lesser. The changes in the rents of the greater leasehold are comparatively straightforward and are set out in Appendix 13.5. A rental of £35. 7s. 4½d. in 1563 was increased to £144. 16s. in 1584. The most dramatic increase, from £6. 6s. 8d. in 1563 to £50 in 1584, was produced by the disparking of Castle Park and the leasing of the herbage as pasture.[112] Owing to the difficulty in establishing an exact figure for the non-leasehold in 1563, the total of the lesser leasehold rents, included in the commotal totals, can only be estimated. The Leicesterian rentals produce totals for all leasehold between £240 and £250 and suggest that the lesser leasehold ultimately produced about £100 per annum. The 1563 revenue from lesser leasehold may in turn be estimated as something just over £50.[113]

The initial reports of Leicester's surveyors suggest that they considered that there was substantial undervaluation of the leasehold lands, which would enable rents to be increased without causing hardship to the tenants. Their immediate target was the steward's leases; in 1563–66 tenants were encouraged to surrender their earlier leases and accept new ones from Leicester.[114] The details of the revivals made in 1563 are found in the survey of that year. There was an increase of some £40 in leasehold rents, the greater part of which came from the parks, several of which had answered to no rent at all in 1563. The other increases were as follows:

	Old			New			Fines		
	£	s.	d.	£	s.	d.	£	s.	d.
Farm of Mancote (40 acres common)		10	4	1	0	0	8	0	0
12 acres in Segrwyd		3			11	0	1	0	0
12 acres in Melai		5	7		10	0	1	0	0
200 acres waste in Meifod	2	10	0	10	0	0	20	0	0

Source: Langleat, Dudley xvi, fols. 72–72ᵛ. The place-names are those of townships.

If these increases are seen as average for the first period of revivals (they were set as a precedent), the general policy seems to have been to double the existing rents of the steward's leases. By contrast, the leases granted in continuation of Crown leases appear to have maintained the previous rents.[115] The relationship between the rents and the economic value of the land can be assessed if the valuations made in the survey by Toby Matthew in 1583–85 are considered accurate. To cite examples: the 37 acres held by Fulk Salusbury as a tenant at will in the township of Segrwyd were valued at £6. 8s. 9d. per annum, he paid a rent (revived in 1563) of £2. 6s. 4d.; the manor or farm of Ystrad held by John Myddelton as a lessee of both the Crown and Leicester answered to a rent of £8 per annum, its 303 acres were valued at £51 per annum.[116]

Leicester's leases were all standard leases by indenture for twenty-one years. Tenancies at will were employed, but only as a temporary measure while a final arrangement was reached.[117] Rack-renting does not appear to have been part of the estate policy of the lordship.[118] The only information we have as to fines comes from the revival of 1563; with one exception they appear to have been the standard two years' rent. Fines became more controversial in the period after the deaths of Leicester and Warwick, when the lordship reverted to the Crown. Elizabeth also inherited the mortgage of £17,000 Leicester had raised on the security of the lordships of Denbigh and Chirk to finance some of his expenses for the expedition to the Netherlands in 1585, and raised part of the cost of the redemption from the lordships.

When the lessees were granted new leases in Denbigh in 1592–93 the Leicesterian rents were maintained but £6000. 10s. 10d. was raised from fines.[119] John Salusbury of Lleweni, for example, paid a fine of £83. 3s. 4d. on lands leased at £5. 0s. 4d. per annum.[120] If an economic motive is to be sought for the turmoil in Denbighshire in the 1590s, this burden on the lordship may provide an answer.

The initial revival of leasehold rents coincided with the compilation of the survey book, the leasehold portion of which was completed in 1569.[121] The lands included were those declared as leasehold, leaving a second category of leasehold lands to be settled. In the Composition Leicester had excluded from consideration as freehold those lands which had been leased between the first day of the reign of Henry VIII (22 April 1509) and 26 September 1564. A considerable amount of land in this category was suspected of being concealed and falsely claimed as freehold. The bond of obligation issued with the enfeoffments rendered the tenants liable to Leicester in the event of a false claim of freehold.[122] The bond stated that an inquisition was to be taken in those lands within seven years of the enfeoffments.

The first steps in this inquisition coincided with the final stages of the enfeoffments and the compilation of the rental of 1583. A presentment of a jury of inquisition held by the steward of the lordship on 4 April 1582 declared a number of rentals of Henry VII and Henry VIII to be accurate and advised any remaining eligible tenants to compound for their enfeoffment with Leicester.[123] A warning that this was not to include leasehold land was probably made in preparation for a commission issued on 1 August 1583 to Sir John Huband, Anthony Dockwra, and Jevan Lloyd of Yale (the steward of Chirk) to investigate the concealment of leasehold between 22 April 1509 and 26 September 1564. The presentments of the juries of survey were made at the manorial court in Denbigh on 5 October.[124] $699\frac{1}{2}$ acres were presented as concealed leasehold: 18 in Ceinmeirch, 115 in Isaled, 276 in Isdulas, $239\frac{1}{2}$ in Uwchaled, and 51 in Uwchdulas.[125] One of those found guilty of concealment – of ten acres in Lleweni – was Robert Salusbury of Galltfaenan, whose bond of obligation we possess.[126]

Concurrently with this inquisition another survey of the 'Parkes [and] certayne other farms' – i.e. the greater leasehold – was undertaken by Toby Matthew.[127] In one sense this was a revision of the survey book of 1569 in that fuller descriptions, based on perambulations, were made of the lands, and economic valuations were attempted. The survey was itself to be employed as a survey book and to confirm the results of the inquisition of 1583. In several instances Matthew records livery of seisin being delivered to him on Leicester's behalf for lands previously concealed and the proposal of new rents.[128] He also notes lands suspected of being encroached. Perhaps his most interesting observation illustrates amply the limitations under which the inquisition was made. While the jury may have found that a certain acreage was concealed leasehold, the existing rentals and surveys were not sufficiently detailed to provide an accurate description. The tenants were permitted to 'exchange' so many acres for the leasehold claimed with the result that 'this Tearme land [i.e. leasehold] yt is found is the worst of every mans landes'.[129]

The results of the inquisition appear to have satisfied neither Leicester's officers (Matthew notes that further leasehold was probably concealed) nor the tenants.[130] On 7 September 1585 Leicester made a second composition with the tenants, whereby for £1200 he would grant them the concealed lands as freehold.[131] On 20 September another inquisition was held at Denbigh before two of the justices of Great Sessions (Henry Townshend and Fabian Philipps) and the officers of the lordship. It was later claimed that between 800 and 1000 acres were presented as concealed leasehold.[132] According to the recorder in 1590, the second composition was never implemented owing to Leicester's absence in the Netherlands; but there are references in Matthew's survey book to certain plots being confirmed as freehold under this composition.[133]

Another of Leicester's major concerns was to regain control of leasehold lands which had been granted for excessively long terms by the Crown or its agents in the 1540s and 1550s. Ample illustrations of this problem are provided by his disputes with Sir John Salusbury over two of the larger portions of the demesne. In July 1544 Salusbury had obtained a lease for forty years in reversion of Kilford Manor and park, the reversion to begin at Michaelmas 1571. He had previously leased the manor for 21 years from 1528.[134] While the intervening tenant, Humphrey Orme, held the manor in 1563, Salusbury may have purchased the remainder of his lease in the late 1560s.[135] By the autumn of 1571 Salusbury was engaged in negotiations with Leicester for a grant of the manor in free socage. A draft indenture, similar to the feoffments, of 28 September 1571 survives.[136] This agreement appears to have fallen through, probably because Leicester and Salusbury were involved in political contest at the time.[137] A year later Salusbury was reported as attempting to use the influence of Sir Nicholas Bagnall with Leicester to obtain the manor.[138] In his will Salusbury made elaborate provisions to keep the lease in his family; in 1592 it was in the possession of his grandson John.[139]

Shortly after the grant of the lordship to Leicester, Salusbury purchased the remainder of a ninety-two-year lease of Castle Park made to Bartholomew Garroway by Sir Richard Sackville in 1549/50.[140] During the initial survey he offered to compound with Leicester for the disparking of the park and its conversion to tillage and by December 1570 he was successful.[141] At that time he sold the remainder of his lease to William Clough for £450, although by the late 1570s the park had returned to the Salusburys.[142] About the time of Sir John's death in 1578, Leicester offered to exchange his interest in the wardship of Salusbury's grandson and heir Thomas for the return of the park. The dispute between Leicester and the executors of Salusbury's will, after they had secretly arranged a marriage for Thomas without his consent, probably caused the family to surrender the original lease, for in 1584 Thomas Salusbury held the park only as a tenant at will.[143] Some years later, probably after Thomas Salusbury's execution for treason, Leicester leased the park to the burgesses of Denbigh for pasture.[144]

IV

The Earl of Leicester's estate policy in the lordship of Denbigh should be evaluated in the light of both local and regional conditions. The Composition of 1564, in particular, should be seen as complementary to the Crown's campaign to reverse the erosion of its rights and revenues in north Wales. The Bromfield and Yale composition of 1562 provides the most valid comparison. The surveyors of Bromfield and Yale also found evidence of decayed rents: £101. 14s. 10d. per annum. To revive these and to resolve the confused tenurial situation, copyholders (either for years or by inheritance) and other customary tenants were offered forty-year renewable leases at increased rents.[145] While there was no direct reference to the claims of the possessors of former bondland, these appear to have been included among the customary tenants, for the Charter of Henry VII was blamed for the confusion in tenures.[146] This solution was, however, to prove unsatisfactory and in 1624–26 a second composition was made in which these tenants were granted the freehold of their lands at twenty-five years' purchase.[147] The decision of 1562 remained the guide for exchequer practice for the remainder of the century, for the judgement of 1603 offered possessors of former bondland in the principality forty-year renewable leases.[148]

By this comparison Leicester's Composition is impressive. It resolved the tenurial confusion immediately by granting all tenants the freehold of their lands and it was to establish the tenurial structure of the lordship for over a century. Moreover it displays a confidence in reform not typical of Elizabethans; the parliamentary surveyors later noted that the tenures in free socage of Denbigh Castle were a new form of tenure.[149] Nor, when compared with the two compositions of Bromfield and Yale, does the cost to the tenants appear excessive. The Bromfield and Yale composition does not, however, provide us with a comparison with Leicester's policy over the traditional renders, which are mentioned in none of the surviving surveys. The interest shown by the inquisition of 1561 in the Denbigh renders suggests that Leicester's policy was not, on the other hand, without precedent.

Another important aspect of Leicester's Composition was its effect on enclosure. While they may not have been as successful as they would have wished, Leicester's officers appear to have made substantial efforts to control enclosure of wastes and commons.[150] In 1563 the surveyors reported that 'improvement of your Lordship's waistes and commons with the contentatione of the tenants' would be worth £100 per annum.[151] An example of this kind of enclosure was the 'certen half marsch being in Abergelley letten to . . . Thomas Rolfe to thend he should enclose the same and defend the seas from other lands there adjoyning which is continually overflowed with the sea'.[152] The Composition appears to have had the effect of securing both the tenants' rights of common and the boundaries of the commons. The most revealing commentary on this effect of the Composition is found in a legal dispute of the 1590s. In 1594 John Morris, lessee of certain lands in Isdulas, brought a suit in the equity jurisdiction of the exchequer against William ap John Lewis and John ap Robert, who, he claimed, had torn down his hedges and driven their cattle across his fields. The defendants in turn claimed that they had unlimited rights of common under Leicester's Composition and that the Composition had set the limits of the common, so that any portions of common afterwards let could not lose their previous identity.[153] It was left to the court to decide whether Morris's lands had ever been common. Apparently losing their case, the defendants returned to the exchequer in 1597 to claim that Morris had concealed encroached common and fraudulently claimed it to be leasehold with the assistance of a suborned jury of survey.[154] In both cases, however, all parties accepted that the Composition had established liberty of common. The limits placed on enclosure may have been the basis for the statement made in 1610 that 'much of the freehold land and farms within the lordship of Denbigh and all the county adjoyning were not heretofore until of late enclosed'.[155] The parliamentary surveyors of 1649 claimed that the enclosure that had taken place during the Civil War was in violation of Leicester's 'charters'.[156]

The success of the Composition can be gauged from the request of the tenants of Chirk to be 'In the case that Denbighland be'.[157] A similar composition was made in Chirk and in the 1570s with the tenants of the lordships of Arwystli and Cyfeiliog in Montgomeryshire.[158] One of the reasons for the bitter reaction to the Forest of Snowdon inquisitions may well have been the decision to proceed through the forest laws and the absence of any advantage to the tenants in compounding.

Apart from the Composition, Leicester's practice in Denbigh followed standard contemporary estate policy. The increases in revenue during his tenure of the lordship probably only countered the effects of inflation during the previous decades; there is no ground for seeing him as rapacious or unscrupulous. Consideration of his policy in Denbigh should also suggest a wider reappraisal of his career and ambitions. High among them was the re-establishment of the house of Dudley as a leading territorial family. The lordship of Denbigh was 'a great parte of thinheritaunce of the said erle'; he sought to establish a firm base there through a mutually profitable relationship with his tenants.[159] The emphasis in the Composition on 'good lordship' was, if old-fashioned, not hypocritical. On the other hand, the response of the tenants was mixed. This may be attributed to suspicions of a new and powerful landlord after a long period of liberty and 'self-government'.[160] A comparison can be made with the outright hostility displayed in Caernarvonshire towards the Forest of Snowdon inquisitions and the relative amicability found among the tenants of Bromfield and Yale; their only recorded response to the composition of 1562 was a request to have it confirmed by Act of Parliament.[161] This may reflect a greater subservience to direct actions of the Crown than to those of a private landlord however powerful; or it may reflect a greater independence and entrenched hostility to 'interference' encountered nearer the periphery. Also important in Denbigh was the political aspect of Leicester's lordship. To the greater squirearchy interference with their 'self-government', a subject which lies outside the confines of this essay, was probably of greater concern than estate policy. Yet this should not be allowed to obscure Leicester's attempt to act as their 'good lord' in the Composition; for, in the words of the parliamentary surveyors, 'Robert, earle of Leicester by licence from Queen Elizabeth for small considerations passed very many great things away'.[162]

APPENDIX 13.1: THE SURVIVING INDENTURES OF FEOFFMENT RESULTING FROM THE COMPOSITION OF 1564

Document	Date	Recipient	Commote or borough	Acreage	Consideration		Rent		
					s.	d.	£	s.	d.
A.									
UCNW Gwynsaney 741	4 March 1579	Edward Conway of Bryneuryn, Esq.	Uwchdulas	128	Nil		2	16	0
B.									
NLW Bachymbyd 325	1 July 1568	Robert Lloyd ap David of Sgeibion, gent.	Ceinmeirch	27		4		10	11
NLW Bachymbyd 123*	2 June 1571	Thomas ap Robert, Thomas ap David ap Madog, husbandmen	Ceinmeirch	71½		4	1	6	0½
NLW Coed Coch 156*	1 March 1574	Richard ap David ap Rees ap Jevan of Abergele, gent.	Abergele	8 acres, 3 burgages		4		10	8
CRO Galltfaenan 589*	4 March 1574	Robert Salusbury of Galltfaenan, gent.	Isaled and Isdulas	78		4	1	19	9½
CRO Nercwys Hall 771	20 June 1574	Griffith ap David ap Griffith ap Llewelyn of Dinas Cadfel, gent.	Isaled	6		4			5½
NLW Coed Coch 158	20 June 1574	Maurice ap John ap Robert Goch of Prys, gent.	Isaled	69		4		17	11½
UCNW Kinmel 686	1 March 1575	Piers Holland, gent.	Isdulas	545		4	6	11	5
NLW Coed Coch 159	1 May 1575	John ap Rees Wynn ap Jenkin ap David Lloyd of Cilcen, gent.	Isdulas and Uwchdulas	127		4½		19	4
UCNW Maenan 111	2 May 1575	Geoffrey ap Sir David of Petrual	Uwchdulas	28		4		6	4

Reference	Date	Name	Place				
NLW Coed Coch 160	2 May 1575	Griffith ap Howell ap Rees of Trofarth, yeoman	Isdulas	46	4	7	4
NLW Deed 914	1 June 1575	Thomas ap John Lloyd ap David Arwylls	Uwchaled	67	4	6	10
UCNW Mostyn 1880	1 June 1575	Robert ap Griffith Lloyd ap Meredith of Denant, gent.	Uwchaled	90	4	10	0

C.

Reference	Date	Name	Place				
NLW Bachymbyd 124	20 June 1574	Richard Lloyd ap David Lloyd of Llewesog, yeoman	Ceinmeirch	40½	9	9	5
NLW Ruthin Lordship 1114	1 May 1575	Robert ap Hugh, Jevan ap Harry, John Gardner, yeomen	Uwchaled	29	13	13	10
CRO Peake of Perthewig 3	1 May 1575	Ludovick ap Rees ap David ap Roger of Bodfari, Flints., clerk	Isaled	16	10	10	6
CRO Nercwys Hall 848	1 May 1575	William ap John ap Evan ap David Lloyd of Cilcedig; Thomas ap Robert ap Llewelyn of Llewesog, yeomen	Ceinmeirch	10 / 8	17 / 0	6	11¼
UCNW 2003	1 May 1575	Thomas ap David ap Jevan / John ap Griffith ap David / Jevan ap David ap Robin / John ap Robert ap Madog	Abergele	18 / 9 / 10 / 10½	18	18	5¼
UCNW 17045	1 May 1575	Henry ap William of Penporchell	Isaled	202	11	11	7

* Indicates that the accompanying release has also survived.

APPENDIX 13.2: PRE-LEICESTERIAN RENTS

	A Assessment 1553			B Survey 1559			C Valor 1563			D Survey 1563		
	£	s.	d.	£	s.	d.	£	s.	d.	£	s.	d.
Leasehold	18	11	4½	–			–			35	7	4½ (including Dinmael)
Borough	–			–			–			6	5	8
Ceinmeirch												
ringild	3	2	0½							3	19	11
commote	80	8	4½							80	10	0¼
total	83	10	5	–		–				84	9	11¼
Isaled												
ringild	1	17	9¾							6	5	6
commote	100	11	7¾							105	14	0½
total	102	9	5½	111	0	7¾	–			111	19	6½
Uwchaled												
ringild	7	5	7½							–		
commote	18	4	2½							–		
total	25	9	10	24	0	6¾	–			28	1	4
Isdulas												
ringild	2	19	7½							6	6	7¾
commote	61	16	1½							61	15	11¾
total	64	15	9	70	8	7	–			68	1	9½
Uwchdulas												
ringild	10	10	4½							13	9	10½
commote	25	13	5½							25	5	9½
total	36	3	10½	32	4	8½	–			38	15	0
Total			*	320	0	11½	265	17	0¾			*
Dinmael	5	17	0	5	17	0	90	15	10	81	19	7¾
Borough	6	5	8	6	5	8	[salaries]			[revival 1563 and perqs. of court]		
Amended total	353	3	8½	332	3	7½	356	12	10¾	453	6	5¾

* Totals are not given in manuscripts.

APPENDIX 13.3: LEICESTERIAN RENTS

	E. Rental 1583			F. Survey 1584			G. Valor 1590		
	£	s.	d.	£	s.	d.	£	s.	d.
Perquisites of Court	[20	0	0]	[20	0	0]	20	0	0
Leasehold	239	4	10	144 [inc. Dinmael, Llysfaen, Penmaen]	6	0	140 [prob. inc. Dinmael, Llysfaen, Penmaen]	17	0
Borough	[inc. in Isaled]			6	3	0	6	3	0
Ceinmeirch									
old	39	11	$1\frac{1}{2}$						
new	36	17	$10\frac{1}{4}$						
total	76	8	$11\frac{3}{4}$	135	1	3	121	0	0
Isaled									
total only	196	11	$1\frac{1}{2}$	206	17	$11\frac{1}{4}$	209	0	0
Uwchaled									
old	21	18	$0\frac{3}{4}$						
new	42	15	8						
total	63	13	$8\frac{1}{4}$	71	2	$11\frac{3}{4}$			
Isdulas									
old	47	1	$7\frac{1}{2}$				314	3	8
new	47	4	$4\frac{1}{2}$						
total	94	6	0	127	15	$0\frac{1}{4}$			
Uwchdulas									
total only	106	2	$4\frac{1}{2}$	117	6	$9\frac{3}{4}$			
Total	[796	7	0]	827	18	$10\frac{3}{4}$	810	3	8
Dinmael	5	17	0						
Llysfaen, Penmaen	7	0	0						
	809	4	0						

APPENDIX 13.4: ASSESSMENTS: MINISTERS' ACCOUNTS, 1581–84

	Denbigh Borough			Ceinmeirch			Isaled			Uwchaled		
	£	s.	d.	£	s.	d.	£	s.	d.	£	s.	d.
Rent and Farm	6	3	0	80	10	2½	105	14	0½	18	4	0¾
Ringild				5	2	11	10	6	0¾	8	7	4¼
Twnc rents				1	4	0	3	0	0¾	3	10	8¾
Increase in leasehold, 1563–69 revival				7	13	9	8	2	2¼	8	9	
Increase in freehold rents after Composition				34	14	10½	109	4	11	38	6	4¼

APPENDIX 13.5: INCREASES IN MAJOR LEASEHOLD RENTS

	1553			1563			1563 (revival)			1584		
	£	s.	d.	£	s.	d.	£	s.	d.	£	s.	d.
Castle Park	6	6	8	6	6	8	–			50	0	0
Moel-y-wig Park	–			No rent paid			17	17	8	20	0	0
Garth Snodyog Park	–			No rent paid			10	0	0	10	0	0
Postney Park	2	0	0	3	0	0	–			3	0	0
Galch Hill Park	[alienated from the lordship, restored 1584]									14	0	0
Kilford Park [and manor]	10	0	0	20	0	0	–			20	0	0
Dinmael	–			5	17	0	–			5	17	0
Penmaen and Llysfaen	[obtained from the Crown, 1567]									7	0	0
'le auditors liveries'	–			–			5	0	0	5	0	0
Lands in the charge of the escheator	–			–			–			4	19	0
Tenements in Abergele	4		8½	4		8½	–			–		
Total	18	11	4½	35	7	4½				144	16	0

NOTES

1 They are part of the Galltfaenan Collection, deposited with the Clwyd Record Office [hereafter C.R.O.] at Hawarden (formerly the Flintshire R.O.). I should like to thank the owners of the collection, Mr and Mrs R. K. L. S. Mainwaring, for their kind assistance.

2 (Wrexham, 1860), pp. 109–13. The Gwenynog muniments have since disappeared.

3 The main sources of relevant archives are the collections of estate papers deposited at the C.R.O., the Library of the University College of North Wales [hereafter U.C.N.W.], and the National Library of Wales [hereafter N.L.W.]; the manorial records of the Denbighshire lordships in the Public Record Office, either in the Special Collections (Rentals and Surveys) Class [hereafter P.R.O., S.C. 11 or 12], or the Land Revenue Office Class [hereafter P.R.O., L.R.]; and the Dudley Papers at Longleat House [hereafter Longleat, Dudley]. The P.R.O. material and some from the N.L.W. are listed in M. Richards, 'Some Unpublished Source-Material for the History of the Lordships of Denbighshire', *Transactions of the Denbighshire Historical Society*, xiv (1965), 197 ff. I should like to thank the Marquess of Bath and his librarian for permission to employ material from the Dudley Papers.

4 Of the two parts of the original indenture, one was kept with the estate papers of the Earl of Leicester and is mentioned in a register of his papers made after his death (Longleat, Dudley xx, fol. 2). The tenants' part was kept either with records of the lordship or the shire, both of which have disappeared.

5 Lord Robert Dudley was not created Baron of Denbigh and Earl of Leicester until 28 and 29 September 1564 (*Calendar of the Patent Rolls, 1563–66*, p. 178). With one exception, reference will be made to him as Earl of Leicester throughout this essay.

6 The Charter of 20 July 1506. As the entry in *Cal. Pat. Rolls, 1494–1509*, p. 147 is only a synopsis, reference should be made to the original enrolment, P.R.O., C. 66/599, memb. 18 (4). The Welsh renders (see also below, p. 265) are identified in T. P. Ellis, *Welsh Tribal Law and Custom in the Middle Ages* (Oxford, 1926), i, pp. 307 ff.

7 (d. 1581). A cousin of Leicester and a lawyer by profession, who served both the Dukes of Northumberland and Leicester as a legal and financial officer (see his will, P.R.O., Prob. 11/63, fols. 117ᵛ–118). He was a close associate of Glasier; M.P. for Helston in 1563, and clerk of the signet of the Council in the Marches from 1565. See also S. L. Adams, 'The Gentry of north Wales and the Earl of Leicester's Expedition to the Netherlands, 1585–1586' [Ch. 12], p. 245.

8 Glasier (d. 1588). A Chester lawyer, associated with Leicester from 1553; M.P. St. Ives 1563, Chester 1571, 1572–83; vice-chamberlain of the county palatine of Chester, and member of the Council in the Marches (see Ch. 12 above p. 245); steward of the lordship of Denbigh *c.* 1565 to *c.* 1580.

9 Lawyer (Middle Temple, 1545), recipient of several leases in the lordship (see below, p. 276).

10 Chester lawyer, M. P. Chester 1563. In Leicester's service from 1559 (Longleat, Dudley i, fol. 44); receiver of the lordship of Denbigh after 1564, later receiver-general of Leicester's estates in north Wales.

11 Thomas Davies, Bishop of St. Asaph 1561–73.

12 Of Lleweni (d. 1578), the leading landowner in the shire, acting steward of the lordship of Denbigh in 1563 (Longleat, Dudley xvi, fol. 74ᵛ).

13 Of Plas Iolyn (1512?–1594?), previously a partisan of Northumberland, later to be the most notorious follower of Leicester in north Wales (Longleat, Dudley ii, fol. 307); steward of the lordship of Denbigh from *c.* 1581 to *c.* 1590. See Ch. 12 above p. 242.

14 Steward for the Crown of the lands of the former monastery of Aberconway (N.L.W., Wales 4/3/5 [Great Sessions, Denbigh Circuit, Gaol Files, *nomina ministrorum*, 13 Elizabeth]). With the exception of Wynn, the commissioners for the tenants were the leading members of the Denbighshire commission of the peace.

15 *Cal. Pat. Rolls, 150–63,* pp. 534–43.

16 P.R.O., L.R. 2/252; undated, but internal evidence suggests a date no earlier than 1540.

17 P.R.O., S.C. 11/948.

18 Longleat, Dudley xvi.

19 See statute 28 Henry VIII, c. 39, 'An Act concerning the assurance of certain lands unto the King's Majestie ... belonging unto the earldom of March'. The grant to Prince Arthur is found in *Cal. Pat. Rolls, 1485–94,* p. 453. The classic study of the early history of the lordship is Vinogradoff and Morgan, *Survey of the Honour of Denbigh, 1334* (Oxford, 1914), but this has been superseded by D. H. Owen, 'The Lordship of Denbigh, 1282–1425' (unpublished Ph.D. thesis, University of Wales, 1967). The importance of the earldom of March in the estates of the Crown is discussed in B. P. Wolffe, *The Crown Lands, 1461–1536* (1970), pp. 50 f.

20 Chirk and Bromfield and Yale escheated to the Crown after the attainder of Sir William Stanley in 1495; Ruthin was purchased from the Greys in 1506–7. All the Denbighshire lordships were granted similar charters by Henry VII.

21 Henry VIII, c. 17.

22 Leicester's impact on local politics and government will be discussed in a future paper entitled 'Court and Country in Elizabethan Wales: the Earl of Leicester and the lordship of Denbigh, 1563–1588'.

23 See the note on the exemplification of a fine of the exchequer of 9 Elizabeth, declaring Penmaen and Llysfaen to be part of the lordship of Denbigh, in Longleat, Dudley xx, loc. cit. Cf. B.M. Lansdowne MS. 62, fols. 118–19, W. Sparke (recorder of the lordship) to Lord Burghley, 24 August 1590. Penmaen and Llysfaen were leased as a separate parcel; see N.L.W. Wynnstay MS., Box 106, no. 127.

24 A. D. Carr, 'Medieval Dinmael', *Trans. D.H.S.* xiii (1964), 9. See N.L.W. Bachymbyd MS. 426, lease to John Salesbury of Rûg, 13 July 1573, and recital of previous leases. Cf. E. A. Lewis and J. C. Davies, (eds), *Records of the Court of Augmentations relating to Wales and Monmouthshire* (Cardiff, 1954), p. 365 [hereafter *Aug. Proc. Wales*]; and T. I. J. Jones, (ed.), *Exchequer Proceedings concerning Wales in tempore James I* (Cardiff, 1955), p. 175 [hereafter *Exch. Proc. James*].

25 Cf. P.R.O., L.R. 2/252, fol. 5, 'the said parkes and pastures before declared ... are taken to be parcell of the demesne belonging to the said castle'.

26 For the Salusburys and Kilford Manor, see below, pp. 274–5. In 1614 David Holland of Kinmel achieved his family's ambition by purchasing the freehold of Dinorben Fawr from James I for £512. 3s. 4d., U.C.N.W., Kinmel MS. 617.

27 Owen, op. cit., p. 122.

28 It had been sold to the leading cadet branch of the Myddeltons and Leicester repurchased it from Richard Myddelton of Wepra for £200 in 1584. See N.L.W. Ruthin Lordship MS. 54 and A. H. Dodd, 'Mr. Myddelton the merchant of Tower Street', S. T. Bindoff *et al.* (eds), *Elizabethan Government and Society* (1961), pp. 250, 266–7.

29 P.R.O., L.R. 2/252, fol. 5.

30 *Ibid.*, fol. 4ᵛ.

31 P.R.O., S.C. 11/948, entries under Isaled.

32 Longleat, Dudley xvi, fols. 72–72ᵛ. As late as 1583 it was noted of Garth Snodyog that 'the pale is greatly in decaie and so the parke lyeth open and the deare lye abroade in daunger and to other mennes hurtes', P.R.O., L.R. 2/238, 'Survey of Parkes and certaine farmes', by Toby Matthew, 1583–85, fol. 37. For the disparking of Castle Park see below, pp. 271, 274–5.

33 P.R.O., S.C. 11/948. Cf. *Exch. Proc. James*, pp. 177–8.

34 Owen, op. cit., p. 252. Owen's thesis concludes with a discussion of the rental of 1437 (N.L.W. Wynnstay MS. 86ʙ); the more dramatic changes no doubt occurred in the century 1450–1550.

35 J. Beverley Smith, 'Crown and Community in the Principality of North Wales in the Reign of Henry Tudor', *Welsh Hist. Rev.* iii (1966), esp. pp. 169–70.

36 T. Jones Pierce, 'Landlords in Wales', in J. Thirsk (ed.), *The Agrarian History of England*, iv (Cambridge, 1967), 368–9.

37 Owen, op. cit., p. 170. In the fourteenth century there were eleven castle-guard tenants in Isaled.

38 P.R.O., L.R. 2/270, fol. 10. Cf. S.C. 11/948, Ceinmeirch, quest. 11, 'and for the charterers . . .'

39 S.C. 11/948, loc. cit.

40 *Ibid.*, Ceinmeirch, quest. 3.

41 P.R.O., L.R. 2/252, fols. 30 ff.

42 A fuller discussion of the stewards of Denbigh will appear in an article entitled 'Office-holders of the Borough of Denbigh and the Stewards of the Lordships of Denbighshire in the Reign of Elizabeth I' [Ch. 14].

43 *Aug. Proc. Wales*, p. 90.

44 See the leases recited in the grant to Leicester, *Cal. Pat. Rolls, 1563–66*, pp. 534–40 *passim*.

45 *Letters and Papers, Foreign and Domestic of the Reign of Henry VIII*, xiii, pt. ii (1538), no. 734 (11). A list of Blount's leases, all for twenty-one years, can be found in N.L.W. Wynnstay MS. 86c. References to these leases can be found in many of the Leicesterian manorial records.

46 *Aug. Proc. Wales*, p. 71. Although Ruthin was not part of the earldom of March, it was attached to it in Blount's licence.

47 *Ibid.*, p. 85.

48 See below, p. 263.

49 For the claims of the tenants of Chirk, see Longleat, Dudley xvii, fol. 186 (survey of Chirk, 1566). This claim may have its origins in the fact that the charters to the

Denbighshire lordships were probably the product of a survey of decays in rent begun in 1503, see *Cal. Pat. Rolls, 1494–1509*, p. 332.

50 P.R.O., S.C. 11/948, Ceinmeirch, quests. 13–15.

51 On Caernarvonshire, see T. Jones Pierce, 'Notes on the History of Rural Caernarvonshire in the Reign of Queen Elizabeth', in J. Beverley Smith (ed.), *Medieval Welsh Society* (Cardiff, 1972), pp. 62–3. Cf. Eric Kerridge, *Agrarian Problems in the Sixteenth Century and After* (1969), pp. 41–2.

52 Longleat, Dudley xvii, fols. 180 ff.

53 P.R.O., L.R. 2/252, fols. 30 ff.

54 Longleat, Dudley xvi, fol. 73. Cf. *Aug. Proc. Wales*, pp. 71–3; see also n. 116.

55 P.R.O., S.C. 11/948, Ceinmeirch, quest. 16.

56 *Ibid.*, final membrane. The freeholders were led by Sir John Salusbury.

57 N.L.W. MS. 4576E; since this was an *inspeximus* it was not enrolled in the patent rolls. Beverley Smith, art. cit., pp. 170–1, notes that the validity of the charters was questioned in the reign of Henry VII, but the king died before the issue could be resolved. Cf. S. B. Chrimes, *Henry VII* (1972), p. 256.

58 P.R.O., S.C. 12/27/30. Some form of survey for the Crown appears to have been taken in Arwystli and Cyfeiliog in 1564, see B.M. Add. MS. 36925, fol. 11.

59 *Cal. Pat. Rolls., 1560–63*, pp. 278–9. The surveys are P.R.O., S.C. 12/27/30 and L.R. 2/234. There are also subsidiary surveys, e.g. for Holt (S.C. 12/17/93) and Esclusham (S.C. 12/26/71).

60 *Cal. Pat. Rolls, 1560–63*, loc. cit.; P.R.O., L.R. 2/234.

61 *Royal Commission on Land in Wales and Monmouthshire*, v (1896), 383.

62 The commission is summarised in a lease of 1 October 1566 (N.L.W. Coed Coch MS. 1023). In their discussion of revivals of rent in the summer of 1563, the commissioners referred to a 'new commission at your lordship's pleasure to be granted to take surrenders and [make] new leases' (Longleat, Dudley xvi, fol. 73ᵛ).

63 For the initial revivals see below, pp. 272–3, and Longleat, Dudley xvi, fols. 73ᵛ–74ᵛ.

64 Given the delay between the grant of Chirk and the major inquisition and survey of 1566, it is probable that such an inquisition was not made in Denbigh in 1563.

65 Longleat, Dudley xvi, fol. 73ᵛ.

66 *Ibid.* xvii, fol. 186; see also the leasehold survey book of 1569 (P.R.O., L.R. 2/235A) *passim* and N.L.W. Coed Coch MS. 1023.

67 Longleat, Dudley xvii, fol. 186. It is interesting that the tenants of Chirk were still confident in their Charter in 1566 and ready to contest the issue with Leicester's legal counsel. But, probably on the precedent of Denbigh, they were ready to 'conform' if its validity was not upheld.

68 Cf. the role of the gentry in the disputes over lands in the township of Dinorwig, Caerns., discussed in Jones Pierce, 'Notes', pp. 67–9. Another example of the difficulties encountered with Welsh tenants at this time can be found in a letter of Edward Norris to the Marquis of Winchester of 17 November 1564 (B.M. Add. MS. 36925, fol. 11), regarding collection of the Crown's rents in Arwystli and Cyfeiliog.

69 There were bondmen in Chirk in the 1550s, however; see *Aug. Proc. Wales*, pp. 309–10; and *Cal. Pat. Rolls, 1560–63*, p. 536.

70 P.R.O., S.C. 11/948, Ceinmeirch, quest. 16. W. J. Smith (ed.), *Calendar of Salusbury Correspondence* (Cardiff, 1954), p. 24, Salusbury to Norris, 6 Nov. 1564. Cf. B.M. Add. MS. 36926, fol. 8, H. Norris to Sir W. Norris, 30 March 1564.

71 Longleat, Dudley xx, loc. cit. Cf. the Bromfield and Yale mise of 600 marks in exchange for which the tenants were granted a pardon of all fines and arrears in rent, often the equivalent of a year's rent. A. N. Palmer and E. Owen, *A History of the Ancient Tenures of Land in North Wales and the Marches* (1910), pp. 209–10.

72 In *The Council in the Marches of Wales under Elizabeth I* (Cardiff, 1958), p. 238, Penry Williams states that Leicester's Composition in Denbigh produced forty-year leases. His source is an erroneous entry in E. Gwynne Jones (ed.), *Calendar of Exchequer Proceedings (Equity) concerning Wales: Henry VIII–Elizabeth* (Cardiff, 1939) [hereafter *Exch. Proc.*], p. 171. Examination of the originals (P.R.O., E. 112/60/79) discovers no reference to forty-year leases, but only to free socage of Denbigh. Jones was probably misled by the composition in Bromfield and Yale (see below, p. 275).

73 Longleat, Dudley xvii, fols. 156–156^v: 'Notes of Remembrances of the conditions and peticions of the iurie to us the said commissioners at this presentment of the verdictt with the some of the talk passed amonge us' [15 September 1566].

74 The survey is included in Longleat, Dudley xvii; the petition has not survived. As a result of this settlement, Sir John Throckmorton discharged the appearance of the jury before the Council at Chester. In Dudley xx, loc. cit., there is an item entitled ominously 'supplications of the mutynous tenaunts of Denbigh', which may relate to this incident, or possibly to the disputes over concealed leasehold in the 1580s. The later disputes are discussed below, pp. 273–4.

75 See below, p. 289 n. 111.

76 *Cal. Pat. Rolls, 1566–69*, p. 922. The licence was necessary to evade the restrictions of the statute of *Quia Emptores* on subinfeudation.

77 Military obligations on the tenantry are discussed in Ch. 12 above, pp. 240–1 and in a further article 'Military Obligations of Leasehold Tenants in Leicesterian Denbigh: A Footnote', *Trans. D.H.S.* xxiv (1975), 205–8.

78 Those releases which have survived with the feoffments are indicated in Appendix 13.1. Some strays have also survived; N.L.W. Coed Coch MS. 1109, McEwen MS. IA. The releases were usually dated the day after the feoffment. The surviving releases do not mention the contributions to the £1000 assessed on individuals; but two enrolled in the Close Rolls record that the recipients, both gentlemen, each paid £20 (P.R.O., C. 54/815 [12 Elizabeth, r. 31]).

79 C.R.O. Galltfaenan MS. 757.

80 Owing to the dispersal of estate papers, some have probably made their way into English repositories, e.g. there is a Chirk feoffment in the British Museum (Add. Charter 8487). Only thirteen Chirk releases survive among the Dudley Papers at Longleat (Boxes ii–iii, nos. 20–32), although Dudley xx, loc. cit., contains references to bags containing the bonds of obligation and releases for Denbigh.

81 Longleat, Dudley i, fol. 245. Prior to 1574 only ten feoffments were enrolled in the Close Rolls (see below, p. 269).

82 *Ibid.*, fol. 32, Snagge to Leicester, 23 July 1571.

83 Glasier's eccentricity as vice-chamberlain of Chester is discussed in W. J. Jones, 'The Exchequer of Chester in the Last Years of Elizabeth I' in A. J. Slavin (ed.), *Tudor Men and Institutions* (Baton Rouge, Louisiana, 1972), pp. 129–32. Cf. the complaints of Yerwerth to Leicester in 1579 (Dudley i, fol. 206). Snagge's letter hints that Glasier wished him to take the blame for the delays in Chirk.

84 Huband was appointed steward of Leicester's estates in the Marches and Mont-gomeryshire in 1573 and entered the Council in the Marches in 1574. From then till his death in 1583 he was Leicester's most important officer in Wales, see Ch. 12 above, pp. 244–5.

85 Longleat, Dudley xvii, fols. 156–156ᵛ, and i, fol. 32.

86 In a surviving fragment of the roll of the court baron of the lordship (U.C.N.W. Garthewin MS. 2693ʙ), there is a presentment of 4 April 1582 in which any outstand-ing eligible tenants were encouraged to compound with Leicester. This may be regarded as the final stage of the process of enfeoffment.

87 C.R.O. Nercwys Hall MS. 848 contains a consideration greater than a year's rent; this may be an error.

88 Longleat, Dudley xvii, fol. 186. Evidence that transformation of copyhold to freehold occurred in Chirk can be found in *Exch. Proc.*, p. 112.

89 P.R.O., E. 317/Denbighshire/3, memb. 1.

90 Longleat, Dudley xx, loc. cit.

91 P.R.O., C. 54/773 [10 Elizabeth, roll 17]; C. 54/815 [12 Eliz. r. 3].

92 C. 54/956–7 [17 Eliz. r. 5 and 6]; P.R.O., Index 10781, fol. 15.

93 Made on 20 February 1575, C. 54/964 [17 Eliz. r. 3]; this enrolment is repeated in C. 54/1014 [19 Eliz. r. 12].

94 N.L.W. Wynnstay MS. 86ᴀ.

95 P.R.O., S.C. 12/26/27.

96 B.M. Lansdowne MS. 45, fols. 188–9.

97 Longleat, Dudley xvi.

98 P.R.O., L.R. 2/270, compiled by the deputy-recorder William Sparke, who as recorder compiled [G.] in 1590.

99 Longleat, Dudley iii, fols. 69 ff. This survey includes Galch Hill Park which was only restored to the lordship in 1584, see n. 28. There is another copy of this survey in the De Lisle and Dudley MSS., see *Historical Manuscripts Commission, De Lisle and Dudley Manuscripts*, i. 301.

100 B.M. Lansdowne MS. 62, fols. 118–19 (printed in Williams, *Records of Denbigh*, pp. 115–18); the valor was enclosed in a letter from William Sparke to Lord Burghley of 24 August 1590.

101 N.L.W. Lloyd Verney MS. 19; it is incomplete, containing only the returns from the borough, Ceinmeirch, Isaled, and Uwchaled together with returns from Chirk. An earlier series of ministers' accounts, for the years 1575–78, exists; but it is defaced by damp (N.L.W. Chirk Castle MS. F. 13666).

102 The larger leasehold properties are found in Appendix 13.5.

103 In [D.] and [G.] perquisites of court were estimated at £20 per annum; this figure has been used in Appendices 13.2 and 13.3. Evidence from the ministers' accounts suggests that this was a low estimate; returns from the borough, Ceinmeirch, Isaled, and Uwchaled alone came to £57. 8s. 10½d. in 1581, £19. 13s. 3¾d. in 1582, £10. 5s. 3d. in 1583, and £22. 7s. 9d. in 1584.

104 This total was that recorded by the surveyors in [D.], it is not the correct sum of the commotal rents. Owing to the suspension of the greater offices, only £5 was to be deducted for salaries.

105 See Appendix 13.4. The comparatively higher assessments levied on the poorer western commotes were the result of their greater development before 1283; see Owen, op. cit., p. 46.

106 Cf. Penry Williams, op. cit., p. 238, and his references.

107 The total for salaries outstanding is drawn from *Cal. Pat. Rolls, 1560–63*, pp. 542–3. Of the total, £62. 0s. 8d. was paid to the nominal steward Charles Wingfield for his various offices.

108 See Appendix 13.4.

109 P.R.O., L.R. 2/235A, discussed below, p. 273.

110 The source for the sum of £333. 6s. 8d. appears to be one-third of £1000. In the 1563 survey the potential increase from a general revival of rents was estimated to be £200.

111 This figure is obtained by estimating from the assessments of the increases in freehold rent found in the ministers' accounts. They are lower than those in [E.] but have been preferred since they appear to have been employed in the actual levying of rent. It has been assumed that the increase in Isdulas was in the region of that given in [E.], while Uwchdulas was probably treated similarly to Uwchaled, i.e. an increase of double the old rent or something in the region of £60.

112 See below, p. 274. The totals are those given in the accounts; the actual totals are £35. 8s. 4½d. and £139. 16s.

113 [E.] gives a total for leasehold of £239. 4s. 10d. A valor compiled after Leicester's death (P.R.O., S.C. 11/949) produces a total of £252. 19s. 6d.: a major component of the difference may have been the £14 rent for Galch Hill Park, which was not included in [E.].

114 Longleat, Dudley xvi, fol. 73ᵛ.

115 The manor of Dinorben Fawr was leased by Henry VIII for £8 per annum and by Leicester for the same, see U.C.N.W Kinmel MSS. 616, 617; P.R.O., L.R. 2/235A, fols. 21–2. The manor of Ystrad (see below, p. 272) also remained stable at £8 per annum.

116 P.R.O., L.R. 2/238, fols. 39, 50ᵛ. The survey is discussed in more detail below.

117 See, e.g., P.R.O., L.R. 2/238, fol. 50ᵛ. An interesting aspect of Leicester's leases was the obligation on the tenant to plant a certain number of trees to remedy the situation discovered in 1563. A lease of 1564 (N.L.W Coed Coch MS. 1023) required the tenant to plant 180 trees, either oak, ash, elm, poplar, or walnut. This obligation is also referred to in the leases issued by the Crown to replace the Leicesterian ones in 1592–93, see n. 119.

118 The only contemporary reference to rack-renting I have found is a comment by the steward of 1590 on the practices of the greater tenants towards their sub-tenants; see B.M. Lansdowne MS. 62, fol. 118.

119 Two assessments were made in 1592; the second assessment (P.R.O., S.C. 12/27/27) records the value of the leasehold lands as £970, annual rents as £276. 12s. 6d., and fines as £6000. 10s. 10d. The new leases granted by the Crown are calendared in *Aug. Proc. Wales*, pp. 354–74.

120 *Aug. Proc. Wales*, p. 359. One man who profited from the 'queen's composition' was the future Sir Thomas Myddelton, who increased his influence in the lordship through loans to the more penurious tenants (on the security of their leases) to meet their fines. See Dodd, 'Myddelton', pp. 267–8.

121 P.R.O., L.R. 2/235A, which contains many references to leases made in 1563–66 by Leicester's commissioners. The survey was made by Henry Dynne, auditor of the lordship, John Yerwerth, receiver, and Robert Snagge. One of the presentments of the jury of survey survives (N.L.W. Bachymbyd, MS. 124).

122 C.R.O. Galltfaenan MS. 757, see above, p. 267.

123 U.C.N.W. Garthewin MS. 2693B.

124 The commission is found in P.R.O., S.C. 12/27/27; the presentment in N.L.W. Lleweni MS. 369.

125 Both S.C. 12/27/27 and Lleweni MS. 369 have schedules attached; the P.R.O. schedule is in better condition.

126 See schedule.

127 P.R.O., L.R. 2/238. The survey was undertaken in three stages: 16 September–17 October 1583, 4–25 September 1584, and 12 August–28 September 1585.

128 P.R.O., L.R. 2/238, fols. 58, 60.

129 *Ibid.*, fol. 54ᵛ.

130 *Ibid.*, fol. 41ᵛ. It is possible that the 'mutiny' of the tenants was a product of these events.

131 N.L.W. Ruthin Lordship MS. 1400 is a copy of the presentment of the jury of survey; there is also a reference to the composition in Longleat, Dudley xx, loc. cit. The commissioners for the tenants were Thomas Salusbury, Esq. (grandson and heir of Sir John Salusbury), Robert Wynn ap Tudor, Edward Conway of Bryneuryn, Fulk Lloyd of Henllan, William Wynne, Piers Holland of Kinmel, Peter Owen of Abergele, Edward Thelwell, Griffith Wynn, John Myddelton of Ystrad, and William ap Jenkin Lloyd.

132 The presentment of the inquisition and jury of survey and the schedule of lands are found in P.R.O., L.R. 2/235B; since the presentment is worn and illegible, reference should be made to the copy, Ruthin Lordship MS. 1400.

133 B.M. Lansdowne MS. 62, fol. 118. Sparke recommended to Lord Burghley that the Crown proceed with the second composition. During his tenure of the lordship from September 1588 to February 1590 the Earl of Warwick had tried to implement the composition. *Calendar of the Wynn (of Gwydir) Papers, 1515–1690* (Aberystwyth, 1926), no. 119. See also P.R.O., L.R. 2/238, fol. 44.

134 *Letters and Papers, Henry VIII*, xix, pt. i, no. 1035 (139). P.R.O., L.R. 2/252, fol. 4ᵛ.

135 Longleat, Dudley xvi, fol. 37. Salusbury is listed as tenant in the survey book of 1569, L.R. 2/235A, fol. 3.

136 N.L.W. Lleweni MS. 243.

137 Another reason may be related to a reference in Longleat, Dudley xx, loc. cit. to legal proof that Salusbury was a tenant of Denbigh Castle, which suggests there had been conflict over the question.

138 Longleat, Dudley ii, fol. 117, John Yerwerth to Leicester, 2 October 1572.

139 N.L.W. Lleweni MS. 247. P.R.O., S.C. 11/286.

140 Salusbury later claimed that he purchased the lease on 1 September 1564, but he was negotiating with Leicester's commissioners as tenant in 1563.

141 Longleat, Dudley xvi, fol. 73. N.L.W. Lleweni MS. 242.

142 Lleweni MS. 242. The sale may have been part of the redemption of a debt Salusbury owed to Clough and his brother Sir Richard; by 1574, however, the lands Salusbury had conveyed to the Cloughs were settled on his grandson Thomas. See R. G. Jones, 'Sir Richard Clough of Denbigh, c. 1530–1570', pt. III, *Trans. D.H.S.* xxii (1973), 52–3.

143 For the dispute see Longleat, Dudley iii, fol. 69ᵛ and *Calendar of Wynn Papers*, nos. 84–6, esp. the original of no. 85, N.L.W. Add. MS. 464ᴇ, no. 85, John Wynn to Arthur Atye [spring 1578]. In the *Calendar* Atye, Leicester's chief secretary from c. 1574, is mistranscribed as 'attorney'.

144 P.R.O., L.R. 2/238, fol. 30.

145 *Cal. Pat. Rolls, 1560–63*, pp. 278–9; P.R.O., S.C. 12/27/30. Cf. Palmer and Owen, op. cit., pp. 204 ff.

146 *Cal. Pat. Rolls, 1560–63*, loc. cit.

147 Palmer and Owen, op. cit., pp. 213–14. The survey of this settlement is found in P.R.O., L.R. 2/205.

148 Kerridge, *Ag. Probs.*, p. 42.

149 P.R.O., E. 317/Denbighshire/3, memb. 1.

150 P.R.O., S.C. 11/949 refers to 'sundrie encroachments within the said lordship sithence the first composicion'.

151 Longleat, Dudley MS. xvi, fol. 74.

152 P.R.O., S.C. 11/949.

153 *Ibid.*, E. 112/60/60.

154 *Ibid.*, E. 112/60/79.

155 *Exch. Proc. James*, p. 166.

156 P.R.O., E. 317/Denbighshire/2, memb. 6.

157 See n. 88. Evidence of the success of the composition in Denbigh can also be found in Thomas Pennant's *Tours in Wales*, although garbled by the legend of Leicester. After relating Leicester's iniquities, Pennant comments 'The various disorders which arose from those practices were so great that Elizabeth interposed, and by charter confirmed the quiet possession of the tenants, and allayed the discontents' (quoted in J. Williams, *Ancient and Modern Denbigh* (Wrexham, 1856), p. 98). This is undoubtedly a description of Leicester's enfeoffments, although Pennant may have been misled by the reference in the indentures to the queen's licence to alienate.

158 E. Evans, 'Arwystli and Cyfeiliog in the Sixteenth Century: An Elizabethan Inquisition', *Montgomeryshire Collections*, li (1949–50), 27. Something similar occurred in the lordship of Ruthin, see R. I. Jack (ed.), 'Records of Denbigh and its Lordships, III: The Lordship of Dyffryn Clwyd, 1630–5', *Trans. D.H.S.* xix (1970), 14.

159 Longleat, Dudley MS. Box iii, no. 52, assignment by Leicester of the revenues of the lordship to the Earls of Warwick, Huntingdon, and Pembroke and Sir Henry Sidney on 6 January 1580 to redeem mortgage owed to the Crown (not executed).

160 The response of the tenants was not dissimilar to that encountered in other cases of 'feudal reaction', see Kerridge, op. cit., p. 30.

161 P.R.O., S.C. 12/27/30.

162 P.R.O., E. 317/Denbighshire/2, memb. 1.

———

Chapter 14

Office-holders of the borough of Denbigh and the lordships of Denbighshire in the reign of Elizabeth I

The loss of the great majority of the records of the institutions of sixteenth-century Denbighshire has seriously inhibited the study of one of the most interesting periods in the county's history. The records of the Court of Great Sessions for the Denbigh circuit are, however, largely intact for the reign of Elizabeth I and could be more fully exploited than they have been. The *nomina ministrorum* in the gaol files, which list all the officers who owed attendance at the court, provide us with a source for the identities of members of the commission of the peace, constables, various stewards, and officers of the borough of Denbigh.[1]

After the J.P.s and the sheriff, the stewards of the four lordships and the aldermen and bailiffs of the borough were the most important office-holders in the county. The present paper will provide lists of these officers together with a discussion of the functions and political significance of their offices. Particular attention will be paid to the influence of the Earls of Leicester and Warwick on appointments. The lists begin in the early 1560s with the earliest surviving *nomina ministrorum*: that of the stewards will be taken to 1588; that of the borough officers to 1597–98, when the Record Book of Convocation begins.[2] The main source is the *nomina ministrorum*, but where gaps in the gaol files are filled, or confirmation provided, from other sources, these will be indicated.

THE STEWARDS OF THE LORDSHIPS OF DENBIGH

The creation of the shires of eastern Wales from the multitude of marcher lordships under the statute 27 Henry VIII c. 26 could only have been undertaken because 'dyvers and many of the said lordships marchers be nowe in the hands and possession of our sovereigne lord the Kinge, and the smaller number of them in the possession of other lordes'.[3] The four lordships of

Denbighshire had been in the possession of the crown since the beginning of the sixteenth century: Denbigh since the reversion of the earldom of March on the accession of Edward IV in 1461, Chirk and Bromfield and Yale since the attainder of Sir William Stanley in 1495, and Ruthin after purchase from the Greys in 1506/7. A previous interest in amalgamation may possibly be seen in the grant of Ruthin, Chirk and Bromfield and Yale to Henry Fitzroy, Duke of Richmond (Henry VIII's bastard son), in 1529, but, despite their 'union' in the crown, the four lordships remained distinct and auto-nomous in their internal administration.[4] Since they had provided the primary organs of local government for two centuries, a strong sense of corporate identity had evolved which lasted long after the creation of the shire in 1536. The geographical influences which had determined the boundaries of the lordships had a similar effect on post-1536 local government.[5] The six hundreds created under section 20 of the statute of 1536 were identical to the lordships: Denbigh was divided into two hundreds, while Ruthin, Bromfield, Yale, and Chirk each became a single hundred.

The records of the lordship of Denbigh provide a clear picture of the structure of the administration of the lordship. The central institution was the *curia baronis*, over which the steward presided. The tenants of the lord-ship owed suit of court every three weeks, or to seventeen courts a year in each of the five commotes: Ceinmeirch, Isaled, Uwchaled, Isdulas, and Uwchdulas. Two of these courts were courts leet (the first after Easter and the first after Michaelmas), in which a grand jury was impanelled 'to inquire of all Tresons, murthers, and all other offences which then [before 1536] were tryed before the steward and now before the Justices of Assise [Great Session]'.[6] At one of the courts leet a view of frankpledge was taken.[7] Apart from the criminal jurisdiction of the courts leet, the jurisdiction of the *curia baronis* included all the tenurial questions and other issues directly pertinent to a court baron as well as all civil pleas and actions.[8]

The two statutes for Wales made massive inroads into the jurisdiction of the *curia baronis*. Although section 9 of the statute of 1543 (34/5 Henry VIII c. 26) permitted the lordships to retain their courts leet, section 10 denied them any jurisdiction over presentment for felony.[9] Presentments were hence-forth to be made by Quarter Sessions and felonies tried before the Court of Great Sessions. The Denbigh inquisition, quoted above, suggests that pre-sentments by grand juries of the courts leet were still being made in the 1560s, but no evidence of this survives in the records of Great Sessions. The civil jurisdiction of the *curia baronis* was limited to personal and real actions of under 40s in value, although the surviving Elizabethan court roll of the lordship (that for 1580) reveals that pleas of debt and trespass involving sums of up to £40 were heard.[10] Untouched, on the other hand, was the 'private' jurisdiction over tenurial relationships within the lordship.

The combination of manorial jurisdiction and corporate identity gave the lordships continued significance after 1536, but a major revision of their importance occurred after Denbigh and Chirk were granted to Lord Robert Dudley, afterwards Earl of Leicester, on 9 June 1563, and Ruthin to his brother Ambrose, Earl of Warwick, on 23 June 1564.[11] The brothers were magnates of major political importance and their interests and influence would not be confined to the narrow jurisdiction left to them by statute. Leicester's jurisdiction in the lordship of Denbigh was granted 'in as large and ample manner . . . as was used when it was a lordship marcher with as large wardes as council learned could devise'.[12] The precise effects of the revival of the lordships are not, however, easy to determine. The statutes for Wales were not reversed and such financial rights as Leicester claimed as a lord marcher, the receipt of the fines of Quarter Sessions and Great Sessions, for example, were only an extension of principles established in 27 Henry VIII c. 26, section 19.[13] Although the jurisdiction of Quarter Sessions over-rode that of the lordships, this did not present a challenge, because Leicester could easily control the membership of the commission of the peace.[14] The *quo warranto* proceeding against the borough of Denbigh in 1585, discussed below, might be considered a clash between lordship and shire, but other influences were probably at work. Nonetheless, as the immediate instruments of Dudley influence, the political role of the lordships in the shire was revived and this is reflected in the appointment of the stewards of Denbigh, Chirk, and Ruthin.[15]

Prior to 1563 the stewardship of the lordship of Denbigh had been mainly in the hands of the Salusburys of Lleweni and the office had been of considerable importance to them before the statutes for Wales. Sir Roger Salusbury had held the stewardship from 1508 to his death in 1530 and he was succeeded by his brother John 'y bodiau' from 1530 to 1549.[16] The cadet branch of Lleweni, the Salesburys of Bachymbyd and Rûg in Merioneth, became stewards of Ruthin in the 1530s. Piers Salesbury held the office in 1536 (he had been appointed by the Duke of Richmond) and he was succeeded by his son Robert in the 1540s.[17] In 1549 the stewardship of Denbigh was granted to Sir Anthony Wingfield, vice-chamberlain of the household, and in 1551 it was re-granted in survivorship with his son Charles. By 1563, however, the office was effectively in the hands of Sir John Salusbury.[18] In the 1550s the stewardship of the other lordships was granted to the first Earl of Pembroke.

The Dudley tenure of the lordships initiated a new policy towards the stewardships. The office (as were most of the offices in their three lordships) was held during pleasure, and the numerous alterations made reflected the development of Dudley patronage.[19] At Leicester's entry into the lordship of Denbigh, Sir John Salusbury solicited the office, but instead Leicester appointed William Glasier, a Chester lawyer and a member of the council in the marches whom he had known for some time. Glasier was also appointed steward of Chirk in the 1560s and his immediate successor there, John Price of Eglwysegl, was another legal member of the council.[20] The appointment of lawyers as stewards was standard estate practice. In the 1570s, however, Leicester used the office in a more political sense. Evan Lloyd of Bodidris in Yale, steward of Chirk from 1572 to his death, on his return from Leicester's expedition to the Netherlands in 1587 rose from the ranks of the middling gentry to considerable prominence in the shire owing to Leicester's influence. He was succeeded by his son John, who also played a leading, if controversial, role in the shire in the 1590s.[21] In the lordship of Denbigh, Leicester employed further important local partisans: John Salesbury of Rûg from 1578 to his death in 1580 and then Ellis Price of Plas Iolyn. Price was continued in the office by the queen until his death in 1594.[22]

Ambrose Dudley employed a particularly involved system of joint and even rotating appointments in Ruthin. His officers included the same mixture of lawyers, like Glasier and Robert Snagge, and prominent local followers: Salesbury of Rûg from 1565 to 1569 and his son Robert from c. 1586, and Simon Thelwall of Plas-y-Ward from 1575 to his death in 1586 and then his son Edward.[23] The use of a common pool of officers provides clear evidence that the Dudley brothers exercised a joint influence in the shire.

The importance of the stewards declined again after the collapse of Dudley power following Leicester's death in 1588. In 1585 he had mortgaged the lordship of Denbigh to a group of London merchants to raise £15,000 for his Netherlands expedition and had died with the mortgage unredeemed. Warwick, his heir, undertook the redemption, but died shortly afterwards in February 1590 and it was the queen who eventually redeemed the mortgage in 1592–93 and restored the lordship to the crown.[24] The reversion of the stewardship to a primarily legal office followed the restoration. In July 1594 Sir Thomas Egerton, the attorney-general, was appointed as successor to Price.[25]

THE OFFICE-HOLDERS OF THE BOROUGH OF DENBIGH

The governing charter of the borough of Denbigh at the beginning of the reign of Elizabeth I was the charter of 25 April 1551, under which the borough was made fully incorporate and its two aldermen granted quarter-sessional jurisdiction within the borough and its precincts.[26] Their jurisdiction was as full as that exercised by justices elsewhere in England and Wales and the borough was freed from the intervention of the justices of the shire.[27] The new authority was superimposed upon the previous manorial jurisdiction within the borough and marks the culmination of two centuries of corporate evolution. The first major step in this process, following the creation of the borough by the Earl of Lincoln at the end of the thirteenth century, was the charter of 22 February 1401, in which the borough was recognised as a free borough with a guild merchant and at least some of the liberties of the royal boroughs of Conway and Rhuddlan.[28] A charter of 1484 defined the role of the borough court (its presiding officer was the steward of the lordship of Denbigh) and granted further privileges, including control of commerce in the commotes of Ceinmeirch, Isaled, and Uwchaled, the inhabitants of which were prohibited from buying or selling victual or merchandise except within the borough.[29] The Henrician statutes for Wales created the borough the shire town of the new county and granted it the right to send a burgess to parliament.[30]

The examination of the constitution of the borough should begin with the *curia burgonis et ville de Denbigh*, the original town Court and an integral part of the *curia baronis* of the lordship of Denbigh. Under the charter of 1551 the presiding officers of the Court were the two bailiffs of the borough, replacing the steward of the lordship. But although the bailiffs were elected annually by the burgesses, they were still officers of the lordship and were charged, for example, with the rents and casualties accruing to the lordship from the borough.[31] The *curia burgonis* functioned similarly to the commotal courts of the lordship; it sat every three weeks, with two courts leet and view of frankpledge. Under the second statute for Wales (1543) the jurisdiction of this court was limited to civil suits under 40s value, but, as with the commotal courts, the Court roll of 1580 records cases involving far larger sums.[32] After 1551 any residual criminal jurisdiction was absorbed by the aldermanic Quarter Sessions and we may assume that, since both aldermen and bailiffs were drawn from the same borough oligarchy, disputes over jurisdiction were settled amicably.

Under the charter of 1551 the two aldermen were elected annually at Michaelmas. While the election of bailiffs is not mentioned in the charter, it is evident that the same course was followed with them. The borough also elected two coroners, although it appears to have been customary to appoint the retiring aldermen.[33] The main permanent officers were the recorder, who in the Leicesterian period and probably before was the recorder of the lordship, and the clerk of the peace.[34] The process of election is not easy to extract from the surviving records. Under the charter of 1551 the burgesses were to elect two of their *comburgenses* aldermen (and bailiffs by implication) even if they were victuallers or innkeepers. This suggests a fairly open corporation in which all burgesses were eligible for election and all had a voice. The charter of 1597 provided for the same franchise, but also created a common council of twenty-five capital burgesses, who soon afterwards 'interpreted' the right of all burgesses to stand as officers to apply to capital burgesses only.[35] The charter of 1551 does not mention a common council,

TABLE 14.1 The stewards of the Denbighshire lordships

	Denbigh	Chirk	Ruthin	Bromfield and Yale
1560	Charles Wingfield	William Herbert, Earl of Pembroke	William Herbert, Earl of Pembroke	William Herbert, Earl of Pembroke
1561 Spring Term	Wingfield	Pembroke	Pembroke	Pembroke
Autumn Term	Wingfield	Pembroke	Pembroke	Pembroke
1562	[no nomina ministrorum]			
1563	Wingfield	Pembroke	Pembroke	Pembroke
1564	[no nomina ministrorum]			
1565 S.T.	William Glasier	Pembroke	John Salesbury of Rûg	Pembroke
A.T.	Glasier	Pembroke	Salesbury	Pembroke
1566 S.T.	Glasier	Glasier [?]	Salesbury	Pembroke
A.T.	[no nomina ministrorum]			
1567 S.T.	Glasier	Glasier	Salesbury	Pembroke
1568 S.T.	Glasier	[not given]	Salesbury	Pembroke
1569 S.T.	Glasier	[not given]	Glasier	Pembroke
A.T.	Glasier	John Price of Eglwysegl	Glasier	Pembroke
1570	Glasier	Price	Robert Snagge	Edward Herbert of Montgomery
1571 S.T.	Glasier	Glasier	John Williams	Herbert
A.T.	Glasier	Price	Glaseor/Snagge	Herbert
1572 S.T.	Glasier	Evan Lloyd of Bodidris	John Williams	Herbert
1573	[not extant]			
1574 S.T.	Glasier	Lloyd	Williams	Herbert
A.T.	Glasier	Lloyd	Glasier	Herbert

1575				
S.T.	Glasier	Lloyd	Williams/Simon Thelwall of Plas-y-Ward	Herbert
A.T.	Glasier	Lloyd	Glasier/Thelwall	Herbert
1576				
S.T.	Glasier	Lloyd	Williams/Thelwall	Herbert
A.T.	Glasier	Lloyd	Glasier/Thelwall	Herbert
1577 A.T.	Glasier	Lloyd	Glasier/Thelwall	Herbert
1578 A.T.	[no *nomina ministrorum*]			
1579				
S.T.	Glasier/John Salusbury of Rûg	Lloyd	Williams/Thelwall	Herbert
A.T.	Glasier/Salusbury	Lloyd	Williams/Thelwall	Herbert
1580				
S.T.	Glasier/Salusbury	Lloyd	Williams/Thelwall	Herbert
A.T.	[no *nomina ministrorum*]			
1581				
S.T.	Ellis Price of Plas Iolyn	Lloyd	Glasier/Thelwall	Herbert
A.T.	Price	Lloyd	Thelwall	Herbert
1582	[not extant]			
1583	[no *nomina ministrorum*]			
1584				
S.T.	Price	Lloyd	Thelwall	Herbert
A.T.	[no *nomina ministrorum*]			
1585	[no *nomina ministrorum*]			
1586 A.T.	Price	Lloyd	Robert Salesbury of Rûg/Edward Thelwall	Herbert
1587				
S.T.	Price	John Lloyd of Bodidris	Salesbury/Thelwall	Herbert
A.T.	[no *nomina ministrorum*]			
1588				
S.T.	Price	Lloyd	Salesbury/Thelwall	Herbert
A.T.	Price	Lloyd	Salesbury/Thelwall	Herbert

TABLE 14.2 Aldermen, bailiffs, and coroners of the borough of Denbigh

Year	Aldermen	Bailiffs	Coroners
1563–64	Simon Thelwall Hugh Lloyd[a]		
1564–65		John Dryhurst William Clough	
1565–66	John Williams Richard Myddelton	William Spen	
1566–67	Robert Salusbury William Clough		
1567–68		Robert Rutter John Dutton	
1568–69	Jenkin ap Richard David Burchinshaw	Robert Lathom John Matthew	
1569–70		John Mersh Peter Wynway	
1570–71	Thomas Lloyd John Matthew	Robert ap Hugh Thomas ap Robert	
1571–72*			
1572–73	Hugh Lloyd Robert Lathom	John Ireland Thomas Walton	William Clough[b] Thomas Lloyd
1573–74	John Lloyd William Knowles	David ap Robert Humphrey Clough	Hugh Lloyd[c] Robert Lathom
1574–75	Robert Salusbury William Clough	Peter Lloyd Thomas Evans	John Lloyd William Knowles
1575–76		Thomas Knowsley David ap Harry	
1576–77*			
1577–78*			
1578–79	Robert Salusbury Thomas Lloyd		
1579–80	John Salesbury of Rûg Thomas Salusbury	Robert Lathom[d] Thomas Lloyd	
1580–81	Thomas Salusbury Hugh Lloyd	John Dryhurst[e] John Lloyd	
1581–82*			
1582–83*			
1583–84*			
1584–85		John Mersh[f]	
1585–86		Robert Salusbury William Clough	
1586–87	Robert Dolben Henry Rutter	Thomas Lloyd[g] Jenkin ap Richard	
1587–88	John Lloyd John ap Rees	Richard Lloyd[g] Humphrey Dolben	

TABLE 14.2 (*cont'd*)

Year	Aldermen	Bailiffs	Coroners
1588–89	Robert Salusbury	Robert Knowsley[g]	
	Thomas Lloyd	Robert Mutton	
1589–90	John Salusbury of Lleweni	Richard ap Rees[g]	
	Thomas Salusbury	John ap Rees	
1590–91	John Salusbury	Robert Lloyd[g]	
	Thomas Salusbury	Thomas Barber	
1591–92*			
1592–93*			
1593–94	Robert Knowsley	Richard Price[h]	
	Hugh Clough	Hugh Pigott	
1594–95*			
1595–96*			
1596–97	Hugh Myddelton	Robert Lathom	Robert Salusbury[i]
	John Dryhurst	Richard Clough	Fulk Myddelton
1597–98	Robert Salusbury	Humphrey Clough	Hugh Myddelton[i]
	Robert Lathom	Robert Lloyd	John Dryhurst

The term of office runs from Michaelmas to Michaelmas.
Unless otherwise specified the source for identification is the *nomina ministrorum* of the gaol files of the court of Great Sessions.
* indicates a year without extant records
[a] C.R.O. BD/A/109.
[b] Longleat, Dudley, ii, fo. 117.
[c] R. Flenley, ed., *A Calendar of the Register of the Queen's Majesty's Council in . . . the Marches [of Wales]* (Cymmrodorion Record Soc., vii, 1916), p. 133.
[d] C.R.O. BD/A/113.
[e] N.L.W. Lloyd Verney MS. 19, ministers' accounts, lordship of Denbigh, 1581–84.
[f] P.R.O. STAC 5, M 12/16.
[g] P.R.O. STAC 5, C 41/24.
[h] P.R.O. STAC 5, L 23/25.
[i] Record Book of Convocation, C.R.O. BD/A/1.

but there is clear evidence of a 'council of sixteen' in the middle years of Elizabeth's reign.[36] It is probable that it possessed a similar control over elections because the account of the election of Michaelmas 1572, discussed below, relates that nominations approved by the 'chief of the town', probably the council, would receive the approbation of the burgesses. On the other hand, aldermen in this period were not necessarily previous members of the council, although the majority appear to have been so. After 1597 the common council also had the right both to fill vacancies among its members by co-option and grant freedom to potential burgesses, even if they were not residents of the borough.[37] It is probable that similar control had existed in previous years, though by 1597 there were pressing reasons for tightening the corporation. The Elizabethan council was undoubtedly composed of men with interests outside the borough as well as within, but a detailed examination of the membership would be necessary before more definite conclusions could be reached.

Despite its incorporation in 1551, the borough was dominated almost entirely by Sir John Salusbury of Lleweni in the 1550s and 1560s. We know that he would attend the aldermanic elections with his followers and it is probable that most successful candidates were dependent on his sufferance. His influence also extended to the election of parliamentary burgesses, for several Salusburys sat for the borough in the 1550s, while Simon Thelwall who sat in 1552, 1553, and 1571 was no enemy to Salusbury. The grant of the lordship of Denbigh to the Earl of Leicester created a direct challenge to Salusbury's influence. Not only did Leicester inherit the remaining manorial jurisdiction within the borough but his less tangible influence far exceeded anything Salusbury could muster. While there is no evidence that Leicester wished to threaten the borough's incorporation, his tolerance of a Salusbury-dominated town was limited.[38]

The most revealing information concerning Leicester's relations with the borough comes from the year 1572 and chronicles a growing crisis. On 16 March 1572 Leicester wrote to the justices of Denbighshire giving his support to the construction of a shirehall within the borough and making a gift of the site.[39] Some weeks later, on 30 April, the borough received an angry letter complaining of their failure to consult him in the election of the burgess for the parliament of 1572, despite 'the many good tournes and commodities which I have bene allwayes willinge to procure you'.[40] On 2 October John Yerwerth, receiver of the lordship, reported to Leicester on the conduct of the aldermanic election at Michaelmas.[41] This letter is worth quotation at length.

> Maye yt please your honor to be advertysed that according to your lordship's lettres unto me and other your officers lately addressed for our repare unto your lordship's towne of Denbigh at the day of ellecions of ther newe officers, to thende that ther myght not any be chosen officers by the practyze and devyse of the Salysburys (as hitherto hathe bynne accustomed) for the servinge of ther owne turnes and suche as upon them depended, but rather suche as shall have special regard to the administration of justice and the good government of your lordship's towne. Even so I made my repare to Denbigh upon their ellecion daye and fyndynge the chef of the towne ther assembled in the open and common hawle suggested unto them your lordship's pleasure touchinge theyre officers to be made. And did name unto them Mr. Hugh Lloyd and Mr. Lathom your lordship's servant to be

theyr aldermen, John Ireland and Thomas Walton bayliffs, Mr. William Clough and Thomas Lloyd your lordship's servant coroners, which personnes were presently ellected with great contentment of all the burgesses ther present. But yet this muche I have thought yt my dutie [to inform you] that Sir John Salusbury (who was wont to be ther present) with all his followers, were all absent and came not to the ellecions, rather as I think to pleasure Sir John Salysbury then to yelde their voyce accordynge to ther duties with your lordship's friends.

Leicester's intervention in the aldermanic elections and his determination to see the return of reliable officers was probably the result of his clash with the borough over the parliamentary election. But it is quite evident that the object of his hostility was not a group of 'upstart burgesses' but the influence of Salusbury. Denbigh was a battleground in the struggle between the two for pre-eminence in the shire. The fact that Leicester was ultimately victorious in the parliamentary election (the burgess for Denbigh in 1572, Richard Cavendish, was one of his followers) as well as in the aldermanic election suggests that there was at least a division within the council between followers of Leicester and Salusbury.[42] The core of Leicester's followers were probably his candidates at Michaelmas. As a group they share certain interesting characteristics. They were neither 'new men' nor outsiders, but members of the borough establishment who had held office before. It is possible that resentment of the Salusbury hegemony may have been among the motives for their allegiance to Leicester, for several of them reappear in anti-Salusbury factions in the 1590s. Robert Lathom (d. 1613) and Thomas Lloyd may have been retainers of Leicester, for the title 'servant' often indicates this. Lathom clearly profited from his association with Leicester, while Lloyd and his brother Hugh were nephews of Fulk Lloyd of Henllan, forester of the lordship.[43] William Clough's allegiance may have been encouraged by his brother Sir Richard's association with Sir Thomas Gresham, who had close relations with the Dudleys. Salusbury's faction cannot be so easily identified, but it probably included his brother Robert (alderman 1566–67) and David Burchinshaw (alderman 1568–69), whose family had close associations with Lleweni.[44]

Sir John Salusbury appears to have regarded his defeat as substantial. According to Yerwerth he was retiring to London on the ground that he had been driven from his 'country' by Leicester. Certainly by the time of Sir John's death in 1578, Leicester's pre-eminence in both shire and borough was complete. In 1579–80 the bailiffs of the borough were Lathom and Lloyd, while the aldermen were John Salesbury of Rûg, steward of the lordship, and Thomas Salusbury of Denbigh Castle, a younger son of Sir John, both of whom had thrown in their lot with Leicester after 1578. The later M.P.s for the borough, Cavendish in 1584–85 and Robert Wrote in 1586–87, were both Leicesterians.

It is remarkable, therefore, that only a few years later anti-Leicesterian feeling in the borough was strong enough to force him to bring a *quo warranto* proceeding against the borough in 1585, in which all the liberties of the charter were lost.[45] The suit was provoked by the borough's refusal to permit Leicester's officers any further jurisdiction within its precincts.[46] In the absence of further evidence it is tempting to see the restlessness in the borough related in some degree to the restlessness of the new squire of Lleweni, Thomas Salusbury, who was playing an important role in the county in 1585.[47] His participation in the Babington Plot a year later was largely motivated by hatred for Leicester and resentment at the reduction in his family's prestige.[48] It is revealing that one of the town's attorneys in the case, Hugh Clough, was elected alderman in 1593–94 as a Salusbury candidate.[49]

No further challenge to Leicester before his death in 1588 is recorded. However, in the 'interregnum' following the death of Warwick in 1590, while the queen was negotiating for the redemption of Leicester's mortgage, a determined and successful Salusbury counter-attack was made. John Salusbury, Thomas's brother and the new squire of Lleweni, and his uncle Thomas, who joined the family after Leicester's death, both obtained election as aldermen of Denbigh at Michaelmas 1589. In the spring of 1590 they quickly re-established Quarter Sessions within the borough and drove out the Leicesterian recorder, John Challenor, threatening him with violence if he attempted to reassert his authority. Challenor brought suit in the Star Chamber against the Salusburys, but without apparent success.[50]

During the next few years the Salusburys re-established their hegemony over the borough – 'sole and absolute rule and government', as one complainant later alleged – and held Quarter Sessions in defiance of the *quo warranto* decision.[51] Simultaneously they were struggling against the former Leicesterian families (Lloyd of Bodidris and Salesbury of Rûg) for preeminence in the shire. In 1594, however, their control of the borough was challenged. A second Star Chamber suit, brought by Thomas Lloyd (the coroner of 1572), accused the Salusburys of having made six score burgesses 'all being countrymen, their servants and friends . . . some dwelling five miles away . . . and not artificers' in 1593. These burgesses 'servants to labour their voices for electing officers at their service' elected men at Michaelmas 1593 (among them Hugh Clough) who were all tenants, servants, or kinsmen to the Salusburys. Lesser borough officers were also purged and replaced by 'carriers, ploughmen, sycemakers, [and] surgeons'.[52] There were also economic disputes between the Salusburys and the borough. During the 1560s Sir John Salusbury had obtained a lengthy lease of Castle Park, part of the demesne of the lordship. The family lost it after the attainder of Thomas Salusbury, and the park was leased by Leicester to the borough for pasture. Although the queen had confirmed Leicester's lease, Thomas Myddelton informed Sir Robert Cecil on 20 September 1593 that the Salusburys were attempting every means to deprive the borough of the park.[53]

The second Star Chamber case together with the Salusburys' involvement in other strife in the county forced the crown to take action. In January 1595 the queen withdrew the liberties of the borough and on 20 June 1597 granted a new charter.[54] The intervention of the crown may also have been due to the influence of Thomas Myddelton, who had been assisting the borough since 1593 at the latest. The Myddeltons had been moderately Leicesterian in sympathy (Richard Myddelton of Galch Hill had been constable of Denbigh Castle from *c.* 1563 to his death in 1575) and Leicester's death was the signal for Myddelton to attempt to take his place. While he was unable to purchase the lordship outright from the queen, he gained considerable influence in the county, as well as profit, by advancing large sums to leaseholders hard-pressed to meet the fines of the queen's composition of 1592–93.[55] By 1597 he had succeeded his father as constable of Denbigh Castle.[56] Myddelton may also have had a hand in the new charter. The queen nominated both the officers to serve until Michaelmas 1597 and the new common council. Fulk Myddelton, Thomas's brother and his main agent in Denbighshire, was a coroner in 1597 and an alderman in 1599–60; Hugh Myddelton the goldsmith was an alderman in 1597.[57]

Together with the Myddeltons, the new régime in the borough also included a number of former Leicesterians. Robert Lathom was a bailiff in 1597 and an alderman in 1597–98; Thomas Lloyd was an alderman in 1598–99. The struggle with the Salusburys was not yet over, however, for in 1598 John Salusbury was informed that a group of burgesses, including Lathom, allied with Myddelton was complaining against him to the Privy Council.[58] In March 1600 Salusbury and a band of his followers marched into the borough and assaulted Fulk Myddelton the alderman and several of the Lloyds. This incident reached the Privy Council and was the subject of a third Star Chamber suit brought in 1602 by Humphrey Lloyd, Thomas's son.[59] Lloyd claimed that Salusbury had publicly declared that he was willing to spend £500 to overthrow the borough and the incident in 1600 was intended to create sufficient disorder to bring the magistrates into disrepute. Salusbury admitted that he had attempted to remove 'such lewde persons as were perjured men and forgatherers dwelling within the town and to have them put out of the corporation'.

The turmoil in the borough was in large part a reflection of the turmoil within the shire. From *c.* 1570 to 1588 Leicester had wrested pre-eminence in the shire from the Salusburys; in the 1590s the Salusburys fought the former Leicesterians to regain it. The borough was a focus for the conflict. Before 1563 it is doubtful whether the borough had any independence from Lleweni; only with the support of a powerful outsider, Leicester or Myddelton, could the Salusburys be overcome. The struggle in the borough has, however, a further aspect, which the surviving accounts only hint at. In several places the Salusbury faction are accused of being 'countrymen'; it was claimed by Humphrey Lloyd that the charter of 1597 had restored to the borough government by its tradesmen.[60] Since the 'tradesmen' included the Leicesterian faction it is possible that the significant feature of Leicester's relations with the borough was not the restoration of the powers of the lords of Denbigh but the freeing of the town from the control of the country.

NOTES

1 National Library of Wales [hereafter N.L.W.], Wales 4/1/1 et seq.

2 Convocation was the annual meeting of the common council instituted under the charter of 1597 for the election of officers. The record book is Clwyd Record Office [hereafter C.R.O.], BD/A/1.

3 *Statutes of the Realm* (1810–1828), iii, p. 563ff.

4 The grant to Richmond was made by statute: 22 Henry VIII c. 17, *ibid.*, p. 338ff.

5 The geographical influences on the social history of Elizabethan Denbighshire have been discussed by Professor A. H. Dodd, in 'north Wales in the Essex Revolt of 1601', *English Historical Review*, lix (1944), pp. 348–52.

6 Public Record Office [hereafter P.R.O.], SC [Special Collections] 11/948, an inquisition of the lordship of Denbigh in 1561. Together with the seventeen sessions of the *curia burgonis* of the borough of Denbigh, some 102 courts were held in the lordship annually. Before the building of the shirehall in the borough in the early 1570s, the court was peripatetic. In 1523 Robert Dolben, the recorder, complained bitterly of the burden of his duties. *Records of the Court of Augmentations concerning Wales and Monmouthshire*, ed. E. A. Lewis and J. C. Davies (Cardiff, 1954), p. 90.

7 A view of frankpledge for both lordship and borough, taken in 1580, survives; University College of North Wales Library [hereafter U.C.N.W.] Garthewin MS. 2693A.

8 In 1523 the recorder claimed he had to call and declare 140 pleas and actions, *vide supra*, note 6. The *curia baronis* of the lordship was originally an honourial court, to which freehold and military tenants owed suit. Some military tenants survived into the late sixteenth century (*vide* the rental of 1583, P.R.O. LR [Land Revenue Office] 2/270, fo. 10); but by then the court had a primarily manorial jurisdiction. The leet jurisdiction of the commotal courts was similar to the leet jurisdiction of English hundredal courts in private hands.

9 *Stat. Realm*, iii, pp. 926ff.

10 U.C.N.W. Garthewin MS. 2693 B. The last known location of the full Leicesterian Court rolls was the library at Llannerch in 1778, *vide* the Llannerch library list, N.L.M. *Journal*, VII, pt. 4 (1952), p. 331.

11 *Calendar of the Patent Rolls, 1560–1563*, pp. 534–43, *1563–1566*, p. 59.

12 U.C.N.W. Gwysaney MS B 744, a seventeenth-century note drawn up by [?] Ralph Davies of Gwysaney.

13 These privileges were granted by the exchequer in 1569, *vide* Manuscripts of the Marquess of Bath, Longleat House [hereafter Longleat], Dudley papers, box 1, H, exemplification of a fine in the exchequer, 29 June 1569. The receipts are included in the ministers' accounts of the lordship of Denbigh for 1581–84, N.L.W. Lloyd Verney MS. 19.

14 This point will be discussed in further detail in a future article entitled 'Court and Country in Elizabethan Wales: the Earl of Leicester and the Lordship of Denbigh, 1563–1588'.

15 Bromfield and Yale, which remained in the possession of the crown throughout the reign of Elizabeth, will not be discussed here.

16 *Cal. Pat. Rolls, Henry VII*, ii, p. 605. *Letters and Papers, Domestic and Foreign, of the Reign of Henry VIII*, iv, no. 6490 (10). The Salusburys had held a number of the minor offices of the lordship before 1508.

17 *Letters and Papers, Henry VIII*, xii, no. 1202. Aug. *Records Wales*, p. 71.

18 *Cal. Pat. Rolls, Edward VI*, iii, pp. 163–4, 311. Longleat, Dudley, xvi, fo. 74v.

19 British Museum, Lansdowne MS. 62, fo. 118v.

20 Glasier's career is discussed in further detail in S. L. Adams, 'The Composition of 1564 and the Earl of Leicester's tenurial reformation in the lordship of Denbigh' [Ch. 13], p. 283, n. 8. John Price had been deputy to Pembroke before 1563, *vide* Longleat, Dudley, xvii, fo. 186. The end of his tenure as steward coincides with his censure by the Privy Council for bringing an unwarranted suit against Sir John Throckmorton, chief justice of Chester, P. Williams, *The Council in the Marches of Wales under Elizabeth I* (Cardiff, 1958), pp. 150–1.

21 *vide* S. L. Adams, 'The Gentry of north Wales and the Earl of Leicester's expedition to the Netherlands, 1585–86' [Ch. 12], pp. 239–40.

22 For Price, *vide* Ch. 13 above, p. 284, n. 13, also P.R.O. SP 12 (State Papers, Domestic, Elizabeth I) 231/57.

23 John Salesbury may have been deputy to Pembroke before 1564; he was receiver for the crown in Ruthin in 1563, Brit. Mus. Additional MS. 36926, fo. 79. For Warwick's relations with the Thelwalls *vide etiam* R. Newcombe, *An account of the Town and Castle of Ruthin* (Ruthin, 1829), p. 61. Snagge was a Puritan lawyer prominent in the parliaments of the 1570s and very much a Dudley follower. In 1571 he was steward of Kenilworth and he served Leicester on commissions of survey in Denbigh and Chirk during the years 1568–72.

24 *vide* P.R.O. SP 12/224/34; Historical Manuscripts Commission, *Report on The Manuscripts of the Marquess of Salisbury*, iv, p. 182.

25 *Calendar of State Papers, Domestic Series*, 1591–1594, p. 525.

26 *Cal. Pat. Rolls, Edward VI*, iv, pp. 102–3. Also worth consulting is U.C.N.W. Gwysaney MS. 1168, 'An abstracte of all and singular the liberties . . . granted by point of charter to the aldermen . . . of Denbigh' [dated 1589].

27 Freedom from shire intervention was the Webbs' definition of full incorporation, *vide* S. and B. Webb, *English Local Government*, II, *Manor and Borough* (1963 ed.), pp. 279, 281–2. The records of Great Sessions provide evidence of aldermanic exercise of their jurisdiction.

28 *Cal. Pat. Rolls, Henry IV*, i, p. 440.

29 *Cal. Pat. Rolls, Edward IV, Edward V, Richard II*, p. 504.

30 Certain functions of the shire-town, sessions of Great Sessions for example, were shared with Wrexham. Wrexham and some of the lesser boroughs were contributory boroughs for the parliamentary elections, but they do not appear to have exercised their right during Elizabeth's reign.

31 *vide* the ministers' accounts for 1581–4, N.L.W. Lloyd Verney MS. 19. The borough paid Leicester a fee-farm rent of £6 3s per annum.

32 The *curia burgonis* roll is part of the *curia baronis* roll, *vide supra*, note 10.

33 The entry for the charter of 1597 in the signet office docquet book (*Cal. S.P. Dom., 1595–97*, pp. 443–4) states that this was a new privilege, but examination of the officers for 1572–74 suggests that coroners were drawn from retiring aldermen previously. The practice was followed until the dissolution of the old corporation in 1835, *vide Report of the Commission on Municipal Corporations* (Parliamentary Sessional Papers, 1835, vol. 26), v, pp. 2559ff.

34 During the 1570s the clerk of the peace for both shire and borough was John Challenor, one of Leicester's local followers, *vide infra*, note 50.

35 *Report of the Commission on Municipal Corporations*, loc. cit., *vide etiam* the enrolment of the charter in the patent rolls, P.R.O. C 66/1469 [36 Elizabeth, roll 28].

36 C.R.O. BD/A/110, 112, 113 [indentures of the corporation, 1568, 1575, 1579]. Indentures of 1560 and 1563 (BD/A/108, 109) refer only to common burgesses.

37 *Rept. of the Municipal Corporations Comm.*, loc cit.

38 Under Leicester Denbigh corporation indentures continued to be made in the name of the aldermen and burgesses, not, as in a manorial borough like Ruthin, in the name of the lord. For a Ruthin example, *vide* E. D. Jones, ed., 'Register of the Corvisers of Ruthin, 1570–1671', *N.L.W. Journal*, vii (1951–52), pp. 238–45.

39 C.R.O. BD/A/19.

40 Two eighteenth-century copies survive: N.L.W., *Calendar of the Wynn of Gwydir Papers, 1515–1690* (Aberystwyth, 1926), no. 44, and C.R.O. DD/PH/150. J. Williams, *Ancient and Modern Denbigh* (Wrexham, 1856), p. 98, prints a transcription.

41 Longleat, Dudley, ii, fo. 117.

42 For Cavendish, *vide* Ch. 12 above, pp. 245–6.

43 For Lathom, *vide* N.L.W. Ruthin Lordship MS. 54; Longleat, Dudley, iii, fo. 70.

44 For the Burchinshaws, *vide* W. J. Smith, ed., *Calendar of the Salusbury Correspondence* (Cardiff, 1954), no. 21.

45 The *quo warranto* case, the judgement in which was reached in Queen's Bench in Michaelmas Term 27 Elizabeth (1585), is referred to in most of the Star Chamber cases involving the borough in the 1590s. The fullest description is that of Robert Lloyd, public notary of St Asaph, one of the borough's attorneys in the case, part of his testimony in the Star Chamber case of 1590, P.R.O. STAC 5/C 41/24. My own examination of the King's Bench Placita Rolls and Conterrollment Rolls has failed to discover the records of the case.

46 P.R.O. STAC 5/C 64/33.

47 *vide* N.L.W. Ruthin Lordship MS. 1400, in which Thomas Salusbury was the leading member of a commission of the tenants of the lordship of Denbigh of September 1585.

48 J. H. Pollen, *The Confessions of Babington and other papers relating to the last days of Mary Queen of Scots*, Scottish History Society, 3rd ser., iii (1922), pp. 76 and 87.

49 Robert Lloyd, the other attorney, may have been the bailiff of that name in 1590–91.

50 P.R.O. STAC 5/C 64/33, C 41/24. Challenor had been clerk of the peace for shire and borough in the 1570s and escheator for the lordship in the 1580s, Brit. Mus. Lansdowne MS. 62, fo. 119.

51 P.R.O. STAC 5/L 23/25. Little effort appears to have been made to enforce the *quo warranto* decision by the autumn of 1590, *vide* Brit. Mus. Lansdowne MS. 62, loc. cit.

52 P.R.O. STAC 5/L 23/25.

53 The Salusbury lease of Castle Park is discussed in Ch. 13 above, pp. 274–5, *vide etiam* Hist. MSS. Comm., *Salisbury MSS.*, vii, p. 185.

54 'Robert Parry's Diary', *Archaeologia Cambrensis*, 6th ser., xv (1915), p. 120.

55 On Myddelton, *vide* A. H. Dodd, 'Mr. Myddelton the merchant of Tower Street', S. T. Bindoff *et al.*, eds., *Elizabethan Government and Society* (1961), especially pp. 267–8. The queen's composition, which raised £6000 from fines on leaseholders to meet some of the costs of the redemption, is discussed in Ch. 13 above, pp. 272–3.

56 Hist. MSS. Comm., *Salisbury MSS.*, vii, p. 185.

57 The nominations are given in P.R.O. C 66/1496.

58 *Cal. Salus. Corres.*, no. 52. Another example of the association between the Myddeltons and the anti-Salusbury faction in the borough is the list of murders committed or abetted by John Salusbury, compiled in 1599. It was printed by W. J. Smith in 'The Salusburies as maintainers of murderers. A Chirk Castle view, 1599', N.L.W. *Journal* vii (1951–52), pp. 235–8. Smith assumed that it originated with Sir Thomas Myddelton, but it is endorsed 'Thomas Lloyd's note'; Lloyd was the complainant in the Star Chamber case of 1594. Lloyd's legal costs may have been subsidised by Myddelton, *vide* Dodd, 'Mr. Myddelton', p. 275.

59 *Acts of the Privy Council, 1599–1600*, p. 216. P.R.O. STAC 5/L 38/22, L 19/4.

60 P.R.O. STAC 5/L 38/22.

Chapter 15

'Because I am of that countrye & mynde to plant myself there': Robert Dudley, Earl of Leicester, and the West Midlands^a

In September 1571 Robert Dudley, Earl of Leicester, paid his second recorded visit to the borough of Warwick. The visit culminated in the flamboyant celebration at St Mary's Church on Michaelmas Day of the feast of St Michael the Archangel, the patron saint of the French order of chivalry to which he had been elected six years previously. Thanks to the detailed narrative that John Fisher, the town clerk of Warwick, entered in the 'Black Book', his precedents book and journal, we possess a unique account of the visit and its consequences. Of the latter the best-known was the suggestion that Leicester use the borough's guild hall for his proposed hospital. Two months later Fisher went to court to deliver to Leicester the corporation's agreement to the conveyance of the guild hall. On 27 November he had an interview at Greenwich, in the course of which the two men discussed the town's economy at some length and Leicester offered his assistance in stimulating local industry:

> And therefore many such poore as I perceive you have, I woold to God you woold some wayes devise that they may in sort be relieved and yor comonwealth proffited. And because I am of that countrye & mynde to plant myself there I woold be glad to further any good device with all my hart.[1]

This episode reveals much about the complexities of the relationship between Leicester and the West Midlands, a subject that has not, to date, received the attention it deserves. Throughout the greater part of the reign of Elizabeth I, Leicester and his brother Ambrose, Earl of Warwick, presided over the largest aristocratic interest in the region, an interest that was in turn the successor to the one that their father, the Duke of Northumberland, had created. Thanks to the Dudley family's unique position in Tudor politics and society, this was no typical noble interest; it was not a regional powerbase, but only one of a range of concerns. From this perspective, it can only be studied adequately as part of a fuller biography. On the other hand, the extensive nature of the Dudley impact on the region demands a work of local history on the scale of the studies of fifteenth- and seventeenth-century War-wickshire that Christine Carpenter and Ann Hughes have undertaken.[2] All that can be attempted within the scope of even a largish article is basically an exploration of the main outlines. However, in his remarks to Fisher about being of the country and minding to plant himself Leicester did, to some extent, reveal his hand, and they thus provide a useful starting place. The significance of the former and the manner in which he went about the latter therefore form the first two sections of this article. They will be followed by a survey of the composition of his local clientele, the impact of his patronage on local institutions, both civil and ecclesiastical, and brief accounts of the more controversial episodes of his planting. The fate of the Dudley interest and its wider significance will form the conclusion.

The range of issues necessitates the tight drawing of the parameters. Northumberland and Warwick are not the subjects of this article, yet Leices-ter's influence cannot meaningfully be discussed without some reference to theirs, however cursory. Leicester's territorial interest in the West Midlands was only a part – if a major one – of a web of lands and offices that extended into practically every county in England and much of Wales. Although the full network does not break down naturally into self-contained sections, we will be concerned here primarily with four concentrations of estates. The main one was centred on Kenilworth Castle in north-central Warwickshire; next in importance was Cleobury Mortimer and its associated lands on the Worcestershire–Shropshire border; the third was the Drayton Bassett estate on the Warwickshire–Staffordshire border; and the last a looser group of manors roughly focused on the vale of Evesham, in southern Worcester-shire, northern Gloucestershire and southern Warwickshire.[3] Leicester's interests in the immediately surrounding counties will receive only passing reference.[4] In the absence of detailed local studies for the reign of Elizabeth, let alone works on the scale of Hughes or Carpenter, the present discussion of local politics must be considered both summary and speculative. The more complex episodes – such as the 'Great Berkeley Law-Suit' or the Drayton Bassett riots – can only be introduced.

The available sources also define the parameters of what is possible. Leices-ter's own papers have been discussed in detail elsewhere; those of most immediate relevance to this essay are found in the remains of his central archive now in the collections at Longleat House and Penshurst Place.[5] There was also an 'evidence house' at Kenilworth Castle, which may have served as a repository for the records of his other manors in the region. In 1590 Leicester's widow was accused by his illegitimate son, Sir Robert Dudley, of removing documents from it.[6] This incident may account for those Kenilworth muniments now among the central collection.[7] A considerable body of Drayton Bassett records also survive at Longleat, owing to the countess of Leicester's residence there after 1594–95, but many of the other estate papers were dispersed when the manors themselves were sold off. Some court rolls for three of his Warwickshire manors, Knowle, Balsall and Honiley, together with legal papers relating to Long Itchington, are now to be found in Warwickshire family collections.[8] The greater part of the Kenilworth muniments have disappeared, however; they were probably lost after Sir Robert Dudley sold the castle to Henry, Prince of Wales, in 1612.[9]

Greater difficulties are presented by Warwick and Northumberland. The present Warwick Castle collection is almost entirely Greville in origin, and there is evidence that on Warwick's death in 1590 the castle muniments were then transported to London and later dispersed and destroyed together with his other papers after the death of the countess of Warwick in 1604.[10] Northumberland's papers were confiscated by the crown after his attainder in 1553; whether they were then lost or whether they were later returned to his sons and ultimately destroyed with Warwick's own papers is unclear.[11] Nor are collections of relevant local correspondence plentiful. The fullest are the Bagot of Blithfield and Paget collections, followed by the scattered fragments of the Ferrers of Tamworth correspondence and the remains of the Devereux archive at Longleat.[12] This imbalance in favour of Staffordshire is in part to be explained by the destruction of the Staunton of Longbridge Collection in 1879, which included a number of Warwickshire family collections, among them the Digby of Colshill correspondence.[13]

I

Leicester's claim to be 'of that countrye' cannot be taken literally. Precisely where he was born is unknown, but it was probably in London or the Home Counties.[14] His claim does, however, reflect a central ambition of the Tudor house of Dudley, the recognition of their descent from the Beauchamp Earls of Warwick and thus their ranking among the ancient nobility, an ambition that was not undisputed. At the expense of an heraldic excursus, the Dudley descent and the controversies surrounding it deserve some comment, for the family obsession with its genealogy had a major influence on the process of planting. Robert Dudley's claim to noble blood was essentially the same as his father's, for his mother's relations were gentle-born, with the exception of her own mother's family, the Wests, lords de La Warre.[15] Northumberland's claims to nobility of blood came through both his parents. His paternal grandfather, John Dudley (d. 1500) of Atherington, Sussex, was the second son of John Sutton (1400–87), 1st Lord Dudley of Dudley Castle; his mother, Elizabeth (d. c. 1530), was the daughter of Edward Grey, Viscount Lisle

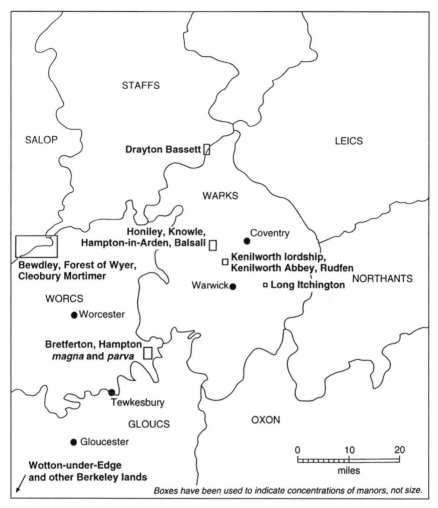

FIGURE 15.1   The Earl of Leicester's permanent estate

(1435–92), and descendant through the female line of Richard Beauchamp, Earl of Warwick.

The best introduction to the controversies surrounding the Dudley pedigree is the often-quoted passage in Sir William Dugdale's history of the barony of Sutton de Dudley in *The Baronage of England*.

In the time of Q. Elizabeth when the Earls of Warwick and Leicester powerful men in their day did flourish most learned and expert genealogists of that age spared not their endeavours to magnifie the family whence these great men did by a younger son derive their descent. Some [*marginal note:* William Harvey and Robert

Cooke, Clarencieux] deducing it from Sutton of Sutton in Holdernesse, Some [Sampson Erdeswick] from the Suttons of Sutton Madoc in Shropshire; but others from Sutton of Sutton on Trent near Newark in Com. Nott. . . . of which opinion was the right learned and judicious Robert Glover then Somerset Herald and Henry Ferrers of Badley-Clinton in Com. Warr. Esq. . . .[16]

Given that the Elizabethans in general were supposedly engaged in the extensive manufacturing of fictitious genealogies, this passage has been the basis for the assumption that a number of bogus pedigrees were created for Leicester.[17] But it deserves closer attention, for it is derived almost entirely from Sampson Erdeswick's *Survey of Staffordshire*. In his description of Dudley Castle, Erdeswick discourses at some length on the disputed origins of Hugh de Sutton, the father of Sir Richard Sutton, who married the heiress of the lordship of Malpas in the reign of Edward I, and whose son Sir John married the heiress of John de Somery, lord of Dudley in that of Edward II. Erdeswick notes that Harvey and Cooke, whom he identifies as clients of Northumberland and Leicester, had advanced the Sutton in Holderness descent; that Glover had traced the Suttons to Worksop; Henry Ferrers to Sutton on Trent; while he himself believed them to be of Shropshire origin. He goes on to claim that Northumberland had created the descent of John Dudley of Atherington from John, Lord Dudley; that Glover had told him 'he saw a descent wherein the duke with his own hand had put it down'; and that he himself had heard locally from one 'of good credit' that John Dudley of Atherington was in fact only the son of a carpenter from the town of Dudley.[18]

The Survey of Staffordshire was compiled in the 1590s, but Erdeswick's comments undoubtedly reflect an earlier dispute over Leicester's origins. It is possible to establish a rough date for his discussions with Glover. Glover conducted the heraldic visitations of Cheshire in 1580 and Staffordshire in 1583, and Erdeswick was among the gentlemen who appeared before him at Stafford in the summer of 1583. Although the visitations were not concerned with the descendants of noble houses, Glover had undertaken some research into the Suttons of Malpas in the Cheshire visitation.[19] The obvious place to look for a disparagement of Leicester's descent is *Leicester's Commonwealth*, which was published in 1584, but in fact it makes only two passing references to it. The first is that he was 'noble only in two descents and both of them stained with the block', and the second: 'He hath not anything of his own, either from his ancestors or of himself, to stay upon in men's conceits; he hath not ancient nobility, whereby men's affections are greatly moved. His father John Dudley was the first noble of his line'.[20]

These comments were enough, however, to spark a near-hysterical reaction from Sir Philip Sidney, who in his 'Defence' of Leicester reveals, despite some errors of fact, a considerable knowledge of, and sensitivity to, the issue. Having conceded that the Dudley claim to nobility of blood came through

Elizabeth Grey, Sidney advances a general defence that 'the mother being an heir hath been in all ages and countries sufficient to nobilitate'. But he then goes on, 'Let the singular nobility of his mother nothing avail him, if his father's blood were not in all respects worthy to match with her', which leads him to claim that the lords of Dudley Castle were of great antiquity. He traces the Suttons back to a Sir Richard Sutton who married the heiress of Dudley Castle in the reign of Richard I: 'And that Sutton was a man of great honour and estimation, as that very match witnesseth sufficiently, it being a dainty thing in that time that one of Saxon blood, as Sutton's name testified he was, should match with such an inheritrix as Dudley was . . .'. He concludes by defending the descent of Edmund Dudley's father (whom he calls Piers Dudley) from Lord Dudley.[21] Echoes of the dispute can also be found in seventeenth-century works, though their conclusions were by no means uniform. William Camden, who employed *Leicester's Commonwealth* selectively and who knew Erdeswick well, placed the disparagement of Leicester in the mouth of the Earl of Sussex, who 'to detract him would say that he could cite only two of his pedigree, that is to wit his father and his grandfather'.[22] On the other hand, Sir Robert Naunton, usually so reliant on Camden, allowed Edmund Dudley to be 'of a noble extract', as did Thomas Fuller, though oddly enough on the authority of Erdeswick.[23] Dugdale quoted Erdeswick at length in the *Antiquities of Warwickshire*, but while he too had doubts about Edmund Dudley's noble origins, he also queried the 'John Dudley the carpenter' story. In the later *Baronage*, however, he accepted Edmund Dudley's descent from Lord Dudley.[24]

The parentage of John Dudley of Atherington is no longer in dispute, for references to his brothers in his will have established that he was indeed a younger son of the 1st Baron Dudley.[25] Similarly, that the Suttons had inherited the lordship of Dudley Castle from the marriage between Sir John Sutton and Margaret the sister and heiress of John de Somery, lord of Dudley in 1322 was never in question.[26] More controversial was the claim to the earldom of Warwick, which in turn followed the descent of the barony of Lisle, one of the most complex in the history of the peerage, yet one central to the Dudley ambitions.[27] The barony was originally the lordship of the Isle of Wight, but by the fourteenth century it had become linked to the barony of Teyes or Tyas. On the death of the last Warenne Lord de Lisle and Teyes in 1391 the baronies descended to his daughter and her husband Thomas, 4th Lord Berkeley of Berkeley Castle. Following Berkeley's death in 1417 the Lisle barony was inherited by his only daughter, the first wife of Richard Beauchamp, Earl of Warwick. However, Berkeley also claimed that his other estates were part of the lordship of Berkeley Castle and devised them on his nephew and heir male, the 5th Lord Berkeley. The refusal of Warwick and his wife to accept this division of the Berkeley lands initiated the 'Great

Berkeley Law-Suit'.[28] Following his wife's death (1422) Warwick continued to hold the Lisle estate for life, and, thanks to a settlement with Lord Berkeley in 1426, certain of the Berkeley lands as well.[29]

On Warwick's death in 1439 the Lisle barony descended to the elder of his three daughters from this marriage, Margaret, the second wife of John Talbot, Earl of Shrewsbury; it was not, therefore, involved in the complex settlement of the Beauchamp estate that followed the death in 1446 of Warwick's son by his second marriage, Henry, Duke of Warwick. On the other hand, the countess of Shrewsbury also retained the Berkeley lands held by her father and later seized the lordship of Drayton Bassett from the main Beauchamp estate.[30] Her son by Shrewsbury, John Talbot (d. 1453), was created Baron Lisle in 1444 and the 1st Viscount in 1452. The viscountcy was inherited by his son Thomas but extinguished following Thomas's death in 1469. The barony then descended to his sister Elizabeth (d. 1487), the wife of Sir Edward Grey, who in turn was created Viscount Lisle in 1483. The Greys had four surviving children: a son, John Grey, Viscount Lisle (1480–1504), and three daughters, Margaret, Anne and Elizabeth, of whom Elizabeth (Edmund Dudley's wife) appears to have been the youngest. On Lisle's death the barony was inherited first by his posthumous daughter Elizabeth (1505–19), who shortly afterwards became the ward of Charles Brandon. Brandon was created Viscount Lisle in 1513 in the right of his wife, having contracted to marry his ward, but then retained the title despite breaking the contract.[31] Elizabeth Dudley married her second husband Arthur Plantagenet in 1515, and in March 1523 (presumably because her elder sisters had both died by then) Henry VIII persuaded Brandon to resign the viscountcy, which he then granted to Plantagenet and his heirs male in the right of his wife. Only three daughters survived from this marriage and the viscountcy was extinguished on Plantagenet's death in March 1542. It was at this point that Henry created John Dudley, Viscount Lisle, Baron of Malpas and Lord Bassett of Drayton and Tiasse in the right of his mother.[32]

It was as the descendants of Margaret, countess of Shrewsbury, that the Dudleys also claimed the inheritance of the Beauchamp earldom of Warwick. The issues at stake become clearer when contemporary heraldic opinion is surveyed. Four pedigrees that belonged to the Dudleys can presently be traced. The earliest, and the only one known to have been drawn up for the Duke of Northumberland, was compiled by William Harvey, Norroy King at Arms, and is dated 15 April 1553.[33] The remaining three were all prepared for Leicester. The second was drawn up by William Bowyer, keeper of the Tower records, in November 1567. It is not, strictly speaking, a pedigree, but rather a collection of historical records of Leicester's titles and estates.[34] The third pedigree can be dated from internal evidence to 1573–76, and from its style was probably by Robert Cooke.[35] The fourth was drawn up by Cooke in

1581.[36] Both the Cooke pedigrees thank Leicester for the loan of other pedigrees and documents, and therefore some degree of involvement can be assumed.[37] Three further pedigrees by Cooke can also be found among heraldic miscellanies.[38] Robert Glover's views can be discovered in a Dudley descent dated 1581 and the relevant sections of several other volumes of heraldic notes.[39]

Before proceeding further a comment on the heralds should be made. Both Erdeswick and Dugdale emphasise the dependency of Harvey and Cooke on the Dudleys and imply that their pedigrees were drawn up to gratify their patrons. Glover, who was generally more respected as a herald, is portrayed as an independent, and therefore more sceptical, expert. However, before being tempted by a factional explanation, it should be noted that Glover as well as Cooke received Leicester's patronage.[40] The 1553 pedigree has been heavily damaged by damp, and the section on the Lords Dudley has been obscured. Its emphasis, however, is on the recent Beauchamp descent. It also contains notes on Northumberland's children added after 1557, in a hand that may be Leicester's.[41] The Bowyer *Eulogia* does not address the issues of descents, but rehearses the history of the earldom of Leicester, in which it emphasises its historic association with the lord stewardship.[42] The earlier Cooke pedigree is concerned with the relationship between Leicester and a number of other Elizabethan peers, which it takes back to Earls created at the Conquest. The 1581 pedigree concentrates on the descent of the earldom of Warwick from the Saxon Earl Guy. Both the Cooke pedigrees trace the Suttons back to a Seyre or Sayer, Lord Sutton of Holderness at the time of the Conquest, although his notes are more cautious.[43] In his Dudley descent Glover observes that nothing specific can be advanced prior to Hugh de Sutton, and simply records the Sutton in Holderness and Worksop theories.[44] However, in a collection of pedigrees of Earls he credits Leicester with a descent from a Serus created Lord Sutton of Holderness by William Rufus.[45]

The main issues in the controversy can be reduced essentially to two. The first is the descent of the Suttons from the lords of Sutton in Holderness, the significance of which is clearly the putative Saxon ancestor Sayerus, Lord Sutton. He is in fact one of three Saxons who appear in these heraldic commentaries, the other two being Earl Guy of Warwick and Dudd or Athelstan Dodo, the builder of Dudley Castle.[46] If obviously mythological, these shadowy ancestors were still legitimate subjects of contemporary historical debate, and if there is a distinction between Cooke and Glover on the issue it is that Cooke appears to have been more willing to accept them than Glover.[47] However, the more interesting question, which unfortunately cannot be addressed here, is why Leicester and Sidney were so concerned to emphasise their Saxon ancestry, for the Saxon theme is also found in the Kenilworth festivities of 1575, which introduces a fourth mythological figure, Kenulph, king of Mercia, the putative builder of Kenilworth Castle.[48]

The second issue is that of female descents, for it was through the female line that the Dudleys claimed both the Lisle barony and the earldom of Warwick.[49] This was also an issue of particular interest to the Sidney brothers, for their own claim to any Dudley inheritance came through their mother.[50] What complicated the descent of the Lisle barony was the distinction between the barony and the viscountcy, for the viscountcy was granted in tail male and was thus extinguished on the failure of each of the male lines. The barony could descend through the female line, although it was also argued that the original barony had reverted to the crown on the death of Richard Beauchamp because it could not be divided among his three co-heiresses. The later grants to Talbot, Grey, Plantagenet and then Dudley had recognised the rights of wives or daughters, but ultimately they rested on 'princely pleasure'.[51] John Dudley's creation as Viscount Lisle was therefore no less legitimate than the earlier ones. More tenuous was the claim to the earldom of Warwick, for earldoms descended only in tail male, though there was a general acceptance that claims through the female line carried some moral weight. In this respect the Dudley claim was no different to those made by other members of the Tudor 'new nobility', for example Sir Anthony Browne's to the Neville viscountcy of Montague or the Devereux to the Bourchier earldom of Essex.[52]

The influence of the Dudley descent on their ambitions and actions cannot be over-emphasised. The 1553 pedigree provides the only direct evidence for Northumberland's own claims, but we can see an awareness of his descent at work at least two decades earlier, although the process can only be sketched here. He received his rights to his father's estates when he was restored in blood in 1512 (3 Henry VIII, *c.* 15) and to his mother's when she died in 1530.[53] Although most of these lands were in Surrey and Sussex, by 1532 he held the lordship of Drayton Bassett and in that year was appointed constable of Warwick Castle jointly with Sir Francis Bryan.[54] By then he had also lent £6000 to John, 3rd Lord Dudley, on the security of Dudley Castle and his other lands and this mortgage was foreclosed in 1537. In the following year financial pressure forced him to sell Drayton Bassett to Sir Thomas Pope, but he seems to have regained it several years later, for it was included in his wife's jointure in 1546.[55] His West Midlands holdings were further expanded by the grants of the large ex-monastic estates of Hales Owen in 1538 and Dudley Priory in 1541. The style he adopted at his creation in March 1542 was a curious mixture of 'Beauchamp' (Lisle, Tyas and Bassett of Drayton) and 'Dudley' titles (Malpas); in the following year he assumed the further Dudley title of lord of Somery, and in 1547 that of lord of Dudley as well.[56]

It was on 16 February 1547, as part of the settlement of the 'unwritten will' of Henry VIII, that he was created Earl of Warwick – though, curiously enough, Henry's initial proposal appears to have been the earldom of Leicester.[57] Several weeks later, in requesting the grant of the lordship of Warwick, he specifically claimed a right to it by descent: 'And because of the name I am the more desirous to have the thing and also I come of one of the daughters and heirs of the right and not defiled line', a reference presumably to the Neville–Clarence line that descended from Anne, Richard Beauchamp's daughter by his second marriage.[58] When he finally received the lordship of Warwick in June 1547 he also obtained two other Warwickshire manors formerly attached to the earldom, Budbrooke and Haseley. In December he was granted Claverdon and the former Beauchamp manor of Henley in Arden.[59] By 1549, if not earlier, he had adopted the old Beauchamp device of the bear and ragged staff.[60] Even his later promotion to the dukedom of Northumberland in 1551 was justified in part by the Beauchamp descent.[61] The series of grants and exchanges that he undertook during the early 1550s is too complex to be discussed here, but it is worth noting that Kenilworth Castle was among them. He finally obtained the castle in 1553, and appears to have begun work on the gatehouse and the stables, buildings which were later attributed to (and probably completed by) his son.[62]

As Northumberland rose through the peerage his cadet titles devolved on his eldest son, John, who married the Duke of Somerset's daughter Anne (d. 1588) in June 1550. The marriage settlement included several Warwickshire manors and it is possible that Northumberland was intending to 'plant' the Earl of Warwick (as he became in 1551) in the county.[63] However, whatever plans Northumberland may have had died with him and in 1553, with only two exceptions, the entire Dudley estate disappeared. One was the duchess's jointure lands and Hales Owen, in which she possessed an estate of inheritance.[64] The other was the jointure lands of the countess of Warwick, who was widowed in 1554.[65] The greater part of Northumberland's estate was retained by the crown, but the lordship of Dudley Castle was restored to Edward, 4th Baron Dudley (d. 1586), in November 1554 and accompanied by Dudley Priory and the manors of Balsall and Budbrooke.[66] Balsall had formerly belonged to the Knights of St John and had been part of the dower lands of Catherine Parr. It came temporarily into Northumberland's possession (the manorial court was held in his name in 1551), but then was granted to the Earl of Warwick in July 1553.[67] The reversion to the manor was later included in Mary's re-endowment of the Hospital of the Knights of St John in April 1558.[68]

In the act of parliament that repealed their attainders in 1558, Northumberland's surviving sons renounced any claim of right to their father's former lands and titles.[69] As a result their 'restoration' was by no means a straightforward process. Lord Robert retained the most direct interest in the West Midlands thanks to a family compact in the autumn of 1555, in which his

brothers gave him their interests in the Hales Owen estate, which had descended to them on the duchess's death at the beginning of the year. However, this he sold in 1558, probably to pay his debts, and retained only lands
with a rental of £25 in Oldbury and Langley as a jointure for his wife. In the
summer of 1558 he was contemplating settling in Norfolk on the Robsart
estate.[70] The accession of Elizabeth obviously transformed his position, but
this in turn raises the question why it took her until December 1561 to grant
Ambrose Dudley the earldom of Warwick and the barony of Lisle, and until
September 1564 to create Robert Dudley Earl of Leicester and Baron of Denbigh.[71] A nervousness about reviving the controversies surrounding Northumberland's fall is both detectable and understandable, yet Elizabeth signalled
her favour to the Dudley brothers publicly in the immediate appointment of
Robert as master of the horse and Ambrose as master of the ordnance, the
election of Robert as Knight of the Garter in the spring of 1559, and then his
appointment as lord-lieutenant of Worcestershire and joint lord-lieutenant of
Warwickshire (with Sir Ambrose Cave) in the summer.[72]

One consideration was undoubtedly the necessary landed endowment,
without which neither brother could support a major title of nobility. Ambrose
Dudley received the manor of Kibworth Beauchamp in 1559, one substantial
grant of Northumberland's lands in 1562 (including the lordship of Warwick,
Henley in Arden and Claverdon), and a second in 1564 (several of Northumberland's other manors and the lordship of Ruthin in Denbighshire).[73] These
formed the core of his estate. Lord Robert's position was more curious. Apart
from the gift of the house at Kew in December 1558 and then the customs
concessions that kept him financially afloat during the early 1560s (and which
were declared to be temporary measures pending the settlement of a landed
estate), initially all he received from Elizabeth were the site of the monastery
of Watton in the East Riding of Yorkshire (which had belonged to Northumberland) in January 1560, and then a number of Northumberland's outlying
properties on 1 March 1561. Two of these, the site of the monastery of Meaux
and the lordship and borough of Beverley, were also in the East Riding.[74] It is
tempting to see the Sutton in Holderness descent behind this interest in the
East Riding, possibly as a basis for a creation. Lord Robert divested himself
of most of these properties soon after becoming Earl of Leicester.[75]

At the same time, however, Lord Robert was actively engaged in re-
establishing the family interest in the West Midlands on his own account. By
the autumn of 1559 he was attempting to purchase Budbrooke from Lord
Dudley, who agreed to sell it if he could obtain the fee simple of Balsall,
presumably to reverse the entail. In November 1560 Lord Dudley reported
that one of Lord Robert's servants had proposed the exchange of Dudley
Castle for lands in fee simple elsewhere. He answered that he had rejected a
similar proposal the previous year because 'it is mine ancient inheritance',

and that he would agree only to the sale of Budbrooke.[76] In early 1560 Lord Robert also approached Sir Robert Throckmorton of Coughton to purchase the constableship of Warwick Castle and the stewardship of the lordship of Warwick that Mary had granted him after Northumberland's fall. Here he was more successful, and the sale was concluded on 26 February 1562.[77]

Of Lord Robert's personal fascination with the Beauchamp descent there is no shortage of evidence. He greeted his brother's creation as Earl of Warwick with the significant phrase, 'it hath pleased the queen's majesty . . . to restore our house to the name of Warwick'.[78] In the spring of 1562 both brothers re-adopted the bear and ragged staff device.[79] References to his Beauchamp descent appear regularly throughout his life, most explicitly in the instruction for his burial in his will of 30 January 1582: 'And for the place I doe not precysely accompt of albeyt in respect that manny of my ancystors doe remayn enterred within the paryshe Church of Warwyk towen, I doe rather wysh yt to be ther than ells where'. This instruction is repeated in his last (1587) will: 'I have always wished as my dear wife doth know, and some of my friends, that it might be at Warwick where sundry my ancestors doe lye'.[80] Yet another reference can be found in the deed of incorporation of his Hospital (21 November 1585), which recalls 'the good and charitable deedes and workes of Richard Beawchampe late earll of Warwick and other our ancestors beinge provyded and intended for the relief of the poore within the saide town of Warwick'.[81] As has already been noted, he possessed a number of relevant pedigrees and when he revived the Berkeley law-suit in 1572 he displayed a detailed knowledge of the Lisle descent.[82]

On 9 June 1563 Lord Robert received *inter alia* what would become the core of his own estate: the lordships of Kenilworth, Denbigh and Chirk, and the manor of Cleobury Mortimer.[83] The most curious aspect of this grant is the fact that it was a year later, 28 and 29 September 1564, that he was created Baron of Denbigh and Earl of Leicester. To his creation only the manor of Kenilworth (formerly of Kenilworth Abbey) was attached, to provide the traditional £20 of land granted with earldoms. Whatever the immediate connection between his creation and Elizabeth's proposals for a marriage with Mary, Queen of Scots, in the autumn of 1564, there can be little doubt that, given the historic association between Kenilworth and the earldom of Leicester and the obvious connection between the lordship of Denbigh and the barony, the creation and the grant of 1563 were closely related.[84] No less curious is why the earldom of Leicester was chosen.[85] The letters patent of the creations do not reveal much, for that for the barony simply mentions Dudley's stature and a general need for noble councillors, and that for the earldom solely his descent from the Earls of Warwick.[86] There was an ancient association between Leicestershire and Warwickshire initiated by the first post-Conquest Earls (Henry de Beaumont, 1st Earl of Warwick

(1048–1119) was the brother of Robert de Beaumont, 1st Earl of Leicester (1046–1118)) and this was reflected in the common sheriffwick the counties shared until 1567.[87] The Sutton–Somery descent created a distant connection with the Beaumonts, as a result of which Dudley bore the blue cinquefoil of Leicester on his armorial, but the association between the earldom of Leicester and Kenilworth had been forged by the Montford Earls and maintained by the duchy of Lancaster, and no claims to either feature in any of the Dudley pedigrees.[88]

In some senses the negative case is more revealing. Assuming Dudley was to be raised to comital rank, what were the alternatives? Although there were a number of other historic peerages vacant, there were existing claimants to most of them and four (the earldoms of Kent, Nottingham, Essex and Lincoln) were to be granted during the course of the reign. There is considerable evidence that Elizabeth vacillated over Dudley's creation for several years, and it must be assumed that the various alternatives were weighed. A dukedom appears to have been discussed, and at least one other earldom, that of March.[89] What makes this alternative significant is the fact that three of the estates in the 1563 grant, Denbigh, Cleobury Mortimer and Clifford (Herefs.), had been part of the earldom of March and Kenilworth alone part of Leicester. It is possible that an initial preference for March may have been reconsidered in the light of possible malicious references to the new Mortimer.[90]

The possible reasons for Elizabeth's vacillations over Dudley's creation lie outside the scope of this essay, but one is relevant. With the exception of the similar 'restoration' of Edward Seymour to his father's earldom of Hertford in 1559, Leicester and Warwick were the only men she raised directly to earldoms; indeed throughout the sixteenth century it was extremely rare for men who were not already barons to be promoted into the higher peerage. If one brother could be granted the core of Northumberland's former lands, the other would require a further endowment from the already stretched royal estate. Ambrose Dudley's seniority made it virtually impossible to grant Northumberland's titles to Lord Robert and, given the very real affection between the two brothers, it is doubtful whether Lord Robert would have desired Elizabeth to do so. But there might also have been an expectation that he would succeed his brother as Earl of Warwick. The significance of this will emerge in the following section.

II

The expansion of Leicester's West Midlands estate after 1563 falls into three quite distinct phases: the first from 1563 to the end of 1569, the second from the beginning of 1570 to 1578, and the last from 1578 to his death, though to all practical purposes until his departure for the Netherlands in 1585. The process was a complex one, which involved both extensive grants from the crown and private purchases. Many of the lands granted to him were sold off fairly rapidly, but a core, those discussed here, were retained on a permanent basis. After 1563 the major grants were technically exchanges, but this was by no means a straightforward exercise for a number of the estates that he returned to the crown were then leased back to him.

The 1563 grant was soon followed by further negotiations with the crown. In the autumn of 1564 he offered to exchange Knole (Kent) for the manor of Rudfen (now Redfern), which had formerly belonged to Kenilworth Abbey, and a share of the manors of Balsall and Budbrooke. Rudfen was granted to him in September 1565.[91] In June 1566 he obtained in his first large exchange with the crown the reversions of Budbrooke and Balsall and, *inter alia*, three manors near Evesham: Bretferton (now Bretforton), Great and Little Hampton, and Dry Marston (Glos., now Long Marston, Warks.).[92] The grant of the reversions of Budbrooke and Balsall was clearly related to his earlier attempts to buy out Lord Dudley, yet, given that Dudley held them in tail male, the reason why Leicester requested a share in 1564 is unclear unless there was some prior agreement with Dudley. As it turned out, Lord Dudley retained possession of Budbrooke until he sold the manor in 1589, and Leicester may have sold the reversion in 1581.[93] Leicester did finally purchase Balsall from Lord Dudley in 1572, but the situation there was more complex. The reversion that Mary had granted to the Knights of St John had been regained by the crown in 1559; this, presumably, was what was granted to Leicester in 1566. However, in his proposal of 1564 he stated that the countess of Warwick held the manor for life with the reversion to Lord Dudley.[94] It is possible that it was part of her jointure, but the Marian grants to Lord Dudley make no reference to her jointure rights.[95]

For all this interest in his country, Leicester remained a distant figure until the end of the 1560s. It is not known whether he had visited the region previously. He may have accompanied Northumberland when he passed through Warwick on his northern tour in 1552, and his coat and conduct money for the St Quentin campaign in 1557 was paid to and from Hales Owen, though what that signifies is unclear.[96] He attempted to visit in the spring of 1566, but he was diverted by the illness or possible miscarriage of his sister, the countess of Huntingdon, and then recalled to Court by Elizabeth.[97] His first known visit was therefore in the royal progress of 1566.[98] The progress of 1568, when he and Elizabeth appear to have spent several days at Kenilworth, provided the next occasion, though it is possible that he was there in the spring as well.[99]

The 1570s saw a dramatic change. In January 1570 he and his sisters went to meet Warwick at Kenilworth on the latter's return from the North and he thereafter visited on a regular basis. The September 1571 visit to Warwick has already been mentioned; the royal progress of 1572 included both Kenilworth and Warwick; he was there on his own in the autumn of 1573, and possibly in the autumn of 1574 as well.[100] 1575 saw the famous entertainment at Kenilworth, and he was there again in April 1576 and then in June and July 1577 en route to the baths at Buxton.[101] The single most important change to the estate in this period was the famous rebuilding of Kenilworth. Some work had already been undertaken by the summer of 1568, but 'Leicester's Buildings' appear to have been initiated during his visit in January 1570 and to have been completed by 1575.[102] The estate itself also underwent a considerable expansion in the early 1570s. In May 1571 he obtained the lease of Bewdley (Worcs.) from the crown. In 1572 he was granted the rectory of Kenilworth and the reversion of Honiley, and purchased Long Itchington from Sir John Throckmorton and Balsall from Lord Dudley.[103] In July 1573 he was granted the manors of Hampton in Arden and Knowle, and then his share of the two Gloucestershire manors that Lord Berkeley lost in the revival of the Berkeley law-suit, which Leicester had initiated during the previous winter.[104] Most of these lands appear to have been deliberately chosen to round out the estate, for Long Itchington was intended to supply Kenilworth; Balsall, Hampton in Arden and Knowle were contiguous; and Bewdley was adjacent to Cleobury Mortimer.[105]

The final phase was also characterised by annual visits, though now they were frequently part of longer journeys of his own. He appears to have stopped briefly at Kenilworth in May or July 1578 during a second visit to Buxton. He was there again in October 1579, July 1580, September 1581 (the occasion of a major banquet at Coventry on 1 October), and September 1582.[106] Although there is no evidence for 1583, he began his longest journey at Kenilworth in May 1584. This took him to Denbighshire and Chester (the only occasion he ever went there) and then on to Buxton. He was at Kenilworth again in August 1585, when he was summoned to take command of the Netherlands expedition.[107] It is not clear whether he stopped at Kenilworth on his journey to Bath and Bristol in April 1587, but he was *en route* when he died at Cornbury House in September 1588.[108] The estate continued to expand. His major purchase was the lease of Drayton Bassett in 1579, but in 1581 he also bought Honiley from Francis Throckmorton and then the site of Kenilworth Abbey from John Colbourne, with the intention of making both permanent additions to the lordship of Kenilworth.[109] In 1582 he obtained the manor of Ernewood (Salop. and Worcs.), and the following year he leased the manor of Langley (Oxon.) from the jointure lands of the countess of Warwick after she was declared a lunatic.[110] In 1584 he leased the forest of Wyer from the crown and then made some further purchases in Worcestershire (Abberley and Alton Woods) in 1588, which were not completed before his death.[111] The 'Berkeley law-suit' was revived again and he and Warwick obtained a second tranche of Berkeley lands in 1585; in 1588 he was preparing a third round of litigation.[112]

The Midlands estates were not, of course, Leicester's only significant territorial interest. The 1570s saw both a major expansion and an internal reformation of his Welsh lordships.[113] Following his purchase of Wanstead House in Essex in early 1578 he spent a considerable sum to create an estate around it. Nevertheless the central role of the West Midlands lands emerges when the value of his overall estate is considered. On the basis of assessments made during the settlement of his will, Lawrence Stone has estimated his annual landed income to have been £2544, a figure which accords with a further posthumous valuation of £2600 18s.[114] It is clear, though, that this is an underestimate, partly because various individual manors may have been undervalued, but more importantly because the leasehold lands were not included.[115] A more accurate valuation is not easy, however, for the sources are erratic.[116] On the basis of the *Brevis Abstract*, the most extensive of the valuations and one roughly contemporary with his death, it would appear that the West Midlands revenue alone was in the region of £2000.[117] The Worcestershire-Shropshire lands produced at least £500, his share of the Berkeley lands £83, the Drayton Bassett estate upwards of £400, the central Warwickshire estates nearly £1000, and the vale of Evesham lands about £50.[118] To put these revenues in perspective, his largest single estate was the lordship of Denbigh, which was worth slightly over £900 p.a.; the total value of his Welsh lands (including Denbigh) was in the region of £1500; and a rough estimate of the income from his lands elsewhere would be in the region of £1000. His total landed income in 1587–88 was thus somewhere around £4500.

Of the various Midlands concentrations, the vale of Evesham manors were the least important. The report his surveyors made on the manor of Bretferton in 1566 makes interesting reading. This was noted as 'very good & profitable land for tillage ground', but not of great profit to the lord: 'The tenants belonging to this manor are not above xxtie in all, fewe of them personable men, but verie mean for the most part and overcome with contynewall drudgery and labour'. The surveyors advised selling the manor to the tenants, but they were 'so glad that they are your lordship's tenants and so loath that your honour should depart with them that they offer to give your lordship anything they have not to depart with them . . .' In the later rentals Bretferton was valued at £4 a year, although Ralph Sheldon sold it for £220 in 1595.[119]

The Worcester-Shropshire lands around Cleobury Mortimer were, by contrast, the most exploited. In 1563 his surveyors drew attention to the potential profits of the woodlands, and recommended that the timber be exported as barrel staves through Bristol, which they estimated would bring in £400 a year.[120] In November 1565 he obtained a licence to export barrel staves, and the accounts of his factor in Spain in 1576–79 reveal a lucrative trade between Bristol and Sanlúcar de Barrameda, in which Leicester employed two ships of his own, the *White Bear* and a flyboat named the *White Lion*.[121] During the 1570s the timber was also used to fuel iron works at Cleobury which in 1588 were leased at £400 p.a.[122] By then there were claims that the woods had been exhausted, and the need to find fresh supplies of timber probably accounts for his expansion in the immediate environs.[123]

The central Warwickshire lands were treated quite differently. At their greatest extent they formed a compact estate around Kenilworth Castle, which combined with Warwick's lands to the south gave the brothers an uncontested pre-eminence in the county. Yet they were not as economically exploited as the others; if anything the reverse was true. Many of the demesnes were leased on favourable terms to his household officers as rewards.[124] The fluctuating series of leases and rent charges partly explains why in 1578 Henry Besbeeche reported that although Leicester estimated his lands in Warwickshire to be worth £700 p.a., they were in fact worth only about £500 clear.[125] Nor was much improvement undertaken, in marked contrast to his Welsh lordships. The lordship of Kenilworth itself, which had a large number of freeholders and few customary tenants, had been valued at £29 a year by the crown in 1563, and was worth only £52 in 1588.[126] The major improvement was the composition he made with the tenants, later held to be to his loss, to expand the deer park.[127] He also obtained a licence to hold a market for the town of Kenilworth.[128]

The attraction of the Berkeley manors and the lease of Drayton Bassett clearly arose from the Beauchamp inheritance, and led to two of the more controversial episodes of his planting. In the case of the Berkeley manors, which he shared with his brother, the financial benefit was a minimal return for the effort he made to obtain them. Similarly, the Drayton Bassett lease, substantial as the income was, may not have compensated for his outlay. He was said to have spent £6000 in purchasing the lease and the fee simple lands from Richard Paramour, 1000 marks to buy out the other interests, and a further 1000 marks in the expenses of ejecting the rioters. It is revealing that £4778 of the £6000 paid to Paramour came from the receipts of his farm of the customs on sweet wines.[129]

A meaningful assessment of the ultimate value of the West Midlands estates can only be made in the context of Leicester's overall finances, a subject which can only be alluded to here. Of most immediate relevance is the cost of the rebuilding of Kenilworth Castle and the expenditure on the entertainments there in 1566, 1572 and 1575. For these expenses no accurate figures survive.[130] Dugdale's claim of £60,000 for the rebuilding of the castle was based on hearsay – 'I have heard some who were his servants say' – and was doubtless an exaggeration, but the capital value of the castle and the lordship combined was assessed by Jacobean surveyors at about £40,000.[131]

It is difficult not to suspect that the two large grants of miscellaneous lands in 1574, intended for immediate resale to raise capital, and the loan of £15,000 from the crown for which Denbigh was mortgaged in 1576 were associated with the completion of the rebuilding.[132] This level of expenditure is of a piece with the general extravagance of his enthusiasm for his country in the early 1570s. The decision to found a hospital in either Kenilworth or Warwick early in 1571 and then the celebration of the St Michael at Warwick (the only occasion he is known to have done so after 1566) certainly announced his planting in dramatic form.[133] According to John Fisher, Leicester's purpose in visiting Warwick was simply to stay with Thomas Fisher at The Priory, but, if the scale of the St Michael celebration was anywhere as lavish as Fisher describes, it could not have been a spur of the moment decision and his officers at Kenilworth were preparing for his arrival as early as June.[134] The symbolism of celebrating a French order of chivalry with a protestant service amid the memorials to the Hundred Years War embodied in the various Beauchamp tombs in St Mary's could not have been lost on at least some of those present. The founding of his hospital was also clearly on Leicester's mind when he arrived and before the guild hall was proposed he was looking at a site adjacent to St Mary's churchyard.[135] It is difficult not to see the whole exercise as a deliberate attempt to celebrate himself publicly as the heir of the Beauchamps.

More enigmatic is the scale of the Kenilworth entertainment of 1575, given that Elizabeth had already visited in 1566, 1568 and 1572 and would never do so again. Without entering into the various literary controversies surrounding the accounts of the entertainment, one explanation might be that it was intended to celebrate the completion of the building works. However, the whole question of Kenilworth's role in the royal progresses raises a number of further issues. The 1575 progress, which lasted from May until October, was the longest of the reign – though this was due in large part to the queen's decision to spend almost all of September at Woodstock. It also marks the end of the series of major progresses that began with the first visit to Kenilworth in 1566. Outside this period (1566–75) only the East Anglian progresses of 1564 and 1578 and those of 1591–92 were of any scale; between 1579 and 1590 the progresses were reduced to a circuit round Windsor and Hampton Court. There is evidence that by 1575–76 the expense of the grander progresses was considered to have got out of hand. There were hostile comments on Leicester's extravagance at Kenilworth, and Elizabeth appears to have turned down a further invitation to visit in 1577.[136] Moreover, she had more convenient means for being entertained by him. She visited Leicester House in London (which he bought from Lord Paget in 1570) in 1573, 1576, 1577 (twice), 1578, 1579 and 1585, and Wanstead House in 1578 (twice), 1579 (on three occasions), 1581, 1582 and 1588. To the extent that Kenilworth was rebuilt to house the queen on progress, after 1575 that purpose had (ironically) become redundant.

This brings us to the further question of why Leicester decided to spend so much money and effort on his country after 1570. It may have been the consequence of a final appreciation that the possibility of being a royal consort was now over, or it may have been a response to the 1569 rebellion. The latter to some degree depends on the rumours that he was fortifying Kenilworth, which appear to have been inspired by the initiation of the building works in 1570. As completed, the rebuilding does not reveal a defensive purpose, though one may have been present in the original plans, which in turn may also have some connection to further contemporary rumours that Mary, Queen of Scots, was to be lodged there.[137] However, there is a further issue to be considered, and that is his relationship to his brother Warwick and the future of their combined estates. The major grants to Warwick in 1562 and 1564 were made in tail male with a remainder specifically to Leicester, while his estates (with the odd exceptions of Cleobury Mortimer, Great and Little Hampton, and Hampton in Arden) were all granted in fee simple or East Greenwich tenure. Warwick's first wife, Ann Whorewood, had died in childbirth in 1552 and his second, Elizabeth, Lady Tailboys, in 1563, also without issue. At the time of the June 1563 grant Warwick was commanding the garrison at Le Havre in the last stages of the siege. Had he too died then, Leicester would have been his heir, and the expectation that he would succeed his brother as Earl of Warwick might in turn have been a reason for the delay in granting him his own earldom.[138]

In 1565 Warwick married the young Anne Russell, and might reasonably have been expected to father an heir, but by 1570 it was clear that he would remain childless, and there is evidence of Leicester's growing concern that both would be heirless. The early 1570s saw his affair with Douglas Sheffield (who did bear him a son, the future Sir Robert Dudley, in 1574), and a legitimate heir was the avowed motive for his eventual marriage to the countess of Essex in 1578.[139] This hope was realised in the birth of the little lord of Denbigh on 6 June 1581, only to be quashed in 1584.[140] In the years prior to 1581 Philip Sidney seems to have been generally regarded as heir to both Leicester and Warwick; if his hopes were revived after 1584 his own death two years later ended them as well. Sidney's death coincided with Leicester's increased affection for his illegitimate son, to whom, although he could not create him full heir, he bequeathed Kenilworth and much of the West Midlands estate after the death of Warwick.[141]

Between 1570 and 1584, therefore, the creation of an estate of inheritance or at least the leaving of a permanent memorial in Warwickshire would appear to have been Leicester's primary ambition. This brings us back to the role of his own descent. The earldom of Leicester appears to have been of no great interest, but the Beauchamp inheritance mattered greatly. The Beauchamp descent inspired his revival of the Berkeley law-suit and (probably) the purchase of the lease of Drayton Bassett. The pursuit of this dynastic interest together with the circumstances of the purchase of Long Itchington, Honiley and Kenilworth Abbey lay behind the charges of sharp practice gleefully related by his enemies. The versions found in *Leicester's Commonwealth* and Dugdale are no doubt exaggerated, but they share the common theme of the pressuring of impoverished local families by a ruthless courtier. Both had a political motive for portraying Leicester in this light, but the energy with which he planted himself gave the accusations some substance.[142]

III

Before looking at Leicester's political impact the existing structure of power and then the influence of both Northumberland and Warwick need to be outlined. The destruction of the old earldom of Warwick and the fall of the Duke of Buckingham in 1521 left the West Midlands without a major resident peer during much of Henry VIII's reign. While a number of non-residents held estates there, in Staffordshire there were only two small Barons, Dudley and Ferrers of Chartley, and in Gloucestershire the weakened Lord Berkeley.[143] Warwickshire appears to have been a gentry republic dominated by the extensive Throckmorton clan.[144] The reign of Edward VI saw a number of creations and promotions in the local peerage, of which Northumberland was the most important. Not only did his rise cause the eclipse of the older Sutton line, but, apart from the ephemeral career of Thomas, Lord Seymour of Sudeley, and the partial restoration of the Staffords in the person of Henry the 11th Baron in 1547, the other two new peers, William, Lord Paget (initially at least), and Walter Devereux, Viscount Hereford, were allies of his. Nor did any of the later changes pose a challenge to the Dudleys. While Mary restored estates to Lord Dudley, Lord Berkeley and Lord Stafford, she created only one new peer, John Bridges, 1st Lord Chandos; Elizabeth limited herself to the promotion of the 2nd Viscount Hereford to the earldom of Essex and the creation of Sir Henry Compton as the 1st Baron (both in 1572). The absence of a major resident peer was of no small importance to the Dudley planting, for there was no established figure to provide a focus for resentment, and by providing an otherwise missing connection to the highest levels of the Court the Dudleys had positive attractions. Moreover, of the Elizabethan resident peers only the Devereux had protestant sympathies and none of the others were trusted with major office. Indeed, as Marian restorations, Dudley, Berkeley and Stafford had grounds for apprehension.

With Henry, the scholarly and Catholic 11th Lord Stafford (1501–63), Leicester appears to have been on quite friendly terms.[145] With his successors,

Henry the 12th Baron (d. 1566), and Edward the 13th (d. 1603), the relationship was more distant, though he held their proxies in the parliaments of 1566 and 1584.[146] The 4th Lord Dudley may have resisted the attempts to buy him out, but otherwise he was content to exploit the family connection to advantage, and he gave Leicester his proxy in the parliaments of 1571, 1572 and 1584. Moreover, not only was his controversial brother Sir Henry among Leicester's followers, but a more intimate connection was formed by his marriage after 1569 to Mary Howard, Douglas Sheffield's sister, as a result of which Douglas Sheffield was a frequent visitor to Dudley Castle in the early 1570s.[147] Leicester was sufficiently close to the Bridges in 1559 to be appealed to in the notorious witchcraft case of Elizabeth, Lady Throckmorton.[148] The 2nd Lord Chandos gave him his proxy in 1566, and the 3rd Baron together with the 5th Lord Dudley attended his funeral.[149] Leicester's relations with Lord Berkeley prior to the re-opening of the Berkeley law-suit at the end of 1572 appear no less friendly. Berkeley used Caludon Castle near Coventry as his second residence and hunted regularly at Kenilworth. In March 1571 he asked Leicester to obtain leave of absence from parliament for him on grounds of ill health and offered his proxy in exchange. He, Dudley and Chandos attended Leicester at Warwick in September.[150]

With Paget and Essex relations were more complex. Whatever the nature of the clash between Northumberland and the 1st Lord Paget in 1551–52, it did not destroy close relations between the families. Paget seems to have protected Robert Dudley during Mary's reign, and according to one source was his evil genius during the first years of Elizabeth's.[151] The 2nd Lord Paget, who spent much of the 1560s abroad, was a boyhood friend of Leicester's.[152] With Thomas, the 3rd Baron, who succeeded in 1569, relations were initially no less friendly, and Leicester stood godfather to his son in 1572.[153] Thereafter, however, they steadily deteriorated. Religion was undoubtedly one issue, but so too was Paget's estrangement from his wife, Nazereth, who was Leicester's cousin. By 1580 Paget's increasingly open recusancy had led to a truculent hostility and ultimately his flight into exile in 1583.[154] With Essex too the initial relationship was amicable (Dudley was godfather to the future 3rd Earl), but there was an estrangement during Essex's Irish venture, whether or not an adulterous liaison with the countess was involved.[155] After 1576 the Devereux affinity, who appear to have retained an impressive solidarity, regarded Leicester with some suspicion.[156] But Leicester's marriage to the countess initiated a *rapprochement*. He took all her children under his wing, and his own close relationship to the young 3rd Earl led to cooperation both at Court and at the local level, as, for example, when Leicester and Essex jointly obtained the licence for the free school at Tamworth in 1588.[157]

Northumberland was a power in the region for some twenty years, and its leading peer for the last ten. Although his local clientele cannot be discussed in detail here, its surviving members – Sir Henry Dudley, Sir Nicholas and Sir Ralph Bagnall, John Fisher of Packington and Thomas of Warwick, Sir John Throckmorton of Feckenham, and possibly Sir Nicholas and Clement as well – provided the first generation of his sons' following.[158] The central figures, curiously enough, were in fact relations of his wife, in particular Sir James Croft of Croft Castle and the Blounts of Kinlet. The latter had divided into three branches after the death of Sir Thomas Blount of Kinlet in 1524. Sir Thomas's grandson in the senior line, Sir George Blount of Kinlet (1513–81), was, like Croft, a member of Northumberland's military clientele. He was later an executor of the duchess's will and a tenant of Cleobury Mortimer; one of his sons may have been in Leicester's household. Walter Blount of Astley (d. 1562), Sir Thomas's second son, and Edward Blount of Kidderminster, his third, were both in Northumberland's service.[159] Edward's son, Thomas Blount of Kidderminster (d. 1568), was perhaps the most important of them all. He too may have served with Northumberland on campaign; by 1553 he was the Duke's comptroller. During Mary's reign he was Leicester's steward at Hales Owen; thereafter he was his leading household officer and probably steward of Kenilworth as well.[160]

A major similarity between Northumberland's and Leicester's impact on the region was their prior involvement at the highest level of the Court. Whatever importance they may have assigned to their local interests, neither was a resident. Nor was Ambrose Dudley, even if he did not play the same role in Court politics as his father and brother. Although he had been constable of Kenilworth for the duchy of Lancaster between 1549 and 1553, the estates of his second wife, Lady Tailboys, were concentrated in Lincolnshire, and in 1562 he was as much an outsider as his brother.[161] His nominal status in Warwickshire was recognised in the lord-lieutenancies of 1569–70 and 1585, but his infirmity caused him to spend most of his time at his house at Northaw, and of his recorded visits to Warwickshire, the majority were in his brother's company.[162] However, his absence had the important consequence of sustaining a united Dudley influence, for, so far as the surviving sources reveal, it is clear that he employed the same pool of estate officers as his brother.[163]

At the centre of Leicester's regional clientele were the officers of his administration, both central and local. Unfortunately, his surviving household records do not include chequer rolls or other formal lists of his servants or officers, and they can only be identified from casual references.[164] As a result, the structure of his administration is not easy to outline. In 1559–60 his central household was clearly quite small and fairly informal, but even when it expanded, determining precise offices is difficult. All too frequently there are simply general references to 'my lord of Leicester's officers', as, for example, in an answer from Arthur Atye (Leicester's chief secretary) to a request from Burghley in 1589 for information about Leicester's finances: he referred Burghley to Thomas Dudley, William Baynham and Charles Wednester 'eche for his porcion', without describing what these were.[165] Having said this, it is nevertheless possible to identify a coherent group of lawyers, men-of-business and estate officers who formed the central administration. The initial generation – Thomas Blount, the brothers John and Thomas Dudley, William Glasier, William Kynyat, and William Grice – had, in the main, been servants of Northumberland's.[166] As they died out they were replaced by a younger group: Sir John Hubaud, John Nuthall, William Baynham, Charles Wednester, Richard Sutton, William Gorge and Jasper Cholmley.[167]

At the regional level, the surviving Court rolls make possible the identification of the stewards of some manors.[168] The Kenilworth administration, on the other hand, poses greater problems. As noted above, Thomas Blount of Kidderminster was probably the steward from 1563 to his death in 1568. On 1 February 1566 Leicester appointed the Earl of Shrewsbury chief steward of his lands in Warwickshire, Shropshire, Denbighshire and Yorkshire, practically all his permanent estate at the time. The office would appear to be purely honorific, but on Leicester's death Shrewsbury claimed £230 of unpaid fees from his estate.[169] The succession to Blount at Kenilworth is unclear. In 1571 the steward was the lawyer Robert Snagge, who was also active in the administration of Leicester's Welsh estates between 1568 and 1573, and who served Warwick as steward of the lordships of Ruthin in 1570–71 and Warwick in 1571–72.[170] However, between 1567 and his death in 1572 John Butler of Warwick held the chief resident office at Kenilworth, probably that of keeper.[171] In 1572 Leicester issued another large commission, this time to Sir John Hubaud, whom he appointed constable of Kenilworth and steward of his lands in Warwickshire, Worcestershire, Shropshire and Montgomeryshire. Until his death in 1583 Hubaud was not only Leicester's leading officer in the West Midlands and Wales, but also in his central administration.[172] No one appears to have succeeded to his overall influence, but Edward Boughton of Cawston may have done so on the regional level.

After 1571 it is possible to identify the main subordinate officers at Kenilworth. The oldest in service (he received livery in 1567) was Thomas Underhill (1545–91), the son of Hugh Underhill the keeper of Greenwich Palace, and nephew of Edward Underhill the celebrated hot-gospelling gentleman pensioner. In 1590 he described himself as of Leicester's wardrobe and his office was probably that of keeper of the wardrobe at Kenilworth.[173] The numerous surviving inventories of Kenilworth reveal that during the 1580s Underhill was responsible for the wardrobe at Grafton House as well and also make it possible to identify some of his subordinates.[174] Next in seniority of service was Anthony Dockwra, who was undoubtedly the compiler of the Game Book, and, on the evidence of it, entered Leicester's service in 1568.[175] He was initially the keeper of the Chase, but by 1580 appears to have become keeper of the Castle as well, an office he held until his death in November 1586.[176] The last was Henry Besbeeche (b. 1534), who was of Kentish birth and entered Leicester's service in 1570.[177] By 1571 he was the keeper of Kenilworth Park, but may have been clerk comptroller as well by 1578. In a letter of March 1580 he complained that Dockwra (with whom he appears to have feuded consistently) and William Edmundes 'rule the roost now', which suggests that he had been displaced by them. However, on Dockwra's death he appears to have succeeded him in the keepership, for in 1590 he described himself as ranger-general of Kenilworth and joint-keeper together with Edward Boughton.[178]

Of the junior staff, the long-serving bailiff Francis Phipps (b. 1512) can be identified, as can several of the lesser keepers, William Richmond (b. 1536), Thomas Forrest and John Duck, the latter two of whom may have been in Leicester's service as early as 1559.[179] A more mysterious figure was William Gorge, who was in service in 1567, described as Leicester's steward in 1571, and was certainly an officer of the central household.[180] In 1588–89 he was keeper of the castle for the countess of Leicester, and supervised the disposal of the household contents there, but whether he held this office or any other at Kenilworth before Leicester's death is unclear.[181]

The most convenient (though not exclusive) guide to Leicester's wider regional clientele is provided by the gentlemen (at least forty-five) who obeyed his summons to serve with him on the Low Countries expedition in 1585.[182] They include a number of members of the second generation of the older Dudley clientele, the most obvious being the sons of Thomas Blount, Christopher and his elder brother Edward, Blount's son-in-law Francis Clare, and Clement Fisher, the son of John Fisher of Packington.[183] However, continuity with the older Dudley clientele was not the sole determinant. During the 1570s and 1580s the key figures in Leicester's regional following were four men who had no obvious earlier connection. The most important of the four was Hubaud. The earliest reference to him in Leicester's circle is found in the visit to Warwick in 1571, though the connection may have been at work in his election as knight of the shire earlier in the year.[184] Hubaud inherited lands in both Warwickshire and Herefordshire, but it was probably his marriage to Sir George Throckmorton's daughter Mary (c. 1564) that brought him into the upper circles of the Warwickshire gentry.[185]

Hubaud would appear to have introduced two younger men to Leicester's service by the end of the 1570s: George Digby of Colshill and Edward Boughton of Cawston. Digby's mother was another of Sir George Throckmorton's daughters; he was a cousin of both Clement Fisher and Hubaud and an executor of Hubaud's will. He succeeded to his father's estate in 1571, and was associated with Leicester by 1576. In 1581 and 1584 he served as knight of the shire for Warwickshire, and was appointed sheriff in 1581–82. Digby had been a ward of Sir Francis Knollys, and this association with the countess of Leicester's family may help to account for his being nominated an overseer (together with Hubaud) of Leicester's 1582 will and a trustee for the countess's jointure settlement in 1584. He accompanied Leicester to the Netherlands where he was knighted, but he died at a relatively young age in 1587.[186] Boughton is first encountered in Leicester's service in 1579, when he was appointed a surveyor of Drayton Bassett. He was sheriff of Warwickshire in 1580–1 and M.P. for Coventry in 1584. He served Warwick as well as Leicester, and may, as has been suggested above, have succeeded Hubaud as their central officer in the region. He too accompanied Leicester to the Netherlands and died in 1589.[187] The last figure of this generation was the more flamboyant, if wayward, Henry Goodere of Polesworth, who was knight of the shire for Staffordshire in 1563, sheriff of Warwickshire in 1570, and M.P. for Coventry in 1571. His earliest recorded connection to Leicester was in 1571, and he also accompanied him to the Netherlands, where he commanded his guard and was knighted. He occupied a prominent place in both Sir Philip Sidney's and Leicester's funerals.[188]

Possibly the most striking feature of the structure of the clientele is the complex relationship between local and central and the absence of a rigid distinction between the two levels, whether central is taken to mean the Court or Leicester's own household and central administration. Some of those mentioned above, Sir James Croft or Sir Nicholas Throckmorton being the most obvious, had their own careers at Court. The two key regional officers, Thomas Blount and Hubaud, were also the leading figures in Leicester's central administration. We lack sources for the personnel of Leicester's immediate household for the 1570s, but in the 1580s we can discover there members of several West Midlands families, of whom the best known are Christopher Blount, then Leicester's master of the horse, and the sons of Sir John Tracy of Toddington (Glos.).[189] The men-of-business came from a variety of backgrounds. The brothers John and Thomas Dudley, the two most long-serving (both began in Northumberland's service), were the descendants of a grandson of the 1st Lord Dudley who had settled in Cumberland at the end of the fifteenth century.[190] Glasier, Yerwerth and Nuthall were lawyers from Chester, Baynham came from Gloucestershire and Wednester from Herefordshire. Some, especially the Cheshiremen, held office in Leicester's Welsh lordships as well, but just as Richard Sutton can be found presiding over Warwickshire manorial courts, so Hubaud and later Boughton can be found undertaking business in Wales. A number also held office under the crown. Glasier was the vice-chamberlain and customer of Chester, Baynham was the crown's receiver-general for the West Midlands and the Marches,

Cholmley clerk of Queen's Bench, and both Wednester and Sutton became auditors of the Exchequer, though apparently after Leicester's death. Blount, Hubaud, Glasier, and Sir John Throckmorton were members of the Council in the Marches of Wales, and John Dudley joint clerk of the Signet to the Council.[191]

Although most of the men-of-business (the main exceptions being the Cheshiremen) appear to have resided in or about London, many held tenancies in Leicester's various estates or had other interests in the West Midlands. No less important were the connections formed on the personal level, of which only fragmentary evidence survives. Thomas Dudley, for example, held land in Warwickshire and Worcestershire and was Warwick's nominee as M.P. for Warwick borough between 1572 and 1589. He had some involvement in the Kenilworth administration, was an overseer of John Butler's will and was left a legacy by Hubaud.[192] In 1566–67 Leicester assigned several manors to Thomas Blount, John Dudley and John Tamworth (the keeper of the privy purse and Leicester's deputy-lieutenant at Windsor Castle between 1562 and his death in 1569), probably to settle debts that he owed them. When they sold off lands in Dry Marston in 1567, William Sheldon of Beoley acted as their collector.[193] This should not be taken to mean that all operated in harmony – just as Besbeeche and Dockwra at Kenilworth appear from their correspondence to have spent all their time bickering, so Glasier was notoriously quarrelsome – but the network was one that bound centre and locality together and was connected to the wider Elizabethan political nation at a number of levels.

IV

That men associated with Leicester achieved prominence in local government is perhaps only to be expected. However, limitations in the sources make a more precise analysis difficult. The evidence for the M.P.s has been discussed elsewhere.[194] Leicester's appointment to the lieutenancies of Worcestershire and Warwickshire in 1559–60 initiated his direct political influence in the region. In these years there were only informal deputies, Sir Thomas Russell of Strensham and William Sheldon of Beoley serving in Worcestershire, and the young Thomas Lucy and Sir Robert Throckmorton of Coughton for Warwickshire. John Fisher of Packington was also proposed for Warwickshire, but given doubts whether as a gentleman pensioner he would be able to serve, Sir Richard Verney of Compton Verney was suggested as a substitute, though in the end Fisher appears to have served.[195] Thomas Blount was appointed muster-master for Warwickshire.[196] When the lieutenancies were revived in 1569, Warwick appointed Lucy and Sir Fulk

Greville (who were reappointed in the final revival in 1585) in Warwickshire, and Leicester Russell and Sir John Lyttleton of Frankley in Worcestershire.[197]

There are a number of references to Leicester's influence on the appointment of sheriffs in the years 1578–80 (mainly in Wales), and Walter Bagot reported in November 1579 that: 'Som report that the Queen was somewhat displeased because most of them which were put in election were belonging unto my Lord of Leicester and my Lord of Warwick'.[198] Certainly the list of Warwickshire sheriffs of 1578–84 reads like a roll-call of Leicester's and Warwick's friends and officers, but the picture is less clear in Staffordshire and Worcestershire. With the J.P.s the evidence is not sufficient as yet to reach any conclusions over Leicester's possible manipulation of appointments.

Leicester's influence in the local towns is better recorded and thus more revealing. It was strongest in Coventry, owing partly to proximity to Kenilworth, but also to a tradition of Dudley patronage and an important intermediary in the person of the city's recorder, Sir John Throckmorton. Together with Throckmorton, Leicester had some involvement in the city's obtaining of the tithes of Holy Trinity Church in 1565, but it was in March 1568 with the grant of the reversion of Cheylesmore Common that the relationship was sealed.[199] In 1549, at the city's request, Northumberland had obtained the manor of Cheylesmore from the duchy of Cornwall, and had given the mayor and corporation a ninety-nine-year lease of the Common for the benefit of the poor. In 1551 he gave the fee simple to his son Warwick, who in turn included the city's rent (£9 p.a.) in his wife's jointure. Although the countess retained her life interest, the fee simple reverted to the crown in 1553. At the city's further request Leicester obtained in 1568 the reversion of the manor in fee farm after the countess's death.[200] His benefaction is commemorated in the 'Brass Lease' in St Mary's Hall, which emphasises the continuity of Dudley benevolence.[201] In July 1572 he was also instrumental in obtaining a licence for the endowment of Bablake Hospital as a poor house.[202] Leicester enjoyed no formal status in the city – it did not have a high steward in the sixteenth century – but the close relationship was reflected in the annual exchange of gifts, particularly during his visits to Kenilworth. The high point was the great banquet in 1581, although precisely what occasioned it is unclear.[203]

The near farcical proceedings that took place in Warwick during his visit in 1571 appear to have been an attempt to follow Coventry's example.[204] However, despite Leicester's decision to found his hospital there rather than at Kenilworth, and the prominence of several of his officers within the borough, he appears to have interfered little in Warwick, probably because he regarded it as his brother's town.[205] He was also elected high steward of Tewkesbury and steward of Evesham, both probably at local request. He obtained a charter of incorporation for Tewkesbury in April 1575, and in

c. 1579 was petitioned to obtain a licence for a market.[206] The intermediary was undoubtedly Gabriel Blike (c. 1520–92), one of Tewkesbury's principal burgesses and an active client of Leicester's but an otherwise shadowy figure.[207]

The concern with the local economy that Leicester expressed to John Fisher in 1571 can be detected most clearly in Coventry. He was probably involved in the grant to the city of the monopoly to manufacture Armentières cloth in 1568, although he is not referred to in the letters patent.[208] His most beneficial act of patronage may have been the introduction of the Lancashire clothier Henry Breres, whom he recommended as freeman to the city in 1574. Breres became the city's leading cloth manufacturer for the remainder of the century.[209] In 1571 his benevolence to Coventry was cited in Warwick as an example of the benefits he might bring to the borough.[210] He was also a patron of the Sheldon of Beoley tapestry works (he owned at least two Sheldon tapestries) and recommended it as a model for Warwick to follow.[211] However, his urban patronage, however extensive, was undoubtedly more a response to local pressures than a sustained policy of his own devising.[212]

Leicester's estates spanned the dioceses of Worcester and Coventry and Lichfield. In the case of Worcester, the first Elizabethan Bishop, Edwin Sandys, was an old Dudley protégé, and relations were cordial.[213] Sandy's initial successor, James Calfhill (who died before he could be installed), may have owed his promotion to Leicester, and his ultimate successor Nicholas Bullingham (1571–76) very probably did.[214] On the other hand neither John Whitgift (1577–83), nor Edmund Freake (1584–91) were obvious followers.[215] At Coventry and Lichfield, Thomas Bentham (1559–80) seems to have had no Dudley connection, but his successor, Richard Overton (1580–1609), was a former chaplain and probably Leicester's nominee.[216] Sandys appointed Leicester high steward of the diocese in succession to Sir Robert Throckmorton in 1570, and Overton appointed him master of the game of Coventry and Lichfield on his election, but these appear purely honorific gestures.[217] Leicester's direct influence on the diocese of Worcester appears to have been limited; he presented to no livings in the diocese, and had no open influence on the leases registered by the dean and chapter, although at least two canons of the cathedral, John Bullingham and Griffith Lewes, probably owed their benefices to him.[218]

In Coventry and Lichfield his influence was more extensive. Thomas Lever, the first archdeacon of Coventry (1560–77), owed his promotion to Cecil, but by the time of the Vestiarian Controversy he was turning to Leicester for assistance. His successor, William James (1577–84), was one of Leicester's favourite chaplains. James resigned in 1584 on becoming Dean of Christ Church; his successor William Hinton attended Leicester's funeral though there is no other known connection.[219] A clash with Edward Boughton over the mastership of Rugby School, which resulted in a Star Chamber case in 1582–83, ruffled Overton's relations with Leicester, but his influence was not diminished.[220] He was undoubtedly behind the granting of the prebend of Eccleshall to Antonio del Corro in 1585, and in February 1586 another of his favourite chaplains, Humphrey Tyndall (who had officiated at his marriage), was appointed chancellor of the cathedral and archdeacon of Stafford.[221]

Leicester's major influence on the religious life of the region was probably his general encouragement of the preaching clergy.[222] This is first detectable in the later 1560s in his patronage of the proposed corporation of preachers of Warwickshire, which also involved the Earls of Warwick and Huntingdon, Sir Ambrose Cave, Sir Richard Knightley, Sir Thomas Lucy, and Sir Nicholas and Clement Throckmorton.[223] The scheme does not appear to have got off the ground, but it may have been related to the proposal that survives among his papers for converting the collegiate church of St Mary's, Warwick, into a preaching centre.[224] A travelling chaplain of his preached in Warwick in 1568, but it is not clear whether this was by design.[225] In 1579 he communicated his alarm at the revival of Catholicism in Warwickshire to Burghley, and this may have inspired him to use his tours in the 1580s to encourage the local godly, as appears to have been the case in Northamptonshire in 1581.[226] To what extent he was further inspired to appoint Thomas Cartwright master of his Hospital in 1585 as part of the same campaign is an interesting question.[227] Little, in fact, is known about the Hospital prior to the drafting of the statutes in November 1585.[228] By then its purpose had been changed from the relief of the poor in general to the support of old soldiers, and specifically men from Warwickshire or Wotton-under-Edge maimed while serving under his command.[229] What does emerge is his power to protect the non-conformist clergy, as their vulnerability to episcopal counter-attacks after his death reveals.[230] In this context his influence on the appointment of the local archdeacons was of some significance, for it is doubtful whether his protégés would have engaged whole-heartedly in the disciplining of the clergy.

Despite the general denunciation of his harrying of the Catholic gentry found in *Leicester's Commonwealth*, the religious allegiance of his clientele was by no means uniform. That of the older generation was distinctly mixed. In the 1564 episcopal survey Sandys included only Thomas Blount and Sir Thomas Russell among the favourers of religion in Worcestershire; William Sheldon he described as indifferent. In Warwickshire he included John Fisher, Thomas Lucy and Clement Throckmorton among the favourers, but Fulk Greville he considered indifferent and Thomas Fisher an adversary. Bentham considered Sir Ralph Bagnall a favourer among the Staffordshire gentry, but for his part of Warwickshire he relied on Edward Aglionby, who included Sir Richard Verney, Clement Throckmorton, Lucy and Henry Goodere among the favourers. Sir George Blount was considered an enemy by Bentham, but a neuter by John Scory of Hereford. Scory in turn listed Sir James Croft as a favourer and Sir John Throckmorton as an enemy. John Hubaud was described as not favourable by Scory and indifferent by Aglionby.[231]

As the reign progressed, the religious allegiance of the local magistracy was shaped by three trends that left the more openly protestant the dominant force *faut de mieux*. The first was the exclusion from local government of the most openly Catholic of the established families, Sir Robert Throckmorton or Sir George Blount, for example. Secondly, other members of the older generation who served the regime loyally during the first decade became compromised, Croft, for example, or Sir John Throckmorton. Thirdly, there was a pronounced rise in recusancy among the younger generation as can be seen in the cases of Francis Throckmorton or Ralph Sheldon of Beoley.[232] To some extent the same trends also shaped Leicester's own clientele, although religious allegiance was never absolute, as is best illustrated by the example of Christopher Blount, though it is not clear how open Blount was about his Catholicism. Leicester's 'friends' included the leading Puritan gentry in Warwickshire – Sir Thomas Lucy, Clement and Job Throckmorton, John and Clement Fisher – but neither Hubaud, Digby, nor Boughton was among the greater Puritan patrons. There is therefore a significant divergence between Leicester's clerical and lay patronage – the lay following never shared the 'ideological coherence' of the clerical – which is found at a number of other levels as well.

The extent to which there was a wider political *cum* religious tension in the region is of importance in any assessment of the three most controversial episodes of Leicester's 'planting': the Berkeley law-suit, the Tamworth high stewardship, and the Drayton Bassett riots of 1578. All were complex disputes over title (which can only be summarised here), and in two cases they were of considerable antiquity, but that may not have been the whole story. In the case of the Berkeley law-suit we are largely dependent on the account of John Smyth of Nibley, one very much coloured by his own allegiances. That Leicester decided to revive the old Lisle claim is clear, but what moved him to do so in late 1572 is not, and why the queen assisted him, which was essential given that the Dudley claim had reverted to the crown in 1553, even less so.[233] Smyth's account is, however, contradictory in this key issue. On the one hand, he portrayed Leicester's pursuit of the Berkeley lands as a longstanding ambition, which was made possible by the execution of Lady Berkeley's brother, the Duke of Norfolk, in 1572. On the other, he claimed it was an act of revenge provoked by Lady Berkeley's persuading of her husband to reject Leicester's proposal of a marriage between their daughters and the Sidney brothers. Smyth also blames Lady Berkeley for rejecting any compromise with Leicester and for alienating the queen, apparently by blaming her for her brother's death.[234] What other evidence survives reveals very friendly relations in 1571, but then Leicester pursuing the case with some energy at the end of 1572, although his need to research the pedigrees at that stage suggests it had not been planned in advance.[235]

Even less clear are Leicester's motives for reviving the suit in the 1580s.[236] The influence on Smyth's account of *Leicester's Commonwealth* may account for a further internal contradiction. On the one hand, he claims that Leicester's attack on Berkeley was part of a more general attack on the ancient nobility in which Berkeley received at least the moral support of Leicester's enemies.[237] On the other, Berkeley is portrayed as the almost isolated victim, with all his former friends manipulated against him by Leicester. In the first phase Leicester's allies were the 2nd Lord Chandos (his 'inward friend') and Henry Goodere, in the second they included such key figures in the Gloucestershire gentry as Sir Nicholas Poyntz and Sir Thomas Throckmorton of Tortworth.[238]

The Tamworth high stewardship dispute did not involve Leicester's immediate interests, but stemmed from Humphrey Ferrers' revival of a claim to the stewardship which had been contested since the division of the lordship of Ferrers of Chartley in the previous century. The affair in fact arose from an error of Burghley's, who, on the death of the 1st Earl of Essex, first confirmed the 2nd Earl's right to it, but then apparently forgot and at Leicester's request granted it to Ferrers. In the spring and summer of 1578 the dispute reached the Privy Council, who settled it in Essex's favour. One of Essex's servants. Richard Broughton, has left a vivid account of the dispute in which George Digby and Edward Holt, identified as Leicester's men, supported Ferrers, while he and his fellows loyally defended the young Earl's interests.[239] However, Ferrers' defeat in the affair suggests that whatever support Leicester may have given him initially was counterbalanced by his growing closeness to Essex.

Ferrers' prominence in the Drayton Bassett riots several months later raises questions about the possible effects of the earlier dispute on the later.[240] The issue here was the seventy-seven-year lease of Drayton Bassett, with effect from either 1556 or 1560, which had been granted to George Robinson by Sir Thomas Pope in 1538. As noted above, the fee simple appears to have been regained by Northumberland several years later, for the manor was included in the duchess's jointure of 1546, and therefore it presumably reverted to the crown on his attainder.[241] Robinson's son William died while serving under Warwick at Le Havre in 1563 and the lease was inherited by his grandson, Thomas, who mortgaged it to the London merchant tailor Richard Paramour in 1575. When Paramour foreclosed in 1576, Robinson contested bitterly, and Paramour only finally obtained possession in June

1578.[242] He was then besieged by a large body of local gentry. In the foreground were the Harcourts, who were closely related to the Robinsons, and already notorious for their recusancy. Behind them was a much larger body of sympathisers, led by Sir Francis Willoughby of Wollaton, and including a number of Leicester's own followers, among them Henry Goodere.[243]

Frightened off the estate in July 1578, Paramour appears to have appealed to Leicester, who then sent Humphrey Ferrers and George Digby to regain possession.[244] Following a struggle for the house in August and early September, they were eventually driven off and one of Ferrers' men was killed. On receipt of the news of the death, the Privy Council ordered Lord Dudley and Lord Stafford and the other J.P.s of Staffordshire into action and the rioters then abandoned the house. The council attempted to trace those involved, but only a rump eventually stood trial at Star Chamber in 1580. Leicester's involvement is possibly the most mysterious aspect of the whole affair. He did not purchase the lease from Paramour until 17 April 1579 and was not, therefore, on the surface directly involved in the initial dispute.[245] A letter from Paramour to Ferrers of 15 September 1578 relaying Leicester's instruction for him to 'further me much in my proceedings in law and justice against them, which is his lordship's only meaning thereby' implies that he was still intending to retain possession and that Leicester was merely assisting.[246] However, the extent of Leicester's involvement, for he was clearly the driving force behind the council's intervention, does leave open the question whether an informal agreement to purchase the lease had already been reached. His intervention certainly had the effect of persuading a number of the rioters (especially his own followers) to abandon their cause, and then of inhibiting Thomas Robinson from reviving the case during his lifetime – although the expense Leicester incurred in buying out the interests of those involved suggests that intimidation was not the whole story.[247] The easiest explanation is that Paramour, exhausted and demoralised by the events of 1578, decided during the winter to cut his losses and that Leicester then took the opportunity to regain an old family estate. However, the very scale of the riot raises interesting questions about the state of Staffordshire at the end of the 1570s.

V

Leicester's death brought none of these disputes to an end; if anything, it gave them new life. A final settlement of the 'Great Berkeley Law-Suit' was at length negotiated by James I in 1609. Humphrey Ferrers was forced to suspend his claim to the Tamworth stewardship during the 1590s, but revived it again in 1602.[248] Thomas Robinson renewed his suit for Drayton

Bassett after 1588, and the dispute became further embittered once the countess of Leicester made it her home in the mid-1590s; it was only when the
Attorney-General barred him from further actions unless he produced 'new
matter of title' in 1608 that her possession was freed of challenge.[249]

John Smyth's jubilant observation on the victory of Lord Berkeley –
'Whereas on the other part there is not one lymme discended from the
loynes of either of those Earles to pisse against a wall' – provides a trenchant
epitaph on the Dudley interest.[250] Leicester's sudden death in 1588 followed
by Warwick's eighteen months later without a direct male heir destroyed the
Dudley interest in the same way that the heirless death of the Duke of Warwick terminated the Beauchamp interest a century and a half before. However, the process of destruction was slightly more complicated than such
a bald conclusion would allow. As noted above, Leicester did try to endow a
further generation in the person of his illegitimate son, Sir Robert Dudley, to
whom after Warwick's and his own widow's death he wished his remaining
estate to descend. What Leicester had not allowed for was the extent of his
(and Warwick's) indebtedness, which forced the sale of so many of his lands
and left Sir Robert with only Kenilworth itself.

No less important was the enmity between Sir Robert Dudley and the
countess and her ally Sir Robert Sidney, the one legitimate male descendant
of the Duke of Northumberland, whose ambition to succeed to the Dudley
titles and lands was notorious. A running dispute between the countess
and Sir Robert Dudley broke out after Warwick's death in 1590, when she
attempted to challenge his right to Kenilworth.[251] What gave it a wider significance was her reliance on her son for the protection of her interests. The
alliance between mother and son undoubtedly hastened the absorption of
the Dudley into the Devereux clientele. The process was a complex one in
which a number of factors were involved, not least Essex's wider role as
Leicester's political heir. By this time too most of the central figures of
Leicester's regional following were dead; only Goodere (who died in 1595)
survived him for very long. Those involved were thus a younger generation,
many of them possibly closer to Essex personally. The key figure was undoubtedly the countess's third husband. Sir Christopher Blount, but among
those who gravitated to Essex were Charles Wednester (who became his
auditor general), the Tracy brothers and Clement Fisher. The antagonism
with Sir Robert Dudley, who in turn looked to his mother's family for support, became part of the wider hostility between Essex and the revived house
of Howard. Given that the rump of Leicester's estate was now divided between Dudley and the countess's jointure lands, the fragmentation of the
clientele was inevitable.

The final disintegration took place in the reign of James I. After 1601 the
Essex clientele went into abeyance, and when it was revived by the 3rd Earl in

the 1620s it involved a new generation. Sir Robert Dudley's departure for Italy following the failure of his attempt to prove his legitimacy in 1605 – an episode that placed great strains on the allegiances of Leicester's surviving friends and servants – and then his sale of Kenilworth to Henry, Prince of Wales, eliminated the remaining Dudley landed interest. Sidney received the Lisle viscountcy, and eventually the earldom of Leicester, but much to his disappointment failed to obtain that of Warwick, which was purchased by Lord Rich. His son's claim to an interest in the countess's jointure lands also failed despite prolonged litigation.

The destruction of the Dudley interest, although the product of a number of private disputes, can also be seen as an example of the wider severing of the connections between the historic earldoms and their estates that followed the Stuart expansion of the peerage. In this respect Leicester's planting marks the end of an era. But there is also another reason for the rapid disappearance of the Dudley interest, and that is that it had not involved any major alteration to the social or political structure of the counties concerned. If men like Blount or Hubaud enjoyed an enhanced stature as Leicester's officers, they were also firmly established within their counties. The same would apply to Edward Boughton, Digby or Goodere, let alone Lucy or Greville. Thus Leicester did not, as in Denbighshire, leave behind him a group of 'new men' to be the targets of the revenge of his and their enemies.[252] Moreover, whatever tensions Leicester may have caused were transcended by the larger ones provoked by Essex in the following decade.

What Northumberland, Leicester and Essex shared and what acted as a common feature of their impact – despite Essex's possibly more legitimate claim to be an established regional peer – was their combination of regional influence with wider political interests. For this reason, as noted above, it is impossible to draw a meaningful distinction between their local and 'national' followings. Moreover, their regional interests were only part of a much wider range of concerns and not necessarily the most important. Therefore the time and attention they could devote to local matters was both limited and sporadic. The 'Black Book' provides two revealing examples of this problem. When Fisher went to see Leicester in November 1571 and later when a delegation from Warwick went to see him in May 1585 over a dispute about the corporation's government, they found great difficulty simply in obtaining an interview. This was not due to any arrogance on Leicester's part, but in 1571 because 'the lords being trowbled with many waightie matters the said Fisher could then have no tyme for conference with the said Earle', and in 1585 because 'my Lord of Leycester [was] greatly occupied in matters of state & cam seldome abroad'.[253] Reference has already been made to Burghley's 'double' granting of the stewardship of Tamworth. The same occurred over the tithes of Budbrooke, which Leicester in February 1581 requested the borough of Warwick to grant to Sir John Hubaud's brother Ralph and then clearly forgot and asked again three months later, this time on behalf of William Baynham.[254]

As a patron, therefore, Leicester suffered from a major weakness, which he shared to some extent with the crown itself. However potentially effective his influence, he was unable to organise his patronage systematically amid the pressure of greater issues. As a result his regional impact was a series of responses to pressures from below, mediated undoubtedly through his own favourites, and not the implementation of a self-conscious or consistent policy. Where he did have a policy was in the advancement of his own interests, in particular his revival of the Beauchamp inheritance. However, this combination of antiquarianism and dynasticism was not a political – in the utilitarian sense – exercise; it was not an attempt to create a power-base for influence at Court. The same can be said about his policy towards his estate, for while there is evidence of quite active economic exploitation of parts of it, it was never his sole, nor necessarily his major, source of income. His estate policy was primarily that of creating an estate of inheritance, which was also essentially dynastic in motive.

Where Leicester might have been expected to have had a more self-conscious policy was in religion. Yet this was essentially one of support for the preaching clergy. Moreover, it took also the form of the advancement and protection of individuals, rather than the deliberate expansion of his means of religious patronage. Nor did religious allegiance determine his relations with the local gentry in any absolute sense. Thus while his attitude towards the clergy displays a certain consistency, this was not the case with the gentry, and thus there were significant contradictions between the two 'halves' of his religious policy. These inconsistencies were of wider impact, because while Leicester was neither a fool, nor lazy, nor totally self-indulgent, his actions could easily appear hypocritical or self-serving. His professions of Puritan piety appeared to be contradicted by the extravagance of his tastes and his tangled private life; his expressions of concern for the public interest by his pursuit of his own immediate ends. The now legendary comparison with his brother, 'the good earl' of Warwick, was based largely on Warwick's more retiring and possibly more austere personal life, for as can be seen here his impact on the region was very much shared with his brother.

In some ways the spirit of Leicester's attitude to his country is best captured in four lines from the inscription in St Mary's Hall, Coventry, that Philemon Holland composed to celebrate the Brass Lease:

And Leicester, mid thos great affaires whereto high place doth call,
His father's worthy steppes hath trac'd, to prop that els might fall.
On forth in Prince and Countrie's cause, hold on this your dayes;
Such deedes do noble bloud commend, such win immortal praise.[255]

Both Anne Hughes and Christine Carpenter have emphasised Warwickshire's fluid politics and the absence of a discrete county community or identity. The same might also be said for its neighbours. But, as Carpenter also observes, a certain identity was provided by the Beauchamp earldom.[256] The Dudley revival of the earldom had a similar effect, the fluidity of regional politics working to their advantage. As non-residents their influence was always at one remove, but they compensated for their absence by effective patronage at Court. This is not to say that Coventry would not have gained Cheylesmore Common or the Amentières patent, Tewkesbury its incorporation or Kenilworth its market without Leicester, but they would not have done so in the same way. Similarly, it is doubtful if four royal progresses would have reached the West Midlands without Leicester's connection to Kenilworth. However mixed his motives or however disparate his influence, Leicester's combination of enthusiasm for his country and pre-eminence at Court brought Court and country together rather than drove them apart. In this respect his interest formed one of the major strands in the fabric of the Elizabethan political nation.

APPENDIX 15.1: THE EARL OF LEICESTER'S OFFICERS[a]

A) CENTRAL ADMINISTRATION[b]

	Period of service	Office[c]
William Glasier M.P. (1525–88)	1556–88[d]	
Thomas Blount M.P. (d. 1568)	1556 to death	
John Dudley M.P. (1526–80)	1559 to death	
Thomas Dudley M.P. (d. 1593)	1559–88	Comptroller 1571[e]
William Kynyat (d. by 1574)	1559 to death	Auditor 1562
John Yerwerth M.P. (d. 1587)	1559 to death	Receiver-General 1579–83[f]
Robert Hutton	1562–88	Comptroller 1582–83
Charles Wednester M.P. (d. 1597)	1566?/1583–88[g]	Auditor 1583
Henry Dynne M.P. (1533–86)	1569 to death	Auditor 1569–74
William Gorge	1567–88	Comptroller 1585
Sir John Hubaud M.P. (1544–83)	1571 to death	
Jasper Cholmley M.P. (1539–87)	1573 to death	
John Nuthall M.P. (d. 1586)	1573 to death	Solicitor 1574
William Baynham M.P. (d. 1597)	1578–88	Surveyor-General 1579–83 Auditor 1580
William Sparke	1580–88	Solicitor 1580
Richard Sutton M.P. (d. 1634)	1581–88	Solicitor-General 1581
Robert Wrote M.P. (1544–89)	1582–88	

B) LOCAL ADMINISTRATION

Place	Office	
Kenilworth	Constable	Sir John Hubaud, 1572–83 Constable of Kenilworth, Steward Warks., Worcs., Salop., Mont. 1572
	Steward	Thomas Blount, 1563?–68 Robert Snagge M.P. (d. 1605) 1571[h] Edward Boughton M.P. (1545–89)?, 1586?–88[i]
	Keeper	John Butler M.P. (1503/ 4–72), 1569 to death Anthony Dockwra (d. 1586), 1580? to death Henry Besbeeche (1534–?), 1586?–88
	Keeper of the Wardrobe	Thomas Underhill (1545–91), 1567–88
	Wardrobe Staff[j]	Humphrey Cole, 1583–85 Thomas Cole, 1584–88 Anne King, 1583–88
	Ranger-General	Henry Besbeeche, ?–1588
	Keeper of the Chase	Anthony Dockwra, 1568–78?
	Keeper of Kenilworth Park	Henry Besbeeche, 1570–88
	Keepers	Thomas Forrest, 1559/ 1575–88[k] John Duck, 1559/1573–88 William Richmond (1536–?), 1568/75–88[l]
	Bailiff	Francis Phipps, 1581?–88[m]
	Office Unknown	William Edmundes, 1574–80[n]
Drayton Bassett	Steward	Humphrey Ferrers, 1579–88[o]
	Keeper of the Park	William Blacknoll, 158?–88[p]

Cleobury Mortimer	Steward	Edward Blount, 1587 (and all Salop manors)
	Keeper of the Park	Walter Blount of Sillington, 1576[q]
Knowle[r]	Steward	John Hugford M.P. (1543–1602), 1579–88 (1581 with Richard Sutton)
Balsall[s]	Steward	Henry Hugford, 1586 John Hugford, 1587 Richard Sutton, 1588
Honiley[t]	Steward	Richard Sutton, 1588

Notes

[a] This table is intended as a provisional handlist only and limitations of space prevent full references. Those supplied here are supplementary to the notes to the text. However, for the sake of convenience, all M.P.s have been identified.

[b] This is not a full list of the officers of Leicester's central household, but only of those who had some involvement in the West Midlands estates. An Index of Servants will be published in *Household Accounts*. They are ranked in order of seniority of service, but the dates are the earliest that can be established, and are not definitive. The Dudley brothers, Blount, Kynyat, and possibly Glasier and Grice as well, had been in Northumberland's service, and it can be assumed that they were in Leicester's before 1559, although precise evidence is available only for Blount, Glasier and Grice.

[c] Offices and the dates are derived from specific references, and are also not definitive.

[d] Glasier, John Dudley, Kynyat and Yerwerth undertook the 1566 survey of Leicester's estates (Longleat, DP XVII); John Dudley, Kynyat and the lawyer Thomas Rolfe that of 1563 (*ibid.*, DP XVI).

[e] *Black Book*, p. 36.

[f] Yerwerth held a number of offices, among them the receivership of the lordship of Denbigh. In several documents of the 1580s he is identified as receiver-general, but whether this was for all Leicester's estates or only those in Wales is not clear.

[g] In a letter to Humphrey Ferrers of 28 July 1566 (B.L., Stowe MS 150, fo. 5), Wednester refers to his work on 'my lord's business' and then to the Earl of Warwick by name. It is reasonable to assume that my lord was Leicester, but no further reference to Wednester can be found prior to 1583.

[h] Snagge was in Leicester's service between 1569 and 1575, and possibly as early as 1567.

[i] Given Besbeeche's statement in his deposition in 1590 (P.R.O., C 2 I/ElizI/D/5/2) that he 'had charge of his [Leicester's] household affaires at Kenilworth aforesaide jointly with Mr. Edward Boughton', it could be assumed that they shared a joint keepership. However, Boughton's wider involvement in Leicester's affairs would suggest his office was more that of steward, while Besbeeche acted as keeper.

[j] Identified from the household inventories, as noted in the text. All held leases on the Kenilworth estate.

[k] A Thomas Forrest and a John Duck were in Leicester's service as a dog-keeper and a huntsman in 1559–60 and were given livery in 1567 (see *Household Accounts*). It is reasonable to assume that Thomas Forrest and John Duck, the keepers at Kenilworth

(K.G.B., fos. [2v], [6v]), were the same men. Forrest held a lease in Rudfen and Duck in Honiley.

[l] Richmond was a deponent in 1590, in which he stated he had known the Kenilworth estate since 1568; he is referred to as a keeper in 1575 in the K.G.B., fo. [6].

[m] Phipps also deposed in 1590. He is identified as bailiff in Baynham's 1581 survey (P.R.O., LR 2/185/37).

[n] Although his office cannot be established, there are numerous references to Edmundes in the Kenilworth correspondence of the late 1570s, as well as in the *Black Book* (p. 221). One letter of his own to Leicester survives (Longleat, DP II, fo. 200, 10 Dec. 1580). He was related to John Butler and undoubtedly the William Edmundes who signed the Wars. Parliamentary return for the election of 1584 (P.R.O., C 219/29/157). The absence of later references suggests that he died shortly thereafter.

[o] I have not discovered any formal reference to Ferrers as steward of Drayton Bassett, but the detailed discussions of the estate found in his correspondence with Leicester after 1578 suggests that he was.

[p] His appointment as keeper of Drayton Park is referred to in a now missing letter from Leicester to Humphrey Ferrers of 22 July 1580; he was also a leaseholder of Drayton Bassett. He served on the Netherlands expedition and attended Leicester's funeral.

[q] His commission (12 July 1576) is Longleat MS 4110.

[r] Knowle Court Rolls (W.C.R.O., CR 1886/2284–2300).

[s] Balsall Court Rolls (W.C.R.O., CR 112/BA307/1–3).

[t] Honiley Court Roll (S.B.T.R.O., DR 18/30/12/3).

APPENDIX 15.2: WEST MIDLANDS GENTRY WHO SERVED IN THE LOW COUNTRIES EXPEDITIONARY FORCE, 1585[a]

County

Warwickshire   Sir Thomas Baskerville of Goodrest M.P.
Edward Boughton of Cawston M.P.
William Boughton [of Long Lawford?]
William Butler [of Kenilworth?]
Thomas Catesby
Walter Clopton
Sir John Conway of Arrow
Sir George Digby of Colshill M.P.
Sir Clement Fisher of Great Packington M.F.
John Fisher [of Great Packington?]
John Fullwood
Sir Henry Goodere of Polesworth M.P.
William Goodere [of Polesworth?]
Sir John Harington of Combe Abbey and Exton, Ruts. M.P.
William Harmon of Hampton
William Hartoppe [of Kenilworth?]
Ralph Hubaud of Ipsley
Sebastian Osbaston of Long Compton
George Turville [of Kenilworth?]

                William Wayte
                Christopher Wright

Worcestershire   Charles Acton [of Elmley Lovett?]
                Richard Acton of Elmley Lovett
                Sir Christopher Blount of Kidderminster M.P.
                Sir Edward Blount of Kidderminster
                Sir Francis Clare of Caldwell
                Sir John Russell of Strensham M.P.
                William Walsh of Abberley

Staffordshire   William Blacknoll of Drayton Bassett
                John Breton of Tamworth M.P.
                Nicholas Breton [of Drayton Bassett?]
                Michael Harcourt of Ellenhall and Leconfield, Bucks.
                John Robinson
                Ralph Sneyd of Keele
                Francis Trentham of Rocester

Shropshire   Francis Bromley of Hodnet M.P.
                Edward Grey of Buildwas
                Thomas Leighton of Wattlesborough M.P.
                Sir Walter Leveson of Lilleshall and Trentham, Staffs. M.P.
                Charles Walcot of Walcot M.P.

Gloucestershire   Sir John Poyntz of Iron Acton M.P.
                Nicholas Poyntz [of Iron Acton?]
                William Poyntz of Iron Acton
                Giles Tracy of Toddington
                Sir John Tracy of Toddington M.P.

Note

[a] For the sources for the expedition's membership, see Adams, 'A Puritan Crusade? The Composition of the Earl of Leicester's Expedition to the Netherlands' [Ch. 9], pp. 184–6. The main source employed here is the muster list of the horse at the Hague on 10 January 1586 (P.R.O. SP 84/6/79ff, printed in E. M. Tenison, *Elizabethan England* (Leamington Spa, 1933–61), vi, 45–7). Some of the identities are still provisional. All M.P.s have been identified and knighthoods have been included even when conferred after 1585.

NOTES

a An initial version of this article was delivered at the 'Who Ruled the Midlands, 1400–1914' Conference (Keele University, 7 Nov. 1992) and 'The Higher Nobility in Britain and Europe *c.* 1000–1700' Conference (St. Andrews University, 15 May 1993). I should like to thank the Most Honourable the Marquess of Bath for permission to cite the Dudley Papers (DP) and other MSS in the collection at Longleat House; the Most Honourable the Marquess of Anglesey for permission to cite the Paget Papers and the Staffordshire Record Office (S.R.O.) for making available their photocopies; the Right Honourable the Viscount

De L'Isle for permission to cite the Penshurst Papers now deposited at the Centre for Kentish Studies (C.K.S./U1475), and the Right Honourable the Lord Montagu of Beaulieu for permission to cite the MS volume 'Orders, Papers and Commissions'. I should also like to thank the following repositories for their assistance: the Archivo General de Simancas (A.G.S.), the Bibliothèque Nationale (B.N.), the Birmingham Reference Library (B.R.L.), the Bodleian Library (BD.L.), the British Library (B.L.), Christ Church Library (C.C.L.), the College of Arms (C.A.), the Coventry Record Office (C.R.O.), the Cambridge University Library (C.U.L.), the Folger Shakespeare Library (F.S.L.), the Gloucestershire Record Office (G.R.O.), the Henry E. Huntington Library (H.E.H.L.), the Hereford and Worcester Record Office (H.W.R.O.), Lambeth Palace Library (L.P.L.), Magdalene College Library (M.C.L.), the National Library of Wales (N.L.W.), the Pierpont Morgan Library (P.M.L.), the Public Record Office (P.R.O.), the Shakespeare's Birthplace Trust Record Office (S.B.T.R.O.), the Warwickshire County Record Office (W.C.R.O.), and Worcester Cathedral Library (W.C.L.). My research has been made possible by generous grants from the British Academy, the Carnegie Trust for the Universities of Scotland and the Wolfson Trust. To avoid unnecessary repetition of biographical information, members of parliament are indicated (M.P.) at the first reference and in the appendices; personal details are to be found in P. W. Hasler (ed.), *The House of Commons 1558–1603* (1981), supplemented by Adams, 'The Dudley Clientele in the House of Commons, 1559–1586' [Ch. 10]. In the spelling of surnames, the usage of *The House of Commons* has been followed with the exception of the vexed issue of Sir John Huband or Hubaud, where Hubaud has been preferred on the advice of the archivist of the S.B.T.R.O., Mr. Robert Bearman.

1 T. Kemp (ed.), *The Black Book of Warwick* (Warwick, [1889]). The account of Leicester's visit and Fisher's interview is found on pp. 26–51. Comparison of Kemp's text of the interview with the original (W.C.R.O. PG 3381) reveals only one error of significance; where Kemp (p. 48) quotes Leicester as saying 'But I doo greve that every man is only carefull for himself', he has misread as 'grieve' the abbreviation of 'perceive'. Leicester's earlier visit took place during the progress of 1566.

2 C. Carpenter, *Locality and Polity: A Study of Warwickshire Landed Society, 1401–1499* (Cambridge, 1992). A. L. Hughes, *Politics, Society and Civil War in Warwickshire, 1620–1660* (Cambridge, 1987). I have benefited greatly from both.

3 See Figure 15.1, Leicester's Permanent Estate.

4 These interests can be summarised briefly. In Oxfordshire, Leicester leased the manor of Langley and Cornbury Forest in 1583 (see above, p. 324). In Northamptonshire he was steward of the honour of Grafton from 1571. In Leicestershire he held only the manor of Burton Lazars (the site and lands of the former hospital). In Cheshire he held no lands but was chamberlain of the county palatine. He received three manors in Herefordshire (Snowshill, Clifford and Ewias Lacy) in the grants of 1563 and 1566 (see above, pp. 321, 323), but all were sold off by 1567.

5 S. Adams, 'The Papers of Robert Dudley, Earl of Leicester', 'I. The Browne-Evelyn Collection', 'II. The Atye-Cotton Collection', 'III. The Countess of Leicester's Collection', *Archives*, xx (1992), pp. 63–85; xx (1993), pp. 131–44; xxii (1996), pp. 1–26 (hereafter 'Leic. Pap. I–III'). The Longleat and Penshurst collections are discussed in Pt. III. Mention should be made here of two MS volumes of particular importance, which survive in two copies, one in each of these collections: 'A General View of the Evidences' (hereafter G.V.E.), a schedule of Leicester's deeds and other muniments of title (Longleat, DP XX and C.K.S., U1475/E91, future reference here will be to the

Longleat copy, because the Penshurst is unfoliated), and the 'Brevis Abstract et collectio Redd. et Reven. prenobilis Robt. Comt. Lecestrie' (hereafter B.A.), a summary valor of his estates (Longleat, DP III, fos. 69–80, and C.K.S., U1475/E90, calendared in *Historical Manuscripts Commission, Report on the Manuscripts of Lord De L'Isle and Dudley*, i (1926), pp. 301–2; future reference here will also be made to the Longleat copy, because, although the Penshurst is the better known, it is missing the leaf containing most of the Warwickshire entries). Both are discussed at some length in 'Leic. Pap. III', where it is argued that they were compiled immediately before or after his death.

6 The accusation features in the interrogatories issued by Dudley in the Chancery case of 1590, discussed above, p. 342, according to which the court rolls of Balsall were said to have been deposited in the Kenilworth evidence house. Depositions in answer were taken from four of the officers of Kenilworth and twelve tenants (P.R.O., C21/ Eliz I/D/5/2), which provide invaluable information about the Castle at the time of Leicester's death.

7 There are some Kenilworth deeds at Longleat (MSS 4611, 4669–73, 46760), and fragments of correspondence from the Kenilworth staff. The 'Game Book' of 1568–78 is now in the Penshurst Papers (C.K.S., U1475/E93, hereafter K.G.B., discussed below, n. 178).

8 The Knowle manorial rolls are found in W.C.R.O., CR1886 [Warwick Castle deposit], the Balsall rolls in CR112 [Lady Katherine Leveson's Hospital deposit], the Honiley rolls in S.B.T.R.O., DR18 [Leigh of Stoneleigh deposit] and B.R.L., MSS 437901–2, and the Long Itchington papers in W.C.R.O., CR136 [Newdegate of Arbury deposit].

9 The Duchy of Lancaster records [e.g. the receivers' accounts and the register, P.R.O. DL 29/464/7603 and DL 42/23] cease at the grant to Leicester in 1563; the later collection of Kenilworth muniments (W.C.R.O., CR 311 [Hyde-Villiers deposit]) begins at the Restoration. The G.V.E. provides an invaluable guide to what has disappeared.

10 Henry Archer is said to have seen Warwick Castle muniments circulating in London in the reign of James I (information kindly supplied by Mr G. M. D. Booth of the W.C.R.O.). The main exception is the survey of the lordship of Warwick of 1576 (W.C.R.O., CR 1886/Cup 4/8), discussed below.

11 The confiscation of Northumberland's papers is noted in B. L. Beer, *Northumberland: The Political Career of John Dudley, Earl of Warwick and Duke of Northumberland* (Kent State Univ., Ohio, 1973), p. 172. Entries in the G.V.E. and survivals at Longleat suggest that some items came into Leicester's possession; if there was an extensive restitution the majority would have gone to Warwick in the first instance.

12 The Bagot correspondence is now F.S.L., MS La. The Ferrers of Tamworth correspondence was dispersed in the nineteenth century. The largest single group is found in B.L., Stowe MS 150, but individual letters from Leicester to Humphrey Ferrers can now be found in the P.M.L., the H.E.H.L. and the Lichfield Joint Record Office.

13 See the discussion of the Staunton of Longbridge collection in 'Leic. Pap. I', p. 77. The Digby correspondence is referred to in a note on the collection in the *Birmingham Weekly Post* for 8 May 1886, filed in the B.R.L.'s volume of cuttings on the Staunton Collection, p. 46. Only a few muniments can be found in the B.R.L., Wingfield Digby MSS. Some MSS of Leicester's were lost on this occasion, but they are not of direct relevance to this essay.

14 All that is known of Leicester's birth is the day (24 June), whether in 1532 or 1533 is still disputed. Derek Wilson, *Sweet Robin: A Biography of Robert Dudley, Earl of Leicester 1533–1588* (1981), p. 10, suggests it was at Ely Place, but not much is known of the future Duke of Northumberland's movements in those years.

15 She was, however, related to several West Midlands families later prominent in the Dudley clientele, see above, p. 331.

16 *The Baronage of England* (1675), ii, p. 214. Dugdale himself supported the Sutton on Trent descent.

17 For a general discussion, see L. Stone, *The Crisis of the Aristocracy, 1558–1641* (Oxford, 1979 ed.), pp. 23–7, and Felicity Heal and Clive Holmes, *The Gentry in England and Wales, 1500–1700* (Oxford, 1994), pp. 34–7, and for Leicester himself, R. C. McCoy, *The Rites of Knighthood: The Literature and Politics of Elizabethan Chivalry* (Berkeley, Ca., 1989), p. 37, and H. R. Woudhuysen, 'Leicester's Literary Patronage: A Study of the English Court 1578–1582' (Oxford Univ. D.Phil. thesis, 1981), p. 259.

18 T. Harwood (ed.), *A Survey of Staffordshire containing the Antiquities of that County by Sampson Erdeswick Esq.* (1844), pp. 332–9. For Erdeswick himself, see M. W. Greenslade, *The Staffordshire Historians* (Collections for Hist. of Staffs., 4th, ser. 11, 1982), ch. 3. I am grateful to Dr Richard Cust for bringing both these works to my attention.

19 The Cheshire visitation is now C.A., MS M.J.D. 14 (Visitation of Cheshire 1580 by William Flower, Norrey, with Robert Glover, Somerset, as Marshall), see p. 56 for Glover's work on Malpas. The Staffordshire visitation has been published: H. S. Grazebrook (ed.), *The Visitation of Staffordshire by Robert Glover Marshall to William Flower, Norrey, Anno Dom. 1583* (1883). See p. 9 for Erdeswick's appearance. He and Glover were in correspondence by 1586, Greenslade, *Staffordshire Historians*, p. 25.

20 D. C. Peck (ed.), *Leicester's Commonwealth. The Copy of a Letter written by a Master of Art of Cambridge (1584) with related documents* (Athens, Ohio, 1985), pp. 80, 193. The editor notes (p. 249) the 'extremely minor part' the disparagement of Leicester's ancestors plays in this work. The implication in Wilson, *Sweet Robin*, 1, that the 'John Dudley the carpenter' story originated in *Leicester's Commonwealth* is wrong. The only contemporary source I have discovered is Erdeswick, but see below, n. 50.

21 K. Duncan-Jones and J. A. van Dorsten (eds), *Miscellaneous Prose of Sir Philip Sidney* (Oxford, 1973), pp. 134–9.

22 W. Camden, *Annales* (1625 ed.), p. 121. Camden's use of *Leicester's Commonwealth* is discussed in Adams, 'Favourites and Factions at the Elizabethan Court' [Ch. 3], pp. 53–6. For Erdeswick's relations with Camden, see *Survey of Staffs*, p. 342, and Greenslade, *Staffordshire Historians*, p. 26.

23 Sir R. Naunton, *Fragmenta Regalia or Observations on Queen Elizabeth, Her Times and Favorites*, ed. J. S. Cerovski (Washington D.C., 1985), p. 49. T. Fuller, *The History of the Worthies of England*, ed. P. A. Nuttall (1840), iii, p. 132. Fuller garbles Erdeswick completely, first citing him as an authority for Edmund Dudley's noble descent, and then assigning the carpenter story a general currency.

24 Cf. *The Antiquities of Warwickshire* (1731 ed.), i. pp. 419–20, and *Baronage*, ii, p. 216. Dugdale's reversal of his earlier opinion is noted in H. S. Grazebrook, 'The Barons of Dudley', *Williarn Salt Arch. Soc.: Collections for the Hist. of Staffs.*, ix, pt. ii (1888),

pp. 73–4. Dugdale also claimed to have seen the pedigree that Northumberland amended, then in the possession of John Rous, see *Antiquities, loc. cit.*

25 Grazebrook, 'Barons of Dudley', pp. 74–7. D. M. Brodie, 'Edmund Dudley: Minister of Henry VII', *Trans. of the Royal Hist. Soc.*, 4th Ser. XV (1932), pp. 134–5.

26 See Grazebrook, 'Barons of Dudley', pp. 6–7 *et seq.* Dugdale (*Baronage*, ii, p. 214) noted that the dispute was solely about Sir Richard Sutton's descent.

27 See the discussion in G. E. Cockayne, *The Complete Peerage of England* (1910–59), viii, esp. pp. 61–8. One of the issues in dispute, whether it was a barony by tenure of the manor of Kingston Lisle (Berks.), is not relevant here. The accounts of the Lisle descent in the three recent biographies of Leicester, Wilson, *Sweet Robin*, A. Kendall, *Robert Dudley, Earl of Leicester* (1980) and A. Haynes, *The White Bear: The Elizabethan Earl of Leicester* (1987), contain numerous errors. In 1595 Richard St. George, Clarencieux King of Arms, compiled a survey of the evidence for Sir Robert Sidney to support his claim to the viscountcy (C.K.S., U1475/F19). This was later employed in the claim of Sir John Shelley Sidney to the viscountcy in the 1820s, a copy of which can be found in W.C.R.O., HR 40.

28 The *locus classicus* for this dispute is John Smyth of Nibley, 'The Lives of the Berkeleys' in *The Berkeley Manuscripts*, ed. J. Maclean (Gloucester, 1883–85), vols i–ii, upon which J. H. Cooke, 'The Great Berkeley Law-Suit of the 15th and 16th Centuries. A Chapter of Gloucestershire History', *Trans. of the Bristol and Gloucs. Arch. Soc.*, iii (1878–79), pp. 305–24, is largely based. For the earlier period, see now A. Sinclair, 'The Great Berkeley Law-Suit Revisited 1417–39', *Southern Hist.*, ix (1987), pp. 34–50.

29 Two of the manors that Warwick retained in this settlement (Wotton-under-Edge and Simondshall) were the initial target of Leicester's revival of the suit in 1572–73.

30 Carpenter, *Locality and Polity*, pp. 439–47. M. A. Hicks, 'Descent, Partition and Extinction: the "Warwick Inheritance"', *Bull. of the Inst. of Hist. Res.*, lii (1979), pp. 116–28, and 'The Beauchamp Trust, 1439–87', *ibid.*, liv (1981), pp. 135–49, esp. p. 138. Lord Berkeley did not regain the manors in question until 1473, Cooke, 'Berkeley Law-Suit', p. 317.

31 S. J. Gunn, *Charles Brandon, Duke of Suffolk 1484–1545* (Oxford, 1988), pp. 20–1, 28–9. See also Helen Miller, *Henry VIII and the English Nobility* (Oxford, 1986), p. 14.

32 Miller, *Henry VIII and the Nobility*, pp. 18, 32–3. J. Gardner *et al.* (eds), *Letters & Papers . . . Henry VIII* (1864–1932), xvii, p. 72. Beer's argument that the viscountcy should have descended to Dudley from his mother by right (*Northumberland*, 9) overlooks the distinction between the barony and the viscountcy (see p. 318 below), which had been granted to Plantagenet and his heirs male. However, there has been a debate whether the letters patent limited the descent of the viscountcy to Plantagenet's heirs male by Elizabeth Dudley or to Elizabeth Dudley's heirs male in general, see Cockayne, *Complete Peerage*, viii, pp. 64–5.

33 C.A., Muniment Room, Roll 61/5.

34 H.E.H.L., MS HM 160, *Heroica Eulogia Gulielmi Bowyeri Regine Maiestatis archivorum infra Turrem Londinensem Custodis ad Illustrissimum Robertum Comitem Leigrescestrensem.* There is an eighteenth-century description of this MS in BD.L., MS Rawlinson D 378, fos. 282–302. Bowyer may have made more than one of these collections; on 11 April 1567 the Marquess of Winchester informed Sir William Cecil that he had

just shown Leicester a book Bowyer had made for him 'declaring my armes and petegree wch I think be well doon . . . whereof will grow a great Reformacion among the heraulds that maketh ther books at adventure and not by the records' (P.R.O., SP 12/42/101).

35 C.A., Muniment Room, Roll 13/1. The dating is derived from the internal references: Charles, Lord Howard of Effingham, had succeeded his father and the 1st Earl of Essex is still alive. It contains a cartouche listing the evidences, which is copied in BD.L., MS Rawlinson B. 283, fo. 116, with the note that the original was then (June 1591) in the possession of the countess of Warwick. The descriptions it gives of the children of the Duke of Northumberland suggest that it (or a copy) may have been the 'Stemmate apud Penshurst' that Arthur Collins employed in *Letters and Memorials of State . . . written and collected by Sir Henry Sidney* (1746), i, pp. 31–2 (hereafter *Sidney Papers*).

36 The Cooke pedigree is presently in the Library at Longleat House; it is the one referred to in McCoy, *Rites of Knighthood*, variously as MS 249 and 149b.

37 In the Longleat pedigree Cooke refers to the 'monny and sondry very auntient evidences which are also remaining with the Erle of Leicestre for whom chiefly this book was drawn and made by me the said Clarencieux'. The cartouche listing the sources on C.A., Roll 13/1, includes pedigrees of the Earls of Shrewsbury and Warwick in Leicester's possession. Cooke also took notes from the 'the Book of the Abbey of Kenilworth' in 1579 (C.A., MS L 7, fos. 72v–3), which was lent to him by Mr. Morley of the Exchequer. This was John Morley (M.P.), who had close financial associations with Leicester in the 1580s, and who leased the site of Kenilworth Abbey from the crown in 1572 (Longleat, MS 4674); for the fate of this lease, see p. 324 below and n. 109. The 'Red Book of Kenilworth' is listed in the G.V.E. (fo. 30v.), but no evidence of Leicester's possession can be found in the original, now B.L., Addit. MS 47677.

38 C.A., MS M 1bis, fos. 18–24, appears to be a draft or abstract by Cooke of the Longleat pedigree. Both BD.L., MS Rawlinson D 807, fo. 19, an incomplete Beauchamp and Talbot pedigree (dated 1574), and C.A., MS L 9bis, pt. ii, Cooke's study of common ancestors, have similarities to Roll 13/1.

39 B.L. Harleian MS 6182, 'Dudleici Generis ut Nobilissimi ita et Antiquissimi origines et prolongationes'. This book was later owned by Peter le Neve who removed some of the pedigrees. The other Glover descents can be found in C.A., MS L 9bis, pt. i, fo. 43–v; B.L., Harleian MSS 807, fos. 17–20; and 1160, pt. ii, fos. 51v–53.

40 The professional abilities of the two are compared in A. R. Wagner, *English Genealogy* (Oxford, 1960), pp. 314–16. For Leicester's support of Glover, see his letter to Shrewsbury, 19 June 1580, on the eve of the Cheshire visitation, Longleat, Original [Talbot] Letters, i, fo. 13. Glover dedicated to him a MS collection of European dynastic disputes in January 1581/2 (C.A., Vincent MS 76).

41 These include a reference to the death of Lord Henry Dudley at St. Quentin in 1557. It is tempting to see these notes as the origins of Glover's observation to Erdeswick.

42 H.E.H.L., MS HM 160, fos. 10v–12v. It is not clear what connection can be drawn with Leicester's later appointment as Lord Steward of the Household in 1587.

43 C.A. MSS L 9bis, pt. ii, and L 15, fos. 80–90, go back only to the 1st Lord Dudley. C. A., MS L 15, fos. 66–8 (possibly a draft of Roll 13/1) stops at Sir Richard Sutton. Only C.A., MS M 1bis, fos. 18–24, goes back to Lord Sutton of Holderness. This also

traces the descent of the Earls of Warwick from Guy, 'who lyved in the year of our Lord God 924'. Another collection of descents, dated 1642 (B.L., Harleian MS 6071, fo. 178v), also claims that Sir Richard Sutton was descended of Seyrus, Lord Sutton of Holderness.

44 B.L., Harleian MS 6182, fo. 2. Note that Glover does not claim the Worksop theory to be his own. This genealogy was employed by Grazebrook, see 'Barons of Dudley', p. 46.

45 C.A., MS L 9bis, pt. ii, fo. 43–v. See also B.L., Harleian MS 1160, pt. ii, fos. 52v–3, a collection of descents said to be based on an original by Glover.

46 Athelstane Dodo is named as the first Lord Dudley (at the Conquest) in B.L., Harleian MS 1160, fo. 52v, and Harleian MS 6071, fo. 178v. It is interesting that Erdeswick did not attribute the building of Dudley Castle to Dudd (*Survey*, p. 336) though Camden did (Grazebrook, 'Barons of Dudley', p. 2).

47 Glover claims that Serus was created Lord Sutton of Holderness by William Rufus (C.A., MS L 9bis, fo. 43v), while Cooke describes him as living 'in the conquest time' (Longleat pedigree, p. 5).

48 F. J. Furnivall (ed.), *Robert Laneham's Letter* (1907), p. 3. W. R. Orwen, 'Spenser's "Stemmata Dudleiana"', *Notes and Queries*, cxc (1946), pp. 9–11, suggests that this lost (or never completed) work may have been influenced by the heraldic debate. However, the only reference I can find to the Saxon descent in the work he proposes as Spenser's immediate source, Gabriel Harvey's *Gratulationem Valdinensem Libri Quattuor* (1578), is the epigram on Warwick in book ii, p. 12, but see also n. 88 below. Heal and Holmes, *Gentry*, p. 36, note that the 'alleging of a pre-Conquest origin for their families' was fashionable among the Caroline elite.

49 See, in general, B. Coward, 'Disputed Inheritances: Some Difficulties of the Nobility in the Late Sixteenth and Early Seventeenth Centuries', *Bull. of the Inst. of Hist. Res.*, xliv (1971), pp. 194–215, esp. pp. 198–9.

50 Sidney's sensitivity on this issue in the 'Defence of Leicester' is worth noting. His defence of Edmund Dudley's descent definitely suggests that there was some contemporary disparagement.

51 Thus St. George (C.K.S., U1475/F19), according to whom the original barony by writ was extinguished by the death of the last Warenne Lord Lisle. The barony created for John Talbot in 1444 could descend by heirs general, but not the viscountcy of 1452.

52 For sources see my essay, 'The Patronage of the Crown in Elizabethan Politics; the 1590s in Perspective' [Ch. 4], p. 73. Other examples can undoubtedly be found.

53 The G.V.E., fo. 16v, lists a licence for Northumberland to enter his mother's lands, but dated 25 November 38 Henry VIII (1546). Northumberland's estate is surveyed in the appendix to Beer, *Northumberland*.

54 Drayton Bassett appears to have descended with the Lisle barony, Erdeswicke, *Survey of Staffs*, p. 419n (Erdeswick himself, pp. 418–19, is wildly out). Edmund Dudley was appointed steward for the crown in May 1506 (presumably during the minority of Elizabeth, Lady Lisle), *Calender of the Patent Rolls, Henry VII* (1914–16), ii, p. 464. It was in Northumberland's possession by 1532, *Letters and Papers Henry VIII*, v. p. 676, and as early as 1531 he was referred to as an interested party in the fate of the Berkeley lands, *State papers published under the authority of his majesty's commission*, i (1830), p. 381.

55 For the mortgage of Dudley Castle, see *Letters and Papers Henry VIII*, v, p. 719; vi, p. 211. For the sale of Drayton Bassett, *ibid.*, xiii (i), pp. 545–6; and for the duchess's jointure, B.R.L., Hagley Hall MS 351609, on which see also below, n. 64.

56 See the discussion of Northumberland's assumptions in Cockayne, *Complete Peerage*, iv, 481; viii, 65; ix, p. 723. The lordship of Malpas was held by Lords Dudley to the reign of Henry VIII, see Visitation of Cheshire, 56. When appointed steward to the dean and chapter of Worcester in 1546 John Dudley was styled Viscount Lisle, Baron of Malpas and Somery, Lord Baset and Tyas, W.C.L., Dean and Chapter Register A (i), fo. 93v.

57 H. Miller, 'Henry VIII's Unwritten will', in E. W. Ives *et al.* (eds), *Wealth and Power in Tudor England* (London, 1978), p. 96.

58 P.R.O., SP 11/1/104, to Paget, 24 March 1547. Cf. Hicks, 'Beauchamp Trust', pp. 146–7.

59 *Cal. Pat. Rolls. Edward VI* (1924–29), i, pp. 170–1, 252. According to a valor of 18 Henry VIII (P.R.O., SC 12/16/47), all were part of 'Warwick's lands', but Claverdon had not been part of the Beauchamp estate.

60 Hist. MSS Comm., *Report on the MSS of the Duke of Rutland*, i (1888), p. 48.

61 Beer, *Northumberland*, p. 181.

62 *Ibid.*, p. 180. N.L.W., Chirk Castle MS F 13310, a fragment of an undated survey of Kenilworth Castle refers to the stable, tiltyard and gatehouse, 'which my lordes grace your fader made'. Dugdale, *Antiquities*, i, p. 249, assigned them to Leicester.

63 References to the settlement, dated variously 8 and 28 June 1550, can be found in *Cal. Pat. Rolls, Philip and Mary* (1937–39), iii, p. 303, and *Cal. Pat. Rolls, 1563–66* (1961), p. 503. It was agreed between Northumberland and Somerset and involved the devising on trustees of lands of Northumberland's to be held in survivorship by John Dudley and his wife, with the remainder to their heirs male. Warwick was joint-lord lieutenant of Warwickshire with his father in 1552, and appointed to a number of county commissions.

64 For the Hales Owen estate, see Adams, 'The Dudley Clientèle, 1553–1563' [Ch. 8], pp. 159–60. The Hagley Hall MSS (B.R.L.) are an invaluable source for the Dudley tenure of these lands. The duchess's jointure lands of 1546 included a life interest in Drayton Bassett and an estate of inheritance in Hales Owen (B.R.L., Hagley Hall MS 351609, inspeximus of Dec. 1553); her jointure rights were the subject of considerable negotiation with Mary's government, and a final settlement of 19 June 1554 (*Cal. Pat. Rolls, Philip and Mary*, i., pp. 128–9) gave her a life interest in the manors of Claverdon, Shenston (Staffs.), Henley in Arden and Kibworth Beauchamp (Leics.) *inter alia*.

65 The countess's jointure was established in the settlement of 1550, but other lands appear to have been added. The jointure included the old Beauchamp manor of Langley (Oxon.) (see p. 324), Malvern Chase (see p. 361, n. 110), Cheylesmore Park, Coventry (see p. 336), the monastery of Combe, and possibly the manor of Balsall (see p. 323). Following her husband's attainder in 1553 the reversions were held by the crown.

66 *Cal. Pat. Rolls, Philip and Mary*, ii, pp. 22–3. These lands were regranted on 31 Dec. 1555, on the eve of Dudley's marriage to Katherine Bridges; Budbrooke was to be held by Dudley, his wife and their heirs male, and Balsall by Dudley and his heirs male, *ibid.*, iii, p. 37. There was an old association between the Lords Dudley and Mary; the

2nd Baron had been her chamberlain in 1525–26 (BD.L., MS Rawlinson B 146, fo. 222).

67 See S.B.T.R.O., DR 18/3/6/1–3 for Catherine Parr; W.C.R.O., CR112/BA306/1–2, for 1551; and *Cal. Pat. Rolls Edward VI*, v. pp. 242–3, for the grant to Warwick.

68 *Cal. Pat. Rolls, Philip and Mary*, iv, p. 315.

69 Noted by St George (C.K.S., U1475/F19). I overlooked this important point in Ch. 8 above, see p. 160.

70 *Ibid.*, p. 163.

71 In Ch. 8 above, p. 000, I stated erroneously that Ambrose Dudley was created Viscount Lisle, but he only received the barony. St George (C.K.S., U1475/F19) noted that as this creation was in tail male, Robert Sidney had no claim of right to the barony.

72 Ch. 8 above, pp. 163–4.

73 *Cal. Pat. Rolls, 1558–60* (1939), p. 86. Kibworth Beauchamp, an old Beauchamp manor, had been held by the Lords Lisle (Hicks, 'Beauchamp Trust', p. 146) and then Northumberland and his wife. Ambrose Dudley was granted it for service as chief pantler at the coronation. For the latter two grants, *Cal. Pat. Rolls, 1560–63* (1948), pp. 291–3, *Cal Pat. Rolls, 1563–66*, pp. 59–62. In the 1564 grant, the only former Beauchamp manor was Shenston, the others were ex-monastic. The three grants were all in tail male, with, the remainder of the first two to his brother.

74 For Watton, see Ch. 8 above, p. 163; for the 1561 grant, *Cal Pat. Rolls, 1560–63*, pp. 189–91. These lands were granted in fee simple. Among Leicester's papers is a valor of Northumberland's former lands in the possession of the crown (including some in the countess of Warwick's jointure) dated from internal evidence between 1560 and 1564 (C.C.L., Evelyn MS 16, art. 2).

75 Most reverted to the crown in the exchange of 1566, see p. 323 above.

76 Longleat, DP I, fos. 84, 108, 171, Lord Dudley to Lord Robert, [Aug?, 1559], 30 Jan. 1560, 25 Nov. 1560.

77 The initial negotiations for Sir Robert Throckmorton's stewardships were conducted by Ralph Sheldon and John Fisher (Longleat, DP I, fo. 154, Fisher to Dudley, 18 Mar. 1560). For the sale, see DP, Box 2, art. 9. Thereafter Leicester appears to have given the offices to Warwick.

78 L.P.L., MS 3206 [Talbot P], fo. 409, to Shrewsbury, 27 Dec. 1561. The letters patent refer to restoring the titles to the ancient family in Ambrose Dudley as legitimate descendant of the former Earls of Warwick. Robert Dudley possessed a copy, M.C.L., Pepys MSS, Letters of State, i, p. 29ff.

79 B.L., Addit. MS 35831, fo. 32, R. Jones to Sir Nicholas Throckmorton, 25 May 1562.

80 The 1582 will is now Longleat, DP Box III, art. 56, see rot. 2. The original of the 1587 will is W.C.R.O., CRI600/LH [Leicester's Hospital deposit] 4.

81 W.C.R.O., CRI600/LH 1.

82 Apart from the pedigrees referred to in n. 37 above, he also possessed the receiver's account of the earldom of Warwick for 1427–28, see 'Leic. Pap. III', n. 73. His recital of the Lisle pedigree is found in his letter to Shrewsbury of 10 Dec. 1572, L.P.L., MS 3197 [Talbot F], fo. 73.

83 *Cal. Pat. Rolls, 1560–63*, pp. 534–43. Most, including Kenilworth, Denbigh and Chirk, were granted in fee simple, Cleobury Mortimer was granted in fee tail, and others in East Greenwich tenure. According to a draft of the grant dated 30 May (B.L., Landsdowne, 45, fos. 188–9), a number of the manors of 1561 were to be exchanged for them, but this was not done.

84 For my doubts about the account of his creation derived from Sir James Melville, see Adams, 'The Release of Lord Darnley and the Failure of the Amity', in M. Lynch (ed.), *Mary Stewart: Queen in Three Kingdoms* (Oxford, 1988), 126, n. 22. The purpose of the grant of the manor of Kenilworth is made explicit in a note by Cecil on a valor of the manor dated Oct. 1564 (P.R.O., SP 12/35/34).

85 Cockayne, *Complete Peerage*, vii, 549, notes 'his connection with Leicestershire is not clear'.

86 P.R.O., C66/1007/19–20. The phrasing of Leicester's descent from the Earls of Warwick is almost identical to that used in his brother's letters patent.

87 D. Crouch, *The Beaumont Twins: The Roots and Branches of Power in the Twelfth Century* (Cambridge, 1986), p. 6. I am very grateful to Professor Crouch for bringing this relationship to my attention.

88 The Somerys had inherited the lordship of Dudley from a marriage in the reign of Henry II between John de Somery and Hawyse, sister and heir of Gervase Pagenal, lord of Dudley, whose wife was the daughter of Robert de Beaumont, the 2nd Earl of Leicester. Although the Beaumont Earls are noted by Cooke in C.A., Roll 13/1 and MS M 1bis, fo. 18, and by Glover in B.L., Harleian MS 6182, fo. 27, the only contemporary work I have found that draws any connection between the Dudley brothers and the Beaumont brothers is the poem by Edward Grant in Harvey's *Gratulationem Valdinensem*, book 2, p. 14.

89 *Calendar of State Papers, Spanish, 1558–67* (1892), p. 190, a despatch from the Bishop of Aquila of 25 Oct. 1562. A valor of the honor of Leicester was compiled in 1562 (P.R.O., SP 12/26/100–1); it is not clear whether it is of any relevance.

90 However, the only contemporary comparison to Mortimer that I have found is in Thomas Rogers, *Leicester's Ghost*, ed. F. B. Williams (Chicago, 1972), p. 19.

91 There are two versions of Leicester's offer: P.R.O., SP 12/35/35, for Rudfen, Balsall and Budbrooke, and SP 12/35/37, for Rudfen alone. For the grant of Rudfen, see *Cal. Pat. Rolls. 1563–66*, p. 312.

92 *Cal. Pat. Rolls, 1563–66*, pp. 457–66. Most of these lands were ex-monastic (Bretferton and the Hamptons had formerly belonged to Evesham Abbey). The Hamptons were to be held in tail male, the remainder in fee simple or East Greenwich tenure. R. W. Hoyle, *The Estates of the English Crown 1558–1640* (Cambridge, 1992), p. 14, n. 38, notes that grants in fee simple rather than tail male would make the lands easier to sell on; this was certainly the intention with many of the manors of this grant and those of 1574 (see p. 327).

93 The manorial court was held in Lord Dudley's name in 1556 and thereafter until he sold it, W.C.R.O., CR 895 [Dormer of Grove Park deposit]/Bundles 1 and 7 [Budbrooke Deeds and Court Rolls]. Grove Park and other parts of the manor were, however, leased to Leicester's officers and friends, initially Thomas Blount (who had obtained his lease from Northumberland) and later Thomas Butler and William Baynham.

94 Some confirmation of her tenure is found in two copies of the court roll of 14 Apr. 1567, which, although they do not name the lord, are signed by Edward Aglionby

(M.P.), the recorder of Warwick and an established Dudley follower, presumably as steward (S.B.T.R.O., DR18/30/4/6–7). The countess's second husband, Sir Edward Unton (M.P.), certainly had an interest in the manor when Lord Dudley sold it to Leicester in 1572 (G.V.E., fos. 33–v).

95 A possible explanation is supplied by the grant by the crown in July 1558 of an annuity of £50 to Lord Dudley during the life of the countess of Warwick (*Cal Pat. Rolls, Philip and Mary*, iv, p. 400). The countess had been granted an annuity of £100 in May 1554 (*ibid.*, i, p. 308); had she exchanged half of it for a life interest in Balsall?

96 For Northumberland's visit, see W.C.R.O., CR1618/WA1/1 [Warwick Borough Accounts, 1548–69], fo. 37v. For Dudley's coat and conduct money, see Ch. 8 above, p. 161, n. 79; he recruited some of his retinue from Hales Owen, and may have gone there to do so.

97 P.R.O., SP 12/39/125, to Cecil, 20 Mar. 1566, 'since my coming into the country, I have not at all seen my house or anything I have thereabout . . . the only cause was my sister, with whom I tarried continually, because I would do her all the comfort I could for the time'.

98 Not 1565, as stated in several otherwise reputable sources (see below, n. 197).

99 The queen's visit in 1568 is an obscure episode, see M. H. Cole, 'The Royal Travel: Elizabethan progresses and their Role in Government' (Univ. of Virginia Ph.D. thesis, 1985), p. 174, n. 49. However, the K.G.B. (fo. [1]) records both her and Leicester hunting there in 1568, and the visit, 'unlooked for', is noted in B.L., Harleian MS 6358 [Humfrey Wanley's collections of Coventry History], fo. 36, and in the Warwick borough accounts, W.C.R.O., CR1618/WA1/1, fo. 93. It would appear to have been in mid to late August; Sir Henry Sidney, writing to Leicester from Kenilworth on the 8th, refers to some bream he had caught, 'to be kept for you, till your lordship's coming', *Sidney Papers*, i, p. 34.

100 For 1570, see his letters to Elizabeth of 10 and 16 Jan., P.R.O., SP 15/17/51–v, 83–v. On 13 Nov. 1573, the Earl of Morton acknowledged receipt of a letter of his from Kenilworth, B.L. Cotton MS Caligula C III, fo. 468; Leicester's letter to Shrewsbury from Kenilworth, dated only 10 Oct. (P.M.L., Rules of England Box III, no. 29), should therefore be assigned to 1573. According to John Smyth ('Lives of the Berkeleys', ii, pp. 290–1) he also visited Wotton-under-Edge in 1573. In 1574 the royal progress went to Bristol; Leicester is recorded visiting Tewkesbury (G.R.O., Tewkesbury Borough Records, A/1/1, p. 361), and, according to Smyth (*ibid.*), Wotton-under-Edge as well. A casual reference in a letter to Walsingham of 8 Mar. 1575 (P.R.O., SP 53/10, art. 17) suggests that he had been at Kenilworth recently.

101 For 1576, see the *Black Book*, pp. 221–2; for 1577, C.R.O., A16 [Coventry Treasurers Accounts, Book of Payments, 1561–1653], p. 33, and K.G.B., fo. [12].

102 In general, H. M. Colvin et al., *The History of the King's Works*, iii, pt. 1 (1975), p. 259. Evidence that work had been undertaken before 1568 can be found in Sir Henry Sidney's comment in his letter to Leicester of 8 Aug. 1568, 'I was never more in love with an olde house, nor never newe worke could be better bestowed, then that which you have done', *Sidney Papers*, i, p. 34. The main sources for the work in progress, undoubtedly 'Leicester's Buildings', are two letters from John Butler, 18 and 25 June 1571 (Longleat, DP II, fos. 4, 9), and two from the architect William Spycer, 15 July 1571 (Longleat, Thynne Papers LVIII (Records of Building III), fo. 161) and 26 June (DP II, fo. 321), undoubtedly 1571 as well. The reference to 'your old yll lodging' in

Leicester to Elizabeth, 16 Jan. 1570 (P.R.O., SP 15/17/83) provides a possible clue as to the motive for the construction of 'Leicester's Buildings'.

103 *Cal. Pat. Rolls, 1569–72* (1966), pp. 240, 426, 444, 460, 472. Extensive lists of the muniments relating to these conveyances can be found in the G.V.E. For Balsall, see also above, p. 323. The surviving court rolls from Leicester's period date only from 1586–88 (W.C.R.O., CR 112/BA 307/1–3). Long Itchington had recently been mortgaged to Throckmorton by John Odingsells, who still retained an interest, Dugdale, *Antiquities*, i, p. 344.

104 Hampton in Arden, a former Montford manor, was granted in fee tail, Knowle, a former Westminster Abbey manor, in fee simple, *Cal. Pat. Rolls, 1572–75* (1973), pp. 16–17. In the same letters patent the Worcestershire Hamptons were re-granted in fee simple. The Berkeley manors of Wotton-under-Edge and Simondshall were originally regained by the crown and then granted to Leicester and Warwick jointly on 25 July 1573, *ibid.*, p. 104. The law suit is discussed on, pp. 339–40.

105 Knowle and Balsall had originally been part of the manor of Hampton in Arden, see J. C. Adams, *Hampton in Arden. A Warwickshire Village* (Birmingham, n.d.), pp. 19, 27, and *V.C.H. Warwicks.*, iv, p. 83. For the function of Long Itchington, see the reference to the lands used for feeding his house in Leicester's assignment of the wardships of Margaret and Frances Wilkes, 27 Nov. 1577, Longleat, DP Box III, art. 42.

106 For 1578, see Longleat DP II, fo. 193, H. Besbeeche to Leic., 23 Oct. 1578; for 1579, B.L., Harleian MS 6992, fo. 112, Leic. to Burghley, 20 Oct.; for 1580, P.R.O., SP 12/140/46–7, Leic. to Burghley, 20 July. The records of the banquet at Coventry in 1581 are considerable, see C.R.O., A16, p. 45, and A7b [Chamberlains and Wardens Accounts, 1575–1636], pp. 59–62. See also T. Kemp (ed.), *The Book of John Fisher (1580–1588)* (Warwick [1899]), p. 71. For 1582, see the reference to Sir Thomas Throckmorton's being at Kenilworth with Leicester and Warwick on 9 Sept., O.R.O., Gloucester Borough Records, B2/1, fo. 100.

107 For 1584, see P.R.O., SP 12/170/142, Leic. to Elizabeth, 22 May, and C.R.O., A7b, p. 110. The 1585 visit is discussed in detail in *Household Accounts*. [See the introduction, p. 3, for 1583.]

108 It is just possible he was there in June 1588. In the 1590 depositions (P.R.O., C21/ElizI/D/5/2, see n. 6 above) there are several references to Leicester ordering a survey of Honiley 'not long before his death', though no specific date is given.

109 For the licence to alienate Honiley (1 April 1581), see *Cal. Pat. Rolls, 1580–82* (1986), p. 92. Many Honiley documents are listed in the G.V.E. or are to be found in S.B.T.R.O., DR 18/3/25. The addition of Honiley to Kenilworth featured in the 1590 Chancery case (P.R.O., C21/ElizI/D/5/2) and several deponents agreed that it was Leicester's expressed purpose. The site of Kenilworth Abbey had been obtained by Northumberland in 1549 (*Cal. Pat. Rolls, Edward VI*, iii, pp. 2–4), and purportedly sold to his follower Sir Andrew Flamock. John Morley leased the site from the crown in 1572 (see n. 37 above), but his lease was successfully contested by Flamock's granddaughter Katherine and her husband John Colbourne in 1573, see Longleat MS 4668, and Beer, *Northumberland*, 180. According to Dugdale (*Antiquities*, i, p. 242), Colbourne was intimidated into selling to Leicester. Leicester also made a further small purchase in Kenilworth in July 1585, S.B.T.R.O., DR18/1/500.

110 For the purchase of Ernewood, see G.V.E., fo. 28v. I have not yet been able to examine the Ernewood muniments in the Childe deposit, transferred from the B.R.L.,

to the Shropshire R.O. For the lease by the Court of Wards (10 July 1583), see Longleat MS 3283, and G.V.E., fo. 33v. On 8 July 1584 he asked Burghley for the keepership of Malvern Chase as well, 'Hit lieth not far from a lordship and a little house I have. I would be careful of the game and the rather being once my fathers and of the ancient inheritance of the earls of Warwick' (B.L., Harleian MS 6993, fo. 70).

111 The lease of the forest of Wyer (16 July 1584) is found in P.R.O., C66/1238/40–1. For the Abberley and Alton Woods purchase, see Longleat MS 3022.

112 The second tranche of the Berkeley manors, a third part of Cam, Slimbridge and Hinton, was granted to Leicester and Warwick jointly on 2 July 1585 (P.R.O., C66/1264/10). For Leicester's initiation of the third round, see Hist MSS Comm, *Rutland MSS*, i, pp. 236 and 238, Leic. to Rutland, 7 Jan., and Michael Purefey to Rutland, 29 Jan. 1588. This may be the same as the suit Smythe ('Lives', ii, p. 315) states Leicester was preparing to have the shares of the second tranche held in severalty. See also the further discussion on p. 340.

113 See Adams, 'The Composition of 1564 and the Earl of Leicester's Tenurial Reformation in the Lordship of Denbigh' [Ch. 13]. The lordship of Chirk and the Montgomeryshire lordships of Arwystli and Cyfeiliog were similarly reformed. Much effort was also expended on the notorious commission for encroachments in Snowdon Forest.

114 'The Anatomy of the Elizabethan Aristocracy', *Economic Hist. Rev.*, xviii (1948), p. 42. His source appears to be part 17 of the probate inventory (B.L., Harleian Roll D 35), the 'Rental of lands of inheritance', though my computation produces only £2,483. H.E.H.L., Ellesmere, MS 5845, 'The value of the Earl of Leicester his lands', gives £2,600. 18s.; Ellesmere MS 763, which bears the same title, and is endorsed by John, Goodman and Thomas Dudley, 20 Dec. 1588, gives £2,294. 17s. ¾d. plus £301.22d. The lands were brought into the probate jurisdiction by Leicester's attempt to settle his estate through his will, see below, p. 328.

115 The leases were separated for purposes of probate. Professor Stone assigned them a capital value of £7,314.

116 Apart from the surveys undertaken after his death and the B.A. (see above n. 5, and the following note), the other main sources are the notoriously low valuations placed by the crown at the time of the grants; the valuations made by Leicester's surveyors in the two general surveys of 1563 and 1566 (Longleat, DP XVI and XVII); and a survey made by William Baynham in 1579–81 of Kenilworth, Drayton Bassett and Cleobury Mortimer (of which two copies survive, Longleat DP XVIII and P.R.O., LR 2/185/24–97). A list of Leicester's surviving surveys can be found in 'Leic. Pap. III'.

117 This is a very rough computation based on the Longleat copy of the B.A., which values the various manors individually and contains no totals. Clear values have been used wherever indicated. To give an indication of the difficulties: Baynham valued Drayton Bassett at £422 in 1579 (P.R.O., LR 2/185/68), the B.A. at £381 minus reprises of £104, and the probate inventory included it among the leases.

118 My computation of the total of the clear valuations of the central Warwickshire estates in the B.A., fos. 73v–76, is £994 and comprises: Kenilworth lordship £52, manor of Kenilworth £71, Honiley £65, Fernhill (part of Honiley) £30, Rudfen £24, Long Itchington £235, Hampton in Arden £153, Hampton in Arden rectory £8, Napton-on-the-Hill rectory £135, and Balsall £221.

119 Longleat, DP XVII, fo. 39v–40. The sale by Sheldon, who purchased it from Warwick, is B.R.L., MS 167622. The concerns of Dudley's surveyors are revealed by their
comments on Chirk, 'at least fyve hundred tall men that hold of your Lp. both able
and redie to serve' (DP XVII, fo. 186).

120 Longleat, DP XVI, fo. 24.

121 For the licence, *Cal. Pat. Rolls. 1563–66*, p. 473. The accounts of his factor, John
Barker, are C.C.L., Eveleyn MS 257.

122 In the B.A. (fo. 71v) the ironworks are recorded as leased to Edward Blount for four
years for £1,600. Professor Stone (*Crisis of the Aristocracy*, 350) has assumed £1,600
to be the annual rent, but it is clear that it was the total over the four years. B.L.,
Harleian Roll D 35, pt. 17, values the iron works at £500 p.a. There is a reference to
an earlier lease (1576) in the G.V.E., fo. 27v. The manor itself was valued by Baynham
in 1580 at £70 p.a. (P.R.O., LR 2/185/95v); the B.A. values it at about £60.

123 Stone, *Crisis*, p. 350. It is revealing that Cleobury Mortimer and the neighbouring
lands (the Forest of Wyer, Ernewood and Bewdley) were brought under the single
stewardship of Edward Blount in 1587 (Longleat MS 4109), if not before.

124 At various times Astell Grove (part of Kenilworth lordship lying within Coventry) was
leased to John Butler, Long Itchington to William Spycer, the parsonage of Napton
on the Hill to Spycer, Thomas Underhill and Sir John Hubaud, parts of Rudfen to
Anthony Dockwra, Underhill and Henry Besbeeche, and the manor of Kenilworth to
Besbeeche. In the *post mortem* survey of Leicester's lands in Warwickshire (P.R.O., E
178/2350, 17 Aug. 1590) the herbage of Kenilworth is entered as leased to Besbeeche
and Underhill.

125 Longleat, DP II, fo. 183. Besbeeche to Leic., 23 Oct. 1578. Besbeeche observed that
£100 was accounted for by various annuities, and that during his last visit Leicester
had exhausted the receipts in hand on his own expenses.

126 Leicester's surveyors in 1563 estimated the total rental as £66, and hoped to increase
it by wood sales of £236, though it is not clear whether they meant annually (Longleat,
DP XVI, fos. 6v, 8). In 1581 Baynham gave the clear rental as only £24. 10s. (P.R.O.,
LR 2/185/36v).

127 There are a number of contemporary references to the composition: Baynham's
survey in 1581 (P.R.O., LR 2/185/37v); J. R. Dasent (ed.), *Acts of the Privy Council of
England* (N.S. 1890–1964), xxi, 441 (1591); *Leicester's Commonwealth*, pp. 118–19; and
Dugdale, *Antiquities*, i, p. 249. However, the only copy I have seen of its terms is
found in the appendix to *A Concise History and Description of Kenilworth* (Warwick,
1827), p. 37. It is dated 12 Elizabeth, but no source is given. In expanding the parklands
and chases Leicester was following the precedent of Henry VIII, see the late Henrician
survey, P.R.O., SC 12/16/22.

128 *Cal. Pat. Rolls, 1575–78*, p. 93 (30 July 1576). The only other 'improvements' are the
customal of Knowle compiled in 1574 shortly after he obtained the manor (S.B.T.R.O.,
DR98/1217), and (according to Smyth, 'Lives', ii, p. 319) the erection of a hundred for
Wotton-under-Edge.

129 The expenses are outlined in B.L., Lansdowne MS 62, fo. 127, 'A brief of the controversy by the countess of Leicester against Thomas Robinson', 31 Jan. 1590. The
payment to Paramour is found in B.L., Harleian MS 167, fos. 135–7, Thomas Smythe's
account to Leicester for the Sweet Wines Farm, 1578–80.

130   None of Leicester's central accounts for the 1570s can presently be traced.

131   *Antiquities*, i, p. 249. B.L., Cotton MS Tiberius E VIII, fos. 212–13, gives £21,000 as the capital value of the manor and £20,401 as that of the castle.

132   For the grants of 5 April and 19 July 1574, see *Cal. Pat. Rolls, 1572–75*, pp. 181–5, 270–5. Longleat, DP Box IV, arts. 73–6, are four bonds made by prospective purchasers to Leicester in advance of these grants. The mortgage of 7 Dec. 1576 is listed in G.V.E., fo. 2, but the original has not survived. Its later history is too complex to discuss here, but to repay the first instalment in 1580, Leicester sold the fee simple of Knowle and the fee simple lands of Drayton Bassett to the queen.

133   The statute for the hospital (13 Eliz., c. 17) was passed in the spring. John Fisher, then M.P. for Warwick, claims to have informed the borough about it at the time (*Black Book*, pp. 28–9); and Leicester sought John Hales's advice about the foundation in the summer, see B.L., Addit. MS 32091, fo. 249v, Hales to Leic., 28 July. On Michaelmas Day 1566, a year after the order was conferred, he and the Duke of Norfolk celebrated it together, see N. Williams, *Thomas Howard Fourth Duke* of *Norfolk* (1964), p. 100.

134   *Black Book*, p. 29. See also John Butler's letter of 18 June, Longleat, DP II, fo. 4.

135   *Black Book*, p. 38. Leicester wrote to Elizabeth on Michaelmas Day (P.R.O., SP 15/20/173), but apart from a reference to his urgent business in Warwickshire, it is chiefly concerned with the infirmity of the Marquess of Northampton, who died at The Priory shortly afterwards.

136   For the hostile comment, see the unfortunately anonymous letter, B.L., Harleian MS 7002, fos. 14–15. In 1566 Elizabeth is said to have hesitated about going to Kenilworth on the ground that Leicester would spend too much on entertainment, B.N., fonds français 1570, fo. 19, Jacob de Vulcob to Robert de La Fontaine, 6 Aug. 1566. For the 1577 invitation, see F.S.L., Xd 428 [Cavendish-Talbot Corres], fo. 125, Richard Topcliffe to the countess of Shrewsbury, 9 July 1577.

137   The reports of Mary going to Kenilworth and the fortifying are found in *Cal. State Papers Span. 1568–79*, pp. 214, 233, despatches of Guerau de Spes, 3 Dec. 1569, 30 Jan. 1570. A further reference to the fortifying is found in an anonymous letter to the countess of Shrewsbury of 31 Aug. 1570, E. Lodge, *Illustrations* of *British History* (2nd edn. 1791), i, 511. J. E. L. Clerk, 'The Buildings and Art Collections of Robert Dudley, Earl of Leicester' (Univ. of London History of Art M.A. diss., 1981), 11, disputes convincingly any defensive purpose in the rebuilding.

138   The possibility of Leicester succeeding Warwick was noted by the Bishop of Aquila at the time of Warwick's creation. A.G.S., E 815, fo. 126, to the duchess of Parma, 27 Dec. 1561.

139   See his comments in his letter to Douglas Sheffield, c. 1570–74, H.E.H.L. Ellesmere MS 253, published by C. Read, 'A Letter from Robert, Earl of Leicester to a Lady', *Huntingdon Lib. Quart.*, ix (1936), 24ff, and as reported by the witnesses at his wedding in their depositions of 13 Mar. 1581, P.R.O., SP 12/148/75–85.

140   The previously unknown date of Denbigh's birth is found in the Cooke pedigree at Longleat. Its implications I shall be discussing elsewhere.

141   Discussed in 'Leic. Pap. III'.

142 *Leicester's Commonwealth*, pp. 117–23, lists among his tyrannies the Kenilworth com-position, the Drayton Bassett affair, and the Berkeley law-suit. Dugdale adds the persecution of John Colbourne, *Antiquities*, i, p. 242. However, to some extent Dugdale was influenced by *Leicester's Commonwealth*, as was Smyth, who is explicit about it in 'Lives', ii, p. 335. In several cases, the original possessors, the Odingsells of Long Itchington and the Robinsons of Drayton Bassett, for example, had mortgaged them-selves heavily, and Leicester bought out the mortgagee. There were similar problems at Honiley, see the complaints of Thomas Hill to Leicester against his officers, 8 Aug. 1581, S.B.T.R.O., DR 18/3/25/10. In Leicester's favour, the G.V.E. reveals the great expense he went to in buying out the residual interests.

143 In 1487 William, Marquis Berkeley, had granted Berkeley Castle and its related man-ors to Henry VII and his heirs male. The crown's right having expired with Edward VI, they were restored to Henry, the 11th Lord Berkeley in Dec. 1554 (*Cal. Pat. Rolls. Philip and Mary*, ii, pp. 9–10).

144 Sir George Throckmorton and his son Sir Robert held jointly the stewardship of the bishopric of Worcester from 1529 (W.C.L., Dean and Chapter Register A7(iii), fo. 85), the preceptory of Balsall (n.d., W.C.R.O., CR1998 [Throckmorton of Coughton deposit]/Box 59/4), and from 1531 many of the Warwick lands (*ibid.*, Box 59/13). Sir Robert was granted the constableship of Warwick Castle by Mary in 1553 (*ibid.*, Box 72/14), which he held until he was bought out by Leicester in 1562. Hughes, *Politics, Society and Civil War*, p. 28, notes the consolidation of the Warwickshire gentry during the sixeenth century, and, pp. 21–6, the recent establishment of the Caroline peerage and the absence of a dominant one.

145 See Stafford's letters to Dudley, Longleat, DP I, fos. 40 (18 July 1559), and 173 (1 Dec. 1560). According to the first, his son was in Dudley's service, possibly the Richard Stafford who appears in a livery list for 1559 (Longleat, DP Box V, fo. 280, on which, see also n. 164 below). The second contains historical discussions. A. H. Anderson, 'Henry, Lord Stafford (1501–63) in local and central government', *Eng. Hist. Rev.*, lxxviii (1963), pp. 225–42, discusses the antiquarianism but supplies no other con-nection to Dudley. Dudley also obtained Stafford's licence to be absent from Parlia-ment in 1563 on grounds of ill health, though the gloss put on this by G. R. Elton, *The Parliament of England 1559–1581* (Cambridge, 1986), p. 361, is debatable.

146 Proxies are taken from the relevant lists in the *Journals of the House of Lords* (1846), i–ii. Their significance is, of course, a subject of some debate.

147 As well as the correspondence of 1559–60, see also Lord Dudley's letters of 11 Nov. 1566 (C.C.L., Evelyn MS 1, art. 4), and post 1569, Longleat, DP II, fos. 289–90. For Sir Henry Dudley, see Ch. 8 above, pp. 152, 155.

148 B.L., Addit. MS 32091, fo. 176, Lady Chandos to Dudley, [24 Aug. 1559?, cf. her letter to Cecil of that date, P.R.O., SP 12/6/24].

149 See the funeral list, B.D.L., MS Ashmole 818, fo. 38. For Leicester's relations with the 2nd Lord Chandos, see also p. 340 above.

150 Longleat, DP I, fo. 222, Berkeley to Leic., 14 Mar. 1571. Whatever his state of health, Berkeley hunted energetically at Kenilworth that summer (*ibid.*, II, fos. 34, 38, A. Dockwra to Leic., 23, 29 July 1571). Smyth ('Lives', ii, p. 292) claims that the invita-tion to hunt was a practice to win Berkeley's confidence. The K.G.B. does not record Berkeley's hunting in 1571, but does so for 1569 and 1574 (fos. [3], [5]); he and his wife

were also sent deer in 1571, 1575, 1577 and 1578 (fos. [2], [7], [13v], [16]). For the attendance at Warwick, see *Black Book*, p. 33.

151 See Ch. 8 above, p. 158. The anonymous history, B.L., Addit. MS 48023, fos. 350–69v, makes numerous critical references to Paget's influence, see e.g. fo. 360v.

152 A number of items from their correspondence in the early 1560s survive: Paget's in Longleat, DP I, fos. 42, 144, 153, and M.C.L., Pepys Letters of State, i, p. 671, and Dudley's in Paget Correspondence, Box V, arts 1, 3, 5.

153 Paget Corres., Box IV, art. 11, Leic. to Paget, 19 Dec. 1572.

154 The deterioration in relations can be traced in the extensive surviving correspondence between them in the Paget Corres.

155 I am unable to substantiate the statement in E. W. Dormer, 'Lettice Knollys, Countess of Leicester', *Berks. Arch. Jnl.*, xxxix (1935), p. 83, that Leicester obtained Essex's earldom for him.

156 See the Tamworth high stewardship dispute of 1577–78 discussed above, p. 340. A certain wariness of Leicester is also detectable in the Bagot correspondence for this period.

157 The Tamworth licence (P.R.O. C66/1307/33–4) was granted on 10 Oct. 1588, after Leicester's death, but see the reference to him on m. 34.

158 See Ch. 8 above, pp. 151, 154–5.

159 *Ibid.*, pp. 155–6 (Croft), 159 (Sir George Blount, both M.P.s). See also A. J. Perrett, 'The Blounts of Kidderminster', *Worcester Arch. Soc.*, NS xix (1942), pp. 11–13. A Mr. George Blount is found in the 1559 livery list and a second in 1567 (see n. 164 below).

160 For Blount in general, see Ch. 8 above, pp. 153–5, and for his stewardship of Hales Owen in 1556, B.R.L., Hagley Hall MSS 346869 and 346501. There is no formal reference to his office at Kenilworth, but in his letter to Leicester of 8 Aug. 1568 (*Sidney Papers*, i, p. 34), Sir Henry Sidney referred to the 'entertainment that my cousin Thomas Blount and other your servantes gave me' at Kenilworth, and the effigy on Blount's tomb in St. Mary's, Kidderminster, bears a chain of office normally associated with stewardships, see Perrett, 'Blounts', pp. 13–14. His will of 28 Nov. 1568 (P.R.O., PROB 11/51/51v) contains no reference to Leicester, but does mention his leases in Wedgenock Park and Cleobury Mortimer. In 1565 Blount was described as a servant of Warwick's as well (*Black Book*, p. 8).

161 He was appointed constable in December 1549 on the death of Sir Andrew Flamock, P.R.O., DL 42/23/47v.

162 Apart from the progress of 1566, there is no evidence of his visiting Warwickshire prior to his journey there to assemble the army against the northern rebellion in 1569. As noted above, p. 323, he joined Leicester at Kenilworth on his return from the North in January 1570. He was with Leicester in 1571, 1576, 1577 and 1582.

163 I first made this point with reference to their Welsh estates in 'Office-Holders of the Borough of Denbigh and Stewards of the Lordships of Denbighshire in the Reign of Elizabeth I' [Ch. 14], p. 296. See also Ch. 10 above, p. 197, and Ch. 8 above, p. 153. Confirmation that the same applied in Warwickshire can be found in the *Black Book*, and the 1576 survey of the lordship of Warwick. Warwick's officers will be identified in passing.

164 The membership of his household can be reconstructed to some extent from a number of livery lists (see n. 145 above), embarkation lists for the Netherlands, and funeral lists. They are published in *Household Accounts*.

165 B.L. Lansdowne MS 61, fos. 206–7, Atye to Burghley, 9 Dec. 1589.

166 Ch. 8 above, p. 154.

167 See Appendix 15.1: The Earl of Leicester's Officers. A. Central Administration.

168 See Appendix 15.1: B. Local Administration.

169 The grant of the office is B.L., Harleian Charter 83 e. 26. Shrewsbury's claim for the fees can be found in Harleian Roll D. 35, pt. I, rot. 62.

170 Snagge refers to being steward of Kenilworth in a letter to Leicester of 23 July 1571, Longleat DP II, fo. 32. For his stewardship of the lordship of Warwick, see the 1576 survey (W.C.R.O., CR1886/Cup 4/8), fos. 23v, 27, and his Welsh offices, Ch. 14 above, p. 296.

171 Butler was a principal burgess of Warwick and figures prominently in the *Black Book*. He was granted the lease of Astell Grove in reversion in 1567 (G.V.E. fo. 30v), and in October 1569 Leicester referred to sending 'to John Butler to stay my servants coming as also to look to my house' (H.E.H.L. Hastings MS 2375, to Huntingdon, 24 Oct.). His correspondence with Leicester in June 1571 (Longleat, DP II, fos. 4, 8) reveals him to be the central household officer at Kenilworth. He nominated Thomas Dudley and John Hubaud overseers of his will (25 Sept. 1572, P.R.O., PROB 11/55/54).

172 The commission was discovered by Dugdale (*Antiquities*, ii, p. 737) among the Hubaud family papers; its fate is unknown. Hubaud was also steward of the lordship of Warwick in 1574–75 (W.C.R.O, CR1886/Cup4/8, fos. 26, 37). A brief account of his service to Leicester in Wales can be found in Adams, 'The Gentry of North Wales and the Earl of Leicester's Expedition to the Netherlands, 1585–86' [Ch. 12], pp. 244–5. See also the extensive references to him in the *Black Book*. His will (1 April 1583, P.R.O., PROB 11/66/232), to which Leicester was overseer, endowed a remarkable range of civic charities, the 'Hybbotts Charity' of Stratford-upon-Avon and elsewhere (*V.C.H. Warwicks*, iv, p. 312). Only two letters by him survive, P.R.O., SP 12/142/10, to Arthur Atye, 9 Sept. 1580, and B.L., Cotton MS Galba C VII, fo. 37, to William Herle, 22 Mar. 1581.

173 See the biographical sketch in J. H. Morrison, *The Underhills of Warwickshire* (Cambridge, 1932), pp. 66–8, 79–85, based in part on Underhill's deposition in the 1590 Chancery case (P.R.O., C 21/ElizI/D/5/2). Although Morrison did not know of the Longleat Dudley Papers, his research into the other sources for the Kenilworth administration was pioneering.

174 There is a list of Leicester's household inventories in 'Leic. Papers III'. For Underhill's subordinates, see Appendix 15.1.

175 The K.G.B. is entitled simply 'Dear kild syns my fyrst coming to my L.' and begins in 1568. It includes the Chase and several other parks, but not Kenilworth Park, and concludes with a proposal by Dockwra for farming Rudfen and complaints against Henry Besbeeche. Morrison (*Underhills*, pp. 80–1), who had discovered that Besbeeche was a ranger but did not know of Dockwra, drew the understandable conclusion that it was kept by Besbeeche, although that meant ignoring Besbeeche's own statement that he entered Leicester's service in 1570 (see n. 176 below). Dockwra's letters to Leicester in July 1571 (Longleat, DP II, fos. 34, 38) reveal that he was then keeper of

the Chase, the Great Park and Rudfen Park. On every ground Dockwra is a better candidate for the compiler of the K.G.B. than Besbeeche.

176 Longleat, DP II, fo. 212v, Besbeeche to William Baynham, 22 Mar. 1580. There are numerous references to Dockwra in 1584–85 in *Household Accounts*. Dockwra's will (7 Nov. 1586, proved 21 Nov., P.R.O. PROB 11/69/461) contains only family references. I have not been able to establish his relationship to the Berks. M.P. Edmund Dockwra, who was lieutenant of Windsor Castle for Leicester in 1569–76. [Mrs Doreen Agutter has since informed me that they were brothers.]

177 Together with Besbeeche's deposition in the 1590 Chancery case, Morrison (*Underhills*, pp. 86–1) discovered a second Chancery case in which he was involved, a dispute with his step-brother in 1592 (P.R.O., C 2/ElizI/B8/52). The latter concerned a property in Kent that Besbeeche claimed his father had given him for his wife's jointure in April 1569; a year later 'this defendant being called to the service of the . . . Earl of Leicester deceased and having an house and keeping of a park with the herbage of the same in Kenelworth', he leased it back to his father.

178 According to the *post mortem* survey of Leicester's Warwickshire estates (P.R.O., E 178/2350) the herbage of Kenilworth Park was leased to Besbeeche on 1 July 1572, but it is clear from Dockwra's letters that he was keeper of the Park in the summer of 1571. Besbeeche's letter to Leicester of 1578 about his rents (Longleat, DP II, fo. 193, see p. 236, above) suggests that he held some form of comptrollership by then. For his displacement see his letter to William Baynham, 22 Mar. 1581, Longleat, DP II, fo. 212v, and for his later offices, his deposition in P.R.O., C 21/ElizI/D/5/2. For William Edmundes, see Appendix 15.1.

179 See Appendix 15.1. Given Phipps's age, the Francis Phipps mentioned in the Jacobean survey (see n. 131 above) must have been a son or grandson.

180 For the reference as steward, see *Black Book*, p. 36; he is listed under the household officers at Leicester's funeral.

181 For his activities in 1588–89 see the depositions of Underhill, Phipps, and Besbeeche in 1590 (P.R.O., C21/ElizI/D/5/2). They are corroborated by the references to Gorge in the 1588 inventories of Kenilworth (Longleat, DP XI, and BD.L. MS Malone 5).

182 See Appendix 15.2: West Midlands Gentry who served in the Low Countries Expeditionary Force, 1585.

183 (Sir) Edward Blount (d. 1630) was appointed steward of Cleobury Mortimer and its related manors on 29 Mar. 1587, Longleat MS 4109. (Sir) Francis Clare of Caldwell (d. 1608) married Thomas Blount's daughter Agnes. (Sir) Clement Fisher (M.P.) served both Warwick and Leicester, and appears to have remained a close friend of the countess. All three attended Leicester's funeral, Blount was one of the bannerol-bearers and Fisher a bearer of the coffin. John Fisher of Packington is discussed further in n. 195 below.

184 *Black Book*, p. 34. He appears first in the K.G.B. in that year (fo. [2]) as Mr Hubaud, but from 1573 simply as Sir John.

185 He thus became a brother-in-law to Sir Robert, Sir Nicholas, Sir John and Clement Throckmorton. Note Dugdale's jibe that although the Hubauds were of some antiquity, 'I have not seen anything very remarkable of this family relating to their publique ymployments until Q. Eliz. time' (*Antiquities*, ii, p. 737).

186 In 1576 he purchased the manor of Sheldon, Warks., from Leicester, B.R.L., Wingfield Digby MSS A810–11. The overseers of his will (drafted 1 April 1586, Wingfield Digby MS A871) included his cousin Clement Fisher and Edward Holt (sheriff of Warks., 1583–84). He was prominent in the disputes over Tamworth and Drayton Bassett in 1577–78, see pp. 340–1.

187 None of his papers survive in the Ward-Boughton-Leigh deposit, W.C.R.O., CR162. For his appointment as a surveyor of Drayton Bassett, see B.L. Stowe MS 150, fo. 19. He is described in the *Black Book* (p. 354) as Warwick's steward for his lands in the county in 1585, but note also his reference to departing for Wales on Leicester's business. For his position in 1588, see the depositions of Underhill and Besbeeche in 1590. In 1589 Warwick described him as his receiver-general in the county of Warwick, W.C.R.O., CR1600/LH51/3. For his dispute with the Bishop of Coventry and Lichfield, see below n. 220.

188 See Ch. 10 above for references. He surveyed Drayton Bassett for Leicester in 1584, see Longleat, DP XIX. His curious behaviour during the Drayton Bassett riots is discussed above, p. 341. No less strange is the apparent contest between him and Digby for election as knight of the shire in the Warwickshire by-election of 1579 (see Ch. 10 above, p. 198), given that they have been described as friends, see T. W. Whitley, *The Parliamentary Representation of Coventry* (Coventry, 1894), p. 56.

189 See *Household Accounts*.

190 W. Jackson, 'The Dudleys of Yanwath', *Traits. Cumberland and Westmorland Hist. and Arch. Soc.*, ix (1887–88), pp. 318–32. For further biographical information on the brothers, see Ch. 8 above.

191 For sources, see the relevant entries in *House of Commons, 1558–1603*, and Ch. 10 above.

192 See their wills, nn. 171–2 above.

193 A number of deeds from these sales survive: W.C.R.O., L3 [Tomes of Long Marston Collection]/78, B.R.L. MSS 357601–2, and S.B.T.R.O., ER/2838.

194 Ch. 10 above.

195 For the Warks. lieutenancy, see Longleat, DP I, fos. 36, 121, 158, Sir Ambrose Cave to Dudley, 16 July 1559, John Fisher to Dudley, 18 Mar., 29 Aug. 1560. For the Worcs. lieutenancy, *ibid.*, fos. 4 (Dudley to William Sheldon, 1 Aug. 1560), and p. 149 (Sheldon to Dudley, 5 July 1560). Fisher (d. 1571) was the steward of the lordship of Warwick in 1562 (1576 survey, fo. 23v), and served with Warwick at Le Havre. Sheldon may have a connection with Northumberland (he was receiver of Worcs. and Salop. for the Court of Augmentations in 1549), and he later helped Leicester's surveyors in 1566 (Longleat, DP XVI, fos. 32, 41). For Leicester's patronage of his tapestry works, see p. 337 above.

196 In Ch. 10 above, p. 241, I referred to Blount as deputy-lieutenant of Worcs. in 1559–60. Closer examination of my source (Longleat, DP I, fo. 158, Fisher to Leic., 29 Aug. 1560) reveals that his office was in fact in Warks., and thus he can be identified as the Blount referred to as muster-master of Warks. in F. Peyto to Sir N. Throckmorton, 9 May 1560 (printed in P. Forbes (ed.), *A Full View of the Public Transactions in the Reign of Queen Elizabeth*, i (1740), p. 443). Peyto describes the muster-masters as men of skill, which implies that Blount had previous military service.

197 For the appointment of Lucy and Greville in 1569, see W.C.R.O., CR 1886/2823, and for the Worcestershire deputies, P.R.O., SP 12/67/52–3, Russell to Leic., 20 Mar.

1570. Both Lucy and Greville were knighted during the 1566 progress, Greville at Kenilworth and Lucy at Charlecote (not 1565 as stated erroneously in R. E. Rebholz, *The Life of Fulke Greville* (Oxford, 1971), 5, and *House of Commons, sub* Lucy), both appear in the K.G.B., and both attended Leicester's funeral. There are numerous incidental references to both in Leicester's correspondence, but only one letter from Lucy to Leicester survives (Longleat, DP I, fo. 95, undated [pre 1564]). Greville was a keeper of one of Leicester's parks (see P.R.O., SP 12/142/22, Hubaud to A. Atye, 9 Sept. 1580, and Montagu of Beaulieu MS 'Orders, Papers and Commissions', art. 95, Greville to Leic., 25 Mar. 1588).

198 F.S.L., MS La 97, to Richard Bagot 19 Nov. [1579?].

199 For Throckmorton, see Ch. 8 above, p. 169, n. 29, and Ch. 10 above, p. 204. For the tithes of Holy Trinity, see Whitley, *Parl. Representation*, p. 54.

200 The city's requests are C.R.O., A79/63C and A79/89D; the grants to Northumberland and Leicester, *Cal. Pat. Rolls, Edward VI*, iii, 2–4, and 1566–69, p. 253. On 4 April 1568 the terms for pasturing on the Common were agreed and Leicester was given some rights of common, see Longleat MS 4664.

201 The text of the Brass Lease is printed in B. Poole, *Coventry: Its History and Antiquities* (1870), pp. 17–18. It was erected in 1571, B.L., Harleian MS 6383, fo. 37.

202 *Cal. Pat. Rolls, 1569–72*, p. 362.

203 The city usually gave a yoke of oxen or other cattle, Leicester venison for the mayor and aldermen. The city's gifts begin in 1568 (C.R.O., A16, p. 14 *et seq.*). Leicester's gifts can be found in the K.G.B., and references to the mayor and aldermen dining on them in C.R.O., A7b, p. 6 *et seq.*

204 The gift of a yoke of oxen in particular. We are, of course, totally dependent on John Fisher's account (*Black Book*, pp. 31–2), which lays the blame for the whole affair on John Butler, who had dissuaded the corporation from following Fisher's advice.

205 Leicester described Warwick as his brother's town in 1571 (*Black Book* p. 34). Although John Butler was a leading burgess, John Fisher considered himself his man, and the Recorder, Edward Aglionby, became Coventry's Recorder as well in 1581 after Throckmorton's death (C.R.O., A7b, p. 49); Leicester's main involvement was in minor matters of patronage. According to Fisher, it was his idea that the borough should persuade Leicester to found his hospital there, and John Butler's that he should use the guild hall.

206 For the grants of appointment by Tewkesbury (28 May 1578) and Evesham (n.d.), G.V.E., fo. 49–v. At Tewkesbury there had been an earlier appointment, for Sir Henry Jerningham had resigned the high stewardship in 1570 and Leicester had visited in 1574. He obtained the charter (*Cal. Pat. Rolls, 1572–75*, pp. 526–8) as chief steward. The borough thanked him with the gift of an ox, and he visited again in 1582 (G.R.O., TBR, A1/1, pp. 361, 352). The petition for the market is P.R.O., SP 12/151/77; it does not appear to have been successful.

207 Blike (M.P.) was under-steward of Tewkesbury in 1580 (*Acts. P. Council*, xi, p. 415) and attended Leicester's funeral. He appears to have held some of his lands (Churcham and Lower Court, Glos.) by a lease from Leicester for life, which was later said to have 'coste the Earl of Leyc as it is to be proved vj^cli., besides other good turnes done to the owner' (B.L., Harleian Roll D 35, pt. xiv). See also nn. 218, 238 below.

208 He is not mentioned in the agreement of 22 Mar. 1568 (C.R.O., C 220) that accompanied the letters patent granting the monopoly either, but he received gifts of cloth from Coventry in 1569 (A16, pp. 17–18) and there is a memorandum on cloth addressed solely to 'your honour' in Commercial and Freemanship Records, Box 1.

209 C.R.O., A17, p. 25 (11 Mar. 1573), noting receipt of his freemanship fine and Leicester's letter of recommendation. Breres (d. 1619) was later an M.P. for Coventry.

210 In the discussions over the proposed hospital, reference was made to Leicester doing good for Warwick 'as he had done to Coventry', and he recommended to Fisher in November the obtaining of 'skilful men' from Coventry, *Black Book*, pp. 30, 49.

211 This is the earliest reference to the tapestry works, J. Humphreys, *Elizabethan Sheldon Tapestries* (1929), pp. 12, 22. For Leicester's close relations with William Sheldon see n. 195 above.

212 A. L. Beir, 'The Social Problems of an Elizabethan County Town: Warwick 1580–90', in P. Clarke (ed.), *County Towns in Pre-Industrial England* (Leicester, 1984), pp. 46–85, comments that Leicester's 'grasp of the economic situation was inadequate . . . and his thinking traditional', but his argument assumes the hospital to have been Leicester's main contribution to Warwick's economy (on which, see above, p. 338) and does not take his involvement in Coventry into account.

213 See Longleat, DP I, fo. 139, and B.L., Addit. MS 32091, fo. 185, Sandys to Dudley, 14 April and 20 July 1560.

214 Calfhill was on Leicester's short-list for the vice-chancellorship of Oxford in 1567, see M.C.L. Pepys MSS, Letters of State, i, p. 549, Leic. to Oxford, 17 Mar. 1567. For Bullingham, see Longleat, DP I, fo. 211, Bullingham to Leic., 23 Mar. [1561]. Note that Bullingham came from a Worcestershire family.

215 Leicester's relations with Whitgift are too complex a subject to be discussed here.

216 Longleat, DP I, fo. 237, Overton to Leic., 22 May 1571, referring to himself as chaplain. The reference to the recommendation for Mr Overton in Walsingham to Leic., 15 July 1580 (B.L., Cotton MS Caligula E VII, fo. 149), would appear to be a reference to his promotion. Leicester does not appear in Bentham's letterbook for 1560–61, edited by R. O'Day and J. Berlatsky, *Camden Miscellany XXVII* (1979).

217 W.C.L., Dean and Chapter Register, A7(iii), fo. 85. The mastership of the game for Coventry and Lichfield (8 Oct. 1580) is referred to in G.V.E., fo. 49v.

218 No reference to him can be found in the H.W.R.O., Index to Presentations in the Diocese of Worcester, 1526–1602, though Warwick, Thomas Blount and Hubaud were active. For John Bullingham, see Longleat, DP II, fo. 146, Bullingham to Leic., 21 June 1572. In 1597 Bullingham was said to have owed his later election as Bishop of Gloucester (1581) to Leicester through the brokerage of Gabriel Blike, see *House of Commons 1558–1603*, sub Blike. Lewes was said to have been a chaplain to Leicester, C.U.L., MS Mm. 1.39 [Anon., 'Life of Sir John Packington'], fo. 223.

219 Information on appointments drawn from J. Le Neve, *Fasti Ecclesiae Anglicanae* (Oxford, 1854 edn) I have not been able as yet to work through the archives of the diocese. For Leicester's chaplains, see Adams, 'A Godly Peer? Leicester and the Puritans' [Ch. 11].

220 P.R.O., STAC5, B53/13 and B69/35. The undated and anonymous accusations against Boughton (P.R.O., SP 12/146/179) were part of this dispute and emanated from

Overton. Boughton was accused of being simultaneously a papist, a Puritan and a keeper of harlots.

221 He also obtained a benefice in the diocese for Arthur Dudley (d. 1577?), a brother of the 3rd Lord Dudley, who had been a prebendary of Lichfield since 1531 and a canon of Worcester since 1553. See Longleat, DP II, fo. 111, Dudley to Leic., 16 Mar. 1573.

222 Discussed in Ch. 11 above.

223 See the undated draft, P.R.O., SP 12/44/148.

224 C.C.L., Evelyn MS 16, art. 1, 'A foundation for Prebendaries in Warwick' (n.d.). It is difficult to say whether such proposals influenced the erection of his hospital. Note also the detailed discussion about the tithes of St. Mary's between Fisher and Leicester in Nov. 1571 (*Black Book*, pp. 45–6).

225 W.C.R.O., CR1618/WA1, fo. 92v. A note suggests he might have been Christopher Goodman. Thomas Sampson also preached at Warwick that year.

226 B.L., Harleian MS 6992, fo. 112, to Burghley, 20 Oct. 1579. P.R.O., SP 12/150/180–2, Sir Richard Knightley to Leic., 17 Oct. 1581. Knightley was organising a subscription to support the lecturer Andrew King at Towcester. Leicester's contributions in 1584–85 are recorded in *Household Accounts*.

227 Ralph Griffin, the first master, was elected dean of Lincoln on 17 Dec. 1584 and installed in April 1585. Cartwright was presumably appointed in the spring of 1585, which in turn would have occasioned Leicester's attempt in July to persuade Whitgift to grant him a preaching licence.

228 See E. G. Tibbetts, 'The Hospital of Robert, Earl of Leicester, in Warwick', *Trans. Birmingham Arch. Soc.*, lx (1940 for 1936), esp. pp. 122–3. Under the statute of 1571 the hospital was to be endowed with lands not held in knight service to the value of £200 p.a. In the late 1570s and early 1580s Leicester appears to have been meeting the costs partly from rent charges (see P.R.O., LR 2/185/51) and partly out of pocket. He assigned lands for the endowment in his 1582 will and in 1585 was collecting others, but the endowment was not complete by his death and had to be settled by Warwick.

229 The provision for old soldiers is not present in the 1571 act of parliament, but the statutes of 26 Nov. 1585 (W.C.R.O., CR1600/LH/2, art. 7) are explicit about the priority to be accorded them.

230 For example, the well-known case of Cartwright and Humphrey Fenn (*V.C.H. Warwicks*, viii, 372). Contrast the portrait of Cartwright safe in Leicester's protection bearding Bishop Freake in 1585 in the fiercely anti-Puritan 'Life of Sir John Packington': C.U.L., MS Mm. 1.39, fos. 223v–4.

231 M. Bateson (ed.), 'A Collection of Original Letters from the Bishops to Privy Council 1564', *Camden Miscellany IX* (Camden N.S. liii, 1895), pp. 4–8, 12–19, 42, 45–6. Blount presented Leicester's former chaplain Thomas Willoughby (see Ch. 8 above, p. 164) to St Mary's Kidderminster in 1561.

232 Sheldon (M.P.) had married Sir Robert Throckmorton's daughter Anne, and Dudley had used him as an intermediary in the negotiations over the constableship of Warwick Castle in 1560 (see above, n. 77), he may have been in his service then. However, there is no reference to Leic. in his 1586–88 household account (W.C.R.O., CR 2632), though William Baynham and Jasper Cholmley appear. The

precise reason for the appeals to Leicester for liberty by such prominent imprisoned Catholic gentlemen as Sir Thomas Tresham (B.L., Addit. MS 39828, fo. 93, 1 Oct. 1583), or Sir Thomas Throckmorton (W.C.R.O., CR1998/60/3/3, 17 Jan. 1588) is unclear.

233 According to Smyth, Northumberland was about to lay claim in 1553. On his attainder, his interest reverted to the crown, which showed some interest in pursuing it in Mary's reign and early Elizabeth, but nothing appears to have been done until Leicester took up the case in the winter of 1572–73, ' Lives', ii, pp. 288–9. I have not as yet been able to examine the Berkeley Castle Muniments.

234 *Ibid.*, ii, pp. 289–90, 335–7.

235 Evidence of Leicester's research for the case is found in his letter to Shrewsbury of 10 Dec. 1572 (see n. 82 above), and Lord Latimer's to him of 26 Mar. 1573 (Longleat, DP, ii, fo. 156).

236 According to Smyth (p. 300), this action was begun by the crown in 1580; Berkeley lost the case in 1584, and the lands in question were granted to Leicester and Warwick in 1585 (see n. 112 above). Leicester's correspondence with Rutland in 1588 (also referred to in n. 112) supplies corroboration for the last stage, but there is no external evidence for the early 1580s.

237 *Ibid.*, ii, p. 335.

238 *Ibid.*, ii, pp. 294, 306. Gabriel Blike was also involved; he was a juror in the survey of Wotton-under-Edge of 1 July 1573 (C.K.S., U1475/L3/5/83).

239 Longleat, Devereux Papers V, fo. 25v (I owe this reference to Dr Paul Hammer). See also *Acts P. Council*, x, pp. 200–1, 214, 259.

240 The brief account of D. C. Peck, 'The Earl of Leicester and the Riot at Drayton Bassett, 1578' (*Notes and Queries* NS xxiii (1980), pp. 131–5), is based on the numerous Star Chamber depositions and the items of Ferrers correspondence in American libraries. Much important information on this very interesting affair is also to be found in the Bagot correspondence, the Ferrers correspondence in B.L., Stowe MS 150 and the Drayton Bassett muniments at Longleat. Erdeswick, *Survey of Staffs*, p. 418, is both curiously reticent on the subject and largely in error.

241 In the valor of Northumberland's lands of 1560–64 (C.C.L., Eveleyn MS 16, art. 2) the fee simple is said to be held by the crown. According to Baynham's survey of 1579 (P.R.O., LR 2/185/67v) and Longleat MS 4494, the Robinson lease began in 1560; according to B.L., Lansdowne MS 62, fo. 127, it began in 1556.

242 Robinson's case throughout was that since a debt of £1,200 had led to the loss of an estate worth £8,000 the mortgage was usurious.

243 A list of those accused of aiding the rioters can be found in P.R.O. STAC 5, A4/26, pt. ii. Goodere was accused of both supporting them and helping them to escape. He had also been a witness for Thomas Robinson in Paramour's action for debt in 1576, see Longleat MS 4503. Was there a connection between his involvement in the Drayton Bassett riot and his contesting of the Warwickshire by-election of 1579 against George Digby (see Ch. 10 above, p. 198)?

244 Paramour was already known to Leicester; he had supplied him with cloth for liveries c. 1567, Longleat, DP Box V, fos. 284–8. He initially appealed to Richard Bagot, then sheriff of Staffs. (F.S.L., La 671, 3 July 1578), but thereafter Bagot appears to have been conspicuous by his absence.

245 Longleat MS 4494. The terms were agreed between John Dudley and Paramour on 31 Mar. 1579 (Longleat MS 4635). Robinson also held some fee simple land in the lordship; this had been sold to Paramour, who sold it to Leicester as well.

246 B.L. Stowe MS 150, fo. 15, Paramour to Ferrers, 15 Sept. 1578. Leicester's own instructions to Ferrers of 13 Sept. (P.M.L., Rulers of England, Box III, No. 29.5) are printed in Peck, pp. 133–4.

247 For Leicester's expenses, see p. 326 above.

248 B.L., Addit. MS 28175, fo. 64.

249 Longleat MS 4504.

250 'Lives', ii, p. 325.

251 This led to the Chancery case of 1590. In the depositions (P.R.O., C 21/ElizI/D/5/2), Dudley sought primarily to establish that the countess had assigned all her interest in Kenilworth to Warwick in the summer of 1589; he also claimed that she had removed muniments and some of the contents from the castle, that Honiley was now part of Kenilworth, and that Charles Wednester had cut down timber in Rudfen on her instructions. There is a summary account of the legal battle over Leicester's estate in 'Leic. Pap. III'.

252 Discussed briefly in Ch. 14 above, pp. 304–6.

253 *Black Book*, pp. 44, 357.

254 *Ibid.*, pp. 305–7.

255 Printed in Poole, *Coventry*, 124. Holland was paid for the inscription in 1583 (C.R.O., A7b, p. 87); it may have been commissioned for the 1581 banquet.

256 *Locality and Polity*, pp. 317–18.

Chapter 16

Baronial contexts?
Continuity and change in
the noble affinity, 1400–1600[a]

The title 'continuity and change' has been employed so regularly that it has almost become a confession of failure to find a better one. However, there is a justification for its use here. The purpose of this exercise is a straightforward one: to compare a late sixteenth-century noble affinity, that of Robert Dudley, Earl of Leicester, with its predecessors. The reason for doing so is no less obvious. The affinity is understood to be one of the pillars (if not the central pillar) of aristocratic power in the late medieval period; changes in the affinity should therefore reflect any changes in the overall structure of politics. The areas of comparison – composition, structure and function – present no difficulties. The wider context, on the other hand, particularly the role and effectiveness of the sixteenth-century affinity, raises some complex questions.

Until relatively recently, these questions were not even considered worth posing. Following the publication of Lawrence Stone's monumental work, it was regarded almost as axiomatic that there was an absolute decline in noble power between the fifteenth and the seventeenth centuries.[1] In the late 1970s this attitude began to change, as Barry Coward noted in his study of the Stanleys: 'Only recently have a few historians begun to question whether Stone's concept of a crisis in the peerage's power, prestige and self-confidence might be equally unfounded as his economic crisis hypothesis.' He referred in particular to Conrad Russell, Kevin Sharpe and Clive Holmes.[2] The immediate stimulus for this revived interest was the attempt by Russell and Sir Geoffrey Elton to reshape the parliamentary history of the period by 'restoring' the House of Lords to its primacy over the Commons. In the 1980s, however, a different group of early-modernists began to re-examine the wider role of the sixteenth-century peerage: David Starkey, Steven Gunn, George Bernard and the contributors to Bernard's 1992 collection, *The Tudor Nobility*.[3] Most dramatically, and controversially, at the beginning of the 1990s,

John Adamson advanced a new interpretation of Civil War politics, which saw the peerage as the pivotal force on the parliamentary side, with its power apparently undiminished.[4] Adamson's approach owes much to the Elton–Russell re-emphasis on the House of Lords, but (like Starkey) he sees the politics of the Lords as derived from a tradition of aristocratic constitutionalism.

The 1980s and 1990s have also witnessed an intense debate over the power and political role of the late medieval nobility. Christine Carpenter has recently drawn attention to what appear to be 'different agendas' in the two periods, quoting with approval Steven Gunn's reference to a 'fault-line of mutual incomprehension'.[5] On one level there is something to this. Much work has been undertaken on the noble affinity in the fourteenth and fifteenth centuries.[6] By contrast, my own research into the Earl of Leicester and his affinity has been carried out almost *in vacuo*, there being no comparable studies of other Elizabethan peers when I began.[7] Coward's book on the Stanleys certainly addresses many of the issues, but in a very general and thematic way.[8] Of the historians of the early sixteenth century only Gunn has studied affinities in any detail.[9] Even more important is the fact that there is practically no work at all on this aspect of the early seventeenth-century peerage, which creates serious difficulties for the overall Adamson thesis.[10] The 'fault-line' is also reflected in the terminology. My approach to Leicester was very much shaped by the fascination of early modern historians in the 1970s and 1980s with factional politics. Searching for a more neutral term than faction to describe Leicester's following, I adopted clientele.[11] By contrast late medieval scholarship has employed the term affinity almost exclusively. To simplify matters, affinity will be employed here as well, as the basic characteristics are the same, and any wider significance of the term clientele can be left for a future occasion.[12]

On another level, however, Carpenter may have drawn the contrast too sharply, for the thrust of her argument is that the basic issues are common to both periods. She makes little reference to recent sixteenth-century work, and it could be argued that her comparison of the late medieval debate with the 1970s debate over the 'county communities' and the Civil War is an extreme one.[13] The wider intellectual influences may be more pervasive than she allows for; I know for a fact that I am not the only early-modernist who would admit to being inspired by Namier, Syme and McFarlane.[14] Recent sixteenth-century scholarship is fully aware of fifteenth-century work, not least Carpenter's own.[15] The basic issues are straightforward enough. No one denies that some form of transformation of noble power took place between the fifteenth and the seventeenth centuries, with the gentry republics of late Elizabethan and seventeenth-century politics as the apparent result. What are debated are the chronology and causes of this transformation. For Carpenter lordship was the 'norm' of early fifteenth-century politics, the change coming at the end of the century with the rise of 'court-centred politics'. She is outspokenly dismissive of the existence of a county community or 'county identity' in Warwickshire or 'any midland county created artificially out of Mercia' in the fifteenth century.[16] Nigel Saul and Simon Payling, on the other hand, have argued that counties dominated by the baronage were the exceptions even then; the early fifteenth century (to use Saul's words) 'saw the emergence of the social order that characterised England in the age of the Tudors'.[17] Felicity Heal and Clive Holmes, approaching the subject from a third perspective, claim that 'a traditional political community, a fraternity or caste defined by lineage, military virtue and, personal honour' still existed, though under threat, at the end of the sixteenth century.[18]

The mechanisms of change are no more straightforward. Since the late nineteenth century the symbol of the decline of noble power was the Crown's apparently successful attack on indentured retaining. However, the picture is now a good deal more nuanced.[19] Formal retaining was of decreasing importance throughout the fifteenth century and it declined naturally rather than as a result of the Crown's campaign. Retaining disappeared into the less formal but more complex affinity.[20] The relationship between the nobility and the Crown is equally debated. Much of the evidence for the early Tudor monarchy's hostility to the nobility is drawn from the Tudors' curious, persistent, yet still unexplained suspicion of the Percies.[21] Other noble families, the Stanleys or the Talbots, for example, were left with their local power undiminished.[22] Related to this is the question of the creation of a 'new nobility' by the Tudors. The distinction between old and new takes its origin in a contemporary political debate, but its modern usage begins with Tawney.[23] The most recent attempt to discuss Tudor politics in such terms can be found in David Loades's biography of the Duke of Northumberland, in which he argues that Northumberland was an example of a Tudor 'service nobility', epitomised by Thomas Cromwell. This nobility was distinguished from the 'traditional nobleman' by the absence of an established local affinity.[24] The distinction may rest on a romanticised view of the Stanleys (who were hardly old in fifteenth-century terms) and the Percies, the more so as neither of these affinities has been studied closely.[25]

It could be argued that K. B. McFarlane's major achievement was to revise the ingrained belief that the nobility was a uniquely destructive force and to see it as but a part of a society that as a whole was competitive and belligerent.[26] Carpenter describes Warwickshire politics in almost military terms.[27] The 'gentry' were not possessors of superior civic virtue; the gentry republics of Elizabeth's reign were not uniformly successful systems of local government.[28] What distinguished the nobility was its superior power, as manifested in its affinities. The lord ruled his country almost as the king ruled the kingdom.[29] Carpenter argues that security of property was the motivating

force for, and the cement of, the affinity.[30] The affinity was the main stabilis-
ing force in local politics because it provided the means for the mediation
and peaceful resolution of disputes. The incidence of violence and cases
reaching the courts becomes almost an index of the affinity's effectiveness.[31]
However, there is also a certain tension in this definition of the affinity. On
the one hand it was unstable, dependent very much on the personal effectiveness of the lord.[32] On the other it was to some extent natural, held together
by local social connections rather than financial reward, access to royal
patronage or a commitment to military service.[33]

At this point we should turn to the Earl of Leicester's affinity. What makes
it particularly interesting in this context is that it was both late and the
creation of a supposedly 'new' nobleman. As mentioned at the outset, it will
be examined under the broad headings of composition, structure and function. Before doing so, some comments on the sources are necessary, for they
are obviously much richer than those for fifteenth-century peers. In Leicester's case there is a voluminous, if widely scattered, range of surviving
papers, including an extensive correspondence and a number of accounts,
household lists and muniments of title.[34] His papers are not, of course,
complete. Missing are his central household records for the 1570s, the bulk
of the Kenilworth estate records and all but a few fragments of the papers of
his brother, Ambrose, Earl of Warwick.[35] Of very real value, therefore, are the
surviving collections of the correspondence of gentry families in the affinity:
the Ferrers of Tamworth papers,[36] the Wynn of Gwydir papers[37] and the
More of Loseley papers[38] being of particular importance.

For the reconstruction of the composition of Leicester's affinity there is a
unique source: the membership of the 1000-strong cavalry contingent of the
Netherlands expedition of 1585. The circumstances under which it was raised
have been discussed in *Household Accounts*.[39] The process began with a series
of some 200 circular letters from Leicester in late September 1585. The horse
were mustered first at Tothill Fields, Westminster, in late October or early
November, and then a second time at The Hague on 10 January 1586. On
both occasions they were mustered by retinue, and after The Hague muster
they were formed into companies or cornets. Some 400 horsemen were
mustered at Westminster and 750 at The Hague. This, of course, amounted
to only three-quarters of the contracted total and the remainder was raised by
other means during 1586.

Two lists of these retinues have been in print for some time. One was an
enclosure in a despatch to Madrid from the Spanish ambassador in Paris. It
is a Spanish translation of an English original, and it assigns the men and
horses to specific ships.[40] The second is a list of the retinues mustered at The
Hague in January 1586, but it is a copy made at least a year later, for it
includes under the knights men who were knighted by Leicester during the

course of 1586.[41] The first reconstruction of 'Leicester's train' was undertaken by Sir Roy Strong and Professor J. A. van Dorsten in the 1960s.[42] On the basis of this I concluded in the early 1970s that the lists would be central to a study of Leicester's affinity and they have served that purpose ever since.[43] At Bangor in 1973 I discovered in the Wynn of Gwydir papers the first of two copies of Leicester's circular letters to survive.[44] Several years later, two further lists of the retinues in collections in the Bodleian Library came to my attention, one in the Rawlinson MSS,[45] and the other in what had once been a section of the Gurney MSS.[46] Although they are not exactly identical, there are sufficient similarities between them and the 'Spanish list' to suggest that all three have a common origin.

The lists have been used previously in studies of the Welsh contingent of the expeditionary force and its overall religious orientation, and to identify the M.P.s of the 1584 Parliament and the members of the West Midlands affinity who took part.[47] However, this essay provides a suitable occasion for an examination of the whole, and a complete list is supplied in Appendix 16.1. The four lists are all ordered by rank, led by three peers, the 2nd Earl of Essex, the 2nd Lord North and the 11th Lord Audley, but thereafter there are some interesting differences.[48] The Hague list is the largest, with 199 retinues and the names listed in a completely different way from the others. The two Bodleian lists are almost identical in number (the Rawlinson 167 retinues, the Gurney 160), with the Spanish less at 122.[49] The smaller total in the Spanish list was reached by excluding men found mainly at the end of the Bodleian lists, so that its earlier sections are identical to them with two significant exceptions. All three divide the men into categories, but not identically, and the Gurney list uniquely includes one of retainers, a category missing entirely from the other two, although the same names are present and in the same order. Both the Spanish list and the Rawlinson move one large group of names to a different position in an identical manner, which suggests that there is some direct connection between them.[50]

The Gurney list is reproduced in part A of Appendix 16.1, with the names found only in the other lists gathered in part B. Identities, where known, have been supplied, together with attendance at Leicester's funeral, the one other occasion when one might expect the affinity to have been present *en masse*.[51] The degree of overlap between the Netherlands expedition and the funeral is considerable but not overwhelming, and for this several reasons may be advanced. Members of both the household (of all ranks) and the West Midlands affinity were heavily represented at the funeral, while some of those in the 1585 lists were dead by 1588 and others were still serving in the Netherlands.[52] Although the 1585 lists themselves provide no guide to the connection with Leicester, they confirm what is known from other sources.[53] Overall, despite the absence of a number of household officers who remained in England (as did both the recipients of Leicester's surviving letters), they give a remarkably complete snapshot of the affinity as it existed in 1585.[54] A list of Leicester's own of the men to whom the 200 letters were sent would obviously be of considerable assistance in explaining why these particular men were chosen. In its absence we are dependent both on a comment he made at the time that they were 'most of them gentlemen of good likings and callings in their countries, though my servants', and on the terms of his summons. The relevant clause of the letter to Wynn reads:

> I am to make choice of such my good friends and servants, as I may make an assured accompte of, amongst which number yourself are one. And therefore I do not doubt, but that according to the shew of your good will always toward me, and my good opinion of you, you will now manifest & perform the same ... to serve your sovereign under me. . . .[55]

As revealed here, the composition of the affinity was conventional, with the usual overlapping groups of family, household and estate officers at the core. There is a strong contingent of members of the household, both past and present. Leicester appears to have employed some form of rotation of young gentlemen in his household (as he did with his chaplains), and a considerable number of the men in the lists had been gentlemen of the household at an earlier date.[56] John Wynn himself falls into this category, for a close reading of the surviving Wynn correspondence reveals that he was a gentleman of Leicester's household in 1577–80 and in attendance during Leicester's visit to Buxton in June 1578.[57] The other contingents are largely defined by the geographical pattern of his estates and offices.[58] The two largest, the Welsh and the West Midlands, have already been mentioned. The Welsh was based on the lordships of Denbigh and Chirk (granted in 1563) and Arwystli and Cyfeiliog (1572). The West Midlands came from Kenilworth (1563) and its surrounding manors, and others in Worcestershire, Gloucestershire and Shropshire.[59] The East Anglians belonged to the old Robsart connection; those from Essex were associated with the Wanstead estate (1578); the Lancashire and Cheshire connection was formed by his chamberlaincy of the county palatine of Chester (1565); the Berkshire, Buckinghamshire and Surrey from the constableship of Windsor Castle (1562); and the Northamptonshire from the stewardship of Grafton (1571).

As well as a few Dudley relatives, there is also a group of men for whom the connection was supplied by the countess and her family.[60] Three other aspects are worth noting. First, despite a long-established legend, there are very few 'courtiers' to be found here. There are only two sons of senior officers of the court or Household (Richard Ward and Francis Fortescue), while Francis Castilion was the son of Elizabeth's Italian tutor and Groom of the Privy Chamber, Giovanni Baptista Castiglione.[61] On the other hand, two of the gentlemen of Leicester's household (George Brooke and Edmund Carey) were the younger sons of important peers, both usually considered enemies of his. The second aspect is the presence of a considerable number of sons or brothers of an earlier generation of the affinity: John Glasier, Christopher Blount, Ralph Hubaud, Thomas Price, Edward Jobson and Clement Fisher all fall into this category. The last aspect is a group of men who held no formal estate or household office (as far as can be ascertained), but who were clearly among Leicester's intimates. In lieu of a better description (though cronies would not be unjustified) they have been identified as 'entourage'.[62]

One further aspect should also be addressed at this stage: the retainers. In August 1565 Leicester received a licence to retain 100 men, one of a series of licences granted to privy councillors and other leading officers of the Crown during the first twelve years of the reign.[63] The precise reasons why they were granted and the use made of them are unknown. Elizabeth's hostility to retaining was open and consistent, but she sought to regulate it by proclamation rather than by fresh legislation. Two proclamations on the subject were published, one in January 1572 and the second in April 1583.[64] Both claimed that unlawful retaining was on the increase and ordered the justices of assize to see that the statutes on the subject were enforced. As well as referring to the existing statutes in general, both also mentioned specifically the Statute of Liveries of 1487 (3 Hen. VII, c. 12) and the 1583 proclamation the Statute of Liveries of 1468 (8 Edw. IV, c. 1).[65] Precisely why the proclamations were felt to be necessary is not clear, although the reference in the 1572 proclamation to retaining leading to unlawful assemblies suggests that it may have been a response to the agitation over the trial of the Duke of Norfolk.[66] Both proclamations barred retainers from serving on juries, and on several other occasions Elizabeth ordered that retainers also be barred from serving on the commissions of the peace. In 1595 the Earl of Essex stated that the latter prohibition prevented him from retaining gentlemen.[67] In some respects it is tempting to conclude that formal retaining more or less disappeared during Elizabeth's reign, except for the odd survival. However, there is evidence of continued retaining in 1583 in the form of a letter from Viscount Montague dismissing a retainer after the proclamation (which at least suggests that it was obeyed) and a list of the Earl of Hertford's retainers.[68] Leicester himself complained of 'patriotic' retaining interfering with the militia system when commanding the army at Tilbury in 1588.[69]

No indentures of retainer by Leicester have been discovered, but since the last known indentures date from the 1480s, this may not be particularly significant.[70] Only two direct references to his retainers have been encountered. One is the category of gentlemen retainers in the Gurney list. The other is found in another document from the expedition, a list of his guard compiled by Henry Goodere, the captain, on 12 January 1586.[71] This divides the guard into three categories: 'ordinary servants in your house' (thirteen men), 'old retainers' (twelve), and twenty-four men preferred to the guard by third parties. However, we also have lists of his servants given badges and liveries in 1559–60 and 1567–68.[72] The later lists are dramatically larger than the earlier, but this should be seen as a consequence of the expansion of his household in the interval.[73] Gentlemen are found in both sets of lists, but no knights, and the later lists also include a number of tradesmen. The 're-tainers' in the Gurney list are gentlemen of some stature and among them are a number of Leicester's officers (though not all) as well as past and present members of his household. They are certainly the sort of men one might expect to have been retainers in a fifteenth-century affinity, but a Gentleman Pensioner (and possibly a second) and an officer of the Stables, whom, as servants of the Crown, it was illegal to retain, are also found among them. Seven of the twelve 'old retainers' in the guard can be identified. Three, and possibly a fourth, attended Leicester's funeral.[74] One of them, William Blackwell, was the keeper of the park at Drayton Bassett and the only one of the twelve also included in the list of retinues.[75] Another, Toby Mathew, was a household servant of some prominence, who undertook a survey of the lordship of Denbigh.[76] Of the remainder, one may have been a steward of Balsall, and one, and possibly a second, was given livery in 1567.

It is not easy to reach a firm conclusion on this evidence. If we assume that those granted livery in 1567–68 included retainers, then the retainers were undoubtedly yeomen. The presence of the tradesmen in the lists may be sig-nificant, for a number of the Earl of Hertford's retainers in 1583 were also tradesmen. But were these the licensed retainers? Given the absence of any other reference to retainers we must assume that they were, and this in turn would suggest that Leicester was obeying at least the spirit of Elizabeth's opposition to retained gentry. Yet if this was the case, why was the licence, which allowed him to retain men who were not his officers or household servants despite the statutes, necessary? One would expect the licence to have been used to retain gentlemen similar to those found in the Gurney list, but many of these men had household connections, while servants of the Crown were specifically excluded from the licence. Similar difficulties exist over a related issue, that of obligations of military service on his tenants.[77] Military service clauses in his leases can be found, but, so far as I have been able to ascertain, they appear to be limited to his Welsh lordships, where military service was still a customary tenurial obligation.[78] In 1566 Leicester's surveyors drew attention to the military potential of the lordship of Chirk: 'There be in Chirkland at the least fyve hundred tall men that hold of your Lordship both able and readie to serve.'[79] This potential was realised in 1585, when Leicester raised two companies of 200 foot each from his Welsh tenants (and was prepared to raise more), though not apparently from any of his other estates.[80]

Turning to the overall structure of the affinity, the central household is discussed in *Household Accounts*. It numbered between 30 and 50 at the beginning of Elizabeth's reign and rose to between 100 and 150 in 1585, roughly average for a peer of his rank and prominence.[81] The structure of his estate administration is more difficult to describe with precision because few of his patents of office survive, and therefore the terms of office, remuneration and function are unclear.[82] The Welsh lordships, given their more developed administration, provide the most detailed evidence of their officers, and Court rolls, where they survive, supply the stewards of individual manors.[83] Several features stand out. Firstly there was a central pool of leading officers, whose responsibilities and range of employment were extremely wide; manorial stewards were drawn either from this pool or from local gentlemen.[84] Secondly, most of the initial generation of officers were inherited from the Duke of Northumberland, and many of them (and their successors) served Warwick as well. There is a distinctly Dudley, as against Leicester, aspect to this branch of the affinity.[85] By background, the officers were a mixture of gentlemen and professionals, either practising lawyers or men of legal training seeking a career in administration.

There were three pre-eminent officers: Thomas Blount of Kidderminster until his death in 1568, Sir John Hubaud of Ipsley (Warks.) from *c.* 1572 until his death in 1583, and (probably) Edward Boughton of Cawston (Warks.) from 1584 until 1588.[86] All were of established gentle rank (Blount was a cousin) and all served Warwick as well. All headed the Kenilworth administration, but also ranged more widely; Hubaud's role in Wales is well known.[87] All obtained prominence in local government and served as Members of Parliament, though not before they entered Leicester's service. Hubaud appears to have occupied a position similar to that of Sir Richard Shireburn in the administrations of the 3rd and 4th Earls of Derby, or Sir John Chichester with the 2nd Earl of Bedford.[88] Boughton does not appear to have possessed the same degree of intimacy, though his importance was certainly growing after 1584. He was the most formally employed of a group of Warwickshire gentlemen close to Leicester in the 1580s, which included George Digby, Henry Goodere, Clement Fisher and, at a further remove, Sir Thomas Lucy and Sir John Harington.

With regard to rewards and remuneration, we have only one surviving wages book, and that for the central household in 1559–61.[89] As might be expected, it includes wages for yeomen servants and expenses only for the gentlemen. Leicester appears to have made relatively little use of annuities and rent-charges. In his earlier accounts the annuitants were mainly former servants of his mother, the Duchess of Northumberland, and their annuities were clearly the honouring of bequests in her will. Two of his officers received annuities, but one was undoubtedly also a bequest from the duchess.[90]

In his later accounts a few annuities can be found, but in the main they appear to have been used to buy out the claims of interested parties in land settlements and (occasionally) to retain lawyers.[91] In the absence of patents of office there is not sufficient evidence to draw any conclusions about the value of salaries or fees attached to the offices on his estates. Rewards to his officers tended to take the form either of leases of his own lands or shares in grants from the Crown.[92]

Less formal rewards are by their very nature difficult to pin down. The accounts of towns doing business with Leicester include the occasional reward to his servants, but it is not clear whether these were demanded, expected or simply proffered.[93] Even more difficult is the question of a 'cut' in more dubious transactions.[94] Similar problems are encountered over Leicester's exploitation of his access to royal patronage to reward his own men. There are a number of clear examples of promotions into the Crown's service: at least two of his men became officers of the Stables (which is not surprising) and others included the keeper of the gardens at Hampton Court and a groom of the Privy Chamber.[95] However, it is difficult to quantify them overall or (in the present state of our knowledge) draw meaningful comparisons with his peers. The same can be said for his influence over appointments to offices in local government. It was clearly at work in the appointments of sheriffs and J.P.s in the West Midlands and in north Wales, especially in the late 1570s and early 1580s, but it cannot be assumed that it was absolute.[96] His household accounts reveal that he was generous in reward, and there was some competition to enter his service.[97] Yet the overall conclusion (if a tentative one) is that Leicester's affinity was not 'patronage-driven'; his men worked for their rewards. What this involved brings us to the subject of function.

A discussion of Leicester as a territorial lord cannot avoid addressing certain mysteries surrounding the circumstances of his creation, for it was the first major grant of lands to him (July 1563) that established the broad outline of his estate, particularly the West Midlands–north Wales axis.[98] Lands obtained later, either by grant from the Crown or by private purchase, merely fleshed out this skeleton. There was only one major exception, the estate he built up round Wanstead House in western Essex after he purchased it in 1578. There is no doubt that Leicester was the recipient of Elizabeth's generosity to an unrivalled degree. In the overall history of Elizabeth's treatment of the peerage, the cases of Leicester and Warwick were unique; no one else was raised directly to an earldom.[99] But Leicester's creation can be viewed from several angles. There is the obvious one of the queen's indulgence of a favourite. On the other hand, it can also be seen as her establishment of a senior officer of the Household and a loyal supporter, whose estate at the beginning of the reign was minimal, complicated by the fact that those lands to which he had any claim were granted to his elder brother after he was 'restored' to the earldom of Warwick in 1561. Lastly it can be seen as part of a wider Edwardian restoration.

What is particularly mysterious about the first grant is that it preceded his creation by a year, yet the lands and titles were directly related (Kenilworth and the earldom of Leicester and Denbigh and his barony). The precise circumstances surrounding the choice of both lands and titles are unclear. Kenilworth was the only part of the old earldom of Leicester granted to him, and the only other connection between the various estates is that some had once been part of the earldom of March. Leicester himself had a considerable knowledge of, and fascination with, the Dudley claim of descent from the Beauchamp Earls of Warwick, but no other real territorial ambitions.[100] Indeed it is possible that the terms of the grants made to both brothers at this time may have reflected an assumption that Leicester would succeed his brother as Earl of Warwick in the immediate future, particularly given Warwick's weakened health following his command at Le Havre in 1562–63. If this was the case then the grant to him in 1563 was to some extent a provisional one, and not intended to form a permanent endowment. On the other hand, the fact that both Leicester and Warwick were ultimately to be ephemeral peerages is not in itself significant. If Leicester may have been expected to succeed Warwick in 1563, it is doubtful that anyone in 1565 would have predicted that Warwick's marriage in that year to the young Anne Russell would have been childless. Elizabeth may have wished Leicester himself to have remained unmarried, but he, on the other hand, was deeply concerned to perpetuate the house of Dudley and came close to doing so. His own estate policy reveals a clear intention of creating a permanent estate of inheritance.[101]

These considerations must be borne in mind if any purpose in creating a lordship for Leicester in these particular counties is to be discovered, other than the cobbling together of a selection of lands to provide a certain level of income.[102] In the case of the West Midlands, and Warwickshire in particular, Leicester's lands would reinforce his brother's (or, given their respective political importance, it should probably be the other way round), and moreover this was a region to which they had a strong sentimental attachment. Yet there is no evidence of any obvious need for the Crown to create a powerful lordship there, only perhaps an appreciation that since there was no resident major peer the Dudley intrusion would not cause any great disturbance. Wales, however, was a different case, because the Crown's immediate possession of the majority of the marcher lordships since the beginning of the century had been seen as a cause of the perceived lawlessness of the region and had inspired both the creation of the Council in the Marches and the extension of the shire system.[103] Yet the planting of Leicester in north Wales cannot be considered part of any broader policy of restoring lordship to

Wales, for apart from the grants to him and the lordship of Ruthin to Warwick, Elizabeth appears to have made no other major grants of marcher
lordships. If there was a 'policy' at work, it may have been a purely financial
one, for there is evidence both of a perception on the Lord Treasurer's part
that the rents of the marcher lordships were now grossly out of date and of
the possible beginnings of a campaign to revive them. Since Leicester initiated just such a revival after taking possession of the lordships of Denbigh
and Chirk, it is possible that it was expected that he would do so.[104] In this
respect the grants represent a form of delegation in which the increased
income he would derive from his Welsh lordships would (hopefully) make
further grants from the Crown unnecessary and save the Crown the expense
of revising the rents itself. The attractive aspect of this argument is that it
explains why the Crown later granted him the Montgomeryshire lordships of
Arwystli and Cyfeiliog and then the keepership of Snowdon Forest (1574),
with the celebrated encroachment commission to follow.

Leicester's three other major territorial offices under the Crown, the
constableship of Windsor Castle, the chamberlaincy of Chester and the stewardship of Grafton, were all in counties where he possessed no land of any
consequence. Windsor Castle and Grafton (which was, it might be noted,
within easy distance of Kenilworth) basically involved the administration of
extensive royal forests, an established form of patronage to courtiers. They
certainly added to his affinity (as can be seen in the Netherlands expedition)
but any power, other than patronage, that they conferred is not immediately
obvious. Chester is more ambiguous. It could be seen as a bolstering of his
position in north Wales, but it had also become an established perquisite of
the Earls of Derby. However, there is no evidence of Elizabeth's (or Leicester's)
hostility to the 3rd Earl of Derby, and once again the precise motive for the
appointment is unclear. By planting the Dudley brothers in Warwickshire,
Elizabeth made possible the revival of the affinity formed by Northumberland and to some extent maintained by his sons during Mary's reign. The
displacement they caused appears to have been minimal. Wales was, once
again, a different matter, for here there were few existing Dudley followers.
The appointment of their brother-in-law Sir Henry Sidney as President of
the Council in the Marches in 1560 certainly eased the process. The Council
became closely associated with Leicester's business; many of his officers sat
on it (most prominently Hubaud, who nearly became vice-president) and he
employed members of it in his estate management. However, it is doubtful
that Sidney's appointment was made in anticipation of the planting of Leicester
in north Wales. Similarly the fact that Leicester's legal agent, the Chester
lawyer William Glasier, was appointed vice-chamberlain of the county palatine in 1559 cannot be seen as an anticipation of Leicester's appointment as
chamberlain either.

Leicester took some time to establish a personal physical presence in Warwickshire. An initial visit in early 1566 proved abortive, and the first occasion was during the progress later in the year. There was a second visit during the progress of 1568, but from 1570 he visited regularly until 1585, the sole exception being 1583.[105] The outlying estates were a different matter, though his trips to the spa at Buxton in 1577 and 1578 certainly provided opportunities to meet the Denbighshire gentry.[106] The year 1584 saw his most extensive tour, which took him to Denbigh for the only time, via Shrewsbury and, on return, Chester. His purpose is not clear, though the visits to Shrewsbury and Chester may have involved an attempt to mediate the dispute between them.[107] On the other hand the employment of young gentlemen from the counties in his household provided a major point of contact for the affinity, and his officers, Hubaud in particular, travelled extensively. It may not be irrelevant to note that Leicester possessed a map of Denbighshire with instructions on how to read Welsh.[108] However, non-residence was not without some importance. A comparison of Leicester's involvement in the affairs of King's Lynn and Great Yarmouth with the Duke of Norfolk's reveals how much more regularly Norfolk was consulted about local business.[109]

Our present knowledge of Warwickshire politics in the sixteenth century is so limited that it is difficult to be precise about the effects of the Dudley planting.[110] Some displacement did occur, notably the semi-retirement of Sir Robert Throckmorton of Coughton, though here religion undoubtedly played a major role. The Protestant wing of the extensive Throckmorton clan certainly became more prominent, as did such other Protestant gentlemen like Sir Thomas Lucy and Sir John Harington. Yet Leicester's affinity was far from being a Protestant, let alone Puritan, monopoly; there were semi-Catholic elements in it (notably Christopher Blount) and even Hubaud's leanings were ambiguous. In Wales the situation was dramatically different, for Leicester's appearance on the scene soon challenged the dominance Sir Thomas Salusbury of Lleweni had possessed over Denbighshire for several decades.[111] This led to a major reshaping of county politics, in which Leicester attracted the lesser gentry hostile to the Salusburys, and they soon formed his local affinity. The result was the participation of Salusbury's grandson and heir in the Babington Plot of 1585–86, and then a major power struggle after Leicester's death in which the plotter's brother Sir John regained the family's control of the county from the former Leicesterians. Members of Leicester's local affinity joined his officers in the Forest of Snowdon encroachment commission, but the extent to which the opposition to the commission was related to the struggle with the Salusburys is still unclear.

The realities of Leicester's local power have been distorted by a powerful historiographical tradition originating in the celebrated Catholic tract *Leicester's Commonwealth*. This was an example, and possibly the most powerful, of a strand of Catholic polemic that portrayed the Reformation as the displacement of the ancient nobility by new men.[112] It compared him to the fourteenth-century favourites, but not so much as the beneficiary of an over-indulgent monarch than as a faction leader who ruled all and kept the queen a near captive.[113] There may have been a polemical purpose in making this comparison, yet it created an internally contradictory image. On the one hand Leicester was hated by all except the queen, on the other his faction was everywhere. Not surprisingly, Leicester's own rapacity was the main cause of dissension and discord. Evidence is supplied by a number of well-known episodes of the 1570s: the revival of the 'Great Berkeley Law-Suit' in 1572–3, the Snowdon Forest commission of 1574, and the Drayton Bassett riot of 1578. *Leicester's Commonwealth* also had a major influence on the county histories written during the subsequent century, in particular Samson Erdeswick's *Survey of Staffordshire*, John Smyth of Nibley's 'Lives of the Berkeleys' and Sir William Dugdale's *The Antiquities of Warwickshire*. Both Smyth and Dugdale refer to it directly.[114] They also had political or personal reasons for finding its portrait of Leicester sympathetic: Erdeswick was a semi-recusant, Smyth a servant of Lord Berkeley's, proud of his role in the restoration of the Berkeley fortunes, and Dugdale a committed royalist. Moreover, Dugdale's patron, who subsidised the lavish illustration of the *Antiquities*, was Lady Catherine Leveson, one of the daughters of Leicester's illegitimate son, Sir Robert Dudley, who could claim to have been cheated of her rightful inheritance by her grandfather's infidelity to Douglas Sheffield. Moreover, the emphasis in these histories on the antiquity of the established county families further shaped their view of the favourite's local impact.[115] Leicester's men were portrayed as upstarts as well, Dugdale's snide comments on Hubaud's family being a case in point.[116]

The reality behind the various embellishments of the legends of these incidents is thus difficult to disentangle, and this is not the place to discuss any of them in detail, but some general points can be made. A central feature of both the Snowdon Forest commission and the revival of the Berkeley Law-Suit is that they took place under the authority of the Crown. The Snowdon Forest commission was in the queen's name and it was the Crown that raised the suit against Berkeley.[117] There was certainly a degree of collusion. Leicester was forester of Snowdon Forest, his officers (led by Hubaud) headed the commission and he was to receive the immediate profits. Likewise, after regaining the Berkeley lands the queen granted them to Leicester and Warwick by letters patent and in the interval appointed their officers as stewards for the Crown.[118] Leicester may have had his own reasons for wishing to revive the Berkeley Law-Suit, but he could not have done so without Elizabeth's connivance, and therefore the real question is why she turned against the Berkeleys, something John Smyth could never resolve.[119] Likewise, the origin of the Snowdon Forest commission is also unknown; if Leicester were the immediate beneficiary the Crown would gain in the long term. In both of these episodes Leicester's initial desire was to reach some form of compromise. It was the absolute resistance of the gentlemen of Llŷn that caused the Snowdon affair to blow up.[120] Similarly the effect of Berkeley's (or possibly more accurately Lady Berkeley's) rejection of the offer of the marriage of Philip and Robert Sidney to his daughters on the revival of the law-suit is unclear. Lastly, both episodes saw Leicester's affinity fully deployed. Another of Smyth's difficulties was explaining why, if Berkeley was so established in his country, so many Gloucestershire gentlemen assisted Leicester. In Wales the situation was more nuanced. Maurice Wynn of Gwydir, whose surviving correspondence is one of the main sources for the Snowdon Forest affair, was unhappy at being caught between Leicester and his 'country'.[121] John Wynn was later warned by one of Leicester's officers that he was seen as too protective of his countrymen.[122]

The Drayton Bassett riot of September 1578 was a different affair altogether.[123] Here the Crown was not directly involved. On the surface this was a dispute over a foreclosed mortgage between the mortgagee (the London merchant Richard Paramour) and the well-connected mortgagor (Thomas Robinson), which had been through the courts for some years. When Paramour's attempt to take possession in June 1578 was resisted by Robinson's friends, the sheriff of Staffordshire (Richard Bagot) proved ineffectual and various mediation efforts failed, Humphrey Ferrers of Tamworth was ordered to gain possession for him.[124] This he did in August with the assistance of George Digby. However, on 2 September, when he and Digby were away hunting, Robinson's allies seized the manor house by surprise. Ferrers' attempt to regain the house led to the death of one of his men and he withdrew, reporting the incident to Leicester and the Privy Council. The Council ordered a massive intervention, but in the meantime the rioters dispersed and the upshot was a long-drawn-out investigation by Star Chamber and a separate trial for murder in 1580.

There are a number of fascinating aspects to this affair, not the least of them the extensive local support for the rioters both at the time and during their subsequent flight. The affair may also be connected to several other incidents in local politics.[125] However, Leicester's involvement is particularly curious. Six months after the riot (April 1579) he bought out Paramour, whose willingness to be rid of the property is quite understandable. The controversial aspect was Leicester's concern to keep his role concealed, which raises the question of whether he had been Paramour's sleeping partner all along.[126] His involvement in September is clear enough, but the June to September period is more obscure. Ferrers and Digby were unmistakably his men, but under whose authority was Ferrers acting? This remains unclear.

Ferrers referred at the time to 'the trust I had to keppe the grounds not only by a lettre of attorney from Paramour but most chefely from your lordship for whom I entered'.[127] Two years later he complained, 'The burden hath layn on my back when your lordship would not have it known you mynded further to deale in it. Then your lordship well knows I dealt not for the merchant [Paramour] and what I dyd att the fyrst was uppon the Lord Chancellor's letters that now is [Sir Thomas Bromley] to frend hym which I did or els he had never devysed the possession unto your lordship's use.'[128] The ambiguity of Leicester's position was later claimed to have been one of the causes of the riot.[129] It certainly did not see his affinity deployed in strength. In early September 1578 Hubaud was in Beaumaris dealing with the Snowdon Forest enclosures; he returned to Kenilworth ill in early October and took to his bed for the rest of the month.[130] More importantly, while Ferrers was supported by some of Leicester's men, notably Digby and William Horton, at least two members of affinity, Henry Goodere and William Harman, were accused of aiding the rioters.[131]

The wider significance of this incident is found in two further aspects. Leicester informed Ferrers of the Council's reaction to the 2 September riot in the following terms: 'My lords having since more delyberately considered of the matter & finding hit so rare & straunge a cause as hath not happened in the tyme of her majesty's [reign?] as well for the notorius royatt as for the murder [of one?] of her subiects.' The Council had ordered the 'lords Dudley and Stafford to be your better assistants in such a cause as this ys, being the principal noblemen of that shire' and he was confident that 'Thomas Trentam & Rafe Aderley, with others such as you know to be my frends will help with ther best'.[132] No less interesting were the efforts to restore good relations after the affair was over. Leicester himself spent a considerable sum in buying out the other claims on the estate.[133] Ferrers interceded with Paramour for two of the rioters for 'I am not to forgett ther old frendshipp and good neighbourhood'.[134] Later, after Leicester preferred William Blackwell as keeper of Drayton Park to one of his own men, Ferrers complained that he hoped that Leicester 'would not have my country see much into my discredit to have hym displaced that bothe deserved well and was of my placing before your lordship had shewen me your pleasure'.[135] Not least significant is the fact that practically all the principal figures in the affinity involved, except Ferrers, later took part in the Netherlands expedition.

Leicester's comments on the novelty of the riot, give or take a certain hyperbole, are possibly the most important comment on the affair. For all that is said about violence in Elizabethan society, this was clearly not business as usual. Neither the Berkeley Law-Suit nor the Snowdon Forest enclosures resulted in violence. Nor did the simultaneous dispute between the Earl of Shrewsbury and his Glossopdale tenants, though the coincidence of the

Council's major intervention in this affair in the spring of 1579 is interest-ing.[136] Tudor historians have assumed a lower level of violence than fifteenth-century historians, as is revealed by Geoffrey Elton's mischievous introduction to a collection on crime and society:

> The exercise seems the more desirable because such conclusions as do get estab-lished tend to be somewhat unsurprising. Dr. Cockburn tells us that homicide was rare and most murderous violence occurred within families. Though it is satis-factory to have the more lurid notions of a people forever battering one another disproved, this remains what one would have expected. Similarly Dr. Curtis finds that violence was usually casual and unpremeditated: were we to think that the realm was full of professional hitmen?[137]

Having said this, on another level, that of enforcement, there are strong similarities. The Council was still dependent on the leading noblemen and Leicester's affinity. If this affair ended as a Star Chamber case, did this make any difference? Should we not simply see Star Chamber as replacing a fea-ture of fifteenth-century government, the issuing of noblemen with commis-sions of oyer and terminer?[138] There is some instructive evidence relating to the involvement of Leicester's affinity with Star Chamber. In 1579, during one of the interminable disputes surrounding his deputy in Chester, William Glasier, Glasier's own deputy (and Leicester's officer) John Yerwerth wrote: 'we have no other means but to complain before the lords of her majesty's Star Chamber, which were a thing not meet to be dealt withal in that place, growing among your lordship's people and where you are our chief officer.'[139] Resort to Star Chamber clearly represented a failure of internal resolution within the affinity. This gives an added interest to the two Star Chamber cases in which members of Leicester's affinity were directly concerned. One was the dispute in 1582–83 between Edward Boughton, then a rising figure in Leicester's administration, and the Bishop of Coventry (Richard Overton, a former chaplain of Leicester's) over the mastership of Rugby School.[140] The issue at stake was the right of appointment, with Boughton standing for local choice, and Overton for episcopal authority. There was a clear element of personal animus involved, with Overton accusing Boughton of being simul-taneously a Puritan, a papist and a keeper of harlots, and Boughton attacking a tyrannical Bishop. There are similarities here to the Bishop-baiting going on in East Anglia at the same time, and Overton claimed that Boughton was being sustained by the favour of a great man (clearly Leicester). Just what Leicester's role was is unclear. The other case was a dispute in the same period (1582–84) between Humphrey Ferrers and a neighbour, John Breton. What makes this particularly interesting is that Breton was Warwick's man, and the two Earls tried to mediate the dispute between them. It was their failure that led to the case ultimately being heard in Star Chamber.[141]

In this respect Carpenter's argument that the resort to law represented the failure of noble mediation is still valid for the sixteenth century. The affinity was still alive and well. So too was its military function, if the Netherlands expedition is anything to go by. To raise over 700 horse, of whom at least 100 were members of the gentry, was no mean feat, as some immediate comparisons reveal. In 1475, the Dukes of Clarence and Gloucester provided retinues of 120 each, the 3rd Duke of Buckingham a mixed retinue of 500 horse and foot in 1513, and the Duke of Suffolk mixed retinues of 1800 in 1513 and 1700 in 1523, although only 100–150 horse in 1544.[142] In the St Quentin expedition of 1557 none of the retinues of horse was larger than 200.[143] On the other hand, there were special circumstances at work in 1585. Only three other peers were directly involved (so there was less competition), and Leicester was a senior member of the government acting directly as the queen's deputy. If there was some scepticism about her commitment, his was unquestioned, and he certainly pulled out all the stops.

However, there are two novel aspects to the affinity detectable; one that strengthened it and one that weakened it. The first was the role of religion. Here there is an element of ambiguity, given the semi-Catholicism of some of Leicester's family connections, and the absence of any clear evidence of a religious test on entry, although conformity to the queen's proceedings was clearly the base. However, there is a gravitation to Leicester among the more 'Puritan-minded', who might not otherwise have entered his orbit, and which to some extent may have affected participation in the Netherlands expedition.[144] By the same token, the contrary may have been true, that Leicester's power may have frightened Catholics into conformity. This is certainly the implication of *Leicester's Commonwealth*, and it is found in other Catholic accounts, although they had a polemical purpose in making this case.[145]

The second aspect is the clear tension between loyalty to the affinity and loyalty to the county community. This can be seen in both Wynn's and Ferrers' attempts to balance their service to Leicester with their allegiances and standing within their counties. Not unrelated to this is a detectable unwillingness by several of his followers in later years to admit that they had ever been in his service. Some did though; an early seventeenth-century poem on Sir Hugh Cholmondley's widow referred proudly to Cholmondley's service as treasurer of Leicester's household in the Netherlands.[146] On the other hand, John Wynn's history of his family and memoirs of his friends and contemporaries make no mention at all of his having been in Leicester's household. Particularly curious in this respect is his memoir of William Thomas of Caernarvon, the commander of one of the companies of Leicester's tenants, who was killed at Zutphen: 'a brave, courageous and wise gentleman as any in this country produced in his time'. Thomas was clearly a personal friend, but what is omitted is that he and Wynn had been closely associated in Leicester's service.[147] The late seventeenth-century life of Sir Richard Bulkeley of Beaumaris makes great play of his defence of his country against the tyrannical favourite in the Snowdon Forest affair, but does not mention that he too had once been in Leicester's household.[148] After Sir Thomas Bodley died, John Chamberlain sardonically observed that he had left a memoir:

> written by himself on seven sheets of paper with vanitie enough, wherein omitting not the least *minutezze* that might turne to his glorie, he doth not so much as make mention of . . . Mr Secretarie Walsingham, nor the Earl of Leicester; who were his maine raisers, whereby may be seen, what mind he caried to his best benefactors.[149]

Wynn's *History* was inspired by the often-quoted sentiment: 'Yet a great temporall blessing it is and a greate hearts ease to a man to find that he is well descended.'[150] The increased gentry concern with their own lineage and stature has long been seen as one of the reasons for the decline of the traditional affinity.[151] Yet there was no immediate reason why it should have been. Leicester's fascination with his own descent was no different, and in that sense there was a definite community of self-regard. Indeed the very point about having gentlemen servants was precisely the honour of being served by men well descended.[152] However, an aspect of gentle pride was being an established member of a county community. Leicester himself saw no conflict in theory between being a member of his affinity and being of local standing, as his description of the men he summoned to the Netherlands makes clear. Indeed he recommended his household servant Richard Browne to the electors of Maldon in 1584 as their countryman and one who would serve their interests.[153] Yet in practice the two may not have been so compatible and the heightened sensitivity to membership of the community made it no longer so easy to give precedence to the demands of the lord.

The fact that it is in seventeenth-century memoirs that this reticence about service is found may also be significant. There is a case to be made that the late medieval peerage effectively came to an end in 1603, for the Stuart expansion of the peerage – which raised it from the consistent 40–60 after 1399 to 126 in 1628 – transformed it entirely. However, if this has been noted, its effects have yet to be explored.[154] It does, however, raise question marks about the continuity of noble power that underpins the Adamson thesis. The most dramatic aspect of this thesis is the evidence for the interesting experiments in aristocratic constitutionalism in the 1640s. More controversial, and to some extent contradictory, are two further arguments, one for a revival of aristocratic self-consciousness in the 1630s, the other for a continuous tradition of aristocratic constitutionalism. The latter is based on some inaccurate Elizabethan examples.[155] This is not to deny that there was a rise in aristocratic constitutionalism in the seventeenth century, which would turn to medieval precedents; nor that some elements can be found in Elizabeth's reign, notably in the various regency schemes. Foreign examples, particularly Scotland or the Netherlands, may have played a role, and Essex may have dabbled with it. But it is difficult to see a self-conscious tradition at work.

Underlying this thesis is an assumption of a continuity of aristocratic power. But before this can be accepted, much more work on the situation before and after 1603 needs to be done. Indeed it could be argued that the expansion of the peerage reduced many peers to the rank of greater gentlemen and if there is a greater self-consciousness among the peerage in the 1630s this was the result of a need to bolster their weakened status. Membership of a noble affinity was no longer reputable and therefore the possibilities for a great affinity similar to Leicester's would disappear. A question mark hangs over Buckingham, but there is reason to doubt whether he attempted to form such an affinity rather than a series of Court alliances. In this respect Leicester (or possibly Essex) does mark the end of an era. It is not so much that his affinity itself was changing, for it still shared the main characteristics of the late medieval affinity, but the wider context in which it operated was doing so, and in consequence its effectiveness was threatened. In the following century these wider changes would accelerate.

APPENDIX 16.1: THE NETHERLANDS RETINUES*

A. THE GURNEY LIST

Knights[a]

Sir William Russell	[*c.* 1553–1611, 4th son, 3rd Earl of Bedford, M.P.]
Sir Robert Jermyn	[*c.* 1540–1614, of Rushbrooke, Suff., M.P.]
Sir Arthur Bassett	[1541–86, of Umberleigh, Devon, M.P., relative]
Sir Thomas Shirley	[*c.* 1542–1612, of Wiston, Suss., M.P.]
Sir Henry Berkeley	[*c.* 1547–1601, of Bruton, Som., M.P.]
Sir John Harington*	[*c.* 1540–1612, of Combe Abbey, Warks., M.P., entourage]
Sir Robert Stapleton	[*c.* 1547–1606, of Wighill, Yorks., M.P.]
Sir Richard Dyer	[cousin of Sir Edward Dyer]
Sir John Conway	[of Arrow, Warks., Governor of Ostend 1587–90]
Richard Huddleston[b]	[d. 1589, Treasurer Netherlands 1585–87]
William Knollys[a]*	[*c.* 1545–1632, M.P., brother-in-law]
William Bassett	[1551–1601, of Blore, Staffs., M.P., poss. household]
George Digby[a]	[1550–87, of Colshill, Warks., M.P., entourage]
Richard Ward	[of Hurst, Berks., son of Richard Ward, Cofferer of the Household]

John Peyton[a]	[1544–1630, of Beaupré Hall, Norf., M.P.]
John Watts*	[of Blakesley, Northants.]
George Farmer[a]	[d. 1612, of Easton Neston, Northants., entourage]
Michael Harcourt*	[d. 1597, of Leckhampstead, Bucks., M.P., tenant]
Thomas Arundel	[poss. son of Sir Matthew Arundel]
Philip Butler[a]*	[d. 1592, of Watton Woodhall, Herts., m. Catherine Knollys]
Robert Sidney[a]*	[1563–1626, M.P., nephew and godson]
Captain William Selby	[d. 1612, M.P., officer of the Berwick garrison]

The Earl's gentlemen, retainers[c]

William Harman*	[of Hampton, Warks., estate officer]
John Fullwood	[of Warks., poss. tenant]
William Pearson	
Roger Brereton*	[household]
Edward Bourchier	
Ralph Hubaud*	[d. 1605, of Ipsley, Warks., brother of Sir John Hubaud]
Clement Fisher*	[c. 1539–1619, of Great Packington, Warks., M.P., entourage]
Thomas Denys	[1559–1613, of Holcombe Burnel, Devon, M.P., household]
Henry Jones	[household, tenant in Denbigh]
Ambrose Butler	
Richard Weston	[1564–1613, of Sutton Place, Surr., M.P.]
George Tuberville*	[of Warks., tenant/estate officer]
William Skipwith	[1564–1610, of Cotes, Leics., M.P.]
Walter Tooke	[poss. son of Northumberland's servant George Tookey of Worcs.]
Richard Acton*	[of Elmsley Lovett, Worcs.?, household]
David Holland	[d. 1616, of Vaerdrey, Denbs., son of estate officer]
Edward Avelin*	[household]
John Glasier*	[son of William Glasier of Lea, Ches., M.P., officer]
Charles Acton*	[of Worcs., ward of Thomas Blount, father of John Acton, M.P.]
Edward Barrow	[of Hants., Captain, Netherlands 1586]
John Breton	[c. 1530–87, of Tamworth, Staffs., M.P., tenant, servant of Warwick]
Nicholas Breton	[d. 1624, son of John]
William Green	[household, gentleman usher 1580s]
William Tatton*	[of Cheshire]
George Booth*	[of Cheshire?]
George Leycester*	[c. 1566–1612, of Toft, Ches., M.P.]
Edmund Trafford*	[c. 1560–1620, of Trafford, Lancs., M.P.]
William Gorge*	[household officer 1567–88]
Richard Browne*	[1538–1604, M.P., household officer 1566–88]
John Wake*	[d. 1621, of Salcey Forest, Northants., keeper of Grafton]

Edward Watson	[*c.* 1549–1621, of Rockingham, Northants., M.P.]
John Wotton*	[Gentleman Pensioner, Captain, Netherlands 1586]
George Brooke*	[1558/9–1604, son of Lord Cobham, household 1580s]
John Hynde*	[household, gentleman of horse]
Thomas Parker[b]	
Michael Dormer[b]	[of Oxon.?, servant of Warwick]
Edward Jobson[b]*	[household 1560s, relative]
Henry Barington[b]	[poss. M.P., Gentleman Pensioner, of Essex, d. *c.* 1590]
Arthur Berners	[Captain, Netherlands 1586]
Edward Pinchon	[poss. son of John Pinchon, of Writtle, Essex, M.P.]
John Fisher	[of Warks., poss. brother of Clement Fisher]
Thomas Harrison	[poss. officer of the Stables]
Henry Goodere[a]*	[1534–95, of Polesworth, Warks., M.P., entourage]
John Poyntz*	[*c.* 1560–1633, of Iron Acton, Glos., M.P., tenant]
Mr Chester	[poss. William, of Almondsbury, Glos., former page]
Mr Smith	

The Earl's gentlemen, servants

Arthur Atye[d]*	[d. 1604, M.P., chief secretary 1574–88]
Hugh Cholmondley*	[1552–1601, of Cholmondley, Ches., M.P., household officer]
Richard Bold*	[*c.* 1541–1602, of Bold, Lancs., M.P., household 1570s]
Walter Leveson*	[1551–1602, of Trentham, Staffs., M.P., officer]
George Fearne*	
Thomas Stafferton*	[officer of Grafton]
Walter Parsons	
William Clarke	[d. 1604, of Watford, Northants.]
Thomas Catesby	[poss. M.P., of Whiston, Northants., d. 1592]
William Walsh	[*c.* 1561–1622, of Abberley, Worcs., M.P.]
Thomas Chaloner	[*c.* 1564–1615, of Steeple Claydon, Bucks., M.P.]
Francis Bromley	[*c.* 1556–91, of Hodnet, Salop., M.P., m. Thomas Leighton's sister]
Thomas Leighton	[*c.* 1554–1600, of Wattlesborough, Salop., M.P.]
Francis Clare*	[d. 1608, of Caldwell, Worcs., entourage]
William Helmes	[Captain, Netherlands 1586]
Robert Dymoke*	
Edward Cave	[household]
Christopher Goldingham	[brother? of Henry Goldingham, entourage]
Francis Fortescue	[*c.* 1563–1624, of Salden, Bucks., M.P., son of Sir John Fortescue]
Thomas Price	[*c.* 1564–1634, of Plas Iolyn, Denbs., son of Ellis Price, M.P.]
Humphrey Stafford	
George Turfield	[Captain, Netherlands 1586]
Sebastian Osbaston	[of Long Compton, Warks., tenant of Warwick]
Mr Zouch	[poss. household, poss. Richard Zouch, M.P.]

Thomas Cottington
William Sprint*
George Ashby   [poss. of Quenby, Leics.]
Philip Babington   [household 1570s]
Robert Hill*   [of Shilton, Devon, household 1570s]
Edmund York*   [household, son of Sir John York]
Stephen Thornhurst*
George Bingham*
Nicholas Poyntz*   [of Alderley, Glos., tenant, poss. household]
William Waight*   [of Warks., household]
John Hughes   [poss. tenant of Kenilworth]
William Goodere*   [brother of Henry]
William Heydon*   [household, gentleman usher 1580s]
Bernard Whetston*   [household]
Edward Barker   [of Little Ilford, Essex, household, tenant of
                                    Wanstead]
George Noel*   [brother of Henry Noel, M.P.]
Christopher Wright*   [J.P., Warks.]
George Kevitt*   [poss. related to Thomas Kevitt, tenant of Balsall,
                                    Warks.]
William Sneyd   [of Keele, Staffs.?]
Francis Trentham*   [son of Thomas Trentham of Rocester, Staffs., M.P.,
                                    entourage]
Rowland Selby   [connection to Captain William Selby unclear]
Mr. Fardshel
Anthony Flowerdew   [son of William Flowerdew of Hethersett, Norf.,
                                    estate officer]
Anthony Nott
John More*
Walter Clopton   [of Clopton, Warks.?]
Richard Lloyd*   [1545–?, secretary, poss. M.P.]
Thomas Chatterton   [Captain, Netherlands 1586]
John Leventhrop   [of Herts., former ward]
Hampden Paulet   [1550–?, of Nether Wallop, Hants., M.P.]
John Knight   [poss. M.P.]
Edmund Carey[a]   [1558–1637, 6th son of Lord Hunsdon, M.P., officer
                                    of Grafton]
James Hobson*   [poss. son of James Hobson, M.P., of Suss.]
Henry Parker
Edward Lomner
William Butler   [poss. tenant of Kenilworth]
Isaac Wincoll
Rowland Mills
Thomas Smith   [Captain, Netherlands 1586]
William Highgate
John Carrell
Alexander Morgan*
Henry Unton[b]   [c. 1558–96, of Bruern Abbey, Oxon., M.P.]

Richard Holney	[household]
William Goslett*	
John Leigh*	[Captain Netherlands, 1586]
Robert Hutton*	[household officer]
Thomas Fairfax	[1560–1640, of Denton, Yorks., M.P., household 1580s]
Thomas Bickley	
William Rogers	
Jenkin Lloyd	[*c.* 1560–1628, of Berthlwyd, Monts., tenant]
Cadwaladr Price	[1561–?, of Rhiwlas, Merion., M.P.]
William Penrhyn*	[of Rhysnant, Monts., recorder, lordship of Chirk]
John Wynne Edwardes	[of Cefn y Wern, Chirk, tenant]
Thomas Morrell	
Richard Morris	[of Rhiwsaeson, Monts., tenant]
Robert Spring	
Edward Boughton*	[*c.* 1545–89, of Cawston, Warks., M.P., officer]
Sylvanus Scory*	[d. 1617, M.P., son of the Bishop of Hereford, household 1570s]
Thomas Salusbury	[of Denbigh Castle, tenant]
John Marvin	[of Wilts., poss. M.P.]
William Hopton*	[household]
Mr Gwin	[poss. reference to men sent by John Wynne of Gwydir]
Captain William Reade	[d. 1604, M.P., officer of Berwick garrison]
Christopher Blount	[d. 1601, M.P., master of horse, son of Thomas Blount]

B. RETINUES FOUND IN THE OTHER LISTS

Henry Appleyard	[of Bracon Ash, Norf., nephew of Amy Robsart, poss. household]
William Blackwell*	[keeper of Drayton Basset, 'old retainer']
Edward Blount*	[d. 1630, estate officer, brother of Christopher]
Peter Boiles	
William Boughton	[of Long Lawford, Warks., cousin of Edward]
John Brock	
Francis Castilion*	[1561–1638, M.P., poss. household, son of G. B. Castiglione]
Thomas Chetwynd	
William Clavell	[poss. brother of John Clavell, M.P., of Dorset]
William Cowper	
Henry Day*	[poss. household]
Jasper Dering	
William Downhall*	[secretary and gentleman of the horse]
Lawrence Fenwick	
John Flackett	
Richard Flowerdew	[relationship to Anthony unclear]
Thomas Fowler	[poss. household servant of that name]

Robert Fulford*   [household, of Devon?]
Gilbert Gerard*   [prob. M.P. Chester 1593, son of Sir William]
Bernard Grenville   [1567–1636, M.P., son of Sir Richard]
Edward Grey   [of Buildwas, Salop., household and relative]
Nicholas Hardlow
William Hartop   [servant, tenant]
George Harvey*   [household, steward in Netherlands]
Richard Hodges
Piers Holland   [d. 1596, of Dinmael, Denbs., brother of David]
Reginald Hollingworth*   [lieut. of Leicester's guard 1586]
Richard Holte   [of Aston, Warks.?]
John Hornedge
William Horton   [relative of William, M.P., of Catton, Derbs. and
                           Caludon, Warks.]

Henry Isley*   [of Kent, household, relative]
William Jermyn   [of Suff., brother of Sir Robert]
John Lamplaugh   [of Cumberland?]
Philip Lappe
Arthur Longfield*
Jerome Markham*
Thomas Peniston   [prob. son of Thomas, M.P., of Oxon., d. 1601]
Christopher Pescott
Thomas Powlewhele   [household]
William Poyntz*   [household, brother of Nicholas]
Anthony Puleston   [of Denbs.?]
Ambrose Rogers
William Rowse   [poss. household]
Christopher Saunders
Edmund Stafford   [household]
Thomas Storey   [rider of the Stables, household Netherlands]
George Tipping   [of Oxon.?]
Giles Tracy   [household, brother of John]
John Tracy*   [c. 1561–1648, of Toddington, Glos., M.P.,
                           household]

Thomas Turner
Henry Vaughan   [either of Hergest, Herefs., or Cors y Gedol,
                           Merion.]

Hugh Vere*
Charles Walcot   [c. 1542–96, of Walcot, Salop., M.P., poss. tenant]
William Walker*
Robert Williams
William Wood   [household]

* List A is derived from the Gurney list and follows its order and structure, omitting only the numbers of men and horses. List B comprises those men omitted from the Gurney list, the great majority found only in the January 1586 muster list, and is arranged alphabetically. There are, of course, numerous variations of spelling between the lists (particularly in the Spanish list, where the clerk had some difficulty with English

names) and this has been standardized. (*) indicates attendance at Leicester's funeral. The identities supplied are as brief as possible, emphasizing any known connection to Leicester. For those identified as servants or members of the household, see the Index of Servants in *Household Accounts*. As was my practice in *Household Accounts*, membership of the House of Commons has been indicated; biographical information will be found in *The House of Commons 1559–1603*, though only occasionally the connection to Leicester. Further information on the Midlands and Welsh contingents can be found in my articles. Many of these men also appear casually in *Household Accounts*.

^a The Spanish list omits Dyer and Conway. The Rawlinson adds Sir Thomas Cecil and Sir Philip Sidney. The Hague muster includes all except Conway, but in a different order and Sir Robert Stapleton twice. It also includes those knighted during 1586, indicated (^a). Many others were to be knighted after 1586.

^b The Spanish list identifies this group as Esquires and adds the six names marked (^b). The Rawlinson list runs this group on from the knights with no gap or identification, omits Hurleston and adds the section Thomas Parker to Thomas Smith as well as Jasper Dering.

^c A similar gap exists in the Spanish list, but the rest of the names are simply identified as the Earl's Gentlemen. The Rawlinson has here a group of four 'Officers': Hurleston, George Harvey, Captain Read and William Gorge, and heads the remainder 'My Lords Servants'.

^d Both the Spanish and the Rawlinson lists vary the order of names of this section in the same way. Both begin with Atye, but between Francis Clare and William Helmes insert the section William Harman to John Hynde. The Spanish list ends with John Leigh, but the Rawlinson continues as the Gurney.

NOTES

a Reference to the Longleat House, Berkeley Castle and Bedford Estate MSS is made with the kind permission of the Marquess of Bath, the Berkeley Trustees and the Marquess of Tavistock and the Trustees of the Bedford Estate. I am extremely grateful to the editor for his forbearance and his stimulating comments on earlier versions of this essay; he of course bears no responsibility for the views expressed here.

1 Lawrence Stone, *The Crisis of the Aristocracy 1558–1641* (Oxford, rev. edn, 1979). M. E. James adopted a more nuanced approach, see *Society, Politics and Culture: Studies in Early Modern England* (Cambridge, 1986), esp. 'The concept of order and the Northern Rebellion', 'English politics and the concept of honour, 1485–1642', and 'At a crossroads of the political culture: the Essex revolt, 1601'. The combined influence of Stone and James can be found in Felicity Heal and Clive Holmes, *The Gentry in England and Wales 1500–1700* (Basingstoke, 1994).

2 Barry Coward, *The Stanleys, Lords Stanley and Earls of Derby 1385–1672. The Origins, Wealth and Power of a Landowning Family* (Cheetham Society, xxx, 1983), p. xiii. He also notes the origins of the crisis of the aristocracy in the rise of the gentry debate.

3 (Manchester, 1992). The contributors include the author, Steven Gunn and Richard Hoyle. Starkey is best known for his influence on the study of the Court, but his views on the importance of the peerage can be found in the introduction to Starkey, ed., *Rivals in Power: Lives and Letters of the Great Tudor Dynasties* (1990), pp. 8–25. The contributors to this volume include Steven Gunn and the author. Helen Miller's

valuable *Henry VIII and the English Nobility* (Oxford, 1986) should not be overlooked, although it does not deal directly with these issues.

4 'The Baronial Context of the English Civil War', *TRHS*, 5th ser., xl (1990), 93–120, and 'Parliamentary Management, Men-of-Business and the House of Lords, 1640–49', in Clive Jones, ed., *A Pillar of the Constitution: The House of Lords in British Politics, 1640–1784* (1989), pp. 21–50.

5 Christine Carpenter, 'Who Ruled the Midlands in the Later Middle Ages?', *Midland History*, xix (1994), 1–2.

6 To select only a few of the major titles out of many, Carole Rawcliffe, *The Staffords, Earls of Stafford and Dukes of Buckingham, 1394–1521* (Cambridge, 1978); C. Carpenter, 'The Beauchamp Affinity: a study of bastard feudalism at work', *EHR*, xcv (1980), 514–32, and *Locality and Polity: A Study of Warwickshire Landed Society, 1401–1499* (Cambridge, 1992); Simon Walker, *The Lancastrian Affinity 1361–1399* (Oxford, 1990). The extensive periodical literature is surveyed in Michael Hicks, *Bastard Feudalism* (1995).

7 This is changing now, see, for example, Paul E. J. Hammer 'Patronage at Court, faction and the earl of Essex', in John Guy, ed., *The Reign of Elizabeth I: Court and Culture in the Last Decade* (Cambridge, 1995), pp. 65–86; Hammer, 'The Uses of Scholarship: the Secretariat of Robert Devereux, Second Earl of Essex', *EHR*, cix (1994), 26–51; and G. R. Morrison, 'The Land, Family and Domestic Following of William Cecil, Lord Burghley, *c.* 1550–1598' (unpublished D.Phil. thesis, University of Oxford, 1990).

8 See his chapters 7–10. The loss of most of the Stanley archive in the destruction of Knowsley during the Civil War (see p. xii) makes a detailed study of the sixteenth-century Earls of Derby difficult. Claire Cross, *The Puritan Earl: The Life of Henry Hastings, Third Earl of Huntingdon* (1966), an otherwise valuable work, concentrates on Huntingdon's public career and religious patronage.

9 Specifically in *Charles Brandon, Duke of Suffolk 1484–1545* (Oxford, 1988), 'Henry Bourchier, Earl of Essex (1472–1540)', in Bernard, *Tudor Nobility*, pp. 158–66, and his contribution to this volume. 'Bourchier' and my essay, 'The Dudley Clientele 1553–1563' [Ch. 8], are in fact the only studies of affinities in *Tudor Nobility*. The discussion of the Talbot affinity in Bernard, *The Power of the Early Tudor Nobility: A Study of the Fourth and Fifth Earls of Shrewsbury* (Brighton, 1985) is limited to pp. 158–66.

10 An example is Roger Lockyer's otherwise excellent biography, *Buckingham: The Life and Political Career of George Villiers, First Duke of Buckingham* (1981). See my review, *EHR*, xcviii (1983), 625–8.

11 Initially I employed the French form but variant house styles led to abandoning of the accent in some essays, and it will be abandoned here as well. This is not the place to discuss the issues raised by the debate on factional politics or its relationship to the politics of patronage. My own views can be found in 'Favourites and Factions at the Elizabethan Court' [Ch. 3], 'The Patronage of the Crown in Elizabethan Politics: The 1590s in perspective' [Ch. 4], and 'The Eltonian Legacy: Politics' [Ch. 5]. See also the survey of the debate in Gunn, 'The Structures of Politics in Early Tudor England', *TRHS*, 6th ser., v (1995), 59–90.

12 French usage of the term *clientèle* has a heavy bureaucratic emphasis, see the contributions to Charles Giry-Deloison and Roger Mettam, eds, *Patronages et Clientélismes 1550–1750 (France, Angleterre, Espagne, Italie)* (Lille, 1995).

13 With the exception of David Starkey's collection, *The English Court from the Wars of the Roses to the Civil War* (1987), her sources are entirely local studies, chiefly of the seventeenth century, see notes 3, 5 and 8. On the other hand, this is an essay on the Midlands and there has not been much work on the sixteenth-century Midlands with which to make comparisons.

14 See the stimulating discussion of their influence in Edward Powell, 'After "After McFarlane": The Poverty of Patronage and the Case for Constitutional History' in D. J. Clayton *et al.*, eds, *Trade, Devotion and Government: Papers in Late Medieval History* (Stroud, 1994), pp. 1–16. This and Carpenter's own, 'Before and After McFarlane', R. H. Britnell and A. J. Pollard, eds, *The McFarlane Legacy: Studies in Later Medieval Politics and Society* (Stroud, 1995), pp. 175–206, are essays of major historiographical importance.

15 See, for example, Guy's general introduction to *Tudor Monarchy*, pp. 1–8.

16 'Who ruled the Midlands?', 6, 13. See also *Locality and Polity*, pp. 33, 290–1, 318 and conclusions.

17 Nigel Saul, *Knights and Esquires: The Gloucestershire Gentry in the Fourteenth Century* (Oxford, 1981), p. 29. Simon Payling, *Political Society in Lancastrian England. The Greater Gentry of Nottinghamshire* (Oxford, 1991), p. 88. See also the survey of this debate in John Watts, *Henry VI and the Politics of Kingship* (Cambridge, 1996), pp. 91–101, and his reference to the 'normal form of local rule', p. 91.

18 *The Gentry*, p. 194. Their discussion of relations between the peerage and the gentry (pp. 190–214) verges on the anecdotal. It is not entirely clear if they regard the Marquess of Newcastle's well-known description of the 7th Earl of Shrewsbury and his affinity at the beginning of the seventeenth century (quoted on pp. 190–1) solely as 'romantic nostalgia'.

19 The best discussion can be found in the introduction to Michael Jones and Simon Walker, eds, 'Private Indentures for Life Service in Peace and War 1278–1476', *Camden Miscellany XXXII* (Camden Society, 5th ser., iii, 1994), pp. 1–190.

20 Carpenter, 'Beauchamp Affinity', 515–17. Watts, *Henry VI*, p. 93, n. 66.

21 See, for example, Heal and Holmes, *The Gentry*, pp. 195–7. However, they also see the attack on the nobility as more widespread and ideological, see pp. 197–201.

22 See Bernard's introduction to *Tudor Nobility*.

23 For the contemporary debate see below, pp. 386–7.

24 *John Dudley, Duke of Northumberland 1504–1553* (Oxford, 1996), esp. pp. ix, 97, 285–6. Cf. my review in *Parliamentary History*, xvi (1997), 361–3. Hicks draws a similar distinction between a courtier following, which he terms an affinity, and a local territorial connection, *Bastard Feudalism*, pp. 104–8, 222–3.

25 For the difficulties posed by the Stanleys, see above, n. 8. James, 'Concept of Order' is the best introduction to the Percies.

26 See the comments of Powell, 'After "After McFarlane"', pp. 9–10, Carpenter, 'Before and After McFarlane', pp. 192–3, and G. L. Harriss, 'The Dimensions of Politics', in Britnell and Pollard, p. 3. That 'disputes were endemic in this landed society' (p. 393) is one of the axioms of Carpenter, *Locality and Polity*.

27 For example, 'In the vacuum left by the Duchy of Lancaster, he [the Earl of Warwick] could not afford a struggle for control that would have unleashed the well-known fury

of Edmund Ferrers against the inexperienced and untried Sutton of Dudley and Buckingham', *Locality and Polity*, p. 375.

28 The two best-known Elizabethan gentry republics emerged in Norfolk and Suffolk, but after the spectacular collapse of the Howards in 1572, see A. Hassell Smith, *County and Court: Government and Politics in Norfolk 1558–1603* (Oxford, 1974), and Diarmaid MacCulloch, *Suffolk and the Tudors* (Oxford, 1986). However, while Norfolk became faction-ridden, Suffolk saw the creation of an effective county administration.

29 See Watts, *Henry VI*, pp. 65–7, on the analogies.

30 'Beauchamp Affinity', 520–1. *Locality and Polity*, p. 284.

31 An observation made by Harriss, 'Dimensions of Politics', p. 4.

32 See also J. M. W. Bean, *From Lord to Patron: Lordship in late medieval England* (Manchester, 1989), pp. 185–8.

33 Carpenter, 'Beauchamp Affinity', 519–20, 523–4.

34 For his papers in general, see Adams, 'The Papers of Robert Dudley, Earl of Leicester I–IV', *Archives*, xx (1992–93), 63–85, 131–44, xxii (1996), 1–26, forthcoming. The surviving household accounts and household lists are printed in Adams, ed., *Household Accounts and Disbursement Books of Robert Dudley, Earl of Leicester 1558–1561, 1584–1586* (Camden Society, 5th ser., vi, 1995).

35 The importance of Warwick's papers lies in the evidence of the considerable overlap of personnel that to some extent created a joint affinity, see below, p. 382. It is possible that a number of men not identified in the list in the Appendix were Warwick's.

36 In '"Because I am of that Countrye and & mynde to plant myself there", Robert Dudley, Earl of Leicester and the West Midlands' [Ch. 15], p. 312, n. 12, I discussed the dispersal of the Ferrers papers. At the time I was not aware of the large Ferrers collection currently being catalogued in the Folger Shakespeare Library, Washington, DC. See N. W. Alcock, 'The Ferrers of Tamworth Collection: sorting and listing', *Archives*, xix (1991), 358–63. I am most grateful to Dr Alcock for bringing his work to my attention and to Mrs Laetitia Yeandle, manuscripts librarian at the Folger, for supplying me with a microfilm of some of the correspondence. As will be seen in the references below, most of the FSL collection are drafts of Humphrey Ferrers' letters to Leicester and the dates are not always clear. In 1580 Ferrers claimed to have been in Leicester's service for twenty-one years, see FSL, MS Le 634.

37 For convenience, reference to the Wynn Papers will be made to the article numbers in the *Calendar of Wynn of Gwydir Papers 1515–1690* (Aberystwyth, 1926) rather than the actual catalogue references to the various sections of this collection in the National Library of Wales. For (Sir) John Wynn's membership of Leicester's household, see below, p. 379.

38 Sir William More of Loseley was the keeper of several of the walks of Windsor Forest, and his correspondence (Surrey RO, Guildford, and FSL) is a valuable source for Leicester's administration as constable of Windsor Castle. His son (Sir) George was a gentleman of Leicester's household in the 1570s.

39 Pt I, Appendix ii, pp. 388–92.

40 *Calendar of Letters and State Papers . . . preserved in the Archives of Simancas*, iii (1580–86) (1896), pp. 554–6. The editing is not perfect, and the original, Archivo General de Simancas, Estado K 1564, fo. 4, should be consulted.

41 The original is PRO, SP84/6/79ff, which is printed in E. M. Tenison, *Elizabethan England* (14 vols, Leamington Spa, 1933–61), vi, pp. 45–7. The copy was probably made during a later settlement of pay and would include all the horse 'in pay' from 10 January 1586.

42 *Leicester's Triumph* (Leiden and Oxford, 1968). Jan van Dorsten told me in the 1970s that the inspiration for this book came from his discovery of a billeting list for Leicester and his men in Leiden in January 1586. In compiling their general list of the train (Appendix III) they drew on some documents that are not strictly relevant, see *Household Accounts*, pp. 22–3.

43 'The Protestant Cause: Religious Alliance with the West European Calvinist Communities as Political Issue in England, 1585–1629' (unpublished D.Phil. thesis, University of Oxford, 1973), pp. 62–73. This is a very primitive initial sketch.

44 This discovery led to my article, 'The Gentry of north Wales and the Earl of Leicester's Expedition to the Netherlands, 1585–1586' [Ch. 12]. The letter, addressed to John Wynn, is printed there as an appendix. More recently another copy, addressed to one of the Warwickshire Burdetts, has appeared in several manuscript dealers' catalogues, see *Household Accounts*, p. 388, n. 18.

45 MS Rawlinson B. 146, f. 235–v.

46 MS Eng. Hist. C. 272, pp. 82–7.

47 'North Wales', though this was written before the discovery of the two Bodleian lists; 'A Puritan Crusade? The Composition of the Earl of Leicester's Expedition to the Netherlands' [Ch. 9]; 'The Dudley Clientele and the House of Commons, 1559–1586' [Ch. 10], pp. 209–11; and Ch. 15 above, pp. 348–9.

48 As the peers pose no difficulties they have been omitted from Appendix 16.1.

49 The differences between them can be explained as follows. The two Bodleian lists were derived more or less directly from a list of the Tothill Fields muster. The Spanish list (given its references to ships) was a copy of an embarkation list. Since the horse were shipped over to the Netherlands in two contingents, one in November 1585 and the other with Leicester himself in December, it may therefore have been a list of only one of them (see *Household Accounts*, p. 393). The men who appear only in The Hague muster list probably arrived after Leicester did, or possibly even after 10 January, as the purpose of the list was to establish who was in pay from then. The later arrivals do not represent a separate section of the affinity; the range of connections is similar to that found in the main body.

50 See the notes to Appendix 16.1.

51 The 'funeral lists' are printed in *Household Accounts*, pt II, arts i and j.

52 It is probable that a number of those still unidentified, especially the men who also attended Leicester's funeral, were members of the Midlands affinity who cannot be identified owing to the disappearance of the Kenilworth records. Others may have had a connection to Warwick.

53 The principal exceptions are those men who can only be identified as officers of the infantry contingent, who may not have been directly connected to Leicester.

54 In Wynn's case the reason may have been genuine ill health. In a later note to his doctor (*Wynn Cal.*, art. 102), he recorded that 'the last year vid. 1585 in Autumne taken with a sharpe choleric flux in so much that I had within 24 hours 40 stoles'.

55 Ch. 12 above, pp. 246–7, and, for the comment, p. 241. I have only been able to examine a photograph of the Burdett letter in a dealer's catalogue, but I can detect no significant difference in the text.

56 For the 1570s we are dependent on anecdotal evidence for identities, so those noted here are probably an underestimate. For the chaplains, see Adams, 'A Godly Peer? Leicester and the Puritan' [Ch. 11], p. 230.

57 See *Wynn Cal.*, arts 76, 79, 85, 89. Wynn was also engaged on Leicester's business in Wales in 1581 and 1587, see arts 97 and 104.

58 An overall survey of Leicester's offices and estates can be found in Ch. 10 above, pp. 200–1. The occasional geographical grouping of names in the lists may reflect an earlier ordering by county.

59 A map of Leicester's West Midlands estates can be found in Ch. 15 above, p. 313.

60 This group is not as large as it appears from other sources, *Household Accounts* especially, but it would include the Earl of Essex himself, as well as George Digby, one of Leicester's intimates, who had previously been a ward of Sir Francis Knollys. Another connection, the Cumbrian, is represented here only by John Lamplaugh. This was created through a cadet branch of the Dudleys, the Dudleys of Yanwath, Cumb., two of whose members were among Leicester's longest-serving household officers.

61 Castilion may also have served in Leicester's household. He witnessed a deed together with several household officers on 10 June 1583, Berkeley Castle, General Series Charter 5397.

62 Lord North, although excluded for reasons mentioned above, would also fit into this category.

63 BL, Lansdowne MS 14, f. IV, gives a list. See also the discussion in *Household Accounts*, p. 22.

64 Paul L. Hughes and James F. Larkin, eds, *Tudor Royal Proclamations* (3 vols., New Haven, 1969), ii, items 582 and 664. See also J. P. Cooper, 'Retainers in Tudor England' in *Land, Men and Beliefs: Studies in Early-Modern England*, eds, G. E. Aylmer and J. S. Morrill (1983), pp. 89–90.

65 My statement in *Household Accounts*, p. 22, that the proclamations rehearsed the 'Great Statute' of 1504 is wrong as that statute expired in 1509. I am grateful to Dr Gunn for bringing this error to my attention. I was misled by a footnote in Hughes and Larkin (p. 105) to the pardoning of illicit retaining in the coronation pardon proclamation of 1559, which included the 1504 statute among the relevant legislation.

66 Why this proclamation also drew attention to the clause in the 1487 statute barring retaining of officers of the Crown is not clear either.

67 Penry Williams, *The Council in the Marches of Wales under Elizabeth I* (Cardiff, 1958), p. 286, and James, 'Crossroads', p. 424. Stone, *Crisis*, p. 207, n. 1, suggests that an attempt in 1561 to exclude retainers from commissions of the peace had remained a dead letter.

68 Montague's letter (16 May 1583) is Henry E. Huntington Library, San Marino, Ca., Battle Abbey MS 56, f. 6. The list of Hertford's retainers (2 May 1583), undoubtedly related to the proclamation, can be found in Historical Manuscripts Commission, *Report on the Manuscripts of the Marquess of Bath IV: Seymour Papers 1532–1686* (1967), pp. 198–9.

69 PRO, SP12/213/40, to Walsingham, 24 July 1588. This is presumably the complaint to which Hicks refers in *Bastard Feudalism*, p. 132.

70 See Jones and Walker, 'Private Indentures', pp. 30–1.

71 BL, Cotton MS Galba C VIII, ff. 96v–7. See also *Household Accounts*, pp. xiv and 24.

72 Printed in *Household Accounts*, pt II, arts b–e. As will be seen there these lists are, strictly speaking, bills, but fortunately they supply the names of those supplied with liveries.

73 The significance of the numbers in these lists depends to some extent on whether they were inclusive (i.e. the award of livery or a badge to all entitled to one) or supplementary to earlier awards. I would regard the 1567–8 lists as inclusive, see *Household Accounts*, p. 21.

74 'Possibly' (here and below) because the relevant lists give only a surname.

75 The probable reason for his appearing among the horse is given in a note to the list of the guard that he had been licensed to serve as guidon-bearer to Thomas Fairfax's cornet. Blackwell was already a servant when appointed keeper by Leicester in July 1580, see Index of Servants in *Household Accounts*. The letter to Humphrey Ferrers appointing him is now in a private collection and I am grateful to the owner for sending me a photocopy.

76 See *Household Accounts*, Index of Servants.

77 Cooper, 'Retainers', tends to conflate retainers and military tenants. Military service clauses in Elizabethan leases are also discussed in Stone, *Crisis*, p. 216.

78 See Adams, 'Military obligations of leasehold tenants in Leicesterian Denbigh', *Transactions of the Denbighshire Historical Society*, xxiv (1975), 205–8, and Ch. 12 above, pp. 240–1. Of particular interest is the quite specific obligation in the lease of a park in Denbigh to his household officer Robert Hutton, cited there from NLW, Ruthin Lordship MS 71. Unfortunately other leases granted to household servants do not survive.

79 Longleat, Dudley Papers XVII, f. 186.

80 Ch. 12 above, pp. 238–40. The captains, William Thomas of Caernarvon and Evan Lloyd of Bodidris (the steward of the lordship of Chirk), were key members of his Welsh administration.

81 *Household Accounts*, pp. 24–30.

82 The patent of Sir John Hubaud (see below) has disappeared, but it was seen in the seventeenth century by Sir William Dugdale, see Ch. 15 above, p. 332, n. 172. A surviving example is Longleat MS 4109, Edward Blount's patent as steward of Cleobury Mortimer (Salop.) in 1587.

83 Tables of the relevant officers and stewards can be found in Ch. 15 above, pp. 346–8, and Adams, 'Officeholders of the Borough of Denbigh and the Lordships of Denbighshire in the reign of Elizabeth I' [Ch. 14], pp. 297–8.

84 A list of the 'central pool' can be found in Ch. 15 above, p. 345.

85 The continuity of the Dudley affinity is one of the themes of Ch. 8 above. It has been challenged by Loades (*Northumberland*, pp. 274–86), but his arguments and evidence are not convincing. For shared officers with Warwick, see Ch. 15 above, p. 382ff., and Ch. 14 above, p. 296.

86 For a more detailed discussion and references, see Ch. 15 above, pp. 332–5.

87 See the extensive references to him in the *Wynn Cal.*, esp. arts 47, 58, 68–9, 79–80, 83, 85, 89.

88 For Shireburn, see Coward, *Stanleys*, pp. 85–6.

89 Printed in *Household Accounts*, pt II, art. a.

90 *Ibid.*, pp. 69–70, 101–2, 128.

91 Examples of the first type can be seen in the annuities paid out of the rents of the manor of Long Itchington (Warks.), listed in Longleat, Dudley Papers XX [The Complete View of the Evidences], fos. 34v, 36v. An example of the second type can be found in the rent charge of £5 p.a. from Kenilworth granted to Edmund Plowden for legal counsel on 7 December 1565, see HMC, *Tenth Report*, pt IV (1885), p. 409.

92 For examples, see Ch. 15 above, p. 326, n. 124, and pp. 334–5.

93 Examples include the 30s Bristol gave his secretary Arthur Atye in 1577 ('Leic. Pap. II', 133) and the substantial £50 the Vintners' Company gave to his household officer Richard Ellis in 1567 (*Household Accounts*, Index of Servants, *sub* Ellis).

94 Hubaud, for example, left £1,300 owing to him from the complex settlement of the Chester Dean and Chapter lands to a variety of Warwickshire civic charities, see his will, PRO, PROB 11/66/232. Leicester's role in this affair was controversial.

95 See *Household Accounts*, Index of Servants, *sub* Thomas Eaton, William Grice, William Huggins, and Ferdinando Richardson. A number of others entered the Crown's service after his death.

96 See Ch. 15 above, pp. 335–6. For the related subject of his influence on parliamentary elections, see Ch. 10 above. The conclusions reached there are, if anything, an underestimate.

97 Evidence of the scale of casual rewards can be found throughout *Household Accounts*. The one complaint of meanness by Leicester that I know of was made by Jean Hotman, who was to some extent a special case. See G. H. M. Posthumus Meyjes, *Jean Hotman's English Connection* (Medelingen van de Afdeling Letterkunde, Koninklijke Nederlandse Academie, nieuw reeks, liii, 1990), pp. 25–6. For an example of the competition to enter Leicester's service, see Longleat, Dudley Papers II, f. 224, Alexander Neville to Leicester, 23 July 1582.

98 For what follows, see Ch. 15 above, pp. 322–9.

99 See Ch. 4 above, pp. 74–5, for a further discussion.

100 As noted in Ch. 15 above, p. 320, Leicester's obtaining of various lands in the East Riding of Yorkshire in 1559–61 may have been related to a possible creation as Lord of Holderness, as it was claimed that the Sutton Dudleys descended from an Anglo-Saxon Lord of Holderness. It is no less revealing that these lands were sold off immediately after his creation as Earl of Leicester.

101 The fairly rapid sale of outlying lands in later grants from the Crown is evidence of a self-conscious policy in the expansion of his estate.

102 It might be noted that our general knowledge of the way in which Crown lands were granted in Elizabeth's reign is still limited, though a start has been made in R. W. Hoyle, ed., *The Estates of the English Crown, 1558–1640* (Cambridge, 1992). The grantee

certainly petitioned in many cases (there are examples in Leicester's later grants), but this does not appear to have been one of them. Elizabeth was not without her own strong views on specific grants; she resisted a request by the Earl of Bedford for the keepership of a royal forest on the grounds that he 'had not loved game or cared much for the preservation of them' (Bedford Estate Office, 2nd Earl's Papers, no. 5, Leicester to Bedford, 4 August [1583]).

103 Williams, *Council in the Marches of Wales*, p. 6.

104 In 1561 a general commission to survey all the Crown lands in Wales was issued, under which surveys of the lordships of Denbigh and Bromfield and Yale were undertaken in that year, and possibly Arwystli and Cyfeiliog in 1564. See Adams, 'The Composition of 1564 and the Earl of Leicester's Tenurial Reformation in the Lordship of Denbigh' [Ch. 13], pp. 263–4. Leicester's survey of Denbigh in 1563 followed the Exchequer survey closely.

105 See Ch. 15 above, pp. 323–4. Details of the visit in 1585 can be found in *Household Accounts*, pp. 285–301.

106 *Wynn Cal.*, art., 85, Wynn to Arthur Atye [autumn 1578], refers to Catherine of Berain going to see Leicester at Buxton in the summer.

107 The dispute involved the Welsh wool trade. It is discussed in the unpublished paper 'The Earl of Leicester as a patron of boroughs'.

108 General Household Inventory 1582 (Leicester House), n.f. Formerly Christ Church, Evelyn MS 264, now being catalogued at the British Library.

109 Leicester succeeded Norfolk as high steward of Great Yarmouth in 1572 and became King's Lynn's first high steward in the same year. The general conclusion is based on the entries in the King's Lynn Hall Books for 1544–69 and 1569–91 (Norfolk RO, KL/C7/6–7) and the Great Yarmouth Assembly Books for 1560–70, 1570–79, and 1579–98 (Norfolk RO, Y/C/19/2–4). A full discussion will be found in 'Leicester as a patron of boroughs'.

110 See Ch. 15 above, pp. 329–35.

111 This is based on an article on Leicester and the politics of north Wales in preparation for many years; a brief initial account can be found in Ch. 14 above, pp. 302–6.

112 See Ch. 3 above, pp. 47–53.

113 *Ibid.*, pp. 49–51. The comparison is found in Dwight C. Peck, ed., *Leicester's Commonwealth: The Copy of a Letter written by a Master of Art of Cambridge (1584)* (Athens, Ohio, 1985), pp. 188–9.

114 See Ch. 15 above, pp. 312–15, 339–41, for references.

115 I owe this point to Dr Richard Cust. See also the discussion of the gentry concern with lineage in Heal and Holmes, *The Gentry*, pp. 34–42.

116 See Ch. 15 above, p. 333, n. 185.

117 For a brief account of the Berkeley Law-Suit, written before I was able to consult the Berkeley Castle muniments, see Ch. 15 above, pp. 339–40. The Crown's formal role in the Berkeley Law-Suit arose from the terms of the repeal of Leicester and Warwick's attainder in 1558, which included the renunciation of any claim of right to their father's lands or offices, see *ibid.*, 319.

118 See *Wynn Cal.*, art. 58, Hubaud and John Nuthall to the gentry of Caernarvonshire, 6 December 1574, and Berkeley Castle, General Series Charter 5119, commission from the Crown to Nuthall and John Goodman, 30 May 1573.

119 See Ch. 15 above, pp. 339–40.

120 See *Wynn Cal.*, arts 58 and 62.

121 On the other hand, the antagonism between the Wynns and the gentlemen of Llŷn, which continued into the 1620s, may also have played its role in the affair. For references to this see J. G. Jones, *Law, Order and Government in Caernarfonshire 1558– 1640* (Cardiff, 1996), pp. 84–7.

122 *Wynn Cal.*, art. 104.

123 See Ch. 15 above, pp. 340–1, for a brief account, written before the FSL Ferrers Papers were brought to my attention. The extensive sources for this affair make possible a detailed study, which I hope to have the time to undertake.

124 Ferrers was undoubtedly the man on the spot as the manor house at Drayton Bassett would have been visible from Tamworth Castle. Ferrers later blamed the whole affair on Bagot's weakness or collusion, see FSL, Le 544 and 549, to Leicester, 22 September and 24 October 1578.

125 One was Ferrers' clash with the Earl of Essex over the stewardship of Tamworth earlier in the year, see Ch. 15 above, p. 340. Another was the Warwickshire by-election in 1579–80, see below, n. 131.

126 Ferrers, who became acting steward of Drayton Bassett after Leicester's purchase, complained about the difficulties the concealment caused him. See FSL, Le 548 and 634, Ferrers to Leicester [13 April 1579] and [post 22 July 1580], quoted below. Paramour was known to Leicester for some time; he was in fact the supplier of the livery cloth in 1567–8.

127 FSL, Le 633, Ferrers to Leicester [between 3 and 6 September 1578). On 15 September Paramour wrote to Ferrers as though Leicester was simply helping him to regain possession, see Ch. 15 above, p. 341.

128 FSL, Le 634. The acerbity of Ferrers' comments on Paramour was the product of a falling out between them in the meantime.

129 Walter Harcourt offered to surrender possession to Leicester if he made his interest clear, but Ferrers thought this a trick, see FSL, Le 544, to Leicester, 22 September 1578.

130 For Hubaud at Beaumaris (8 September), see *Wynn Cal.*, art. 88, and for his return to Kenilworth, Longleat, Dudley Papers II, f. 193, Henry Besbeeche to Leicester, 23 October 1578.

131 Goodere's house at Polesworth was also just outside Tamworth. In the winter of 1579–80 Digby and Goodere contested a by-election to replace a deceased knight of the shire for Warwickshire, see Ch. 10 above, p. 198. This is an obscure episode, but the coincidence is curious; it would suggest a serious division within the affinity.

132 Pierpont Morgan Library, New York, Rulers of England Box III, Elizabeth I, pt 2, no. 29.5, Leicester to Ferrers, 13 September [1578]. The letter is damaged.

133 Ch. 15 above, p. 326.

134 FSL, Le 548, Ferrers to Paramour [13 April 1579].

135 FSL, Le 634.

136 On this episode, see Steven Kershaw, 'Power and Duty in the Elizabethan Aristocracy: George, Earl of Shrewsbury, the Glossopdale dispute and the Council', Bernard,
Tudor Nobility, pp. 266–95. Was the Council's intervention motivated by fear it might
lead to another Drayton Bassett?

137 J. S. Cockburn, ed., *Crime in England 1550–1800* (1977), p. 9.

138 For examples of the latter, see the comments on the Duke of Norfolk's commission
in Watts, *Henry VI*, pp. 64–5, and the references in Payling, 'Law and Arbitration
in Nottinghamshire 1399–1461', Joel Rosenthal and Colin Richmond, eds., *People,
Politics and Community in the later Middle Ages* (Gloucester, 1987), p. 141.

139 Longleat, Dudley Papers II, f. 206, Yerwerth to Leicester, 8 October 1579. For Yerwerth,
see *Household Accounts*, List of Servants.

140 For references, see Ch. 15 above, p. 338, n. 220.

141 For the mediation efforts, see FSL, Lee 550, 632 and 471, Leicester to [Edward
Boughton], 27 February 1583, Ferrers to Leicester 22 August [1582/3?], and Boughton
to Ferrers, 21 January 1584. I have not yet been able to see the Star Chamber case
papers, but the case is mentioned in P. M. Hasler, ed., *The History of Parliament: The
House of Commons 1558–1603* (1981), *sub* Breton. One of Leicester's sanctions was to
refuse to take Breton's son Nicholas into his service until the dispute was settled.

142 For Clarence and Gloucester, see Michael Hicks, *False, Fleeting. Perjur'd Clarence:
George, Duke of Clarence 1449–1478* (Bangor, 1992), p. 169, and for Buckingham,
Miller, *Henry VIII and the Nobility*, p. 140. For Suffolk's retinues, Gunn, 'The Regime
of Charles, Duke of Suffolk in north Wales and the reform of Welsh Government,
1509–1525', *WHR*, xii (1985), 463–4, and 'The Duke of Suffolk's March on Paris in
1523', *EHR*, ci (1986), 598.

143 HMC, *Fifteenth Report, Pt. V: The Manuscripts of F. J. Savile Foljambe* (1897), pp. 5–6.

144 Sir Robert Jermyn, who had been removed from the Suffolk bench for his participation
in the attacks on the Bishop of Norwich in 1582–83, and Sir Robert Stapleton, notorious
for his involvement in the conspiracy against the Archbishop of York, are cases in point.

145 An example can be found in the account of the Welsh Catholic martyr Richard Gwyn,
see D. Aneurin Thomas, ed., *The Welsh Elizabethan Catholic Martyrs* (Cardiff, 1971),
pp. 229, 251.

146 Cheshire RO, DBC 2309/1/11 [Thomas Lytler, Life of Lady Cholmondley], p. 69.
I owe this reference too to Dr Cust.

147 *The History of the Gwydir Family, written by Sir John Wynne*, ed. Askew Roberts
(Oswestry, 1878), see pp. 98–9 for Thomas. Wynn makes only one or two distant
references to Leicester but he does record the generosity of Northumberland, 'so
good a master', to one of his relatives. For his relations with Thomas, see *Wynn Cal.*,
art. 97, Thomas to Wynn, 11 December 1581.

148 See Ch. 12 above, p. 246, n. 99. I suspect that Bulkeley was the Mr Bulkley in the
1567 livery list.

149 N. E. McClure, ed., *The Letters of John Chamberlain* (Memoirs of the American Philosophical Society, xii, 1939), i. pp. 430–2, to Dudley Carleton, 25 February 1613.

150 p. 57.

151 Jones and Walker, 'Private Indentures', p. 32.

152 This was the point of Newcastle's description of Shrewsbury's affinity, quoted in Heal and Holmes, *Gentry*, pp. 190–2.

153 Essex RO, D/B/3/3/422, art. 9. Maldon had, in fact, already made its decision.

154 Described in Stone, *Crisis*, pp. 97–119, and noted in Hicks, *Bastard Feudalism*, p. 7, but neither draws any wider conclusions. See also my comments in Ch. 4 above, pp. 72–3.

155 Adamson states that Leicester had claimed the Lord High Stewardship ('Baronial Contexts', 96–7). An antiquarian treatise on Leicester's descent by Robert Bowyer (now Huntington Library MS HM 160) does refer to the historic association between the earldom of Leicester and the stewardship of England, but Leicester does not appear to have shown any interest in the claims of his earldom, unlike his fascination with the Beauchamp descent. There is no evidence that his appointment as Lord Steward of the Household in 1587 was the result of pressure on his part. Further on in the same essay (p. 105, n. 56) Adamson refers to Leicester being 'Captain-General' in the 1580s. This can only be explained as a conflation of his commission as captain-general in the Netherlands with his temporary commission as lieutenant-general in the South Parts in July 1588.

Index

Note: 'n.' after a page reference indicates a note number on that page.